Popular Opera in Eighteenth-Century France

Music and Entertainment before the Revolution

This is the first book for a century to explore the development of French opera with spoken dialogue from its beginnings. Musical comedy in this form came in different styles and formed a distinct genre of opera, whose history has been obscured by neglect. Its songs were performed in private homes, where operas themselves were also given. The subject-matter was far wider in scope than is normally thought, with news stories and political themes finding their way onto the popular stage. In this book, David Charlton describes the comedic and musical nature of eighteenth-century popular French opera, considering topics such as Gherardi's theatre, Fair Theatre and the 'musico-dramatic art' created in the mid-eighteenth century. Performance practices, singers, audience experiences and theatre staging are included, as well as a pioneering account of the formation of a core of 'canonical' popular works.

David Charlton is Emeritus Professor of Music History at Royal Holloway, University of London. He has published on topics in opera between Bizet and Purcell. He is author of *Grétry and the Growth of Opera-Comique* (Cambridge University Press, 1986) and *Opera in the Age of Rousseau* (Cambridge University Press, 2012), and editor of *The Cambridge Companion to Grand Opera* (Cambridge University Press, 2003) and also of *The Music of Simon Holt* (The Boydell Press, 2017).

Popular Opera in Eighteenth-Century France

Music and Entertainment before the Revolution

DAVID CHARLTON

Emeritus, Royal Holloway, University of London

Shaftesbury Road, Cambridge CB2 8EA, United Kingdom

One Liberty Plaza, 20th Floor, New York, NY 10006, USA

477 Williamstown Road, Port Melbourne, VIC 3207, Australia

314–321, 3rd Floor, Plot 3, Splendor Forum, Jasola District Centre, New Delhi – 110025, India

103 Penang Road, #05–06/07, Visioncrest Commercial, Singapore 238467

Cambridge University Press is part of Cambridge University Press & Assessment, a department of the University of Cambridge.

We share the University's mission to contribute to society through the pursuit of education, learning and research at the highest international levels of excellence.

www.cambridge.org
Information on this title: www.cambridge.org/9781009011754

DOI: 10.1017/9781009026734

© David Charlton 2022

This publication is in copyright. Subject to statutory exception and to the provisions of relevant collective licensing agreements, no reproduction of any part may take place without the written permission of Cambridge University Press & Assessment.

First published 2022
First paperback edition 2023

A catalogue record for this publication is available from the British Library

Library of Congress Cataloging-in-Publication data
Names: Charlton, David, 1946– author.
Title: Popular opera in eighteenth-century France / David Charlton.
Description: Cambridge ; New York : Cambridge University Press, 2021. | Includes bibliographical references and index.
Identifiers: LCCN 2021034474 (print) | LCCN 2021034475 (ebook) | ISBN 9781316515846 (hardback) | ISBN 9781009026734 (ebook)
Subjects: LCSH: Opera – France – 18th century. | Musical theater – France – History – 18th century.
Classification: LCC ML1727.3 .C53 2021 (print) | LCC ML1727.3 (ebook) | DDC 782.1/0944–dc23
LC record available at https://lccn.loc.gov/2021034474
LC ebook record available at https://lccn.loc.gov/2021034475

ISBN   978-1-316-51584-6   Hardback
ISBN   978-1-009-01175-4   Paperback

Cambridge University Press & Assessment has no responsibility for the persistence or accuracy of URLs for external or third-party internet websites referred to in this publication and does not guarantee that any content on such websites is, or will remain, accurate or appropriate.

*To
Patricia*

One of the most intriguing and least understood aspects of the history of communication involves the power of melody.
Robert Darnton, *Poetry and the Police* (2010), 169

Imagine judging the Broadway revue of today on the basis solely of the printed dialogue! And what a task for the brow-beaten scholar of the twenty-second century to clarify for his breathless reader the countless topical or political allusions!
Edmond McAdoo Gagey, *Ballad Opera* (1937), 10

Contents

List of Illustrations   [*page* viii]
List of Tables   [x]
List of Examples   [xii]
Preface   [xv]
Acknowledgements   [xix]
Notes on the Text   [xxi]
List of Abbreviations   [xxiii]

1 Introduction   [1]

2 Music and Spoken Theatre   [27]

3 Music in Gherardi's Company   [46]

4 Singing and Acting at Home   [77]

5 Opéra-comique *en vaudevilles*   [100]

6 Experiences of Popular Theatre   [134]

7 Comic and Serious Themes   [156]

8 Performance as History   [184]

9 Musical Expansion   [208]

10 Italian Inroads: The King's Company   [236]

11 Six Methods of Synthesis   [262]

12 A 'Musico-Dramatic Art'   [290]

13 Conclusions   [310]

Stage Works Cited   [321]
Bibliography   [330]
Index   [357]

Illustrations

2.1 [Nicolas?] Bonard [Bonnart], engraved by François de Poilly the younger, frontispiece to Lesage, Fuzelier and d'Orneval, *Le Rémouleur d'amour*, in *Le Théâtre de la Foire* (Paris: Étienne Ganeau, 1724), V, 71. [*page 32*]

3.1 Franz Ertinger, frontispiece to Jean-François Regnard, *Les Filles errantes* in *Le Théâtre Italien de Gherardi* (Paris: Jean-Baptiste Cusson, Pierre Witte, 1700), III, 2. [47]

3.2 [Laurent?] Desmarets, engraved by Franz Ertinger, frontispiece to Charles Dufresny, *Pasquin et Marforio*, in *Le Théâtre italien de Gherardi* (Paris: Jean-Baptiste Cusson, Pierre Witte, 1700), VI, 598. [48]

4.1 François Robert Ingouf, *Charles Minart*. [81]

4.2 Pierre-Alexandre Monsigny, *Les Aveux indiscrets, Intermède* (Paris, c.1759, TP missing), pencil markings on pp. 41 and 58. [94]

4.3a Antoine Dauvergne, *Les Troqueurs* (Paris: L'Auteur, c.1753), p. 83. [96]

4.3b Farin de Hautemer, *Le Troc* (Paris: Duchesne, 1756), p. 56. [97]

5.1 Charles-Simon Favart, *La Chercheuse d'esprit*. Versailles, Bibliothèque municipale Ms. Mus. 198, pp. 6–7. [128]

6.1 Unsigned frontispiece to Thomas-Simon Gueullette, ed., *Théâtre des boulevards* (Mahon: Gilles Langlois, 1756), I. [137]

6.2 Philibert-Louis De Bucourt, *Annette et Lubin*. [148]

6.3 François Boucher, *Esquisse d'un décor de scène* (1744). Amiens, Musée de Picardie. [150]

6.4 [Nicolas?] Bonnart, engraved by François de Poilly the younger, frontispiece to Lesage and d'Orneval, *La Princesse de Carizme*, in *Le Théâtre de la Foire* (Paris, Étienne Ganeau, 1721), III, 95. [153]

7.1 [Joseph?] Perdoux, *The Woodman and Mercury*, in *La Fontaine's Fables* vol. I, translated by Robert Thomson (Paris: all the booksellers, c.1805). [164]

7.2 [Nicolas?] Bonnart, engraved by François de Poilly the younger, frontispiece to Lesage, d'Orneval and Autreau, *Les Amours de Nanterre* in *Le Théâtre de la Foire* (Paris: Étienne Ganeau, 1721), III, 269. [168]

7.3 Gabriel de Saint-Aubin, engraved by Augustin de Saint-Aubin, frontispiece to Michel-Jean Sedaine, *Le Jardinier et son seigneur* (Paris: C. Hérissant, 1761). [172]

12.1 Unsigned frontispiece to Robert Dodsley, *The King and the Miller of Mansfield* (London: the author, c.1750). [295]

Tables

1.1 Theatre troupes, 1673–1680. [*page* 4]
1.2 Disruptions to musical Fair theatre. [6]
2.1 Selected musical plays probably intended for the private reader and musician. [28]
2.2 Molière, Lully and mixed forms of French opera. [35]
3.1 Selected revivals seen at the restored Comédie-Italienne. [53]
3.2 Evolution of vaudeville usage in *TIG*. [64]
3.3 Melodies written for *TIG* that remained popular as *vaudevilles*. [69]
4.1 Early appearances of published opéra-comique materials for private use. [92]
5.1 Vaudevilles with the most irregular total number of bars in Connon and Evans's *Anthologie de pièces du Théâtre de la Foire*. [105]
5.2 Narrative scenes in 'royal operas'. [125]
5.3 Sentimental scenes in 'royal operas'. [126]
6.1 Theatre admission prices given in French and contemporary English currency. [141]
8.1 First and subsequent years in which Charles-François Pannard's opéras-comiques were given. [187]
8.2 Operas not seen after 1745, ordered by the period of years in which they were viable. [187]
8.3 Operas not seen after 1745, ordered by the period of years in which they were viable. [188]
8.4 Operas revived after 1751 but not after the merging of companies in 1762, ordered by the period of years in which they were viable. [189]
8.5 Operas revived after 1761 at the Comédie-Italienne or elsewhere, ordered by the period of years in which they were viable. [189]
8.6 Italian *intermezzi* given at the Paris Opéra compared with French works derived from them. [194]
8.7 Selected opéras-comiques and *parodies* in the approach to the merger between the Opéra Comique and the Comédie-Italienne in February 1762. [196]

8.8 Long-lived works created in the final decade of Fair theatre, ordered by the number of years in which they were viable. [200]
8.9 All known records of musical comedies at the Fair theatres, including marionette operas and parodies with music, but not ballets. [201]
8.10 First-period works revived during the 1720s and 1730s, showing original and revival years. [202]
8.11 Apparent reversal of the ratio between new operas and revived operas at the Fair theatres up to the point of closure in mid-1745. [202]
8.12 Most-frequently revived operas between 1740 and summer 1745. [203]
8.13 Ratio of new to revived operas between 1752 and 1762. [204]
8.14 Revivals of older works between 1752 and 1762 ordered by period of origin. [205]
9.1 Online: new music in popular operas in *TF*.
9.2 Named composers in Fair theatre pieces, ordered by number of works to which identified contributions were made. [210]
9.3 Set pieces in first-period *TF* operas, with vocal clef indications. [214]
9.4 Selected Fair theatre works correlated with Concertos comiques or other music by Corrette, ordered by date. [219]
9.5 Selected showpiece uses of 'Jupin du grand matin'. [229]
9.6 Musical and dramatic focus points in Favart. [231]
10.1 Online: Mouret's arias and duets in Italian for the Comédie-Italienne.
10.2 Notable singers at the Comédie-Italienne, listed chronologically. [241]
10.3 Key premieres in 1753. [253]
10.4 Summary of numerical differences between Bouffon versions of four *intermezzi* at the Opéra and their derived *comédies mêlées d'ariettes* at the Comédie-Italienne. [260]
11.1 Music and action in *Ninette à la cour*. [272]

Examples

3.1 Anonymous, 'Ne veux-tu pas, Perrette', *Arlequin et Scaramouche vendangeurs*, *TIG* I, 16–17. [*page* 56]

3.2 Anonymous, 'Une fille bien apprise', Jean-François Regnard, *La Naissance d'Amadis*, Sc. 1, *TIG* V, 100–1. [58]

3.3 Jean-Claude Gillier, 'Époux qui possédez', Jean-François Regnard and Charles Dufresny, *La Foire Saint-Germain*, III/4, *TIG* VI, 303. [60]

3.4 Traditional, 'Lanturlu', Jean Palaprat, *Arlequin Phaéton*, I/1, *TIG*, III, 450. [65]

3.5 Traditional, 'Pierre Bagnolet', Jean-François Regnard and Charles Dufresny, *La Foire Saint-Germain*, III/4, *TIG*, VI, 303–4. [67]

3.6 Anonymous, 'La verte jeunesse', Jean-François Regnard and Charles Dufresny, *La Baguette de Vulcain*, Sc. 5, *TIG*, IV, 297. [68]

3.7 Anonymous, 'On dit que le médecin', Charles Dufresny and Brugière de Barante, *Pasquin et Marforio*, I/7, *TIG*, VI, 617, stanza 4. [74]

3.8 Anonymous, 'Mère dont la fille est jeunette', Charles Dufresny and Brugière de Barante, *Pasquin et Marforio*, III/1, *TIG*, VI, 638. [75]

4.1 François Rebel and François Francœur, *Pyrame et Thisbé*, II/4, Chaconne, arranged anonymously in *Recueil d'airs*, issue 7. [84]

4.2 Jean-Claude Gillier, 'L'uceletto non è matto' in *Divertissement de la Comédie des Folies Amoureuse[s] De la Composition de Mr Gillier*. [90]

4.3 Jean-Claude Gillier, *Divertissement de la Comédie des Folies Amoureuse[s] De la Composition de Mr Gillier*, 'Danse dialogué entre Momus et la Folie'. [90]

5.1 (a) *Air*, 'Quand le péril est agréable', parodied from Jean-Baptiste Lully, *Atys*, I/3. (b) *Air*, 'Non, je ne feray pas', parodied from Jean-Baptiste Lully, *Isis*, II/7. [101]

5.2 *Air*, 'Quitte ta houlette', parodied from Jean-Baptiste Lully, *Le Divertissement royal*. [104]

5.3 *Air*, 'Menuet d'Hésione', from André Campra, *Hésione*, Prologue. [111]

5.4 Anonymous *air*, 'J'entends déjà le bruit des armes' from Ballard, *La Clef* (1717), 191 in Lesage, *Les Petits-maîtres*, Sc. 5. [112]

5.5   Air, 'Menuet d'Exaudet', from André-Joseph Exaudet, *Sonate en trio*, Œuvre II/1 (1751–2), 'Minuetto Gratioso'. [119]
5.6   Lesage and d'Orneval, *La Reine du Barostan*, Sc. 8: Air. [123]
5.7   Lesage and d'Orneval, *Achmet et Almanzine*, III/10. Air. [127]
5.8   Charles-Simon Favart, *La Chercheuse d'esprit*, Sc. 12, F-V, Mus. Ms. 198, p. 98, *Air*. [129]
5.9   (a) 'Dans notre village chacun vit content', *Air* 101 in *TF* I, *Table*, 27 (R/I/121). (b) Charles-Simon Favart, *La Chercheuse d'esprit*, Sc. 8, F-V, Mus. Ms. 198, p. 78, *Air*, 'Dans notre village chacun vit content'. [130]
5.10 'Ces filles sont si sottes', Air 52 in *PNTI* (1738), II, *Table*, 14–15, compared with Charles-Simon Favart, *La Chercheuse d'esprit*, Sc. 2, F-V, Mus. Ms. 198, pp. 25–6. [130]
5.11 Final bars of 'Que je regrette mon amant', *Air* 76 in *TF* VIII, *Table*, 31 (R/II/388) compared with Charles-Simon Favart, *La Chercheuse d'esprit*, Sc. 10, F-V, Mus. Ms. 198, p. 91. [131]
5.12 Final bars of *Air*, 'Je sommeille' in Charles-Simon Favart, *La Chercheuse d'esprit* (Paris: Veuve Allouel, 1741), *Table*, 3–4 compared with version in Sc. 15 of F-V, Mus. Ms. 198, pp. 107–8. [132]
9.1   Louis de Lacoste, 'Comme les Dieux' in Lesage, *La Princesse de Carizme*, II/9. [216]
9.2   Louis de Lacoste, second half of 'Comme les Dieux' distorted by incipient madness in Lesage, *La Princesse de Carizme*, II/11. [217]
9.3   Anonymous, 'Le Père Barnaba', *vaudeville*. [222]
9.4   Michel Corrette, *La Béquille du Père Barnaba*, XIIIe *concerto comique* (Paris: l'Auteur, n.d.), I, showing the 'crutch' theme. [222]
9.5   Michel Corrette, *La Béquille du Père Barnaba*, XIIIe *concerto comique*, III, opening. [223]
9.6   Michel Corrette, *L'Allure*, IIe *concerto comique* (Paris: l'Auteur, etc., n.d.), I, opening, words added from Denis Carolet, *L'Allure, Pièce en un acte*, Sc. 1 (*TF* IX/2, 177 (R/II/601)). [223]
9.7   Alexis Piron, *Le Fâcheux veuvage*, I/11, [*Air*], 'Parodie de l'ouverture de Bellérophon'. [228]
9.8   *Air*, 'Menuet de la Chasse' in Alexis Piron, *Le Caprice*, Sc. 12. [228]
9.9   'Jupin du [de] grand matin' in Denis Carolet, *Le Réveil de l'Opéra Comique*, Sc. 5, *TF* IX/2, 13 (R/II/559) and *Table*, 2 (R/II/691). [229]
9.10 Charles-Simon Favart, *La Chercheuse d'esprit*, Sc. 12, F-V, Mus. Ms. 198, pp. 100-1, *Air*, 'Et la Belle le trouva bon'. [231]
9.11 *Air*, 'Sotto Mettode' = François Couperin, 'Les Calotins et les Calotines', in Charles-Simon Favart, *Le Bal bourgeois* (La Haye: Pierre Gosse Junior, 1750), Sc. 10. [232]

9.12 Jean-Joseph Mouret, *Air* 80, 'Ah! que la forêt de Cythère' parodied in Charles-Simon Favart, *Les Nymphes de Diane* ([Bruxelles], 1748), Sc. 19. [234]

10.1 (a) Jean-Joseph Mouret, 'Sin dal profondo di flegetonte' in the divertissement for Louis-André Riccoboni, *Colombine mari par complaisance* (1719: lost), opening ritornello. Source: Mouret, *Premier Recueil des Divertissemens*, 149. (b) Jean-Joseph Mouret, 'Sin dal profondo di flegetonte', excerpt from middle section of the aria. [240]

10.2 Carlo Sodi, *Baiocco et Serpilla, parodie françoise du Joueur* (Paris: Aux adresses ordinaires, n.d.), III, 48. Duo, 'Règne sur mon âme', final bars. [255]

11.1 Gioacchino Cocchi, *La scaltra governatrice*, III/2, aria 'Gli Sbirri già l'aspettano'. [264]

11.2 Andrea Bernasconi, 'È spècie di tormento' as part of Rinaldo Di Capua, *La zingara* (*La Bohémienne*, Paris, Aux adresses ordinaires, n.d.), II/1, 44–9. French text from Favart, *La Bohémienne* (Paris: De la Chevardiere, n.d.), II/2, 53–8. [270]

11.3 Giuseppe Sellitto, *Il cinese rimpatriato*, 'Io sono una Donzella' parodied by Charles-Simon Favart in *Ninette à la cour*, I/4 as a dialogue duet, 'Tout va vous rendre hommage'. [274]

11.4 Jean-Jacques Rousseau, *Le Devin du village*, opening bars of six solos showing five characteristic style features and the prevalence of a falling stepwise figure. [277]

11.5 Egidio Duni, *Le Retour au village*, I/6, 'Auroit-on cru cela?', 40. [283]

11.6 Egidio Duni, *Le Peintre amoureux de son modèle*, I/2, 17, 'Me promenant près du logis'. [286]

11.7 Egidio Duni, *Le Peintre amoureux de son modèle*, I/2, 24, 'Quand j'étois jeunette, fillette'. [287]

12.1 Pierre-Alexandre Monsigny, *Le Roi et le fermier*, III/12, 148, 'Que le Soleil dans la plaine'. [303]

Preface

I never met the great democratiser of opera Edward J. Dent, but I wish that I had. For a 'long period', he wrote, 'there were two sorts of opera in existence, the formal ceremonious opera of the court, and [...] the comic opera of the people'.[1] Only the second category is covered in this book: opera and music theatre given in medium-sized venues. I will follow a roughly chronological path with themed chapters about the period between Jean-Baptiste Molière and André Grétry (dubbed the 'Molière of French music'[2]), whose career began twenty years before the Revolution. This book is introductory in two ways: first, it asks straightforward questions, and second, the subject it defines is in great need of wider introduction. Topics covered include staging, singing, storylines, performance patterns and making theatre at home. How might this music have sounded? How did the spoken dialogue fit with the music?

Music frequently plays a role in Molière's comedies; comedy and music together were the ingredients of popular opera. By avoiding all-sung works, this book fills in numerous gaps in the history of opera, building on others' research as well as my own.[3] It considers that popular operas belong on the historical map. Rejecting the 'skewed historical picture' offered by Charles Burney, Michael Burden observed that 'for the majority of English theatre-goers, "real opera" *had* spoken dialogue, and was a genre they preferred'.[4] The same sort of preference in France caused a crisis in the 1750s. It followed eighteen months of performances by the Bouffons at the Paris Opéra, familiarising the public with *intermezzi* and adaptations of Italian comic operas.

'Opéra-comique' was the common term for French popular opera, liked by all classes and sometimes performed in London. This book's many connections across the Channel start with Richard Baxter, famous as

---

[1] Edward Dent, *Opera* (Harmondsworth: Penguin, 1940), 32–3.
[2] J.-N. Bouilly, cited in Arnold, *Grétry's Operas*, 170.
[3] See Bibliography for studies by Thomas Betzwieser, Julia Doe, Michael Fend, Erica Levenson, Nathalie Rizzoni, Vanessa Rogers, Herbert Schneider, Jama Stilwell, Downing A. Thomas and others.
[4] Burden, 'The lure of aria', 385, citing Charles Burney, *A General History of Music*, IV (1789).

Arlequin in Paris, and end with an opera adapted from a Drury Lane play. Instead of speculating about the unknowable feelings and frameworks through which people enjoyed these works, I have proposed the idea of a 'binary identity': popular opera as both public and private, made at home everywhere in France. My own observations about specific performances appear in Chapters 2 and 5.

After falling out of the international repertory, pre-Revolution popular opera was discovered by a young Thomas Beecham in 1904: 'One evening I went to hear Grétry's *Richard Cœur de lion* at the Opéra Comique, and, at once attracted by this delicate and delightful music, set out to acquire all I could of the composer's work as well as that of his contemporaries.' Beecham's next remarks are significant: he detected no Italian influence, even though Italian music helped to form this style. In its last three chapters, therefore, this book explains the formation and uniqueness of the new operatic medium:

> This music is markedly individual in that it owes little or nothing to any ancestry but that of the popular song of old France, which in turn took its character from the idiom and accent of the language. [...] Having plenty of time on my hands, I spent some of it in the Bibliothèque Nationale, transcribing those works.[5]

Before the arrival of the Bouffons in 1752, opéra-comique thrived at seasonal performances at the Paris Fairs. One of this book's tasks is to show how these unexplored decades fit together with the better-researched post-Bouffon years, namely the three decades preceding the Revolution. Music at the 'Fair theatres' (usually just outside the actual Fairs) was as varied as the vast range of subject matter in popular opera. Jama Stilwell has discussed the *merveilleux* (supernatural) and the influence of *commedia dell'arte*,[6] but the tradition of Molière's comedy was also basic, rooted in the critique of society. For this book, *parodies* (popular take-offs of serious operas) are not 'the heart of the enterprise':[7] its aim is to discover popular opera's independent identity and development.

Scott McMillin wrote that even if 'most musicals [...] are not overtly political', their aesthetic 'looks towards the political, not with the direct glare of Brecht [...] but with full regard for the principles of difference that we have been finding at the heart of the genre'.[8] That goes too for the repertories in this book. Even 'abduction' operas might contain 'correctives

---

[5] Sir Thomas Beecham, *A Mingled Chime. Leaves from an Autobiography* (London: Hutchinson, 1944), 52–3.
[6] Stilwell, 'A New View', 55–6.   [7] Harris-Warrick, *Dance and Drama*, 256.
[8] McMillin, *The Musical as Drama*, 199–200.

for vice and licentiousness' or 'veiled (or not so veiled) critiques' of French 'political and social structures'.[9]

In some ways there are similarities between early popular opera and musicals. The use of pre-existing melodies in earlier popular opera (including the type of song called *vaudeville*) anticipates the idea of *Mamma Mia!*[10] But if complete source materials are missing, what are the best ways of discussing musical theatre of the past? Much further enquiry is needed into what earlier opéra-comique was like, musically and dramatically. The enormous potential for this was summarised by Erica Levenson: the 'dizzying challenge' of tracking down popular tunes; the provision of editions and recordings to repair our common neglect of 'popular entertainments unattached to a canonic musical figure'. At the same time, popular music and its theatre attract by 'their engagement with the social and political issues of a particular moment in history'.[11]

Some theory is found scattered about this book, yet a near absence of contemporary discourse about popular theatre was the unfortunate rule for France. *Philosophes* and journalists made up for lost time in the late 1750s (still disparaging *vaudevilles*), and Chapter 12 addresses some of their observations. The method of working from first principles allows one to gradually re-enact the pieces, albeit without understanding all their jokes or knowing how coarse or subtle their acting was. The legacy of Alain-René Lesage and Jacques-Philippe d'Orneval, *Le Théâtre de la Foire*, preserves only the cleaned-up face of popular opera. Yet Lesage was a genius and his dedication to this medium urgently requires discussion.[12]

*

English translations of titles of stage works are given on their first appearance in a chapter and are also found in the complete list of stage works on pages 321–9. There are descriptions of *Le Théâtre italien de Gherardi* in Chapter 3 and *Le Théâtre de la Foire* in Chapter 9. Various online resources for this book are listed in the Notes on the Text, and Chapter 10 is linked to a new edition of the 1729 *parodie*, *Le Joueur*, which is accessed similarly from www.cambridge.org/9781316515846. Original French texts of quotations translated in this book are available here too.

Popular Opera complements two books forming part of the same project: the *catalogue raisonné* of musical stage works at the Opéra Comique;[13] and my

---

[9] Stilwell, 'A New View', 81. [10] See 'Jukebox musical' in *Wikipedia* (29 Nov. 2019).
[11] Levenson, 'Traveling Tunes', 11–12. [12] Striker, 'Theatre of Lesage' dates from 1968.
[13] Between 1762 and 1972: Wild*TOC*.

Opera in the Age of Rousseau, abbreviated as *OAR*. The project continues with a planned open-access database of popular opera and its performances to be available from ObTIC (*Observatoire des textes, des idées et des corpus*) edited by Martin Wåhlberg (University of Trondheim) at https://obtic.sorbonne-universite.fr/projet/revolutionary-opera-comique.

Acknowledgements

Friends and colleagues have been generous with answering requests for materials and information, sometimes books, dissertations and iconographical material. I hope to have done them justice, perhaps especially Kent M. Smith (1947–2000), who entrusted his friends with his pioneering thesis on Duni. Underlying multiple aspects of this book's research is the enormous contribution of Herbert Schneider in uncovering, evaluating and publishing new sources for the history of opéra-comique in Europe. He has encouraged this project from the start through both generosity and friendship.

For information, helpful discussions and gifts I thank Annelies Andries, R. J. Arnold, Katherine Astbury, Anne Birberick, Daniel Brandenburg, Bruce Alan Brown, Noël Burch, Donald Burrows, Tim Carter, Jan Clarke, Derek Connon, Elisabeth Cook, Nicholas Cronk, Tili Boon Cuillé, Mark Darlow, Emanuele De Luca, Katharine Ellis, Annegret Fauser, Matthieu Franchin, Jonathan Godsall, Lesley Gould, Laurent Guillo, Catherine Harbor, Rebecca Harris-Warrick, Susan Harvey, Sarah Hibberd, Marian Hobson, Jonathan Huff, Jean-Luc Impe, Janet L. Johnson, Ulla Kölving, Judith le Blanc, Mark Ledbury, Raphaëlle Legrand, Sarah McCleave, Jean Mongrédien, Ruth Müller-Lindenberg, Andreas Münzmay, Barbara Nestola, Kevin O'Regan, Karin Pendle, Andrew Pinnock, Bertrand Porot, Dominique Quéro, Rudolf Rasch, Philip Robinson, Vanessa L. Rogers, Stephen Rose, Françoise Rubellin, Julian Rushton, Paolo Russo, Pierre Saby, Lionel Sawkins, Hendrick Schulze, Denis Smalley, Blake Stevens, Patrick Taïeb, Colin Timms, Jacqueline Waeber, Martin Wåhlberg, John Warrack, Paul Watt, William Weber, Arnold Whittall and Bruce Wood. My apologies are tendered for any inadvertent omissions.

With great generosity Derek Connon and Michael O'Dea read the complete text of the book. Several chapters were scrutinised by Michael Fend, Janet Johnson and Marcie Ray. My thanks to them all for their improvements, and to CUP's own readers, cannot be too warmly expressed.

Julia Doe assisted in many ways, including facilitating my access to Grout's dissertation and sharing facsimiles of documents located by her in the Archives Nationales. John Romey transformed my work on Gherardi by sharing his source materials; Nathalie Rizzoni located a Lesage manuscript, transcribed for me Pannard's manuscript prologue to *Ma Mie Margot*, and gave much help and advice. Susan Harvey presented me with her edition of *La Grand'mére amoureuse, parodie d'Atys*; Yves Jaffrès sent me his scores of Corrette's *Concertos comiques*; Clive Scott made possible full access to *Le Théâtre de la Foire* in book form; Richard Langham Smith made good the literary deficiencies of the capital; Michael O'Dea made me gifts of the *Mémoires secrets*, other materials and his intellectual support. Michel Noiray pointed me to Chamfort's *Dictionnaire dramatique*, discussed ideas and alerted me to many sources. Michael Fend discussed problems and prodded me into action at a key moment. Graham Sadler's generosity, knowledge, patience and fifty-year friendship have been at all times a reminder of what humanity and good fortune are. Colin Homiski (formerly London University Library, Senate House) was of great and unique help. I thank all these friends and colleagues, with special mention of Peter Turner and Hannah Godfrey too for their meticulous bibliographical and database work in the early stages.

My gratitude goes to colleagues who invited me to their conferences, from which I have always benefited: Paolo Russo at Parma; Randi Selvik at Trondheim; the 'Performing Premodernity' research group at Stockholm; Franck Salaün and Patrick Taïeb at Montpellier; Charlotte Loriot at Paris; Martin Wåhlberg at Trondheim; Emanuele De Luca and Andrea Fabiano also at Paris; and Bertrand Porot at Reims.

Acknowledgement is made that the Regents of the University of California granted leave to copy C. D. Brenner's *The Théâtre Italien* (1961); the University of East Anglia Library did that work on my behalf and, much later, made *Le Théâtre de la Foire* permanently available to me. Support from Royal Holloway, University of London, has been indispensable, as has that of Ric Lloyd (musicprep.co.uk) in preparing the music examples.

My engagement with ideas explored in this book owes much to J. Allan Benstead, senior English master at Ealing Grammar School in the 1960s, whose generosity, knowledge and skill brought theatre to life – literally.

[I am] firmly persuaded that every time a man smiles, – but much more so, when he laughs, that it adds something to this Fragment of Life.

Sterne, *Tristram Shandy*

Notes on the Text

'Opéra-comique' denotes the genre and 'Opéra Comique' denotes the company.

Primary sources, print and manuscript, are given in relevant footnotes. Many are available in digital collections such as *Gallica* (Bibliothèque nationale de France: gallica.bnf.fr) or *Internet Archive* (archive.org).

Pre-1800 publications cited in footnotes are given date(s) in parentheses.

Authors, composers and translated titles of stage works mentioned in the book are found in the list of Stage Works Cited, pp. 321–9. The general index includes only their title.

The *Théâtre italien de Gherardi* (abbreviated *TIG*) is referenced exclusively to Gherardi's six-volume edition of 1700, issued under his control. Available on *Gallica*.

Text or music in *Le Théâtre de la Foire* (abbreviated *TF*) is referenced first to the ten-volume issue of 1737 and then to its reprint edition (Geneva: Slatkine, 1968). Each volume concluded with a separately paginated '*Table des airs*'. Thus, *TF* VI, *Table*, 2 (R/II/134) means that an *air* is on page 2 of the *Table* in volume VI of the 1737 issue, corresponding to page 134 of vol. II of the reprint edition.

The online depository for this book is www.cambridge.org/9781316515846. It contains the first modern edition of *Le Joueur* (1729), with an introduction; Table 9.1 (a handlist of new music in popular operas in *Le Théâtre de la Foire*); Table 10.1 (a list of Mouret's arias and duets in Italian for the Comédie-Italienne); an annotated list of the contents of *Le Théâtre de la Foire*; and French-language texts whose translations appear in the book.

Principal online sources consulted:

Burney Collection Newspapers: http://find.galegroup.com/bncn/retrieve.

CESAR: *Calendrier électronique des spectacles sous l'ancien régime et sous la révolution*: cesar.huma-num.fr/cesar2/home.php?lang=french (https://cesar.huma-num.fr).

De Luca, Emanuele, *Il repertorio della Comédie-Italienne di Parigi (1716–1762). Le répertoire de la Comédie-Italienne de Paris (1716–1762)* (Les *savoirs des acteurs italiens*, Digital Collection, ed. Andrea Fabiano) (Paris: IRPMF, 2011). https://hal.inria.fr/IRPMF

Dictionnaires d'autrefois. French Dictionaries of the 17th, 18th, 19th and 20th Centuries: https://artfl-project.uchicago.edu.

Diderot, Denis and Jean Le Rond d'Alembert, eds, *Encyclopédie ou Dictionnaire raisonné des sciences, des arts et des métiers*, 17 vols. (Paris: 1751–72) ed. Robert Morrissey as *ARTFL Encyclopédie* (https://encyclopedie.uchicago.edu).

Le Gazetier universel: French eighteenth-century periodicals are gathered at http://gazetier-universel.gazettes18e.fr/periodiques. The *Mercure de France* is also found on gallica.bnf.fr.

Grove Music Online: oxfordmusiconline.com/grovemusic.

Opéra Baroque: https://operabaroque.fr

RISM (Répertoire International des Sources Musicales): opac.rism.info.

Sgard, Jean, ed., *Dictionnaire des journalistes*, rev. ed.: Voltaire Foundation http://dictionnaire-journalistes.gazettes18e.fr/ Copyright © 2015–2019 IHRIM UMR 5317 / MSH-LSE USR 2005.

Le Théâtre de la Foire à Paris. Textes et documents established by Barry Russell © 1996–2000 www.theatrales.uqam.ca/foires.

Theaville: Database of *vaudevilles* founded by Françoise Rubellin, published by the Centre d'étude des théâtres de la Foire et de la Comédie-Italienne (CETHEFI): www.theaville.org.

Online audiovisual source used in Chapter 10:

Antonio Palomba, Pietro Auletta, *Il maestro di musica*, 1954 television performance in German with Graziella Sciutti, Fritz Wunderlich and Walter Berry conducted by Hans Swarovsky: www.youtube.com/watch?v=W6IdzyVPRB4.

Abbreviations

Note: Books are more fully described in the Bibliography.

ABDA:	Philip H. Highfill Jr. and others: *A Biographical Dictionary of Actors, Actresses, Musicians, Dancers, Managers and Other Stage Personnel in London, 1660–1800* (1973–93).
AL:	[Élie-Catherine Fréron], *L'Année littéraire* (1754 etc.).
AN:	Paris, Archives Nationales.
BCN:	Burney Collection Newspapers.
BNF:	Bibliothèque Nationale de France.
CESAR:	*Calendrier électronique des spectacles sous l'ancien régime et sous la révolution* (https://cesar.huma-num.fr).
CF:	Comédie-Française.
CI:	Comédie-Italienne.
COJ:	*Cambridge Opera Journal*.
Corr. litt.:	F. M. Grimm *et al.*, *Correspondance littéraire*.
DOP:	S. Bouissou, P. Denécheau and F. Marchal-Ninosque, *Dictionnaire de l'Opéra de Paris sous l'Ancien Régime*, 4 vols. (2019–20).
F-LYm:	Lyon, Bibliothèque municipale.
F-Pn (Mus):	Paris, Bibliothèque Nationale, Département de la musique.
F-Po:	Paris, Bibliothèque-Musée de l'Opéra.
F-Po, *Registres*:	*Registres de l'Opéra Comique*, also on *Gallica*.
F-V:	Versailles, Bibliothèque municipale.
FSG:	Foire Saint-Germain.
FSL:	Foire Saint-Laurent.
GB-Lbl:	London, British Library.
Grove:	Grove Music Online (www.oxfordmusiconline.com/grovemusic).
JAMS:	*Journal of the American Musicological Society*.
Mémoires secrets:	Christophe Cave and Suzanne Cornand, eds., *Mémoires secrets pour servir à l'histoire de la*

	République des Lettres en France (2009 etc., in progress).
Mercure:	*Mercure de France*.
MGG:	Ludwig Finscher, ed., *Die Musik in Geschichte und Gegenwart* (Second edition, 2002).
NG/2:	Stanley Sadie, ed., *The New Grove Dictionary of Music and Musicians* (Second edition, 2001).
NGO:	Stanley Sadie, ed., *The New Grove Dictionary of Opera*, 4 vols. (1992).
NOHM:	Egon Wellesz, Frederick Sternfeld, eds, *The New Oxford History of Music*, VII (1973).
OAR:	David Charlton, *Opera in the Age of Rousseau* (2013).
OC:	Opéra Comique
PNTI:	*Parodies du Nouveau Théâtre Italien*: First edition (3 vols., 1731) and Second edition (4 vols., 1738).
RISM:	*Répertoire international des Sources Musicales*.
RMFC:	*Recherches sur la Musique française classique* (*La vie musicale en France sous les rois bourbons*, 2e série) (Paris: Picard, 1960–).
TF:	Alain-René Lesage and Jacques-Philippe d'Orneval, eds., *Le Théâtre de la Foire*, 10 vols. (Paris: Gandouin, 1737). Reprint references (e.g. R/I/7) are to the two-volume edition (Geneva: Slatkine, 1968) containing this ten-volume edition. More detailed information is in the Bibliography and Cordier, *Essai bibliographique*.
TIG:	*Le Théâtre Italien de Gherardi*, 6 vols. (Paris: Jean-Baptiste Cusson and Pierre Witte, 1700).
TP:	Title page.
WildTOC:	Nicole Wild and David Charlton, *Théâtre de l'Opéra-Comique, Paris: Répertoire musical 1762–1972*.

1 | Introduction

Popular opera deserves a history, if only to reveal the origins of today's flourishing musical theatre. Operas with spoken dialogue originated in Paris as well as London some years before *The Beggar's Opera*.[1] In both countries a tradition of social critique was inscribed from the first. The *vaudeville* tradition has changed, but its roots are not actually remote: Marie-Justine Favart, the legendary singer, writer and actress discussed in Chapter 10, created the role of Roxelane in *Soliman II*, a musical play by Charles-Simon Favart: 'The last Roxelane on stage was Madeleine Renaud (1900–94) [...] also one of the first performers in plays by Samuel Beckett (1906–89) and Marguerite Duras (1914–96).'[2]

One might, like Derek Scott, argue that *Die Zauberflöte* (*The Magic Flute*) – even with its spoken dialogue – would have been perceived at the time as an opera, not as a musical (in our sense).[3] Another viewpoint would regard it as a German-language opéra-comique. In either case its mixed musical styles, prose dialogue and moral discussions align it with works covered in this book.

Popular opera in the French capital was permeated by images of society and attended by a wide cross-section of citizens. One journalist in 1754 referred to 'amusing plays set to music', 'portraying the *mores* of our century'.[4] Sustained commercially, it was vulnerable to both market forces and anticompetitive politics. In 1762 it was ordered into the fold of state supervision, but then the cycle of exploration began again elsewhere.

Many differences are found between the worlds of 'opera' and of opera with spoken dialogue, though their origins were closely linked. There are crossover aspects (opéra-comique could be sung throughout in *vaudevilles*), but the rules are different: the nature of spoken dialogue must be considered alongside the music as a piece of drama potentially saying

---

[1] Rogers, 'John Gay'. For Germany, Spain and Sweden, see Keefe, ed., *Cambridge History of Eighteenth-Century Music*, 351, 417, 422.
[2] Moindrot, 'The "Turk" and the "Parisienne"', 429.   [3] Scott, 'Musical Theater(s)', 53.
[4] Chevrier, *Observations* (1755), 83, praising Jean-Joseph Vadé. All translations are by the present author unless otherwise mentioned. See www.cambridge.org/9781316515846 for original French texts.

something about the world. The acted scene joins with various musical forms. Dynamically, the media combine to form some kind of larger experience. They complement each other, successfully or otherwise.

David J. Levin and Reinhard Strohm have both written about understanding opera – as a whole – from a viewpoint fairly measuring literature and drama against music. In 1994 Levin's *Opera Through Other Eyes* presented a wide-ranging challenge to 'opera studies' orthodoxy that remains relevant, as is obvious from reading the *Oxford Handbook of Opera* (for example) two decades later.[5] *Handbook* chapters favour theory and performance criteria (e.g. 'voice', production, gender, costume) over literature, drama, theatre history or libretto studies.[6] Strohm's challenge in *Dramma per Musica* was politely explicit: its starting point was 'the conviction – or some may say, the prejudice – that Italian opera [in the earlier eighteenth century] was theatre in the first place and music in the second'. For an unfamiliar tradition like popular opera, it is yet more important to 'attempt to recover something like a collective feeling of being "within" [an] artistic tradition, through the analysis of social and repertorial patterns of which audiences would have been aware'.[7]

By the early nineteenth century, opéra-comique, now institutionalised, was unofficially 'the national genre' – not, however, for being known only in France: international success had conferred its cultural prestige on the genre. A hundred years before, travelling opéra-comique players had brought numerous pieces to London.[8] Favart premiered *Les Nymphes de Diane* in Brussels. After changing its style in the 1750s, popular opera travelled more: research projects now trace traditions in Spain, Russia, Germany, Poland, Sweden and the Caribbean.[9]

'Opéra-comique' became a common term, but there was always a desire for an alternative name to reflect its varied subject-matter and (see Chapters 11 and 12) its new musical language. 'Why do you call this theatre the Opéra Comique? It's not my fault. Who asks you to keep the name? What does it mean?' asked the writer and librettist, Nicolas-Étienne

---

[5] Levin lambasted 'a history of opera criticism that places music at the centre, and the suppression or banalization of the libretto that has enabled that criticism': *Opera through Other Eyes*, 2; Greenwald, ed., *Oxford Handbook*.
[6] Its most relevant chapters for our subject are by Thomas Betzwieser, Andreas Giger, Vincent Giroud, Derek Scott and John Warrack.
[7] Strohm, *Dramma per Musica*, vii–viii.   [8] Rogers, 'John Gay'; Levenson, 'Traveling Tunes'.
[9] Schneider, 'Übersetzungen'; Marica, 'Rappresentazioni'; Brown, 'La Diffusion'; Kleinertz, 'Zur Rezeption'; Evstratov, *Les Spectacles*; Beaurepaire et al., eds., *Moving Scenes*; Wolff, 'Lyrical diplomacy'; Clay, *Stagestruck*.

Framery.[10] The *Mercure de France* juggled with alternative labels: 'drama of the new type'; 'play mixed with singing'; 'intermède'; 'opéra bouffon'.[11] 'Popular opera' in this book refers to comedy where dialogue occurs in music as well as speech. The term is not limited to any subject-area, place or particular musical style. Opera in the inclusive sense is, in Howard Mayer Brown's words, 'a drama in which the actors sing some or all of their parts',[12] but this book makes a semantic distinction between 'operas' (with some or all dialogue sung) and 'musical comedies' or 'plays' lacking dialogue in music. The historical importance of this will emerge in many chapters to follow.

Ulrich Weisstein's article 'Librettology' considered opera as music theatre, plotted along a continuum between the 'Romantic' model (maximum weighting of musical elements) and the *King Arthur* model (maximum weighting of libretto elements).[13] His open concept could have clarified Herbert Lindenberger's point that 'tragic opera [...] resisted the movement towards contemporary middle-class themes' in the age of Diderot.[14] *Popular* opera certainly did address them.

*

Louis XIV's theatre companies all used music, and, following an established view, this book accepts that their repertories connect with the origins of popular opera; Chapters 2 and 3 will survey plays with music as developed in the seventeenth century.[15] Musical innovation was restricted from 1672 by certain royal orders favouring Jean-Baptiste Lully's monopoly of the Opéra (Académie Royale de Musique) at the expense of rivals. These politics must be understood in context: Louis XIV's suppression of long-standing structures and guilds in order to control cultural output. Effected by his First Minister, Jean-Baptiste Colbert (1619–83), this 'centralizing policy applied not only to the administrative and economic life of the kingdom: with the foundation of the various academies, it had already extended to the intellectual field'[16] – academies of dance (1661); inscriptions and belles-lettres (1663, discussing

---

[10] Framery, 'Sur le genre larmoyant' (1770), 5.
[11] Review of Anseaume and Duni's *Mazet*, *Mercure*, 1761, Oct./1, 192–3.
[12] Thus, only in the 'most narrowly conceived' sense should 'opera' mean an all-sung drama: 'Opera' in *Grove*.
[13] Weisstein, 'Librettology', referring to Dryden and Purcell's *King Arthur* (1691).
[14] Lindenberger, *Opera the Extravagant Art*, 52.
[15] Cucuel, *Les Créateurs*, 14–17; Grout, 'The Origins', *passim*.
[16] Mongrédien, *Daily Life*, 97. See Isherwood 'Centralization', 157–8, and *Music in the Service of the King*, Chap. 4.

the texts of operas); painting and sculpture (1664); music (1669) and architecture (1671).

The anticompetitive orders awarded to Lully when he gained the *privilège* of the Académie Royale de Musique were:

March 1672 '[No-one is permitted] to organise the performance of any piece that is completely sung, whether in French verse or in other languages, without the written permission of the said Sieur Lully.'[17]

12 August 1672 'His Majesty similarly forbids [all companies of actors in Paris] to use musicians [singers] in excess of six in number, or [to use] instrumentalists in excess of twelve in number.'[18]

22 April 1673 'His Majesty has revoked the permission [above] and permits [companies] to use only two singers and six players of string or other instruments. His Majesty expressly forbids all troupes [...] to use any external musicians, nor a larger number of instrumentalists for the entr'actes, nor any dancers, nor any orchestra, on pain of punishment for disobedience.'[19]

Following the death of Molière in February 1673, the king centralised public art once again by imposing a new theatre regime, merging two companies: see Table 1.1. There were to be four official troupes, two giving French plays. One of these, the King's company, shared an erstwhile opera house on the rue Guénégaud with the Italian players.[20] In fact, the Italians were in London from April to September 1673 at Charles II's invitation; they would visit London again in 1675.[21]

Table 1.1 Theatre troupes, 1673–1680.

(a) The King's company at the Hôtel Guénégaud (including actors from Molière's former company and the former Marais company).
(b) Biancolelli's Italian company, sharing the Guénégaud theatre with the players mentioned earlier.
(c) The Hôtel de Bourgogne theatre players.
(d) The Académie Royale de Musique (Opéra) at the Palais-Royal theatre.

---

[17] Ranum, 'Lully plays deaf', 24. Offenders would be fined 10,000 *livres* and have their equipment and theatre confiscated: Isherwood, 'Centralization', 167.
[18] AN, O^1.16, f° 142, ed. in Benoit, *Musiques de cour*, 38–9 and in La Gorce, 'Le Collier de perles'.
[19] Wood and Sadler, *French Baroque Opera*, 8, from AN, O^1.17, f°.72, ed. in Benoit, *ibid.*, 41.
[20] Built for Pierre Perrin and Robert Cambert (see Table 2.2), the Guénégaud held nearly 1,500 spectators: Scott, *Commedia dell'Arte*, 164–5; Mongrédien, *Daily Life*, 93, 99–103.
[21] Scott, *Commedia dell'Arte*, 158–9.

In 1680 the king formed the Comédie-Française by combining the Hôtel Guénégaud and Hôtel de Bourgogne companies. It was substantial enough to perform at Versailles and in Paris on the same day. Royal power could 'make its authority felt more easily' over this company,[22] having created 'a system of state subsidy in which specified kinds and numbers of performances were expected in return for subventions'.[23] Strategically freer, the Italian players received 15,000 *livres* a year plus allowances when playing at court.[24] Louis now passed the Hôtel de Bourgogne theatre over to them; after their suppression (see Chapter 3), it lay empty until the arrival of Luigi Riccoboni's new company in 1716 (see Chapter 10).

The Opéra, Comédie-Française and Comédie-Italienne supplied the monarch's operas, plays or Italian comedies in various palaces, yet life for them also meant competing for audiences: admission charges provided the income needed for their musicians, actors, staff, scenery and pension funds.[25] They had official status, but their degrees and definitions of monopoly were not comparable; this complicated their relations with independent Fair theatres and indeed with each other.[26]

The Opéra had a *directeur* with private financial backers but no regular subsidy: it was a devolved monopoly, able to make management and policy decisions with some independence.[27] Comédie-Française actors formed an association, players taking a direct stake in profits and losses. They were 'eager to see that their monopoly of [spoken] dialogue was respected'[28] and sued Fair theatres regularly, especially if the Opéra Comique attracted such crowds that spoken plays became unprofitable.

Popular opera took the name Opéra Comique and grew up outside the official matrix. It performed seasonally and was managed by entrepreneurs with financial backers. In winter it played during the Saint-Germain Fair (3 February until Palm Sunday) and in summer during the Saint-Laurent Fair (early July to September: exact dates varied). Jurisdiction over these Fairs belonged to their landowners, the Vincentian Order (Saint-Germain) and the clergy of Saint-Lazare.[29] Theatres identified with opéra-comique (see Chapter 6) were often outside the main Fairs with their booths,

---

[22] Mongrédien, *Daily Life*, 97.   [23] Scott, *Commedia dell'arte*, 241.
[24] Scott, *ibid.*, 157, 241; paid only 'when State finances allowed': Moureau, *Gherardi à Watteau*, 21.
[25] Lagrave, *Théâtre et public*, 21–55. Royal bailouts were infrequent.
[26] Lancaster, *Sunset*; Marcetteau-Paul, 'L'Obstacle'; Campardon, *Spectacles*, II, 256–85.
[27] But answerable to the monarch's relevant Secretary of State: see *OAR*, 59–60.
[28] Lancaster, *Sunset*, 22.
[29] Isherwood, *Farce and Fantasy*, 22–3; Fair theatre's evolution: Lindsay, *Dramatic Parody*, 11–26.

Table 1.2 Disruptions to musical Fair theatre. Marionette theatres continued when opéra-comique was prohibited.

Saint-Germain Fair (Winter)		Saint-Laurent Fair (Summer)	
1708–13	Restrictions: see Chapter 5.	1708–13	Restrictions: see Chapter 5.
1719–20[a]	No performances.	1719	No performances.
1722	Marionettes only.	1721	Comédie-Italienne arrives; there is some disruption.
1727–28, 1733	Marionettes only.	1722–23	Comédie-Italienne performs: marionettes only could compete.
1746–51	Closure, except for dance and pantomimes.	1745–51	Closure, except for dance and pantomimes.

[a] On 1720, see J.-M. Hostiou, 'Notice' to *L'Ombre de la Foire* in Rubellin, ed., *Théâtre de la Foire*, 221–41.

marionettes, jugglers and so on; however, rope-dancers originally formed the curtain-up to popular opera.[30]

Legal disputes between free-enterprise troupes and official ones meant disruptions and closures for the former: see Table 1.2.

From 1699 the Opéra began a profitable relationship with Fair theatre that will be seen at several points in this book. It leased out musical rights, normally to one entrepreneur at a time.[31] Fair theatre joked about its reliance on this income:

L'OPÉRA: Sans la Foire, sans ses ducats,   No Fairs, no funds:
   Croyez-vous que je puisse vivre? O how shall I survive without you?[32]

By 1730 the Opéra gained the permanent right to profit from these arrangements.[33] Without such shackles, marquis d'Argenson observed, popular opera would have evolved differently:

[1734] Pontau has resumed as leaseholder of the Opéra Comique, with an extra 3,000 *livres* he gives to the Opéra, which makes in total 15,000 *livres* paid each year: an unjust practice to oblige one theatre to pay tribute to another. It always affects the enjoyment of the public, which would otherwise have more sumptuous shows. Pontau is extremely suitable to direct this company.[34]

---

[30] Isherwood, *ibid.*, chaps. 2, 3, 4; Lancaster, *Sunset*, 317–20.
[31] Marcetteau-Paul, 'L'Obstacle'; Porot, 'Aux Origines', 288–9. The CF disputed this procedure.
[32] Lesage and d'Orneval, *Les Funérailles de la Foire* (1718): TF III, 403 (R/I/362), music from Lully's *Alceste*.
[33] 'Arrêt du Conseil', 1 June 1730: AN, E.2104, ff. 108–15, para. 2.
[34] D'Argenson, *Notices* (1725–57), II, 533.

Documents left by Louis Fuzelier set out the reasons why the Opéra Comique should be made a department of the Opéra;³⁵ this actually occurred in 1744–5, as Chapter 8 will show.

Opéra-comique's great achievements between 1714 and 1718 provoked its suppression, instigated by the Comédie Française. Then the new Italian company moved into the Saint-Laurent Fair during 1721 to 1723, seeking custom by giving spectacular *comédies-ballets* like *Danaé* and *Belphégor* while effectively blocking opéra-comique.³⁶ It is interesting to see how this stalemate was apparently resolved by the young Louis XV just after assuming power at the age of thirteen, 15 February 1723.

Eighteen months earlier, Louis was already being introduced to stage works (Molière, Lully, Italian *commedia*).³⁷ Thus, he might have seen opéras-comiques at the Palais-Royal on 2 October 1721 given for his aunt, the Duchess d'Orléans: in fact, these petitioned for the existential rights of Fair theatre.³⁸ Months later, his uncle the Regent visited the Saint-Germain Fair (after closing time) to see opéras-comiques that the Comédie-Française and the Parlement of Paris had obliged to be given by marionettes.³⁹

As the first king to be crowned since 1654, Louis was a celebrity whose actions were intently scrutinised. To coincide with ceremonies for his birthday and majority, two Fair companies prepared ambitious musical works for the winter season of 1723: *L'Endriague* (*The Dragon*) by Piron, featuring a monster that filled the stage space, and *Les Trois commères* (*Three Married Women*) by Alain-René Lesage, Jacques-Philippe d'Orneval and Alexis Piron involving a prologue, three acts, and elaborate stage sets, see pp. 151, 165.⁴⁰ For *L'Endriague* the Opéra's *directeur* backed the sponsors of a fourteen-year-old prodigy, Mlle Petitpas. Piron recalled that they 'showed off her voice to me and begged me to compose a piece for her'; '[Jean-Philippe] Rameau, then very little known, composed for my

---

³⁵ In 1740: Porot, 'Chants de Momus', 36–9.
³⁶ Details: Viollier, *Jean-Joseph Mouret*, 122–6; le Blanc, *Avatars*, 243ff. Lesage's 1722 comedies for the CI are at the end of *TF*, V.
³⁷ Antoine, *Louis XV*, 94. Louis, whose parents died when he was two, was educated in Paris under the guidance of the Regent, Philippe II d'Orléans (1674–1723).
³⁸ Francisque's troupe gave Lesage and d'Orneval's *Les Funérailles de la Foire* (*The Fair's Funeral*), *Le Rappel de la Foire à la vie* (*The Fair summoned back to life*) and *Le Régiment de la Calotte* (*The Calotte Regiment*); see TP of the latter, *TF* 1 (R/I/528) and Le Blanc, *Avatars*, 217–23.
³⁹ Lesage and Fuzelier, *L'Ombre du cocher poète* (*The Phantom of the Coachman Poet*), *Le Rémouleur d'amour* (*The Sharpener of Love*) and *Pierrot Romulus* (*TF*, V): Parfaict, *Mémoires* (1743), II, 4–6; Cucuel, 'Sources et documents', 255–6; Lindsay, *Dramatic Parody*, 22.
⁴⁰ Parfaict, *Mémoires* (1743), II, 12–13; *L'Endriague* was staged by Dolet & Laplace's troupe and *Les Trois commères* by that of Restier: see p. 138 for theatres.

sake the music of this piece' (he and Piron both hailed from Dijon), the idea being that it should be in a 'lofty style'.[41] This was Rameau's operatic premiere, in fact.

While not attending the Fair himself,[42] the young king contrived to send a signal: after arriving in Paris on 20 February, Louis made ceremonial visits and met elite functionaries but declined to attend either the Opéra or the Comédie-Française.[43] He might simply have feared boredom, having seen *Persée* after his coronation the previous October, but in Oscar Brocket's view it was a snub: 'After this, the official theatres did not dare to object, and although the order against the Fair theatres was not revoked [before 1724] it was universally ignored.'[44]

Thanks to the Orléans family, eleven or more opéras-comiques were given on the stage of the Opéra – adjoining their Palais-Royal – between 1718 and 1726, including *La Princesse de Carizme*, *Les Amours de Nanterre* and *Les Pélerins de la Mecque* (*The Princess of Carizme*, *The Loves of Nanterre*, *The Pilgrims from Mecca*). In fact, the duchess and her sisters-in-law visited the Opéra Comique at the Saint-Laurent Fair in 1725.[45]

Structures, Events and Systems

The plight of popular opera was that its genre and practice were different from those of official theatres and yet threatened those same theatres. We shall benefit, therefore, by understanding these frictions. An essay by Fabrizio Della Seta offers for this purpose the twin notions of 'structure' and 'event'.[46] 'While events are produced or experienced by specific subjects, structures are [...] long-term processes that occur independently.'[47] An idea from Wittgenstein can be useful in understanding performance traditions: 'the strength of the thread does not reside in the fact that some

---

[41] Piron, *Œuvres* (1776), III, 135; Sadler, 'Rameau, Piron', 14; Sylvie Bouissou, 'Petitpas' in *DOP*, IV, 130–2. Petitpas entered the Opéra in 1727. Neither this music by Rameau nor that for Piron's *Les Jardins de l'Hymen ou La Rose* has survived. Banned in 1726, it was successful later: see Tables 8.4, 8.12, 8.14; Sadler, *Rameau Compendium*, 170.

[42] Albert, *Théâtres de la Foire*, 144, misreads Barbier, *Chronique* (1718–63), I, 254, 259, followed by Brocket, 'Fair Theatres of Paris', 261.

[43] Antoine, *Louis XV*, 135–6; Barbier, *Chronique* (1718–63), I, 259.

[44] *Persée* seen on 9 Nov.: Antoine, *Louis XV*, 132. Brocket, 'Fair Theatres of Paris', 261.

[45] See *TF* between 1718 (four works) and 1726 (four works) with others in 1721 and 1725, always indicated on the TP. The duchess's 1725 visit: Parfaict, *Mémoires* (1743), II, 31.

[46] Della Seta, 'Some difficulties', 9.

[47] Reinhardt Koselleck, *Vergangene Zukunft* (Frankfurt, 1979), 146–8, trans. in Della Seta, 'Some difficulties', 9–10.

one fibre runs through its whole length, but in the overlapping of many fibres'.[48]

In opera, a 'structure' might be applied to theatre legislation, but an 'event' to a performance, a revival or act of government. These concepts are 'constructions made by the historian, who assembles fragments [and] decides what is a structure and what an event'.[49] To bring these together, one might apply knowledge concerning audience experience. In Chapter 8 we shall assemble data about events (revivals) to consider audience judgement or expectation, and the possibility of a 'core' repertory – evidence for a type of structural organisation.

The metaphor of 'threads' helps our narrative to overcome certain difficulties presented by an apparent break around 1753 when the musical nature of opéra-comique undoubtedly changed. Questioning this supposedly nodal point, Thomas Betzwieser's critique of earlier opera historians seems entirely correct: it centred on the unacceptable perspective that denies *vaudeville* a legitimate existence in the history of opera.[50] Wittgenstein's metaphor can be applied to various continuities around that point. First are the musical (vocal) forms and their functions that continued in some way after 1752; second are elements like subject matter, character, incident, social critique, typology and humour. And then there are the 'structures' of practice that were common to popular theatre – dance, scenery, *commedia* characters and probably a hundred now-lost conventions of acting and delivery.

'Threads' can exist in forms of words, for example, when denoting a genre. Being unofficial in genre, popular opera was legally heterogeneous, defined in non-Aristotelian terms, yet documents still observe semantic continuity. At the Fairs in 1717 they refer to 'song-and-dance shows with instruments', but after 1721 the consistent legal formula was '*vaudevilles*, dance, stage machines and instrumental music'.[51] In 1751 – see Chapter 8 – a modification of this wording signalled the intentions of the entrepreneur Jean Monnet.

In Paris, theatre structures were not unified, each company constituting a different 'system' by reason of its permitted form and separate repertory. As one result, for example, opéra-comique was impossible at the Comédie-Italienne; only the Opéra Comique had a leased-out permission to use music as its medium of comedies, alongside spoken dialogue. *Parodies* of

---

[48] Ludwig Wittgenstein, *Philosophical Investigations*, trans. G. E. M. Anscombe (Oxford, 1958), 32e, quoted in *ibid.*, 'Some difficulties', 7.
[49] *Ibid.*, 'Some difficulties', 11.   [50] Betzwieser, 'Zu einer Theorie', 135–52.
[51] Campardon, *Spectacles*, I, 95, 155; Marcetteau-Paul, '*L'Obstacle*', 265–75.

opera formed an expedient for the Comédie-Italienne: comedy with dialogue sung in *vaudevilles*. They were newly written yet not wholly new works.[52] In the online supplement to Chapter 10 an exceptional *parodie* from 1729 has been edited, with introduction: *Le Joueur* (*The Gambler*), the Comédie-Italienne's version of Orlandini's *Il giocatore*, recently given by visiting soloists at the Opéra.

But it is wrong to think of *ancien régime* Paris as a place where rules could not be challenged. It was a litigious place, and orders made by the king's Council were not always obeyed. With 'tacit permission' the Comédie-Italienne was able to give opéras-comiques from 1760, as Table 8.7 shows. But no new 'structure' was introduced when the Opéra Comique was merged with it in 1762: ministers instead contrived that the Comédie-Italienne should have access to the former's repertory, its five best singers and its entitlement to give operas with spoken dialogue. Armed by this 'event' the Comédie-Italienne was freed from the limitation that its musical pieces must be *parodies*, versions of some other opera, French or Italian. The 'threads' of the legal and practical definition of repertory remained unchanged, just as the company's inner structure (with profit-sharing members) also did.

Musical *parodies* soon became instruments of rivalry between Fair theatre and the Italian company. They were also staged by marionettes: an accessible example is Susan Harvey's edition of *La Grand-mére amoureuse, parodie d'Atys*, showing how Lully's opera was burlesqued in winter 1726 at the Fair. Because its authors were not working at the time with the entrepreneur who had secured that season's permission to mount opéra-comique with real actors, sophisticated puppets replaced them.[53]

What were *vaudevilles*? Chapter 5 begins with an official definition, and Robert Darnton's *Poetry and the Police* is easily the best modern introduction, linked to free-access recordings.[54] French practice was to constantly invent new words for them so that they became a vehicle for wit and satire, whether privately or on the public stage of opera. Harvey offered a judgement based on practical experience:

The most crucial elements for a successful performance of *La Grand-mére amoureuse* are sensitivity to the dramatic nuances of the text itself, as it careens swiftly

---

[52] Harvey, 'Opera Parody'; Beaucé, *Parodies d'opéra*. 'Parodie' can mean 'version' or even 'translation'; its serious purpose was critical, to pass judgement on the faults of a play or opera.

[53] Harvey, ed., *La Grand-mére amoureuse*, with contextual introduction.

[54] Darnton, *Poetry*, incl. chapter on 'Music', 77–102, with many texts. An associated 'Electronic Cabaret' is intended not as historically accurate but to give aural life to the words: *ibid.*, 174–88 and www.hup.harvard.edu/features/darpoe (30 Dec. 2020).

between satire and sincerity, and an appreciation for the astonishing musical / emotional palette of the *vaudevilles*. They are simple, of course, but like all vernacular art forms, they are very powerful when deployed with respect and imagination.[55]

And the system of using common-source music in spoken drama extended back into the seventeenth century or earlier:

The traditional method of adding new words to well-known melodies [*parodier*] reached its full scope in the eighteenth century. However, the system of '*timbres*' [identifying a melody through a mnemonic phrase, e.g. 'Greensleeves'] had many functions both in literature and music, in very different spheres, theatre among them. So in popular theatre the musical process was always the same. The music had a decorative function and was not specially written for the drama. Being basically vocal, it was borrowed from the commonwealth of *timbres* and adapted to the text of the play. Since the Middle Ages such a process was used in mystery plays and *jeux*. [...] In the comic plays, or *farces*, an often substantial number of songs were inserted either in original form or as *parodies*, the last one very often being taken up by the audience at the close of the piece.[56]

This closing piece became the *vaudeville*-finale, whose origins are traced in Chapter 3.

*

'Opera' is sometimes talked of as a synthesis of the arts, but obviously it does not, if all-sung, comprise the arts of spoken verse or prose. In popular opera, the system was for spoken dialogue to be improvised as well as written and learned. Spoken text overcame the perennial problem that sung words are not completely intelligible. Pierre Corneille (in the preface to *Andromède*, 1651) and others specifically planned for this:

I have taken good care not to have anything sung that was necessary for the understanding of the drama, because as a rule words which are sung are poorly understood by audiences; so the resulting confusion induced by the diversity of voices uttering them together would have made for great obscurity in the body of the work, had their function been to inform the audience of something important.[57]

In our own age of filmic mumbling, it is vital to remember Nicholas Cronk's words: 'The French, even more than the Italians, were especially anxious that music should not detract from the power of the spoken word

---

[55] Harvey, *ibid.*, xiv. [56] Rollin, 'À propos des recherches', 6–7.
[57] Cited in French by Cronk in 'The Play of Words and Music', 11.

[...]. The potency of the tragic declamation was widely appreciated in this period [...] and there was an understandable suspicion that music could only diminish the impact of the spoken word.'[58] Élie Fréron, a critic who championed new forms of opéra-comique, declared of Favart's *Les Chinois* (*The Chinese People*), 'we have replaced the tedious monotony of recitative by scenes spoken rather than chanted'.[59]

Reflections of Society

Authors of popular opera were social observers. Alain-René Lesage (1668–1747) and Jean-François Marmontel (1723–99) also wrote prose fiction and plays; Charles-François Pannard (1691–1765), Charles-Simon Favart (1710–92) and Michel-Jean Sedaine (1719–97) were playwrights. Jean-Jacques Rousseau, whose opera is discussed in Chapter 11, wrote in all these genres and more.

Like the London stage, Fair theatre valued generic freedom, social criticism and burlesque. *Vaudevilles* in opera are well suited to oblique discussion of social matters, sung by characters from all walks of life. Jacques Scherer conceived of popular genres as 'anti-theatre': 'To understand it we must highlight the links between our avant-garde and that of the eighteenth century. Defining the meaning of anti-theatre will be perhaps easier if we study it first in prose fiction.'[60] Another solution is to study the Tales and Fables of Jean de La Fontaine, which inspired so many popular operas (see Chapter 7).

Since it is rarely tested on stage, popular opera in *vaudeville* form remains resistant to a judgement concerning what might be called its symbolic truth: a balance of means or an aesthetic combination that made sense of the world. As T. S. Eliot observed of Joyce's *Ulysses*: '[its] continuous parallel between contemporaneity and antiquity [...] is simply a way of controlling, of ordering, of giving a shape and a significance to the immense panorama of futility and anarchy which is contemporary history'.[61] For all its mysterious artificiality, Fair theatre must have rendered 'shape' and 'significance' to its audiences.

Society was the 'default' subject of popular opera up to the Revolution. In fact, it was born during the years before the French crash of 1720 when

---

[58] Cronk, *ibid.*, 11, adducing Bénigne de Bacilly's *Remarques curieuses sur l'art de bien chanter* (1668).
[59] AL, 1756/VI, 332.   [60] Transl. from Scherer, 'Théâtre et anti-théâtre', 7.
[61] Eliot, '*Ulysses*, Order and Myth' (1923) discussed in Raine, *T. S. Eliot*, 78.

tax and monetary reform under John Law's 'system' collapsed under pressure, producing a type of anarchy described by Montesquieu:

All those who were rich six months ago now live in poverty, and those who were hungry are stuffed with wealth. Never did those two extremes touch one another so closely. The Foreigner [Law] turned the state inside out as an old-clothes dealer turns a coat; he put on top what used to be underneath and up-ended what used to be on top. [...] The consequences of this are frequently bizarre.[62]

Lesage's vision of an anti-classical theatre grew and prevailed; music was as essential to it as the spectrum of society. Its narrative resources were as varied as its mixtures of music and word could allow. Even in *parodies* of court operas, burlesque inversion might reveal the *societal* relationships concealed behind classical pastorals and myths.[63] Moral observation was through laughter: just as Lesage's novel *Gil Blas* announced 'you will find that mixture of the useful with the agreeable, so successfully prescribed by Horace' (*castigat ridendo mores*), readers of *Le Théâtre de la Foire* (henceforth *TF*) were told 'our purpose, no less than that of any other theatre, is the correction of morals'.[64]

Lesage and Favart found that *vaudevilles*, as well as new music, could give characters an emotional history: see Chapters 5 and 9. This was also possible when popular opera borrowed from classicism, as it often did: in *Le Médecin de l'amour* (*The Love-doctor*, 1758) the librettist Louis Anseaume rewrote the ancient story of Stratonice so as to feature not a widowed king Seleucus but a village constable (*bailli*) in the same situation, whose son is secretly in love with his father's young fiancée.[65] The idea distantly parallels *Ulysses*, for we must suppose that audiences thought the story believable with everyday characters.

Critical reflection about society gathered pace in mid-century drama and fiction, especially when English influences grew more decisive. French readers knew of George Lillo's moralistic tragedy *The London Merchant* (1731) since Antoine Prévost praised it, Pierre Clément translated it (coining the phrase '*tragédie bourgeoise*') and Denis Diderot quoted it in the 1750s.[66] British authors knew that their work circulated across the

---

[62] Montesquieu, *Lettres persanes* (1721), 219–20 (Lettre 138); see Velde, 'John Law's System'.
[63] Harvey, 'Opera Parody'; also 'Heroic transposition' in *OAR*, 79, 100.
[64] *Adventures of Gil Blas* (1715 etc.), I, xxiii; 'Préface', *TF* I, [11] (R/I/9).
[65] Music by Jean-Louis Laruette; briefly revived 1762, 1783; re-set by Pierre Van Maldere for Brussels.
[66] Diderot, *Entretiens sur Le Fils naturel* and *De la poésie dramatique*. See Noiray, 'Un opéra-comique "bourgeois"', 159–62. In 1765 Louis Anseaume made an opera of it for Egidio Duni as *L'École de la jeunesse ou Le Barnevelt françois* (Paris: L'Auteur, etc., n.d.).

Channel: Tobias Smollett's *Peregrine Pickle* has the travelling hero sent to the Bastille for embarrassing a nobleman, and his friend deceived into fearing 'a punishment ordained by law, being no other than breaking alive upon the wheel'.[67]

Henry Fielding had opened Book VII of *Tom Jones* in 1749 with 'A Comparison between the World and the Stage' which moved between theatre, life and the novel to propose a moral continuity across all three spheres. Novels and popular operas now wished to represent the conditions of a society and its dialects, costumes and visual details.[68] Fielding's 'A Comparison' was omitted from the first French translation, yet we find a strikingly similar vision for theatre by Carlo Goldoni, whose impact on popular opera we follow up in Chapters 10 and 11. Goldoni's spoken comedies from 1743, beginning with *La contessina* (*The Count's Daughter*), intended a new purpose, which Ted Emery summarised as follows:

> It is the function of the World to stimulate in the author an examination of the defects of contemporary society, while the Theatre furnishes a model, a structure of conventions accepted by both author and theatre-goers, which allows Goldoni's observations to be effectively communicated to the audience. The audience occupies a central position in this scheme, for comedy finds its didactic *raison d'être* only upon being received by the viewers. This, then, is one reason why comedy must be 'natural' or 'realistic' [rather than improvised in *commedia* style]: to allow the public to recognise itself in the on-stage fiction.[69]

Music could have an obvious place here and participate, for example, when it came to staging *tableaux*. *Tableaux* as a resource were both theorised and practised by Diderot. Pierre Frantz's analysis of this technique casts useful light on opéra-comique. A 'static' *tableau* suits the opening of a scene where silent activity creates 'a general atmosphere, a framework for the action': in Diderot's words, 'scenery brought to life'.[70] Thus, at the opening of Act III of *Le Roi et le fermier* (*The King and the Farmer*) Sedaine and Monsigny portrayed three members of the household absorbed in different

---

[67] *Peregrine Pickle* (1751), 251. Pickle befriends a republican doctor who would 'dissolv[e] the chains of slavery' in France and 'give rise to some renowned revolution': *ibid.*, 248. Shortened trans. as *Histoire et avantures de Sir Williams Pickle* (Amsterdam, etc., 1753).

[68] Runte, 'Parallels', 283–99. As a popular opera, *Tom Jones* was written by A. H. Poinsinet, set by F. A. Danican Philidor and revised by Sedaine (1766).

[69] Emery, 'Carlo Goldoni', 182–3, taken from Goldoni's *Il teatro comico* and preface to the Bettinelli ed. of his works (both 1750).

[70] Frantz, *Esthétique du tableau*, 157; discussion of Sedaine's *Le Déserteur* on 162–3.

tasks, singing a static ensemble.[71] But a 'climactic' *tableau*, say at the close of a scene or act, put energy to use in fixing a pathetic or even sublime image with a group of characters. *Tableau* was the word used by Favart to describe such a moment in his *Annette et Lubin* (see p. 146).

When the critic Jean-François de La Harpe discussed Sedaine and Grétry's *Le Comte d'Albert* (*Count d'Albert*), he ventured a theory of opéra-comique involving *tableaux* as a basic element:

> It is a type of proverb in mime; there is no sort of plot complication but more like *tableaux* arranged for the stage and for the composer; but together it all produces an effect [...]. This is a special genre which in some way approaches Shakespeare's dramas and seems well enough suited to the Comédie-Italienne, which is no conventional theatre, and to music which adopts every register and likes to change its register. It is inappropriate to judge such pieces by the rules of conventional art.[72]

In the practice of a 'critical public reflection' (Jürgen Habermas's phrase), authors of popular opera played a literary part, and this coincided with the rapid growth of journal publication.[73] Some added prefaces to librettos (as opera librettists had been doing), informing the public of their methods, principles or thoughts about 'the new genre'.[74] Of twenty-six prefaces known between 1752 and 1764, two by Antoine-François Quétant (1733–1823) are essays and three by Sedaine are equally wide-ranging.[75] Prefacing *L'Anneau perdu et retrouvé* (*The Ring Lost and Found*), Sedaine added: 'I forgot to mention that in one *ariette* I used two lines from La Fontaine, and that Shakespeare's final scenes from *The Merry Wives of Windsor* gave me the idea for those which conclude my comedy.'[76]

Journal publication, however, was equally able to serve the public itself in manifesting criticism of popular opera. When its music changed radically after 1753, there was at first no universal approval, and as Chapter 4

---

[71] *Le Roy et le fermier, comédie* (Paris: Claude Herissant, n.d.), 113; see p. 318.
[72] La Harpe, *Correspondance Littéraire*, V, 138–9; Charlton, *Grétry*, 268–77; Castelvecchi, *Sentimental Opera*, 71–5 (on Diderot's *tableaux*) and 130–43 (on *tableaux* in Dalayrac's *Nina* and Grétry's *Lucile*).
[73] Habermas, *Structural Transformation*, 29; Censer and Popkin, eds., *Press and Politics*; *OAR*, 216–24.
[74] Contant d'Orville, *Histoire*, I, 4.
[75] Quétant, 'De l'opéra-comique en général' (to *Le Maréchal-ferrant*) and 'Essai sur l'opéra-comique' (to *Le Serrurier* (*The Locksmith*)). See Charlton, 'Sedaine's Prefaces', 237–47, also Tables 1 and 3 on 204, 217.
[76] 'Avertissement de l'auteur', *L'Anneau perdu et retrouvé* (1764), in *ibid.*, 'Sedaine's Prefaces', 248.

shows, Philidor's music was the subject of some contention. *Le Maréchal-ferrant* (*The Blacksmith*) was defended by the *Mercure de France*:

The music [...] is new and full of harmonic interest; several *ariettes* containing imitations contribute especially to its success, such as those of the Coachman [La Bride's 'Brillant dans mon emploi' / 'Superbly at work'], the one with the sound of bells ['Quand pour le grand voyage' / 'When for the great journey'] and others no less pleasurable. [...] The beneficial aspect of these *ariettes* is to depict rather than express; their multiple repetitions seem tolerable and often fit the veracity of the images. Moreover the things depicted by music in this opéra-comique are of a type that will always amuse people at this theatre.[77]

Le Maréchal-ferrant begins with the blacksmith working and singing 'Chantant à pleine gorge' ('As I sing out loud'); a stage direction reads, '[Marcel is] working at his forge and striking the anvil'. Hammer blows are detailed in the score, and the bellows must be pumped. Its text has become so unpoetic as to include onomatopœia: 'We strike on! Patatan, / Pan, pan, pan'; 'No use lying asleep!'[78]

Remarkable letters between two friends took opposing sides in discussing these matters and were also published by the *Mercure* (perhaps coincidentally, the *Journal des dames* had just appointed a radical female editor).[79] These friends were obviously used to making domestic opera, but Mme Gastin d'Entreville hated the newer works, while Mme Bouchait de Serée valued them. D'Entreville objected to their 'change of register' as La Harpe had called it and preferred 'a more regular and *univocal*' style: *vaudevilles* in performance offered this. 'We no longer have *vaudevilles*, whose pleasing and natural melodies were suitable for continuity of dialogue; for which reason the hearer, favouring things which seemed to be real, found them less unattractive.'[80] Her reactions to the new style are extremely valuable:

Hardly has the mind fixed on a few spoken words than it is overwhelmed by a frightful noise: the arrival of musical pleasures. The ears are no better treated here: hardly have they started to acclimatise to the *ariette* clinking or clashing with the orchestra than they are left alone except for some words that haven't been properly fitted into the metre of the verse; for this versification is quite strange, and does not take after poetry at all.

---

[77] *Mercure*, 1761, Sept., 215–16.
[78] *Le Maréchal ferrant, opéra comique en deux actes* (Paris: La Chevardiere, n.d.), 3.
[79] Mme de Beaumer: see Gelbart, 'The *Journal des dames*'.
[80] Degastin, femme d'Entreville, 'À M. Delagarde, Pensionnaire au Privilége du Mercure pour la Partie des Spectacles', *Mercure*, 1761, Nov., 165–72 [167–8]. See Chap. 5 for *vaudeville* performance.

'Chantant à pleine gorge' fed her ironic response: 'When the Blacksmith drinks and sings at his anvil, the heroes of Greece and Rome must be silent and the gods themselves must hold their peace on the stage or else speak to a few who cherish the good old days.' These are 'frivolities contrary to all the rules of art'; they signify a national 'effervescence' that is ridiculous and even dangerous. 'This sort of music' is like a 'kind of riot' and can never 'elevate the soul or inspire the imagination'.[81]

But Mme Bouchait de Serée liked all these novelties, and her defence also invoked the nature of society. Older comedies can no longer satisfy modern taste because society has changed. Familiar locutions, steady pace and the old way of satirising fixed characters (as in Molière) are as boring as their excessive subtleties, clever dialogue or accurate portraits.[82] 'Do we see a regular pace in today's pleasures or passions, or even in the progress of our fortunes? You say it yourself: we have never before lived so rapidly, so why should drawn-out plots be of interest?' (160) As a Modern, Mme de Serée believed that genres must rise and fall, move with the times, be regarded like a commodity: 'In Parnassus as in business, each article of merchandise has its Fair' (165). 'This genre is like nothing else, you say? Well, therein lies its sublime relevance' (160).

My house shall be open to creators and connoisseurs of all these new genres. Doubtless they shall have the good sense, like me, to make light of the serious applause they'll be given. You shall laugh with us, Madame, since to annoy you better you will join our group: *ariettes* at the ready, we shall force you to enjoy them. (166)

Chamfort's Overview

The best objective summary of popular opera before the Revolution came from Sébastien Roch Nicolas, called Chamfort (1740–94); he wrote librettos as well as journalism.[83] Chamfort and La Porte's *Dictionnaire dramatique* (1776) formulated excellent summaries that we shall use later.[84] Popular opera was defined by a mixed form of content and technique, and two related forms: Chamfort does not say or imply that the *vaudeville*

---

[81] *Ibid.*, 169, 171.
[82] 'Réponse de Madame Bouchait [de Serée] à la lettre de Madame Gastin d'Entreville', *ibid.*, 1762, Jan./1, 157–166 [159–60]. The following quotations are also from this text.
[83] Sgard, ed., *Dictionnaire des journalistes*.
[84] Chamfort and La Porte, 'Opéra-comique', *Dictionnaire dramatique* (1776), II, 337–45.

has run its course; he just sets it in parallel to a newer form, the one in which 'la Musique' is 'the main object of interest' (343). This twin identity is minimised (the article is undivided by headings) though clearly explained. Between 1770 and 1775 the presence of *vaudevilles* had dwindled in the face of new music,[85] but Chamfort provides a reminder that *vaudeville* comedy was still on the boards and sung in the home.

'The merit of little Dramatic Poems acted at the Opéra Comique resides less in their convention or dramatic design than in the choice of a subject apt for lively scenes, jolly performances and *vaudevilles* containing subtle satire, sung to gay and amusing tunes' (339). Their content included 'satirical depiction of *mores*, ridiculous customs and extravagant fashions; parody, critique of [artistic] works, news of the day, working-class or middle-class plots, allegory, supernatural, pastoral: anything except tragedy and tearful comedy' (340).[86]

[The genre] focuses mainly on faithful represention of simple, naïve *mores* of manual workers and villagers, using an uncomplicated plot about love or something else. Examples of these are *Le Maréchal-ferrant, Le Bûcheron (The Woodcutter), Les Deux chasseurs et la laitière (Two Hunters and a Milk-maid)* etc.; which does not mean that it may not embrace loftier subjects; for none need be excluded. (339-40)

The essence of the genre was summarised as follows:

Opéra-comique is a drama of mixed genre that is basically a play, but which approaches opera by reason of its form. There are two types: opéra-comique *en vaudevilles*, an unpretentious expression of our nation's innate gaiety; and *pièces à ariettes*, whose invention we owe to the Italians. (340)

Speech was discussed in relation to expositions and links, perhaps echoing Lesage's approval of rapid expositions in his Preface to *TF*:

Whatever the chosen subject-matter, it must be simple so that the exposition can be written plainly and clearly: a long exposition in *vaudevilles* would be unbearable; things must go quickly and scenes be short because singing only makes them longer. Some scenes demand more extension, and the art lies in drawing them out properly without overstepping one's self-defined limits. People have felt that spoken prose is necessary for links and transitions. It is also useful for dialogue: certain commonplace things would be in bad taste if sung. (340-1)

---

[85] Matthes, *Vaudeville*, esp. the table on 43.
[86] Chamfort ignored Framery's discussion of 'the tearful genre', though he must have heard incoming styles of sentimental music: Framery, 'Sur le genre larmoyant' (1770), 7, citing Philidor's *Tom Jones* and Grétry's *Sylvain* and *Lucile*.

After advice about composing texts to pre-existing melodies, Chamfort considered the way that they, like *vaudevilles*, served in the home:

The most experienced practitioners have always noted that the majority of songs [*couplets*], although integral to the basis of the comedy, may be separated off and sung in private company. One should thus regard opéra-comique as a flower-bed from which each blossom may be plucked separately, forming an agreeable whole when all are brought together. (342)

Regarding the new type of opéra-comique containing *ariettes*, Chamfort defined essential differences from Italian opera that we shall discuss at the end of this book. One was the desire for texts that did not repeat ('our minds wish to be occupied, as well as our ears; we find empty repetitions painful'). *Tableaux* were seen as integral: 'the libretto [must] provide the composer with opportunities to create *tableaux* that serve both the dramatic impetus and the plot, which must never be lost sight of – that is the great merit of Sedaine'. (343)

Chamfort was emphatic that composers 'must not allow the action to sag by writing ritornellos to arias'; in fact, composers already worked with librettists to integrate music and action in such places (see Chapter 11). Music and spoken dialogue were to share responsibility for the dramaturgy so that potentially either medium could articulate a situation. A feeling of continuity – across music and speech – was what these operas aimed at.

What we must also note is the proportioning of the spoken dialogue to the musical numbers so that the former does not occupy more time than the music; similarly, the music should not entirely absorb the dialogue. One should extend both one and the other according to the subject-matter and dramatic flow. Because verse dialogue has more analogy with music it might seem preferable to use it in this type of work; but it was felt that spoken prose, being more rapid, gave greater movement and warmth to the action. (344)

Defending Popular Opera

With the normalisation of new music came a focus in popular opera on working people and trades: the 'conditions' of life. Charles-Simon Favart had approached this area, and Sedaine foregrounded it in 1756, as Chapter 7 describes.[87] A year later, Diderot advocated 'the conditions of

---

[87] See pp. 179–80 and Ledbury, *Sedaine*, 75–102.

men' as a fitting criterion for drama.[88] 'Low' subject matter was therefore the defining feature for the moment, and the journalist Nougaret sought to problematise it.[89]

Nougaret's *De l'art du théâtre* will always cause puzzlement owing to its use of irony, pulling the occasional rug from under the reader's feet to make things more amusing (as the author says), more apt for *opéra-bouffon*.[90] So it is an anti-classical essay on an anti-classical subject. However, Nougaret's strategies are also a product of the novelty of his task, one related to the problematic nature of popular opera in Western historiography: that is, our own subject in the present book. Dedicating his work to an aristocratic playwright,[91] Nougaret had no difficulty accepting the classical tradition of scholarship and criticism, or Molière as the standard against which comedy should measure itself. However, he wanted to probe the basis of opéra comique because although it was accepted culturally, it still existed outside the 'rules'. His quest fixed him on the horns of two dilemmas.

Lully's tragedies had never been treated as a legitimate branch of (spoken) theatre, and music was in any case classed as inferior, hierarchically speaking, to poetry, meaning the libretto. But the new type of popular opera combined speech with music so convincingly that it logically demanded (said Nougaret) to be treated within the legitimate *theatre* tradition, that of Racine and Molière.

A second dilemma was caused by 'low' subject matter, partly because playwrights in spoken theatre had, in John Lough's words, 'tended to confine their attention more and more exclusively to the portrayal of characters drawn from the upper ranks of society'.[92] To consider popular opera within the spoken tradition would mean accepting working-class characters and stories. How could this be reconciled with the official rankings of art, which deemed peasant scenes to be inferior to classical, historical or religious subjects? Nougaret's readers would recognise the problem because journals constantly advertised paintings and prints depicting village scenes. Writers sometimes cited 'Teniers' when characterising a popular opera or pantomime ballet, always with positive implication.[93]

---

[88] Diderot, 'Troisième entretien sur *Le Fils naturel*', *Œuvres esthétiques*, 167; Furbank, *Diderot*, 140–44.
[89] Nougaret (or Nogaret, 1742–1823), *De l'art du théâtre* (1768). His journalistic career: Sgard, ed., *Dictionnaire des journalistes*, rev. ed. (see p. xxii).
[90] Nougaret, 'Discours Préliminaire', *ibid.*, I, xvii–xxi; also I, 157.
[91] 'le comte de P***', conjecturally Antoine de Ferriol, comte de Pont de Vesle, author of three *comédies* staged between 1732 and 1749.
[92] Lough, *Paris Theatre Audiences*, 243–4.
[93] David Teniers I (1582–1649); David Teniers II (1610–1690). 'M. Vadé est le Teniers de la Halle & des Ports': *AL*, 1755/1, 355. Lacombe used Teniers to argue for the expansion of musical depiction: *Spectacle* (1761), 263.

Marian Hobson's *The Object of Art* showed that the status of 'low' subjects changed as the century progressed.[94] However, she sees Nougaret's satire as inimical to his chosen genre.

> It is as if the sophistication of the artistic medium, opera, offset the low subjects for the eighteenth-century audience: as with the popularity of the *parades* at the fairs, a titillating enjoyment of the socially unseemly is made possible by the highly stylised form in which it is presented. [...]
>
> In satirizing the *opéra bouffon* by turning against it the aesthetic of imitation and illusion, which is its justification, he is showing the feebleness of that aesthetic: this should in turn destroy the grounds of his satire. But does he realise this? The oscillation between [an onlooker's] awareness and illusion can, I have suggested, be translated on a formal level into an oscillation between seriousness and parody. These poles nearly coincide, or rather they are nearly indistinguishable, in Nougaret.[95]

Nougaret apparently argued that popular opera, uniquely equipped to take on the subject of society, could benefit its culture by depicting low-class characters (I, 75–6). Opera placed them at the forefront without describing them as morally inferior, which offered 'a new discovery of the human spirit' (I, 76). Workers were of no less interest than anyone, even monarchs, on stage. Earlier Fair theatre purged itself of 'repulsive and crude' characters in order to banish farce; now the public applauds non-farcical situations and admires the depiction of 'their style of talking'. By 'faithfully copying the ways of the lowest people' (I, 77) while engaging our interest in a woodcutter (*Le Bûcheron*) or a cooper (*Le Tonnelier*), popular opera has discovered its own justification. 'The perfection of the new opera is perhaps found in its very lowness' since it aims *not* to reproduce the sublime seen in other forms of theatre (I, 77, 133) and it should serve to 'accustom rich people to cast eyes on the poor' (I, 111). In a Fielding-like move Nougaret hazards an ethical purpose for the art: 'the sight of their passions should correct our own' (I, 130), for the poor are exposed to the same vices and misfortunes as anyone else; workers in the audience would identify with characters resembling themselves (I, 131).

Nougaret maintains the ironic complexity: popular opera 'should belong by right to the working people, just as the playhouse exists for the elite class'; but yet this genre admirably does its work 'on the quiet' by instructing 'us' while seeming to do no more than entertain (I, 131–2). Popular opera could be superior to other theatre forms by reason of its fidelity to observed nature, so that one observes humanity in a more complete sense

---

[94] Hobson, *Object of Art*, 68. [95] *Ibid.*, 157–8.

(I, 137–40). The means of achieving this might be radical but had been sanctioned by Aristotle:[96] librettists and composers must imagine being coopers, gamekeepers or bakers, must 'counterfeit the motions and gestures of a locksmith, a street-porter, a beggar', must compose their *ariette* while working an imagined forge, field or wine-press; must perspire while cutting wood or opening an oven (I, 155). Even if we take Nougaret as a mere satirist, we are obliged to review arguments that might be taken positively as well as negatively.

Conceptual Problems

When Thomas Beecham encountered Grétry's unfamiliar *Richard Cœur de lion* in 1904 (see Preface), his understanding of its genre was completed at the Opéra Comique, where he saw it. Today, however, false binaries obscure the understanding of popular opera, even though our musicals present one parallel to it. Some people assume plays only ever to be all-spoken (thus trivialised by music), and others think operas are only ever all-sung (thus trivialised by spoken dialogue). Cultural historians and those of opera can be misled.[97]

In 1769 Sedaine and Monsigny's *Le Déserteur* (*The Deserter*) became a world-famous popular opera. According to the records of fourteen German theatres, it was the most frequently performed piece during 1776 *in any genre*, overtaking Lessing, Goethe, Shakespeare and Mozart.[98] Its score contains twenty vocal items – solos and ensembles that run the gamut of expressive possibility, four instrumental items and through-composed finales to Acts I and III. A modern recording logs a playing-time of ninety-seven minutes, to which spoken dialogue would add appreciably more.[99]

Le Déserteur was responding to public issues: crime, punishment and revaluations of the figure of the common soldier.[100] Whether in prosaic reports or else in texts by *philosophes*, 'soldiers [. . .] came increasingly to be viewed and portrayed as dignified, useful to the public good', as Stefano

---

[96] Nougaret cites *Poetics*, Chap. 18 in *ibid.*, I, 154: 'As far as possible, too, the dramatic poet should carry out the appropriate gestures as he composes his speeches', etc.: Aristotle, *On the Art of Poetry*, 55.
[97] Moreover Isherwood, in *Farce and Fantasy*, offered wildly inaccurate discussions of Favart (105–7, 116), Duni (111–12) and *Le Roi et le fermier* (115).
[98] From Johann Friedrich Reichardt's *Theaterkalender*, in Bruford, *Theatre, Drama and Audience*, 199–201. There were fifty performances across eleven theatres.
[99] Opera Lafayette, cond. and ed. Ryan Brown (2010): Naxos 8.660263-64.
[100] Castelvecchi, *Sentimental Opera*, 94–102.

Castelvecchi explained.[101] But Sedaine's protagonist is tragically impetuous: deceived whilst on leave by an obscure caprice, Alexis believes that his fiancée Louise has abandoned him.[102] He loses equilibrium, declares he will leave the village and is arrested for desertion. It is a capital offence, the more foolhardy because every soldier has been ordered back to camp to present arms to the king the next day. Acts II and III find Alexis in the condemned cell, where intense spoken scenes involve increasingly acute expressions of sorrow and loss in music. Responding to the taste for English drama, Sedaine offsets potential tragedy by gallows humour involving the tipsy Montauciel ('Up-to-heaven') and Louise's cousin, Bertrand. Louise finally rescues Alexis by petitioning the king: 'Ah, Sire! He's my beloved, And if he must die, Let me suffer the same fate.' Her words and actions are not staged but reported in the sung music of a witness. She even offers to exchange her life for Alexis's: 'Who am I? Less than nothing on this earth.' The brigadier Courchemin continues: 'Old soldiers wept; even courtiers likewise.' The king accedes; his nobles produce valuables or gold which Louise collects in her apron; she drops everything in order to run and tell Alexis the news.

When she reappears at the prison, she falls unconscious with exhaustion. Alexis sings his last farewell and is led away by soldiers. Louise recovers by degrees, singing in arioso while the orchestra, miming her hazy inner sensations, recalls the music of Alexis's recent farewell. Cries of 'Vive le Roi!' offstage snap her awake: we have already embarked on a spacious finale. As the scene changes to a public square, Alexis is told by the chorus that he is pardoned, although D minor music still conveys uncertainty. When it switches to D major, all can finally rejoice: even Montauciel, who had quarrelled with Alexis, will congratulate him. Monsigny's music of celebration, which also permeates the opera's overture, was popular enough to sound over Bonn when Beethoven was young.[103]

On *Le Déserteur*'s revival in 1843 Delacroix and Berlioz became two of its numerous devotees: the latter commented mainly on the music, the former exclusively on the drama:

Exaggerated love of the natural, or rather the natural carried into accessory details, as in the dramas of Diderot, of Sedaine, and others, has not prevented this form from making real progress: it leaves immense latitude for the development of characters and action, since it permits changes of place, and also great intervals

---

[101] *Ibid.*, 96.
[102] Sedaine, *Le Déserteur, drame en trois actes en prose meslée de musique* (Paris: Veuve Duchesne, 1771), Sc. 2. The unseen local duchess whose caprice this is actually knows Alexis well, because she has brought him up: *ibid.*, 8–9.
[103] Broadcast on the town's carillon: Schiedermair, *Der junge Beethoven*, 137.

[of imagined time] between the acts; and yet the law of progression in the interest, the art with which the actions and the characters contribute to augment the moral effect, is here quite superior to that of the finest tragedies of Shakespeare. [...] By following the French system of tragedies, it would have been impossible to produce the effect of the last scene of *Le Déserteur*, for example. That changing of place for five minutes, in order to show the scene where the deserter is prepared to submit to arrest, makes one shudder, despite one's expectation of seeing his pardon arrive.[104]

Berlioz thought that 'in no musical composition destined for the theatre have truthful dramatic qualities, expression of emotion and character, been taken further'. He confessed astonishment at the rich musical variety, especially the fugal trio in Act II when Alexis's death sentence is made known to his family:

A strange, almost uncouth theme breaks in, then is taken up by the three soloists in the style of a fugal exposition. This style is amazingly apt. We are surprised, even fearful to hear such a sequence of sounds – it ravishes soul and senses alike. And when [Louise's] voice is drawn out in tearful cries over a succession of dissonant harmonies, the hearer suffers the dreadful illusion of experiencing what the characters must be feeling. One's heart seems to break in two, like theirs.[105]

Gathered in an article by Adrienne Hytier are the facts and figures about French military recruitment and desertions, serving her interpretation of dramatic and prose literature.[106] One side of the punishment debate was supported by Voltaire: Candide, after being tricked into joining the Bulgarian army, walked away:

He had not gone six miles before he was caught [...]. At the court martial he was graciously permitted to choose between being flogged thirty-six times by the whole regiment or having twelve bullets in his brain. [...] his eyes were bandaged and he was made to kneel down. The King of the Bulgars passed by at that moment and asked what crime the culprit had committed. [He] granted him a pardon, an exercise of mercy which will be praised in every newspaper and in every age.[107]

The death sentence for deserters was not, however, repealed before 1782, when Louis-Sébastien Mercier's play, also called *Le Déserteur*, was finally permitted to be given in public. It was specifically intended to influence opinion on behalf of reform, so Mercier has the protagonist executed.[108]

---

[104] Pach, ed., *Journal of Eugene Delacroix*, 723–4. Heinrich Heine's review: Heartz, *Music in European Capitals*, 776.

[105] Hector Berlioz, 'Théâtre de l'Opéra-Comique. Reprise du *Déserteur*', *Journal des débats*, 12 Nov. 1843, *Critique musicale*, V, 373–8 [374–5].

[106] Hytier, 'Decline of Military Values'. [107] Voltaire, *Candide* (1759), 24.

[108] *Le Déserteur* (Paris: Le Jay, 1770), V/7, 91. It would be in repertory at the CI.

But between 1769 and 1782, Sedaine and Monsigny's opera was the only public dramatisation on stage; it was an astoundingly popular opera in Paris.[109]

A nuanced view of Sedaine's treatment of comedy and pathos has been written by Manuel Couvreur and Philippe Vendrix.[110] Modern recording allows the complete music to be heard, while on a French radio recording we hear how it was performed sixty years ago.[111] Nevertheless, and ironically for a book on 'sentimental opera', Castelvecchi's account avoids all discussion of Monsigny's music and the daring uses of comedy. (Berlioz testified that nightly laughter ended Act II when the tipsy Montauciel duetted with Bertrand.) But Monsigny's musical power obviously manipulated 'public indignation at the rigour of the laws on desertion';[112] French liberal opinion was already agreed that capital punishment for this misdemeanour was indefensible, which is why Sedaine's unseen king (who is French by implication) is effectively made to accord with this view.

Hytier certainly considered Sedaine's *Le Déserteur* but regrettably judged it to be a 'sweet, sentimental little play with music and comic scenes'. Unaware of its scale and sophistication, she confessed 'it is hard to imagine today the tremendous success of the play [*sic*]' or the fact that it had been translated into foreign languages; its 'criticism of society's harsh dealing with deserters, while very clear, was also indirect'.[113] Her assessment was adopted fancifully by Marisa Linton ('Sedaine's play was a fairly light-hearted affair, with much romantic comedy') and the myth of the Sedaine 'play' went on circulating.[114]

*

Le Déserteur was exceptional, but its technical and musical resources were based on a 'musico-dramatic art' that had already evolved and begun to be theorised. The following chapters will suggest that the path to *Le Déserteur* emerges through the history of popular opera, not that of spoken theatre. Opera with spoken dialogue, whether on the public stage or in the home, was a familiar experience and a concept-model for the eighteenth and nineteenth centuries. People even studied this art outside France, as, for example, in London where the *Morning Chronicle* advertised 'Readings at

---

[109] Given 154 times between 1769 and 1780: Charlton, *Grétry*, 66, 215.
[110] Couvreur, Vendrix, 'Les Enjeux théoriques', 231–2.
[111] ORTF (French Radio) abbreviated studio broadcast, 21 Jan. 1960, cond. Louis de Froment.
[112] Castelvecchi, *Sentimental Opera*, 99, but writing about Mercier's play.
[113] Hytier, 'Decline of Military Values', 153; Michael Robinson, 'Two London Versions' shows modes of presentation there.
[114] Linton, *Politics of Virtue*, 121.

N°. 40, Great Marlborough Street'. Here we find not just a few French or Italian operas on the agenda but a conspicuous group of popular operas with music by Grétry and Dalayrac; even the Duke and Duchess of York came along.[115] The few historians who have written recently about popular opera have been hampered by lack of musical information and evaluation, not to mention recordings.[116] Their initiatives will not develop fairly until opera history takes due account of this wealth of experience.

---

[115] *Morning Chronicle*, announcements from 20 May 1799 to 19 May 1800; *Oracle*, 22 May 1800, seen on BCN.

[116] See Maza, *Private Lives*, chap. 2; Wyngaard, *From Savage to Citizen*, 71–97; Moindrot, *ibid.* (see n. 2).

2 | Music and Spoken Theatre

There may be an argument for thinking that just as the 1670s inaugurated all-sung opera in France (as 'events' and 'structures'), so they also inaugurated popular opera. We can see Molière as a nodal point in this development for two reasons: his comedies had a lasting effect on writers and audiences, which informed opéra-comique (see p. 159); and his uses of music were both integrative and extensive, especially in his last play.

This chapter sets out various solutions found for introducing music within spoken comedy. Comedies up to 1680 are surveyed for their uses of music. Some basic questions will be raised, as, for example, those relating to the allocation of stage-time to music and the provision of actor-singers. In Britain some such problems were being theorised by George Granville in 1710, but he had no equivalent in France:[1] even though French and English genres of musical comedy were closely related, difficulties were caused in France by the Opéra's stringent restrictions placed on musical resources in other theatres. As will be seen, however, even the Comédie-Française in 1680 was staging plays that thrived on the incorporation of music in different styles, heard for different purposes.

Recent Research

> The introduction of musical performance in spoken drama presented technical and aesthetic problems, for which seventeenth-century playwrights found ever-creative solutions. Many dramatists assigned set pieces to characters in the play, thereby making artistic creation one of the play's subjects.[2]

One hundred and fifty-three secular plays with music appeared between 1605 and 1680; they include the fifteen comedies with music written by Molière between *Les Précieuses ridicules* (*The Female Wits Ridiculed*, 1659) and *Le Malade imaginaire* (*The Hypochondriac*, 1673). John S. Powell's

---

[1] Hirschmann, 'The British Enchanters'.
[2] Powell, *Music and Theatre*, 82, with handlist on 435–9.

discovery of hitherto missing parts of Marc-Antoine Charpentier's music for the latter makes possible new assessments of its aims and achievements; his discovery of music for *Le Mary sans femme* (*The Wifeless Husband*, 1663) by Montfleury is also important.[3] *Le Malade imaginaire*, Molière's final play, was quite different in scale and ambition from *Le Bourgeois gentilhomme* (*The Would-Be Gentleman*, 1670).[4]

One group of musical plays is not thought to have been acted publicly, and their domestic role connects directly with popular opera in the private domain. Private music was mentioned in theatre texts themselves: the would-be gentleman, M. Jourdain, learns that the fashionable world organises domestic concerts each week (Act II/1), while a different play has the line, 'Hardly a house is found where one doesn't sing whole opera scenes'.[5] Table 2.1 lists musical plays probably intended to be read or acted in private.

The singer, composer and lutenist Dassoucy (1605–79), who wrote an autobiography and travelled widely, composed both text and music (currently lost) for *Les Amours d'Apollon* (*The Loves of Apollo and Daphne*). It was an ambitious, fascinating '*mélange* of burlesque and pastoral scenes in a variety of modes: ribald, erotic, heroic, serious and tragic', 'scenes sung in their entirety alternat[ing] with spoken or partly-sung scenes'.[6] Dassoucy assigned singing parts to main characters like Apollon, L'Amour (Cupid) and Daphné, while secondary characters had exclusively spoken roles.

Table 2.1 Selected musical plays probably intended for the private reader and musician.

1625	*Antioche*	Le Francque
1640	*La Comédie de chansons*	Charles Sorel (attrib.)
1642	*L'Amante ennemie*	Sallebray
1648	*Le Jugement de Paris*	Dassoucy (Charles Coypeau)
1650	*Les Amours d'Apollon et de Daphné*	Dassoucy
1660	*L'Inconstant vaincu*	Anon.

Antioche is replete with imagined spectacle, ballets and a chorus.[7] Claironde, heroine of *L'Amante ennemie* (*The Lover as Enemy*), finds adventure in a distant land, travelling in male guise and carrying a guitar.

---

[3] Powell, *ibid.*, 92–5.
[4] Powell, 'Charpentier's Music'; 'Music, Fantasy and Illusion'. For 1672 to 1745 see le Blanc, *Avatars*, 713–817.
[5] Charles de Saint-Évremond, *Les Opéra* (c. 1676), II/3, cited in Cronk, 'The Play of words', n. 20. See Powell, *Music and Theatre*, 141–2.
[6] *Ibid.*, 191–3. [7] Powell, *ibid.*, 130.

The association of main characters with sung roles took on importance after Louis XIV's statutes of limitation (1672–3) quoted in Chapter 1 because, if professional singers could not be hired, then the job of singing might fall to a regular actor. This occurred in the work of later playwrights (Poisson, Dufresny, Regnard) and in Gherardi's Italian troupe. After that, music carried much of the drama, and actor-singers were qualified in both areas.

In *La Comédie de chansons* (*The Comedy in Song*), attributed to Charles Sorel and Charles de Beys, songs were knitted together as happens in our own time within 'jukebox musicals'; it was made from pre-existing material and obliged main characters to sing. Powell suggests that it was given at the Marais theatre, but no date is confirmed. Music included a 'Chœur de musiciens' and a grotesque serenade.[8]

> Since the finest *airs de cour* are mingled here with *vaudevilles*, it is as though gold and silk were mixed with straw to make something more exquisite. [...]. Only rustic or crude spirits would hear them and then say: Here are pretty novelties; we have heard them sung a hundred times by our valets and servants. [...] Witty sayings at court, for the most part, are the same sort of thing: a figure of common speech is applied to something else. Verses taken from a song are no less apt [for this process]. On that principle, our intention was to make a play out of song texts whose presence must be very amusing to every person, especially to those who know both old and new songs, being the more surprised by their juxtapositions.[9]

In this interesting passage the authors do two useful things. They explain a comic function that music may supply and then point to the use of that function, one that became fundamental to popular opera. These juxtapositions would create, in effect, 'the pleasure in surprise and the surprise in pleasure' which a joke habitually provides.[10] When *vaudevilles* formed the basis of early opéra-comique, their impact must have been identifiable with the idea that 'the art of comedy' is 'a continuity that [...] builds with – and is built through – interruptions and breaks, a continuity that constructs with discontinuity'.[11] Stylistic contrast, as we shall see, flourished within the Gherardi troupe and then became typical of popular opera. In Mozart's *Die Entführung aus dem Serail*, for example, stylistic contrasts have been argued to play a structural role in the exploration of its particular 'binary oppositions'.[12]

---

[8] 'Alidor will arrange a serenade with a troupe of grotesque Musicians playing a Guitar, a hurdy-gurdy, cymbals, regals, flageolets and anything of use in a Charivari': [Charles Sorel and Charles de Beys, attrib.], *La Comédie de chansons* (Paris: Toussaint Quinet, 1640), 113–16, on *Gallica*.
[9] 'Avertissement aux Lecteurs', *La Comédie de chansons*, [ii–iii].
[10] Zupančič, *The Odd One In*, 132, from Lacan, *Le Séminaire Livre V*.   [11] Zupančič, *ibid.*, 140.
[12] Matthew Head, *Orientalism, Masquerade and Mozart's Turkish Music* (London: Royal Musical Association, 2000), 21.

Twenty years after the *Comédie de chansons*, *L'Inconstant vaincu* (*The Defeat of the Cheat*), a 'Pastorale en chansons', referenced the earlier piece in its preface. Interest, however, focused on the poetry; humour was limited to 'rustic' accents in Scene 5. Dramatic functions were given to music both in the beautiful 'Au secours, ma raison' (II/2) and in the drinking-song of Célimène in V/2, but the evidence suggests domestic performance. The nuns of the Récollets convent in Paris who once owned the copy now seen on *Gallica* would have noted its preface: 'poetry for the most beautiful *airs* to have been issued to date has been written into this play. [...] Such will be evident if you take the trouble to *read* this text.'[13]

Powell finds twelve thematic areas in which music functioned in plays between 1605 and 1680 – types of musical moment which formed a repository and a burgeoning set of conventions: 'When introduced as a natural part of the action, such musical episodes make the play itself appear all the more realistic.'[14] Even performative shortcomings were factored into the dramatic illusion: 'I have a slight cold and so cannot sing, / I say this to satisfy you.'[15] For Powell,

amateur performance can make a fictional character seem more true-to-life by endowing him with human virtues and frailties. In Molière's *Le Médecin malgré lui* (*The Unwilling Doctor*, 1667) the drinking-song 'Qu'ils sont doux, Bouteille jolie' in Act I/5 portrays a moment of intimate, lyrical reflection [...]. Composed by Lully in the style of a popular *chanson* this song has a charm of its own which could be enjoyed purely for its own sake. [...] Sganarelle remains blissfully unaware that his song is being overheard by Valère and Lucas. Suddenly noticing his audience, Sganarelle [becomes] self-conscious and flustered.[16]

In other words, the performance was an expression or revelation of character. It is useful here to quote W. H. Auden: discussing Shakespeare, he identified 'called-for' songs and 'impromptu' songs. 'Qu'ils sont doux' would fall into the latter group:

A called-for song is a song which is sung by one character at the request of another who wishes to hear music, so that action and speech are halted until the song is

---

[13] Italics mine: 'Le Libraire a qui le lira', *L'Inconstant vaincu* (Paris: Jean Guignard, 1661), [ii–iii]. See title page of BNF Yf 4039 on *Gallica*: 'Ex libris Recollectorum Conventus Parisiensis'.

[14] Powell, *Music and Theatre*, 82. The thematic areas, systematically treated within Powell's Chapter 7, are: 'The set-piece'; 'The play within the play'; 'Musical exoticism'; 'Ballet as a dramatic device'; 'The musical world of lovers'; 'The serenade and serenade-complex'; 'The farcical serenade and the charivari'; 'The musical powers of lovers'; 'Musical performance and dramatic irony'; 'Enchantment and illusion'; 'Apparitions, dreams and the supernatural'; 'Madness and delusion'.

[15] L. C. Discret, *Alizon, comédie* (Paris: Jean Guignard, 1637), 69.

[16] Powell, *Music and Theatre*, 82; for dramatic irony, see *ibid.*, 111–20.

over. [...] On the stage, this means that the character called upon to sing ceases to be himself and becomes a performer. [...] The impromptu singer stops speaking and breaks into song not because anyone else has asked him to sing or is listening, but to relieve his feelings in a way that speech cannot do, or to help him in some action. An impromptu song is not [construed as] art but a form of personal behaviour. It reveals, as the called-for song cannot, something about the singer.[17]

'Called-for' songs naturally respond to group situations (e.g. drinking-songs) while love-songs fall naturally into the impromptu group. In popular opera later we find impromptu songs linked thematically to a trade – stylised work-songs – or a way of life. Thus in 1722 the knife-grinder Pierrot, seen working in the first scene of *Le Rémouleur d'amour* (*The Sharpener of Love*), sang the 'Gagne-petit' song (quite close to Papageno's bird-catcher song in *Die Zauberflöte*): see Figure 2.1.[18] In 1782 Mozart opened *Die Entführung* with Osmin singing 'Wer ein Liebchen' while harvesting figs, unaware of watchers.[19] A called-for song could in later years involve narrative description, story-telling, or the answer to a simple question. Marforio, 'doctor of morals', is singing advice shown in Example 3.8 on p. 75 when questioned (in a later scene) by the young woman seen on p. 48.

In the context of spoken dialogue any song is liable to be heard in a double way if its lyrics or music refer to experience outside the comedy. 'The popular songs introduced in Discret's *Alizon* (1637) serve to delineate the social class and upbringing of its characters'.[20] Thus the merry widow Alizon Fleurie sings a refrain, presumably not heard on the public stage: 'Nous pissons dans mesme pot, / Nous nous baisons à gogo, / Nous chantons tan-tire-li-ra-lire / Sans jamais nous dire mot' (In one pot we piss, In frenzy we kiss, We sing tire-lire, And give talk a miss).[21]

Extrinsic factors invite the audience to draw on its own experience when interpreting popular music.[22] On a virtual level, audience members become, as it were, surrogate singers; their memory and interpretation join with the stage performance in hand. Furthermore, the spoken context, having created a normative response to text as such, seems to continue on one special level into the next sung episode; we may feel, in fact, that two

---

[17] Auden, 'Music in Shakespeare', 511, 522.
[18] Sc. 1: *TF* V, 73 (R/I/547), *Air* 90 in Table, 27 (R/I/645). Papageno's 'Der Vogelfänger bin ich ja' has the same metre, mode, contour and repeated notes.
[19] *Ninette à la cour* uses the same technique: see pp. 271–2.   [20] Powell, *Music and Theatre*, 83.
[21] Discret, *Alizon*, 68 (also on *Gallica*). No music is yet known for the five songs performed by main characters in *Alizon*; its preface permits actors to use their own material.
[22] This paragraph draws on experience of a musical play involving two actor-singers performing a range of music evoking politics of the 1930s: *Dare-Devil Rides to Jarama* by Neil Gore (Townsend Productions), Feb. 2017.

Figure 2.1 *Le Rémouleur d'amour* (*The Sharpener of Love*), Sc.1: Pierrot the knife-grinder ('gagne-petit'), represented by a marionette, sings his theme-song. Cupid appears and takes him to the Gardens of Cythera.

levels of communication are present simultaneously. A third element of reception may respond to memories of other contexts where the song might have been heard. Borrowed music, in short, seems to involve various layers of hearing and to make various demands of the hearer.

Solo song functions differently from music involving two people, especially any dialogue in music, for plays avoid the impression that characters are thinking while singing in a cause-and-effect way. Saint-Évremond's argument would retain speech for 'Conversation, all that relates to Intrigues and Affairs, all that belongs to Council and Action':

I pretend not, however, to banish all manner of singing from the Stage: there are some things which ought to be sung, and others that may be sung without trespassing against reason or decency: Vows, Prayers, Sacrifices, and generally all that relates to the service of the Gods, have been sung in all Nations, and in all times; tender and mournful Passions express themselves naturally in a sort of querulous tone; the expressions of Love in its birth; the irresolution of a soul toss'd by different motions, are proper matters for Stanzas, as Stanzas are for Musick.[23]

Unfortunately, Saint-Évremond, who was exiled in London from 1661 and never saw Molière's productions or Lully's, avoids determining whether a main character in a drama should be permitted to sing anything.

At this point a related question arises: how do we know what were the actual proportions between music and speech? Chamfort (see p. 19) considered that speech in popular opera should occupy less than half the length of a performance. For the century before Chamfort we are not often in a position to decide about proportions because musical sources tend to be lost, unpublished or incomplete. No opera can be judged unless all its music is available for scrutiny; when this happens, the results are surprising.

Antoine de Montfleury's *Le Mary sans femme* (1663) incorporated music in three out of five acts, including *airs* expressive of identity and others with narrative purpose.[24] Two young lovers captured by corsairs become subject to the whims and cruelties of the vaguely oriental Fatiman, Governor of Algiers, and Célime, a Turkish lady. Four leading actors of the performing troupe at the Hôtel de Bourgogne were singers; one was also a lutenist.[25] Innovative use of local colour was made through *lingua franca*, an actual hybrid language used by traders and sailors around the Mediterranean: 'O Giornata Fortunata! / Ringrasciar Mahometa', and so on.[26] Music for this play was discovered a decade after Forman's 1985 edition was published, revealing the key fact that brief references made to music in the text concealed the extensive presence of music in the theatre.[27]

Six other discoveries echo this pattern. The first is Beauchamps' score for *Le Collier de perles* (*The Pearl Necklace*, 1672), discussed later; the second is Charpentier's for Raymond Poisson's *Les Foux divertissans* (*The Amusing Madmen*, 1680), also discussed later. The next is a duet of 113 bars in *Arlequin et Scaramouche vendangeurs* (*Harlequin and Scaramouche Grape-Pickers*, 1681), discussed and quoted in Chapter 3; the fourth is Dancourt's *Angélique et Médor* (1685), which omits mention of Charpentier's musical

---

[23] 'To the Duke of Buckingham' [1678] in Hayward, ed. *Letters of Saint Evremond*, 209; also Weiss, *Opera*, 53–6.

[24] Antoine Jacob de Montfleury, *Le Mary sans femme*, ed. Edward Forman (Exeter: University of Exeter, 1985). It held the stage for nearly a century.

[25] Forman, *Le Mary sans femme*, xv.   [26] Forman, *ibid.*, 95, 118–19.

[27] Powell, *Music and Theatre*, 92–5; 'O Giornata Fortunata' was joined by an unexpected song at line 1631; an *Air pour les Turcs*; 'O le bon Païs'; two dances; 'S'il ne falloit' (line 1643); and a *Contredanse en rondeau*.

'Dialogue' opening Act IV – this music is still in manuscript.²⁸ The fifth is Dancourt's *Les Trois cousines* (*The Three Cousins*, 1700) for which Gillier's newly edited score reveals 1,848 bars of music, lasting twenty-five minutes.²⁹ And the sixth is *Le Malade imaginaire*: Charpentier's score, now recovered, points towards opera by reason of relative proportions and variety of functions:

> Villégier's production [1990] cast a radically new light on the architecture of the work and on its structural coherence, as the overwhelming impact of the music compelled us to reconsider the interrelationship of music, dance and speech. The performance lasted some four hours, two of which were dialogue, and two music and dance: the long prologue and the three *intermèdes*, though they might seem short on the page, double the length of the 'play'. It is inconceivable therefore to regard the musical sections of the work as mere interludes; it might be more accurate to say that in the theatre, the spoken scenes function as interludes between the more spectacular musical scenes – this is the sense of the writer in the *Gazette de France* (18 October 1670) who described *Le Bourgeois gentilhomme* as 'a ballet in six *entrées* accompanied by a play'. Certainly the musical scenes establish (or ought to establish) the keynote of the performance as a whole, determining the rhythm and style of the spoken scenes, for there is subtle interplay between the techniques of the ballet dancer and those of the *commedia dell'arte* actor. [...] Villégier's production [...] challenges us to redefine the nature of the spectacle which Molière and Charpentier were aiming to create.³⁰

The history of popular opera will depend on more such discoveries. There cannot be a single formula, but when music intervenes for half the time, the result in London at least would qualify for the label 'opera'.³¹

*

Between 1645 and 1662 seven Italian operas were introduced to France by its first minister, Jules Mazarin.³² The last two were Cavalli's *Xerse* in November 1660 (for Louis XIV's marriage) and *Ercole amante* in February 1662. French opera was formalised only from 1669, but different kinds of musical theatre were pursued after that date as well as prior to it, as Table 2.2 suggests. The explicit aim of the first opera librettist, Pierre Perrin

---

²⁸ Le Blanc, *Avatars*, 73–5.
²⁹ Directed in Paris by the editor, Matthieu Franchin, 18 May 2017.
³⁰ Cronk, 'Molière–Charpentier's *Malade imaginaire*', 217.
³¹ From London title pages 'one learns just how generically jumbled the seventeenth-century notion of opera really was': Hume, 'Politics of Opera', 16. Between 1656 and 1707 twenty operas thus designated (including John Dryden's *King Arthur*) involved eleven works with spoken dialogue.
³² James R. Anthony, 'Mazarin' in *NGO*, III, 287.

Table 2.2 Molière, Lully and mixed forms of French opera. Scores are fragmentary or lost other than those written by Lully, Beauchamps or Charpentier. Text = 't', music = 'm'. The opera *privilège* of Pierre Perrin was awarded in June 1669, and Lully's *privilège* was awarded in March 1672.

Date	Author, composer	All-sung forms	Part-sung forms
April 1659 (Issy, then Château de Vincennes)	Perrin (t), Robert Cambert (m)	*La Pastorale d'Issy*	
May 1664 (Versailles); 9/11/1664 (Palais-Royal)	Molière (t), Lully (m)		*La Princesse d'Élide*
1666 (Marais theatre)	Claude Boyer (t), Louis de Mollier (m) (attrib.)[a]		*Les Amours de Jupiter et de Sémélé* (Powell, *Music and Theatre*, 131)
14[?]/2/1667 (Saint-Germain-en-Laye)	Molière, Lully		*Le Sicilien* (in *Le Ballet des Muses*), rev. Palais-Royal, 10/6/1667
13/10/1670, (Chambord, then Palais-Royal)	Molière, Lully		*Le Bourgeois gentilhomme*
17/1/1671 (Tuileries, then Palais-Royal)	Molière, Quinault, P. Corneille (t), Lully (m)		*Psyché*, rev. 1672, 1673
3/3/1671 (new opera house, rue Guénégaud)[b]	Perrin (t), Cambert (m)	*Pomone, pastorale* (146 performances)	
7/1/1672 (Marais)	De Visé (t), de Mollier (m)		*Le Mariage de Bacchus et d'Ariane*
Jan. 1672 (Hôtel Guénégaud)	Gabriel Gilbert (t), Cambert (m)	*Les Peines et les plaisirs de l'amour, pastorale héroïque*	
July 1672 (Palais-Royal)	Girardin (t), Pierre Beauchamps (m)		*Le Collier de perles*. In the following month, Lully first obtained restrictions over music in rival companies.
11/11/1672 (Jeu de paume de Béquet)	Molière, Quinault (t), Lully (m)	*Les Fêtes de l'Amour et de Bacchus, pastorale*	
10/2/1673 (Palais-Royal)	Molière (t), Charpentier (m)		*Le Malade imaginaire*. In April, Lully obtained further restrictions over music in rival companies.
Mar. and Apl. 1673 (Jeu de paume de Bel-Air)	Quinault (t), Lully (m)	*Cadmus et Hermione, tragédie*	

[a] Benoit, *Dictionnaire*, 471; Anthony, *French Baroque Music*, 61.
[b] The Hôtel Guénégaud, provided with an orchestra pit, constructed 'in the tennis court at the sign of La Bouteille' (Mongrédien: *Daily Life*, 93), thus explaining the name sometimes used for this theatre, *Jeu de paume de la Bouteille*.

(c. 1620–75), was to develop a specifically French, superior type of opera; he rejected Italian efforts and mocked their arias and plots. On that basis, Perrin won the first monopoly patent for establishing 'Academies of opera or musical representations in French' in June 1669.[33]

If there was an acceleration of interest in musical theatre before Perrin's *privilège*, 'by January 1672 music and dancing had come to be seen as indispensible to any spectacular production, as well as the most assured way of attracting the theatre-going public'.[34] Music was important in certain comedies from the Italian troupe, alongside magic, diversity and spectacle: *La Rosaura* (1658) and *Le Voyage de Scaramouche* (*Scaramouche's Journey*, 1676). For lack of sources, it is impossible to guess at any proportions between music and spoken dialogue. Charles Mazouer has wondered whether *La Rosaura* was actually 'an opera' containing more music than the twelve or so items discernible from descriptions.[35] The lead character herself performed at least four songs,[36] so the effect may have been no less operatic than was *La finta pazza* (*The Fake Madwoman*), brought over in 1645 by Mazarin, which contained many spoken scenes as well as Francesco Sacrati's Venetian score.[37]

The Italian troupe linked contemporary subjects with musical treatment in *Le Régal des dames* (*The Ladies' Delight*, 1668: its score is lost)[38] and *Le Collier de perles* (*The Pearl Necklace*) in 1672. For this, seventeen dance movements have been found, discussed later. The plot recounted a social scandal: after gambling away his money, a certain youth had stolen a pearl necklace from a woman asleep at a ball. He panicked, swallowed the pearls and was arrested. Having confessed, he was obliged to take laxative enemas. For the stage version the action was moved to Italy and the reprobate Sbroufadel was personified by Arlequin.[39]

Molière and Music

There seem to have been two broad approaches to larger combinations of spoken and musical theatre. One preferred looser action with scene changes and effects to which music should contribute along the way. The other wanted to include complexity and irony in the involvement of music,

---

[33] Co-signed by Louis XIV and Jean-Baptiste Colbert: Isherwood: 'Centralization', 162.
[34] Clarke, 'Music at the Guénégaud', 89, citing De Visé's preface to *Bacchus et Ariane* (1672).
[35] Mazouer, *Théâtre d'Arlequin*, p. 52; Powell, *Music and Theatre*, 266.
[36] Powell, *Music and Theatre*, 30; Scott, *Commedia dell'arte*, 65–70.
[37] Scott, ibid., 53–64; NGO, II, 213. [38] Scott, *Commedia dell'arte*, 195.
[39] Plot: Scott, *Commedia dell'arte*, 202; music: La Gorce, 'Le Collier de perles'.

the possibility of tighter dramatic structure. In the first category was Molière's grandiose collaboration with Quinault and Pierre Corneille, *Psyché* (1671), originally a court commission which mixed spoken dialogue, *divertissements* and transformation scenes.[40] 'Ridiculous, brilliant, touching or frankly tragic, we go through the entire scale [...]. In consequence the play is not presented as a plot whose dénouement one is waiting for, but as an adventure.'[41] *Psyché* constituted 'a new form of multigeneric theatre' which betrayed knowledge of Italian opera too.[42]

Where he could exercise more control, Molière involved music more deeply, seeking structural connections between music and speech, the best methods by which music should bear relevant meaning. It had to be indispensable, not recreational: in James Anthony's view, 'through *intermèdes* he introduced sub-plots that emphasised, mirrored or contrasted with the principal intrigue. This concept [...] is the model for the later *opéra comique*.'[43]

Molière and Lully's *Le Sicilien* (*The Sicilian*) included two main characters who must sing as well as act. The Sicilian Dom Pèdre wants to marry his Greek slave, Isidore. Adraste, being a gallant Frenchman, will rescue her, aided by Hali. Music is used in Scene 3, at night: an elaborate serenade arranged by Adraste to attract Isidore. Hali's spoken introduction prepares the audience for this little *intermède*, binding text and music in a further way. Unnamed singers each have solo verses interleaved with two duet sections. They vanish into the dark, and the Sicilian emerges, sword at the ready.

In Scene 8, Hali accosts Dom Pèdre and Isidore in the street and pretends to entertain them with four dancers representing slaves. But his real task is to establish surreptitious contact with Isidore using action and song: 'Chiribirida ouch alla! / Star bon Turca, / Non aver danara. / Ti voler comprara?'[44] Dom Pèdre loses patience and briefly joins Hali in a realistic, but *sung*, conversation: 'You know, my dear fools, that this song brings my stick to your shoulders.' After mocking Hali's jargon, he sets about attacking him. Thus, music and action were joined together, active characters linked to more-than-passive listeners. Later comedy made use of similar

---

[40] Given eighty-three performances: *Psyché, Tragi-Comédie et Ballet*, ed. John S. Powell and Herbert Schneider (Jean-Baptiste Lully, *Œuvres Complètes*, Series II, vol. 6) (Hildesheim etc.: Georg Olms, 2007), xxi.
[41] Laura Naudeix, 'Introduction to the Livret', *ibid.*,10.   [42] Powell, 'Introduction', *ibid.*, xxvi.
[43] Anthony, *French Baroque Music*, 54.
[44] Parallels with Montfleury's 'O Giornata fortunata': Powell, *Music and Theatre*, 375–6 and Exx. 7.5 and 7.6.

integration, as in Jean-François Regnard's *Les Folies amoureuses* (*Crazy Loves*), discussed in Chapter 4. *Le Sicilien* retained Lully's music in Paris performance, and the play gathered support; Charpentier wrote new music for it in 1679.[45]

George Dandin (1668) has no singing principals, but stories in music represented by pastoral characters create analogies with the human story: 'they are however so well joined to a common subject that they form the same piece and depict but a single action'.[46] For want of funds the music was dropped when the show transferred to Paris, and on revival.[47]

Lully's music is indispensable to *Le Bourgeois gentilhomme* (1670), though not requiring main characters to sing. It was one of the four plays that would regularly continue to be performed with music.[48] Monsieur Jourdain cultivates the nobility, finally thinking to marry his daughter to the son of the Grand Turc: but her lover has adopted that disguise since IV/4, a musical mock ceremony for Jourdain's supposed induction into Turkish religion and nobility.[49] Act I ends with demonstrations by M. Jourdain's music master and dancing master, and Act II has him dressed by four tailors to special music. Dancers represent six cooks in Act III. Act IV/1 stages a banquet for a marquise and her lover when music again helps to exaggerate Jourdain's farcical gullibility.

In 1670 comedies always had fixed stage-settings, so every musical event had to involve visitors to the Jourdain household. This limitation no longer applied in *Le Malade imaginaire*, written in three acts.

Even before his break with Lully, Molière had decided to move towards more elaborate productions, for during the *relâche* of 1671 he initiated an expensive refit of his theatre. [...] *Le Malade imaginaire* was written to exploit the possibilities opened up by the new machinery (and first used in *Psyché*), and three contrasting sets are required: the 'lieu champêtre' of the Prologue, 'une ville' (that is, a street) for the first *intermède*, and 'une chambre' for the remaining scenes. No *comédie-ballet* had required so many set-changes.[50]

---

[45] Powell, *ibid.*, 377; Charpentier's score in Powell, ed., *Music for Molière's Comedies* (Madison, WI: A–R Editions, 1990).
[46] Félibien, *Relation de la Feste de Versailles du 18 juillet mil six cens soixante-huit* (Paris, 1679), 13, in Powell, *Music and Theatre*, 204 (modified). Powell, *ibid.*, Table IIIa, 327–79.
[47] Jean-Baptiste Lully, *George Dandin ou Le mari confondu*, ed. Catherine Cessac (*Œuvres Complètes* Série II vol. 2)(Hildesheim, etc.: Georg Olms, 2013).
[48] Alongside *L'Amour médecin*, *Monsieur de Pourceaugnac* and *Le Malade imaginaire*: Clarke, 'Music at the Guénégaud', 96.
[49] Locke, *Music and the Exotic*, 223–7.
[50] Cronk, 'Molière–Charpentier's *Malade imaginaire*', 218.

Molière called *Le Malade imaginaire* a 'play mixed with music and dance', a phrase that conceals its integral musical character. It received fifty-three dance rehearsals and eighteen acting rehearsals involving fifteen instrumentalists and seven extra singers;[51] Molière and his company defied Lully's arbitrary restrictions which we quoted on p. 4. All combinations of the arts seem to be tried, starting with a wholly musical Prologue; then the first entr'acte resembles 'a short comic opera in seven scenes'.[52] Its epilogue, another *intermède*, resolves Argan's imaginary illnesses within a social satire when he qualifies as a doctor in a musical mock graduation.

The central figure, Argan, was played by Molière in four performances before his death on 17 February. Obsessed by purgations and enemas, Argan is cosseted by his second wife Béline (revealed as treacherous in Act III) and is changing his will in her favour. He wants his daughter Angélique (kept confined) to marry a dunce of a medical graduate, Thomas Diafoirus, his own doctor's son. However, Angélique has recently encountered a young man, Cléante. For the first *intermède* the scene changes to a street. It features Polichinelle (Punch), reportedly the lover of Argan's servant Toinette, and is fantastical but not quite random: Charpentier's manuscript score states that the actor stands 'in front of Toinette's window'.[53]

In Act II, next day, Cléante has adopted the disguise of a music master in order to enter the household. Dr Diaphoirus and his son make a formal visit, and the son makes a ridiculous address to Angélique, gives her a copy of his thesis and invites her to a dissection 'for some amusement'. At this awkward point Argan suggests that Angélique might like to sing something. Cléante offers 'a scene from a small opera recently composed' and passes her some music paper later revealed to contain music but no text. He says their piece will be in 'rhythmic prose or basically free verse' – a necessary excuse since they are going to have to make up the words – 'such as passion and necessity might inspire two persons who utter original thoughts, and utter without prior preparation'.

Cléante explains the piece at great length. Only gradually do we realise that he is recounting the actual story of his chance meeting with Angélique six days before at a playhouse, when she had been allowed out at the behest of an old aunt (II/1). His narration of past events catches up with the situation on stage: their pastoral music, he says, will depict a lover who

---

[51] Cronk, *ibid.*, 218, 220. [52] Powell, *Music and Theatre*, 388.
[53] 'devant les fenestres de toynette': BNF Rés. Vm^1. 259, XVI, ff. 53–5, quoted in Powell, *ibid.*, 235, n.30.

finds his way into the house of his beloved and encounters the 'unworthy rival whom her father's whim has opposed to his tender love'. And so their duet becomes a surrogate love scene between young people who have hardly spoken before. Music could not be more cleverly woven into the drama and the quality of the actor's voice is excused: 'I have no singing voice' (line 210).[54]

At the end of Act II Argan's brother visits the house to cheer him up with a new *intermède*: 'Four Moorish women dancers sing conventionally of young love [...]. What is most remarkable about the scene is that Argan remains present on stage throughout. [...] The therapy of art and music is thus proposed as an alternative to the therapy of medicine.'[55]

Intermède I was far different. In its free dramatic integration of music with spoken word Molière's imagination – Charpentier at his side– reached into realms we would probably class as surreal. But in 1673 the reference terms were Italian comedy. Polichinelle's songs are in Italian with a virtuoso mingling of different styles and registers, the first high-toned, the second a jocular response.[56] Then we plunge into a farcical argument between Polichinelle and offstage strings who represent an invisible comedic force. Charpentier called it 'a fantasy with interruptions'.[57]

Here we see a realm of music and fantasy intersect with spoken reality [...]. Polichinelle's repeated attempts to silence the music, first by shouting at it and then by pretending to play back at it with his lute, provoke first dissonant then impertinent musical responses. Here the laws of the rational world break down.[58]

In the next episode, 'Polichinelle encounters the Night Watch, who are patrolling [...] and speak by singing in chorus. [...] Polichinelle's spoken lines alternate with the choral interrogations and the musically accompanied

---

[54] Powell, ed., *Music for Molière's Comedies*, 76–9, a total of eighty-five bars, with continuo accompaniment. To give the impression of semi-improvisation, Charpentier makes very limited use of repetition and develops the motif in bar 9 ('Vous me voyez, Tircis') into a repeated figure (bars 31–2: 'Oüy, Tircis, je vous ayme': see bars 42 and 54 also). Cléante's nervousness is suggested by effects including awkward passing discords (bars 26, 35, 70) and unexpected prosodic stresses (bar 36).

[55] Cronk, 'Play of words and music', 8–9; see Powell, 'Music, Fantasy and Illusion', 234.

[56] Probably dating from after Molière's death: Powell, *ibid.*, n. 30. Dominique Visse's DVD recording suggests a direct line with Venetian opera: *Le Malade imaginaire*, cond. William Christie, Harmonia Mundi (1990).

[57] Facsimile of MS in Powell, *Music for Molière's Comedies*, [xlvi], Pl. 3.

[58] Powell, 'Music, Fantasy and Illusion', 235. After the 'Fantaisie' a stage-direction appears: 'Polichinelle avec un Luth, dont il ne jouë que des lèvres & de la langue, en disant, plin tan plan, &c.', which explains his monologue just before the entry of the Night Watch: Powell, *Music for Molière's Comedies*, 53. This routine of imitating musical instruments was a speciality later used in *intermezzi*: Scott, *Commedia dell'Arte*, 187.

dance of the Night Watch [...]. His two punishments, a nose-tweaking and a beating with sticks, are both carried out in music and dance.'[59] Whereas Polichinelle had first railed at wordless music, he now converses with constables who sing their texts. These sublimely impossible juxtapositions were doubtless inspired by Biancolelli's company whose acting Molière saw regularly: 'Molière was often our guest' at dinner, according to the playwright Jean de Palaprat (1650–1721).[60]

In the play's finale, the 'burlesque ceremony', Argan's knowledge of various diseases and their treatments is tested, each answer followed by choral responses from the fake doctors. Recommending universal use of enema syringes, he passes the 'examination'. Then (Molière's direction) 'all the surgeons and apothecaries come to do him reverence, to music'. 'In pidgin Latin, Argan addresses the assembly, which responds with choral song and dance'[61] before a last *entrée* whose music, says Molière, should join with banging of apothecaries' mortars.[62]

Little is known about the Italians' music before 1680. However, the seventeen recently discovered dances for *Le Collier de perles* show much sophistication: 'interesting, subtle, imaginative ballet music' as La Gorce writes,[63] attributing the score to Pierre Beauchamps. As happens in Polichinelle's *intermède*, humour was made out of music being oddly interrupted:

In the first act of *Le Collier de perles* the school pupils 'begin to dance' but, says the libretto, 'hearing a noise, and fearing that the Doctor is coming back, they begin again with a precise timing that is very amusing'. With these prominent silences, abruptly interrupting the concerted instrumental music, did not Beauchamps seek to portray [...] the anxious atmosphere that takes hold of the pupils?[64]

After Molière

Intense musical activity in spoken theatre continued during the 1670s. A letter written by Pierre Bayle in June 1675 considered that 'If the Molière troupe were allowed to have music and dance and as many instruments as they liked, *Circé* would have driven away all the operas seen so far.'[65] Thomas Corneille's *Circé* had music by Charpentier, as did

---

[59] Powell, 'Music, Fantasy and Illusion', 235–8. [60] Mongrédien, *Daily Life*, 106.
[61] Powell, *Music and Theatre*, 389. [62] Molière, *Œuvres*, 638.
[63] La Gorce, '*Le Collier de perles*', n. 45. The composer-choreographer Beauchamps also served Molière's troupe in the same theatre.
[64] La Gorce, *ibid.*, 105–6, with music examples. [65] Clarke, 'Music at the Guénégaud', 103.

L'Inconnu shortly after. Janet Clarke observes: 'Nor was the Guénégaud [company] alone in attempting to exploit this passion on behalf of the theatre-going public. Hauteroche's *Crispin musicien*, performed at the Hôtel de Bourgogne in 1674, contained so much music that it was known in the provinces as 'l'Opéra de l'Hôtel de Bourgogne'.[66] Charpentier's connections with the Orléans family kept his operatic ambitions afloat in the private sphere.[67] Professional singers were then disallowed for Corneille and Charpentier's *Le Triomphe des dames* in 1676; so, as Clarke finds, 'two devices [were] used to make up for any lack of skill on the part of the singers: firstly the integration of musical episodes into the plot in such a way that a less than perfect rendition is acceptable or even desirable; and, secondly, the use of music for comic effect.'[68]

Molière's ideas for text–music encounters were put to new purpose in the last musical play to be discussed here; indeed, they were added to in ways he might have enjoyed. But Raymond Poisson's *Les Foux divertissans* (1680) depicts the poorer households of Paris: this urban comedy staged by the Comédie-Française is set in an asylum. 'Subsequently reduced to one act by Dancourt, the comedy became, next to *Le Baron de la Crasse*, the most popular of Poisson's plays'.[69] It was then turned into an opéra-comique, as Chapter 7 will explain, and Poisson's comic style seems to point in that same direction.

Although the three-act plot of *Les Foux divertissans* is sketchier than Molière's would have been, the rhythm of the scenes is quicker, acted on a single set with upstage extension. We feel an insistent concern with money and survival, day to day. These characters are sometimes hungry and sometimes cold: one servant talks of surviving by filching the rations of inmates. The living-quarters consist of two rooms and a kitchen, Angélique says.[70] A hoped-for inheritance fails to materialise.

The presence of 1,414 bars of music by Charpentier plus several Lully excerpts in Act II, alongside the subject matter and setting, makes for a prophetic sort of entertainment. Charpentier wrote an overture, songs, other music and three *intermèdes*, perhaps a minimum of thirty or forty

---

[66] Clarke, *ibid.*, 103; also Hitchcock, 'Marc-Antoine Charpentier', 266.
[67] Ranum, 'Lully plays deaf'.   [68] Clarke, *ibid.*, 106.
[69] 'He presented samples of low-class Parisian manners', was 'quick to make use of [...] recent happenings' and 'especially interested in comic varieties of speech': Lancaster, *History of Dramatic Literature*, 121.
[70] *Les Foux divertissans* (Paris: Jean Ribou, 1681), I/6, II/7, III/3.

minutes to perform.[71] The leading actors, Léandre and Angélique, are both required to sing (warrants for their vocal quality are duly provided), separately and together.[72] Three trained singers, named in the manuscript, represent the performing inmates, while dancers are given principal roles in the *intermèdes*.

We are in a kind of clinic, an institution called the Petites-Maisons on the Faubourg Saint-Germain. It is run by Grognard with his helpers. Angélique's father, the miserly M. Vilain, wants her to marry Grognard so as to earn money and have a place to live: 'money is the cure for all ills' (I/3). Having a nice voice, she will arrange entertainments featuring the inmates to which the paying public will be admitted. Her rescue plan must involve young Léandre, but time is short, so he decides to disguise himself as a musical madman. At the end of Act I the inmates rehearse songs, duets and dances.

Grognard's brother is ill. Before visiting him, Grognard explains to Angélique that they have a new inmate, crazed by opera, who compulsively sings *airs*. This will amuse the future public because he might go into 'a thousand contortions' as he 'expresses all the passions': we are primed for satire. After a scene for two mad poets, the stage opens to reveal the inmates in their *loges*, babbling simultaneously. In II/9 Léandre enters singing music from Lully's *Proserpine*, which had been premiered nine months earlier. Grognard is pleased and encourages Angélique to join him. They sing a duet scene from Lully's *Bellérophon*, which had had great success the previous year. Léandre is incarcerated for trying to take Angélique's hand, but Grognard thinks it is safe to leave. She has a tearful farewell scene with him but actually plans to elope. The inmates are made to sing and dance (*Intermède* II).

A soldier who has been billetted for the night arrives and is assigned to the freezing garret without food. Léandre has had a meal brought in; he and Angélique perform songs to each other. Angélique's *menuet* is twinned with a danced *air* in similar style performed by a gypsy. Unexpectedly, Grognard returns during the feast: his brother has died and left him nothing. The soldier, watching all this, becomes master of ceremonies: after more music, he convinces everyone that he can materialise the devil, whose food they are enjoying. All rush off except Grognard, while M. Vilain

---

[71] Œuvres complètes de Marc-Antoine Charpentier, I. Meslanges autographes. Volume 18. Facsimile du manuscrit Paris, Bibliothèque nationale, Rés. Vm^1.259 (Musica Gallica) (Paris: Minkoff, 2000).

[72] LÉANDRE: 'Though I haven't the most affecting voice, let me sing what I have composed. And that minuet of yours, as though made for our love, would sound beautiful in your charming throat.' ANGÉLIQUE: 'I sing very badly, but let it suffice if it should move you': *Les Foux divertissans*, III/7, 69.

decides to accept his daughter's chosen partner. Music closes the play, sung and danced by eight inmates carrying baubles.

Poisson's style moves towards freedoms that the Italian troupe would shortly develop. All types of song except narrative are present in *Les Foux divertissans*. The inmates, for example, are musically identified in a 'laughing' trio and a disjointed dance in II/16.[73] Burlesque performance is implied by the use of Lully's music, but 'it is difficult to evaluate the degree of satire'.[74] Perhaps the actors decided to mimic the opera's original soloists, an idea that would be repeated in Fair theatre. In the ninety-bar duet from *Bellérophon* (II/2) little exaggeration would be needed to burlesque Lully's verbal repetitions ('Disons-nous cent fois, Je vous aime, Je vous aime, Je vous aime, Je vous aime' etc.).[75] Lully's music is not copied into Charpentier's score: there is a simple rubric. But Poisson's play-text does reproduce all the operatic words originally written to be sung.

Léandre's initial *air* from *Proserpine* III/2 ('Que l'absence de ce qu'on aime') is immediately recognised by other characters as 'from the latest opera'. A continuo accompaniment might have been played for these twenty-one expressive bars, but there is no indication anywhere.[76] Then Léandre sings four lines from II/1 of *Bellérophon* which had originally been sung by the princess, Philinoë ('Cruelles inquiétudes . . .'). Comedy is fuelled by the gender switch, and Lully's music is tricky in its intervals and harmonic turns, easy to burlesque. The ninety-bar *Bellérophon* duet follows this and convinces Grognard that the new inmate will be a public attraction.

Poisson, it might be argued, emulated Molière's adherence to musical plausibility. *Le Malade imaginaire* had made two lovers sing together, justifying the result by their supposed sight-reading and textual improvisation. Poisson in a related situation supposed that his lovers also sing pre-existing music: Lully's. But within the fiction, that music could be argued to have been memorised by them. This special category of verisimilitude may serve as one theoretical reason why popular opera maintained the use of precomposed music during the first half of the eighteenth century.

---

[73] Music examples in Powell, *Music and Theatre*, 139–40 and Hitchcock, 'Marc-Antoine Charpentier', 271–2.

[74] Le Blanc, *Avatars*, 63–7. Powell, *ibid.*, 137, claimed that Léandre adds his own words (with *doubles entendres*).

[75] Lully, *Bellérophon, Tragédie mise en musique*, Seconde Édition (Paris: Christophe Ballard, 1714), 57–8, 61–66. Textually, only the second duet line was changed. Forty-one bars of conversational music precede the duet. If everything from the originals is sung, these excerpts from Lully amount to 165 bars.

[76] *Les Foux divertissans*, 40. Originally sung by the character Alphée, an *haute-contre*: *Proserpine, Tragédie mise en musique*, Seconde Édition (Paris: Christophe Ballard, 1714), 227–8.

The singing ability of Poisson's actors was tested during Act III/8, where audience pleasure seems to be the dramatist's aim; dramatic propriety was stretched and opera was approached. The popular but elegant nature of their verses invites notice:

LÉANDRE:

Ce n'est qu'entre deux Amans	Only true lovers
Que les Concerts sont charmans ...	Feel music's true charm ...
Leurs amoureuses langueurs	Amorous longing
Forment une Symphonie ...	Is musical balm ...
Et la plus douce Harmonie	Harmonies sweet,
Est l'union de deux cœurs.	Two hearts that meet.

*

'The 1680s marked the turning point of royal absolutism'[77] and also a crossroads when Paris theatre attained the form which Louis XIV and Colbert had – as they assumed – made permanent: one Comédie-Française, one Comédie-Italienne and one Académie Royale de Musique showing one type of music-drama. Although comic scenes had been featured in Lully and Quinault's early *tragédies*, *Cadmus et Hermione* and *Alceste* (1673, 1674), they were subsequently 'sacrificed to the demands of unity of action'. '[B]y silencing Lully's comic muse, official French taste delayed the development of any indigenous *opéra bouffe*.'[78]

Life and art were not stilled, of course: 'the new generation of comedy authors [...] were extremely successful and amused the spectators with lighter plays of sometimes doubtful morals, but full of ingenious situations'.[79] However, in July 1682 a further royal edict on Lully's behalf formalised the prohibition of professional singers in spoken theatres.[80] It fell to the Italian company in January 1682 to take a first public step that would slowly lead to a generic expansion in theatre beyond what Colbert had ordained: it inaugurated a combined Franco-Italian form of spoken comedy,[81] which in due course would involve music to a profound extent. This phase of evolution in musical theatre is described in Chapter 3.

---

[77] Isherwood, *Music in the Service of the King*, 310.   [78] Anthony, *French Baroque Music*, 73.
[79] Mongrédien, *Daily Life*, 98.   [80] Hitchcock, 'Marc-Antoine Charpentier', 274.
[81] *Arlequin Mercure galant* by Anne Mauduit de Fatouville.

3 | Music in Gherardi's Company

Repertory and Musical Resources

The first *opéra comique*, so called, made Arlequin into a parody of an opera hero: *Arlequin Roland furieux* (*Harlequin the Raging Roland*). This illustrates the close link between *commedia* tradition and French popular opera. Because *Arlequin Roland furieux* was written for domestic entertainment (see pp. 85–7) it also argues for the 'binary identity' of popular opera, private as well as public.

This chapter offers a new assessment of a legendary period of achievement in musical comedy, the formation of an essential link between France and Italy. It builds on Donald J. Grout's dissertation, discovering what the Gherardi company bequeathed to opéra comique, and follows Virginia Scott and others in accounting for its authors and social critiques.

Italian players had been employed by French kings since 1571: Henri III and IV, Louis XIII and XIV. Actors improvised to a plan, no fixed dialogue was needed, and no dialogue sources remain; early musical comedies are known from descriptions or from various scenarios. A frequently reproduced oil painting ('Molière et les comédiens italiens') shows Molière and French actors together with *commedia* actors who shared the Palais-Royal theatre with them.[1] From 1660 Arlequin was acted by Domenico Biancolelli, stage name 'Dominique' (1640–88): 'well-educated, refined and handsome', he was on familiar terms with the king.[2] By 1686 there were fourteen actors, who 'moved on to Italian [improvised] plays interlaced with scenes in French, and eventually to plays spoken principally in French, written down in advance and learned by heart.'[3] So French character-types evolved alongside Arlequin, Isabelle, Colombine and the rest.

---

[1] Oreglia, *Commedia dell'arte*, 134. Lully's Opéra took this theatre over in 1673 (Table 1.1).
[2] Oreglia, *ibid.*, 60–2.   [3] Scott, *Commedia dell'arte*, 251.

Figure 3.1 *Les Filles errantes* (*Girls astray*), final scene: Italian actors play and sing a parody of Lully's Chaconne from Act I of *Cadmus et Hermione*.

In Figure 3.1, male *commedia* characters perform in a finale first staged in 1690.[4] On the left is the Doctor with hat and moustache (Angelo Lolli), then Mezzetin with colourful costume and soft cap (Angelo Costantini), then Arlequin with his leather mask (Evaristo Gherardi), Scaramouche

---

[4] Regnard, *Les Filles errantes* (*Girls astray*). Identifications from 'Grand Almanach historique' (1689) in Scott, *ibid.*, 312, in Mazouer, *Théâtre d'Arlequin*, Pl. 13, and Moureau, *Gherardi à Watteau*, Pl. 4.

(Tiberio Fiorilli) and Pierrot with his ankle-length pantalons (Giuseppe Giaratoni). Others in the circle possibly include an *amoureux* (young lover) like Octave or Léandre (Bartolomeo Ranieri). In Figure 3.2, a scene dating from 1697, Arlequin and Mezzetin are behaving insolently to Angélique

Figure 3.2 *Pasquin et Marforio*, Act II Sc. 3: Pasquin (Arlequin) as a *petit-maître* (fop) and Marforio (Mezzetin) interview Angélique.

(Angelica Toscano): her costume is similar to those worn by her counterparts Isabelle and Colombine in other engravings (Françoise and Catherine Biancolelli, the daughters of Domenico).

In succession to Dominique came Evaristo Gherardi (1663–1700). His own father had worked with Biancolelli as the musical character Flautino.[5] Evaristo came from Italy as a boy. He was well educated in France and became a language teacher. Doubtless due to that bookish training we possess our main source, his six-volume anthology *Le Théâtre Italien de Gherardi* (*TIG*), graced by many illustrations and 143 pieces of engraved music.[6]

Biancolelli's first French playwright was a wealthy lawyer, Anne Mauduit de Fatouville, who established the comedic 'house-style' between 1681 and 1687 with its satirical exposure of various abuses committed by the professional classes.[7] He and other authors were not from working or commercial backgrounds like Favart, Sedaine or Marmontel in the next century. Jean-François Regnard (1655–1709) inherited a fortune; Charles Dufresny (1648–1724) received lucrative royal patronage; De Losme de Montchesnay (1666–1740) was a lawyer, as had been Eustache Lenoble (1643–1711). The company was officially warned about social commentary – what an earlier English playwright called 'a personating of vices in the present governors and government'.[8]

Satire was to the fore in their most musical comedy, *Pasquin et Marforio*, 3 February 1697.[9] These are names taken from two ancient 'talking statues' in Rome, easily visible now thanks to the Internet. Citizens through the ages had used them as though posting anonymous tweets, especially to launch anti-establishment polemics about injustices or scandals. So, an ironic question on paper stuck at night on Marforio would receive an amusing 'answer' in *doubles entendres* stuck on Pasquin a few hours later, normally implicating someone in power as being to blame for the relevant woe. In the stage comedy, Pasquin and Marforio come from Rome to Paris as 'doctors of morals' offering consultations to ordinary people. Since in real life papal leaders had long sought ways of suppressing the 'talking statues', so perhaps Louis XIV feared that sequels to this comedy might

---

[5] Oreglia, *Commedia dell'arte*, 73–4; Mazouer, *ibid.*, 79–80.
[6] Issued 1700. Publication details: Ravel, *Contested Parterre*, 113–18.
[7] Scott, *Commedia dell'arte*, 280–3, 354; Moureau, *Dufresny*, 281–90; Mazouer, *ibid.*, 163–85.
[8] Fulke Greville (1554–1628), who prudently destroyed his play *Antony and Cleopatra*: Shapiro, *1606*, 264. Additionally, improvised obscenity was reported to the king: Scott, *ibid.*, 325–6.
[9] By Dufresny and Mr B***, thought to be Brugière de Barante.

trade off from it (other sequels had occurred before), speaking truth to power yet more inconveniently.

*

Italian-trained actors retained some of their *commedia* aspects within roles invented by French authors. Angelo Costantini made Mezzetin into a 'half-valet, half-adventurer',[10] whose versatility is apparent in *La Foire Saint-Germain* (*The Fair of Saint-Germain*). His many roles in this comedy may be quoted from an old London translation: 'MEZZETIN, A Pudding–Pye Man, then Squire *NinnyHammer*, afterwards *Tarquin's* Groom, Father Time, a *Petit Maitre* or Fop, as also a *Spaniard*'.[11] Multiple roles remained typical. As for the unique repertory, we find 'mythological and exotic elements', 'ordinary life' and 'an extensive representation of manners' that shifted 'from prose to verse, from French to Italian, and other languages', including an invented one for the Cannibal in *La Foire Saint-Germain*.[12] Gherardi's more musical plays have modern parallels such as the Coen brothers' film, *O Brother, Where Art Thou?* (2000): loose narrative, dry wit, rich use of music performed within the fiction; some supernatural or spectacular elements; characters opposed to the political *status quo* (late 1930s in the American South); and reference to institutional corruption. Gherardi's repertory sometimes reminds us of radio comedy:[13] corny running jokes; a cast of familiar characters; wordplay; performative and even literary parody; topical references from the news. If 'counter-culture' is an apt label, that would include satirical broadcasting within an 'establishment' medium (the BBC in our era, the monarch's troupe in the 1690s). Bruce Griffiths saw the results as 'the beginnings of comic operetta, of the cabaret style, of the music-hall'.[14]

Louis XIV destroyed the company on 14 May 1697.[15] His reasons are not documented; they are thought to have been moral, political and financial. In a country ruined by years of war, the king gained 15,000 *livres* annually by not paying its subsidy. Versailles despised City taste and preferred older Italian comedies to the French-language plays.

Spurred on by pirate editions from Brussels, Liège and Amsterdam, Gherardi devoted his brief final years to re-editing *TIG* in order to preserve

---

[10] Mazouer, *Théâtre d'Arlequin*, 171; Griffiths, 'Sunset', 97–8.
[11] *The Fair of St Germain. As it is Acted at the Theatre in Little Lincoln's-Inn-Fields, by the French Company of Comedians, Lately Arriv'd From the Theatre-Royal at Paris* ([London]: W. Chetwood, 1718), [3]; *TIG* VI, 214. 'NinnyHammer' was Regnard and Dufresny's 'Nigaudinet'.
[12] Lancaster, *A History*, Part V, 136–7.   [13] 'Round the Horne' (1965–8): see Wikipedia.
[14] Griffiths, 'Sunset', 104.   [15] Scott, *Commedia dell'arte*, 326–31.

what he considered best versions.[16] These six volumes made possible the rebirth of a repertory; they spread in 'many pirated or reprinted editions',[17] knowledge of which was taken for granted by Jonathan Swift, for example, in defending *The Beggar's Opera*: 'Whoever hath a taste for true humour, will find a hundred instances of it in those volumes printed in France under the name of *Le Théâtre Italien*, to say nothing of Rabelais, Cervantes, and many others.'[18]

'True humour' was explained in 1698 by the opportunistic publisher Braakman:

> One sees everywhere [in these texts] plain truths that are pleasurable to read, and the human heart is here so well characterised that it is easy to see that these playwrights have studied it with care and success. Utility and enjoyment are found side by side, everything seasoned by small doses of satire in just the right amount. General faults are attacked more than people. However, these characters are so true to life, albeit generalised, that innumerable types of person will easily see themselves in the portraits scattered here and there.
>
> We cannot fail to be surprised, in view of various inconvenient truths being made known as obviously as is the case here – and especially in France, where probity is almost defined by the keeping up of appearances – that the actors were allowed to continue for so long. They mocked not just the most upright people in France but also the most powerful groups in society in the most satirical way, albeit concealed beneath generalised and compliant expressions. So that is why they have just been permanently banned.[19]

Of fifty-five texts in *TIG* some thirty-five call for music.[20] Earlier comedies are preserved in a fragmentary way, yet even in later comedies the exact proportions between scripted scenes, improvised scenes and music can never be known. *TIG* does summarise the improvised actions, however.

Gherardi received permission to print *TIG* on 2 May 1698,[21] so he may have prepared his forty play-texts plus various excerpts in about one year. Presumably the illustrations and music were prepared subsequently, but Gherardi's final preface discusses neither them nor social references: 'I will

---

[16] He died shortly after delivering *TIG* to the court on 31 August 1700: Scott, *ibid.*, 351. His editing procedures: Moureau, 'Un singulier moderne', 284–5, 289–90. Mazouer compares Gherardi's 1694 and 1700 prefaces: *Théâtre d'Arlequin*, 125–32; Scott, *ibid.*, 277–8.

[17] Moureau, *ibid.*, 284; for London, see Levenson, 'Traveling Tunes'.

[18] Swift, 'A Vindication of Mr Gay' (1728), 317.

[19] 'Avertissement', *Supplément du Théâtre italien, ou Nouveau Recueil des Comédies et Scenes Françoises* (Amsterdam: A. Braakman, 1698), [2]–[3].

[20] Scott, *Commedia dell'arte*, 383; Grout, 'Music of the Italian Theatre'; Mazouer, *Théâtre d'Arlequin*, 149.

[21] *TIG* I, after front matter, 'Extrait du Privilege'. See, however, Scott, *ibid.*, 279–80, 354–5.

pass silently over the piquancy and verve of the speeches within: their subtle satire, their intimate knowledge of our century's moral habits.'[22] His music engravers prepared small-format fold-outs on thin paper which were inserted between each comedy. Users must recopy songs and add a bass sometimes because the originals are too small and fragile to play from. Their organisation is occasionally haphazard; music for one comedy can appear in the wrong place or even be divided between two volumes.[23]

Ballard's collections of 'airs from modern plays' contained songs from TIG comedies: *Les Adieux des officiers* (The Officers' Farewells), *La Baguette de Vulcain* (Vulcan's Wand) and *Les Chinois*.[24] Songs from *Pasquin et Marforio* and *Les Fées* appeared separately. Since Italian actors were usually also singers and instrumentalists, their voices and skills formed unofficial supplements to Lully's intended maximum of two (specialist) singers and six (specialist) players. Biancolelli's daughters were musicians, as were Pasquariel (Giuseppe Tortoriti) and those seen in Figure 3.1: Angelo Costantini was a frequent singer and Giovanni Costantini could play eight or more instruments.[25] The finale of *Les Filles errantes* (Girls Astray) shown in this figure depicts six guitars, three wind instruments, a violin, a cello and a percussion player, twelve performers responding to the following directions:

ARLEQUIN: Monsieur, for the sake of this wedding we must enjoy ourselves: come on, bring in the violins, call the whole household. *(All the actors enter, each with a guitar, and play a parody of [Lully's] chaconne from Cadmus.)*
CHORUS: We follow Love, let us love.[26]

In the 1691 *Ulysse et Circé* a useful note describes the instruments seen and heard in an onstage concert given for Circe and Ulysses: flutes, strings and oboe.[27] New stage machinery in 1691–2 encouraged music at the scene-changes. Angelica Toscano was the resident singer-actor, but from 1694 Elisabeth Danneret was appointed as a professional singer rather than as an actor. Touvenelle, a professional *haute-contre*, also worked with the company at this time.[28] Music had a range of purposes, as we shall see.

---

[22] 'Avertissement qu'il faut lire', [xvii]; ed. in Mazouer, *ibid.*, 130–1. Excerpts trans. in Ravel, *Contested Parterre*, 117–18.

[23] Volume I of a critical edition has appeared, ed. Nathalie Marque (Paris: Garnier, 2016). I have used the 1700 text.

[24] Laurent Guillo, 'Musique de scène', 490–1, 493–5.   [25] Scott, *Commedia dell'arte*, 267, 335.

[26] 'Suivons, suivons l'amour' from I/4 of *Cadmus et Hermione* where Arbas and two Africans sing a continuation of the Chaconne before their trio: TIG III, 49–50.

[27] 'Flûtes, Violons, Haut-bois, & une Chanteuse': TIG III, 588.

[28] Nestola, 'L'Air italien', I, 120, 148 citing Parfaict, *Histoire du théâtre français*, V, 494.

Table 3.1 Selected revivals seen at the restored Comédie-Italienne taken from *Le Théâtre Italien de Gherardi*, followed by *TIG* volume number.[29]

Le Tombeau de M. André (V)	1718–22
La Baguette de Vulcain (IV)	1718–33
Les Filles errantes (III)	1719–53
Attendez-moi sous l'orme (V)	1719–31
La Foire Saint-Germain (VI)	1720–33
Le Phénix (III)	1721–31
Ésope à la cour (III)	1722–24
Les Deux Arlequins (III)	1724–25
Pasquin et Marforio (VI)	1724–29
Arlequin Misanthrope (VI)	1726–31

Comedies from *TIG* re-appeared in earlier Fair theatre; revivals also occurred at the restored Comédie-Italienne. Table 3.1 indicates the more successful of these.

Social Themes

The background to everything was a French decline after 1685, when Louis XIV reversed Henri IV's edict of religious toleration and there ensued military defeats, crippling taxation and the loss of half a million inhabitants to emigration or starvation. Reflected in *TIG* is 'a society disrupted, fascinated, destroyed by money'.[30] François Moureau has documented the way *TIG* pilloried exploitative money-men, lawyers, venal abbés and urban bully boys; a musical reference to the wars is mentioned later.

Social hardship appeared on the stage in *La Matrone d'Éphèse, ou Arlequin Grapignan* (*The Widow of Ephesus or Harlequin Grapignan*, 1682).[31] We see Grapignan's office, clients, hangers-on and the man himself signing documents. Arlequin has become a *procureur*, that is, a rich legal advocate.

> Grapignan's mentor [...] swears that if the new *procureur* follows instructions he will have ruined a hundred families and acquired ten houses in Paris within four years. [...] 'Do you love money above all things?' asks the master. 'Will you do anything to get it?' And of course, Grapignan will.[32]

---

[29] Sources: Lagrave, *Théâtre et public*, 342–3; Brenner, *Theatre Italien*; De Luca, *Il repertorio*; d'Origny, *Annales*.
[30] Moureau, *Gherardi à Watteau*, 53–4. [31] *TIG* I, 17–64; Mazouer, *Théâtre d'Arlequin*, Pl. 8.
[32] Scott, *Commedia dell'arte*, 286.

Grapignan's dealings produce money and valuables; eventually he is condemned to death like Macheath in *The Beggar's Opera*. In *TIG* the main characters belong to the entrepreneurial class, renting out their services so that the workings of a society are dealt with more than family-centred lives of private individuals.[33] It is interesting to see how many themes in *TIG* would recur in popular opera: in fact one can say that every one of the following topics was familiar up to 1765 or even beyond:

> Satires of the lesser nobility, especially their pride in noble ancestry. A ridiculous marquis in *La Coquette* sings and dances, combing his wig; Baron de la Dindonnière in *Les Chinois* (*The Chinese People*) enters in hunting-rig holding a cowhorn. In *Pasquin et Marforio*, II/5, family trees are satirised and deficient methods of noble education alluded to.
>
> Satires of professionals. *Procureurs* are targeted, such as M. Jacquemard in *Les Momies d'Egypte* (*The Egyptian Mummies*), and financiers; doctors are too common to mention. Colombine, cross-dressed, burlesques lawyers in *L'Homme à bonne fortune* (*The Lucky Man*).[34]
>
> Paternal or family power over a daughter or ward. Young lovers are contrasted with risible pretenders like Nigaudinet in *La Foire Saint-Germain*. In *Les Chinois* a risible father in his country château awaits the arrival of suitors he has arranged but never previously met.
>
> Ridiculous persons lampooned. These include *petits-maîtres* (fops)[35] and music lovers like La Gamme in *Les Originaux* (*The Eccentrics*) or the opera-mad Mme Prenelle in *L'Opéra de campagne* (*Opera Goes to the Country*); 'crazy poets' included Scaramouche in *Les Promenades de Paris* (*Paris Walks*).
>
> Particular social groups and dialects on display. These include Gascons (*Arlequin misanthrope*) and local boatmen who sing and 'swear out loud in their fashion' in *Les Bains de la Porte Saint-Bernard* (*Swimming at Porte-Saint-Bernard*).[36] Gypsies and fortune tellers regularly appear with their music.
>
> Marriage problems. *Les Mal-assortis* (*The Ill-Matched Couples*) is briefly mentioned later. The Jacquemards in *Les Momies d'Egypte* are openly unfaithful; in *Pasquin et Marforio* most of the advice dispensed by the eponymous pair concerns marriage.

---

[33] Moureau, *ibid.*, 49–51.

[34] Following this comedic thread, Mlle Deschamps acted the part of M. Tousset, *avocat*, in Sedaine's *L'Huître et des plaideurs* (*The Oyster and the Litigants*, 1759), music by Philidor.

[35] 'With their red-heeled shoes and plumed hats, their beribboned coats with gold and silver buttonholes': Garrioch, *Making of Revolutionary Paris*, 274–5.

[36] *TIG* VI, 446. Accents in *TIG*: see Kirkness, *Le Français du Théâtre Italien*.

Paris and its life. This theme was extremely common; in *Arlequin Phaéton* the city appears as if spread out beneath the airborne Phaéton, allowing its inhabitants to be scrutinised.

The countryside, comically stereotyped but occasionally idealised. It is already opposed to city corruption (*Arlequin Phaéton*, III). Rural constables (*baillis*) are present in *La Coquette*, *L'Opéra de campagne* and *Le Retour de la Foire de Bezons* (*Return from the Bezons Fair*).

Music and Musical Roles

Recent summaries have foregrounded *vaudevilles*, *récits*, parodistic songs and Italian material.[37] Although Donald J. Grout's work on detailed contexts was limited, he transcribed all the music in *TIG* and documented a meticulous search for stylistic and formal elements showing continuity with later opéra-comique, as well as its debts to opéra-ballet and Lully's operas. His dissertation was 'not a history [of Lesage's venture] but rather a pre-history' aiming to discover 'How did the opéra-comique come to be what it was in 1715?'[38]

Aiming to identify styles within contexts, the following pages will discuss music in particular areas: an early dialogue duet; music and its functions in one-act comedies; and Italian music. Then the focus moves to *vaudevilles* and *vaudeville*-finales and finally to *Pasquin et Marforio*, the late comedy that comes nearest to opéra-comique.

The anonymous duet 'Ne veux-tu pas, Perrette' stands at the gateway of popular opera and is remarkable for its length and the musical dialogue it contains. It originated in the mainly improvised comedy *Arlequin et Scaramouche vendangeurs* (*Harlequin and Scaramouche Grape-Pickers*, December 1681) whose manuscript scenario shows its position at the end of Act Two.[39] Gherardi himself never published this scenario, but the words of the duet were pirated by Braakman, who fortunately quoted the title of his source.[40] The music – 113 bars long – is printed in *TIG* vol. I after *Arlequin Mercure galant* (January 1682), yet its words identify it with the

---

[37] Nestola, 'L'Air italien', I, 139; Harris-Warrick, *Dance and Drama*, 224 n.9. John Romey's article 'Songs That Run in the Streets' appeared too late to be considered here. Its material intersects with various topics covered later and in Chapter 5.

[38] Grout, 'Origins', Introduction, 1. The earliest *TIG* editions used by Grout dated from 1717 (Paris: P. Witte) and 1721 (Amsterdam: M. C. le Cène).

[39] Dating: Scott, *Commedie dell'arte*, 398–9. Source: BNF, Fonds français 9329, ff. 156–62 [160], on *Gallica*.

[40] *Supplément du Théâtre italien* (Amsterdam, 1698), 494–6.

Example 3.1 (a) Anonymous, 'Ne veux-tu pas, Perrette', *Arlequin et Scaramouche vendangeurs*, *TIG* I, 16–17. LUCAS: 'Perrette, will you not hear me a moment, relieve my torment?' (b) PERRETTE: 'Oh, no, Lucas, I won't. Have more sense than to talk of marriage.' (c) PERRETTE, LUCAS: 'When we love well, a kiss is freely given.'

1681 comedy: see Examples 3.1 (a–c).[41] One inspiration for it may have been the comic rustic scene with Charpentier's music in *La Nopce de village* (*The Village Wedding*) earlier in 1681 at the Comédie-Française.[42]

In Act I of *Arlequin et Scaramouche vendangeurs*, a visit to the country is arranged for Isabelle and Colombine, then Act II shows the exploits of Arlequin and Scaramouche, centred on a grape press. Lucas offers a song (now lost) for the assembled peasants, then follows our duet. In Braakman it was labelled 'Chanson en dialogue d'un Païsan, & d'une Païsanne'. Like the duets in *Les Foux divertissans*, discussed on p. 44, this forms a colloquial scene, though not for the main characters. Lucas and Perrette sing separately, come together, continue in dialogue, then sing together again: thus, the form is ABAB. Its fusion of word, action and music is specifically operatic, on a different plane of dramatic existence from its improvised surroundings.

Lucas pleads: see Example 3.1(a); Perrette resists. They argue: see Example 3.1(b). In bars 51 to 76 the argument resolves into simultaneous voicing, though not old-fashioned *unanime* texture. Again in dialogue, Lucas requests a kiss.

---

[41] *TIG* I, between 16 and 17. Grout, 'The Origins', allocated this duet to *Arlequin Mercure galant*. In *Le Théâtre italien*, ed. Marque, I, 132–9, the correct provenance is noted but not contextualised. In Briasson's 1741 edition of *TIG* this duet was truncated from 113 bars to the opening 36 bars, printed at the end of volume I.

[42] By Marcoureau de Brécourt: Hitchcock, 'Marc-Antoine Charpentier', 273.

The final section resolves matters in unanimity: 'When we love well, a kiss is freely given': see Example 3.1(c). Duets in this basic form were standard in later *intermezzi*. But Lully was experimenting with varied duet textures in the 1680s,[43] and in contemporary Venetian opera, duet designs also led towards simultaneous singing. The concerted (à 2) sections of our duet are French-influenced, their texts solidly vernacular ('Ardé, chamon'). Yet the dialogue sections use repeated notes and stepwise movement, almost all in common metre: this gives them an Italian character, potentially easier to act in a lively, natural way. As Chapter 4 will suggest, other 'rustic' dialogues were available, making it understandable why Gherardi should have issued 'Ne veux-tu pas, Perrette' in 1700.

*

All one-act works in *TIG* contain music, more than was heard in those at the Comédie-Française.[44] One-acters began in 1692, reaching eleven in number. As noted earlier, multiple roles could be taken by one individual, making musical interventions seem both pervasive and varied. Because Elizabeth Danneret did not take character parts, ingenious roles were invented for her. Only in *La Fontaine de sapience* (*The Fountain of Wisdom*) did she alone sing. It culminated in a showpiece where, costumed as a shepherdess, she focused on cynicism in a corrupt society whose vices are normally hidden. Various characters drink from the magic Fountain of Wisdom; songs evoke earlier mention of chicanery, creditors and other woes. Danneret's final six songs conclude with 'Les maris et les loups-garoux', in C minor: 'Husbands and werewolves are roughly identical'.

Vocal planning in *Les Adieux des officiers* was not untypical: three or four singers (Mezzetin, Arlequin and others) shared out seven named parts. Mezzetin's music is sometimes tricky and twice demands a high, held note. Unnamed singers took both acting and walk-on roles. Multiple roles for singer-actors appeared again in *Les Fées* (*The Fairies*), the company's last production: Danneret as a Fairy, then a Nymph transformed into a butterfly; Mezzetin as a Nurse singing a lullaby, then an Old Man. A walk-on singer represented King Croquignolet; C. V. Romagnesi sang as a shepherd; and Arlequin (Gherardi) sang as a valet.

Les Momies d'Égypte (1696) demonstrates how scene-changes, diversions and finales all employed music. A *procureur*, Jacquemard, and his wife (Mezzetin) are looking for amorous diversion at a Fair. In Scene 5, as had

---

[43] Cook, *Duet and Ensemble*, 11–12; but no other duet mentioned here exceeded seventy bars in length.
[44] Scott, *Commedia dell'arte*, 371–5.

Example 3.2 Anonymous, 'Une fille bien apprise', Jean-François Regnard, *La Naissance d'Amadis*, Sc. 1, *TIG* V, 100–1. GALAOR: 'The experienced young woman who goes her own way promises nothing to her neighbour, for fear he will talk. She strikes a better deal with a foreign buyer.'

actually happened in Paris, ancient mummies, tombs and pyramids are displayed.[45] A singing Sibyl (Danneret) ironically compares flighty Parisiennes to famous women in history. Mark Antony suddenly turns into a singing character after much mock-heroic verse dialogue with Cléopatre (Sc. 8). A finale featured 'Le Chœur': Jacquemard is punished in an essentially operatic ensemble. Hoping to dine, he is instead forced under the table and kept there by musketeers who keep their weapons trained on him while everyone else eats. Arlequin sings two mocking stanzas, 'Mr Jacquemard est bénin' and the chorus repeats the last two lines as a refrain each time.[46]

Music diversified its style according to new roles it played, sometimes echoing linguistic jokes like parodies of Racine or play on obsolete medieval words. Example 3.2 from *La Naissance d'Amadis* followed a parodic echo of Racine's *Phèdre* (I/3) reacting in fear to the name of Hippolyte.[47] Wholly different was 'Quelle fierté' sung by Debauched Cupid in *Les Adieux des officiers*

---

[45] Scott, *ibid.*, 373. See frontispiece at *TIG*, VI 329.
[46] *TIG* VI, 358. It is preceded and followed by other songs for Arlequin and the Sibyl.
[47] *La Naissance d'Amadis*, *TIG* V, Sc. 1, 81 ('Ah, malheureux! Quel nom est sorti de ta bouche?'). See le Blanc, *Avatars*, 159–61 for the ingenious parodic jokes played throughout on Quinault and Lully's *Amadis*.

as a reply to Venus:[48] probably composed by Dufresny himself, the refined contour of melody follows the text. Jacqueline (Mezzetin, cross-dressed) sang an expressive song when she passed the test of virtue concluding *Attendez-moi sous l'orme*, and her assertive phrase 'ma mère l'a dit' is sung twice, differently, as though being improvised.[49]

Example 3.2 is also representative of 'comic-moralistic' songs. Others occur in *Les Mal-assortis*, II/2, one from a barman and the other from the god Hymen.[50] Laughter in music is found: Momus's 'Ah, ah, Compère Vulcain' in *Les Adieux des officiers*, for example.[51] We shall see this basically operatic convention in later chapters, and it is present in *Le Joueur* (no. 29 of the online edition).[52] Other songs made use of dance rhythms, trumpet motifs or imitation of non-musical sounds.[53]

*

The following discussion comprises longer as well as single-act comedies. A number remain anonymous, which explains why most of the music also is: the creative result mattered more than any individual's contribution. Playwrights supplied texts gratis and they became company property, as did some music composed for their own texts by Jean-François Regnard and Charles Dufresny (never attributed, however). The only composers named in TIG were Paolo Lorenzani for 'Tornami in petto speranza' (*Arlequin empereur dans la lune / Harlequin Emperor in the Moon*, 1684) and de Masse for songs in *Les Originaux* (1693).[54] 'Philbert' may have written a 'song of the nightingale' for *La Critique de La cause des femmes* (*Critique of The Women's Lawsuit*).[55]

The known compositions of Jean-Claude Gillier, however, were exceptionally dramatic and sought after. When he broke ranks and had his songs for *La Foire Saint-Germain* (16 December 1695) engraved independently,[56] Gherardi's indignant players took legal action; by the time Ballard's print-shop was raided, only seven copies remained.[57] Among this edition's nine pieces, 'Miei spirti amorosi' is now attributed to Carlo Grossi's opera *Giocasta regina d'Armenia* (Venice, 1676).[58] Gillier's music often helps

---

[48] Sc. 4: TIG IV 330. [49] Text by Dufresny: TIG V, 547. [50] TIG IV, 380. [51] TIG IV, 346.
[52] www.cambridge.org/9781316515846. [53] Grout, 'Origins', 214–18; see Chapter 11.
[54] Music split between vols. III and VI, where his name is found: Grout, 'Music of the Italian Theatre'.
[55] TIG II, 105, music lost. Grout conjectured Philbert Gassaud; Marcelle Benoit suggested Philibert Rébillé, a musical colleague of Molière's: *Dictionnaire*, 551.
[56] See *Gallica* and GB-Lbl: B.319 (15). On Gillier and England: Rogers, 'John Gay', 188.
[57] On 8 February 1696: Campardon, *Comédiens du Roi*, I, 137–9.
[58] Nestola, 'L'Air italien', I, 55, 90, 140; II, 173. Seven songs were omitted and are lost: Act I, 'Oranges de la Chine'; 'Prens garde à mes dents'; 'Un air gay' in Act III, 'Après un pareil procès'; 'Dedans tes champs'; 'Pour vous, Monsieur le Sauvage'; and 'Je suis an Apothicaire'.

Example 3.3 Jean-Claude Gillier, 'Époux qui possédez', Jean-François Regnard and Charles Dufresny, *La Foire Saint-Germain*, III/4, *TIG* VI, 303. LA CHANTEUSE: 'Husbands with attractive wives, do not sleep.'

singers, because his tonal imagination suggests meaning and action. In I/7 Danneret's enigmatic 'Venez à nous' was sung as a Talking Head in a fortune-telling booth. This *menuet* shifts from G minor through C minor and E♭ major to B♭ at the double-bar: 'Come and hear your future fate! But ignorance is a great help in the married state!' In III/2 ('Ton temps est passé') Mezzetin as Father Time derides the old Doctor as semi-impotent, repeating 'Ton' as though shouting in his face. A tremolo effect on the final note 'quart' completes the accusation: he might chime the first quarter, but never the full hour.

This leads to a fantastic court scene with exotic animals, humans and flowers: Arlequin is the Emperor of Cape Verde and Scaramouche is his elderly stooge. Dressed as a Sultana, Danneret sings to him the graceful warning 'Époux, qui possédez', seen in Example 3.3. Gillier's vocal embellishments are usefully written out in both repeats, so this is a good example of an *air* made to be taken away and tried at home. Music is often heard amid the fantasy and farce of this act, crowned by Gillier's beautiful 'Vous qui vous moquez par vos ris' which becomes a finale-number (see Table 3.3 on p. 69).

No further duets like 'Ne veux-tu pas, Perrette' are found, but character, acting, text, music and stage directions certainly formed new levels of synthesis. Example 3.2 ended Scene 1 of *La Naissance d'Amadis*, the knight-errant Perion (Arlequin) joshing with his squire Galaor. It is designed as a comic exit aria, as the stage direction shows. It may reference

Quinault's 'maxim' *airs*, but it twists the convention as Galaor repeats the final bars like a 'fade', their clustered quavers implying a gestural response.

Musical expositions were also possible. In Dufresny's *Les Adieux des officiers*, Mars' and Venus' loves are the chosen allegory, ironising the recall of army officers to war in the spring, leaving city wives with their bourgeois husbands. Mars bids Venus adieu; four cupids attend. We hear a trumpet tune for the drummer, Mezzetin:

MEZZETIN [*singing to noisy music*] Saddle up, saddle up, Mars, quickly! to war! Take your sword, it's time. (etc.)
A CUPID [*stops him and sings languidly*:] You can follow Glory and its rewards, Leave Mars and Venus in peace.[59]

These alternations are heard three times before Bellone enters singing, 'It's time to leave, Mars, Go, carry war to the ends of the earth; leave us in peace for at least six months.' Then Vulcan appears and strikes his anvil to annoy the lovers; this is coordinated rhythmically when a cupid again sings, hammering timed with the music.[60] Because singing takes longer to perform than the speeches in between, Dufresny established a proportion in favour of operatic values, which develops throughout. Ten musical numbers are given a wide variety of functions, including the aforementioned solo for Cupid, smoking and probably swigging from the brandy-bottle hanging from his belt.

*

As Chapter 10 discusses, Italian music was long familiar in popular theatre. Thanks to Barbara Nestola we know that five Italian-language arias in *TIG* and the duet 'Mia luce' derive from recent Venetian operas. Three Italian arias remain unidentified; for a few others we have the text but no music.[61] From before Angelica Toscano's debut in 1685 two sectional Italian arias are preserved in *Arlequin Mercure galant* (1681) plus Lorenzani's 'Tornami in petto' for *Arlequin empereur dans la lune* three years later.[62] Their dramatic role is unknown, owing to the fragmentary preservation of these texts; nevertheless the two from 1681 are fully fledged examples of declamatory and expressive Italian style.

---

[59] *TIG* IV, 317. The wider role of this scene in musical planning is shown in Moureau, *Dufresny*, 142.
[60] *TIG* IV, 322: 'Un Amour chante sur l'air des Forgerons, dans le temps que Vulcain frappe sur Enclume'. Also timed to the music, Marcel hammered an anvil in *Le Maréchal-ferrant* (1761).
[61] Nestola, 'L'Air italien', I, 55, 90–1, 140–54.
[62] Marque, ed., *Le Théâtre Italien*, I, 125 ('Risvegliatevi', 60 bars), 129 ('O giorno avventuroso', 60 bars), 492 ('Tornami', 20 bars, sung twice).

Angelica Toscano's first known music is a nocturnal scene within *Les Deux Arlequins* (*The Two Harlequins*): she played her own guitar accompaniment, overheard by the concealed Harlequins.[63] Musically, 'Non ha mai pace' is a graceful da capo aria in A minor, thirty-seven bars long, Venetian in style. Nestola discovered that Toscano's next preserved music, 'Voglio far col mio sembiante', came from *Giulio Cesare in Egitto* (1677), music by Antonio Sartorio (1630–80). It forms a markedly attractive da capo piece in C major whose position and function in *Les Chinois* are unfortunately unknown.[64] Nestola is surely right to claim that, even before Gherardi's leadership, the Italian troupe was positioned to compete musically with opera houses anywhere. This happened before the Paris Opéra introduced Italian *ariettes* in the 1690s.[65]

We can speculate that other dramatic uses for Italian music existed in *TIG* than have survived, so two surviving scenes must be mentioned. In *Ulisse et Circé*, II/11, we have 'Cantiamo compagni la gioia, sù, sù' sung as a finale number by Mezzetin (now a cat metamorphosed by Circe), Arlequin and other various animals.[66] In *Les Mal-assortis*, I/5, Marinette is one of four daughters on a Spanish island, corseted, costumed and made up in order to attract Arlequin's attention.[67] Her song with tambourine contrasts laughter and freedom with marriage bonds.[68]

After Elisabeth Danneret was hired in 1694, Italian music was used in less active ways: rounding off a scene, as we saw, or as part of a *divertissement*. The third-act finale of *Arlequin misanthrope* included 'Mia luce', a love duet taken from the opera *Tito* (1666), possibly by Cesti; the singers were dressed as 'bergers héroïques' ('heroic shepherds'), that is, purely artificial types familiar at the Opéra. Whether or not their costumes parodied Opéra styles would be interesting to know.[69]

Vaudevilles and *Vaudeville*-Finales

A central part of Grout's argument was a perceived 'important change which began during the early 1690s, that from the use of opera music to

---

[63] Act II/11, 1691: *TIG* III, 353, stage direction provided. The music, melody and bass, is found at I/4, where Marinette does not appear.
[64] *TIG* IV, music inserted after 178.   [65] Collasse, *Astrée* (1691); Charpentier, *Médée* (1693).
[66] *TIG* III, 590; no music survives.   [67] Arlequin, the new governor, must marry one of them.
[68] 'Nò, nò, non, che non prendo marito', *TIG* IV, 365; no music survives.
[69] Thirty-six bars long: *TIG* VI, 593–4. Nestola, 'L'air italien', I, 149–50. Its original Italian vocal scoring was adjusted; analogous processes would occur at the Fair theatres.

vaudevilles'.[70] From 1692–3 specifically musical jokes in different comedies became associated with popular tunes or *vaudevilles* which could 'deflate' more pretentious music. In Dufresny's *L'Union des deux opéras* (*The Two Operas United*) (1692) Grout saw 'the contrast of two ideals', namely parody of courtly opera as opposed to 'simple airs, tunes of the people'. Then in *Le Départ des comédiens* (*The Actors' Farewell*) (1694) Grout thought 'the popular basis of the opéra-comique is fully realised' because 'We have set *Bellérophon* to *airs* of the Pont-Neuf', as Pasquariel sings.[71] The Pont Neuf bridge was once a central exchange point for *airs* to be traded (see Figure 4.1 on p. 81).

This is how it works: Dufresny's text specifies seven *vaudevilles* in a burlesque rendition of two scenes from *Bellérophon* that were especially vulnerable to humorous criticism. Indeed the first of these (II/2) is the one that Poisson had included in *Les Foux divertissans*, noted in Chapter 2. Arlequin as Bellérophon sings to the tune 'Sur le pont d'Avignon' (not the modern tune), 'Princess: destiny seems to crown my love for you' and Mezzetin (as Philinoë) replies with the tune of 'Réveillez-vous, belle endormie', 'I have shared your woes, I must share your pleasures.' Pasquariel strikes up in the role of a Priestess and Mezzetin that of a Sacrificateur, burlesquing Lully's III/5 with tunes like 'Ami ne quittons point Créteil', 'Vous m'entendez bien', 'Flon flon' and 'Rossignolet joli'. Arlequin parodies the oracular appearance of Apollo (in the original, as a golden statue), poking his head through a screen before taking on the hero's role in IV/7, mounting a winged horse and combatting the monstrous Chimaera (Pasquariel).[72]

But the one thing the Italians eschewed was any method or formula. Further context is useful when evaluating how far their use of *vaudevilles* anticipated Fair theatre practice by employing pre-existing tunes. Grout's list of *vaudevilles* included cases where music composed originally for TIG went on to become popular and thereby entered the Fair repertory. This research is obviously important because it proves that Gherardi's repertory was a musical source for popular opera. However, once we take out those cases and order the rest chronologically, we discover the use of traditional *vaudevilles* before the point in 1694 when TIG authors embarked on more-structured ideas such as the sequence of seven pre-existing tunes in the little parody of *Bellérophon*.[73]

---

[70] Grout, 'Origins', 167. See also Mazouer, 'L'apparition du *vaudeville*', *Théâtre d'Arlequin*, 145–60.
[71] Grout, *ibid.*, 172–4. Dufresny's *L'Union des deux opéras* was the sequel to *L'Opéra de campagne*, discussed later, burlesquing Lully.
[72] For precise comparisons see the web-based Annexe 3 to Chap. III of le Blanc, *Avatars*, 25–6. Also, Mazouer, *Théâtre d'Arlequin*, 145–60.
[73] TIG distinguishes between pre-existing *vaudevilles* and new material simply by never printing the music for the former, only the latter.

Table 3.2 Evolution of *vaudeville* usage in *TIG*.[a] *Clef* = Ballard, *La Clef* (1717).

Location in *TIG*	Date	Title of comedy	*Timbre* of *vaudeville*	Examples of later usage
I, 412	8/6/1685	*Colombine avocat pour et contre*	'Hélas la pauvre fille' (brief snatch sung in passing).	*TF* I, *Table*, 35. Falk, *Parodies*, no. 93, p. 138.
II, 521	10/1/1690	*L'Homme à bonne fortune*	'Morguenne de vous' (sung by Mezzetin as a parrot).	*TF* I, *Table*, 17; *Clef.*
III, 568, 578, 580	20/10/1691	*Ulisse et Circé*, I/10, II/5	'Et brin, bron, brac' (as a drinking-song); 'Beaucoup de vin'; 'Je mène une agréable vie'.	No sources found.
III, 450	4/2/1692	*Arlequin Phaéton* I/1	'Lanturlu'.	*TF* I, *Table*, 7; *Clef.*
IV, 75	7/6/1692	*L'Opéra de campagne*, III/7	'De mon pot je vous en répons' (sung by Arlequin as Renaud).	*TF* I, *Table*, 26.
IV, 292	10/1/1693	*La Baguette de Vulcain*, sc. 3	'Réveillez-vous'.	*TF* I, *Table*, 1; *Clef.*

[a] This table interprets various information in Grout, 'Origins', 205–7.

In 1685 (see Table 3.2) Arlequin was a 'false Marquis' jeering at Colombine, who has eloquently testified before a judge as to his infidelity. Although only momentary, the *vaudeville* had extra comic value because he sang 'she has a cough' ('elle a le mal de toux') instead of 'everything's wrong with her' ('elle a le mal de tout'). In 1690, again mocking, Mezzetin importuned Colombine. She replied 'Me? I don't want to marry a parrot,' so Mezzetin sang his *vaudeville* and Pierrot reacted diegetically to its origin: 'There goes the ambassador of the Pont-Neuf!' Joining these examples in 1691, 'Et brin, bron, brac' became the finale-song to Act I of *Ulisse et Circé*, performed by Ulysses and his companions. In II/5 Marinette and Mezzetin, having been shipwrecked, cheer themselves up by singing Italian words to the two French *vaudevilles* specified.

Things took a new turn in 1692 when 'Lanturlu' was used for a set piece of derision. Jean Palaprat was a significant playwright, whose freewheeling comedy *Arlequin Phaéton* featured an ambitious aerial view of Paris.[74] Palaprat seems to have originated a basic ironic technique that would be crucial to popular opera. The arrogant Phaéton (Arlequin) mocks his rival

[74] *TIG* III 466 (II/1), with Phaéton and Momus 'in the clouds'. Mazouer, *ibid.*, 187–98.

Example 3.4 Traditional, 'Lanturlu', Jean Palaprat, *Arlequin Phaéton*, I/1, *TIG*, III, 450. PHAÉTON: 'If those brainless cowards make ridiculous obeisance to that son of a cow, I will make my opinion of that good-for-nothing known everywhere, Lanturlu.'

Epaphus, whose mother Io had once been transformed into a heifer by Zeus. Fashionable people have been making sacrifice in Io's temple so Phaéton lashes out in song (I/1) at these 'brainless cowards' and at Epaphus as the 'son of a cow': Example 3.4. The referent and the *vaudeville* receive a more complicated link, what might be called 'double-operational irony': Phaéton, we assume, 'remembers' the tune 'Lanturlu' and 'improvises' new words to it. Comic value is immediate because people actually did sing *vaudevilles* in derision.[75] But a double irony emerges through the original words of 'Lanturlu'; although unsung, they must have been intended to be present in the minds of listeners:

Familiar, unsung words:

Quand mère sauvage / Dit dans ses leçons / Que fille à votre âge / Doit fuir les garçons: / Vous devez répondre, / C'est ce que j'ay résolu, / *Lanturlu, lanturlu, lanturlu*.[76]

When beastly mother lays down the law and says 'A girl of your age must never speak to boys', you should reply, 'That's what I'll do, *Lanturlu*', etc.

New words, as sung:

Si le peuple lâche / Foible du cerveau, / À ce fils de vache / Fait le pied de veau; / Je veux bien qu'on sache / Que je dis de ce tondu:[77] / *Lanturlu, lanturlu, lanturlu, lantire.*

---

[75] Campardon, *Spectacles*, I, 97.
[76] Ballard, *La Clef* (1717), 226. Momus (god of Jollity) walks in later after some stagey mock-heroic alexandrines and says, 'Your singing is lousy, like street-porters, have you no shame?' The youths have mocked sing-song declamation at the CF; their verses were printed in smaller font. The same type of joke was used at the Fair theatres.
[77] 'A 'tondu' literally means, in modern parlance, a 'skinhead'.'

If those brainless cowards make ridiculous obeisance to that son of a cow, I will make my opinion of that good-for-nothing known everywhere: *Lanturlu*, etc.

It surely struck the first spectators powerfully. Although hard to write, this double method flourished and continued. But when *TIG* authors adopted *vaudevilles*, each example involved a diegetic, a derisory or set-piece performance. *Vaudevilles* never functioned as a dialogic medium in their repertory. That watershed development, which evolved around 1709, has been described thus:

The opéra-comique comes into being when by a tacit understanding with the author, the audience admits that one character on the stage, after having expressed himself in prose or verse, may begin singing and then drop back to speaking without the change seeming to be noticed by the other characters.[78]

In promoting derision, *vaudevilles* inherited a ludic pattern known in literature and society from the tenth century. A fifteenth-century example was quoted and glossed by Natalie Z. Davis:

In the text Solomon gave forth rhymed proverbs of high moral tone; Marcolf then answered back in earthy verse, either redoing Solomon's sayings in shrewd practical language, or going him one better in a joke. Thus Solomon observes:

A load upon a mare
May be silver or brass
Which one the beast won't care.

To which Marcolf responds:

The whore doesn't care
Which man jumps on her ass,
To her it's all one fare.[79]

In comedy, a Marcolf 'role' could be played by a *vaudeville*. A song in *TIG* is sometimes performed by a professional singer using a cultivated type of style, after which Mezzetin or Arlequin would perform a 'down-market' equivalent set to a *vaudeville*. Thus 'Époux qui possédez' (Example 3.3) was followed by Arlequin singing 'Pierre Bagnolet', which collapses the moral message into a vulgar form: 'Women form an enemy territory / Which will be besieged sooner or later' (Example 3.5). Because the original

---

[78] Font, *Favart*, 22, trans. in Grout, 'Origins', 20. See pp. 107–13.
[79] *Solomon et Marcolphus collocutores*, undated imprint of unknown provenance: Davis, *Society and Culture*, 227.

Example 3.5 Traditional, 'Pierre Bagnolet', Jean-François Regnard and Charles Dufresny, *La Foire Saint-Germain*, III/4, *TIG*, VI, 303–4. ARLEQUIN: 'Women form an enemy territory which will be besieged sooner or later. Husbands are always shouting, "Who goes there?" Take care if possible: if the sentry sleeps, someone will enter the guard-room.'

text of 'Pierre Bagnolet' was an army song, double-operational irony applied too.[80]

For some in the audience, paired songs might have recalled scenes in Lully's operas where contrasting *airs* followed each other.[81] And 'high–low' antitheses themselves may have created expectation regarding contrasts in style. After all, musical contrasts involving the coexistence of *vaudevilles* and newly composed music remained key issues for opéra-comique up to 1762.

*

Gherardi's company also developed the *vaudeville*-finale, an iconic part of popular opera even found in Classical, Romantic and later opera up to *The Rake's Progress*. 'It is in strophic form and most often has verses of seven or eight relatively short lines with a refrain in which all may join.'[82] Different characters sang different verses, but the refrain, like a moral, was reinforced by everyone. Ending a comedy with a strophic song was presumably ancient practice, taken up by Shakespeare in *Twelfth Night*, for example.[83]

Grout's list of *vaudeville*-finales (p. 199, n. 1) numbers fourteen examples. Whereas *Arlequin homme à bonne fortune* (*Harlequin the Lucky*) closed with merely two stanzas sung to a guitar, *L'Union des deux opéra* ended with four strophes sung by different characters.[84] Within *La*

---

[80] Ballard, *La Clef* (1717), 287.   [81] Rosow, 'The Articulation', 83–4, 96–7, citing *Armide*, V/1.
[82] M. Elizabeth C. Bartlet, '*Vaudeville* final', *NGO*, IV, 905.
[83] For a comprehensive survey of eighteenth-century *vaudeville*-finales: Schneider, 'Das Finalvaudeville'.
[84] In minor mode and duple metre: *TIG* IV, 95–6; music: *TIG* VI, after 376, sheet 2, verso, line 2.

Example 3.6 Anonymous, 'La verte jeunesse', Jean-François Regnard and Charles Dufresny, *La Baguette de Vulcain*, Sc. 5, *TIG*, IV, 297. LE DRUIDE: 'Youth is green, blows with the wind, always lives for the moment. But for feeble old age, pleasure is the remembrance of good things past.'

Baguette de Vulcain in 1693 seven stanzas were sung by different characters all joining in with the refrain: see Example 3.6.[85] Dancing was normal both before and after.

Many finale tunes were like brisk gavottes or else Branles, which could be in either duple or triple metre. Tapping into history, Branles in *TIG* and popular opera recalled 'the solo verse and choral refrain structure of the old French *carole*'.[86] Other finales have four-bar tunes of sometimes extreme gaiety. In one case the play's title appears as a refrain in every strophe: 'Attendez-moi sous l'orme' (*TIG* V), or 'Wait for me till the cows come home' in proverbial French.

Grout's analysis of *vaudevilles* identified those composed for *TIG* and which survived in *Le Théâtre de la Foire*. In Table 3.3 the addition of 'F' denotes material in *TIG* appearing as a *vaudeville*-finale. In Fair theatre practice, *vaudeville*-finales were specially composed and credited to a composer; Mouret's final *vaudeville* for *Le Joueur* at the Comédie-Italienne can be viewed as no. 30 of the online edited source.[87]

---

[85] By Regnard and Dufresny: *TIG* IV, 297; music after 312.
[86] Daniel Heartz, Patricia Rader, 'Branle', *Grove*; branles 'shared some affinities with the *vaudeville*; indeed several 16th-century *voix de villes* were labelled "chanson-branle"': *ibid*.
[87] See www.cambridge.org/9781316515846.

Table 3.3 Melodies written for *TIG* that remained popular as *vaudevilles*.[88]

F	Pata, pata, pata pon (*Colombine avocat*)
	Je sis la fleur des garçons du village (*L'Union des deux opéra*)
F	Mathurin mon compere (*L'Union des deux opéra*)
F	La verte jeunesse (*La Baguette de Vulcain*: Example 3.6)
	Qu'un mari soit pulmonique (*La Foire Saint-Germain*)
F	Vous qui vous mocquez par vos ris (*La Foire Saint-Germain*)[89]
	M. Jacquemard est bénin = Amis sans regretter Paris (*Les Momies d'Égypte*)
F	Comme un coucou que l'amour presse[90] (*Arlequin Misanthrope*)
	Jean-Gille, Gille joli Jean (*Pasquin et Marforio*)
	Robin ture lure (*Pasquin et Marforio*)
	Mère dont la fille est jeunette (*Pasquin et Marforio*: Example 3.8)

Towards *Pasquin et Marforio*

This final section describes musical ambitions in full-length works. The Italians were afraid neither to address the big picture – the theme of society – nor to include music when planning dramas. Thus Charles Dufresny 'deflated' Lully's *Armide* at the end of his three-act farce, *L'Opéra de campagne* (*Opera in the Country*). To a basic marriage-comedy,[91] he added a running joke: Mme Prenelle (Mezzetin) is desperate to see an opera in Paris. Fortunately a travelling opera company arrives on stage in Act I with an incredible collection of grotesque characters, their children, instruments, scenery, costumes and boxes piled into a cart pulled by horses. Very lengthy stage directions make clear that special music was composed for this entrance: 'trumpets and timpani are heard' and 'everyone plays as they go' circling the stage, while a carter sings orders to the horses 'accompanied by all the instruments'.[92] Mme Prenelle and Arlequin (as Renaud) finally perform a burlesque of *Armide* Act II, and this distraction allows her daughter to marry young Octave offstage.

In an elaborate finale to *Les Originaux* (August 1693) Houdar de La Motte wrote a danced *divertissement* with a geopolitical theme.[93] Colombine's suitor Arlequin and her lover Octave present this extravaganza. After musicians have entered playing a march, the inner stage reveals a large 'terrestrial globe revolving' and four singing characters: Marinette (Angela Toscano) dressed as Asia, in an 'amorous pose';

---

[88] Information arranged from Grout, 'Origins', 205–7.
[89] Text: *TIG* VI, 319–21; music in Ballard, *La Clef* (1717).
[90] Text of final stanza. First stanza was 'Comme l'hyver a des roupies'.
[91] The daughter is confined so that she can be married off conveniently. Molière's *L'École des femmes* (see pp. 159–60) was a famous precedent.
[92] *TIG* IV, 15–16. [93] *TIG* IV, Act III/12, 469.

Mezzetin (Angelo Costantini) as America, dressed in a fur coat; Pasquariel (Giuseppe Tortoriti) blacked up, representing Africa; and 'A Singer' representing Europe, dressed in French style. As in courtly opera there was dancing between each of their songs: four different sets of dancers performed *entrées*.

Stylish verses suggested each continent: if this was burlesque, the parody must have been in the delivery. Masse's songs are elegant and sober, often falling into contrasting halves. Dissonant word-painting conveys 'froid' (cold), and Lully-influenced figures infuse 'tremble' (L'Amérique). Never, though, would a Lully *divertissement* have contained the words sung in Europe's solo: 'All Europe feels the cruelties of Mars. Under his colours France alone takes sides with Victory.'[94]

Three months later, various musical forms permeated *Les Aventures des Champs-Élisées* (*Adventures in the Elysian Fields*). Its brilliant conceit viewed society from the perspective of the underworld. 'The play is full of music and spectacle,' wrote Scott; moreover, there is an enormous cast, a unified setting and a consistent theme.[95] Acts I and II start with music; all three end with music. In this version of Hades the shades talk with full knowledge of what has recently happened to them in life. Pluto is courting the ghost of Lucinde, who loves Agénor. Eventually Proserpine and Agénor persuade the god to return the young couple to life. Wit is especially strong when Arlequin, a career thief by family tradition, is in polite discussion with a *procureur* in I/3:

ARLEQUIN: Let me embrace you and ask your friendship. There is too much similarity in our professions for there not to be at least some in our tastes.

PROCUREUR: Similarity in our professions? And in what respect, if you please, Monsieur?

ARLEQUIN: In what respect, Monsieur? Excepting that you work in the city and we in the suburbs, I see no difference at all. [...] *Procureur*, robber, it's as much as to say barber, wig-maker. Whoever mentions the one, supposes the other.[96]

Act I opens as follows: 'Pluto appears with the shade of Lucinde, with whom he is in love. He is in the middle of several Happy Shades who dance, sing and play various instruments.' This music, now lost, involved three different soloists and a chorus; a chorus ending Act II does survive.

---

[94] *TIG* IV, 471, music split between vols. III and VI.
[95] Text anon., by 'L.C.D.V.': Scott, *Commedia dell'arte*, 378–9. [96] *TIG* IV, 481.

Twenty-four lines of verse were allotted to music in I/1; Pluto then says 'Pray withdraw, happy souls; your concerts, so far from alleviating sorrow, serve only to increase it.'

In Scene 4 the Shade of a musician arrives in Charon's boat and performs an eight-line lyric (music lost). Arlequin enters and says 'Oh, oh, Here come the complainants in song' and asks them for news of the 'other world' using the *vaudeville* 'Jean de Vert'.[97] Its catchy tune is in AABB form, running to 8+8+8+8 bars. Initial quatrains are sung by Arlequin to the AA music, then various Shades reply in the BB phrases. Nine times, Arlequin sings a leading question about the world and each time comes a witty answer ending with the 'Jean de Vert' refrain. What all this ironically celebrates is that nothing in society ever improves:

ARLEQUIN: You who come newly embarked from the place of our birth, Tell me, does life go on as it was before my departure?
FIRST SHADE: Interest reigns supreme just now, As in the time of Jean de Vert in France.

There is no proof that audiences sang, but the structure offers an invitation to join in this survey of topics like marriage, bankers, doctors and the law.[98]

Six compact spoken scenes later, we arrive at the finale to Act I, set in the Temple of Hymen. Pluto hopes that a *divertissement* will assist in Lucinde's seduction. At Proserpine's instigation the words instead elaborate on the anguish of marriage, using a parody of Act III/ 1–3 of Lully's *Amadis*. The performers are a Husband, a Wife, a chorus of married couples, Hymen, Florestan and Corisande. The latter pair's undying mutual affection in the original opera becomes undying loathing in the parody.

The names 'Lully', 'Quinault' and *Amadis* do not appear here in *TIG*, but Judith le Blanc convincingly argues that where there is close textual, metrical and rhyming parody of an opera libretto rendered in a smaller type size, then the appropriate original music was heard in some form.[99] The Italians had already arranged Lully's chaconnes to end *Arlequin Jason* in 1684 (*Amadis*), *Les Filles errantes* in 1690 (*Cadmus*, see Figure 3.1) and *Ulisse et Circé* in 1691 (*Armide*). Other examples involved 'situational parody': 'they are integrated within the action and involve close connection with the text of the original'.[100] In *Les Aventures des Champs-Élisées* the Act

---

[97] Ballard, *La Clef* (1717), 212; Jean de Vert was Johann von Werth (Weert), famous mercenary (1591–1652).
[98] Scott, *ibid.*, 384.
[99] Le Blanc, *Avatars*, 155–8, where she reproduces the Quinault text side by side with the parody text.
[100] Le Blanc, *ibid.*, 146.

I parody involves over a hundred lines of text linking I/12 with I/13. Lully's corresponding music involved recitatives, solos, duets, choruses and contrasting musical styles: in fact, if we include the occasional *Prélude*, these sections involved 469 bars of music.[101] Given that a recording of *Amadis* exists, it is possible to time the parody: between eighteen and nineteen minutes are needed.[102] Again we find that where measurable evidence survives, larger proportions of music in spoken comedy were involved than appearance today suggests.[103]

A similar parody in *Les Aventures des Champs-Élisées* closed Act II using music from *Cadmus et Hermione*; yet it was preceded by *new* music sung by two mourners and a chorus of Afflicted Shades. This (anonymous) music and its text are reminiscent of *Alceste*, lasting between eighty-six and 113 bars in length, depending on repeats, notated on two staves. It displays no irony in word-setting. With most of the Italian actors singing, up to a dozen voices might have been heard.

*

So, we end with *Pasquin et Marforio*, the last three-act comedy in *TIG*. As mentioned at the start, the 'talking statues' of Rome were here transformed into eponymous human form. Scholars have seen the clearest evidence of something new:

The play has more music than any of the other mainpieces, partly because Julie, the second of the Doctor's daughters, never speaks but only sings. [...] However, Mezzetin also sings much more than is usual in a play of this genre. *Pasquin et Marforio* is, in many ways, a kind of summary of the changes that took place in the Italian repertory after 1691.[104]

A closer look reveals how different aspects of music have been integrated within its practical plan and thematic tissue – the conception and treatment of the subject; no references to Lully operas are required. The collaboration between an experienced Dufresny and an obscure Brugière de Barante made for a new approach wherein all the solos are carried by only four actors, three

---

[101] Calculated from the 'Nouvelle édition' (Paris: J. B. C. Ballard, 1719), 100–23, excluding 16 recitative bars whose words are not parodied in *Les Aventures*.
[102] Discounting the recitative mentioned in above note; CD cond. Christophe Rousset: Aparté AP094.
[103] For other *parodies*, see Moureau, 'Lully en visite chez Arlequin'.
[104] Scott, *Commedia dell'arte*, 381; Mazouer, *Théâtre d'Arlequin*, 92, 154. Maria Teresa D'Orsi, *pace* Scott, arrived too late to take the part of Julie: Gueullette, *Notes et souvenirs* (1750–62), 21. Ballard's *Pasquin et Marforio* collection contains eleven anonymous songs. An attribution to Lalande in Guillo, 'L'Édition', 97, has been withdrawn (personal communication).

of whom retain their roles throughout: Pasquin (Arlequin), Marforio (Mezzetin) and Julie. This key fact makes *Pasquin et Marforio* different from all its predecessors. It automatically enhances the strength of operatic feeling, and this consistency is paralleled by the fourth singer, presumably Elizabeth Danneret, who represented the non-speaking Slander (La Médisance) in Finale I and then was apparently silent until Finale III, music simply labelled 'La Chanteuse'. Two female actors, neither required to speak at all, matched another 'operatic' pair, Pasquin and Marforio.

A hackneyed plot-type was adopted but expanded in a way that allowed for unity. Le Docteur has two daughters, Julie and Angélique, and a niece, Léonor. Julie, the favourite, loves Leandro, who has persuaded her to sing but never speak: because the Docteur loathes music, he might (so it is hoped) be persuaded not to keep her unmarried (his long-term plan). Angélique is extremely vain, and the Docteur wants her to marry not Octave but a noble. Into this group come Pasquin and Marforio, 'doctors of morals', and their effect is twofold. They encourage Parisians to imitate Romans, to deposit written innuendos and to spread slander; and they invite anyone seeking advice to consult them. Le Docteur asks them to attempt to cure Angélique; in disguise, they denigrate her appearance and behave badly, impersonating a *petit-maître* (Pasquin) and his page (Marforio): see Figure 3.2. Léonor, however, is less impervious than Angélique and eventually runs mad because her numerous love affairs begin to be the subject of public comment.

All these elements are given greater interest by a socio-philosophical question that is foregrounded in Finale I: what is truth, once slander is believed? Today's debates concerning 'fake news' are evidently venerable, and the 'social media' aspect of Léonor's fate is obvious.[105] Truth and Slander are personified in Finale I; in a paired sequence, Slander's pained G minor solo ('Non, ce n'est pas la Médisance' with da capo) was followed by a catchy ensemble sequence of twelve verses: see Example 3.7. Each one is structured as a question-and-response, which makes a musical performance out of the very dynamic of the 'talking statues' tradition. Lines 1 to 3 (seven bars of music) plant a rumour starting 'They say . . .' and conclude, 'It's just slander.' Lines 4 to 7 (eight bars of music) expand the rumour but conclude, 'That's the pure truth.'

They say that doctors are malicious assassins. It's just slander.
    They say that their ignorance causes more deaths than war and plague. That's the pure truth.

---

[105] 'Publicity will ruin a woman's reputation', I/5: *TIG* VI, 607.

Example 3.7 Anonymous, 'On dit que le médecin', Charles Dufresny and Brugière de Barante, *Pasquin et Marforio*, I/7, *TIG*, VI, 617, stanza 4. LA MÉDISANCE: 'They say that doctors are malicious assassins. It's just slander. They say that their ignorance causes more deaths than war and plague. That's the pure truth.'

The flawless matching of word and music within this structure ensured the song's survival. Its clever momentum performs the act of hysterical rumour-mongering itself: one rumour leads to another, and the audience, if joining in, becomes complicit in the spreading of 'false news'.

The twelve strophes were shared between Pasquin, Marforio and Slander. Subsequently, Pasquin and Marforio have other question-and-answer sequences in music. Their propensity to sing matches their status as legendary popular figures: down-market equivalents of the supernaturals of orthodox operas. Their music, Grout wrote, can sometimes be perceived 'as an accepted part of the action itself'. He quoted 'Mère dont la fille est jeunette' in III/1, four stanzas that reply to Angélique's spoken question, 'Tell me the secret of pleasing and seeming attractive': Example 3.8.[106] Marforio's advice endorses coquetry, suggesting help from the mother to ensnare the lover.

With Julie, the ambiguity of convention as between singing and speaking is itself foregrounded. She is not pretending to be crazy (like Agathe in *Les Folies amoureuses*: see Chapter 4); her music emulates the lament style, so that we might identify her as a serious character moving in the realm of opera. In II/4 the seamless transition between her father's speech and her sung reply binds the two media together.

LE DOCTEUR: Parle, je t'en conjure (Speak, I beg you).
JULIE: (singing): Ah, ne me faites point parler (Ah, do not make me speak).

---

[106] Grout, 'Origins', 195–6.

Example 3.8 Anonymous, 'Mère dont la fille est jeunette', Charles Dufresny and Brugière de Barante, *Pasquin et Marforio*, III/1, *TIG*, VI, 638. MARFORIO: 'If a mother wants his young daughter, landerira, to make her fortune, she should discreetly, landerirette, [help make her pleasing.]'

This opening refrain starting on a high f" is heard thrice, in D minor tonality. Her other solo, 'Craignez, pères' in III/6, is a short da capo in A minor also using high f" at the start, thus a plaintive submediant note.[107]

Thanks to the loose style of construction often used in *TIG*, audiences would not perhaps expect Julie's story to be wrapped up neatly, any more than Angélique's or Léonor's are. For a *dénouement* the comedy substitutes a kind of musical finale starting in Scene 8, a farcical advice-surgery between Pasquin, Marforio and an Impatient Man. After the pair sing their quasi-duet 'Mari dont l'impatience' nothing more resolves: La Chanteuse appears unannounced and initiates a series of four or five musical items.[108] A *vaudeville*-finale, 'Quand la colique', sings in praise of remedies like Sirop de Mante and Vin de Mante.[109] The final 'argument' of the comedy is that neither doctors nor spouses can alter destiny, so we must simply enjoy the wait.

Pasquin et Marforio was revived in 1724, as Table 3.1 showed, and it was seen for five more years. We can only guess how many times it was read, sung or acted in the private sphere.

*

The legacy of Gherardi's troupe had influence beyond popular theatre and is still familiar today through the art of Antoine Watteau and his

---

[107] Her music avoids g" (a favourite pitch in Danneret's solos) which argues for Julie's role being taken by one of Orsola Cortesi's daughters: Scott, *ibid.*, 345.
[108] A *unanime* duo, 'L'épouse la plus belle', is in the Ballard print, not *TIG*, just as 'Craignez, pères' is in *TIG* but not Ballard.
[109] 'Sirop' was a low term for 'wine': Grout, 'Origins', II, 137. 'Mante' might be 'Mantoue', Mantua.

followers.[110] Italian themes and comic spirit spread to the Opéra;[111] the Dauphin and his friends sought to have Italian comedy re-established.[112] Fair theatre troupes adapted Gherardi's repertory and absorbed some of his former players;[113] erstwhile Italian colleagues constantly toured around France.[114] Rewriting and adding to *TIG* was a speciality of Louis Fuzelier (ca. 1672–1752): see Chapter 5.[115] Gillier's songs stand as part of the same legacy, memorable music that would be as familiar today as Watteau's paintings if music could have its own living 'gallery'.

Seen against the background of music in purely French plays, music in *TIG* injects great inventiveness to match the surrounding generic freedom. Musical planning gave rise to functions well beyond those seen before in comedy. Molière's musical legacy was defined in part by plausibility – inventing a logic of musical intervention – and in part by inherited convention. Franco-Italian comedies offered the opposite, being unconventional and often implausible to start with. But there was a paradox: when writers like Dufresny acted as their own composer, text and music had the closest, most plausible relationship and fitted the context perfectly. This ideal of unitary authorship continued into the era of Fair theatre, since the author who selects a *vaudeville* and gives it words becomes, in effect, a composer as well as a librettist.

Italian actors formed choruses and quasi-ensembles, as were seen in Fair theatre. Audiences knowing their Lully operas would benefit from a range of jokes and parodic episodes, also as in early Fair theatre. Italian opera arias made for a natural comparison between national styles. Stylistic mixture and contrast were central, and an aesthetic bequest to popular opera: what might be called 'creative discontinuity' and 'multivocal' effects.

Many of the songs in *TIG* remained in the public mind for decades; Chapter 4 investigates the domestic implications of such musical knowledge.

[110] Tomlinson, *La Fête galante*; Heartz, 'Watteau's Italian Comedians'.
[111] Cowart, 'Carnival in Venice'; Rebecca Harris-Warrick, 'Staging Venice', and *Dance and Drama*.
[112] Fader, 'The "Cabale du Dauphin"'. [113] Moureau, *Gherardi à Watteau*, 32.
[114] Pierre-François Biancolelli's career is representative: see S. Le Floch, M. Berjon, 'Notice' in Rubellin, ed., *Théâtre de la Foire*, 41–3; Sakhnovskaia, 'Sur la trace des Italiens'.
[115] Fuzelier wrote forty or more texts for Fair theatres between 1701 and 1716: Trott, *Théâtre du XVIIIe siècle*, 139–46; Cucuel, 'Sources et documents', 253.

4 | Singing and Acting at Home

Contexts

This chapter draws out what Chamfort and Mme de Serée have borne witness to (see pages 17–19): the pleasure of bringing theatre music home.

Here is what has caught on with the most popular pieces [in Monsigny's *Le Roi et le fermier* (*The King and the Farmer*)]: after hearing them twenty times people want to hear them more; they respond vividly when someone else sings them; what if one sang them oneself? They want to memorise them, at least; if they lack a good voice or ears, they hum them quietly; in a word, they are enraptured, yet without reflecting that what makes them so delightful is that they derive from an interesting basis in theatre.[1]

Much in the following pages supports the notion that popular opera had a binary identity: that it was probably more sung and played in private than viewed publicly. 'A lively, easy music attracts the ear and sometimes the soul. [...] The *airs* which people take away from these pieces serve them in private entertainment no less than in the theatre.'[2]

It has been estimated that over 450 publications offered arrangements from Grétry's operas.[3] During earlier periods, as will be seen, raw materials for playing and singing would be arranged individually, but publishers sought to assist arrangers: Rameau had *Les Indes galantes* issued in domestic form, reordering its pieces into five 'concerts', as he called them, for players and vocalists.[4] To think about domestic practice allows us to bring different phases of popular opera together, dissolving fault lines between them that seem large today but might have been irrelevant at the time.

Between 1721 and 1737 the ten compact volumes of *Le Théâtre de la Foire* (*TF*) were published specifically for ordinary people; Lesage and

---

[1] Garcin, *Traité* (1772), 74–5. Example 12.1 shows the Romance from this opera.
[2] La Dixmerie, *Lettres* (1765), 43.   [3] Audéon, 'Des arrangements'.
[4] *Les Indes galantes / Balet, / Reduit à quatre grands concerts / Avec une nouvelle Entrée complette* (Paris: Boivin, Leclerc, l'Auteur, n.d.).

d'Orneval spelled this out in their editorial Preface. Cue numbers allowed users to locate music quickly; comedies aimed at 'the correction of morals'; they were 'suitable to provide a serious man with some distraction from his important duties'; they 'may serve above all most usefully in the country, where one often follows various other pleasures by performing small dramatic pieces within the family'; and readers were urged to *sing* the *vaudevilles*, because contributing one's own effort will inspire an 'indulgent gaiety'.[5]

To whom exactly was this addressed, and with what expectations on either side? We guess that many families would have had nothing to do with theatricals, for within the Gallican Church there was a vociferous line of moral debate against acting and theatre. Bishop Bossuet's *Maximes et réflexions sur la comédie* of 1694 struck a new tone of 'harshness [...] difficult to explain', only gradually finding mitigation as the next century proceeded.[6] Yet numerous clerics involved themselves in theatre, wrote plays, even defended its moral possibilities. Private theatricals were 'led by the duc d'Orléans and spread down the social scale'.[7] The comic masterpiece *Ragonde* was originally a domestic creation.[8]

At the moneyed end of the spectrum, good standards were bolstered by the participation of professional musicians.[9] In more modest environments one supposes that the result was tailored to the talents of a particular gathering. A journalist's account of private theatres is withering in its disdain for poor taste and ignorant audiences far from the capital city.[10] In Paris, the Comédie-Française felt challenged: 'The good times are over, everything has changed / Since twenty new theatres by the Seine / Vie together to rival us.' A barman retorts, 'Thirty, more like. I saw a list in the *Mercure galant*.' 'At that time [1731]', explained the editors of *TF*, 'theatre pieces were given in several well-appointed houses' – which logically included opéras-comiques, inasmuch as almost all Fair texts are labelled 'pièce'.[11] In the company of Voltaire – a dedicated amateur actor – Léopold Desmarets recalled having been 'involved in rehearsing or performing forty-four acts of plays or operas' in the space of two days.[12]

---

[5] 'Préface des Auteurs', *TF* I, [4–13] (R/I/7–9), first issued in 1721.
[6] McManners, 'The Theatre' in *Church and Society*, II, 315.   [7] *Ibid.*, 330.
[8] P. Néricault Destouches and Jean-Joseph Mouret, *Ragonde, ou La soirée de village* for the duchess du Maine at Sceaux, Dec. 1714.
[9] Hennebelle, 'La Vie musicale'.   [10] Chevrier, *Observations* (1755), 58–63.
[11] *Les Désespérés, Prologue*, Sc. 5, *TF* IX, 137 (R/II/429). The only *TF* text with the generic label 'opéra-comique' is Carolet's *L'Isle du mariage, TF* IX/2, 222 (R/II/612).
[12] Connon, *Identity and Transformation*, 11–12; Favart, *Mémoires*, III, 245–6.

We must not forget good humour. The prince de Conti's country house had a small portable stage,[13] whence an eyewitness reported to Favart:

I saw your *divertissement*, *Les Comédiens du Mans* [*The Actors of Le Mans in Flanders*, 1745] given privately at L'Isle-Adam [...]. The stage itself was the spitting image of what one sees at an inn thrown together for jugglers or acrobats. Instead of wings there were four screens of different heights; the backdrop was a serge curtain that the actors lifted by one corner when someone went on stage [...]. The prince's musicians were grotesquely dolled up. The overture was conducted by M. [Josef] Kohaut, lutenist at the Concert Spirituel. He wore a black woollen wig, and with his red camlet suit he looked like one of the Furies at the Opéra; on his nose, which is extremely long, perched a pair of glasses. All the musicians were in the wrong place. Duport [cellist] played violin. Vachon and Trial, excellent violinists, were on cello. And so nature, being thus perverted, very naturally produced the most bizarre comic effects.[14]

Both private and public music knew *quietness*. Female voices, thought François Raguenet, were insufficient to fill a theatre ('Girls that have neither lungs nor wind').[15] J. J. Quantz thought the 'French manner' to be 'more simple than artful, more spoken than sung'.[16] Documents reveal one noble amateur 'lowering his voice when he sings', or another with 'not much voice', and another with 'a small voice'.[17] At the Opéra Comique 'Mlle Nessel has a mere slip of a voice but tender, true and flexible, and her trills are brilliant and light [...]. Besides, [this theatre] can tolerate small voices.'[18]

These sources help us understand a cultural continuity that Charles Perrault refers to in the first-ever public defence of French opera:

ARISTIPPE: I will not gainsay the fine points you make; but I am surely not mistaken in thinking that the little songs that are performed [in Lully's *Alceste*] are very bad.
CLÉON: How can they be worthless if the whole world knows them by heart and sings them everywhere? You can think of them what you please;

---

[13] Vernet, 'Théâtre, musique et société', 81–4.
[14] Antoine-François Quétant, 17 April 1763 in Favart, *Mémoires*, III, 82–3.
[15] Raguenet, *Parallèle* (1702) trans. as *A Comparison* (1709), 38; Nancy, *La Voix féminine*, 181–4. The perceived loudness of the opéra-comique singer Hamoche (see p. 114) should be understood in this context.
[16] Quantz, *Playing the Flute* (1752), 334 (Chap. XVIII, §76): he stayed in Paris for 7 months in 1726–7.
[17] (a) the duc d'Ayen, 1746; (b) the prince de Condé, 1781; (c) Mme de Marchais, undated: Hennebelle, *De Lully à Mozart*, 170.
[18] *Mercure*, 1759, July/2, 198.

but to me it's more than far-fetched that a worthless song could get all Paris singing. Is it the one with the refrain 'Si l'Amour a des tourments' that you don't like, or the one with 'L'Amour tranquille s'endort aisément', or five or six others similar? I should be very sorry not to enjoy them; and I would never disdain these little songs which make perfectly good sense when detached from the main work, are appreciated by many persons, and yet still come together to form the body of that work.[19]

Lully's music was apparently being sold in the street as early as 1660.[20] Street sellers offered new melodies but also new words for older ones, especially on the wide central river bridge, the Pont-Neuf. Urban legend remembered the composer-singer Philippot le Savoyard working here in the seventeenth century.[21] Figure 4.1 shows one of his successors, Charles Minart, in action.

Lully's dance *airs* were commonly sung, taken from *divertissements* or prologues where much musical repetition occurred. Thus Lully 'tutored' audiences as Judith le Blanc says, maximising their exposure to melodies.[22] People then sang along at the Opéra, causing English writers like Joseph Addison to report: 'The Chorus in which [French] Opera abounds, gives the Parterre frequent Opportunities of joining in Concert with the Stage.'[23] Martin Lister noted: 'There are great numbers of the Nobility that come daily to them [the operas], and some that can Sing them all.'[24] La Bruyère satirised the élite amateur in his *Characters*:

Narcissus rises in the morning to lie down at night. [...] Who will let us know that Beaumavielle [an actual operatic bass] died yesterday, and that Rochois [the opera star famous as Armide] has got a cold and will not be able to sing for a week? [...] who will sing at table a whole dialogue of an opera, or the madness of *Roland* in a *ruelle*, as well as he does?[25]

But the universal presence of song in society was what struck Le Cerf de La Viéville (1674–1707) when issuing his defence of opera in 1705–6. 'In poetry and music, etc., time puts its seal on the reputation of works

---

[19] Perrault, *Critique de l'Opéra* (1674), 50–2.
[20] Schneider, *Die Rezeption*, 2; le Blanc, *Avatars*, 549.
[21] Gétreau, 'Philippot le Savoyard'; Isherwood, *Farce and Fantasy*, 3–21.
[22] Le Blanc, *Avatars*, 580. See Examples 5.1 and 5.2.
[23] Addison, *The Spectator*, 3 April 1711: vol. I, 88–9.
[24] Lister, *A Journey to Paris* (1699), 171. Singing took place in the boxes, not just the *parterre*.
[25] La Bruyère, 'De la Ville', *Les Caractères* (1688/1829), I, chap. 7, 163, 165, trans. in Van Laun, *Characters*, 172, 175 (modified). '*Ruelle*' signified a space between a bed and a wall. François Beaumavielle [Baumavielhe] and Marie Le Rochois created many roles: *DOP*, I, 394–5 and III, 541–3.

Figure 4.1 Charles Minart, well-known singer and music-seller on the Pont-Neuf. Source: BnF.

[...]. [Anthoine] Boesset's *air* 'Si c'est un crime d'aimer' is sixty years old. We sing *vaudevilles* every day that are at least the same age: marvellous proof of good quality.'[26] His forceful extension of this reasoning proposed a musical form of social inclusion:

When I heard, for example, the air of *Amadis*, 'Amour, que veux-tu de moi', etc., sung by all the kitchen-maids of France, I was right in thinking that this air was

[26] La Viéville, *Comparaison* (1705–6), II, 318.

already certain to have the approbation of everybody in France between the ranks of princess and kitchen-maid; that this air had passed through all those ranks to reach the lowest [...] and noticing that it had succeeded in touching the kitchen-maid as it succeeded in touching the princess, that it gave pleasure to the learned and the ignorant alike, to minds of the highest order and the lowest, I concluded that it must be very beautiful, very natural, very full of true expression.[27]

This ideal of music and words held in common was defended by Noël-Antoine Pluche in *Le Spectacle de la nature*, rejecting a social exclusion made more obvious by fashionable concerts of instrumental music.[28] The ubiquitous presence of music was described in Laura Mason's 'Songs under the Old Regime', from which the following is taken:

Songs and singing did more, however, than simply entertain and inform. They were fully integrated into the richly aural and visual culture of the eighteenth century. Sound and vision did not exist in opposition to one another, as some scholars have suggested; rather, they formed a sensually complex whole.[29]

Publications and Practices

In 'The Power of Domestication in the Lives of Musical Canons', James Parakilas theorised music-making alongside studies of canon formation.[30] Parakilas problematised the activity of amateur musicians. 'How can we consider a performance that to us represents open distortion, even travesty, of the original – as opposed to hidden transmutation of it [as] "a canonical musical performance"?' 'The wider we open our definitions of musical canons, of arrangements, and of domestications, the more deeply we will be able to understand the role of domestic (including pedagogical) marketing in the history of Western musical canons.'[31]

This is a perfect formulation for approaching popular opera. On one hand, Lesage was giving status to selected opéras-comiques by publishing them. On the other, arrangers' instructions and publicity texts reveal clues about the educational uses of opera music.

[27] Ibid., II, 328, trans. in Strunk, *Source Readings*, 3, 138–9 (modified).
[28] Pluche, *Spectacle de la Nature*, VII (1746) quoted in *OAR*, 136–8.
[29] Mason, *Singing the French Revolution*, 17.
[30] Parakilas, 'Power of Domestication'. William Weber's writing on French operatic life also bridges public and domestic spheres: '"La musique ancienne"' and 'Lully and the Rise of Musical Classics'.
[31] Parakilas, *ibid.*, 14, 18; he theorises individual consumption of manufactured products using Michel de Certeau, *The Practice of Everyday Life*, trans. Steven Rendall (1984).

The first known printing of Lully's music, namely excerpts of *Isis* in 1677, consisted of part-books for home performance. Full scores emerged only in 1679 (*Bellérophon*).[32] The publisher Ballard's twenty-six opera scores in folio format were 'for amateurs to purchase so that they could play and sing their favourite sections of the opera in their homes'.[33] Near-proof of this comes in a full score of the opera *Achille et Polixène* printed at Amsterdam, because the editor boasted that the increased size of its note-heads would comfort 'those who sing in concerts'.[34]

Amsterdam was home to seven publishers arranging music from French operas. Most surviving copies are now preserved outside France, but some could have circulated internally: Carl B. Schmidt found at least thirty-four editions of part-books.[35] *Amadis* was offered in rival sets, each including the chaconne and each with a different decorative title page.[36] International buyers were welcomed with a note in English on five of Pointel's title pages: 'Fit for to sing and to playd uppon all sorts of Instruments.'[37] One arranger told buyers that they had replaced the vocal clefs with one single clef 'for those learning to play the flute or violin'.[38]

Such part-books could have been used to accompany operatic singing at home. Chaconnes, overtures and dances arranged for private singers with added texts were issued as 'Bacchic Parodies', which grew into a three-volume collection by 1702. For example, with a continuous text spread over four pages, the whole *Passacaille* from *Armide*, V/1–2, was parodied as 'Amis, fuyons tous l'Amour'.[39] This was not a momentary fashion. From Examples 4.1(a) and (b) we see how 'a new *parodie*' of the Chaconne from *Pyrame et Thisbé*, all 306 bars, was arranged for solo singers in the late 1740s within a music periodical for domestic performers.[40] In Example 4.1 (a) the opening words refer to 'Rhea and Astræa', ancient divinities

---

[32] Guillo, 'L'Édition', 96–8; it is not true for France that 'virtually all opera scores circulated exclusively in manuscript, and even then, in a bewildering number of versions': Christensen, 'Public Music', 70.

[33] Griffiths, 'Critical Report', 276. Guillo listed Ballard's various scores in 'La musique de scène'.

[34] Edition by Antoine Pointel (1688): Schmidt, 'Amsterdam editions', 134.

[35] Between 1682 and about 1715: Schmidt, *ibid.*, 131–65; Rasch, 'Soixante ans', 108–9.

[36] Heus 4 (1684) and Pointel 5 (c.1687) in Schmidt, *ibid.*, unique copies preserved in GB-Lbl. On p. 71 we saw the same chaconne used in *Arlequin Jason*.

[37] Schmidt, *ibid.*, 137–43.

[38] *Les Trio des Opera de Monsieur de Lully, Mis en ordre pour les concerts*, 2 vols. (Amsterdam: P. & J. Blaeu & A. Le Chevalier, 1690): Schmidt, *ibid.*, 147.

[39] *Parodies bachiques, sur les airs et symphonies des opera. Recueillies et mises en ordre par Monsieur Ribon. Seconde Edition* (Paris: Christophe Ballard, 1696), 210–13. *Les Ouvertures des opéra de Monsieur de Lully* were likewise intended to be sung (Paris: J. P. C. Ballard, 1725).

[40] Rebel and Francœur's opera had been revived in 1740. *Recueil d'Airs, de Contredanses, Menuets et Vaudevilles Nouveaux chantés sur les Théâtres de L'Académie Royalle de Musique et de*

Example 4.1 (a) François Rebel and François Francœur, *Pyrame et Thisbé*, II/4, Chaconne, arranged anonymously in *Recueil d'airs*, issue 7, bars 1 to 13: 'Here dwells Venus and her court, here is the dwelling we dedicate to Love, a safe haven for Rhea and Astræa.' (b) Rebel and Francœur, *Pyrame et Thisbé*, Chaconne, arranged in *Recueil d'airs*, issue 7, bars 137 to 143: 'Finally one tires of suffering: yes, I shall be cured and languish no longer, cruel one, or die faithful; and soon a new lover, tearing off my fateful blindfold [...]'.

possessing Masonic associations at this particular time. Thus, parodic texts might have been vehicles for all kinds of cultural dynamics.[41]

The copying of instrumental parts could help to teach skills, as discussed later. When Ballard issued vocal arrangements of four hundred and one *menuets* 'In every key / Notated for [the use of] instruments',[42] no instrumental parts were actually included. A key table in the form of an index was arranged by seven tonalities, presumably so that users could arrange a personal sequence on the basis of whether their group could best play in one key rather than another.

The *New Grove Opera*'s account of opéra-comique publication was uncontentious for the pre-1752 field but erred in saying that librettos 'to

---

L'Opéra Comique. Lesquels se jouent sur toutes sortes d'Instruments (Paris: Boivin, Leclerc), issue 7 (n.d.), 100–15.

[41] Rhea and Astræa: see *OAR*, 103–4.

[42] *Les Menuets chantants, sur tous les tons; notez pour les instruments*, 2 vols. (Paris: Ballard, 1725).

the 1770s' provide 'the main surviving source for this period'.[43] Printed scores flowed unceasingly from publishers after the success of the first musical comedy on the *intermezzo* model: Dauvergne's *Les Troqueurs* (*The Swappers*) of 1753.[44] At first they might lack wind parts or an overture, but they often included spoken dialogue. Scores appeared of some of the visiting Bouffons' repertory that we shall encounter in Chapters 10 and 11,[45] and of their French-language adaptations. Two were even published retrospectively in order to claim some priority in the development of the new genre: Monsigny's *Les Aveux indiscrets* (*Indiscreet Confessions*) and Duni's *Le Retour au village* (*Return to the Village*), both in 1759.[46] Virtually all new works by Duni, Monsigny, Laruette and Philidor were offered in score, and this was in addition to excerpts, arrangements and librettos.[47] Only catastrophic failures in public theatres were *not* engraved.[48]

The full score of Philidor's *Le Sorcier* (*The Sorcerer*) shows the intimate kind of connection felt between a composer and their domestic public. It was dedicated to 'The Public' in terms that thanked and flattered an 'impartial, enlightened public that encourages and protects' the artist. Philidor was aware that his 'new genre' was something 'that one part of the nation still wishes to oppose' (perhaps he remembered Mme d'Entreville's letter to the *Mercure*). Consequently, 'At the request of several Musicians, the composer has had the score engraved complete.'[49] The traditional function of printed scores was to provide study material, and *Le Sorcier* shows that a popular opera could be meant for study as well as sensation.

Bordelon's *opéra-comique*

It happens that the 'first' opéra-comique to bear that genre label was conceived and published for domestic entertainment: a burlesque issued by *abbé* Laurent Bordelon (1653–1730). As a description of his publication the following (although it concerns another country) could serve well: '[Some] fully scripted [Italian] plays apparently date from around the

---

[43] Richard Macnutt, 'Publishing', *NGO*, III, 1158.
[44] Existence of full scores is shown by 'P' [*Partition*] in Wild*TOC*.
[45] Occasionally claimed as having been engraved from an authentic MS source.
[46] See Chap. 8, p. 198, and Chap. 11, p. 281.   [47] Schneider, 'Publier la musique'.
[48] La Borde's *Les Amours de Gonesse* (CI, May 1765) was withdrawn after four nights but also published. See Wild*TOC*.
[49] 'Au Public' and title page of *Le Sorcier. Comédie Lyrique en deux actes* (Paris: La Chevardiere, etc., n.d. [1764]).

turn of the seventeenth century, and seem to have been attempts by amateurs "to reproduce something like the *commedia dell'arte* experience in private performances among friends".[50] If we believe the publisher's claim that *Arlequin comédien aux Champs Élisées* (*Harlequin Actor in the Heavenly Fields*) was a text never intended for publication, which he persuaded the author to part with, it could be inferred that other amateurs might have written domestic comedies using music.[51]

The first edition of *Arlequin comédien* emerged on 23 April 1691:[52] a three-act comedy with stage directions and humorous ancillary material providing a framework, 'Cardan's Letter Sent from the Heavenly Fields'. Thus it was supposedly written to amuse the shades of philosophers (Aristotle, Xenon, etc.) who took individual roles as shown on the finely engraved frontispiece. The edition sold well, claims the publisher, before a revised and expanded version appeared on 27 August 1694.[53] This is where we find *Arlequin Roland furieux* (*Harlequin the Raging Roland*), 'opéra comique' in ten scenes written in extremely dramatic and concise style. It parodies Lully's *Roland*, ending with the hero roaring drunk and smashing up a tavern instead of running mad as in the tragedy. It transpires that 'there are thirteen extracts from Lully's airs or recitatives, either verbatim or with new words almost all concerning wine'.[54]

In *Arlequin comédien* the hero jokes about bad smells, rushes round the stage and gets drunk; in Act II he starts telling jokes like a stand-up comedian. Fine engravings show imagined scenes for all three acts. Music is included, some pieces on fold-out sheets. This publication, then, was a

---

[50] Grewar, 'Shakespeare', 33–4, citing an unpublished paper by Richard Andrews entitled 'Scripted theatre and the *commedia dell'arte*' (1990).

[51] It had supposedly been penned 'to form an honest diversion for his mind during his hours of recreation and rest': [Laurent Bordelon,] *Arlequin comédien aux Champs Elisées, Nouvelle Historique, Allegorique & Comique* (Amsterdam: Adrian Braakman, 1694): 'Le Libraire au Lecteur', [iii].

[52] *Ibid.*, [131]: 'Achevé d'imprimer pour la premiere fois le 23 Avril 1691', issued by A. Seneuze, Paris.

[53] *Arlequin comédien* [...] *Seconde édition, Revüe, corrigée & augmentée de plusieurs Scenes* [...] *de trois Lettres, d'un Opera Comique, & d'une petite Comédie, intitulée, la Baguette* (Paris: Arnoul Seneuze, 1694), pp. 230: on [231], 'Achevé d'imprimer pour la seconde fois le 27 Août 1694'.

[54] Le Blanc, *Avatars*, 152, writing as if the text (it lacks any documented performance) were in the repertory of the Ancien Théâtre Italien; likewise Barthélemy, 'La Critique', 488. Aside from the whole tenor of the enterprise, private use is obvious when the publisher takes pains to stress in the preface to his second edition that the scene of the pedantic Doctor (II/16) is quite different from the (public) one in '*Colombine Docteur* chez les Italiens', and invites readers to make their own critical comparisons where 'similar cases' occur: they will notice 'une entière différence'. 'Le Libraire au Lecteur', 2nd ed., [v].

template for home use – reading, singing, reciting, excerpting, discussing *parodies*, perhaps acting. According to the publisher, it offered a 'new way of creating diversion, comedy, mockery and laughter, all in a completely comic vein, without offending polite morals'.[55] More specifically, 'I have seen [the first edition] in the hands of people of all classes. Even those who refuse to enter a theatre have had no trouble in accepting it (although it is a play), not minding laughter – for people do laugh when reading it – when there is no danger of compromising either their virtue or their propriety.'[56]

Braakman reprinted it in 1698; parts of it were apparently remembered by writers including Louis Fuzelier.[57] Its prelude featured a street and a man with a ladder, a bucket of glue and a sheaf of posters for the 'new opera'. A passer-by reads out the poster: 'Today will be performed a new opera, *Arlequin Roland furieux*. This opera will be given in verse and in [spoken] prose so that it will not provoke boredom or yawning.'

It is significant that a direction in Scene 2 reads, 'strings should accompany everything that is sung': the user must add the material. Songs in *Arlequin comédien* resemble those issued in Paris;[58] they imply a standard of performance requiring singers who could deal with modulation, accidentals, irregular rhythms as found in art song, and breath control to carry a phrase through a high note. Singers might respond to stage directions: Arlequin's unaccompanied bass solo in Scene 6 is delivered 'childishly', sitting down, a drunkard's address to the bottle which he clutches. Mezzetin's song in III/13 was in the character of a lonely traveller; there are three verses accompanied by a bass-line, not hard to sing but ideally benefiting from some dramatic projection.

Private and Public Music Shared

The appetite for owning music for stage works is obvious in the 1690s, as the rustic dialogue in Example 3.1 shows. Ballard's elegant monthly *Recueil d'Airs Sérieux et à Boire* often reveals music involving such 'dialect'. Michel (?) La Barre's 'Air Paysan' encourages the singer to act vividly, since the

---

[55] 'Le Libraire au Lecteur', 2nd. ed., [v]–[vi].   [56] 'Réponse de Monsieur +++ à Cardan', 34.
[57] *Supplément du Théâtre Italien* (Amsterdam: Adrian Braakman, 1698), II, 432–48. In Fuzelier's *Pierrot furieux ou Pierrot Roland* (1717) the celebrated actor Hamoche ended with a crazy mixture of popular tunes and opera airs to amusing new words, before smashing various pots and glasses: le Blanc, *Avatars*, 153.
[58] Principally by Ballard: Goulet, *Poésie, musique*; Gougon, 'Les *Recueils d'airs*'; Fader, 'The *Goûts-réunis*'.

husband scolds the wife in a stylised *air* from an imagined comedy (September 1695). 'Dialect' for group singing appeared in Montéclair's jolly Branle, 'Boute var la tasse en mair, Morgué que t'és badeine!' (November 1695). An 'Air Paysan' by Desfontaines needs strong characterisation because the narrator is shown to be a rival for the affections of a female neighbour, not a mere observer (March 1696). Two generations later, Pierre de La Garde would still include a 'Duo Païsan' and 'Duo champêtre dialogué' in his *Premier recueil d'airs*. A manuscript cantata 'in lively buffo style', *Le Mauvais ménage* (*The Household in Trouble*), included a 'Carillon' for the wife's protest after her husband goes off to the bar.[59]

From 1698 to 1704 Ballard's subscribers were offered music that had been composed for professional performance at the Comédie-Française. Music for twelve plays was issued,[60] and the story of this company's deep investment in music has been the subject of much research.[61] Playwrights included Dancourt, Dufresny and Houdar de La Motte and composers included Campra, Lalande and Gillier, who was hired at the Fair theatres in 1713. (In London he had written music for Farquhar's last play, *The Beaux' Stratagem*.[62])

Pierre Ribou, a rival publisher, marketed diverse forms of Comédie-Française music in *Airs de la Comédie Françoise* (1703–18). Only four plays represented here overlapped with Ballard's series. Gillier's music to *Le Médecin de village* (*The Village Doctor*, 1704) is perhaps exemplary for this genre: twelve *airs* and instrumental movements in a *divertissement*.[63] *Le Médecin de village* itself is an anonymous effort, tolerably well-constructed.[64] But only seven performances occurred, and it remained unpublished. Gillier's *divertissement*, on the other hand, brimming with life, was put on sale. Thus, we have a situation parallel to that of La Borde's *Les Amours de Gonesse* (*The Loves of Gonesse*) mentioned in note 48. Ribou

---

[59] Music by Reboul: Anthony, 'A Source for Secular Vocal Music'. [60] Gougon, *ibid.*, 49–50.
[61] Moureau, 'Un singulier moderne' and *Dufresny auteur dramatique*. Ballard included CI music in *Recueil d'airs des Comédies modernes*, dated 1706 in Guillo, 'La musique de scène'.
[62] *Mr Gilliers Musick in the Play call'd the Stratagem* (London : J. Walsh and J. Hare, 1707). See Harris, 'Jean-Claude Gillier'.
[63] GB-Lbl, B.319 (6): Marche; Air pour le Viéleur; Mariée de Village pour Colin et Claudine; Air pour Colette; Gavotte pour Mme Argant et le Carillonneur; Menuet pour Eraste et Lucinde [the main characters in the play]; 2e Air pour Colette; Carillon; Air pour un Niais sur la Viéle; 1er Branle; 2e Branle; 3e Branle.
[64] Pitou, '*Le Médecin de village*'. An undated play of the same name by Romanet is in Brenner, *Bibliographical List*.

surely calculated that private groups would use the music – dramatically or otherwise – once word got around that it was excellent.[65]

It has an artful, uninhibited and catchy style. The Branle could be sung by any unaccompanied drinkers, but the evocative hurdy-gurdy song in 'dialect' needs an authentic drone so that the singer can convey the persona of the 'blind beggar' who nevertheless 'sees everything'. Gillier anticipated popular opera's concern with different places, peoples and eras. Equally prophetic was 'Le Carillon', a six-part instrumental ensemble printed on five staves, with voices of girls and boys added in the middle section. The bassline imitates bells, and so do the singers. It even compares with the 'Duo des cloches' in *Ninette à la cour* (*Ninette at Court*: see p. 272) and 'Sans un petit brin d'amour' in Nicolas Dezède's *Les Trois fermiers* (*The Three Farmers*, 1777).[66]

Ribou issued Gillier's memorable music for Regnard's *Les Folies amoureuses* (*Crazy Loves*, 1704), a clever variation on the 'lecherous guardian' theme. At the time of its writing, the Comédie-Française employed specialist singers.[67] Amateur performances nevertheless could have 'much effect', said the *Manuel des châteaux* in 1779.[68] As Molière did in *Le Sicilien*, Regnard made music integral to the course of the plot. Agathe feigns craziness in Act II with a song covertly informing Eraste that she and her maid have been virtual prisoners for six months. Her guardian's nightly searches for amorous intruders are rendered as 'Every night a nasty tomcat roams'.[69] In II/6 she performs an extended song in Italian (Example 4.2) effectively telling Eraste she seeks to be liberated; she manages to pass a note to him. (This comic 'thread' continued in 1761 in Sedaine and Monsigny's *On ne s'avise jamais de tout*: see p. 160).

Finally, in a mock-classical frame, Momus, god of raillery, joins La Folie in a *divertissement* that merges with the principal plot. Gilliers and Regnard devised a dialogue-duet in which Momus and La Folie simultaneously dally and dance: Example 4.3. Almost meaningless without the music, this breathless conversation became a *tour-de-force*, a forerunner of *parlante* episodes as in *La traviata* where the band plays in the background and couples pass each other, their conversations fragmented in the vocal lines.[70]

---

[65] Guillo, 'La musique de scène', 497, assumes public success to be a *sine qua non*.
[66] Itself arranged for domestic performance as *Le Carillon des Trois Fermiers* by Jean-Baptiste Cardon.
[67] J.-B. Salley (Sallé) and Françoise Thoury ('Mlle Sallé'): Moureau, 'Parties et parodie', 89.
[68] Paulmy and Contant d'Orville, *Manuel des châteaux* (1779), 210.
[69] 'Toute la nuit entière un vieux vilain matou': 'matou' means a tomcat or an unpleasant customer.
[70] Schneider, 'Airs de comédie'.

Example 4.2 Jean-Claude Gillier, 'L'uceletto non è matto' in *Divertissement de la Comédie des Folies Amoureuse[s] De la Composition de Mr Gillier*. AGATHE: 'The simpleton is not mad; looking high and low, she will find freedom.'

Example 4.3 Jean-Claude Gillier, *Divertissement de la Comédie des Folies Amoureuse[s] De la Composition de Mr Gillier*, 'Danse dialogué entre Momus et la Folie'. LA FOLIE: 'Momus?' MOMUS: 'How may I serve?' LA FOLIE: 'You have loved me.' MOMUS: 'A little.' LA FOLIE: 'A lot.' MOMUS: 'Too tenderly'.

'Those Who Play Instruments'

Although Lesage and d'Orneval claimed that families performed 'small dramatic pieces', it is hard to find privately owned theatre music collections before c.1750; research has focused on the period when records are more abundant.[71] To judge from published materials, domestic performance was normally in the form of arrangements. Such 'arranger-authority' is seen in the way that (for example) Samuel Pepys's personal library contained no score of any Lully opera but a significant number of excerpts from them, edited for his use by Cesare Morelli.[72]

---

[71] Hennebelle, 'La Vie musicale'; Vernet, 'Théâtre, musique et société', 85–6.
[72] Twenty songs from *Thésée* and thirteen from *Cadmus et Hermione*: Stevens, 'Introduction' and Catalogue no. 2804.

Groups could buy a kind of 'toolkit' for making opera-like ensemble music at home. *Les Charmes de l'harmonie* (1723) by François Chauvon (*fl.* 1710–36) offered a large-format set of ingredients in score for voices and instruments: overture, recitatives, *airs*, duets, plus generic samples of music: 'plaintive', 'Bacchic', 'happy', 'lugubrious', 'warlike', 'triumphal', 'tempest', 'rural'. Chauvon included parts for flute, oboe, bassoon and double-bass.[73]

Published sources for domestic opéra-comique around mid-century were issued in the periodical referenced in note 40; in translation its title reads *Collection of airs, contradances, minuets and new vaudevilles sung on the stages of the Académie Royale de Musique and the Opéra Comique. Which may be played on all sorts of Instruments*. Permission to print was granted on 13 December 1745. At least thirteen issues appeared, the last two containing excerpts – three of them unauthorised – from Rousseau's *Le Devin du village* (*The Village Soothsayer*) and Mondonville's *Titon et l'Aurore*.[74]

It is interesting that this *Collection* began after the suspension of the Opéra Comique in June the same year. Presumably for this reason, its first four issues focused exclusively on Opéra Comique repertory, chiefly in the form of *parodies* (new texts) written in strophic verses. These narratives concerned young love, couched in varying degrees of explicitness and innuendo. Some information about instrumental teaching arrived with Issue 6:

Since these collections have been greatly appreciated, people having found therein everything that seemed most attractive and diverting, the publisher is undertaking to continue them and earn the public's approbation, being eager to give to it whatever is found the best and most amusing. In addition it may be seen that they offer an infinite resource for foreigners and for those who play instruments, since they contain the most attractive airs and those most proper in educating young people and perfecting them in music. All these pieces are sold in fives, whether bound or separate, and very useful for every assembly wishing to act *comédies*.

Because the pages of sources like *Recueil d'airs* are too small to play an instrument from, separate manuscripts must have been prepared; one concludes that families kept libraries of arrangements suited to their own talents.

---

[73] *Les Charmes de l'harmonie, concert de Voix et d'Instruments* (Paris: Ballard, 1723). The GB-Lbl copy contains performance annotations in ink. See also *MGG, Personenteil*, 4, 800–1.

[74] Charlton, 'Spying on Rousseau'.

Table 4.1 Early appearances of published opéra-comique materials for private use

TITLE/YEAR of first performance	VOCAL EXCERPTS	ORCHESTRAL PARTS
Le Diable à quatre (collab., 1756)		Parties séparées [1761]
Le Soldat magicien (Philidor, 1760)	1 *air* issued (n. p., n. d.)	Horn parts available
Le Jardinier et son seigneur (Philidor, 1761)	Ariettes (Paris: Adresses ordinaires), 13 pages	Available [1761]
Le Maréchal ferrant (Philidor, 1761)	Ariettes (Paris: La Chevardière), 16 pages	Available [1762]
Le Cadi dupé (Monsigny, 1761)	Ariettes (Paris: Adresses ordinaires), 9 pages	Available [1761]
Annette et Lubin (La Borde, 1762) [composed for private performance]	[Ariettes] (Paris: Lesclapart), 28 pages, appended to libretto	Available [c.1762]
Annette et Lubin (Justine and Charles-Simon Favart, 1762)	*Recueil de toutes les ariettes d'Annette et Lubin, Avec accompagnement de clavecin ou violoncelle* (Paris: La Chevardière)	Available [1762]
Sancho Pança (Philidor, 1762)	*Ariettes de Sancho Pança* (Paris: La Chevardière), 20 pages; its *Romance* includes figured bass.	Available [c.1762]
Le Guy de Chesne (Laruette, 1763)	*Airs détachés ... avec accompagnement de basse ou clavecin* (Paris: La Chevardière), 16 pages. Cf. *Ariettes du Guy de Chêne*, without accompaniment, 20 pp. (Duchesne)	Available [1763]

That notion is arguably supported by the fact that publishers after 1752 began to sell orchestral parts, advertised together with full scores of popular operas and collections of vocal extracts: see Table 4.1. The title page of Philidor's *Le Soldat magicien* (*The Soldier-Magician*) is revealing in this regard because it announces that horn parts were available separately 'for the convenience of amateurs': private musicians, as normal, could copy or arrange string and woodwind parts, but the score had omitted the horn parts.

The presence of figured bass offers other clues. All one hundred pages of *Recueil de toutes les ariettes d'Annette et Lubin*, the 1762 version by Justine Favart, were engraved for voice and figured bass; so were sixteen *airs* from Laruette's *Le Guy de Chesne* (*The Oak and the Mistletoe*) the following year. The melodic parts of *Annette et Lubin*'s accompaniment are missing: this edition serves the amateur singer trying out the extraordinary range of musical styles found in it, or else learning a role for private stage performance.

This is not to suppose that complete operas were the norm: Hennebelle's conclusion was simply that amateurs performed spoken dialogue freely mixed with music. He writes of the years after 1752, but one is tempted to backdate his assessment: 'The interpenetration of spoken and sung theatre is often to be noted. A large portion of the [domestic] repertory actually consisted of musical interludes (*airs*, ariettes, songs, *vaudevilles*, *divertissements*, etc.) placed inside spoken dramatic texts.'[75]

Pierre Laujon, librettist and socialite, recalled that certain of 'these entertainments much resembled the old opéra-comique style by their mixture of prose, poetry, *vaudevilles* and songs'.[76] Other evidence suggests that musicians used printed scores as performance sources: see Figure 4.2. These handwritten indications are representative of markings found regularly in old copies, as mentioned earlier, such as expressive markings and repeat signs.[77]

Domestic Operas

Perhaps the first complete opera in *vaudevilles* to be printed up with all its music, obviously for domestic use, was Favart's *Les Nymphes de Diane* (*Diana's Nymphs*), described on pp. 167–9 and 233–4. A music supplement of forty pages was issued in Brussels in 1748, the year after its premiere there. The *vaudevilles* are not underlaid with their new words but cued by number to the libretto.

Around 1756, in the same compact format, appeared another type of semi-score: *Le Troc* (*The Exchange*) by Farin de Hautemer (dates unknown), a professional actor and playwright. No public performance is documented, but professionals would not have required such a publication as this. It has a decorated title page designed and engraved by Anne Fonbonne, which can be seen on *Gallica*. Sixty pages long, *Le Troc* cost only three times a single issue of the *Recueil d'Airs*.[78]

---

[75] Hennebelle, 'La Vie musicale', 59.
[76] Pierre Laujon, *Œuvres choisies*, 4 vols. (Paris: Patris, 1811), IV, xii, cited in Hennebelle, *ibid.*, 59.
[77] The copy in Figure 4.2 was owned by 'F. Mainebeau'. Missing tempo indications were entered in pencil on 28 ('Gratieux'), 35 ('Un peu vitte') and 41 ('Gratieux. Leger. Pas trop vitte'). Four small cuts are indicated.
[78] LE TROC Opera-Comique, Parodie DES TROCQUEURS, Par M. Farain de Hautemer (Paris: Duchêne, n.d.); the price is entered in ink at 3 *livres* 12 *sols* (author's coll.). Brenner, *Bibliographical List* no. 7370 reports perf. at the FSL in 1756. But no documentary evidence has verified this. The copy on *Gallica* is dated 1756, omits Hautemer's name and substitutes 'Représenté sur les Théâtres etc.', that is, private stages.

Figure 4.2 F. Mainebeau's copy of Monsigny, *Les Aveux indiscrets* (*The Indiscreet Confessions*) with performer indications on p. 41 ('Gratieux. Leger. Pas trop vitte') and the start of a 9-bar cut on pp. 58–9.

Le Troc's source was *Les Troqueurs* (*The Swappers*), the groundbreaking musical comedy by Joseph Vadé and Antoine Dauvergne which guided the course of opéra-comique after 1753.[79] Its runaway success caused the

---

[79] See p. 170 (plot) and pp. 279–80 (music); also *OAR*, 287–92.

authorities to limit performances in 1754, such was its damage to the Opéra's attendance figures.[80] Perhaps *Le Troc*, a new type of *parodie*, is evidence not just of the binary identity of popular opera but also of resistance to the rationing of public performances of *Les Troqueurs*.

Derived from La Fontaine (see Chapter 7), *Les Troqueurs* was modelled on *intermezzi* seen at the Opéra in 1752–3. Lubin is engaged to Margot (the fiery one) and Lucas to Fanchon (the turbid one). On a whim, the men decide to exchange fiancées without even informing the latter. Margot plots revenge and, by the final quartet, she and Fanchon force Lubin and Lucas into asking forgiveness, literally on their knees, begging to be taken back.

In adapting this comedy, Hautemer retained its cast of two non-married couples but reshaped the conflict by setting youth against age: a widower and his son, a widow and her daughter. There are obvious parallels with *La Chercheuse d'esprit* (*The Girl Who Sought Wit*; see Chapter 5). Langlois *père* deludes himself into thinking he could marry Mme Anroux's daughter Lucresse, who loves Langlois *fils*. It is done with such dexterity that it sometimes manages to recall Vadé's original rhyme schemes or even exact phrases within the totally new set-up. In the final quartet of conflict and resolution, the acts of kneeling even parody Vadé's stage actions, making Dauvergne's jocular musical accompaniment serve a different comic purpose. We see how it works from Figures 4.3 (a) and (b), which compare this same passage in the original finale with Hautemer's parody. Whereas in *Les Troqueurs* Lubin and Lucas are being forced to kneel again, in *Le Troc* Mme Anroux and Langlois *père* are preventing their children from leaving. Stage directions are footnoted in *Le Troc* but not present in the score of *Les Troqueurs*: as was normal practice, they are found in the libretto at this point.

Le Troc contains all Dauvergne's vocal music in single-line form with Hautemer's reconceived text; the keys are identical. Whereas Dauvergne used recitative, Hautemer used *vaudevilles* for the conversations, identifying their melodies by *timbre*. Theoretically Duchesne had no need to publish the music at all because Hautemer's new words were matched so cleverly to music which Dauvergne had issued already in full score. Yet it was engraved to a high standard, like a collector's item. The six solos, two duets and two quartets might have been reckoned to be daunting, but they must relate to the skill of amateur groups. Private performers attempting *Le Troc* would need to copy or borrow the parts for strings and oboes, not apparently sold separately.

---

[80] MS news-sheet, 15 April 1754, in Munich Staatsbibliothek MS 401 f°. 13: Prod'homme, 'La Musique à Paris', 576, showing that Monnet installed extra seating for the 1754 pre-Easter performances; La Borde, *Essai* (1780), III, 379–80.

Figure 4.3 (a) *Les Troqueurs* (*The Swappers*), finale, bars 110 to 116. Lubin and Lucas try to rise from their kneeling position but are forced down again by Margot and Fanchon. (b: see opposite page) Equivalent passage in *Le Troc* (*The Swap*) with footnoted stage directions: Lucresse and Langlois *fils* 'make as if to leave'; Mme Anroux and Langlois *père* sing 'to the children', then 'to each other'.

Someone might have written a continuity score for the *vaudevilles*, as Favart did for *La Chercheuse d'esprit*, seen in Figure 5.1.

Grimm reported around 1752 that 'Paris can now boast as many as a hundred and sixty theatre groups'.[81] Figure 4.3 provides a possible snapshot of their standards: *Le Troc* required less subtle acting than *Les Troqueurs*, but Hautemer's parodic mastery would have added much pleasure. Subsequent full scores like *Le Cadi dupé* (1761) often included acting instructions, perhaps with amateurs in mind: 'The Aga makes a very respectful oriental greeting by touching his turban with both hands, then remains with his arms crossed over his chest.'[82]

*

The existence of *Le Troc* makes the extraordinary case of *Annette et Lubin* easier to understand. Two different operas with spoken dialogue bearing this title came out at the same time, February and March 1762. Justine Favart's version for the Comédie-Italienne became the familiar one, carefully avoiding direct reference to Annette's condition.[83] She is a teenager,

---

[81] Kavanagh, *Enlightened Pleasures*, 175.
[82] P. R. Lemonnier and P. A. Monsigny, *Le Cadi dupé, opéra bouffon en un acte* (Paris: De La Chevardiere, 1761), 27. Engraved orchestral parts were advertised, as Table 4.1 mentioned.
[83] Favart and Blaise, *Annette et Lubin* (1762), ed. Münzmay: see Chapters 6, pp. 146–8, and 7, p. 181.

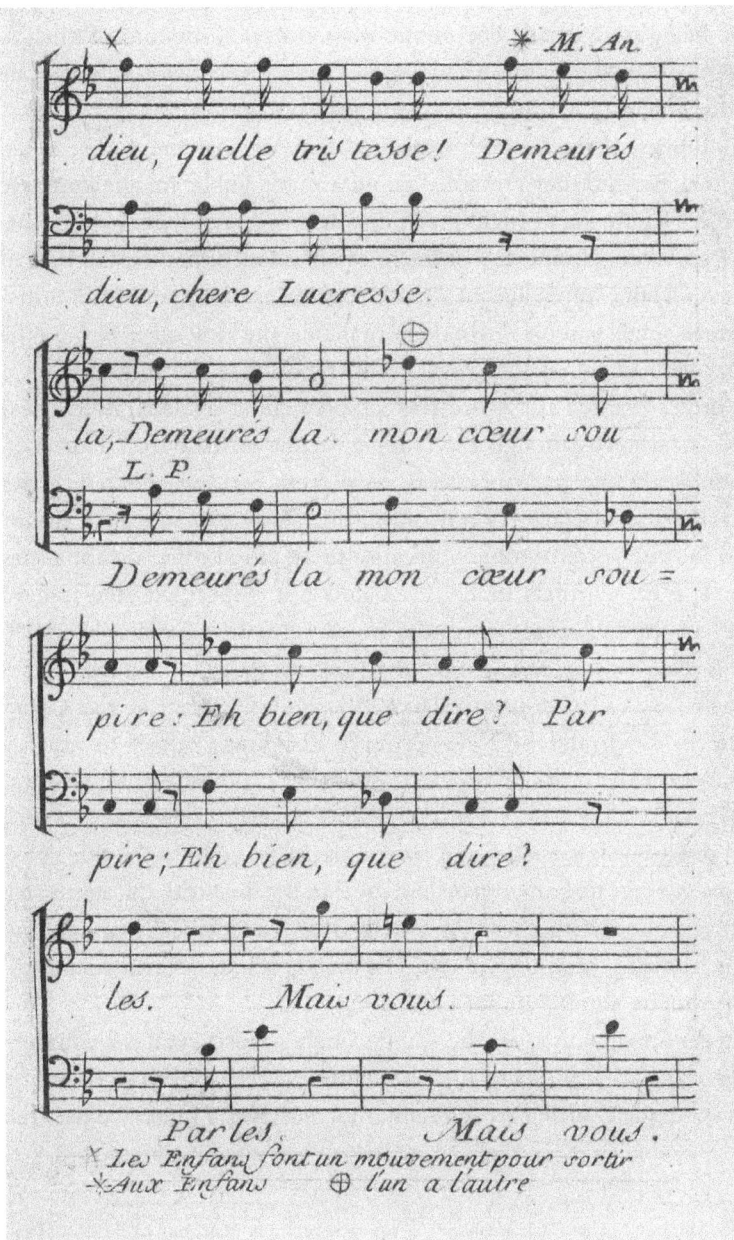

Figure 4.3 (cont.)

living in a poor cottage with her cousin and pregnant by him. They are orphans as well as lovers. Jean-François Marmontel's version, taking his own Moral Tale as its source, was limited to private performance because its open references to pregnancy could not be made on public stages, Annette being unmarried. The public version used a mixture of musical sources, whereas Marmontel's had a score composed by Jean-Benjamin de La Borde, which some thirty private groups were performing.[84]

Marmontel's *Mémoires* later explained that his characters were taken from actual life, and they remained familiar in the public imagination: see Figure 6.2.[85] Their story caught the moment: young love; happiness threatened by social constraint; the problem of abandoned infants; the cost of permission from Church authorities for cousins to marry; and rural measures against single parents. As in the Moral Tale, the local *seigneur* pays the necessary fees, an act reflecting real events reported to the author.

La Borde's printed full score was supplemented by separate orchestral and vocal parts, though the latter omit the ensembles.[86] However, the composer made no concessions to players, writing energetic parts and making use of clarinets not only in the fiery overture in F minor but also in four vocal numbers. Because these are in different tonalities (E♭, C, A, e/E), clarinets in B♭, C, A and E are specified (the last on page 107 of the full score, where the music turns to the major mode).[87] La Borde had written the first known clarinet parts in popular opera, namely in *Gilles Garçon-peintre* (*Gilles, Assistant Painter*) at the Opéra Comique in 1758, and here he seems to encourage others to employ them: much of the clarinets' music is doubled on other instruments, but some is not.[88]

Most of La Borde's *ariettes* and two of his duets involved the title roles. The *seigneur* sings just one *ariette* and joins in the final trio; the aggressive Bailli sings a difficult duet with Annette and joins a technically demanding D minor trio with the young couple. His unique solo is a stormy denunciation of Annette and her unborn child.[89]

Often sentimental in style, the young couple's music creates a counterbalance to that of the authority figures. In music and in spoken sections, the cousins are made to articulate humanitarian messages: Lubin eulogises the

---

[84] Favart to Durazzo, 7 May 1762: *Mémoires*, I, 267; background in Charlton, 'La Borde's ironic pastoral'.
[85] Marmontel, *Mémoires* (1799), Livre VII, 246–7 and 520, n. 420.
[86] RISM series A/I/5, items L62 and L63; vocal parts (Paris: Lesclapart, 1762), Cambridge, King's College.
[87] *Annette et Lubin, Pastorale* (Paris: Moria, n.d.), on *Gallica*.
[88] See Sc. 7, 'Pour s'aimer de bonne foi', 66, and 'Entre nous deux', 70.
[89] Professional singers Mlle Nessel and J.-B. Clairval took the leading parts at the duke de Richelieu's theatre: *Mémoires secrets*, I, 54 (31 March 1762).

seigneur as a father figure.[90] A kind of hymn of defiance is sung by him against the Bailli, invoking the support of heaven and nature on behalf of innocence and love.

*

Of course, all this was voiced by privileged actors for privileged audiences, with Marmontel's verse dialogue sounding even more sententious in effect than his original Tale. But some wealthier people had long identified with villagers, for whatever motives: 'Women of quality often dress as peasants and appear thus in public, in their carriages and on their walks.'[91] Evidence is lacking for the motives of any singer who participated in society opera, but those in role as Annette and Lubin were at least articulating Marmontel's image of rural poverty and its human consequences. If singing was part of daily existence in France and had once been proposed as an image of its society as a whole, how ready were later groups to approve the opera's message of social responsibility? One answer is provided by Simon Smith, concluding his study of *Musical Response in the Early Modern Playhouse*:

The kinds of playfulness proposed by this study rely upon the seemingly contradictory juxtaposition of opposing instincts, attitudes and behaviours, most fundamentally in the way that 'play' is simultaneously frivolous and entirely serious: a game of imaginative identification that is initiated in order to engage closely, personally and critically with dramatic performance. Playful encounters with music should not, then, be seen as incompatible with – or opposed to – the sophisticated, serious and often subversive subject matter with which much early modern commercial drama wrestled.[92]

---

[90] See Figure 6.2 for the equivalent moment in Justine Favart's version.
[91] Desfontaines, *Observations* (1743), 329.   [92] Smith, *Musical Response*, 186.

5 | Opéra-comique *en vaudevilles*

Raw Materials

Opéra-comique was built originally on singing-culture in the form of *vaudevilles*. These were defined as 'A song that runs through the town, is easy to sing and whose words normally report some adventure or current intrigue.'[1] But the context in which they functioned was wider and can be described as follows:

Most societies in early modern Europe possessed an equivalent of British broadside culture: a wide-ranging, universally shared body of knowledge. This mass of ballads, broadsides and chapbooks functioned not only to provide musical entertainment, but also to spread news, gossip, religious messages and propaganda. Though the uses might vary from case to case, the 'texts' themselves constituted a culture uniting all strata of society. The elite culture that existed at the time tended to build on and supplement this universal material rather than displace it, making the shared layer a truly communal 'popular' culture in a sense of the word that disappeared later.

In the narrowest musical sense, melodies themselves were the lowest common denominator of this shared, popular material. In London around 1720, many ballad-singers might have been beggars, but they drew a diverse crowd and they sang the same melodies that were heard in fashionable theatre pieces attended by nobility and gentry, and that were available inexpensively on printed half-sheets.[2]

Those sold by Charles Minart (Figure 4.1) would have favoured an ironic edge: 'The French, born shrewd and malicious, invented *vaudevilles*: jolly indiscretions sung by one person to another, embroidered all the while.'[3] New words were constantly embroidered for the 'shared layers' of popular music. Revolutionary songs during the Fronde (1648–53) had incited support against Mazarin's government; a century later students, teachers

---

[1] *Dictionnaire de l'Académie française*, 1st ed. (1694).
[2] Gelbart, *Invention of 'Folk Music'*, 17–18. See Romey, 'Songs that Run in the Streets'.
[3] Nicolas Boileau Despréaux, *L'Art poétique*, Canto II (Paris: Thierry, 1674), 118.

Examples 5.1 (a) *Air*, 'Quand le péril est agréable', parodied from Jean-Baptiste Lully, *Atys*, I/3. (b) *Air*, 'Non, je ne feray pas', parodied from Jean-Baptiste Lully, *Isis*, II/7.

and their friends were passing round politically sensitive poems and songs. The unexpected reward for this was arrest, exile and ruin.[4]

Vaudevilles deriving from Lully or his successors number over seventy:[5] 'Quand le péril est agréable' is from *Atys*, Example 5.1(a); 'Non, je ne feray pas' is from *Isis*, Example 5.1(b); 'Quitte ta houlette' is from Lully's *Divertissement* to Molière's *Les Amants magnifiques*, Example 5.2. Thirty others were derived from Gherardi's troupe: see Tables 3.2 and 3.3.[6] Daniel Heartz identified some that went back to Renaissance styles yet seem to fit their new contexts, implying that empirical enjoyment of a *vaudeville* opera might be possible today.

'Du Cap de Bonne Espérance' ('Cape of Good Hope') [...] was particularly favoured by Lesage for purposes of exposition. The three-measure phrases that mark this tune identify it as a descendent of the old *branle simple*, whose step pattern led to a phrase structure of 3 x 4/4 [giving eight three-bar phrases in common time]. Its singsong quality makes an oddly satisfying match with the dry economy of Lesage in telling a tale at once complicated and piquant.[7]

---

[4] In 1749: Darnton, *Poetry*, 53.
[5] Le Blanc, *Avatars*, 705–12; Barnes, '*Théâtre de la Foire*', 178–88; le Blanc and Monnier, 'Le Devenir'.
[6] Grout, 'Origins', 205–8.
[7] Heartz, 'Terpsichore at the Fair', 141; music in Ballard, *La Clef* (1717), 66.

The *vaudeville* fashion meant that by 1702 they had become 'more saleable than [older] parodied *airs*'.[8] '*Vaudevilles*' began to appear in the monthly *Airs sérieux et à boire*.[9] In 1717 three hundred *vaudevilles* were anthologised as *La Clef des chansonniers* (*The Keys to Song-making*), a title referring to their music: users 'will hold the key, i.e. the *airs* notated', the point being that most publications omitted the actual music but simply quoted the tune's title, or *timbre*. Their editor, Ballard, stated: '*Vaudeville* simply means an *air* circulating publicly. You will thus find a number that were printed in different collections and a number that might be unknown; this is the normal fate of pieces that appeared many years ago.'[10] But *La Clef* also included '*airs* [...] which remain in our memory [and] shall never cease to give pleasure' even after a century of use. Indeed citizens sang *vaudevilles* through to the nineteenth century.[11]

'Manufactured' popularity could occur:

It is likely that the replacement of political words in several seventeenth-century songs with more banal, or *grivois* [vulgar], lyrics, represents a deliberate attempt on the part of the Paris authorities, who are known to have employed song-writers, to suppress the opinions which the songs in question represent. The use of such songs in the theatre is therefore not neutral.[12]

Vaudevilles acquired spheres or auras of association either because of origins in dance or by repeated use in parallel circumstances. Any *menuet* meant a likely association with love: Examples 5.1(a) and 5.7 for instance. Recent musicology teaches that later eighteenth-century *menuets* constituted 'a specifically aristocratic dance',[13] but *menuets* in popular opera signified the presence of love without any association with social class. So, in *Les Eaux de Merlin* (*Merlin's Waters*, 1715) Merlin offers Arlequin and Mezzetin the chance to make a fortune in Paris by selling water. He 'shows them the fountain of Love' which he has built and explains by singing the *Menuet de M. de Grandval*:

MERLIN: Dès qu'on en boit, on sent son ame   You drink from it and straight away
S'enflammer d'une vive ardeur.   Your spirits are consumed by love.

---

[8] 'Avertissement', *Nouvelles parodies bachiques, mêlées de vaudevilles ou rondes de table...Tome III* (Paris: Christophe Ballard, 1702), 13 (on *Gallica*).
[9] In May, June and November 1709.
[10] Ballard, *La Clef* (1717), vii. Thirty items came from *Nouvelles parodies bachiques* and over twenty from Lully's works.
[11] Schneider, ed., *Chanson und Vaudeville*, vi–vii.   [12] Darlow, '"Peindre sa voix"', 129–30.
[13] Frits Noske, *The Signifier and the Signified* (The Hague: Nijhoff, 1977), 32.

MEZZETIN: Ah! Voilà donc pourquoi ma flamme   Ah! That's the reason why I still
           Vient encore embraser mon cœur!   Feel ardour rising in my heart![14]

Other spheres of association were linked to fashion and politics: 'Monsieur le Prévôt des marchands' generally ridiculed authority, while 'Dirai-je mon Confiteor' was linked to anti-government texts in the 1740s.[15] But could an opera always count on its audience to make these associations, say between 'Confiteor' and reform of the State, or between 'Lanturlu' and mockery of the Jesuits, or between *Nouvelle fanfare en menuet* and the riches spent on keeping King Stanislaus of Poland in royal comfort?[16] Derek Connon concluded that many tunes 'were used so often that they must surely have become too familiar as simple melodies for the audience to be reminded of the original text at every repetition'.[17] Robert Darnton observed that 'the fungibility of words and tunes presents a problem: if the same melody could be adapted for many disparate subjects, how is it possible to trace a consistent pattern of themes associated with the music?'[18]

Style of performance was crucial because 'by varying the tempo and the manner of performance slightly, [*vaudevilles*] can [...] lend themselves to the expression of a variety of emotions.'[19] Darnton concurred with this insight as follows:

Anthropologists often stress the 'multivocal' aspect of symbols, which can convey many meanings within a shared cultural idiom. Multivocality inheres in singing, both literally and figuratively. Associated messages can be grafted on to the same song as different composers add new verses [or dramatists supply new texts] and successive singers give voice to its tune.[20]

Analysis of *vaudeville* collections convinced Darnton that a sort of 'core' of *vaudevilles* existed, juxtaposed with shifting 'peripheries'. Most lasted 'one or two decades', while others 'spread rapidly for a few months and then died out', a phenomenon we shall encounter in Chapter 9.[21]

On the popular stage the ironic power of *vaudevilles* was exploited, as Chapter 3 described, in 'double-operational irony', and this was especially

---

[14] *TF*, I, 92 (R/I/154).   [15] Robinson, 'Les Vaudevilles'; Darnton, *Poetry*, 95–102.
[16] Barbier and Vernillat, *Histoire de France*, 15–16, 65, 99.
[17] Connon, 'Music in the Parisian Fair Theatres', 122. He sees the music as 'the medium carrying the message' via 'the emotional neutrality of the tunes': *ibid.*, 129–30.
[18] Darnton, *Poetry*, 89–90.   [19] Connon, *ibid.*, 122.   [20] Darnton, *ibid.*, 101–2.
[21] *Ibid.*, 169–73. See Barberet, *Lesage*, 94–5, for further thought on Lesage's choice of *vaudevilles*.

Example 5.2 *Air*, 'Quitte ta houlette', parodied from Jean-Baptiste Lully, *Le Divertissement royal*. ISABELLE: 'What terrible misfortune! Why is he so heartless?' COLOMBINE: 'He plans to exercise his rights.'

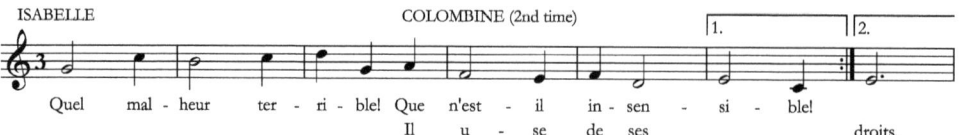

useful for 'singing the unspeakable', a phrase adopted by Jama Stilwell.[22] Her discussion addressed the lack of self-determination of women in the society for whom the Fair offered an environment of escape and disguise. In *Arlequin sultane favorite* (*Harlequin Sultana and Favourite*) occur 'frank sexual messages that could never have been stated outright on stage': 'Isabelle's sung response to the Sultan's advances communicates one thing ["What terrible misfortune! The Sultan is so cruel!"], while the erotic metaphor laced throughout the original text of her tune [the *air* "Quitte ta houlette"] implies that she is *really* saying something else':[23] see Example 5.2.

One must emphasise the individual character of all *vaudevilles* as music. Their immense variety – their moods and internal design – sometimes goes with an epigrammatic quality, especially up to about 1720: the average length of the 120 *vaudevilles* in Connon and Evans's anthology is 15.35 bars.[24] But there is startling diversity in their dimensions and especially in their range of expression. The majority in this sample contain even numbers of bars: in descending order of frequency, totals of 16, 12, 8, 24, 20 and 18 bars (93 cases). The other twenty-seven cases are irregular and singular in length, some having mixed time signatures (Table 5.1).

Major and minor modes are both found, but *vaudevilles* like 'Je ne suis né ni roy ni prince' obey modal inflexions with lack of polarity between a tonic and a subsidiary key.[25] Above all, internal rhythm and metre are driving factors as much as contour or mode and seem endlessly varied. The results form expressive musical miniatures, self-contained and individual

---

[22] Stilwell, 'A New View', 77.

[23] Stilwell, *ibid.*, 76–8. The unheard text envoices Nanette's invitation to Tircis to lie on the grass with her.

[24] Found in *TF* between 1713 and 1722 plus one from 1726: Connon and Evans, *Anthologie de pièces*, 285–333, omitting pieces by Gillier, L'Abbé, Aubert and long excerpts from Lully etc. For other observations, see Barnes, 'Théâtre de la Foire', 138–45 and Grout, 'Origins', Supplement III, 'Introduction', i–xx.

[25] Grout, *ibid.*, sampled 143 *vaudevilles*: 85 were in major, 55 in minor, and 3 in Dorian or Æolian modes.

Table 5.1 *Vaudevilles* with the most irregular total number of bars in Connon and Evans's *Anthologie de pièces du Théâtre de la Foire.*

11 bars in total: 5 cases	13, 14 or 26 bars: 3 cases each
10, 22 or 23 bars: 2 cases each	3, 4, 7, 9, 17, 21, 28 bars: 1 case each

worlds. They have a narrative feel, a 'semantic implication' sometimes reminiscent of folk song or, say, a piano piece by Grieg. Some are graceful, some quick and humorous, others blunt or sad. They usually move into a contrasting area, sometimes abruptly, with new motifs, micro-rhythms or modes. Only a few make use of repeated notes, and sequences are quite rare.[26]

Their beginnings set up expectation in different ways, sometimes by means of paired opening phrases; some do this by apparently starting halfway through a phrase. One is the 'Cap de Bonne Espérance' tune, which ends in semi-uncertainty too.[27] It begins by inverting the expected order of note-values, moving from smaller (crotchet) values into larger ones (minims). There is no rule to say on which particular beat a *vaudeville* starts, except for gavottes and *menuets*. Quite a few end with a catchphrase – perhaps in nonsense syllables – tending to imply an ironic subversion of whatever has gone before: we saw on p. 65 'Lanturlu' in Example 3.4. Another ends with 'Talaleri, talaleri, talalerire', another with 'Un certain je ne sais quoy' ('A certain nameless something').

Vaudevilles on Stage

Introducing his own popular operas, Denis Carolet repeated Lesage's message: 'Fair theatre texts are made to be sung'.[28] Visually speaking they emphasise speech, since the music is usually absent or at the end, even today. We still have to construct our scores. Help with musical identification comes in digital form as well as books.[29] Lesage and d'Orneval were exceptional in publishing accurately engraved music from the start. All ten volumes of *Le Théâtre de la Foire* (*TF*) contain a musical appendix, with original compositions alongside borrowed material. As a formula, it

---

[26] Barberet, *Lesage*, 91–2, attempts a classification. [27] Music in Ballard, *La Clef* (1717), 66.
[28] Carolet, 'Préface', *TF* IX/2, [vi] (R/II/555).
[29] *Theaville*: www.theaville.org/kitesite/index.php; Falk, *Les Parodies*; Ballard, *La Clef* (1717). But a century ago Georgy Calmus issued *Télémaque, parodie* as a readable score: *Zwei Opern-Burlesken aus der Rokokozeit* (Berlin: Liepmannssohn, 1912), now in reprint.

succeeded; volumes IV and V (said the censor) 'should be received with the same pleasure by the public as the first three'.[30]

Volumes I to III (1721) contain works staged between 1713 and 1718, which will be discussed in Chapter 9. Volumes IV to IX/2 appeared between 1724 and 1737.[31] Dates are important since each volume relates differently to the evolving Fair. Although they look similar, *TF* volumes include, in addition to the majority of opéras-comiques, three 'lyric pantomimes' (discussed later) in Volume I; seven plays (some with music) in Volumes IV and V;[32] and three marionette operas in Volume V, written in 1722 when Lesage could not use actors (see Table 1.2). Favart began publication only with the 1739 *parodie*, *Moulinet Premier* (*Moulinet the First*) and remained selective in deciding what to release; thus his earlier choices of *vaudeville* are known from rare editions, some issued at The Hague. One has constantly to be aware of musical changes within later editions of Favart's works. Piron and Pannard, who were not concerned to publish their opéras-comiques at the time of staging, left us the greatest number of problems in finding the music to which certain *timbres* refer.

As the music examples have shown, *vaudevilles* were printed in keys like C, G or F major, or G minor and D minor. However, the impression of fixity is a deception. In performance, the key was selected to suit the performer(s), as will be proven later. Direct lines of performance information have been lost (or await rediscovery) except for the revelatory manuscript discussed at the end of this chapter.

*

Chapter 3 described the legacy of Gherardi's company, whose *vaudevilles* were used ironically, but not for dialogue. In the early eighteenth century official eyewitnesses at the Fairs reported new *vaudeville* uses in extraordinary detail, as shown later. The first report dates from 1707, not long before spoken dialogue, then monologue, then even singing, were temporarily banned.[33] *Vaudevilles* thereupon entered an experimental dramaturgy – here called 'lyric pantomime' – using Italian-influenced acting.[34]

---

[30] Signed Danchet, *TF* V, 434 (R/I/638).
[31] Cordier, *Essai bibliographique*, 252–67. Lesage's final contribution was labelled Vol. IX (1737) and Carolet's (1734) renumbered IX/2.
[32] Four for Francisque's troupe in vol. IV and three for the CI in vol. V.
[33] *Arlequin écolier ignorant*, FSL 1707, 'canevas en 1 acte en prose et *vaudevilles*' by Fuzelier, Dolet and Laplace: BNF Ms f.fr. 25476; Le Blanc, *Avatars*, 731.
[34] Briefly mentioned in Lagrave, 'La Pantomime'.

The Alard brothers had been in show business at the Fairs for three decades and were favoured by the king. In winter 1708 the Opéra agreed that Alard and Veuve Maurice could use dancers and singers in *divertissements*.[35] In summer 1708 the same entrepreneurs persuaded the Comédie-Française to allow plays with 'changes of scene, machines, music and ballet'.[36] Then in winter 1709 officials reported on a new form of sung dialogue that Alard's team had introduced, presumably using *vaudevilles* since the report's key phrase 'couplets de chansons en vers' would cover those:

[Pierrot Roland] sang several different songs to which the second character [a boy in the role of his son] replied, also singing. Several more actors entered, dressed variously as Arlequin, Scaramouche or classical actors; they sang in the same way, answering each other on stage with various songs in either French or Italian, one serving normally as a question and the other as an answer. Consequently, the actor of Pierrot Roland sometimes defied the prohibition on dialogue by singing in prose and without rhyme.[37]

The Comédie-Française decided to challenge this perceived infringement of their monopoly over dialogue. Officials reported likewise on the troupe of Dolet and Laplace, whose *La Fille capitaine* (*The Girl Commander*) concluded with other sorts of musical dialogue: 'several actors and actresses sang solo and the others replied in chorus'.[38] Circumstantial evidence that these cases were judged to be *operatic*, musical, and therefore no infringement of spoken convention is that on 17 April 1709 the Comédie-Française obtained an injunction preventing the Opéra from licensing any 'comedies wholly sung'.[39] As so often, they were not prepared to compete, only to crush. However, the breakthrough seems to have been made: viable sung forms of comedy now existed.

A revolutionary development around 1709 circumvented the ban on spoken or sung dialogue: written signs or scrolls (*écriteaux*). Two plays called *Astrée et Thyeste* and *Les Poussins de Léda* (*Leda's Chicks*) are said to have employed scrolls which actors drew from a pocket to show to the

---

[35] Parfaict, *Mémoires* (1743), I, 74.
[36] Campardon, *Spectacles*, I, 3; Parfaict, *ibid.*, I, 74, 78–9. Isherwood, *Farce and Fantasy*, 81–91, provides a different overview.
[37] Campardon, *ibid.*, II, 121, 7 Feb. 1709.
[38] *Ibid.*, I, 259–60 (19 Feb. 1709). The entrepreneurs had been fined 1,300 *livres* on 2 January, damages payable to the CF: Barthélemy, 'L'Opéra-comique', 33.
[39] 'Aucune pièce entière en musique', quoted in Barthélemy, *op. cit.*, 33; my interpretation diverges completely at this point from his. Marcetteau-Paul, 'L'Obstacle', 268; Darlow, '"Peindre sa voix"', 118.

audience, perhaps like captions in a silent film.[40] Yet in winter 1710 Alard's troupe still made use of song,[41] and Rauly's made extensive use of music:

A comic *divertissement* consisting of *airs* parodied from *Phaéton* and other *airs*, beginning like that opera with a prologue and dances and continuing the sequence of acts. The actors and actresses conversed and replied in song, accompanied by the musicians who played for the choruses and duos.[42]

This was from Louis-Jérôme Daminois' second report of 6 February 1710. His first report that day – probably of an earlier performance – mentioned 'obscene songs' used in conversation between Pierrot and Arlequin, adopting 'scandalous gestures and postures'. We know for sure that by next winter scrolls displayed *vaudeville* texts: *Les Avantures comiques d'Arlequin* (*Harlequin's Comic Adventures*, now in a modern edition) prescribes signboards on stage. For example, in Scene 1 after extensive comic mime, 'A *vaudeville* is displayed by the side of the throne, which everyone sings when the violins have given the note.'[43] Audiences themselves were to sing the words that actors simply mimed. Here we have the conditions for 'lyric pantomime'.[44]

By summer 1711 Alard's team used *écriteaux* in a three-act lyric pantomime whose *timbres* (titles) and texts for *vaudevilles* appeared in a well-printed scenario: *Arlequin Énée ou La prise de Troyes* (*Harlequin-Aeneas or The Siege of Troyes*).[45] The Fall of Troy was burlesqued, so satirical humour in the *vaudeville* texts was readily understandable. These do not constitute conversation: the audience's music acted as comment, spiced with references to *procureurs*, doctors and others. It is significant that prologues were being introduced as if to emulate French opera, setting the action in context. The two comedies just mentioned each have one, and so did *Harlequin à la guinguette* (*Harlequin at the Tavern*) at the same Fair.[46]

---

[40] Brenner, *A Bibliography*, nos. 6153, 6154, attributed to Faroard or Lenoble, asserted to have used *écriteaux*; both parodied plays. Parfaict credited their invention to two part-time Fair authors, Rémi and Chaillot: *Mémoires* (1743), I, 109, 133–4; II, 299, 317. *Arlequin grand Vizir* might have used scrolls as early as winter 1709: le Blanc, *Avatars*, 732.

[41] Campardon, *Spectacles*, I, 6–7, 85–9. Parfaict, *ibid.*, I, 108–9, asserts their use of scrolls explaining the action: perhaps this was done in summer 1710, as le Blanc supposes in *Avatars*, 734.

[42] Campardon, *ibid.*, II, 299.

[43] Martinuzzi, 'Pièces par Écriteaux', 227, Dolet & Laplace's troupe.

[44] *Jupiter curieux impertinent* at the same Fair given by Alard's troupe enlivened comic sketches with *vaudevilles*, but no *écriteaux* are mentioned: dated 3 February on printed copy (Paris, 1711), on *Gallica*.

[45] *Arlequin Énée* (25 July 1711); its preface (see *Gallica*) noted that more *vaudevilles* were sung than were printed.

[46] Spelled *Harlequin à la guinguette* (Paris: Rebuffé, 1711: on *Gallica*) presumably because he was acted by Richard Baxter: its Preface reports that he and Saurin had been hired.

On 7 August a new form of *écriteaux* was seen, facilitating dialogue in *vaudeville* form:

[The actors] play silent scenes on different subjects using *écriteaux* held by two small boys who are suspended and lifted by ropes within the stage machinery. These display the songs that are sung by several in the *parterre* as soon as the tune has been given on a violin; the texts, written on both sides, usually serve for conversational responses or else explain the action.[47]

Soon after, an inspector saw large lettering that made these signs 'very readable', carrying *airs* 'that the spectators sang and repeated'. The *Harlequin* Prologue was set in Paris: Jupiter and Momus descended from the heavens.

MOMUS [sung by the audience] to the *air* 'Des Pellerins de S. Jacques':

Although fate gives you power over us all, I am the god of satire, everything is allowed to me. Are you hoping for adventure in these beautiful surroundings?

JUPITER [sung by the audience] to the same *air*:

I know the residents of this city. I have come to vent my anger at their over-indulgences [etc.].

And pantomime action continued, interspersed with similar dialogue. A dramatised description was provided by Lesage much later:

CHEVALIER: During that time, we saw two small boys as cupids, who went up and down all the time.
COUNTESS: So what?
CHEVALIER: Well, it was entertaining.
COUNTESS (LAUGHING): Very pretty!
CHEVALIER: And as these children constantly changed over the *écriteaux*, it offered us a kind of moving picture.
COUNTESS (LAUGHING): Very nice!
CHEVALIER: The spectators themselves became actors. As each *écriteau* was unrolled the band gave the note and immediately we had the most joyful, discordant chorus in the world.[48]

Even expressive music could be sung by an audience, like the laments in *entrée* II of *Harlequin à la guinguette* when Harlequin and Colombine mime a parodic farewell-scene. First, they 'sang' Gillier's haunting Sarabande from

---

[47] Campardon, *Spectacles*, I, 91 (7 Aug. 1711).
[48] Prologue to *Arlequin Endymion*, FSG 1721: *TF* IV, 222–3 (R/I/454). *Écriteaux* were occasionally needed later to circumvent injunctions.

L'Inconnu (*The Stranger*);[49] then Colombine planned serious vengeance for which the audience sang Gillier's 'Vous qui vous mocquez', from *La Foire Saint-Germain* (Table 3.3).[50] Its new words required the musical repeats to be sung, producing forty-six bars in which all could share its haunting beauty.

When we reach 1712. we see different expressive uses of music alongside frequent physical comedy and slapstick; orchestras accompanied dances and added ritornellos.[51] Innovations included mimed duets and ensembles: in *Les Fêtes parisiennes* (*Festival in Paris*) by Fuzelier the third *entrée* contains *vaudevilles* 'sung' together by rival amorous shopwomen during another nocturnal *imbroglio*.[52] A 'sextet' was tried out in *Arlequin baron allemand* (*Harlequin German Baron*) when dancers performed 'a characteristic *entrée*',[53] possibly burlesquing the fact that the Opéra was currently linking dancers' roles and singers' roles.[54]

*

Alain-René Lesage offered his formidable talents to the Fair theatres when already an established novelist and playwright famous for *Crispin rival de son maître* (*Crispin His Master's Rival*) and *Turcaret*. The play *Turcaret* was controversial because its wealthy comic object is a tax collector.[55] His 'caricature of the financier, apparently based on inside knowledge or close observation, gave offence.'[56] No one could be certain that Fair actors would be allowed to sing again, but Lesage threw in his lot with them at this point, beginning with the 1712 lyric pantomime, *Arlequin et Mezzetin morts par amour* (*Harlequin and Mezzetin Die for Love*).[57] Brief and undeveloped in comparison with its successors, it reveals an affecting choice of music in Scene 6: five minor-mode *vaudevilles* interrupted only by the all-purpose 'Réveillez-vous'. Example 5.3 shows one of them, derived from Campra's *tragédie*, *Hésione* (1700), often to be used in *TF*. Lesage's operatic instincts are announced here: his desire for music to expand and articulate a scene that is concerned with emotion.

---

[49] Ballard, *La Clef* (1717), 357.
[50] Gillier's own edition, 18 (on *Gallica*); Ballard, *La Clef* (1717), 420.
[51] Martinuzzi,'Pièces par Écriteaux', 161, 172–3.   [52] *Ibid.*, 246–8.
[53] *Ibid.*, 272, attrib. Lesage, d'Orneval and Fuzelier.
[54] As in Campra's *Les Fêtes vénitiennes* (1710): Harris-Warrick, *Dance and Drama*, 248–9, 281–2.
[55] *Crispin* (15 Mar. 1707) stayed in the CF repertory until 1874. *Turcaret* (14 Feb. 1709) was quickly dropped but returned in 1730 and survived 200 years: Lancaster, *Sunset*, 254–62.
[56] Brereton, *French Comic Drama*, 192.
[57] Rubellin, ed., *Théâtre de la Foire*, 17–37 (omits *Les Petits-maîtres*); Martinuzzi, 'Pièces par écriteaux', 183–203.

Example 5.3 *Air, 'Menuet d'Hésione', from André Campra, Hésione, Prologue.*

As a curtain-raiser to this piece stood *Les Petits-maîtres* (*The Fops*), set 'In the Fair', which also points to Lesage's values: abandonment of old-style obscenity, with inclusion of valuable music. Scene 4 advertised the Bel-Air company's programme, using 'Réveillez-vous', still sung by the audience: 'Come inside, ladies and gents, it's a really nice show. The women won't be offended, nor innocent folk neither.'[58]

And Arlequin – for specifically *musical* reasons – questions a rival company offering 'new scenes from the old Italian theatre': 'Yes, but in *vaudeville* matters I'm actually a bit fussy. Do you have those lovely songs so popular in town?'[59] These words, sung on his behalf by the audience, are applied to the attractive melody shown in Example 5.4.[60]

Lesage's lyric pantomimes of 1713, *Arlequin roy de Serendib*, *Arlequin Thétis* and *Arlequin invisible*, show that he conceived the ebb and flow of dramatic rhythm in conjunction with appropriate music, built into a solid frame. Perhaps their quality was inspired by his ongoing contact with Richard Baxter, taking Arlequin roles in all three alongside Saurin.[61] Baxter is portrayed in the frontispiece to *Le Tombeau de Nostradamus* (*Nostradamus' Tomb*) as a hopeful female dancer for the Opéra, seeking to know her fortune by consulting the philosopher.[62]

During the winter season, *Arlequin roy de Serendib* satirised portions of two operatic *tragédies*, *Callirhoé* and *Iphigénie en Tauride*.[63] One needs neither permission nor articulate actors, implies Lesage, to show how coherent popular art can be in reacting to the pretensions of official theatre.

---

[58] Rubellin, *ibid.*, 24–5; Martinuzzi, *ibid.*, 191.
[59] Martinuzzi, *ibid.*, 192; MS on *Gallica*, BNF f.fr. 9314, f.1ʳ–f.4ᵛ.
[60] 'Oüi, mais en fait du vaudeville / Je suis un peu délicat, moy. / Ces beaux airs qui courent la ville / Les entend-on chanter, chés toy? / Je veux par tout des *il m'enfile*, / Et grand nombre de *j'en connois*.'
[61] Saurin [Sorin] specialised in 'Mezzetins, *travesti* parts, sultans and fathers': Campardon, *Spectacles*, II, 402.
[62] *TF* I, 67 (R/I/48), illustrating Sc. 8; see footnote to *TF* I, 190 (R/I/54).
[63] *Callirhoé* (1712) by Roy and Destouches; *Iphigénie* (1704, rev. 1711) by Duché and Desmarets. The plots of this and eight other early Lesage comedies are summarised in Lancaster, *Sunset*, 324–8.

Example 5.4 Anonymous *air*, 'J'entends déjà le bruit des armes' from Ballard, *La Clef* (1717), 191 in Lesage, *Les Petits-maîtres*, Sc. 5. 'Hear you the sound of arms, and the drum signalling '*Aux champs*'? I sense the fears returning, brought on each year through you. Must I shed tears at every spring's departure?'

Crucially, however, he adopted the structures of French opera: on one side, conversational *scènes* (plot development) and on the other, *divertissements* featuring dance. This was a period of intense competition; already the previous year the Saint-Edme company employed a choreographer directing between eight and twelve dancers.[64] Act I/1 of *Serendib* introduced dance, as also did I/5, Arlequin's ceremonial arrival; II/6, Arlequin selecting a female slave; and III/6, a mock-ritual praising the local god.

For the summer Fair, *Arlequin Thétis* offered a *parodie* aimed at the first two acts of its target opera, *Thétis et Pélée*.[65] We have a sequence in which the nymph herself (Baxter) is seen first with Doris, her confidante, then with a comic (mimed) trio of Sirens, then with the gauche suitor Neptune, tempting her with herring and mackerel, then with Mercure and finally with Jupiter. Even scenes using commoner *vaudevilles* are calibrated: for example, the twice-sung *menuet* by Lully, Example 5.1(a), echoes the ironic amorous banter between Neptune and Thétis in Scene 3. In Scene 6 Lesage designs a moment of reflection: Thétis and Doris, conversing, adopt an objective tone (they prefer ordinary men to gods): 'La jeune Abesse de ce lieu' is a graceful gavotte in G, in regular four-bar phrases. These give way to the banal, repetitive 'Pierre Bagnolet' (Example 3.5) sung to lines cleverly introduced from the target opera. Jupiter descends and Thétis / Baxter 'circles the stage with a handkerchief, imitating the singer in the opera', Françoise Journet.[66] This old joke, famous from *L'Opéra de campagne*

---

[64] F-Po, Rés. 611 in Porot, 'Chants de Momus', 162.
[65] *TF* I, 77 (R/I/24); *Thétis et Pélée* (1689) by Fontenelle and Collasse: Beaucé, *Parodies*, 152–3, 301.
[66] Appearing in the 1712 revival: https://operabaroque.fr (seen 14 March 2021); Philip Weller, 'Journet, Françoise', *NGO*.

(*Opera Goes to the Country*; see Chapter 3), connects with Fuzelier's updated version of the latter during the same 1713 Fair.[67]

In *Arlequin invisible* La Favorite and her lover gain our sympathy (Scenes 4 and 7) with serious texts and appropriately restrained music: 'Nos Pèlerins ont bonne mine' must be sung steadily, evoking love through its *menuet* overtones.[68] Lesage's three lyric pantomimes do not want for humour and topicality, but the varied choice of *timbres* bestows great musical interest: these pieces contain sixty-seven different *vaudevilles*. Whether or not the audience knew them all, the results (so far as the printed sources go) show that lyrical elements were intended to balance out Arlequin's mimetic tricks.

Singers and 'Irrecoverable Sounds'

Early opéra-comique singing may be an obscure 'unknowable' of music history, but we possess some evidence about its 'irrecoverable sounds' and singers.[69] It is worth pondering Bertolt Brecht's advice on singing in *The Threepenny Opera* (1928):

As for the melody, [actors] must not follow it blindly; there is a kind of speaking-against-the-music which can have strong effects, the results of a stubborn, incorruptible sobriety which is independent of music and rhythm. If he drops into the melody it must be an event; the actor can emphasise it by plainly showing the pleasure which the melody gives him.[70]

The return of professional solo singers was in 1713. A large royal party attended Fuzelier's *Les Amours déguisés* (*Love in Disguise*, music by Thomas Bourgeois) at the Opéra, dined after Act II, then moved to the Saint-Laurent Fair and commanded *L'Opéra de campagne* with *vaudevilles* to be shown at midnight. So as Fuzelier recalled, 'the Opéra, persuaded by the Fair's complaints as well as its money, allowed *vaudeville* singing' to Baxter's troupe: Mme Maillard, Saurin, Hamoche, Mlle d'Aigremont and Du Londel.[71] In due course Hamoche became famous, named by marquis

---

[67] See *TIG* IV, Act III, 75–6, where Arlequin parodies Duménil, and Mezzetin (Mme Prenelle) parodies le Rochois as Armide. Fuzelier's updating: Sakhnovskaia-Pankeeva, 'Théâtre de la Foire'. Fuzelier's notes: Cucuel, 'Sources et documents', 253.
[68] *TF* I, 96 (R/1/30).
[69] Giles, 'A Natural Voice?', *COJ* 29/2 (2018), 240, offers consideration of 'irrecoverable sounds'.
[70] 'Notes to *The Threepenny Opera*' in Willett, ed., *Brecht on Theatre*, 45.
[71] F-Po, Fonds Favart, Carton I, C 6: Cucuel, 'Sources et documents', 253; Sakhnovskaia-Pankeeva, 'Théâtre de la foire', 167–8, 191, n.117.

d'Argenson and praised by Charles Pannard: 'Such impact, such lungs, / This peerless voice, these / Pleasing, piercing recitals / Filling the hall.'[72] 'One of the first descriptions of an opéra-comique without *écriteaux*', as Bertrand Porot notes, is provided by a contract dated 9 July 1714:

[It will employ] four different persons to sing *vaudevilles* and songs both separately and between each other, such as previously were conveyed through our *écriteaux*, even [to sing] an individual Italian aria accompanied by our stringed and other instruments not exceeding eight in number [...] and to perform *entrées* designed for six dancers, using the normal scenery.[73]

At least forty-three actor-singers are mentioned or discussed in the Parfaicts' *Mémoires*, especially in the 1730s, with styles of self-presentation, career paths and public reception closely matching those of other singers. Fans could read poems in praise of Fair theatre soloists, not just those at the Opéra,[74] and students could learn about the breath control of Charles Rochard at the Comédie-Italienne.[75] Fair theatre singers also worked at official opera houses:

What drew the crowds [to *Arlequin Hulla*] was the début of the new Colombine. She was the famous Dlle de Lisle who had arrived from the Lyons Opéra in 1715. I do not recall why she was not accepted at the Paris Opéra. Soon after, she was invited into Dame de Beaune's troupe with resounding success. Her reputation was thereafter such that various people were convinced that Paris's rival theatres would be hard put to find anyone equally as good.[76]

Desjardins, real name La Faloye, was Parisian:

In his youth he entered the service of M. Destouches [the composer] who discovered his voice and aptitude, taught him music and paid him favourable attention. Desjardins [...] made use of his talents in the provinces, singing on various opera stages, and returned around 1708. When producing his new version of *Issé*, Destouches got him a place in the Opéra chorus. Through contacts made by his wife, Desjardins met Octave [Costantini] and began his Fair career in 1714 taking lovers' roles and other characters: he had a very beautiful voice and was quite a good actor.[77]

---

[72] D'Argenson, *Notices* (1725–57), 556–7; Pannard, *La Fausse Égyptienne*: Rizzoni, 'Inconnaissance', 142.
[73] Between the Opéra and Jean-Baptiste Costantini: Porot, 'Aux Origines', 289; Paris, AN, Minutier central, XXXVIII, 130, in Marcetteau-Paul, '*L'Obstacle*', 268.
[74] *Les Talens du théâtre célébrés par les Muses* (Paris: Mesnier, 1745).
[75] [Blanchet], *L'Art* (1756), 32.
[76] Parfaict, *Mémoires* (1743), I, 189. She retired in 1740. See also Campardon, *Spectacles*, I, 239–40. Social status and life of Fair actors: Paul, 'Les Théâtres des Foires', 110.
[77] Parfaict, *ibid.*, I, 210–11; Campardon, *ibid.*, I, 284–5; *DOP*, III, 186.

We saw on p. 8, n. 41 that Mlle Petitpas moved from Fair theatre to Opéra: her starry career has recently been documented, including her knowledge of London.[78] In 1738 Mlle Antheaume (or Antiaume) moved from the Opéra to the Fairs, heralding herself with ariettes by Corrette and a 'trumpet *air*', perhaps one by Mouret.[79] By 1744 it was possible for the best Fair singers to earn not much less than famous names at the Opéra, though the personal pressures they experienced on the popular stage were not always preferable.[80] One good way of measuring popularity is to study the *compliments*, that is, verses declaimed on each season's opening and closing night: frequently encountered performers were Mlles Angélique (=Destouches), Julie and Chéret, and MM Rebours, Drouin, Drouillon and Lécluze.[81] Thanks to Corrette's publishing activities we can begin to match singers' names with specific music, such as Mlle des Aigles with a da capo 'Ariete' of 43 bars and a 'Récitatif' setting of a lyric poem.[82] His duet 'Cruelle Sévérine' for Mme Durancy (Mlle d'Arimath) and M. Rebours appeared in Favart's *Les Nymphes de Diane* (*Diana's Nymphs*): see p. 233.

Nathalie Rizzoni's research in 'Inconnaissance de la Foire' emphasised that Fair actors, as those elsewhere, specialised in certain types of role, called *emplois* in French. *Emplois* became visible later when librettos printed singers' names with their roles, but before 1746 this was not normally done.[83] Nonetheless, a few librettos issued by Clousier do include cast-lists. As printed in the 1746 edition of Laffichard's *Les Effets du hazard* (*Just by Chance*) Clousier's cast-list appears to celebrate a Fair season eleven years before which had honoured the art of Charlotte Legrand; she had died in 1740.[84] Back in winter 1731 she had joined the Opéra Comique from the Comédie Française; her success in Barthélemy Fagan's *Isabelle Arlequin* conceivably inspired Lesage to create the Arlequin role of Lizette for her in *Roger de Sicile*.[85]

---

[78] DOP, IV, 130–2.   [79] DOP, I, 202; Parfaict, *ibid.*, II, 128; Viollier, *Jean-Joseph Mouret*, 190.

[80] Payments to Françoise d'Arimath, Marie-Jeanne Brillant, Rose Beauménard: Porot, 'Chants de Momus', 44–9; Legrand, 'Libertines'.

[81] Rizzoni, 'Inconnaissance', 137.

[82] 'Venez, venez, tendres amants' from *L'Isle du mariage* and 'Pourquoi changer' from *Le Départ de l'Opéra Comique*: Corrette, *Recueil des divertissements de l'Opéra Comique* [...] *en 1733*. *Œuvre IX*, 13, 23.

[83] Not a fortuitous date: in mid-1745 the OC had been suppressed; so as happened after 1697 (closure producing TIG) and 1718 (closure producing TF) new editions of theatre texts were made, as if surrogates for the stage itself.

[84] *Les Effets du hazard, opéra comique* (Paris: Clousier, 1746) had been premiered on 19 March 1735. Clousier's cast-list: Dorimène, young widow, Mlle Julie; Clitandre, lover of Dorimène, M. Drouin; Finette, servant of Dorimène, Mlle Legrand; Frontin, Clitandre's valet, M. Drouillon; Jacot, gardener, M. Rebours (seen in Fig. 7.3).

[85] See review in *Mercure*, 1731, March, 591; see Table 5.2.

The winter Fair season of 1735 opened not with a premiere, as was the custom, but with older pieces associated with her artistry: thus she acted in Pannard's *La Comédie sans hommes* (*The Women-Only Comedy*) and *L'Académie bourgeoise* (*The Urban Academy*), Fagan's *La Fausse ridicule* (*Misplaced Ridicule*) and *Isabelle Arlequin*. Then came *Les Effets du hazard*; and when the Saint-Germain Fair closed, Legrand left for Holland, never to return except in the memories of her public or buyers of Clousier's edition.[86]

*

Raguenet and Quantz had noted French quietness of voice – see Chapter 4 – but also superior acting: 'The only distinctive quality of their singers is their acting ability, in which they are superior to other peoples.'[87] These qualities perhaps made circulation between different stages and repertoires easier. It is notable that Nicolas Bergiron, director of the Lyons Opéra, programmed Favart's *La Chercheuse d'esprit* (*The Girl Who Sought Wit*) when it was new alongside *tragédies* from the Opéra repertory.[88] Jean Monnet, his successor, employed the remarkable Mlle Duval *l'aînée* of the Paris Opéra 'to double Princess roles in operas, sing leads if necessary and perform on the spoken stage or in opéra-comique or at the *Concerts spirituels*'.[89]

To begin to understand *vaudeville* singing, let us consider very divergent perceptions of Italian recitative. François Raguenet, an Italophile by persuasion, heard recitative as 'little better than downright speaking, without any Inflexion, or Modulation of the Voice'.[90] But his English translator added: 'they that understand [recitative] reckon it the greatest Beauty in Musick, and I believe they are right, considering how much Art and Knowledge is necessary for the Composing, Playing and Singing it'. A third opinion, found in the margin of one copy of Raguenet's translated *Comparison*, added: 'The beautys I find in the Italian recitative are the simplicity of the composition & of the Performance'.[91] So three observers registered, by turns, near-dullness, great science, beauty and artful simplicity.

---

[86] Parfaict, *Mémoires* (1743), II, 101; Campardon, *Spectacles*, II, 54–6.
[87] Quantz, *Playing the Flute* (1752), xix, 328–9, 334 (Chap. XVIII, §66, §76).
[88] *La Chercheuse d'esprit* (Lyon: Aux depens de l'Académie, 1741) at Lyons, Bibliothèque municipale, Rés. 360173–360179(4).
[89] 3 Oct. 1745: Vallas, *Un Siècle de musique*, 240. Monnet united the Lyons Opéra, playhouse and Opéra Comique: *Mémoires* (1772), 95; DOP, II, 443–6, 814–20: Mlle Duval's opera-ballet *Les Génies* had been staged in 1736.
[90] Raguenet, *A Comparison* (1709), 35–6.   [91] Raguenet, *ibid.*, 35–6 and n. 22.

In a way the dramatic medium of *vaudevilles* is comparable to both French and Italian recitative. Just as French recitative was declaimed according to the poetic interpretation of the singer, so *vaudeville* performance fluctuated according to the dramatic meaning, as we shall see. Free-flow *vaudeville* in popular opera and poetically declaimed recitative in serious opera contrasted with the regular beat of their respective dance sequences. Like Italian recitative, *vaudeville* performance might seem to be close to speech: J.-J. Rousseau thought 'the tune serves only to make the reciting more accentuated'; it had 'no regular rhythm'.[92] In recommendations to domestic players the marquis de Paulmy wrote,

> To play the old opéras-comiques one must be an actor much more than a singer; for *vaudevilles* do not require a great voice or much musical knowledge to be well done. You might even say they should be spoken more or less animatedly, yet bearing in mind the correct tone for the stage situation and the character being played. [...] You must try and discover the style of this singing within the meaning of the words themselves.[93]

A related element was improvisation: proof exists that actors improvised dialogue. Official records describe *Arlequin Mahomet* and *Le Tombeau de Nostradamus*, which in *TF* contain almost no speech; these records mention speech 'in over a hundred places' during public performances.[94] Lesage and d'Orneval failed to add dialogue to printed texts, although there was time to do so. Subsequent *TF* volumes were issued more quickly (volume 6 was passed for publication *before* the premiere of *Achmet et Almanzine*, which it contains). But this does not prove that there was any less divergence between what we read and what audiences heard.[95] Much later, Sedaine changed prose into verse dialogue in *Les Femmes vengées* 'in order that the actors should add the least amount through their contributions'.[96]

Accompaniment

Contradictory evidence exists for accompaniment practices, but part of this inconsistency may be due to differences in performing traditions between

---

[92] J.-J. Rousseau, 'Vaudeville', *Dictionnaire de musique*, 1138–9.
[93] Paulmy and Contant d'Orville, *Manuel des châteaux* (1779), 242–4.
[94] Campardon, *Spectacles*, I, 93. Few speeches are printed in *Arlequin Sultane favorite*.
[95] Martin, *Théâtre de la Foire*, 145–7 discusses BNF Ms. f.fr. 9295, advising actors on improvisation. This has no proven connection with Fair theatre.
[96] Sedaine, 'Quelques réflexions' (1778), 514.

the Comédie-Italienne in its *parodies* and the Fair theatres which habitually used *vaudevilles*. Notably, the 1729 *Le Joueur* at the Comédie-Italienne was said by the *Mercure de France* to have had accompaniments, 'Couplets [...] whose accompaniments gave them new attractiveness.'[97] This agrees with other evidence, namely invoices for the copying of parts and scores when the same company performed at Fontainebleau: we read of *Les Amours de Bastien et Bastienne* with 'accompaniments for the *parodie* [...] and its score' or, for *Les Amants inquiets* (*The Unquiet Lovers*), 'the score of the three-act *parodie*, [and] accompaniments'.[98]

The printed parts issued for Justine Favart's *Annette et Lubin* offered accompaniments for all nine *vaudevilles*, written by or for Adolphe Blaise. As this was created for the Comédie-Italienne, one is unwise to draw general conclusions from it, especially regarding Fair theatre.[99] Seven years later a published letter, as though evoking common knowledge, asserted that *vaudevilles* were still not *automatically* accompanied: its context was a debate about the future of popular opera, spoken dialogue, and music.

Perhaps [one could adopt] dialogue sung to simple *airs* well selected. This would form a brief unaccompanied recitative [...]. Several pieces by Pannard and Favart offer such examples. *Les Amours de Bastien et Bastienne* [...] is a particular case. The whole piece is sung; but the orchestra accompanies the ariettes only, or certain *airs* that function similarly.[100]

Unaccompanied *vaudeville* performance is explained in a letter from Rameau's brother-in-law Jacques-Simon Mangot dated 24 June 1762 at the court of Parma. Mangot directed the duke's French troupe from 1756 after holding directorships at Bordeaux and Lyons, and was helping an unknown correspondent in Vienna.[101] Numerous *vaudeville* comedies performed at the Parma court in 1755–6 have been documented by Marco Marica.[102]

I have the honour of sending you the *airs* and *vaudevilles* that I have copied; I have not added the accompaniments for the Menuet d'Exaudet or the *air* from *Castor*,

---

[97] *Mercure*, 1729, July, 1639. See Chap. 10 and online score.

[98] AN, O¹ 2993, 'Comédie Italienne, fontainebleau, le 3 novembre 1753', single sheet; O¹ 2998, 'Comédiens Italiens six 1ers mois 1755', 22 Janvier.

[99] Favart and Blaise, *Annette et Lubin* (1762) ed. Münzmay p. xxiii. OC actors were not involved: see p. 291 and n. 4.

[100] 'Observations d'un amateur sur la réunion de l'Opéra Comique à la Comédie Italienne', *Mercure*, 1769, Jan./2, 166.

[101] Mangot's roles in the ducal company: Butler, *Musical Theater*, *passim*; also Sadler, 'Mangot', *Rameau Compendium*, 124.

[102] Marica, 'Rappresentazioni', 430–4.

Example 5.5 *Air*, '*Menuet* d'Exaudet', from André-Joseph Exaudet, *Sonate en trio*, *Œuvre* II/1 (1751–2), 'Minuetto Gratioso'.

because it is normal in this kind of piece that the songs we introduce, which are either familiarly known or else *vaudevilles*, are sung by the actor without accompaniment. I have discussed it with Marianno, who has told me that in case one wanted to have an accompaniment, they did have the accompaniments in Vienna, and that then it would be possible in the blink of an eye.[103]

Mention of André-Joseph Exaudet's *Menuet* could not be more revealing: see Example 5.5. Mangot's advice contradicts every instinct now to supply accompaniment to such a classical-sounding composition. But that instinct was also expressed by the cultural critic Jacques Lacombe, whose description of *vaudevilles* was entirely musical in its nature.

[*Vaudevilles*] make a sort of recitative, almost always made hard and disagreeable by the bizarre conjunction of dismembered *airs*, and contradictory and most dissonant changes of key. This crude song is normally unaccompanied, and could not be otherwise. But if the *airs* are complete, sustained and follow logically, they should have a full accompaniment. [...] Without the support or guidance of instruments it is hard for voices to agree; they often wander from the key; the melody and time-signature are then not exactly observed.[104]

Grimm's words in 1764 usefully referred to 'the dialogue' as the unaccompanied element:

This detestable genre was no less odious to people of taste than it was to those who value public decency. If the latter were ashamed to have to endure foolery, obscene or satirical allusions and smutty puns, the former were equally shocked to hear the dialogue performed in *vaudevilles* or songs [*couplets*] without musical accompaniment. This old *opéra comique*, all the rage with young people less than ten years ago, is finished – or rather, has gone out of fashion.[105]

---

[103] Parma, Archivio di Stato, Teatri e spettacolo barbonici, b.1: 1739–178[?]. Document discovered by Paolo Russo, to whom many thanks are due.
[104] Lacombe, *Spectacle* (1761), 187–8.
[105] Grimm, *Corr. litt.* (Furne ed.), IV (15 Sept. 1764), 63–4.

The truth seems to be that *vaudevilles* could serve many different functions. Certain *TF* details suggest that instruments introduced or rounded off solos, perhaps with two or three bars of music (as with the *vaudevilles* arranged for *Annette et Lubin*). After Fanchette has sung two lines of *Air 112* in scene 14 of *Le Rémouleur d'amour* (*The Sharpener of Love*) the band interrupts and 'plays as Ritornello half the following *air* [*Air 24*] to announce the arrival of Cupid'. Fanchette and Pierrot then sing the last four lines of *Air 24*, after which 'The Orchestra plays the reprise of the preceding *air*'.[106] At the close of *Le Temple de l'Ennuy* (*The Temple of Boredom*) Lesage writes 'violins take up the melody' in the text, as though for a ritornello while dancing continues.[107] In the final scene of *Les Funérailles de la Foire* (*The Fair's Funeral*) 'the orchestra plays *Air 134*' but then two actors 'enter singing the same music, after the band has played'.[108]

Olivette juge des Enfers (*Olivette, Judge of the Underworld*) points to a similar thing. In Hades, Olivette (disguised as Minos) greets new arrivals and meets an abbé.[109] After an initial *air* which is shared, the latter begins to weep ('*L'abbé pleure*'). Since Olivette's next sung words are 'This music is so pretty. / What – are you weeping?', we know that the orchestra has played a ritornello that has provoked the abbé's reaction – it was Lully's *menuet* shown in Example 5.1(a).

A rare performance in 1991 of *La Répétition interrompue* (*The Interrupted Rehearsal*, Favart's version) had the singers virtually unaccompanied.[110] My notes made at the time read:

One delights in the very quickness of the switches and skill of word-setting itself, and also the use of responses between characters, which comes over not as a genuine conversation but a sort of conversation between inverted commas, or quotation. Literary at all times, and this reduces the level of the music in a way we are totally unused to. Non-repetition of words becomes crucial in achieving speed and intelligibility, but artificiality outbalances the 'naturalism' of such word-setting. Total absence of ritornellos helps gain flow in acting style, even though 'acting style' means something totally different in *vaudeville* from composed scores – we seem to be dealing in types, akin to Arlequin, rather than individuals, and this throws the interest back from the situation on to the words and word-settings.

---

[106] Sc. 14: *TF* V, 103 (R/I/554).
[107] *TF* II, 274 (R/I/200): '*les violons reprennent l'Air*'; *Air 62*, Table, 15 (R/I/247).
[108] *TF* III, 408 (R/I/363).
[109] Piron, *Olivette juge des Enfers* (7 Sept. 1726) in Rubellin, ed., *Théâtre de la Foire*, 295–6.
[110] 12–23 April 1991, Paris, OC, cond. Christophe Rousset (preceding Duni's *La Fée Urgèle*).

Continuity

Opéra-comique's stock-in-trade was specifically *not* to delay the flow of events. Too many ritornellos would have contradicted the principle that Lesage and d'Orneval defined in their preface to *TF*:

Each piece contains a simple action, so condensed that we see none of those slow transition scenes adopted in better plays. Such preciseness, foreign to other theatres, would in effect be a fault were it not absolutely essential to ours, becoming the first rule in our book. We noted that any scenes containing music, no matter how rich their sources, were tedious as a result of the languishing effect of the singing. That is why we preferred to entertain with a light-touch treatment of the material, rather than working it to exhaustion.[111]

Conversational texture could mould together speech, wit and *vaudeville*, as shown in Scene 1 of *L'École des amants* (*The School for Lovers*, 1716) by Lesage and Fuzelier. Anticipating *Così fan tutte* (whose subtitle was *La scuola degli amanti*) its plot will detach Isabelle and Olivette from their established lovers, Léandre and Arlequin. The enchanter Friston sets up the exposition in a narrative told to Pierrot, who interrupts repeatedly.[112]

FRISTON   *Air 7*:   'Tu croyois, en aimant Colette'
Porté sur un char invisible,   [sings:] Borne aloft on my invisible chariot
Je passois sur Florence un jour....   I passed over Florence one day....

PIERROT, *l'interrompant*.

C'est une belle ville que Florence. Continuez.   [speaks:] A fine city, Florence. Go on.

FRISTON

Mon cœur, depuis long-tems paisible   [sings:] Long since untroubled, my heart
N'y croyoit pas trouver l'Amour.   Never thought to find love there.

PIERROT

Oh, dame! L'amour est un petit Drôle   [speaks:] Oh no! The little rascal lurks
qui se fourre partout.   everywhere.

Then Pierrot's interruptions invade the *vaudeville* level, comically taking over Friston's words and music:

---

[111] 'Préface des auteurs', *TF* I, [7] (R/I/8).
[112] *TF* II, 321–2 (R/I/212): *TF* always makes clear what is to be sung by using a smaller typeface for *vaudevilles*.

FRISTON *Air* 50: 'J'ai fait souvent résonner ma musette'

| Je résolûs de ravir Isabelle | [sings:] I resolved to carry Isabelle away |
| A ce Rival qui régnoit dans son cœur. | From the rival she cherished. |

PIERROT [continues the *vaudeville*]

| Un pauvre Amant en a bientôt dans l'aîle | [sings:] Your poor lover gets fixed up |
| Quand pour Rival il trouve un Enchanteur. | Then finds his rival is an enchanter. |

Friston then says, 'Will you not keep quiet, babbler?' and Pierrot answers, 'Sorry, sir, I shan't say anything more.' Clearly the actors worked freely together, the absence of accompaniment allowing them to switch medium at a moment's notice.[113]

The same fluidity is even more marked in the Prologue of *Les Trois commères* (*Three Married Women*). Three wives are walking in the Luxembourg Gardens in Paris; they find a diamond ring but soon return it to an Englishman who is obviously searching for it. He decides to make a present of the ring, moving in mid-sentence from speech to song:

LE CAVALIER Hé bien, je ferai présent de mon diamant   Very well, I'll give my diamond

Air: 'Quand on a prononcé ce malheureux Oui' [sings:]

A celle de vous trois,	To whichever of you three,
Qui, montrant plus d'adresse	With the most skill
A son Époux fera	Creates the funniest situation
La plus plaisante piéce.	For her husband.

COLOMBINE [continues the song]

| Monsieur, nous acceptons la proposition. | Sir, we accept the proposition. |
| Nous allons travailler d'imagination.[114] | We'll set imagination to work. |

There are many places where TF inserts a series of suspension-dots at expressive moments within music which must signify pauses where the actors were allowed time to change their expressions and bodily disposition before continuing with the next phrase.[115] A very clear example is Scene 8

---

[113] Barberet, *Lesage*, 93, also discusses these points.   [114] *TF* IX, 435 (R/II/503).
[115] But when dots occur in the middle of a word, they indicate a melisma on the relevant vowel: see *Les Routes du monde*, *TF* VIII, 140 (R/II/323) *Air* 6, 'Voïelles anciennes', regularly found.

Example 5.6 Lesage and d'Orneval, *La Reine du Barostan*, Sc. 8: *Air*, 'Branle de Metz'. ALMORADDIN: 'When we see Love's flame there ... The most heavenly features ... A heart ... My tender wishes ...'; NOUR: 'His feelings have taken possession!'

of Lesage and d'Orneval's *La Reine du Barostan* (*The Queen of Barostan*), containing a *vaudeville* for four main characters. Prince Almoraddin is introduced at the court of Barostan; the queen, seeking a husband but also desiring to be valued as a person, is dressed as her own lady-in-waiting, Nour. Nour is costumed as the Queen. Struck with instant emotion for the supposed lady-in-waiting, Almoraddin fails to give an adequate response. So the music is constantly and freely interrupted, raising tension even while all four actors participate: see Example 5.6.

NOUR *le regarde, ce qui l'oblige à baisser*   Nour looks towards him; he averts his eyes.
           les yeux.

AMORADDIN, *troublé*:   *Air*: 'Branle de Metz'

Lorsque l'on y voit la flamme	When we see Love's flame there ....
Les plus célestes attraits	The most heavenly features .....
Un cœur .... Mes tendres souhaits	A heart .... My tender wishes .....
NOUR: Quel transport saisit son ame!	His feelings have taken possession!
ALMORADDIN: Ah! Si mon bonheur obtient	Ah! If my happiness could obtain ...
LA REINE, *à Nour*: Vous l'avez troublé, Madame.	You have troubled him, Madame.
ALMORADDIN, *se reprenant*:	*Starting again*:
Oui, si mon amour obtient	Yes, if my happiness could obtain ...
PIERROT: Oh! C'en est fait, il en tient.[116]	Oh! That's it, he fancies her.

---

[116] *TF* VII, 372 (R/II/247).

Vaudevilles Structured in Lesage's 'Royal Operas'

The new term 'royal operas' designates eight works involving noble characters. Lesage and d'Orneval here expanded musically expressive episodes, grouping *vaudevilles* into longer narratives or scenes of pronounced sentiment. Expressive episodes were not limited to these eight pieces, but their particular presence demonstrates a type of musical structure within the dramaturgy. First seen between 1720 and 1732, these eight works include four that Chapter 8 will show to have enjoyed revivals: *La Statue merveilleuse* (*The Magic Statue*), *Les Pèlerins de la Mecque* (*The Pilgrims from Mecca*), *Achmet et Almanzine* and *La Reine du Barostan*.

Each is set in a different, distant part of the world. Their unifying factor is a concern with ruling families, sometimes dwelling on the responsibilities of rulers or the problem of a noble who wishes to set aside his or her nobility in order to love (or be loved by) a person for whom nobility is irrelevant. Yet the 'royal operas' were not *parodies* of other works: they offered parallels to courtly operas, even to the extent of duplicating themes known to us from Metastasio, couched in quite sententious language. Long before Metastasio's *Il re pastore* (*The Shepherd King*), *Zémine et Almanzor* staged a monarch, Timur-Can, who has had his own son brought up as a shepherd in ignorance of his true birth. The 'shepherd king' theme is articulated by the supposedly noble Zémine, who loves the supposed commoner, Almanzor:

La Vertu n'a-t-elle donc pas / Des Bergers fait des Potentats?
Did virtue never make a ruler of a shepherd? (*Zémine et Almanzor*, Sc. 7)

And in *Roger de Sicile*, II/2, the king of Damascus says to Roger, king of Sicily: 'Everything in Palermo pictures the gentleness of your reign'. Roger replies in song, referring to his subjects: 'I am more their father than their king'.[117] Three years later Metastasio put similar words into *La clemenza di Tito*, culled from Seneca.[118]

All 'royal operas' except *Achmet et Almanzine* involve events from the past which must be explained to the audience; some give rise to a narrative scene where *vaudevilles* are grouped together: see Table 5.2. Often, these past events concern a misfortune or mistake followed by a character's decision to travel in search of resolution or closure. One example is *Roger de Sicile*, which also contains the fullest narrative sequence, spanning eleven *vaudevilles*. Stories of

---

[117] *TF* IX, 45 (R/II/406).
[118] 'My children will be my subjects, and I keep all of my affections for them': Cotticelli and Maione, 'Metastasio', 74.

Table 5.2 Narrative scenes in 'royal operas'.

1720 *La Statue merveilleuse*	I/6: Zéyn, king of Kashmir, narrates a dream and its momentous aftermath. Vizier Mobarec interprets its significance and explains what actions are required.
1726 *Les Pèlerins de la Mecque*	I/6: The valet of Ali, prince of Balsora, narrates his master's background story. II/6: Rezia, princess of Persia, explains how since her confinement she has avoided the Sultan's attentions.
1729 *La Princesse de la Chine*	I/6: Elmazie narrates how the Chinese princess Diamantine [Tourandocte in the source] has come to resist marriage and caused the death of unsuccessful suitors. I/8: Zerbin, tutor of the executed prince of Basra, narrates the story of the prince's obsession.
1730 *Zémine et Almanzor*	Sc. 1: Pierrot, confidant of the vizier Almanzor, narrates the story of the vizier's upbringing and describes his character.
1731 *Roger de Sicile*	I/1–7: personal narratives are related by Zerbin, Zerbine, Mezzetin (valet of the king of Damascus) and Lizette (disguised as Arlequin, king Roger's clown). II/6: Lizette narrates the central background events surrounding the vicious enchantment of the Queen by a corrupt ambassador.

this type resemble patterns in certain novels, for example those of François-Thomas Baculard d'Arnaud (1718–1805). David Denby observed that

> Baculard clearly opts for one of the central imaginary clichés of the sentimental novel throughout the eighteenth century. Sentimental love, the spontaneous experience of the heart, dictated by nature, is pitted against the social prejudice which sets obstacles of birth and fortune in its way, and the sentimental identification of the text is all on the side of the victims. [...] Misfortune, then, is the prime moving force of the narrative, the obstacle to happiness.[119]

Popular opera borrowed later from fictions like Baculard d'Arnaud's *La Nouvelle Clémentine*.[120] Denby also observed the way that 'the economy of sentimentalism' in novels involves 'an explicit denial of the validity of a social hierarchy' (p. 18), and it is plain to see that, later on, Marmontel's *Moral Tales* or popular operas from them can sometimes adopt this matrix – for example, in *Annette et Lubin*. Social references found in Lesage and

---

[119] Denby, *Sentimental Narrative*, 13.
[120] Inspiration for the famously sentimental *Nina ou La folle par amour* (*Nina, or The Woman Crazed by Love*) by Marsollier and Dalayrac, 1786. Other popular operas from Baculard d'Arnaud: WildTOC, 484.

Table 5.3 Sentimental scenes in 'royal operas'.

1726 *Les Pèlerins de la Mecque*	II/6: the lovers (Ali, prince of Balsora and Rezia, princess of Persia) rediscover each other after two years of unhappiness.
1728 *Achmet et Almanzine*	II/4: the main lovers converse alone for the first time. III/9–11: an extended *dénouement* centres on the nascent affection between the Turkish emperor Soliman and the Grand Vizier's daughter, Attalide.
1730 *La Reine du Barostan*	Sc. 9: Almoraddin, prince of Achem, declares his love to Zélica, queen of Barostan, thinking that she is only a commoner. Sc. 13: Zélica avows her love to Almoraddin, though she is still disguised.
1732 *Sophie et Sigismond*	Sc. 2: at night, Sophie sings in anticipation of meeting her lover Sigismond, prince of Hungary. Sc. 3: he arrives: their love is mutually declared.

d'Orneval, however, do not extend beyond qualities deemed desirable in noble rulers.

Roger de Sicile includes a sentimental thread in the lost-and-found story of Lizette and Mezzetin, whose musical expressions of regret and compassion in III/11 are affecting, if concise. The regular phrase structures and refined, beautiful melodies heard here are typical of sentimental scenes: *airs* 'Quand on a prononcé' and 'Je me plaignois d'une Inhumaine'.

Table 5.3 shows where *menuets* and lyrical gavottes were heard, and Example 5.7 reproduces 'Plus inconstant que l'onde' which featured in both *Achmet et Almanzine* and *La Reine du Barostan*. In Act III of *Achmet* it occurs within a sequence of no fewer than six *menuets* during Scenes 9 to 11. We can imagine fine voices performing these passionate declarations of sentiment.[121]

La Chercheuse d'esprit

A manuscript containing this, Favart's perhaps most-cited opéra-comique, appears to show how actors subtly changed the music of *vaudevilles* to enhance

---

[121] 'Je ne veux point sortir'; 'Plus inconstant que l'onde'; 'Si ma Philis'; 'Quand je vous ai donné'; 'Mon Amant me serre la main'; 'Menuet de M. de Grandval', followed by 'Quand le péril' (Ex. 5.1(a)). On *menuets* sung as *airs-vaudevilles*: le Blanc, *Avatars*, 568–71. It is worth mentioning that Striker believed that *La Reine du Barostan* 'actually satirises, albeit gently, the cult of sensibility which was already appearing in French society' and that in the same year, 1730, in *Les Routes du Monde*, Sc. 1, Lesage 'considered *galanterie* a mask for debauchery'; ultimately 'he felt alien to the new world of refined sensibility' brought about by Marivaux and La Chaussée: 'Theatre of Alain-René Lesage', 169–70. Nevertheless, as Table 5.3 suggests, his own sentimental scenes dated back to 1726.

Example 5.7 Lesage and d'Orneval, *Achmet et Almanzine*, III/10. *Air*, 'Plus inconstant que l'onde'. SOLIMAN: 'Know the power of your beauty. Atalide, your triumph is complete. Your father does not offend me, his crime is of no effect, nor is young Achmet's behaviour. The love which has suddenly burgeoned in my heart leaves no place for anger.'

the dramatic flow, but in ways that modernised their musical character. The story drew on two sources: an expurgated echo of La Fontaine's tale about the seduction of Lise (see p. 166); and an echo of Claude-François Desporte's *La Veuve coquette* (*The Coquettish Widow*). In this Comédie-Italienne play staged from 1721 to 1748, the widow Flaminia loves her own daughter's suitor: 'thus while the young man stammers through his request to marry Sylvia, Flaminia misunderstands him and thinks that he has come to ask for her own hand'.[122] The same misunderstanding besets Favart's widow, Mme Madré. Her old friend M. Subtil wants to marry Mme Madré's apparently dull-witted daughter, Nicette, but also suggests that Mme Madré should make a second marriage to his own son, Alain. During her search for wit, Nicette discovers the art of gentle deception, falls for Alain and finally outsmarts her mother.

Versailles, Bibliothèque municipale, manuscript Mus. Ms. 198, is unique.[123] Unsigned, but headed with the date of first performance, 20 February 1741, it is anterior to the first printed edition.[124] Moreover, it

---

[122] Ray, *Coquettes*, 49.
[123] It also contains the *Compliment* for the close of the 1741 FSG. It was studied from the holding library's online facsimile (April 2018: deleted subsequently) at: www.bibliotheques.versailles .fr/simclient/Integration/DOSSIERSDOCS_VERSAILLES/DossiersDoc/voirDossManuscrit .asp?INSTANCE=DOSSIERSDOCS_VERSAILLES&DOSS=BKDD_BMVMsmus_000024_ MSMUS198. The writing may not be Favart's, according to Dominique Quéro (personal communication), but I think that no one else could have been responsible for the particular modifications to be described.
[124] First ed.: *La Chercheuse d'esprit, opéra comique* (Paris: Veuve Allouel, 1741), pp. 61 + unpaginated *Approbation* (22 March 1741) and music supplement. The proof of anteriority lies in Sc. 5 where, for publication, small cuts were made and retained thereafter.

128 *Opéra-comique en vaudevilles*

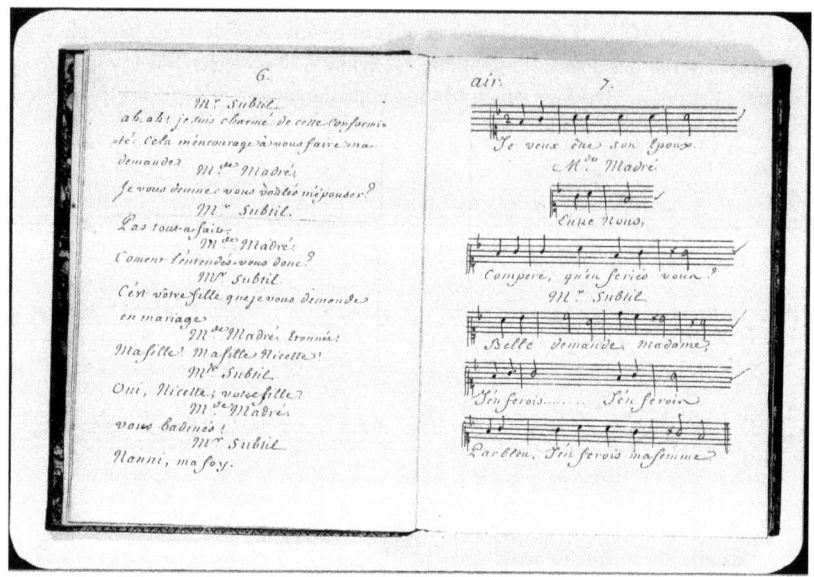

Figure 5.1 Charles-Simon Favart, *La Chercheuse d'esprit*, Sc. 1, F-V, Mus. Ms. 198, p. 7, Air, 'Des Feüillantines'. © Bibliothèque municipale de Versailles.

contains music for the entire collection of seventy *vaudevilles*, set out within the dialogue. No hint is present of accompaniments or ritornellos. It is a professional document, not a public one, since every verse begins on a new line, allowing for soloists to learn their parts either from exact copies or character-specific copies made from it: Figure 5.1 shows this.

Numerous subtle changes in the *vaudevilles* are revealed by comparison with the same *vaudevilles* printed elsewhere, including Allouel's original edition,[125] suggesting that Favart's singers modified the usual rhythms, pitches, contours and metres; even sang versions that were shorter or longer than familiar ones. This is not to say that those without access to Ms. 198 could not have used the *vaudevilles* found in printed sources: Favart's published words were mostly performable with 'textbook' versions of the *vaudevilles* but would sometimes need changes.

The manuscript source might imply that singers *always* improvised in role. And it proves that keys and clefs in published *vaudevilles* have no particular authority.[126] This is because its literal notations, for any given

---

[125] Allouel's 1743 ed. is on *Gallica*. Thirty-four of Favart's *vaudevilles* are on *Theaville*, its sources being *TF* and *PNTI*. None of the music for the thirteen *vaudevilles* issued by Allouel is on *Theaville*.

[126] Clefs and keys in Ms 198 frequently differ from those in the printed sources. Scholars formerly assumed the accuracy of notated keys in published *airs*. Barnes, 'The Théâtre de la Foire', 141, noted that *TF* sometimes prints the same *air* twice in different keys.

role, demand impossibly wide vocal ranges: only by transposition could some *vaudevilles* be sung. The manuscript usefully translates suspension-dots within the published libretto into precise musical notation, and in the very first *vaudeville*, Ms. 198 also asked M. Subtil to repeat the actual phrase, 'J'en ferois', that causes him embarrassment: see Figure 5.1. This extra 'I would … ', making three in all instead of the two found in the printed libretto, contradicts all other sources.

   Air: 'Des Feüillentines'
M. SUBTIL   I wish to be her husband.
M. MADRÉ   Between ourselves, old friend, what is she to you?
M. SUBTIL   Good question, Madame, I would. . . . . I would – zounds, I would make her my wife.

Vivid brief alterations occur in Scene 12: we see a lovers' disagreement between Nicette's cousin Finette and her fiancé, L'Éveillé. The *vaudeville* 'Diversité flatte le goût' is supposed to continue without a break into its middle section, but Favart introduces an action: L'Éveillé tries to steal a kiss. '*He tries to kiss Finette, she pushes him away*'. The manuscript stretches the incident, introduces Finette's riposte 'Steady on!' ('Tout doux!') and allows time for her stage reactions to register: Example 5.8.

In Scene 8 the jovial mood of the familiar melody 'Dans notre village' changed significantly when Favart's new contours transformed it into a musette: the comparison is made in Example 5.9.[127] Alain's and Nicette's music now expresses calm happiness; the original dominant chord implied in bar 8 no longer fits because a heard or imagined tonic pedal is to function throughout. In effect, as all through, Favart was using *vaudevilles* as 'raw material' to construct forms of subjectivity, a more operatic flow of music.

Example 5.8 Charles-Simon Favart, *La Chercheuse d'esprit*, Sc. 12, F-V, Mus. Ms. 198, p. 98, *Air*, 'Diversité flatte le goût'. L'ÉVEILLÉ: 'Steal a kiss on your chin, or on your pretty mouth.' FINETTE: 'Steady on!' L'ÉVEILLÉ: 'What's got into you, then?'

[127] Traditional version also found in Ballard, *La Clef* (1717).

Examples 5.9 (a) 'Dans notre village chacun vit content', Air 101 in *TF* I, *Table*, 27 (R/I/121). (b) Charles-Simon Favart, *La Chercheuse d'esprit*, Sc. 8, F-V, Mus. Ms. 198, p. 78, Air, 'Dans notre village chacun vit content'. NICETTE: 'Let's look for it together; when we find it we'll share it.' ALAIN: 'You're right, seems to me, I'll find it better when we be two.'

Example 5.10 'Ces filles sont si sottes', Air 52 in *PNTI* (1738), II, *Table*, 14–15, compared with Charles-Simon Favart, *La Chercheuse d'esprit*, Sc. 2, F-V, Mus. Ms. 198, pp. 25–6. M. SUBTIL: (to Mme Madré) 'They [Nicette's responses] prove to me her chastity. (To Nicette) 'Yes, my little heart, you have treasures that astound me.'

In dialogue duets Favart tightened the exchanges and in Scene 2 even altered the metre from triple to common time in the *air*, 'Ces filles sont si sottes': see the comparison in Example 5.10. The new metre hides the jocular sexism, for Monsieur Subtil does seem serious about Nicette.

Example 5.11 (a, b) Final bars of 'Que je regrette mon amant', *Air* 76 in *TF* VIII, *Table*, 31 (R/II/388) compared with Charles-Simon Favart, *La Chercheuse d'esprit*, Sc. 10, F-V, Mus. Ms. 198, p. 91. MME MADRÉ: '[You present her] in a loving way with a bouquet of lily-of-the-valley or carnations, which you fix to her bodice.' ALAIN: 'Yes, yes, I'll remember.'

Favart's manuscript omits the traditional repetition of bars 1 to 4; singers elsewhere would presumably include them.

For Scene 10, where Mme Madré gets carried away by her passion for Alain, unexpected manuscript additions heightened the stage action. She is teaching Alain how a suitor should fix a bouquet to the beloved's bodice (Example 5.11), whereupon Favart provided four extra bars and eleven extra words, 'un bouquet de muguet ou d'œillet qu'on luy met'. These are the comic means for an actress to exaggerate the misunderstanding under which Mme Madré labours, and the audience would laugh at the musical joke for itself. But what did non-Parisian performers do when they encountered text that does not fit into the conventional *air*, 'Que je regrette mon amant'?

Alain soon puts precept into practice with Nicette, who is feigning sleep: she hopes thereby to find wit (*esprit*) as her cousin Finette and L'Éveillé had recalled in Scene 12 having done, overheard by Nicette: see Example 9.10 and p. 230. Alain, desperately wanting to present his flowers, sings his *vaudeville* three times (*Air*, 'Je sommeille') with different words each time but always ending with 'réveille', 'awaken':

Avec ces rubans ornons-la;	Let's put these ribbons on her
Mais prenons garde que cela	But let's beware that this
Ne la réveille.	Does not awaken her.

Example 5.12 (a, b) Final bars of *Air*, 'Je sommeille' in Charles-Simon Favart, *La Chercheuse d'esprit* (Paris: Veuve Allouel, 1741), *Table*, 3–4 compared with version in Sc. 15 of F-V, Mus. Ms. 198, pp. 107–8. ALAIN: 'But let's beware that this does not awaken her.'

Example 5.12 illustrates how in the Versailles manuscript 'réveille' is expanded from five notes to fourteen, making the result even more of an operatic solo than it was already. The critic Desfontaines saw early performances and announced in his review that *La Chercheuse d'esprit* should become a model for its genre. Manuscript 198 helps us to understand what he meant by 'voices that show it to best advantage':

Such is the plot of this entertainment, which is shot through with subtle lines and jovial allusions. I would willingly quote some of them, except that this type of graceful humour loses its charm on the page, deprived of the melodies and the voices that show it to best advantage.[128]

*

Vitiated by uncertainties for want of documentary evidence, this chapter has pushed open the door at least a little. In subsequent chapters we shall find more solid evidence for the history of comedy *en vaudevilles*: the ambition of its themes and its life on the stage. We have seen that Favart and Lesage both linked musical repetition with narrative description, sometimes using stories that fitted into the wider plot. L'Éveillé's strophic tale in Scene 12 about Finette pretending to sleep (Example 9.10) is probably the direct origin of the *romance* or ballad tradition as 'backstory' which benefited both Mozart and nineteenth-century opera. In Chapter 6 we will see an elaboration of this in Gaviniès' *Romance* in *Le Prétendu* (*The Intended Husband*: see pp. 154–5). But even in Gherardi's company, repetition of *vaudevilles* could generate meaning, as Chapter 3 showed.

---

[128] Desfontaines, *Observations* (1741), 141–4.

As will be recounted in Chapter 8, Favart and his company became too successful by 1744–5. Manuscript 198 suggests new reasons why this was so: their specialised performances in an authoritative house style effectively made them a popular equivalent to the Paris Opéra. That is, the Opéra Comique had become the official representative of a mature operatic culture, whether by virtue of what it performed or (as we now see) *how* it performed, while originating pieces that were taken professionally outside Paris, for example, to Lyons.

Chapter 5 has not made good the lack of sources concerning instrumental accompaniments (or perhaps sub-ensembles: at the Opéra only a *petit chœur* supported the recitatives). However, it has identified the practice whereby popular opera focused on expressively rich *vaudevilles* at emotive points, and this principle, surely involving the accompaniment group, will be observed again in Chapter 9.

In *La Chercheuse d'esprit* Favart's operatic methods invited audience perceptions of a personal utterance in *vaudevilles*, enhancing a character's own qualities in musical terms. The acting ability of French singers was obviously central to Favart's aims and would remain fundamental to the practice of 'musico-dramatic art' for the next generation (see Chapter 12). More concretely, the revelations of Ms. 198 mean that at last we can draw a detailed musical connection between the two halves of the eighteenth century. Favart, on one hand, was stretching *vaudeville* praxis towards normative musical values of the 1740s; seven years later, Jean-Jacques Rousseau pulled operatic style in *Le Devin du village* towards normative musical aspects of *vaudevilles*. This evidence is to be explored in Chapter 11. Favart and Rousseau were approaching a common stylistic position from different parts of the operatic world.

Charles Collé's journal shows us where, in terms of actual singing, these tendencies led. Writing just after the departure of the Bouffons, Collé rails against a modern taste in comedy that Nivelle de La Chaussée's plays had begun:

He is one of the reasons why gaiety has disappeared from the theatre – seeking to imitate him, writers try to dignify everything [...]. Even the Opéra Comique is desperate to dignify its comedies; no other types are written; and the actors, in order to dignify themselves as well, sing their *vaudevilles* as though they were Jéliote singing a fine *air*.[129]

---

[129] Collé, *Journal*, I, 408–9 (March 1754). Pierre Jéliote was the most famous of *hautes-contre* at the Opéra.

6 | Experiences of Popular Theatre

This chapter leaves musical details aside and turns to material factors. New research is insisting that the Opéra Comique and Comédie-Italienne were neither small, ill-equipped nor poorly provided for in musical matters.[1] In what follows, three contributions are made to the revisionist movement: a synthesis of evidence regarding buildings, orchestras and admission prices; unfamiliar descriptions by visitors; and a synoptic account of scenery, staging and lighting, together with dramatic contexts. The Fair theatres and the Comédie-Italienne will be treated alternately here; ultimately they merged in 1762 within one building, the crowded Hôtel de Bourgogne theatre dating from 1548. After 1762 this had two names (Comédie-Italienne, Opéra Comique) and offered three genres: *commedia*, French plays and popular operas.[2]

At both Fairs, entrepreneurs regularly financed the construction or refurbishment of theatre spaces. There were competing troupes, but 'thanks to prohibitive decrees, implemented by heavy fines and actual demolition of theatres, all producers at the fairs except those holding the directorship of the Opéra Comique were forced either to shut down or to give *pièces à écriteaux* or marionette plays'.[3] Marionette-operas (see Figure 2.1, p. 32) were no different in musical character from shows using human actors, so far as is discernible from *TF*.[4] The only recent musical edition of a *vaudeville* opera from this period (1726) is of such a work.[5] Documents show the care with which Fuzelier commissioned scenery to be painted for his marionette theatre, whose string band sat below the stage.[6] From 1717 to 1744 'Nicolas Bienfait produced at both Fairs over fifty marionette

---

[1] Rizzoni, 'Inconnaissance'; Porot, 'Aux origines'; Golder, 'Hôtel de Bourgogne'; material in the CESAR database. The best documentary basis for imagining the social experience in Paris theatres is *The Contested Parterre*, Jeffrey Ravel's historical study.
[2] Other surveys: Beaucé, *Parodies d'opéra*, 34–48; Lagrave, *Théâtre et public*, 361–413.
[3] Lindsay, *Dramatic Parody*, 20.
[4] *L'Ombre du cocher poète*, TF V, 47 (R/I/540); *Le Rémouleur d'amour*, TF V, 70 (R/I/546), *Pierrot Romulus*, TF V, 107 (R/I/556); see Lindsay, *Dramatic Parody*, 122–31.
[5] Harvey (ed.), *La Grand-mére amoureuse*.   [6] Porot, 'L'organisation', 130, 136–43.

plays, – some parodies of comedies and operas, others *pièces en vaudevilles* after the fashion of opéra-comiques'.[7]

Modern writers differ widely in their accounts of comic experience. Readers of Isherwood's *Farce and Fantasy* find a carnivalesque celebration of vulgar comedy, whereas those of Lancaster's *Sunset* find that 'Except for an occasional reference [in Lesage] to a "pot de chambre", there is little vulgarity' besides the colourful array of spectacle, dance, gymnastics and so on.[8] Change is suggested by the fact that in *La Chercheuse d'esprit* there are no *commedia* characters or jokes; by 1741 Favart had been refining his art for ten years.

Theatre Size and Ambience

There was relatively little difference between the capacity of the main popular theatres, but their locations were vastly different. The Comédie-Italienne, the oldest performance space, was 'situated between the throbbing arteries of the commercial heart of the capital, in the noisiest, most noisome, congested and dangerous area of Paris': 'an extremely crowded quarter where traffic disputes caused by the proximity of the market threatened bad accidents on a daily basis.'[9] The Fairs themselves were agreeable places, especially the summer fair with its open-air layout by the church of Saint-Laurent, near today's Gare de l'Est. '[Its] grounds were lined with acacia trees, and after 1706 chestnut trees from India were planted'; boutiques sold 'pots of rich soil and sandstone, crockery, crystal and toys'.[10] The winter Fair was, in today's terms, a substantial shopping mall, rectangular rows of booths selling 'a sumptuous array of products' including luxury food, everything sheltered under a timbered roof.[11]

Fortunately, we have eyewitness accounts of social aspects of popular opera. The first was by Joachim Nemeitz (1679–1753), observing matters during the first period of opéra-comique.

---

[7] Moore, *The 'genre poissard'*, 220–1; Isherwood, *Farce and Fantasy*, 43–4.
[8] Lancaster, *Sunset*, 328.
[9] Golder, 'Hôtel de Bourgogne', 485; second quotation (c.1780) derives from F-Po, *Registre* 1; Lagrave, *Théâtre et public*, 116.
[10] Isherwood, *Farce and Fantasy*, 23, moving inside and outside the performance spaces, suggesting a continuum of vividness and excitement.
[11] Isherwood, *ibid.*, 23–4. The Fair was destroyed by fire in March 1762, but not the former OC. The frontispiece to *La Foire Saint-Germain* shows its retailing represented on stage: *TIG* VI, opp. 215.

[Chapter 12: Theatres] The [Italian] actors are almost all good, especially Lelio and Arlequin [...]. But the theatre's future must seem in doubt since few people frequent it unless they live in the Marais district.

[Chapter 19: Fairs] At Saint-Germain, rope-dancer troupes are the most popular. Sometimes they number four or five different companies, erecting theatres both in the courtyard and outside. [...] Sometimes, I notice, these five are at full capacity, just like the Opéra and other official playhouses. [...] Rope-dancing is thought less worth consideration than the drama that follows it, some troupes employing actors from the former Théâtre Italien. (*Footnote*: The Duke of Orleans allowed them to sing or declaim their plays, as they preferred; however, these are mainly sung.) Their comedies are mostly from the Gherardi repertory [compare Table 3.1] and the actors are sometimes able to give the same one for fifteen consecutive days. These rival troupes move heaven and earth to attract the most spectators. The best Arlequin, however, gets the most supporters and his vulgar words, jokes and sometimes obscene gestures are no barrier to these audiences. I was frequently astonished to see fashionable women see and hear such dirt without any shame [...] they laugh heartily.[12]

Nemeitz issued no proviso that enjoyment of opéras-comiques was limited to those knowing the French language or popular music. The diplomat Sir Andrew Mitchell (1708–71) reported on the reason and how rival theatres copied each other:[13]

The Italian Comedy is much followed because of the Harlequin who certainly excells. His gesture is so comick & so well accommodated to his odd tone of voice, that one can't help laughing even without knowing what he says. [...] The Opera Comique differs but in a few degrees from this, viz. more dancing & singing & less Harliquinades than in the Italian Comedy.[14]

Fair companies became solid operations whose actor-singers, as Chapter 5 suggested, sometimes moved to official stages or transferred from them. Fair theatre tickets were cheaper than elsewhere, with a greater differential between low and high prices: see Table 6.1. We read of the presence of titled audience members such as the duchess of Meilleraye, the chevalier de Mesmes, and 'several lords and ladies of the court' in 1712 at Biancolelli's summer theatre. Evidence for these and other descriptive details comes from sworn eyewitness statements by *commissaires*, policing officers.[15] The theatre represented in Figure 6.1 is unidentified, but its general size is corroborated by other images.

---

[12] Nemeitz, *Séjour* (1718), 80, 138–44; *ibid.* (1727), 98, 172–4.
[13] That is the theme of *Les Comédiens corsaires* (FSL, 1726): *TF* VI, 231 (R/II/66–72).
[14] Diary entry of July 1731: GB-Lbl, Add. MS 58314, f° 28^r.
[15] Campardon, *Spectacles*, II, 346, from AN series Y (Châtelet de Paris) 1629. This evidence was collected when theatre practice was asserted by a complainant to be illegal.

Figure 6.1 A pre-entertainment *parade* outside a Fair theatre. Source: BnF.

We begin with Saint-Germain, whose theatres were situated both outside the main complex and within the courtyard area, called the *préau*. Some in the courtyard were described as 'large' or 'very large', one having 'several boxes right and left'.[16] An eight-strong ensemble was noted at one

---

[16] *Ibid.*, II, 116 (1706); *ibid.*, I, 257–8 (1708).

in 1712,[17] and eight players agreed for at least one of the new theatres erected here in 1713 by Costantini.[18]

Outside the main complex we know of six theatres, or else sites for them: the point being that these were all refurbished or rebuilt over time.

(Grand) Jeu de Paume d'Orléans, corner of rue du Cœur-Volant and rue des Quatre-Vents, already existing in 1701.[19] In 1710 it was described as having three tiers of boxes on either side, with an ensemble of eight – which by 1715 (perhaps with more players) also had a functioning sub-group of three which accompanied songs and *vaudevilles*.[20] An extra stage area could be revealed when the backdrop was opened (1712).[21]

Jeu de paume de Bel-Air, rue de Vaugirard, created 1670, used for Lully's first opera in 1673.[22] As described then and in 1710 it had three tiers of boxes. Nine players were reported: six *violons*, two *basses de violon* and a bassoon.[23] Another report defined a *parterre* and *amphithéâtre*, i.e. a raked and seated area behind the standing *parterre*.[24]

A small theatre (*loge*) for the dancer Nivelon was built in 1711 next to the gate of the Fair at the end of the rue de Tournon.[25]

Opéra Comique de Bel-Air, described in 1718: on the rue des Quatre-Vents but next to the Fair entrance opposite the rue de Tournon. Decorated with chandeliers and boxes, it had 'about twelve' musicians on 15 March, but only eight on 28 March; scene-changes were provided when *Les Animaux raisonnables* (*The Animals Endowed with Reason*) was given.[26] Plans for a 1722 season allowed for up to fifteen instrumentalists, nine actor-singers, two specialist singers and nine dancers.[27]

Jeu de paume, rue de Bussy [Buci], opened 19 February 1726 with boxes; rebuilt in 1728 by Boizard de Pontau, the incoming Opéra Comique entrepreneur; then refurbished by him in 1730; then replaced by him in 1734.[28] No ensemble statistics are known.

Cul-de-sac, rue des Quatre-Vents. Pontau built this in 1735 with superior decorations in the front-of-house; d'Argenson thought it 'magnificent and in

---

[17] *Ibid.*, II, 187. [18] Marcetteau-Paul, '*Obstacle favorable*', 268.
[19] 'Jeu de paume' = a tennis-court. Parfaict, *Mémoires* (1743), I, 22; Campardon, *Spectacles*, II, 116.
[20] Campardon, *ibid.*, I, 6 and II, 223.
[21] *Écriteaux des Festes Parisiennes*, IV, ed. in Martinuzzi, '*Pièces par écriteaux*', 249.
[22] See Table 2.2. Plan and description: *Le Théâtre de la Foire à Paris* (www.theatrales.uqam.ca/foires, seen 23 August 2020).
[23] Campardon, *ibid.*, II, 298–301. [24] *Ibid.*, I, 88: not dissimilar to Lully's configuration.
[25] Parfaict, *Mémoires* (1743), I, 118.
[26] Campardon, *ibid.*, II, 403–5: not the same location as the first-mentioned theatre, above, as is verifiable from maps of the period seen on *Gallica*.
[27] Porot, 'Rameau', from Fuzelier's 'Éclaircissements'.
[28] Lagrave, *Théâtre et public*, 99; *Mercure*, 1728, Dec./I, 2711; *Mercure*, 1730, Jan., 151; Parfaict, *Mémoires* (1743), II, 32–3, 65–8, 91; *Mercure*, 1734, Feb., 368.

good taste, in spite of its modest size'.[29] Mme Du Boccage (see later) described this building after its refurbishment by the next entrepreneur, Jean Monnet, in 1744.[30] It remained the winter home of the Opéra Comique between February 1752 and Easter 1761, the final season.

The orchestra of the Opéra Comique rose to fifteen players in 1744 with seventeen in 1753, disposed as twelve strings and five winds (one oboe, two bassoons and two horns).[31]

Verging on open country, the Saint-Laurent Fair had more space available in its *préau*, illustrated in *TF* showing double-height buildings with pitched roofs.[32] Correlating the same type of information as earlier, we find the following:

In the *préau* area in 1702 the 'Cabanne de Mde Morice [Maurice]', entrepreneur, measured an estimated 43 m. by 11 m, making it longer than either the Comédie-Française or Comédie-Italienne, but narrower than both.[33] By 1707, Veuve Maurice's 'large hall' was recorded as having two tiers of boxes, a *parterre*, a seated *parquet*, chandeliers and perspectival sets.[34] By 1710 she had sold her theatre and equipment to two entrepreneurs who leased or let it to the Saint-Edme couple, after having 'made it extremely brilliant'.[35]

Also in the *préau*, in 1711, perhaps on the same site, Maurice's daughter, Dlle Baron, built or converted a theatre space for her Bel-Air troupe, 'raised up 4 or 5 feet', with two tiers of boxes, three rows of upholstered benches, crystal chandeliers and décors, with a reported ensemble of between six and eight musicians.[36]

A theatre was built in 1711 by chevalier Pellegrin abutting the *ruelle* Saint-Laurent. It was still used when the Comédie-Italienne leased it for their summer seasons (Table 1.2). From their still-surviving *Registres* the number of tickets sold is known: at least 1,262 places were available. Approaching the Hôtel de Bourgogne in size, this theatre had two tiers of boxes plus a third level (the 'paradis'), an amphithéâtre, seats on the sides of the stage and (in 1714) ten orchestral players.[37] In 1724 the entrepreneur Honoré lavished much money on the theatre;

---

[29] D'Argenson, *Notices* (1725–57), 554. No information in *Mercure*, 1735, Feb., 365.
[30] Monnet, *Mémoires*, 87.
[31] Porot, 'Chants de Momus', 150, 153. He calculates an average of eighteen players during the 1750s.
[32] *TF* IV, 353 (R/I/479), frontispiece to *La Fausse-Foire*; in Venard, *La Foire*, 90 who also shows (*ibid.*, 48) smaller *loges*, perhaps serving marionettes: cf. Campardon, *Spectacles*, I, 132 (1717).
[33] AN, N III Seine 271 analysed in *Le Théâtre de la Foire à Paris* (www.theatrales.uqam.ca/foires) 'Iconographie' (28 April 2020).
[34] Campardon, *Spectacles*, II, 117–19. [35] Parfaict, *Mémoires* (1743), I, 117.
[36] Campardon, *Spectacles*, I, 91–4.
[37] On 8 August 1723, for the standing *parterre* and *paradis* together 652 tickets were sold, plus 248 tickets for the second-level boxes and amphithéâtre. On 2 August 362 tickets for the first-level boxes were sold: Lagrave, *Théâtre et public*, 98–9. Parfaict, *Mémoires* (1743), I, 128; Campardon, *ibid.*, II, 222.

we presume that this is the structure called the 'Opéra-Comique' in a 1729 report.[38] In 1743 Jean Monnet arrived, moved the *parterre* and put in an extra seated *amphithéâtre*.[39] François Boucher, the royal painter, created sets and costumes for 'Les Fleurs' in Favart's *Les Indes dansantes*; Rameau was hired for this item as *maître de musique*.[40] In the following year Favart planned an orchestra of sixteen and up to twenty actor-singers, and thirteen dancers.[41]

By 1714 the Saint-Edme team had built a theatre in the *préau* with machines, chandeliers and various sets, with 'nine or ten' in the orchestra. In 1716 it was 'honoured with the most brilliant audiences' and employed twenty orchestral players.[42]

Also by 1714 Baxter and Saurin constructed a theatre in the *préau* with 'decorations, chandeliers and different machines'; used by the Bel-Air company, it employed twelve in the orchestra for Lesage's *Le Tombeau de Nostradamus* (*Nostradamus' Tomb*) and *Arlequin Mahomet* (*Harlequin-Mahomet*), rising to fourteen in summer 1716.[43]

In 1752 Monnet built a renowned summer theatre whose acoustics were so good that after 1762 the building was taken to the royal workshops (Menus-Plaisirs) and used for rehearsals and concerts. Its structure measured ca.100' (30.5 m) by 48' (14.6 m); the stage's depth reached 40' (12 m). Its orchestra pit was 24' (7.3 m) wide by 5' (1.5 m) deep, next to which was a strip of seats (the *orchestre*), 4' 6" (1.4 m) deep; behind this was the standing *parterre*. Two tiers of three boxes each went along the sides, completed by five semicircular rows of raked benches at the end opposite the stage (*amphithéâtres*).[44]

Denis Carolet, author of all the popular operas in the final volume of *TF*, claimed in 1734 that the Opéra Comique had 'in effect become the theatre of gentlefolk',[45] but only under Jean Monnet's tenure was anyone specifically excluded. The *Mercure* announced: 'All manner of gentlefolk, bourgeois and others may sit unencumbered by liveried servants; the king's order of 17 June [1743] prohibits them and lackeys from admission henceforth, even upon payment,' at both Fairs.[46] This was in line with the

---

[38] Campardon, *ibid.*, II, 196; Porot, 'Chants de Momus', 27.
[39] Lagrave, *ibid.*, 100; Campardon, *ibid.*, II, 196; *Mercure*, 1743, July, 1631; Oct., 2282; Porot, *ibid.*, 86.
[40] Monnet, *Mémoires*, 86; Sadler, 'Rameau, Piron', 27–8; Porot, 'Rameau'.
[41] Porot, 'Chants de Momus', 44–5, 143, 165. This building was apparently demolished after 1745.
[42] Campardon, *Spectacles*, II, 349–50, 355, 360; Parfaict, *ibid.*, I, 187.
[43] Campardon, *ibid.*, I, 101–2 and II, 402–3; Parfaict, *ibid.*, I, 162–4.
[44] Drawings: Lagrave, *Théâtre et public*, Fig. 19; figures from Prod'homme and de Crauzat, *Les Menus-Plaisirs*, 46.
[45] 'Préface de l'auteur', *TF* IX/2 (R/II/554).
[46] *Mercure*, 1743, July, 1629–32. Lackeys were 'liveried adolescents who did little more than run an occasional errand, brawl in taverns, and eat', advertising their masters' wealth: Fairchilds, 'Masters and Servants', 369.

Table 6.1 Theatre admission prices given in French and contemporary English currency.[a] There were 20 *sols* in a *livre*; 's' = shillings; 'd' = pence.

Name of theatre	Best boxes or seats downstairs	Second-level box	Third-level box	*Parterre*
Opéra				
1716	7 *livres* 7 *sols* / 6s 1½d	3 *livres* 12 *sols*/3s	36 *sols* / 1s 6d	36 *sols* / 1s 6d
1749	10 *livres* / 8s 4d	4 *livres* / 3s 4d	2 *livres* / 1s 8d	2 *livres* / 1s 8d
Comédie-Italienne				
1716	4 *livres*/3s 4d	2 *livres*/1s 8d[b]	30 *sols*/ 1s 3d	1 *livre* / 10d
1776	5 *livres*/ 4s 2d	3 *livres*/ 2s 6d		2 *livres*/ 1s 8d
1783 (new building)	6 *livres*/ 5s	3 *livres* / 2s 6d	36 *sols* / 1s 6d	24 *sols* / 1s
Fair theatres:				
Godard's troupe, 1709	30 *sols*/1s 3d	12 *sols* / 6d		5 *sols* / 2½d
Dolet & Laplace, 1709	3 *livres*/2s 6d	20 *sols* / 10d		5 *sols* / 2½d
Opéra Comique, 1745	3 *livres*/2s 6d	30 *sols* / 1s 3d		6 *sols* / 3d

[a] Condensed from Lagrave, *Théâtre et public*, 46–52 with 1776 prices from Bentley, *Journal* and 1783 prices from Campardon, *Les Comédiens*, I, xlvi.
[b] Amphithéâtre price.

Comédie-Italienne's 1716 regulations, but Monnet maintained that the servants 'controlled the *parterre*, decided the fate of new pieces, hissed the actors and sometimes even their own masters'.[47] *Parterre* standing places at the Fairs remained much cheaper than those elsewhere – see Table 6.1 – and yet no special evidence of disorder is recorded.[48]

A craftsman in a city earned only between 15 and 30 *sols* a day, while a family was reckoned to need 52 *sols* a day or more to get by.[49] Lesser servants could hardly have replaced those who had been excluded: the spectrum of wages generally was between 10 and 40 *livres* a year up to about 1750, often not regularly paid.[50] 'There was a world of difference between the well-educated, well-paid stewards and house managers at one end of the scale and the cooks' assistants and stable-boys at the other.'[51] Theatre seats must be thought of as luxuries within this scenario.

---

[47] CI rule: Campardon, *Les Comédiens*, II, 238–9; Monnet, *Mémoires* (1772), 78–9.
[48] Fewer arrests (7) between 1717 and 1765 reported than at the CI (19) or CF (44), but Fairs were seasonal and, as Table 1.2 shows, the OC shut for 13 seasons: Ravel, *Contested Parterre*, 146.
[49] Roche, *History of Everyday Things*, 58, 63.   [50] Fairchilds, 'Masters and Servants'.
[51] Garrioch, *Making of Revolutionary Paris*, 36.

Descriptions

The longest text descriptive of popular theatre was published in winter 1745 and was centred on the Opéra Comique, rue des Quatre-Vents: *Lettre de Madame* +++ *à une de ses amies sur les spectacles, et principalement sur l'Opéra Comique*, forty-four pages long. Fair theatre was at a high point of popularity, thanks to Favart's genius. Anne-Marie Du Boccage's anonymously issued tract explicitly aimed to shut down this company and could be classed as a pamphlet, such as seen during the 'Querelle des Bouffons'.[52] The actual suppression of the Opéra Comique between June 1745 and the end of 1751 (detailed in Chapter 8) resulted from pressure by the Comédie-Française, which is strongly defended in *Lettre de Madame* +++. Its unnamed publisher began with an apologia:

> If sometimes she [the author] departs from her usual tone of moderation, we easily see that her motive demonstrates zeal for the glory of the French nation, that her aim is the abolition of the Opéra Comique; in truth, what must visitors in Paris think of our moral standards when they see such a show? (5–6)

These words silently refer to the fact that 23 February 1745 was the wedding day of the Dauphin of France and Maria Teresa, Infanta of Spain. Lully's *Thésée*, an opera associated with 'legitimate succession in an absolute monarchy',[53] had been revived for the occasion in December. Some fashionable visitors to Paris might have attended a *parodie*, *Arlequin Thésée*, on 30 January at the Comédie-Italienne, which ran for nine performances; but more must have attended the rival *parodie*, *Thésée*, at the Opéra Comique from 17 February, which ran for much longer.[54] Its vulgar ridicule at a sensitive moment was a main object of Boccage's attack, which also targeted Favart's *L'Amour au village* (*Love in a Village*) in the same programme.

Anne-Marie Lepage, later Mme Du Boccage, was soon to be a published poet, playwright, translator and denizen of the cultural scene in Venice and London.[55] Born in Rouen in 1710, she married, and moved to Paris in 1733.[56]

---

[52] No publisher was mentioned. Du Boccage's authorship is accepted by Gill-Mark, *Une Femme de lettres*, 172. On pamphlets, see Arnold, *Musical Debate*, Chap. 3.

[53] Couvreur, *Jean-Baptiste Lully*, 357.

[54] The OC *parodie* was by Favart, Laujon and Parvi; *Arlequin Thésée* at the CI was by Valois d'Orville; Beaucé, *Parodies*, 334–6.

[55] *Recueil des Œuvres de Madame Du Boccage*, 3 vols. (Lyon: Perisse, 1762). Her *Les Amazones* was staged at the CF in 1749.

[56] Little is known of her early career: Gill-Mark, *Une Femme de lettres*. Her husband Joseph Fiquet Du Boccage translated English plays.

I arrived before starting-time; it was very cold, so I went to warm myself in the foyer.[57] My surprise may be judged from what struck me on entering: a young musketeer kneeling at the foot of a pretty actress, declaiming in tragi-comic tones and kissing a hand that she freely released to him. Another actress struggled feebly with a dull councillor who insisted on putting back her garter, which she had removed so that he could admire its beauty. A third one joked with an impudent fop [*petit-maître*] whose hand was on her breast. No-one took notice when I appeared, none of the youths round about bothered to make room. I wanted to retreat, but the door was blocked by new arrivals. I asked the person next to me to allow me through; it was the Duke of +++, as I only subsequently recognised. 'Why, Madame, it's you!' he said, turning, 'I am most surprised! What might you have come for?' I said I was freezing cold and wanted to warm up. He gave me his hand to lead me near the fire, but [...] had much difficulty finding me a place. [...] Everyone looked at me with such effrontery that I had to look away, so my embarrassment gave rise to unpleasant jokes that were loud enough for me to hear: I lost all composure, so that the actresses burst out laughing. [...] The councillor went on with his amorous attempts; he took them so far, and was sitting so near me, that I could not ignore him any more, got up suddenly and asked the duke for his arm. Everyone promptly burst out laughing. [...]

I entered my box in very dissatisfied state with the duke's explanations, and annoyed with you. Hardly had I sat down when I noticed twenty opera-glasses trained at me. I had certainly seen people ogled at the playhouse and the Opéra, but not with such effrontery as here. [...] Soon they were whispering, asking about my name, which no-one knew; they discussed what had happened in the foyer [...]; luckily a pretty young creature, dressed coquettishly, drew attention away from me when she noisily entered a box opposite mine. I imagine she knew everyone there, smiling at them in turn, simpering, taking snuff, whispering to a sort of servant she had with her [...]. [Finally] she leaned her head on her arm and remained for some time in this interesting pose.[58]

These experiences compare with the fictional Rica's report in *Persian Letters* (1721): 'If I was in a theatre [wearing Persian costume] I straightaway found a hundred lorgnettes trained on my face'.[59] Du Boccage's description of acting in *parodie* is valuable:

The High Priestess hears the sounds of combat and rushes on crying 'What a din, what an un-hole, what an unholy noise is here', [...] carefully emphasising the words 'un-hole, unholy' with expressive gestures and a meaningful smile to show her wit.[60]

---

[57] We have no plans for this theatre. The *foyer* at the CI had doors at either end but also a door leading to the stage; there was no other 'green room'. Golder, 'Hôtel de Bourgogne', Fig. 3.
[58] [Du Boccage], *Lettre* (1745), 9–16. [59] Montesquieu, *Lettres persanes*, 65 (Letter 30).
[60] *Ibid.*, 31.

The *foyer* of the rival Comédie-Italienne was described by Casanova after a visit in 1751. Whereas Garrick called this space 'a wretched Hole', the Italian felt completely at home:[61]

During the intermissions the greatest noblemen are to be found [in the green-room], for they go there to get warm in winter and at all seasons to amuse themselves by talking with the actresses who sit there waiting for their turns in the parts they are playing. I was sitting beside Camille, Coraline's sister, keeping her laughing by flirting with her. A young councillor, who did not like my monopolizing her attention, attacked me in a conceited tone [etc.].[62]

At the same theatre, seen merely at distance, Coraline's effect on Restif de la Bretonne was violently sexual.[63] In 1782 Laclos referenced the same *foyer* as 'petit salon' at the close of *Les Liaisons dangereuses* when Madame de Merteuil is humiliated; she 'saw an empty space on one of the benches and sat down; whereupon the other women already sitting there rose immediately, as of one accord, and left her absolutely alone'.[64]

Mme Du Boccage's text implies that the Opéra Comique had the same gendered division of spaces as other theatres, here summarised by Henri Lagrave:

The distance separating boxes from the [standing] *parterre* meant not just a social polarity but gave rise to a gendered confrontation. The *parterre*, reserved for men, remained strongly aware of its masculinity. Sometimes crude jokes, flying up for the benefit of the boxes, relayed its group psychology to the female audience looking down. These separate groups did not react in the way that they would have done had they been mixed together, as now, throughout the theatre.[65]

On reopening in February 1752, the Opéra Comique attracted the police's interest: the best boxes were occupied by people like the theatre-loving comte de Clermont, the princes of Turenne and Soubise, marshal Richelieu and ambassador Wenzel Kaunitz of Vienna.[66]

---

[61] Garrick, *Diary* (1751), 19.
[62] Casanova, *History of My Life*, III, Chap. 9, 164–5 (modified). The marquis de Marigny and the duke of Maddaloni were also in the green room. Coraline (Anne-Marie Veronèse) was about 21 and her sister about 16. Camille's portrait is in Oreglia, *Commedia dell'arte*, 124. Both were famous actors and dancers: Campardon, *Les Comédiens*, II, 187–202.
[63] Reported in his autobiography *Monsieur Nicolas*: Scott, *Women on the Stage*, 269.
[64] Choderlos de Laclos, *Les Liaisons dangereuses*, Letter 173, 389. See Wåhlberg, 'L'opéra-comique'.
[65] Lagrave, *Théâtre et public*, 663.
[66] Paris, Archives de la Bastille: Pré, 'Livret d'opéra-comique', 22; Brown, *Gluck*, 44–5.

In 2009 John Golder revealed the plans and elevations he had discovered of the Hôtel de Bourgogne, drawn in 1760. With three tiers of boxes and a standing *parterre* calculated at 630, the theatre's capacity could have reached 1,489.[67] This includes 150 seated in the stalls *parquet* and 95 seated in the rear *amphithéâtre*. We saw earlier that 1,262 places are estimated for Pellegrin's theatre at the Saint-Laurent Fair, used until 1745. The old 1548 Hôtel was cramped both for its audience and especially for the performers, with poor conditions and sparse facilities persisting until the company moved into a custom-built theatre, the Salle Favart, in 1783.[68] Thomas Bentley (1731–80), Josiah Wedgwood's partner in manufacturing, left a description of the original theatre that is good on detail:

[29 July 1776] The house is long, narrow and badly lighted. The ornaments are in a poor style, very heavy and extremely old and tarnished. The lower part of the house has three divisions. The first, which answers to our pit, next to the music, is called the orchestre, and is the best place in house for those who would see and hear well – price 5 livres. Here the Court sit. Behind this is a large space called the *parterre*, without seats, in which all the people stand and can scarcely see over the heads of those in the orchestre. The price 2 livres. The third division behind the pit is raised a little above it with seats and the price is 3 livres. It is called the amphitheatre.

All round the house there are rows of lodges or boxes, I think 4 or 5 stories high, and in these, and especially in those that are nearest the stage, the ladies make a very brilliant figure. Their heads are dressed out like Indian queens with plumes of feathers interspersed with diamonds and other stones, so that many of them seem more like generals fit to command an army. [. . .] But I see many ladies who dress in a very moderate and becoming manner, just as reasonable and modest ladies dress in England.

The scenes were very bad, and the actors middling; the music agreeable. I lost much by not understanding French half so well when I hear it spoken as when I read.[69]

Visits to the Hôtel de Bourgogne by Laurence Sterne in the 1760s emerge in the semi-fictional *A Sentimental Journey* (1768) whose purpose, he confided in a letter, 'was to teach us to love the world and our fellow creatures better than we do'.[70]

---

[67] Golder, 'Hôtel de Bourgogne', 481.
[68] Description: Brenner, *Théâtre Italien*, 17–22; illustrations: Legrand and Wild, *Regards*, 46, 60.
[69] Bentley, *Journal* (1776), 37–8.
[70] Ian Jack, 'Introduction' to Sterne, *Sentimental Journey*, xv.

> There was no body in the box I was let into but a kindly old French officer. [...] I have a predilection for the whole corps of veterans; and so I strode over the two back rows of benches, and placed myself beside him. The old officer was reading attentively a small pamphlet, it might be the book of the opera, with a large pair of spectacles. As soon as I sat down, he took his spectacles off, and putting them into a shagreen case, return'd them and the book into his pocket together. I half rose up, and made him a bow. [...]
>
> At the end of the orchestra, and betwixt that and the first side-box, there is a small esplanade left, where, when the house is full, numbers of all ranks take sanctuary. Though you stand, as in the parterre, you pay the same price as in the orchestra. A poor defenceless being [of restricted height] had got thrust some how or other into this luckless place—the night was hot, and he was surrounded by beings two feet and a half higher than himself. The dwarf suffered inexpressibly on all sides; but the thing which incommoded him most, was a tall corpulent German, near seven feet high, who stood directly betwixt him and all possibility of his seeing either the stage or the actors. [...]
>
> The old French officer [leaned] a little over, and nodding to a centinel, and pointing at the same time with his finger to the distress—the centinel made his way up to it.—There was no occasion to tell the grievance—the thing told itself; so thrusting back the German instantly with his musket—he took the poor dwarf by the hand, and placed him before him.[71]

Sterne's private reports describe extreme enthusiasm for popular opera in its newest guise: 'the whole City of Paris is bewitch'd with the comic opera'.[72] *A Sentimental Journey* suggests currents of sympathy and humanity found at this juncture; Sterne might have seen *Annette et Lubin*, where Lubin's offstage rescue of Annette by force was followed, upon his reappearance, by a *tableau* (Favart's own term): 'he holds her in one hand and scatters the last of the seigneur's men with the other'.[73] After his aria the seigneur returns and Lubin, 'seized with respect', utters a passionate speech which was 'constantly applauded' after being 'rendered by M. Caillot with a truth to life impossible to attain even by the greatest study'.[74]

> I admit I was wrong, but I say it again,
>   Monseigneur, take care of Annette.
> If I must take my leave of Annette come what may
>   Let me serve under arms in your own regiment. [...]

---

[71] From 'The Translation' and 'The Dwarf', *A Sentimental Journey* (1768), 56–61.
[72] March 1762: Cash, *Laurence Sterne*, 145, 162.
[73] Favart, *Correspondance*, I, 243, details not found elsewhere.
[74] Contant d'Orville, *Histoire* (1768), I, 223–4.

>   When seeing those less fortunate
>   You act in their best interests:
> You say to yourself: they are no different,
>   Yes, those poor souls are people too.

This is represented in Figure 6.2. When a performance was judged badly, though, the audience mood could be antagonistic:

> [13 June 1770] In the evening I heard two pieces performed at the *Theatre Italien* [...]. One of these pieces was new [...]. And this piece was as thoroughly d[amne]d as ever piece was here. I used to imagine that a French audience durst not hiss to the degree I found they did upon this occasion. Indeed quite as much, mixt with horse laughs, as ever I heard at Drury Lane, or Covent Garden. In short, it was condemned in all the English forms, except breaking the benches and the actors' heads; and the incessant sound of *hish* instead of *hiss*.[75]

Staging

It has well been noted that 'part of the charge levelled against [Fair theatres] by their privileged competitors' concerned the popular stage's 'efforts to reproduce the physical experience' of going to official theatres: 'the loges, pit, stage seating, perspectival stage sets and elaborate ornamental decorations'.[76] When reading librettos and studying the engraved frontispieces in *TF* a vivid enough world comes alive. 'The spectacular element is considerable' in the early years,[77] even if popular opera always throws the primary emphasis on to the living figure – acting, movement, costume, song, dance. The Hôtel de Bourgogne building had five sets of wings.[78] Fair theatres must have used similar methods; by 1712 for *Arlequin empereur dans la lune* (1684: *TIG* I) Costantini had installed quick-change mechanisms for his sets, using pivots: an operator could change the whole décor with a hand movement.[79]

Diagonal wings completed the stage picture in front of a painted backdrop. Recent restoration of painted sets and their use in performance have revealed a memorable blend of form, colour and perspective. Those

---

[75] Burney, *Present State ... France and Italy* (1771), 16–17: he saw *Alvar et Mencia*, now lost, text by A. G. Cailly, music by L. J. Saint-Amans.
[76] Ravel, *Contested Parterre*, 120.   [77] Lancaster, *Sunset*, 328.
[78] Golder, 'Hôtel de Bourgogne', Plan 1.   [79] Parfaict, *Mémoires* (1743), I, 134.

Figure 6.2 Marie-Justine Favart, *Annette et Lubin*, final scene: Lubin convinces the Seigneur to let him remain with Annette. The medallions depict a peasant couple identified with Marmontel's story and given a benefit performance in 1787. Source: BnF.

for *Le Roi et le fermier* (*The King and the Farmer*, discussed in Chapter 12) took the viewer into the forest where the king is lost and from which he is escorted to safety. In the set for Act III inside the farmhouse, skilful perspective painting offered the illusion of a three-dimensional space.[80]

Librettos before 1745 refer not to the word *ferme* (which denoted any piece of scenery at the back) but rather to *aîles*, wings.[81] Nine of the ten volumes in TF supply engravings, frontispieces to each opera or play which often show diagonal flats on each side, leading one's eye towards the backdrop by using perspective. Interpretation of these is needed, for they squeeze the visual impression into a small upright 'portrait' format. In reality, of course, their theatrical impact was in 'landscape' format, as we see from the oil-painted set design by François Boucher for the Saint-Laurent production of *L'École des amours grivois* (*Love on the Battlefield*) in 1744: Figure 6.3.[82] Boucher's harmonious image combines the effect of three elements: the painted backdrop with cannons being fired during the bombardment of Flanders; two diagonal wings showing realistic high frontages of village buildings that lead the eye inwards, using perspective; and a number of stage props in the middle – tables, chairs, a tray, a jug.

Favart used the term *aîles* in his detailed specification of this very décor in the 1744 libretto, from which we can extrapolate backwards when we interpret the TF images and their frequent depiction of wings which look squashed. The first specification of such wings dates back to *Arlequin traitant* (*Harlequin the Financier*, 1716): 'a country house seen in the wings'. This second volume of TF (1721) also showed wings in frontispieces for *Les Eaux de Merlin* (*Merlin's Waters*), a Paris shop, and *Arlequin défenseur d'Homère* (*Harlequin Takes Homer's Side*), a domestic library.

How does other evidence affect one's interpretation of TF engravings? These volumes appeared at various times after the premieres of the works portrayed. Nevertheless, their frontispiece images may imply that instead of being based on artists' impressions of the sets during production, they were based on drawings made by the set designer before production. This reasoning is based on two things: first, discrepant frontispieces which show plain interior sets when the relevant stage instructions demand highly decorated sets;[83] second, an extant frontispiece for a work never actually staged, though it was prepared: Carolet's *L'Amour désœuvré* (*Cupid*

---

[80] Gousset and Masson, 'Les décors historiques' showing sets used in 2012 at Versailles, originally painted by P.-L.-C. Cicéri in 1836 for the Trianon theatre but found to include eighteenth-century materials.
[81] Clarke, 'Aîle, coulisse et cantonade'.
[82] Legrand and Wild, *Regards*, 32. 'Grivois' later meant 'vulgar'.
[83] E.g. *Arlequin Traitant*, TF II, 132 (R/I/164) or *Le Temple de l'Ennui*, TF II, 259 (R/I/196); note also *Les Routes du monde*, TF VIII, 135 (R/II/321) whose left-hand gateway is labelled 'Richesse' instead of 'Fortune'.

Figure 6.3 François Boucher: set-design for Favart's *L'École des amours grivois* (*Love on the Battlefield*) in 1744. Photo © RMN-Grand Palais/Agence Bulloz.

Unemployed, 1734):[84] Venus and Cupid are seen reclining in front of a curving palace on Cythera, the sea in the background.

The unique involvement of Jean-Nicolas Servandoni at the Fairs suffers likewise. The famous stage designer created the décor for *La Pénélope moderne* (*The New Penelope*) in 1728. Lesage's libretto prescribes the intended location in Anjou: 'The stage represents an old château at the back and an avenue in the wings.'[85] In the frontispiece, this building is beautifully detailed. A press description is fuller:

Much was spoken of this décor. It was by Chevalier Servandoni [...] and represented an open space edged by a wood with a château in the distance; and to one side a torrent of water that fell by cascades on to the open ground. This was very ingeniously imagined and well constructed, notwithstanding the small size of the available space.[86]

No image of water appears in *TF*, and only three trees on each side represent the avenue or wood; the frontispiece looks formulaic, whereas

---

[84] *TF* IX/2, 491 (R/II/678). Carolet claimed that it was written by early August and 'could have been staged by the end of the same month' but for the oversupply of works in general.
[85] *TF* VII, 1 (R/II/152).
[86] *Mercure*, Sept. 1728, 2094; reprod. Parfaict, *Mémoires* (1743), II, 47–8.

the staging itself inspired admiration. So *TF* engravings must be expanded and adorned in our minds.[87]

Because the Hôtel de Bourgogne remained in use until 1783, popular opera's basic style of staging could be only modestly updated prior to that year. Perhaps changes in its lighting units might account for the brighter tonality of a coloured engraving that survives to show the setting for Grétry's *Silvain* (1770).[88] Structurally, its painted wings and perspective backdrop are no different to what was utilised half a century earlier. The routine quality of the image may have an only indirect connection with the original staging. Nonetheless there exists a blistering public attack on the quality of scenery at the Hôtel de Bourgogne made by Masson de Pezay when he worked with Grétry.[89] On the other hand, the same company reportedly spent 20,000 *livres* on sets and costumes for *La Fée Urgèle* (*Fairy Urgèle*, 1765).[90]

Many earlier operas needed just a single set and many were in one act.[91] But they might involve two sets each, even if programmes consisted of three separate works. As we saw, there could be an inner area concealed by a curtain (*La Statue merveilleuse*/*The Magic Statue*)[92] or an inner 'theatre within a theatre' as demanded by Piron.[93] Lesage's trilogy of 1714 (*La Foire de Guibray* (*The Fair at Guibray*), *Arlequin Mahomet* and *Le Tombeau de Nostradamus*) required seven different sets in all, while Fuzelier's contemporaneous *La Matrone d'Éphèse* (*The Widow of Ephesus*) required five sets for its two acts and a prologue. Lesage, Piron and d'Orneval's three-act *Les Trois commères* (*Three Married Women*) needed six sets. Lesage's final three-act opera, *Roger de Sicile* (1731), demanded five sets:

I/1 Palermo: a public square, the king's palace in the background and a town-house represented by one of the wings;
II/1 The royal gardens, later with 'a troupe of English dancers';
II/3 The queen's apartment;
III/1 A landscape in the background and a road depicted by the two wings;

---

[87] Parfaict, *ibid.*, II, 144, 156–7 mentions two other set designers, Le Maire and Charmoton. Le Maire created a spectacular Palace of the Sun at the Hôtel de Bourgogne: Beaucé, *Parodies*, 349–50.
[88] Legrand and Wild, *Regards*, 72. An etching of a different scene is at the Musée Carnavalet: www.parismuseescollections.paris.fr/fr/musee-carnavalet, G.11854.
[89] Masson de Pezay, 'Réflexions', *La Rosière de Salenci* (Paris: Delalain, 1774), vii–xxvii: see Charlton, *Grétry*, 125–6 and *idem*, 'Sight meets Sound', 46–7.
[90] By Favart and Duni: Grimm, *Corr. litt.*, Dec. 1765, ed. Tourneux, VI, 446.
[91] Rizzoni, *Pannard*, 451–75; Favart produced only four three-acters in thirty years of activity.
[92] Act I/6: *TF* IV, 21 (R/I/404).   [93] *L'Âne d'or d'Apulée*, II/3 in Piron, *Œuvres* (1758), III, 424.

III/2 A wood represented by the wings, with a statue of a white marble giant set on grassy steps at the back.

Settings in general represented extremely diverse geographical locations, appealing to the imagination with images of distance and difference across the world just as our entertainments now do. Backdrops served the appearance of local characters, members of imagined societies in – for example – Quebec, Cairo, Gujarat, Spain, Peking (Beijing), Astrakhan, Livorno, Dieppe, Belgrade and the Moroccan city of Salé.[94]

We can nevertheless see a system of visual conventions behind these fictions. Island settings were frequent, often with a temple. Paris itself was frequently portrayed, sometimes as an exterior, more often as a bourgeois interior. By 1730 many operas featured bourgeois characters without any caricatural content; a good number of these avoid any stage description. Favart often specifies merely 'a village' in the 1740s, as did the often-revived *Les Amours de Nanterre*, illustrated in Figure 7.2, p. 168. Classically referenced settings representing temples, Mount Parnassus, deserts, caverns or Hades were intended to frame an ironic and jovial comedy, alerting audiences to potential moral and critical judgements. Similarly, exotic or picturesque decors invited audiences to make ironic comparisons or connections with Europe. Strange or fantastic settings sometimes provided imaginative escape and intellectual pleasure: *Le Monde renversé* (*The World Upside Down*) demanded a very elaborate painted set with 'grotesques' and 'animaux extraordinaires' echoing the spirit of the Fairs themselves.

The large statue in *Roger de Sicile* reappeared in *Les Désesperés* (*Entertainers in Despair*) the next year, 'painted in gold, on laths [...] on a pedestal of white marble'.[95] Excellent TF engravings show, for example, the towers detaining love-crazed suitors in *La Princesse de Carizme* (Figure 6.4) or trees which sang, declaimed and moved using actors inside them, their green faces occasionally exposed through shutters (*La Forêt de Dodône* / *The Forest of Dodona*). Characters could enter or leave the stage via doors or windows at the back, or from below using a trap-door. A double-height scene in *Achmet et Almanzine* had three characters on a balcony upstage facing the sea below while a *divertissement* with fishermen took place on the shore itself. A large practicable rock and fire-breathing dragon adorned Fuzelier's *La Matrone d'Éphèse*. Piron's

---

[94] Respectively seen in *Les Mariages du Canada*, *Les Pèlerins de la Mecque*, *Le Jeune-Vieillard*, *La Robe de dissension*, *La Princesse de la Chine*, *Zémine et Almanzor*, *La Force de l'amour*, *Les Enragez*, *Sophie et Sigismond* and *Le Corsaire de Salé*.
[95] TF IX/1, 119 (R/II/425).

Figure 6.4 *La Princesse de Carizme*, Act I: the Prince of Persia and his confidant, Arlequin, discover love-crazed suitors imprisoned.

monstrous dragon in *L'Endriague* (see pp. 7–8) could swallow the teenage heroine Grazinde and later her rescuer Arlequin (Francisque) who jumped 'in one perilous leap' into its jaws, which 'opened nine or ten feet wide'.

Shifting the dragon around needed four men concealed inside, since its legs were twice the size of those of real elephants.[96]

Fair theatre was a 'theatre of marvels', especially before it lost some of its spontaneous fantasy and its *commedia* characters. In 1711, spectacle enlivened the mime shows: 'three fountains of fire erupt from the earth'.[97] In Pellegrin's theatre the Comédie-Italienne staged *Le Jeune-Vieillard* (*The Old Young Man*) set in Gujarat: 'The sky darkens, the winds whistle, thunder roars [...] the palace changes into a desert.'[98] Frightening effects of lightning hurled from an aerial machine are seen in the frontispiece of *Arlequin Mahomet*.[99] Other operas used smoke effects. The footlights could be lowered for a quick or a slow fade; Piron demanded that 'the darkness ends and a great light fills the cavern'.[100] 'Night' scenes formed part of popular opera across the whole century, and the illustration for Scene 8 of *Le Tombeau de Nostradamus* shows both the penumbra and a conventional lamp, lantern or torch.[101] Music and darkness had already merged in Act II/11 of *Les Deux Arlequins* (1691, rev. 1724): see pp. 53, 62. In the gardens of Basra, Scene 9 of *Arlequin Mahomet* (1714), Arlequin by lamplight showed the princess a portrait of the Prince of Persia. Eighteen years later *Sophie et Sigismond* opened with a nocturnal garden scene in Hungary as Sophie read a letter, holding a lamp.[102] Thirty-three years later still, Favart's *Isabelle et Gertrude* opened in a nocturnal garden as Dorlis waited to meet Isabelle.[103]

One scenic influence from Italy to Paris was the darkened *imbroglio*, when candles are snuffed out, amusing mistakes are made and physical acting is needed: Fuzelier's version of *La Matrone d'Éphèse* (1714) opened with a prologue like this for Arlequin and Mezzetin.[104] In mid-century an *imbroglio* in the Bouffons' *Bertoldo in corte* (*Bertoldo at Court*) was made into a quartet in dialogue in *Ninette à la cour*: see Table 11.1, p. 272. Antoine Riccoboni planned a different night-time scene in *Le Prétendu* (*The Intended Husband*), its score composed by Pierre Gaviniès.[105] The room is lit by two candles on a table. Waiting at midnight in Act III, Marine sings 'On craint un engagement' which she calls 'our new Romance', whose

---

[96] Lurcel, ed., *Théâtre de la Foire*, 449, 461–2, 469.
[97] *Les Avantures comiques d'Arlequin*, II, ed. in Martinuzzi,'Pièces par écriteaux', 229. In *Télémaque* (1714) Lesage specified the overture and storm music from Marais' *Alcione* (1706).
[98] FSL, 1722: Act I/8: *TF* V, 164 (R/I/570).   [99] FSL, 1714: *TF* I, 133 (R/I/40),
[100] FSL, 1725: Piron, *Le Fâcheux veuvage*, Sc. 7.   [101] FSL, 1714: *TF* I, 167 (R/I/48).
[102] FSL, 1732: *TF* IX/1, 155 (R/II/434).
[103] Aug. 1765: *Isabelle et Gertrude* (Paris: Veuve Duchesne, 1765), [5] with lengthy stage direction.
[104] Rubellin (ed.), *Théâtre de la Foire*, 97–100.
[105] See Table 8.7: Pierre Gaviniès, *Le Prétendu, Intermède en trois actes* (Paris: L'Auteur, etc., n.d.).

words – as though fortuitously – reflect her actual situation. Then she snuffs out the lights and falls asleep, music tailing away; low lighting and a new popular style functioned as one. In the 1760s alone, fifteen other popular operas would use structured lighting effects.[106] Marine's Romance soon entered wider circulation in Justine Favart's *Annette et Lubin*, to the words 'Lubin, pour me prévenir'.[107]

*

Vaudevilles might be hard for us to imagine as a theatre medium, but we have seen that the theatres themselves and even their audiences are relatively easy to visualise. Popular opera during the Fairs was not given with meagre facilities: one would have found a varied cluster of theatres making themselves attractive, musically and visually. Entrepreneurs refurbished or rebuilt structures; orchestra sizes stabilised; similar numbers of players were heard at the Fairs as were heard at the Comédie-Italienne.[108] Opéra-comique was associated with investment as well as topicality. The Hôtel de Bourgogne's inferior conditions, scenically as well as front-of-house, must have thrust Monnet's new summer theatre into extra relief in 1752, the start of the final decade of rivalry: see Chapters 8 and 10.

The green rooms at Fair theatres and the Comédie-Italienne were obviously not polite places, and the attack by Mme Du Boccage certainly used audience morality as a weapon; but little seems to suggest that, inside the auditorium, actors were not attended to. When a new generation of visitors like Laurence Sterne left us their impressions, they chose to stress order and civility, whether upstairs where diplomats might be found or in the *parterre*. Sound-levels of singing, speaking and playing were modest, as will be seen again on pp. 245–6. Fair theatre soloists would be judged, by comparison, to be less audible than their new Comédie-Italienne colleagues.

---

[106] Heartz, 'Beginnings of the Operatic Romance', 149–78; Charlton, 'Sight meets Sound', 55–6, 69ff.
[107] Favart and Blaise, *Annette et Lubin*, ed. Münzmay, 56.
[108] Charlton, 'Orchestra and Chorus'.

7 | Comic and Serious Themes

No area of early popular opera is so regularly misconstrued as that of subject matter. The range of stories told on stage was far greater than is usually imagined.[1] In order to suggest this range as well as the changing temper of the critiques contained in popular operas, the method will be to focus on two key areas, one defined by a common source (the poet Jean de La Fontaine, 1621–95) and the other by a common theme (marriage). The chapter begins and ends with topics already written about by others, but which seem to invite further work: the practice of recycling and the nature of the 'abduction' theme.

Introduction

Moral issues were never far from popular opera. Rereading a 1730 prologue, marquis d'Argenson noted that 'the Opéra Comique is still consumed by morality'.[2] There were even allegorical morality tales, reminiscent (to us) of John Bunyan's *The Pilgrim's Progress*: *Ways Through the World* by Lesage, Fuzelier and d'Orneval and *The Pit of Scruples* by Charles-François Pannard.[3] Titles like *The World Upside Down* (*Le Monde renversé*: discussed later) or *Hope* (*L'Espérance*) advertised a likely social and moral framework. For subject matter and approach, the year 1715 – when solo singing had returned – proved a turning point. Musical aspects were part of this, as Chapter 9 will show: Lesage commissioned a duet by Elisabeth Jacquet de La Guerre for *La Ceinture de Vénus* (*Venus's Girdle*) in the winter season.[4] Months later, theatre directors met audiences' evident desire for higher standards of comedy: Saurin at the Bel-Air theatre and Dominique Biancolelli at Saint-Edme's company both issued policy statements. Biancolelli even used the phrase 'this glorious

---

[1] The true range is evident in Müller, '"Il faut s'aimer"', and Pré, 'Le Livret d'opéra-comique'.
[2] D'Argenson, *Notices* (1725–57), 571, reviewing *L'Indifférence* by Lesage, Fuzelier and d'Orneval.
[3] *Les Routes du monde* (1730), *TF* VIII, 135 (R/II/321); *Le Fossé du scrupule* (1738), Pannard, *Théâtre*, III, 69: see p. 187.
[4] 'The Reconciliation of Nicole and Pierrot', *TF* I, 311–13 (R/I/84).

reform': he would respect 'difficult-to-please audiences' dismayed by vulgar entertainments. Saurin's text was printed in the *Mercure*: 'You want new ideas, original scenes' appealing to the mind, though it would be hard, he warned, to include *commedia* characters without 'grimaces' or 'crude acting'.[5] One of the new ideas was *Arlequin défenseur d'Homère* (*Harlequin Takes Homer's Side*) which alluded to the current climax in the quarrel over the existence of Homer, led by Anne Dacier and Houdar de La Motte.[6] Fuzelier set this *vaudeville* comedy in 'a fine house' near Paris.

Startling change arrived the following winter, after Louis XIV's death. D'Orneval's *Arlequin traitant* (*Harlequin the Financier*) broached themes of contemporary politics and financial corruption. As its rubric in *TF* would explain, it celebrated the arraignment of tax collectors and financiers (*traitants*) that the new Regent had sanctioned.[7] A modern summary gives the essentials: 'Arlequin, a *traitant* of low birth, obviously a crook, has willingly signed a pact with Belphégor [a devil] with the aim of getting rich. [...] He exhibits a revolting bad faith, and humiliation meted out to his employees emphasises the powerless status of the humblest classes.'[8] It contains the most socially critical lines anywhere in *vaudeville* opéra-comique. When another money man admits swindling the rich, the financier Arlequin boasts:

ARLEQUIN [spoken:] Voler des gens riches!   Swindled the rich!
[sung:] *Air*: 'Tu croyois, en aimant Colette'

Oh! Voilà de belles prouesses!	Amazing achievement!
N'ai-je pas, moi, mieux mérité?	Haven't I been cleverer?
J'ai puisé toutes mes richesses	Every penny that I make
Dans le sein de la pauvreté. (I/8)	Is plucked from the poorest.

Then Belphégor makes a violent entrance, double-crosses Arlequin and takes him to the Underworld, the setting of Act II. Arlequin, however, escapes: Pluto knows that France after the former régime 'breathes again', so that Arlequin will be adequately punished there. Recovering his riches in Act III, the financier is rejected by Isabelle and finally arrested after hiding in a barn: straw is seen on his clothes. By this detail the audience knew that

---

[5] Parfaict, *Mémoires* (1743), I, 170–5; *Mercure*, 1715, July, 281.
[6] FSL, 1715: *TF* II, 1 (R/I/131); background in DeJean, *Ancients against Moderns*, 95–108; Lancaster, *Sunset*, 330–1.
[7] *TF* II, 132 (R/I/164); Parfaict, *ibid.*, I, 185–6. The Regent had initiated enquiries quickly, in September 1715.
[8] Martin, *Théâtre de la Foire*, 225–6.

one particular financier was being laughed at.⁹ *Arlequin traitant* follows in the radical tradition of *Arlequin Grapignan*, seen earlier in Chapter 3.

Any theatre reform emerges from latent materials but also from a philosophical base. Fuzelier, d'Orneval and Lesage gave opéra-comique its 'founding myths', a set of identities that would continue to flourish. Its responses to society drew on theatrical precedent, but Lesage also developed its links to literary fiction, a generic connection that it never abandoned.¹⁰ His public probably expected this, since his first novel was very well known: *Le Diable boiteux* (*The Devil on Two Sticks*) set in Madrid.¹¹ The devil Asmodeus surveys the world, spying with his student friend Don Cleofas into house after house discovering greed, vanity, violence, cynicism and hypocrisy. Asmodeus preaches, 'Really, I admire the folly of mankind, whose own faults seem trifles to them, while they look at those of others through a microscope'; 'Were I not a devil I would be an inquisitor'; 'I have a much greater pleasure in troubling consciences than in setting them at rest.'¹²

French society is often implicated: 'adventures of this kind [...] happen every day in France to abbés, to gentlemen of the long robe, and rich farmers of the revenue'.¹³ Like popular operas on the 'revue' principle, *Le Diable boiteux* moves from one story to another, held together by the narrator.¹⁴ It gave the public a social mirror very different from what Montesquieu's *Persian Letters* offered.¹⁵ Popular opera did, however, ask a question defined by Montesquieu, one which the present chapter also addresses: 'What is at stake for political power in the relation between the sexes?'¹⁶

Besides La Fontaine, popular opera drew on a burgeoning subgenre called *poissard*, which has been called 'a democratic art which constitutes a parallel to eighteenth-century neo-classic achievement.'¹⁷ The word is derived from *poix* (pitch: thus dirt, thievery, corruption), and *poissard* language is street dialect.¹⁸ Its language and characters can be traced back to the Gherardi period, especially Act III/2 of *Les Bains de la Porte Saint-Bernard* (*Swimming at Porte-Saint-Bernard*, the boatmen's scene) and subsequently Pannard's *Le Temple du Sommeil* (*The Temple of Sleep*,

---

⁹ *TF* II, 223, footnote (R/I/187). ¹⁰ Charlton, *French Opera*, II: 'Continuing Polarities'.
¹¹ Lesage, *Le Diable boiteux* (1707/1726). ¹² *Ibid.*, trans. by W. Strange, 26, 90, 27.
¹³ *Ibid.*, 90. Nobles 'of the robe' held official positions of state.
¹⁴ Runte, 'Parallels', 296; 'revue' or 'tiroir' form aggregates scenes without plot development.
¹⁵ Montesquieu, *Lettres persanes* (1721). ¹⁶ Grosrichard, *The Sultan's Court*, 30.
¹⁷ Moore, *The 'genre poissard'*, 126.
¹⁸ Not the same as the generalised or regional peasant dialect found in village comedies, and those of Favart: Moore, *ibid.*, 13–19.

1731), where Alizon complains about her drunken husband.[19] Moore considered that *poissard* figures gradually took the place of earlier *commedia* roles 'and with far greater realism', appearing in pieces before and after 1752: 'Madame Engueule, the newly rich *Poissarde* [...]; the fishwife's daughter, always in high need of a speedy marriage'; press gangs (*racoleurs*); the alcoholic shoemaker and his unfortunate wife; and Janot the simpleton.[20]

Recycling

Thematic recycling was (is) basic to popular as well as serious theatre; then, as now, recycling was a topic of critical discourse.[21] Molière's effect on opéra-comique was inevitable, for writers and critics in succeeding periods remembered his ideas, scenes and characters. Almost as a matter of course, the historian Barberet asserted in 1887 that La Guerre's 'Reconciliation' duet (see note 4) came from Act IV/3 of Molière's *Le Dépit amoureux* (*The Amorous Quarrel*) even though the characters and situation seem unrelated.[22] In 1912 Max Achenwall investigated the connection further.[23] He noted the influence of Molière through generalised comic themes and through Sedaine's use of specific features from *Le Sicilien* (*The Sicilian*) and *L'École des femmes* (*The School for Wives*) in writing *On ne s'avise jamais de tout* (*Impossible to Think of Everything*). Sedaine's obsessive doctor, Monsieur Tue, is clearly a version of Arnolphe in *L'École des femmes*: both confine young females, preparing them for marriage, and both are outwitted by the young son of a friend.[24]

At the same time, it could be said, Sedaine was recycling La Fontaine's *On ne s'avise jamais de tout*. All four main characters and one central incident stem from this Tale, with the cardinal differences that Monsieur Tue was originally a husband, unnamed, and Dorval was just one of his wife's lovers.

---

[19] Ibid., 179–80.   [20] Ibid., 5, 361.
[21] Thus, D'Origny noted thematic links between *La Vengeance comique* (CI, 1718), *Le Double tour* (FSG, 1735) and *Le Cadi dupé* (FSG, 1761): *Annales* (1788), I, 49–50.
[22] Barberet, *Lesage*, 43.
[23] Achenwall compared *Le Cocu imaginaire* with d'Hèle and Grétry's *Les Fausses apparences ou L'amant jaloux*, then discussed education, Don Juan, miserliness and the grotesque: *Studien*, Chap. 3.
[24] On *L'École des femmes*: DeJean, *Reinvention of Obscenity*, 84–121.

One day, as she [the wife] was coming back from church
Someone threw a bucket of rubbish over her.
There were apologies. The wretched woman,
Covered in filth, was invited to go in [...].
The refuse had been aimed deliberately
In order to give a plausible excuse
For sending the old woman [the wife's chaperone] back to the house.[25]

Sedaine adopted Molière's jokes featuring an instruction book: Arnolphe in Act III made Agnès read ten paragraphs from *Maxims for Marriages, or, Duties of the Married Woman*. In Scene 5 of *On ne s'avise* Monsieur Tue orders Margarita, the newly hired duenna to Lise, to read from *Compendium Cythereum*, likewise going through its teaching on 'how to supervise a girl', as it says, especially to prevent her access to reading and writing materials. Tue remembers that Maxim 12 has been set to music (i.e. as a supposed *vaudeville*) and forthwith sings its nonsensical lines in Monsigny's song 'Un chanteur n'est pas un Caton'.

Humorously pointing to his other source, Sedaine made Margarita into a Sicilian, although the action is set in Paris; she introduces herself with a comic song in which 'buse' (fool) is made to rhyme with 'Raguse' (Ragusa in Sicily) and 'Syracuse'. (This role was created by Mlle Deschamps, pictured in Figure 7.3; also see p. 286, note 91.) Scene 8 of *On ne s'avise* exactly reproduces the situation in Scene 8 of *Le Sicilien*, described earlier on p. 37: a fake street-singer contrives to pass a message to the young woman being closely guarded. Like Molière's Hali, Dorval uses jargon language as a distraction:

HALI		DORVAL
Chiribirida ouch alla!	[sung to Lise:]	Aladdin, fils de Noraddin,
Star bon Turca,		Un jour entra dans son jardin.
Non aver danara: [etc.]	[to Margarita:]	Harsëinam robek milon semur.
Parlara, parlara:	[to Lise:]	En revenant passez le long du mur,
Ti voler comprara?	[to Margarita:]	Harsëinam robek milon semur.

Writing at the very end of the stage-life of crabby tutors and guardians, Sedaine realised that he could parallel in modern musical terms the comic power of Arnolphe's tenacious reluctance to admit defeat. When Tue is faced by the combined challenge of family protest and civil law in the shape

---

[25] From 'Impossible to Think of Everything', *Some Tales of La Fontaine*, 95; *Contes et nouvelles*, 147.

of Le Commissaire, Monsigny's lengthy, fast and emphatic quintet drives home the old doctor's stubbornness. Five parallel columns of text were printed across the libretto page to clarify the words of Dorval, Lise, Tue, Margarita and the Commissaire.[26] Sedaine and Monsigny translated Tue's denials, a key element of Molière's psychology, into modern operatic terms.[27]

The next example also involves a double recycling, but not Molière. Raymond Poisson's play *Les Foux divertissans* (*The Amusing Madmen*, 1680) which we described on pp. 42–5 was shortened in 1691 by the playwright Dancourt and became a success entitled *Le Bon soldat* (*The Good Soldier*). This subsequently became an opéra-comique by Anseaume and Philidor, *Le Soldat magicien* (*The Soldier-Magician*) in 1760.[28] The final scenes of Poisson's play had shown Grognard's unexpected return from visiting his brother. A billetted soldier comes downstairs and pretends to have power over the supposed devil who produced the lovers' feast; when he summons the devil (in fact Léandre) out of his hiding-place, Grognard turns his back in fear and the lovers escape.

Dancourt reworked these scenes into a one-act farce helped by new characters: a valet, a caterer and a barber. In his other comedies, 'plot and characters are subordinated to singing, dancing and spectacle',[29] and the soldier in *Le Bon soldat* is required to sing during the supper scene. Anseaume retained this plot but converted Grognard into the quarrelsome *bourgeois* M. Argant and Angélique into the frustrated Mme Argant. Léandre became M. Blondineau, a lawyer specialising in divorce cases who wants to marry Mme Argant and orders the supper to be delivered. Anseaume's caterer enters unexpectedly, wanting payment for the food. A new character is Crispin, valet to M. Argant, who pays off the caterer with cash he has received in advance for spying on Mme Argant. Following a trend revitalised in the 1740s (see Chapter 10) Crispin's part was cross-dressed, Dorothée Luzy being the actor – she was, it seems, only thirteen or fourteen at the time.[30]

Philidor wrote a quartet for one scene that audiences would potentially be expecting (that is, for the meal being consumed) but also a quintet for the surprise appearance of the caterer. Anseaume was also inspired to make

---

[26] Shown in Cook, *Duet and Ensemble*, 123.
[27] On comœdic psychology: Zupančič, *Odd One In*, 49.
[28] Favart, *Mémoires*, I, 82–4. Table 8.8 documents its success and that of *On ne s'avise*.
[29] Lancaster, *Sunset*, 150. [30] Campardon, *Spectacles*, II, 81.

Scene 1 into an argumentative duet for the Argant couple playing *tric-trac*, a type of backgammon, where Philidor could write imitative music for the throwing of the dice. In his letter to Count Durazzo, Favart vented some dissatisfaction with Anseaume: it was not the existence of the quintet itself which displeased, but the illogic of the caterer appearing unannounced after midnight. Even in a comic work, Favart said,

> the means employed for working up an *imbroglio* must be natural ones, notwithstanding the surprise that they are to cause, and the audience must believe that the stage action occurs out of necessity, even something unforeseen. [...] Philidor was reproached for having repeated himself a little; be that as it may, this piece is giving pleasure: people demand less of the Opéra Comique than they do of other theatres.[31]

Operas from La Fontaine

Lesage's social attitudes inherited the example of La Fontaine, whose work was crucial to popular opera over six decades. Stage adaptations of La Fontaine were written by every main author, making for a strong conceptual thread. The Tales formed the basis of fifty-four popular operas and many plays.[32] 'Lesage read La Fontaine's *contes* [Tales] as well as his Fables. We note that entire [operas] like *La Matrone d'Ephèse* (*The Widow of Ephesus*) and *Les Trois commères* (*Three Married Women*) rely on La Fontaine for inspiration. [...] Like La Fontaine, he saw man engaged in a power struggle in which the strongest would rule.'[33] This was a unique popular heritage; the Fables and Tales gave opéra-comique a literary and moral identity from the Grand Siècle, parallel to the classical identities of *tragédie en musique*.

The Tales retold venerable stories about sex and deception. The Fables were for both young and old, yet the use of birds, animals and insects permitted sociopolitical references far too virulent for the stage. A lion king invites deputies of subaltern powers to his 'Louvre', a lair which stinks like a charnel-house: any comment at all is liable to be punished.[34] Plague strikes the land, so the lion calls a council to discover whose sin might be to blame. Meat eaters with claws are exculpated; the ass, having nibbled a little churchyard grass, is executed.[35] The 'law of nature', said La Fontaine

---

[31] As for n. 28.   [32] Brenner, 'Dramatizations'.   [33] Runte, 'Parallels', 294, 297.
[34] *Selected Fables*, 7/6, 'At the Court of the Lion'.
[35] Ibid., 7/1, 'The Animals Sick of the Plague'.

elsewhere, means people helping each other.[36] His philosophy allowed the reader to infer a 'highly ironic and critical' attitude to the wars of Louis XIV.[37]

Earlier popular operas favoured the Tales, duly censored; later ones, derived from Fables, staged a rural world where 'Life is particularly hard on the small and weak [...] who in the long run are likely to be the victims'.[38] A Woodcutter struggles in one Fable against hunger, work, soldiers, taxes, debts and Death.[39] He also features in 'The Woodman and Mercury', a Fable illustrated in Figure 7.1 from an English translation of 1805.[40] The same emblematic figure inspired Philidor's opera *Le Bûcheron* (*The Woodcutter*), adapted from Charles Perrault's story, *The Ridiculous Wishes*.[41] One enthusiast found its effect strong enough to be compared to the most famous of novelists:

What Richardson was in his books, I want a composer to be in the theatre. When a woodcutter drags himself on stage exhausted, confides in me his troubles, describes his work, the details of his domestic griefs, and naively admits to me (taking a bottle from his bag) that he finds consolation in wine, I repay his confidence with genuine interest.[42]

*

The early years produced wide contrasts in adaptation. At one extreme was Fuzelier's *La Matrone d'Éphèse* (1714), from La Fontaine's eponymous Tale derived from Petronius' *Satyricon*.[43] A widow sits grieving in her husband's tomb; a soldier gradually manages to cure her depression; the soldier's life is saved because the husband's remains are passed off as those of a criminal the soldier was meant to be guarding. After an unrelated first act, Fuzelier exploits gallows humour and physical jokes. Arlequin appears both as the soldier and sometimes as himself; La Fontaine serves the farce as much as the farce serves La Fontaine.

At an opposite extreme stands *Les Animaux raisonnables* (*The Animals Endowed with Reason*, 1718) by Fuzelier and Marc-Antoine Le Grand. It

---

[36] Ibid., 8/17, 'The Donkey and the Dog'.
[37] Ibid., 7/17, 'An Animal in the Moon'; Grisé, 'The Optics of Relativism', 131.
[38] Ibid., 'Introduction', xxvii.
[39] Ibid., 1/16, 'Death and the Woodcutter': 'Rather to suffer than to die'.
[40] Fable 5/1 in *La Fontaine's Fables. Now first translated from the French* by Robert Thomson (Paris: All the Booksellers [Chenu; Brochot], n.d.), I, frontispiece.
[41] Perrault, 'Les Souhaits ridicules', *Histoires ou contes du temps passé* (1697); J. F. Guichard & N. Castet, *Le Bûcheron, comédie mêlée d'ariettes* (Paris: Herissant, 1763).
[42] Garcin, *Traité* (1772), 120. Thomas discusses Garcin in *Aesthetics*, 233–8.
[43] Rubellin, ed.: *Théâtre de la Foire*, 89.

164 Comic and Serious Themes

Figure 7.1 Illustration of La Fontaine's Fable, 'The Woodman and Mercury' ('Le Bûcheron et Mercure'), Book 5 no.1.

derived from *Ulysses' Companions*, the Fable in which Ulysses' entire crew prefers to remain in the animal state caused by Circe's magic: 'Their chief delights were liberty, the wild, to which their lusts all led.'[44] The libretto explores both sides of the dialectic set up by the poet: how can humans reconcile society with individual instinct and appetite? Different aspects of La Fontaine were expanded so that specific professions could be satirised by

[44] *Selected Fables* 12/1, 301; *TF* III, 1 (R/I/261).

reference to the Wolf (formerly a *procureur*, or legal officer) and the Pig (formerly a *financier*). Ulysses questions two female characters not found in La Fontaine. The Hen is happy to remain separated from her unfaithful human partner and to escape the dangers of childbirth; the Linnet, formerly a young girl, is happy to avoid the rigours imposed by her moralising governess.

Ulysses' Companions, dedicated to the king's grandson, resolves in favour of law and order; the opera declares that a 'reasonable animal' is anyone who gives in to social pleasures and avoids conflict and prudery. But the opera's title suggests also that Fuzelier and Le Grand pointed to La Fontaine's public quarrel with Descartes, whose theory it was that animals are merely machines.[45]

Les Trois commères, ambitiously produced when the new king was welcomed in Paris, echoes the structure of *opéra-ballet*: three separate but linked stories, each with a different cast, framed by a prologue and epilogue.[46] La Fontaine's Tale consists of a wager between three wives as to which of them will devise the most extravagant way to trick her husband. These all involved sexual adventures, for which Lesage's team substituted three new tales: each husband is tricked and punished for fecklessness and drinking. Elaborate disorientations are the means. During Act I a Paris street façade is changed to appear like a different one, then returned to its first form; in Act II the husband wakes up to find himself apparently in Hades. In Act III the third husband (Arlequin) wakes from a drunken sleep to find himself dressed as a soldier apparently in Germany amid the rumpus of field exercises, nearly suffering a summary execution ordered by the Grand Provost on horseback. Within the hilarity and carnivalesque dialogue are references to the slippery problem of appearance and reality; Piron's other work regularly uses this theme, as we see later.[47]

When opéra-comique taste changed, leaving *commedia* jests behind, La Fontaine adaptations took on new aspects. In 1734 *Le Fleuve Scamandre* (*The River Scamander*) by Laffichard and Pannard made a bourgeois comedy from the poet's classical setting near Athens.[48] In the Tale, bathing in the river Scamander, the heroine is seduced into believing that a talkative

---

[45] Ganim, 'Scientific Verses', 107–10.
[46] See Chap. 1: FSG, 1723; by Lesage, d'Orneval and Piron: TF IX, 422 (R/II/500). See 'Three Ladies Make a Wager' in *Some Tales of La Fontaine*, 76.
[47] Connon, *Identity and Transformation*, 131. Piron's own *Colombine-Nitétis* alludes to the collaboration and his authorship of Act II.
[48] La Fontaine, *Contes et nouvelles*, 421. The source was Æschines, c. 390–314 BC. Laffichard, Pannard, *Le Fleuve Scamandre, opéra comique* (Paris: Clousier, 1746).

youth is a river god who has chosen her as his bride. He promptly forgets about her, but when she sees him trying to marry someone else, her friends chase him out of town. In the opera, the student Pamphile has a valet who overhears Calhirée (the central role) narrate her dream of marrying a god. After civilised adventures Pamphile turns out to be the marriage partner whom both sets of parents had intended all along. The authors humoured polite sensibility through textual references to La Fontaine while, on another level, its classical details evoked courtly opera: divinities, dreams, seductions of mortals, dancers, chorus, two *divertissements*.

Charles-Simon Favart's engagement with La Fontaine in 1740–41 resulted in a brilliant trilogy that turned its back on bourgeois comedy. The first two to be seen were *La Servante justifiée* (*The Justified Servant*) in 1740 and *La Chercheuse d'esprit* (*The Girl Who Sought Wit*) in 1741. The third, *Les Nymphes de Diane*, was planned for the summer of 1741 but was banned before being seen. After its premiere in Brussels (1 June 1747) it was given at the Saint-Laurent Fair of 1753.[49] Of La Fontaine's Tale *La Servante justifiée* nothing is left except the 'justified servant' herself; yet its sexual content persisted on the edge of consciousness because people remembered the original *Servante justifiée*.[50] The source of *La Chercheuse d'esprit*, La Fontaine's *Comment l'esprit vient aux filles*, was likewise expurgated,[51] so that the teenage Nicette (as Chapter 5 explained) finds independence through her attraction to Alain; she thwarts her mother's aim to marry her to Monsieur Subtil, the widowed lawyer.

These two Favart works are embedded in rural communities and should be classed as popular operas about people who work, or else as 'soft pastorals' (Geoffrey Chew's term).[52] Certainly Favart created sympathy for older female characters. In many ways he drew on an opéra-comique not derived from La Fontaine that was one of the longest-serving titles of the half-century: *Les Amours de Nanterre* (*The Loves of Nanterre*), 1718, by Lesage, d'Orneval and – probably – Jacques Autreau.[53] Developed through

---

[49] Favart, *Les Nymphes de Diane* (n.p., 1748). Paris premiere: *Mercure*, 1753, Nov., 174. Revised without spoken dialogue on 22 September 1755 (Paris: Duchesne, 1755).

[50] A wealthy husband seduces his servant on the lawn: *Some Tales of La Fontaine*, 72; D'Argenson, *Notices* (1725–57), II, 605.

[51] Lise was quickly seduced by Father Bonaventure: see 'How Girls Acquire Intelligence' in *Some Tales of La Fontaine*, 128.

[52] Geoffrey Chew, 'Pastoral' in *NGO*, III, 910–13 [912], describing *Le Devin du village* and its epigones. Favart's adaptations might echo the social dynamics of town *versus* village: Tocqueville, *Ancien Régime*, 99.

[53] Autreau is credited in Parfaict, *Mémoires* (1743), I, 213. Its success in London (1734): Levenson, 'Traveling Tunes', 68. See Ray, *Coquettes*, 52–4.

a substantial single act, the comedy concerns villagers with jobs and economic relations. Arlequin appeared only near the end, as a soldier: the plot involves a recruiting officer as the main *amoureux*, Valère. Valère's hoped-for marriage to Colette is opposed by her mother, Mme Thomas, the widow of a rich farmer. In Figure 7.2 we see her farm manager Lucas in the course of being deceived by Colette and her cousin into thinking that Colette loves him.

The type or figure of Mme Thomas was used by Favart in both aforementioned adaptations: in *La Servante justifiée* Mme Bertrand runs a mill and wants to marry her assistant, Colin; in *La Chercheuse d'esprit* Mme Madré is a well-off farmer and wants to marry Alain. All three might relate to the rich *poissarde* as a type, but they also reflect the fact that many widows ran businesses like linen weaving, brewing, baking, barrel-making or shopkeeping.[54] In the dynamics of comedy such figures replace the Doctor or tutor from Italian comedy whose plans for a love match must be overcome. Mme Thomas's role was not burlesqued by a cross-dressed actor, as might have been expected.[55]

Les Nymphes de Diane, situated at an opposite thematic extreme, invites our particular attention. It derives from La Fontaine's Tale 'Les Lunettes' ('The Spectacles'): a beardless youth joins a convent as a nun, fathers a child, and is discovered when all are required to undergo physical inspection. Memories of this obscene episode presumably caused the opera's original prohibition, since Favart retained only two details from La Fontaine: the offending youth Cliton, apprehended and chained to a tree, tricks a stranger into taking his place; and spectacles are worn by the opera's matronly Gangan, a cross-dressed role.[56] Favart's method was based on decontextualisation: everything occurs in the realms of classical pastoral and all the characters' names seem classical. Few other opéras-comiques had relinquished outward reference to modern society. Moreover, *Les Nymphes* confused expectation by employing rhymed verse for its spoken dialogue; it had the ambience of pastoral opera, smoothing the differences between speech and song.[57]

---

[54] Garrioch, *Making of Revolutionary Paris*, 70–1.
[55] Mlle Aigremont ('La Camuson') took the part: Parfaict, *ibid.*, I, 209. In *La Servante justifiée* the role of Commère Cliquet, the chatty neighbour, was cross-dressed. We lack casting information for Mme Bertrand and Mme Madré.
[56] La Fontaine's Mother Superior wears spectacles for the inspection. They are referred to in Sc. 4 of the opera and portrayed on the right of the frontispiece to the 1748 ed.
[57] Ledbury, *Sedaine, Greuze*, 66–9. See below, pp. 233–4, for a musical description.

Figure 7.2 *Les Amours de Nanterre* (*The Loves of Nanterre*), Sc. 12: Colette and Mathurine allow themselves to be overheard by Lucas.

But all this classicism masks a second inspiration, namely La Fontaine's attitude to convent life. He wrote six Tales about nuns, a recent study of which has proposed regarding them as a cycle, developing his 'criticism (and satire) of confining young women to convents against their will'.[58] In effect Favart's opera is a comic precursor of Diderot's novel *La Religieuse* (*The Nun*), the 'anti-cloistral satire that argues for human rights and self-determination'.[59] Favart shows the connection through a motif serving as the mainspring of his plot, set in Diana's forest: initiation. The High Priestess of Diana, Séverine, presides over a ceremony in which her acolytes must reject an aspiring lover, face to face. The present lover is Agénor, who has caught sight of Thémire (the protagonist) earlier. Deeply troubled, Thémire fails to complete her ceremonial speech. Her subsequent feelings for Agénor are validated by Cupid himself (in Brussels, a child actor), who leads an attack on Diana's followers and defeats them offstage, finding lovers for them all. And as Corinne Pré noticed, Favart's revised 1755 text pointed to the real world when Agénor assured Thémire, 'The cry of nature tells you that you must love'.[60]

All La Fontaine's Tales of nuns deal in sexuality, but as a correlative of the fact that the education and life prospects of better-off women in France were determined by the convent system. This was the route to education for bourgeois and noble women, and the convents performed what John McManners called a 'marriage-agency role': 'girls stayed until a husband was found for them'.[61] Nevertheless there was pressure to change the fact that 'the age at which binding religious vows could be taken was regulated by the state at sixteen', something the king did not repeal until 1768.[62] The protagonist of Diderot's *The Nun* is devastated when, at sixteen, she is pressured into taking the veil; Thémire, who is fifteen, escapes from her vows just in time.

*

After the closure of the Opéra Comique from summer 1745 to February 1752, explained in the following chapter, La Fontaine inspired new forms of comedy. Jean Monnet, the new director, encouraged two writers of genius capable of matching Favart: Jean-Joseph Vadé (1719–57) and Michel-Jean Sedaine (1719–97). Table 8.7 provides an overview of this period.

---

[58] Birberick, 'From World to Text', 186.
[59] Goulbourne, 'Introduction' to Diderot, *The Nun*, xvii. It remained semi-private until 1796.
[60] *Les Nymphes de Diane* (Paris: Duchesne, 1755), 49; Pré, 'Livret d'opéra-comique', 724; cf. 'natural cry' in Thomas, *Music and the Origins of Language*, 65–80.
[61] McManners, *Church and Society*, I, 536. [62] Tancock, 'Introduction', 11.

Les Troqueurs (*The Swappers*) was introduced at the end of Chapter 4. Vadé brilliantly reworked La Fontaine's story of two rural couples who persuade a friendly lawyer to legalise their exchange of spouses: a successful experiment. Whereas La Fontaine had, unusually, introduced some social background (civil and religious authorities are left wondering how to unpick the contract), Vadé excluded it all, being influenced by the new wave of Italian *intermezzi*. Lubin and Lucas are not yet married and they are punished for their stupidity, chiefly through the strategies of the fiery Margot acting as judge, jury and probation officer combined. La Fontaine's morality was cleverly reversed, if not critiqued.

In his masterly adaptation *en vaudevilles*, *Nicaise* (1756), Vadé farcically expanded on La Fontaine's cast of two: the dull-witted Nicaise and a fiancée who gives up on him when he fails to act at a crucial moment. Vadé's Nicaise acquired a rival, and Angélique received an aunt and an uncle who are risible, each wanting different husbands for her. The uncle urges Nicaise to abduct Angélique, and when the dullard delays, his rival neatly steps in to replace him.

The farcical tendency continued in *Le Maître en droit* (*The Master at Law*) in 1760, adapted by a new writer, Lemonnier, for the composer Monsigny.[63] It was an immense success, mixing *vaudevilles* (twenty-three in number) with new music (solos and ensembles, nineteen in all). Both Tale and opera are set in Rome, where a French student learns from his pupil-master how to locate female companions. Only in the Tale does the master discover that his own wife is meeting the pupil. Hoping to meet the female friend himself, the master is guided through dark passages unexpectedly leading to the Faculty of Law where he is publicly unmasked. Lemonnier stages this by a change of scene to a lecture-room, complete with students in chorus. They humiliate their teacher, who has been unwittingly disguised in women's clothes by the elderly matchmaker, Jacqueline.

Where did its success lie, given that the Doctor is just another lustful greybeard, the text is ungrateful to read, the plot is poorly managed, the characters seem unexceptional and one *ariette* is excused with almost no motivation? Surely in Monsigny's score, the love of farce, of singing and of surprise – a darkened stage allows the Doctor to be dolled up. Lively solos and ensembles together carried the whole weight of character interest, so *Le Maître en droit* held strong against the best that was on offer (Tables 8.7 and 8.8).

---

[63] From the Tale *Le Roi Candaule et Le Maître en droit*. Lemonnier was a theatre practitioner.

These attractions were a desecration for lovers of the wit and speed of 'univocal' *vaudeville* comedy (see p. 16), a loss bemoaned by a journalist reviewing Audinot's farce *Le Tonnelier* (*The Cooper*): 'It's another imitation of *Le Cuvier* (*The Wash-Tub*) by La Fontaine, who serves as the current warehouse for Opéra Comique librettists, and from whom they empty out all the seasoning in order to stuff the audience full of ariettes, duos, trios, loaded with music and devoid of sense.'[64]

On ne s'avise jamais de tout, described earlier, was another farce which might have attracted equal opprobrium. Then Philidor and Sedaine produced two La Fontaine adaptations set in everyday environments where farce linked up with social satire. In La Fontaine's *Blaise le savetier* (*Blaise the Cobbler*),[65] the indolent husband and his long-suffering wife pay off their rent by blackmailing the landlord; in the Fable of *Le Jardinier et son seigneur* (*The Gardener and his Lord*) the trusting Simon is ruined when the squire's retinue, summoned to drive out a ravaging hare, tramples his smallholding and raids his wine cellar.[66] Sedaine's added characters, female associates of the squire, tempt Simon's daughter Fanchette with the lure of the fashionable world.

The jokes often derive from Sedaine's characters: Simon's blind deference and obsequiousness towards the squire; his wife's cynicism; the squire's indifference towards anything except Fanchette. Simon intervenes to protect his property, but the village syndics (not in La Fontaine) interrupt with a ceremony for the squire. Figure 7.3 preserves this memorable incident: Maître Thomas (leaning forward) is singing his speech to the squire while Maître Jacques (holding the paper) corrects his mistakes. Lacking his toupée (another joke), Simon cringes in embarrassment.

Table 8.8 shows that the Sedaine–Philidor operas entertained Parisians for twenty-five years, and presumably private groups too. But the success of Anseaume and Duni's *Les Deux chasseurs et la laitière* (*Two Hunters and a Milk-maid*, 1763) enters another dimension entirely. It became the most performed opera of any kind during the Revolutionary decade, with 355 or more performances in twenty-one different theatres.[67] Fusing together two La Fontaine Fables, it balanced hope against despair, comedy against grimy reality.[68] The destitute villagers Colas and Guillot have sold a bear's skin to

---

[64] *Annonces, Affiches et Avis divers* (*Affiches de Province*), 7 October 1761, 160.
[65] From 'Something That Happened at Château-Thierry', *Some Tales of La Fontaine*, 33.
[66] *Selected Fables*, 4/4.
[67] Kennedy, *Theatre, Opera and Audiences*, 94, 382, 389. Julia Doe's 'Two Hunters, a Milkmaid' presents an important exegesis. CD recording available, cond. Roberto Balconi.
[68] *Selected Fables*, 5/20, 'The Bear and the Two Companions'; *ibid.*, 7/9, 'The Milkmaid and the Jug of Milk'.

172 Comic and Serious Themes

Figure 7.3 *Le Jardinier et son seigneur* (*The Gardener and his lord*), Sc. 18: Maître Thomas (Claude-Antoine Bouret) delivers his harangue to Le Seigneur (Jean-Baptiste Clairval) watched by the bald gardener Simon (Nicolas-Médard Audinot) and Mme Simon (Mlle Deschamps). Source: BnF.

a friend but have still not managed to kill the animal; the opera is entirely occupied by their doomed efforts to defeat it. When their neighbour Perrette appears in Scene 4, she carries a pitcher of milk on her head (thus the stage direction). Later she trips up and loses the milk, offstage, ruining her dreams of accumulated riches.

No opera of the period went further in depicting material poverty; Guillot's clothes are so rough that they repulse Perrette when he makes her a marriage offer near the end of Scene 4. Alone in Scene 3, he smokes his pipe, spits on the ground and then sings. The bear finally chases Colas on to the stage; Guillot clambers up a tree, but Colas plays dead instead, exactly as in the Fable. Rejected by Perrette, Guillot meditates suicide; a ruined hovel half-collapses as he prepares to use it for this purpose. For us, the black humour foreshadows *Waiting for Godot*.[69]

Some audiences were discomfited. Diderot, or a journalistic colleague of his, defended the opera's integrity:

Our judges say, 'Why did [Anseaume] not send away these poor characters happy, by adding the Fable of the treasure-trove to the others?'[70] [...] M. Anseaume has shown far more judgement than his critics. [...] Nothing is commoner than to see people cradle themselves with false hopes, only to be rewarded with worry and care; treasure is always illusory. M. Anseaume has given us the story of life whereas his critics want him to tell us a tale.[71]

Les Deux chasseurs appeared not long after Voltaire's *Candide, or Optimism*, and the prevailing optimism of Duni's music was the perfect narrative counterbalance to Anseaume's terse dialogue.[72]

Marriage as a Measure of Society

The theme of marriage always constituted a mirror of social morality. Popular opera, as perhaps befits 'anti-theatre', reveals many paths of

---

[69] Further La Fontaine adaptations in Table 8.7 not considered here are *Le Quiproquo* and *Mazet*. In the 1790s *Mazet* gained 115 performances and Anseaume and Duni's *La Clochette* (also from La Fontaine) gained 116.
[70] *Selected Fables*, 9/16, 'The Treasure and the Two Men'. The man with nothing left decides to try and hang himself, but as the old wall collapses it reveals hidden gold.
[71] Grimm, *Correspondance littéraire*, ed. Tourneux, V, 349–52 (1 August 1763). Diderot was an anonymous contributor at this time.
[72] In Sc. 2 Guillot's *ariette* in D minor, 'So long as a glimmer of hope remains', combines stoicism and optimism: *Les Deux chasseurs et la laitière, comédie* (Paris: l'Auteur, etc., n.d.), 32.

resistance to this institution.[73] Ordinary plots reconciled parental approval with the preferences of young love. But there were other approaches. What if partners proved incompatible or the husband had a propensity for violence? How could lives proceed when divorce was too difficult to obtain?[74] Could young love face parental opposition so strong that it forcibly removed a daughter or son from France by deportation?

Spoken and sung comedy in France and England discussed marriage in terms of definite questions; in *The Beaux' Stratagem* (1707) Farquhar had incorporated phrases from John Milton's tract on divorce: 'Can radical hatreds be ever reconciled? No, no, sister; Nature is the first lawgiver; and when she has set tempers opposite, not all the golden links of wedlock nor iron manacles of law can keep 'em fast.'[75] Farquhar's couple separates when £10,000 becomes available at the last minute for Mrs Sullen.

When the Comédie-Italienne tackled the same theme in Regnard's *Le Divorce* (1688), the wife and her septuagenarian husband submit to a burlesque trial in the Temple of Hymen; her dowry must be repaid, and he is detained in an institution. In fact, Fair theatres remained more liberal than official ones when they portrayed independent or separated women.[76]

As a kind of anti-comedy, Lesage and Fuzelier wrote *Le Tableau du mariage* (*A Portrait of Marriage*) in 1716; told from two young women's perspective, the opéra-comique is wholly naturalistic. Diamantine is about to commit to marriage with Octave but has a warning dream. Then conjugal cruelty is revealed by visitors to the house: Francœur is a proud wife-beater; the notary seems unmoved by his wife's mortal illness; Diamantine's *confidante* Olivette overhears Arlequin advising Scaramouche to beat her. In the end, Diamantine's uncle and aunt, supposed paragons of felicity, fall into disagreement and attack one another, whereupon their niece cancels her wedding.[77]

Themes of wife-beating and fecklessness became part of *Les Trois commères* in 1723, as mentioned earlier. Almost like portraits of marriage, the three Tales actually promote moral reform, as when Michel-Asne's story in Act I closes with the words: 'Farewell, neighbour; be more wise; give up wine and drink soup'.

---

[73] See Chap. 1 for 'anti-theatre'.
[74] Divorce was not available generally before 1792; separations were possible, usually of property rather than persons: Ray, *Coquettes*, 63–7; Brereton, 'Bourgeois Comedy' in *French Comic Drama*, 214–36.
[75] End of Act III, echoing Milton's *The Doctrine and Discipline of Divorce* (1643/44): Rogers, ed., *18th and 19th-Century British Drama*, 59.
[76] Ray, *Coquettes*, 59, 68–73.
[77] This reached London in 1726: Gagey, *Ballad Opera*, 31–2; Leveson, 'Traveling Tunes', 215.

A different type of opéra-comique avoided realistic fables but challenged the audience with comedies of ideas, sometimes in directly philosophical frameworks. The audience was taken to an imaginary environment and mental work was demanded of it. In Merlin's upside-down world (*Le Monde renversé* by Lesage and d'Orneval),

Pierrot and Arlequin immediately fall in love with Diamantine and Argentine, who [...] demand from them fidelity and a promise of marriage. They also require from them a surprising quality: poverty. Being themselves wealthy, they can marry only poor husbands since, they explain, our laws, to divide wealth up equally, forbid rich families from making alliances.[78]

The provocation is precise: Merlin's magic world is part of 'a political system diametrically opposed to that of France', Pauline Baggio confirms, where wealth was kept in families through marriage alliances. Happiness for Arlequin and Pierrot is attained when Merlin finally removes their rivals in love: contentment and social mixture unexpectedly defeat inherited wealth and family pressure.

In *Amazon Island* (*L'Isle des Amazones*, 1718/20) by Lesage and d'Orneval, audiences faced four propositions: first, that women can derive agency from the use of force; second, that women may organise a republican society according to their own needs and preferences; third, that married men are unattractive though necessary for propagating the species; fourth, that heterosexual marriage has no necessary place in a society. Comic episodes satirise various temporary husbands during their statutory three months on the island: their self-delusions, tediousness and physical habits make for apt comedy. Only one Amazon becomes sentimentally attached to her partner: ironically, he, Dorante, is Parisian and a shameless seducer. Scaramouche provides a running joke ('married'/ *marié* pronounced 'marinaded'/ *mariné*). If any subtexts referred to current debates about women's roles, these were kept well in the background; the power of Lesage's comedy is fully self-sufficient.[79]

Gender roles within marriage regularly fascinated Alexis Piron in fulllength musical comedies of ideas. The legendary Tiresias had experienced life as a woman. Piron's comedy *Tirésias* (1722) explains away this sudden transformation because Jupiter wants him removed in order to seduce Tirésias' wife-to-be, Cariclée. Tirésias is given a friend, Mopse, an overworked innkeeper with a new wife, Cléantis. Tirésias' gender change

---

[78] Baggio, 'The Ambiguity', 622–3; *TF* III, 200 (R/I/311), 1718.
[79] Gender equality was argued for by Poulain de la Barre (1673): Stuurman, *Poulain de la Barre*.

happens in Act I,[80] after which he is too embarrassed to talk to Cariclée and slips away in the dark, leaving her in confusion. During the night Mopse brings him some women's clothes. Cariclée and her confidante Naïs dress as men in Act II, hoping vaguely for some vengeance. When Tirésias encounters Cariclée, neither recognises the other, so they go through a kind of dating scene as experienced from the opposite side of the gender divide.

At the climax of Act III Jupiter and Juno, speaking rather than singing, debate the roles and advantages of either gender in society, whether biologically or socially. Eventually the female Tirésias delivers judgement: 'If a man has the advantage during a quarrel, we have our recompense in the making-up. In brief, perfect happiness would be to be male from morning until night and female from night until morning.' Whereupon Juno changes him back and he recovers his love for Cariclée once she has recovered from the shock.

Fallibility, gender privilege and satirical views of marriage are all found in Piron's *Le Fâcheux veuvage* (*The Trials of Widowerhood*, 1725), set in an invented Eastern society whose law demands that surviving spouses be buried alive after the death of a married partner (see Example 9.7). Balkis is only fourteen, but her father Aboulifar condemns her to marry the sixty-year-old Cadi. As Marcie Ray's account of the piece suggests, this was only a slight caricature of French practice.[81] Using the same strategy as princess Rézia in Lesage's *Les Pèlerins de la Mecque* (*The Pilgrims from Mecca*) one year later, Balkis fakes her own death to avoid marriage. On reappearing, her warrant for the deception is that Arlequin (an Indian savant, thanks to Piron's ingenious plot) is able to raise the dead. Aboulifar's pathological misogyny makes for very particular comedy.[82]

One point of using non-European sources like *Les 1001 Nuits* (1704–17) or *Les 1001 Jours* (1710–12)[83] was that different forms of courtship and marriage could be opposed to the European *status quo*, and that female characters might achieve autonomy or self-realisation. Letellier's *Arlequin sultane favorite* (*Harlequin Sultana and Favourite*) in 1715 offered an interesting model: the plot turns into a 'school for sultans' because the Sultana gives help to the captured Isabelle (predictably desired by the Sultan) specifically in order to reform her husband. Following *commedia* escapades and disguises in Acts II and III, the Sultan adopts the high

---

[80] See Lurcel, *Théâtre de la Foire*, 381 and Connon, *Identity and Transformation*, 158–61.
[81] Ray, *Coquettes*, 54–7.   [82] Connon, *ibid.*, 165–7.
[83] The earlier theory that Lesage was partly responsible for *Les 1001 Jours* has been discredited: Hahn, *Pétis de La Croix*.

ground of remorse: he will forgo his harem, love only his wife and release the French captives.[84]

In *Arlequin Hulla* the following year, Lesage and d'Orneval's closing scenes made comparisons between marriage in European and non-European traditions. The 'hulla' theme refers to the humiliating treatment of wives if rejected by their husband. After repudiating Dardané, the foolish youth Taher regrets his action, which can only be righted after a temporary marriage for her to a 'hulla' (i.e. some other man). Arlequin is conveniently spotted begging in the streets of Balsora. Considering the absence of accessible legal divorce in Europe, Arlequin observes that hullas might be 'very convenient',[85] albeit Parisian habit already allows some wives to take lovers without being thought immoral. So the fable compares inadequate aspects of both Eastern and Western systems.

Non-European stories also provided a source of 'quest' operas where noblewomen resist official rules for the selection of a husband. They construct alternative strategies, going beyond Diamantine in *Le Tableau du mariage*. The Queen of Barostan (*La Reine du Barostan*, 1730) and the Princess of China – more familiar under her original name, Tourandocte – put their aspiring princes to the test or even to death, as in Act I of *La Princesse de la Chine*, 1729. In *La Princesse de Carizme* (1718) the conundrum was that her beauty drove suitors literally mad.[86] Long before the action of *Les Pèlerins de la Mecque* opens, Rézia has desperately staged her own death. Her eventual reunion with the beloved Ali in Act II/6 proves that not only in later operas do we see situations where one could 'laugh and cry at the same time' (these words of Melchior Grimm were written of Act II of Sedaine's *Le Déserteur*).[87]

W. G. Howarth observed that 'dramatists of the Enlightenment seem more concerned to appeal to the sensibility of their audiences than to their capacity for rational thought', especially once tearful family dramas (*comédies larmoyantes*) were initiated by Nivelle de La Chaussée in 1733.[88] One saw escapes, unorthodox births or marriages, coincidences and sentimental endings.[89] Musical theatre, however, showed the way. In Lesage's *Le Corsair de Salé* (*The Pirate of Salé*) in 1729 even piratical husbands knelt for forgiveness before their wives, who have endured

---

[84] Stilwell, 'A New View' and '"A Story altogether foolish"', 80, 126–48.
[85] Sc. 6: *TF* II, 369 (R/I/224).
[86] Guichemerre, '*Princesse de Carizme*' compares the adaptation with its literary source.
[87] *TF* VI, 185–9 (R/II/55–6); see Thomas, *Aesthetics*, 221.
[88] Howarth, 'Playwright as Preacher', 10–11; Brereton, *French Comic Drama*, 223–8.
[89] Lanson, *La Chaussée*, 157–62, 179–93.

their behaviour towards married female captives. Then in 1734 Lesage widened operatic scope, using the theme of marriage to critique a public policy: the government's semi-official method of deporting people at various times to Louisiana, the Caribbean or Canada. Deportation had occurred sporadically since the seventeenth century (thus the *air*, 'De Paris jusqu'au Mississipi', 1718)[90] but not all victims were criminals: families could seek the removal of a son or daughter whose behaviour they considered unforgiveable. Between 1726 and 1734 Quebec received about a hundred deportees each year.[91]

Les Mariages de Canada (*The Marriages in Canada*) is set in Quebec, telling entwined stories of young couples who have been separated in the course of deportations of this sort. Lucile has invented a fresh identity in order to remain faithful to her lost beloved, Damis. An exiled *chevalier* is unexpectedly reunited with his love Clarice, whom he first met working on the Faubourg Saint-Germain.

To survive the harsh climate, marriage is advisable, so an official matchmaker is on hand, Madame Bourdin. Lucile's strategy circumvents Bourdin's plans, happily as it turns out, for Damis has fortuitously arrived in Quebec. Lesage articulates his message: Lucile tells Damis that, like her honorable friend Clitandre, she 'has been unjustly sent to Canada', and Clitandre confirms: 'We have avoided the awful fate, / The inevitable lot [unwanted marriage] / Of French people led by force / To these inhospitable climes.'[92]

The defeat of parental objections to marriage continued as a sentimental theme, with various local colourings. *La Foire de Cythère* (*The Fair at Cythera*) by Pannard and Fagan is one; Marmontel and Grétry's *Silvain* another; the former is set in the world of entertainment and the latter in the depths of nature.

*

With particular consequences for popular opera, a change of temper was promoted by Pierre-Antoine de La Place in 1746 with an influential essay drawing English plays to French attention. Whenever the English stage contains only subaltern characters, he wrote, 'you will see them speak only in very simple prose. Thus [...] style is always fitted to the matter, and never matter to the style'; 'language, according to [the English], must be fitted to the status of those conversing'.[93] The conduit from spoken theatre

---

[90] TF III, 114, *Air* 146 (R/I/290), *Table*, 41 (R/I/385).   [91] Frostin, 'Du peuplement pénal', 87.
[92] TF IX, 327, 331 (R/II/476–7).   [93] La Place, 'Discours' (1746), I, xliii–xliv.

to opéra-comique was an educated lawyer more interested in theatre: Claude-Pierre Patu (1729–58), who lived in London for seven months in 1754, counting Garrick and John Cleland as friends.[94]

Patu's strategy of reform was to issue translations of six musical comedies, including *The Beggar's Opera*.[95] As he wrote (in English) to Garrick: 'How must I lament the state of our scene! It shall, it must fall down, if nobody is bold enough to enlarge our fetters.'[96] Sedaine soon took advantage of Patu's translation of *The Devil to Pay, or the Wives Metamorphos'd*,[97] and then adapted Patu's translation of Robert Dodsley's *The King and the Miller of Mansfield* (see Chapter 12).[98]

The Devil to Pay (which became *Le Diable à quatre*) is a totally different take on the marriage theme: there are two couples, and both are already married.

The *Diable* of the title is a mean and haughty Marquise who inflicts cruelties on persons she considers socially inferior [...]. She was so rude to a doctor-magician who happened by, that he plots revenge: summoning devils from the underworld that same night, he casts a spell by which the she-devil Marquise changes place with [Margot], a shoemaker's wife, so that she wakes the next morning to find herself in the cobbler's bed, looking just like his wife and dressed in her clothes. Meanwhile the real cobbler's wife has been changed to resemble the Marquise. Thus there is a double inversion: the high becoming the low, and the low becoming the high.[99]

Magic in Fair theatre was always intended for 'imparting truth, knowledge and wisdom' as David Buch says.[100] But the language of life in *Le Diable à quatre* has a shock value of its own, as when in Act II Sedaine transmits the growing panic of the Marquise finding herself in a malodorous bed, woken

---

[94] Patu is discussed in Ledbury, 'Sedaine and the Question of Genre'.
[95] Patu, *Choix de petites pièces* (1756).
[96] 25 February 1755: Boaden, ed., *Correspondence of David Garrick*, II, 385. Patu's letters are in the Victoria & Albert Museum.
[97] Using Theophilus Cibber's one-act version: Rodmell, 'Sedaine's *Le Diable à quatre*'. The three-act original (1731) was by Charles Coffey and John Mottley, derived in turn from Thomas Jevons' *The Devil of a Wife*, 1685 or 1686.
[98] Patu's other translations were Dodsley's *The Toy-Shop* and *The Blind Beggar of Bethnal Green* and John Gay's *The What D'ye Call It*. Jean Monnet saw *The Devil to Pay* in London: Monnet, *Mémoires* (1772), 180.
[99] Rex, 'Inversions', 57. See Bruce Alan Brown, 'Vorwort', in Christoph Willibald Gluck, *Le Diable à quatre, ou La double métamorphose* (*Sämtliche Werke*, Abteilung IV Band 3) (Kassel etc.: Bärenreiter, 1992), vii–xviii. Brown prints all known *vaudevilles*; the latest information on these is contained in his 'Sedaine, le vaudeville, et l'opéra-comique'.
[100] Sometimes in the form of 'a magic mirror or statue that exposes sin and moral weaknesses': Buch, *Magic Flutes*, xiv, 104–5, 113. *La Statue merveilleuse* (*The Wondrous statue*) derived from *Les 1001 Nuits* and was revived at least three times: *TF* IV, I (R/I/398).

at 5.00 a.m. by Jacques's rough songs and habitual modes of address. The original of Jacques is called Jobson and we must quote the original English:

LADY: Nay, then, I'll hold no longer; you Rogue, you insolent Villain, I'll teach your better Manner. *(Flings Bedstaff [a stick] and other things at him.)*
JOBSON: This is more than I ever saw by her. I never had an ill word from her before. Come, Strap, I'll try your Mettle; I'll sober you, I warrant you, Quean. *(He straps her, she flies at him.)*
LADY: I'll pull your Throat out; I'll tear out your Eyes; I'm a Lady, Sirrah. Oh Murder! Murder! [etc.]

Sedaine's Marquise hits her servant Lucile when she passes by because Lucile sees and addresses her as Margot. Then Jacques strikes them both and forces the Marquise (as Margot) to her knees. He claims he never uses a stick (*Air*: 'Non, je ne ferai pas') but the act ends with his ugly *Air*, 'A coups de pieds, à coups de poings': if a wife tries to hit back, 'With kicks and punches I'd break her jaw and smash her face in.'[101] *Le Diable à quatre* confronts violent behaviour, class and character within marriage, ingeniously insisting that they are mutually exclusive, for the Marquis is portrayed as a kind man, a counterpart to the forbearing Margot.

*

Among several turning points for popular opera was the rise of the Moral Tale in the 1750s, especially those of Jean-François Marmontel (1723–99), who was already a librettist; he would even develop Tales with future stage adaptation in mind.[102] Marriage is sometimes threatened by a dilemma whose resolution would involve a change or modification in behaviour or social convention. The impediment to happiness becomes social as well as individual. *Lucile*, for example, depicted an elderly peasant, Blaise, who walks into a bourgeois household on Lucile's wedding day and informs the family that he is her true father. He and his story are accepted. The radical message was enhanced because

---

[101] *Le Diable à quatre* (Paris: Duchesne, 1757), 38, 40. This had no equivalent in Patu's translation, and Patu did not include many song texts or discuss music in his Preface. But stage cruelty, even to disabled characters, was traditional in London, and *The Devil to Pay* was 'the most-performed afterpiece of the eighteenth century': Dickie, *Cruelty and Laughter*, 62.
[102] Astbury, *Moral Tale*, 17–36; Couvreur, 'Opéras-comiques de Marmontel'.

the actor Caillot, in Grétry's operatic setting, appeared in actual peasant clothing, apparently bald.[103]

Annette et Lubin, another Moral Tale, was discussed at the end of Chapter 4. It was an outstandingly successful example of Marmontel's art, and its benefits extended to popular opera in the same way as C. S. Favart's *Acajou* had quickly benefited from Duclos' story *Acajou et Zirphile*. Justine Favart's adaptation of *Annette et Lubin* lived on in six different countries and languages, wherever audiences were ready to accept indigent orphans as main characters.[104] In real life, rural unmarried parents were mercilessly treated: magistrates attempted to uncover the father's identity by questioning mothers as they went into labour. So, it is no surprise that Marmontel's Bailli wants to antagonise Annette and Lubin: it gives him reason to hope he might marry her himself (Sc. 12). The couple's expression of innocence became a catchphrase, still used in Laclos' *Les Liaisons dangereuses*: 'But that's all it was.'[105]

Abduction

The theme of abduction, familiar to us from Mozart's *Die Entführung* (*Abduction from the Seraglio*), spanned the century in France, where it finally absorbed and portrayed violent criminality.[106] Letellier's *Arlequin sultane favorite*, described earlier, has been shown by Jama Stilwell to form a coherent and musically sophisticated response to the vogue for 'Turkish' and 'Chinese' abduction stories.[107] Aristocratic power as related to women (but also the possibility of women's power over aristocrats) returned prominently as a theme in the 1750s when Goldoni's *Bertoldo in corte* was introduced to Paris by the Bouffons. Chapters 10 and 11 will describe its successful reworking by C.-S. Favart as *Le Caprice amoureux ou Ninette à la cour*. Justine Favart, who created the part of Ninette, subsequently added a thwarted abduction to conclude her own *Annette et Lubin*. The apparently trustworthy *seigneur*, like his Bailli, conceives an infatuation for Annette and suddenly has her taken away. Lubin rushes after her, rescues

---

[103] Arnold, *Grétry's Operas*, 28–34; Charlton, *Grétry*, Chap. 4.
[104] Iacuzzi, *European Vogue*, 100–5, 136–40, 321–2, 329, 363.
[105] 'Cependant, voilà tout': Marmontel, *Contes moraux* (Amsterdam, 1761), II, 105. Wåhlberg, 'L'opéra-comique', 298; Favart and Blaise, *Annette et Lubin* (1762), Sc. 7, 74.
[106] Abduction operas have been studied by Betzwieser in *Exotismus und 'Türkenoper'*, Ward in *Pagodas in Play*, Locke in *Music and the Exotic* and several authors in Hüttler and Weidinger, eds., *Ottoman Empire*.
[107] Stilwell, '"A Story Altogether Foolish"' and 'A New View'.

her by force and reappears with her in Scene 15: see p. 146. The moment is celebrated in music with Lubin's *ariette* 'Non, je ne crains personne' borrowed from Leonardo Vinci's *Alessandro nell' Indie* (1730); he delivers the successful appeal that is illustrated in Figure 6.2.

In the same year Sedaine used the abduction theme when adapting Dodsley's *The King and the Miller of Mansfield*: Jenny is tricked by Lord Lurewell and confined in his property, but escapes through a window. After rejoining Richard's family, she gives testimony when (as in the play) her assailant stands accused in the presence of the king: Figure 12.1.

Abduction in popular opera continued to appear as a correlative of social perversion, such as the corrupt exercise of power by authority.[108] The correction of a wrong might take spectacular form as when, after the fall of the Bastille, force was represented on stage. In this way an abducted woman, Camille, together with her young son, is rescued at the point of expiry in *Camille, ou Le souterrain* (*Camille, or The Dungeon*) by Marsollier and Dalayrac (Opéra Comique / Comédie Italienne, 1791). This discovery of abduction and incarceration was unfortunately taken from real life: the unbelievable cruelty of duchess Cerifalco's fate had been made known by her interviewer in 1782.[109]

In conclusion, we must therefore confirm the relevances Jama Stilwell listed as applicable to 'abduction' operas: aristocratic privilege, male sexual desire and general social inequity across lines of gender and class:

An examination of the extensive generic travels of the abduction plot in the eighteenth century may thus go a long way towards uncovering a diversity of new explanations for its popularity. As the plot moved from venue to venue, it could not help but be experienced in ways that were conditioned by the particular musical, dramatic and cultural values implicit in each new genre that took up the tale.[110]

*

Taken together, themes in popular opera were built from an extraordinary number of characters and styles; the foregoing account is selective and could be expanded. Their range extended from *commedia* and farce to the triumph of personal happiness; from Piron's intellectualism to Lesage's novelistic breadth; from private to public; and from marriage woes to

---

[108] Similar issues were explored by Cahusac and Rameau: the abduction of Amélite in *Zoroastre* and the ordeals of Zélide in *Zaïs*.

[109] Stéphanie-Félicité de Genlis, 'Histoire de la Duchesse de C***' in *Adèle et Théodore* (1782). Cerifalco was discovered, a human wreck, after nine years: Mary Trouille, 'Buried Alive'.

[110] Stilwell, 'A New View', 54.

current events. La Fontaine's strength remained with the genre because his social conscience was there to be reflected whenever popular opera took up his stories. An assortment of quack doctors, money men, lawyers, eccentrics and guardians was inherited from the Gherardi era. Aristocrats, seen initially (if at all) as simply risible, became scrutinised more carefully. But so was individual behaviour: of men towards women, of powerful towards powerless. Even social policies were scrutinised; even Church law, disguised through allegory and eroticism. In Chapter 8 we can identify those popular works which were most able to hold the Paris stage and provide further levels of continuity.

8 | Performance as History

Pre-1748 Works

This chapter starts with facts and figures, continues with managerial manœuvres and concludes by bringing both together. It identifies the most popular works, the length of time that they were on stage in Paris, and the possibility of a core repertory. Two central sections focus on the crisis affecting all companies in 1745, and the tactics of the rival companies as they evolved new forms of opéra-comique.

Since opera has a public identity, we often know which pieces were more popular than others. So the idea of a 'canon' (a collection of works regarded as exemplary) might be measured through performance histories. Popular opera in Paris has been studied in this way because daily records exist of performances at the Comédie-Italienne, both before and after it absorbed the Opéra Comique on 3 February 1762. André Grétry's operas, for example, had provable dominance here in the 1770s and 80s; recent work by R. J. Arnold has determined many reasons why.[1] However, regarding the Fair theatres, reception histories of popular opera have remained generally unclear, except for Pannard's.[2] Until now the effort has been to secure accurate data for first performances. The present aim is to discover trajectories of performance.

Written judgements about earlier Fair theatre are rare; one is found within the important review by Desfontaines of Favart's *La Chercheuse d'esprit* (*The Girl Who Sought Wit*): 'Except for *Les Pèlerins de la Mecque* (*The Pilgrims from Mecca*) and [*Achmet et*] *Almanzine*, the Comico-Lyric Stage has not so far produced more than a few passable works'.[3] Desfontaines here intended a provocation since 'lyric' emphasised music's importance and 'Comico-Lyric Stage' acknowledged that the Opéra Comique was much more than a rootless seasonal venture. Only four

---

[1] Arnold, *Grétry's Operas*. [2] Rizzoni, *Pannard*, 451–75, giving revival dates for all his works.
[3] Desfontaines, *Observations* (1741), Letter 351 (29 April), 141.

years later, competition and ill-will succeeded in shutting down Favart's company for six years.

The problem, therefore, is to know whether Desfontaines was correct and which the 'few passable works' might be, judged by the number of times they were seen on stage. Statistical evidence for the Fair theatre is different from data obtained from a day-by-day source. For one thing we have no reliable record of performances, even up to 1762. For another, competing troupes existed until the mid-1720s.[4] Moreover, Fair theatre could not necessarily rely on things that an official theatre had, like a stable group of performers or a library of materials. Each season was managed on a one-off basis: hardly any archival documents survive from before Favart's period.

Allied to this is the question of how far one can justify terms like 'canon'. Fair theatre responded to the rhythms and vagaries of social life and the expectation of novelty and change. Nevertheless, we shall find a definite evolution in the pattern of revivals. What had originally been disparate – whether *ad hoc* offerings within Fair seasons, or different styles between the Fair and the Comédie-Italienne – became similar enough for the two troupes to be merged. After the fusion of 1762 twenty-seven earlier operas continued to be revived or adapted, sometimes for many years. This explains Chamfort's account seen in Chapter 1 which normalised the coexistence of early, mid-century and later pieces at the Comédie-Italienne, a company that worked every day of the year except for three weeks at Easter.[5] The precise fluctuation between older and newer pieces after 1762 remains to be analysed when digital database resources are complete.[6]

This brings us to our method for the period between 1714 and the Revolution. All these factors make a chronological approach desirable. We will use sources describing both individual operas and performance histories. Sources describing works have either primary or secondary status: primary sources consist of ten volumes of *Le Théâtre de la Foire* plus various imprints or manuscripts of individual works. The universal secondary source is Brenner's monumental *A Bibliographical List of Plays*

---

[4] See account of rival companies in Parfaict, *Mémoires* (1743), II, 25–7 (winter 1724). In winter 1727 the promoter Honoré could not find a theatre to hire and borrowed that of the Opéra in Holy Week: *ibid.*, II, 39.
[5] It offered spoken drama (except during the 1770s), *commedia* plays with Italian actors on Tuesdays and Fridays (ceasing in 1780), *parodies*, older *opéras-comiques* and newer *comédies mêlées d'ariettes*: daily listings in Brenner, *Theatre Italien*.
[6] To be mounted on the ObTIC site: see p. xviii.

in the French Language,⁷ which details manuscript and printed sources of every known work given at the Fairs (and at the Opéra and all other theatres as well), plus dates. We also have Emanuele De Luca's *Il repertorio della Comédie-Italienne di Parigi (1716–1762)*, ordered chronologically as a digital *catalogue raisonné*;⁸ and the annotated catalogue of works given from 1762 at the Comédie-Italienne / Opéra Comique by Nicole Wild and the present author.⁹ For Pannard, details are found in Nathalie Rizzoni's monograph (note 2). One may also consult a pioneering list by Carmody.¹⁰

Sources on performance also come in primary and secondary forms. The Comédie-Italienne's monthly accounts and some committee notes are available.¹¹ Primary publications are the *Mercure galant*, the *Mercure de France*, the Parfaicts' *Mémoires* and two trade journals.¹² Secondary sources are Brenner's day-by-day list (note 5) and other publications just mentioned. By collating all these we can develop a picture that is certainly not complete but at least informed by general patterns of repeat performances. Regrettably, the monthly or bimonthly *Mercure* supplies inconsistent records of what was staged at the Fairs (the Parfaicts seem to have relied on these too): levels of detail are unpredictable for new opéras-comiques and minimal for revivals. Thus many accounts of revivals have undoubtedly been lost, as the end of this chapter observes.

Such hazards can be gauged, for example, from d'Argenson's undated note concerning *Achmet et Almanzine*, a work 'that has been the most often given, and repeatedly'.¹³ If he was referring merely to success within its initial season, summer 1728, we can corroborate him from reported evidence that sixty-eight performances did occur.¹⁴ But if d'Argenson was referring to subsequent seasons we are not in a position to corroborate, because *Achmet* was to our present knowledge revived only in 1729 (FSG) and 1744 (FSG) whereas many other operas were repeated in more seasons than two. Was its supposed familiarity based merely on three seasons' performances? This is unlikely: see Table 8.1. All statistical comparisons and assessments of revivals must be provisional.

Because of the Opéra Comique's enforced closure in summer 1745, performance histories during the first thirty years of opéra-comique can

---

[7] Brenner, *Bibliographical List* with musical appendix by Neal Zaslaw and Michael Keller.
[8] In the collection *Les Savoirs des acteurs italiens*, ed. Andrea Fabiano (Paris: IRPMF, 2011).
[9] Wild*TOC* gives duration of performance runs and titles of pre-1762 works taken over after the fusion.
[10] Carmody, 'Le Répertoire'. [11] F-Po, *Registres*.
[12] *Annonces, affiches et avis divers*: from 1752 the *Affiches de province* or '*Grandes affiches*' were issued on Wednesdays; the *Affiches de Paris* or '*Petites affiches*' on Mondays and Thursdays.
[13] D'Argenson, *Notices* (1725–57), II, 534. [14] Parfaict, *Mémoires* (1743), II, 46.

Table 8.1 First and subsequent years in which Charles-François Pannard's opéras-comiques were given.*

La Tante rivale (also called *L'Amant musicien*): 1729, 1733, 1736, 1742
Le Nouvelliste dupé: 1732, 1734, 1742, 1757
Pygmalion first version: 1735, 1736, 1743
Pygmalion second version: 1744, 1745, 1752
Le Magazin des modernes: 1736, 1737, 1741, 1742, 1758, 1759
Le Fossé du scrupule / Le Saut du fossé: 1738, 1739, 1742, 1744

---

* *Sources:* Rizzoni, *Pannard*, 451–75 and references described earlier. Translations of all French titles in this chapter are provided in the list of stage works, pp. 321–9.

Table 8.2 Operas not seen after 1745, ordered by the period of years in which they were viable. These operas were given in at least four seasons ('season' meaning a single FSG or FSL).

Le Tombeau de Nostradamus (Lesage: staged between 1714 and 1733)
L'École des amants (Lesage, Fuzelier: 1716–32)
Les Funérailles de la Foire (Lesage, d'Orneval: 1718–1734)
La Tante rivale/L'Amant musicien/L'Amant maître de musique (Pannard, Thierry: 1729–42)
Le Fossé du scrupule/Le Saut du fossé (Pannard: 1738–44)
La Foire de Bezons (Favart, Pannard: 1735–37)

---

be thought of together. Some works first seen in these decades continued to be given after 1751 and some after 1761. In all the tables that follow, only the more successful pieces are included, namely titles which were revived in at least two seasons subsequent to that which saw their premiere. This is for manageability. If those operas had been included which were revived in only one subsequent season, an extra fifty works would have had to be added. As with films today, both the failure rate and the turnover rate were considerable; many were apparently never revived. Yet as we shall see, a number of favourites existed that were seen in multiple revivals, whether over a long or short time span.

We can begin by grouping *vaudeville* pieces that we know to have been given in four seasons at least (Table 8.2) or three seasons at least (Table 8.3) though not beyond 1745. Given the limits of our knowledge, these are meant to be complementary, not to imply contrast. To compare long-term durability of operas complements the counting up of incomplete references to revivals.

Table 8.4, working across the years of silence, shows the degree to which older operas could compete against new styles of opéra-comique and French versions of Italian *intermezzi* (see Table 8.6). The number of seasons noted to contain revivals represents a minimum of possibilities.

Table 8.3 Operas not seen after 1745, ordered by the period of years in which they were viable. These operas were given in at least three seasons ('season' meaning a single FSG or FSL).[a]

Achmet et Almanzine (Lesage, d'Orneval, Fuzelier: 1728–44) (also 1776, Fontainebleau)
L'Isle des Amazones (Lesage, d'Orneval: 1718–31)
Les Témoins contre eux-mêmes/Les Coffres (Gallet: 1736–45)
Pygmalion (Pannard, version 1: 1735–43)
La Comédie sans hommes (Pannard: 1732–40)
Les Couplets en procès (Lesage, d'Orneval: 1730–38)
Les Animaux raisonnables (Fuzelier, Legrand: 1718–25)
La Mère embarrassée (Pannard, Pontau: 1734–42)
L'Impromptu du Pont-Neuf (Pannard: 1729–36)
Arlequin Mahomet (Lesage: 1714–21)
Les Époux réunis (Pannard: 1736–42)
La Matrone d'Éphèse (Fuzelier: 1714–18)
Le Festin de pierre (Letellier: 1713–16)

[a] *Les Funérailles de la Foire* and *L'Isle des Amazones* were also seen in London: Levenson, 'Traveling Tunes', 68.

Works in Tables 8.4 and 8.5 employed more *vaudevilles* than new music. Those in Table 8.5 showed exceptional staying power against operas having all new music, or mostly new music mixed with *vaudevilles* (for example, *Le Maître en droit*, discussed in Chapter 7). But *vaudeville* opera never actually died out, as Herbert Schneider has long emphasised, and so the Théâtre du Vaudeville was founded in January 1792.[15] Even at the Comédie-Italienne there was a revival phase when Jean-Baptiste Moulinghen was employed to give *vaudevilles* new accompaniments, starting in 1773.[16]

A few popular operas in Tables 8.5 and 8.8 were revived during the Revolution years. Meticulous research on theatre performance between 1789 and 1795 has been issued by André Tissier,[17] while a team under Emmet Kennedy assessed the whole Revolution decade using a much narrower database of journal information.[18] Both revealed that operatic 'tragedies and *pièces de circonstance* that have long drawn attention from the academy formed only a small subset of the overall repertory', which consisted of ordinary and escapist comedies much of the time.[19] Kennedy estimated that Anseaume and Duni's *Les Deux chasseurs et la laitière* and Pierre Baurans's and Pergolesi's *La Servante maîtresse* were the second- and third-most frequently performed theatre works in any genre staged between 1789 and 1799.

[15] Schneider, 'Die Revitalisierung'. [16] Wild*TOC*, 531. [17] Tissier, *Les Spectacles à Paris*.
[18] Kennedy, *Theatre, Opera and Audiences*. [19] Doe, 'Two Hunters', 177.

Table 8.4 Operas revived after 1751 but not after the merging of companies in 1762, ordered by the period of years in which they were viable.[a] A 'season' means a single FSG or FSL. See pp. 205–6 for particulars of updating.

Les Amours de Nanterre (Lesage, d'Orneval, Autreau: 1718–55)[b]	7 seasons
Le Monde renversé (Lesage, d'Orneval, La Font: 1718–53)	4 seasons
La Statue merveilleuse (Lesage, d'Orneval, Fuzelier: 1720–52)	3 seasons
La Reine du Barostan (Lesage, d'Orneval: 1730–60)	8 seasons
Le Mariage du caprice / Le Caprice (Piron: 1724–53)	3 seasons
Le Nouvelliste dupé (Pannard: 1732–57)	4 seasons
Le Magazin des modernes (Pannard: 1736–59)	9 seasons
Le Bal bourgeois (Favart: 1738–61)	6 seasons
La Répétition interrompue (Pannard, Fagan, rev. Favart: 1735–58)	5 seasons
La Fausse ridicule (Fagan: 1731–53)	5 seasons
La Fête [or Les Bateliers] de Saint-Cloud (Favart: 1741–59)	5 seasons
Les Jardins de l'Hymen ou La Rose (Piron, rev. Favart: 1744–60)	7 seasons
Les Jeunes mariés (Favart, Parmentier: 1740–55)	5 seasons
Le Siège de Cythère (Favart, Fagan: 1743–55)	4 seasons
La Coquette sans le savoir (P. Rousseau, Favart: 1744–54)	4 seasons
La Muse pantomime (Pannard: 1737–47)[c]	3 seasons
Pygmalion (Pannard, version 2: 1744–52)	4 seasons

[a] I omit works that were tried out after February 1762 and rapidly dropped.
[b] Given in London, 1734 (Leveson, 'Traveling Tunes', 68) and Lyons, 1750 (Vallas, *Un Siècle*, 250).
[c] 1747: unverified date from Carmody, 'Le Répertoire'.

Table 8.5 Operas revived after 1761 at the Comédie-Italienne or elsewhere, ordered by the period of years in which they were viable. All are by Favart except the last, which is by Pannard. A 'season' means a single FSG or FSL.

La Servante justifiée (1740–94)	7	seasons before 1762
Les Nymphes de Diane (1747–93)	3	ditto
Acajou (1744–88)	3	ditto
La Chercheuse d'esprit (1741–81)	11	ditto
Le Coq de village (1743–80)	6	ditto
La Pièce à deux acteurs (1738–72)	1	ditto

La Servante justifiée had sixty-two performances at the Comédie-Italienne from 1762 to 1773, with a further run using accompaniments by Moulinghen from 1773 to 1793. *Les Nymphes de Diane*, premiered in Brussels, arrived at the Foire Saint-Laurent in 1753.[20] It subsequently had seventy performances at the Comédie-Italienne between 1774 and 1780, also revised by Moulinghen, and six at the Théâtre du Vaudeville in 1793. Moulinghen's revision of *Acajou* had sixty-eight performances at the

---

[20] See Chapter 7, n. 49.

Comédie-Italienne from 1773 to 1788; *La Chercheuse d'esprit* had thirty-one performances there between 1762 and 1781; and *Le Coq de village* twenty-three performances between 1762 and 1780.[21] *La Pièce à deux acteurs* was modernised as *La Ressource comique*, with Pannard's original reworked by Anseaume with music by Lefroid de Méreaux (1772).

The Crisis of 1745

Charles-Simon Favart's influence on popular opera becomes more apparent in our final chapters and at the close of the present chapter. We shall now follow certain events leading to the six-year suspension of the Fair theatres for which he worked. All Paris theatres suffered endemic financial weakness; large debts at the Opéra Comique are evident from about 1737 when Boizard de Pontau as *entrepreneur* needed to deal with competition from dance companies, pantomime-ballets and visiting English practitioners, both winter and summer. His ordinary expenses in summer 1739 amounted to 14,462 *livres*, not counting 15,000 *livres* for the *privilège*.[22] On one hand, Pontau maintained a troupe of ten dancers, their number increasing to about sixteen by 1744.[23] On the other, he hired Henry Delamain's English dancers for both 1739 seasons and still owed them nearly 8,500 *livres* two years later when the law intervened to help Delamain recoup his losses from the Opéra Comique's takings.[24] By 30 September 1741 stone-throwing rioters (presumably creditors) were attacking Pontau's house near the Saint-Laurent Fair: Favart tried to speak to them, and Pontau's servants fought back.[25] When Pontau resigned in 1743, the Opéra Comique owed the Opéra some 33,660 *livres*, debts going back to the 1730s which a subsequent *directeur*, Tréfontaine, was still trying to resolve in 1748.[26]

This situation explains often-quoted remarks in Jean Monnet's autobiography asserting the sad state of an institution he took over in 1743. Yet Monnet does not dwell on the financial reason why he was dismissed by the

---

[21] Some performances of *La Chercheuse d'esprit* from 1 July 1770 consisted of a version with new music by Duni, La Borde and Gottfried van Swieten: Framery, *Journal de Musique*, July 1770, 39–40 (R/I/557).

[22] Fuzelier, 'Éclaircissement au sujet de la Régie de l'Opéra Comique', in Cucuel, 'Sources et documents', 251.

[23] Porot, 'Chants de Momus', 166–8.   [24] Campardon, *Spectacles*, I, 229–31 (15 Sep. 1741).

[25] *Ibid.*, I, 156–8.

[26] *Ibid.*, I, 158–9. Contractual and employment documents analysed in Marcetteau-Paul, 'Les Théâtres des Foires', 50–109.

Opéra's new entrepreneurial director, François Berger, after one year:[27] Berger wished to direct the Fair company himself, retaining Favart at 2,000 *livres* per annum to manage its business. There were no winners under the monopoly system: the Comédie-Française actors from 1742 to 1745 felt obliged to pool one-sixth of their individual income in order to tackle a debt mountain that would reach 486,930 *livres* by 1756.[28] During the period from 1741 to 1746 the Comédie-Italienne actors set aside a quarter of their individual income similarly, and their global debt by 1760 remained at 25,000 *livres*.[29]

Madame Du Boccage's public attempt to ruin the Opéra Comique was issued in late February or March 1745.[30] It followed months of acrimony. The Comédie-Française hated ridicule, and Favart detested the stylised declamation used by its actors. His *Acajou* (18 March 1744) had been a great success, a *cause célèbre*. It derived from a new short story by Charles Duclos which was notorious, *Acajou et Zirphile*. On the surface it read like a fairy story, inspired by (and issued with) a set of fanciful engravings; but it wove in strong flavours of satire regarding the state of aristocratic education.[31] In Act I of Favart's opera the youthful Acajou is visited by tutors, one of whom shows in a long tirade how to declaim heroic verse in the official style. But the actor, Terodac, exactly mimicked the sing-song delivery of one particular player at the Comédie-Française. Although mimicry of actors and singers was traditional, this proved a step too far.[32] Legal action obliged Favart laboriously to remove *Acajou*'s spoken dialogue and substitute continuous *vaudevilles* (28 September). But Berger saw a chance to create extra profit by putting the Opéra Comique on the stage of the Opéra, whose normal performances took place only three or four times a week.[33] The *Mercure*'s journalist mentioned the performance of Saturday 14 November,[34] for which Terodac was contractually free to be present, presumably still in his *Acajou* role.[35]

---

[27] Monnet, *Mémoires* (1772), 78–9; Campardon, *Spectacles*, II, 141: Conseil d'État, 30 May 1744.
[28] Lancaster, 'Comédie Française', 596; Scott, *Women on the Stage*, 263.
[29] Brenner, *Théâtre Italien*, 8–9.   [30] See Chapter 6, p. 142.
[31] Dagen, 'Préface' in Duclos, *Acajou et Zirphile* (1744), 25.
[32] La Porte, *Anecdotes dramatiques* (1775), I, 4–5.
[33] Berger received permission for four shows: Porot, 'Chants de Momus', 55, 171.
[34] *Mercure*, 1744, Nov./1, 171. A copy at F-Po (Liv.18.2289) of *Acajou* (Paris: Prault fils, 1753) is annotated by 'desboulmiers': '1744 [...] reprezantée en 8bre a téatre de l'opéra / a palès royal', confirming that this was one of the unnamed pieces mentioned by the *Mercure*.
[35] F-Po, Fonds Favart, Carton I, doss. C12, docs. 6, f° 1 and 26–7, signed 'Feydeau de Marville'. Terodac's contract at La Rochelle had been cancelled.

Thus antagonised, the French players and their high-level protectors pleaded loss of income and persuaded the government that the Opéra Comique should be stopped. Mme Du Boccage's diatribe was published. A long-term monitoring of the box-office position was agreed on,[36] and a 'verbal decision' was handed down via the chief of police, reporting on 6 June 1745.[37] The players obtained a prohibition of the Opéra Comique for three years and then asked for more time.[38] Their assertions eventually proved groundless but were in any case unfair: a decline in their audiences between 1736 and 1742 was actually thereafter being reversed, as has painstakingly been shown.[39] They acted out of pique. And ironically enough, attendance at the Comédie-Française during the six years when the Opéra Comique went dark increased only marginally in summers and not at all in winters.

Peter Davies considered that the aims of these French players 'were not restricted to suppressing a particular theatre but instead to suppressing a disturbingly popular genre [*parodies*] shared by two theatres'.[40] But a new action against the Comédie-Italienne was launched, rather, by the Opéra's vengeful Berger, accusing it of mounting an excessively musical *parodie*, *La Fille, la veuve et la femme* (*The Woman, the Wife and the Widow*), written mainly by the young Pierre Laujon.[41] On 1 September the government agreed and fined it 10,000 *livres*, simultaneously withdrawing permission for any new musical *parodies*.[42]

These restrictive measures placed on the Comédie-Italienne explain why Favart left Paris in 1745. Not only was his own theatre closed but also the one to which he might have transferred his allegiance was at the same time denied the use of that part of its repertory to which he could have contributed.[43]

Deprived of musical shows, the Comédie-Italienne benefited little from the closure of the Fair theatres: its audiences went down during the months of February and March between 1745 and 1750 and only rose by 2 per cent during summers. In this bleak period, seasonal dance or pantomime companies must have profited most from these machinations.[44]

---

[36] Lagrave, *Théâtre et public*, 379.   [37] Boislisle, *Lettres de Marville* (1742–7), II, 90.
[38] 'les representations [...] seroient sursises pendant trois ans': Boislisle, *ibid.*, II, 90.
[39] Lagrave, *Théâtre et public*, 377–8, 656–8; Lough, *Paris Theatre Audiences*, 174, 272.
[40] Davies, 'Heir to Anacreon', 180.
[41] The target was Mouret's *Les Fêtes de Thalie*: AN AJ/13/3/IX, dated 23 Aug. Copy in F-Po, Fonds Favart, Carton I, Doss. C.2 (4).
[42] Campardon, *Comédiens*, II, 261–3; Beaucé, *Parodies*, 45–6; De Luca, *Il repertorio*. Existing *parodies* of plays were not stopped, only fresh *parodies* of plays or operas.
[43] Davies, 'Heir to Anacreon', 182.
[44] Lagrave, *Théâtre et public*, 377; Leathers, *British Entertainers*, 21–3; Beaucé, *Parodies*, 45–8.

Theatre Politics and the Bouffon Legacy

Early in 1751 d'Argenson noted, 'The Italian players have just won their suit in the [king's] council and obtained permission to give sung *parodies* or opéras-comiques, which have been found not to cause harm to the serious pieces of which they are critical.'[45] So 'upon his return to Paris in 1751, Favart found the Comédie-Italienne very receptive to new talent and leadership. [...] [His] attachment to the Comédie-Italienne was quite different from his previous experiences as manager and régisseur in that he was not officially a part of the troupe'.[46] Davies produced statistics to emphasise the acclaim received by Favart's newly written *parodies* in a completely novel style. Six were premiered between 9 March 1751 and 24 March 1753 (Table 8.7) and are selectively discussed in Chapter 10.[47]

Albeit undocumented, reconsideration in 1751 was obviously being given to the Opéra Comique. It can be imagined that numerous interests were in favour of ending the suspension. In one bid for the future *privilège* we find seven arguments for restitution: the Opéra Comique was a training ground for talent; the Opéra needed its income from the Fairs; Fair traders are losing business; the public wants its entertainment back; money is not being generated for the poor-tax; foreign visitors need more activity in the evening; and the notion of competition with the Comédie-Française is irrelevant because the nature of the entertainment is not the same.[48] Jean Monnet pushed hard while still in London, writing to the marquise de Pompadour and to Bernage de Saint-Maurice, the Provost of Merchants. Bernage was *Directeur* of the Opéra because since 1749 the City of Paris (of which he was the chief) had been vested by the king with its management. Bernage's six-year contract with Monnet was duly signed on Christmas Day, and the winter season began on 3 February 1752.[49]

Not coincidentally, the Opéra obliged Eustachio Bambini's *intermezzo* troupe to perform in Paris for a brief trial period. They arrived in July 1752 from Strasbourg and began performing on 1 August (see Table 8.6). The rest of this book tells the story of how their *intermezzi* changed the course

---

[45] D'Argenson, *Notices* (1725–57), II, 650, after seeing Favart's *Les Amants inquiets* whose 'grotesque' *parodie* of *Thétis et Pélée* he enjoyed.
[46] Davies, 'Heir to Anacreon', 183. Further background in Darnton, *Cat Massacre*, 159–60.
[47] 'Favart's five [=6] works were the most popular and most frequently performed. Of the 525 performances during the same period Favart's work held the stage for 166 of them': Davies, ibid., 184.
[48] Undated 'Mémoire à Monsieur le Procureur du Roy de la Ville' from Sr Tristan, 'Maître d'hôtel chez le Roy': AN AJ/13/3/II, large bifolium.
[49] Monnet, *Mémoires* (1772), 162–4; Charlton, 'New Light', 38.

Table 8.6 Italian *intermezzi* given at the Paris Opéra compared with French works derived from them.[a]

Bouffon works and their Paris première dates.	Opéra Comique: derived operas. None was retained after the merger of 1762.	Comédie-Italienne: derived operas. Square-bracketed works were not retained after the merger of 1762.
La serva padrona: 1 Aug. 1752		*La Servante maîtresse* adapted by Pierre Baurans: 14 Aug. 1754. Held this stage in revivals up to 1937.
Il giocatore: 22 Aug. 1752		[*Baiocco et Serpilla* set to music by Carlo Sodi using their 1729 text: 9 Aug. 1753. (Number of performances uncertain)]
Il maestro di musica: 19 Sept. 1752		*Le Maître de musique* adapted by Pierre Baurans: 31 May 1755. Expanded version: 7 Mar. 1757. Held this stage until 1776.
La donna superba: 19 Dec. 1752		*La Femme orgueilleuse* adapted by Louis Anseaume: 8 Oct. 1759. (24 performances to Dec. 1762)
Tracollo, medico ignorante: 1 May 1753		[*Le Charlatan* by Jacques Lacombe and perhaps Louis-Joseph Francœur: 17 Nov. 1756. A completely new libretto was written. (6 performances)]
Il cinese rimpatriato: 19 June 1753	*Le Chinois poli en France* adapted by Louis Anseaume: 20 July 1754.	*Les Chinois* adapted by Jacques-André Naigeon and C.-S. Favart: 18 March 1756 (73 performances, the last in 1764).
La zingara: 19 June 1753	*La Bohémienne* adapted by Moustou: 14 July 1755.	*La Bohémienne* adapted by C.-S. Favart and Charles-François Clément: 28 July 1755. Held this stage until 1774.[b]
Il paratajo: 23 Sept. 1753		[*La Pipée* adapted by Charles-François Clément: 19 Jan. 1756. (16 performances, all in 1756)]
Bertoldo in corte: 9 Nov. 1753	*Bertholde à la ville* adapted by Anseaume and Pierre-Augustin de Marcouville: 9 March 1754.	*Le Caprice amoureux, ou Ninette à la cour* adapted by C.-S. Favart: 12 Feb. 1755, rev. in 2 acts, 8 Mar. 1756. Held this stage until 1774.

[a] Table 8.6 omits Bouffon works that were not adapted; for further details, see *OAR*, 237–8.
[b] Revived 38 times at the Théâtre des Jeunes Artistes in the 1790s: Kennedy, *Theatre, Opera, and Audiences*, 158.

of popular opera. At first, *vaudeville*-based pieces imported Italian music from *intermezzi*; then in hybrid operas, whole *intermezzi* were translated into French and adapted in various ways, some being fitted with *ariettes* taken from completely unrelated Italian sources, obtained by methods that remain unknown today. Both rival theatres did this.

Of the rival adaptations made of *Il cinese rimpatriato*, *La zingara* and *Bertoldo in corte*, Favart's proved in each case the more durable. Table 8.6 reveals, however, the alacrity with which both troupes responded in 1754: the Fair theatre produced *Bertholde à la ville* in March and *Le Chinois poli* in July, while the Comédie-Italienne produced *La Servante maîtresse* in August. Italian music, now a necessity, was something this company could deal with: *parodies*, their permitted musical genre, could be made out of any pre-existing work. Thus, the Comédie-Italienne was reported by d'Argenson in 1755 as proposing 'to give, little by little, every piece from the Bouffon repertory, and the company is making this its speciality'.[50] By far the most successful adaptation was that of Pierre Baurans, *La Servante maîtresse*, which held the stage for over 180 years.[51] Neither this nor Baurans' *Le Maître de musique* was challenged by a rival adaptation.

Overall, however, there was coalescence, along with competition. As Table 8.7 shows, the Comédie-Italienne was quietly permitted to premiere four popular operas not having any connection with a pre-existing opera: *Le Quiproquo*, *Le Prétendu*, *Mazet* and *Les Deux amies*.[52] Moreover, two of these trespassed on territory hitherto monopolised by the Opéra Comique, since *Le Quiproquo* and *Mazet* were based on La Fontaine's Tales. *Mazet*, furthermore, was written and composed by none other than Louis Anseaume and Egidio Duni, both established Opéra Comique artists. A further sign of coalescence was the inclusion of C.-S. Favart as a co-director of the Opéra Comique in 1758.[53]

The contractual aspect of competition in this final decade is as interesting as the tactical aspect. When Monnet was offered the directorship in 1751, Bernage obviously knew that he had experienced London theatre in the raw. After initial visits to London from 1748, Monnet planned a touring company to appear for a season at the Little Haymarket Theatre. This did not get beyond four performances in November 1749, defeated by anti-French rioters, bad publicity and the withdrawal of his licence. Monnet was bankrupted and placed under guard for a few months, but he was still given 'the liberty of the town'[54] and awarded two benefit performances at Drury Lane: May 1750 and January 1751. He must have attended the second season of Italian operas – comic and serious – at the same Little Haymarket

---

[50] D'Argenson, *Notices* (1725–57), II, 662.
[51] Seen during the 1790s in 353 performances on thirty different stages. Baurans' name remained on the TP of *La Servante maîtresse*, 'Édition conforme à la représentation' (Paris: E. Dentu, 1862).
[52] Derived from *The Merry Wives of Windsor*: Desboulmiers, *Histoire* (1769), VII, 455.
[53] See following and n. 74; Davies, 'Heir to Anacreon', 183–6.
[54] 'Monnet' in *ABDA*, X, 279–83.

Table 8.7 Selected opéras-comiques and *parodies* in the approach to the merger between the Opéra Comique and the Comédie-Italienne in February 1762. All works here, except those asterisked, were taken into the post-merger repertory.

Comédie-Italienne	Opéra Comique
1750s	**1750s**
C. S. Favart: *Les Amants inquiets*, 9/3/1751*	Vadé: *Le Suffisant*, 12/3/1753
C. S. Favart: *Les Indes dansantes*, 26/7/1751*	Vadé, Dauvergne: *Les Troqueurs*, 30/7/1753
C. S. Favart: *Les Amours champêtres*, 2/9/1751*	Vadé: *Le Trompeur trompé*, 18/2/1754
C. S. Favart, Marcouville: *Fanfale*, 8/3/1752*	Anseaume, Marcouville: *Bertholde à la ville*, 9/3/1754*
Gondot: *Les Bergers de qualité*, 5/6/1752*	Anseaume: *Le Chinois poli en France*, 20/7/1754*
C. S. Favart: *Tircis et Doristée*, 4/9/1752*	Vadé: *Jérôme et Fanchonnette*, 18/2/1755*
C. S. Favart: *Raton et Rosette*, 24/3/1753	Moustou: *La Bohémienne*, 14/7/1755*
M.-J. Favart, Harny de Guerville: *Les Amours de Bastien et Bastienne*, 4/8/1753	Vadé: *Les Racoleurs*, 11/3/1756
Baurans: *La servante maîtresse*, 14/8/1754	Sedaine, Baurans: *Le Diable à quatre*, 19/8/1756
C. S. Favart: *Le Caprice amoureux ou Ninette à la cour*, 12/2/1755	Anseaume, Duni: *Le Peintre amoureux de son modèle*, 26/7/1757
Baurans, *Le Maître de musique*, 31/5/1755	Anseaume, Lourdet de Santerre, Duni, Laruette: *Le Docteur Sangrado*, 13/2/1758
C. S. Favart: *La Bohémienne*, 28/7/1755	Anseaume, Marcouville, Laruette: *Le Médecin de l'amour*, 22/9/1758*
Naigeon, C. S. Favart: *Le Chinois*, 18/3/1756	La Ribadière, Monsigny: *Les Aveux indiscrets*, 7/2/1759
C. S. Favart, M. J. Favart, Guérin de Frémicourt, Harny de Guerville: *Les Ensorcelés*, 1/9/1757	Anseaume, Laruette, Duni: *Cendrillon*, 20/2/1759
Favart, Duni: *La Fille mal gardée*, 4/3/1758	Sedaine, Philidor: *Blaise le savetier*, 9/3/1759
C. S. Favart: *La Soirée des boulevards*, 13/11/1758	Vadé, Anseaume, Duni: *La Veuve indécise*, 24/9/1759
1760s	**1760s**
Moustou, Philidor: *Le Quiproquo ou Le volage fixé*, 6/3/1760 *	Lemonnier, Monsigny: *Le Maître en droit*, 13 (or 23)/2/1760
M. J. Favart, Bertrand: *La Fortune au village*, 8/10/1760	Anseaume, Serrière, Philidor: *Le Soldat magicien*, 14/8/1760
A.-F. Riccoboni, Gaviniès: *Le Prétendu*, 6/11/1760	Sedaine, Philidor: *Le Jardinier et son seigneur*, 18/2/1761
Anseaume, Marcouville, Bertin d'Antilly, Duni: *L'Isle des foux*, 29/12/1760°	Lemonnier, Monsigny: *Le Cadi dupé*, 4/2/1761
Anseaume, Duni: *Mazet*, 24/9/1761	Harny de Guerville, C. G. Alexandre: *Georget et Georgette*, 28/7/1761
A. Bret, J. Papavoine: *Les Deux amies ou Le vieux coquet*, 5/12/1761*	Quétant, Anseaume, Philidor: *Le Maréchal ferrant*, 22/8/1761
	Sedaine, Monsigny: *On ne s'avise jamais de tout*, 14/9/1761

Ø A *parodie* of Goldoni's *dramma giocoso*, *L'arcifanfano, re de' matti* (1749).

Theatre, given by G. F. Croza's company in 1749–50. *La serva padrona* was seen here for the first time in England. And he could have studied British composers' responses to the two Croza seasons, both at Drury Lane: Thomas Arne's *Don Saverio* in February 1750 and Charles Burney's *Robin Hood* the following December.[55] These pioneering comic operas ('burlettas') cannot fail to have suggested his own future commissions in response to the Bouffons' programmes in Paris.

All the more interesting, then, is a phrase in Monnet's 1751 contract which was not previously part of the definition of an 'opéra-comique'. After 'vaudevilles, danses, machines, décorations, simphonies' we find the added phrase 'morceaux de chants' (i.e. *airs* or *ariettes*, possibly duets).[56] Following Monnet's London experiences and Favart's first three new *parodies* (Table 8.7), it was agreed that vocal music without particular limits would be allowed at the independent theatre. Cultural politics were to test the practical scope of this contract.

As mentioned in Chapter 7, Monnet discovered an author of exceptional originality in Jean-Joseph Vadé (1719–57). Then he found a composer, Antoine Dauvergne (1713–97), who had absorbed every necessary detail from Bouffon works because he led the Opéra orchestra that accompanied them. *Les Troqueurs* was Vadé and Dauvergne's equivalent of a London burletta, complete with recitatives.[57] While it was being rehearsed secretly, Monnet circulated the rumour that it was by an Italian composer in Vienna.[58] Because Italian singers were still actively making history at the Opéra, Monnet's strategy was indeed audacious; and *Les Troqueurs* rewarded him with instant success in July 1753. Presumably because of those recitatives, Monnet recalled, 'tacit permission' needed to be given by Bernage's office in the Town Hall where the Opéra was administered.[59] As a consequence of its extreme popularity, the Opéra then retracted permission for *Les Troqueurs* at the next summer Fair.[60]

---

[55] *OAR*, 245–9; King and Willaert, 'Giovanni Francesco Crosa'.

[56] Monnet's 1751 conditions are specified in Julien Corby's contract with Rebel and Francœur dated 4 January 1758: AN, Minutier central, ET XXXV, 694, f°.1, discovered by Julia Doe.

[57] Dratwicki, *Dauvergne*, 158–61. After this and *La Coquette trompée* pressure seems to have been placed on Dauvergne not to continue writing comedy. This was a blow, because none of his serious operas was outstanding except *Énée et Lavinie* (1758).

[58] Monnet, *Mémoires* (1772), 174–5. Evidence for the secrecy: AN, O^1 2993, bifolium signed by Francœur headed '1753/Menus/fontainebleau' reimbursing one M. Godard, 'musicien qui a repetté pour M. Jeliote a Paris [...] Et chez M. De Curys *la coquette fixée* et *Les Troqueurs*'.

[59] Monnet, ibid., 182.

[60] Order dated 14 August 1754 recorded in 'Inventaire des papiers et pièces déposées au Greffe de la Ville': F-Po, Ms. Arch.18 (25), 64.

In the aftermath of the Bouffons, Monsigny seems to have offered the Opéra a new comedy: newly unearthed reports claim that he offered it *Les Aveux indiscrets*, based on a La Fontaine Tale.[61] Perhaps it was even commissioned. At any rate the score contains recitatives and mingles Italianate *intermezzo*-like pieces with 'characteristics peculiar to the French tradition such as *petits airs*, a final *divertissement* and dialogue arias'.[62] Shorn of its recitatives, it reached the popular stage in 1759, as Table 8.7 shows. Perhaps the Opéra Comique was refused permission to put it on earlier, or perhaps Monnet thought the libretto too inferior.

Monnet's next two innovations changed the direction of popular opera once and for all. He persuaded Sedaine to write for the stage and encouraged Duni to move to France and develop his long-standing interest in opéra-comique: see Chapter 11.

An accelerated form of competition ensued under the Opéra Comique's next management, but now the Opéra was very nervous. Julien Corby and his associates signed their contract with Rebel and Francœur, incoming *directeurs* of the Opéra, on 4 January 1758. It seems actually more restrictive than Monnet's had been: *written* permission from these officials would be needed before the Opéra Comique could show 'pieces in one or more acts that form continuous works of music such as *Les Troqueurs* and others of similar nature'.[63]

The contract also revealed the desperate opposition of the Opéra's directors to any merger of the smaller theatres, following which it stood to lose its income from the Fairs. Rebel and Francœur bound the signatories 'to prevent on one hand the merging of the Comédie-Italienne with the Opéra Comique and on the other the introduction of *intermezzi* or Italian operas on the stage of the Opéra Comique', and to prevent invitations to performing artists from Italy.[64] Equally significant is the fact that Favart was one of the contract's four signatories and would be working on

---

[61] 'This one-act piece had been written in verse and set to music four years ago because it was destined, as we said before, for the Opéra': *Affiches de Province*, 14 Mar. 1759, 44. The same assertion in *ibid.*, 21 Feb. A note in the libretto (Paris: Michel Lambert, 1759), [iii] simply testifies that Monsigny 'desired [in publication] to retain the recitatives just as they were'.

[62] Michel Noiray, 'Monsigny, Pierre-Alexandre', *NGO*, III, 438.

[63] AN, Minutier central XXXV, 694, f°. 3. Monnet wrongly recorded that Corby could stage 'any type of [comic] opera that he judged appropriate': *Mémoires* (1772), 182. In 1757 Bernage had been replaced as the Opéra's *Directeur*. Rebel and Francœur, *directeurs* and composers, now controlled programming as well as finance: *OAR* 58–9; Wood & Sadler, *French Baroque Opera*, 22–3.

[64] AN, *ibid.*. After this, to help the CI, Joseph Caillot returned from Parma: see p. 246.

programme planning: see following. He had been suspected of strengthening his hand as early as November 1754, when d'Argenson noted:

They talk of sending the Italian actors back; the Opéra Comique would replace them during the Fairs. [...] Ten years ago the Comédies Française and Italienne expelled the Opéra Comique, today this Opéra Comique will hound out the Italians and take over their ballets; so all is governed by the court [...]. Dlle Favart and her husband are in league with Monnet [...] for this operation.[65]

At the very same moment, Chevrier noted this rumour too: '[We should] negate the malign intentions of certain persons who would suppress the Italian Theatre to substitute a permanent Opéra Comique. That absurd plan is an excessive affront to the Nation and its pleasures, and I would never have raised it; yet one must correct small minds.'[66]

The Opéra, for its part, was at such a low point that it believed that popular opera might threaten its survival: that Italian music and new styles had taken irrevocable hold. This fear, expressed in this contract, even antedated popular operas by Monsigny and Philidor. But radical arguments and opinions were in circulation. D'Alembert shocked some members present at the Académie Française when he denigrated traditional French operas as tasteless 'plainchant'; others, however, applauded.[67] A pamphlet in the following year contained these lines:

I am very opposed to the feelings of those who would abolish our Opéra because its music is less good than that of the Italian Operas [now in hybrid form]. It brings together other attractions that make up for the feebleness of its music.[68]

Creating a Repertory

We return in conclusion to patterns of revival and the question of whether the Fair theatres were concerned with 'canonic' pieces that had the status of favourites, if not 'classics'. Table 8.8 shows the long-term success achieved by twenty operas created during the final decade of competition. For the definitive selection of repertory after the merger of the companies, a process of trial and error continued during the months following 3 February 1762.[69] Vadé's best *vaudeville* works as well as some composed

---

[65] D'Argenson, *Journal*, VIII, 367, 8 Nov. 1754.
[66] Chevrier, *Observations* (1755), 56–7, read by censor Crébillon on 28 December 1754.
[67] Fréron, *AL*, 1760/6 (10 September), 174.   [68] Lebeau de Schosne, *Lettre* (1761), 29.
[69] Wild*TOC*, 33–7.

Table 8.8 Long-lived works created in the final decade of Fair theatre, ordered by the number of years in which they were viable. From 1762 to January 1791 these were seen at the Comédie-Italienne / Opéra-Comique and thereafter sometimes at other theatres as well. Pieces in Table 8.6 are not included.

1761–1815	*Le Tonnelier* (Audinot, Quétant) + 7 other theatres from 1791
1761–1802	*Le Maréchal-ferrant* (Anseaume, Quétant & Philidor)
1752–93	*Le Poirier* (Vadé) + Ambigu-Comique
1756–94	*Les Racoleurs* (Vadé) + 5 other theatres from 1791
1756–94	*Nicaise* (Vadé) + 6 other theatres from 1791
1760–95	*Le Soldat magicien* (Anseaume, Serrière & Philidor)
1757–92	*Le Peintre amoureux de son modèle* (Anseaume & Duni) + Ambigu-Comique
1759–93	*La Veuve indécise* (Vadé, Anseaume & Duni) + Ambigu-Comique
1761–92	*Georget et Georgette* (Harny de Guerville & Alexandre) + Ambigu-Comique
1761–92	*On ne s'avise jamais de tout* (Sedaine & Monsigny) + Théâtre Molière
1753–83	*Les Troqueurs* (Vadé & Dauvergne) + Théâtre de la Cité
1760–90	*Le Maître en droit* (Lemonnier & Monsigny)
1761–90	*Le Cadi dupé* (Lemonnier & Monsigny)
1761–89	*Le Jardinier et son seigneur* (Sedaine & Philidor)
1759–85	*Blaise le savetier* (Sedaine & Philidor)
1758–83	*Le Médecin de l'amour* (Anseaume, Marcouville & Laruette)
1758–82	*Gilles, garçon-peintre* (Poinsinet & Laborde)
1756–76	*Le Diable à quatre* (Sedaine; recast with music by G. Porta, 1790–93) + Théâtre des Variétés-Amusantes
1759–79	*Les Aveux indiscrets* (La Ribadière & Monsigny)
1758–65	*Le Docteur Sangrado* (Anseaume, Lourdet de Santerre & Duni & Laruette).

by Duni or Philidor still held the boards during the Revolution. Table 8.8 can also be compared with Table 8.5, showing Favart's long-term successes, and Table 8.6, documenting the longevity of certain hybrid operas based on *intermezzi*.

But what was the nature of revivals, overall? For an overview, Table 8.9 summarises proportions between new and revived works given at the Fair theatres between 1714 and 1740. Revived operas were always a feature of Fair theatre, probably entailing changes. For example, *Le Festin de pierre*, Letellier's Don Juan drama (Table 8.3), was revived twice and survives in three different manuscript versions.[70] Lack of publication was no impediment to a good piece of work. Conversely, there seems to be no correlation between a work's inclusion in *Le Théâtre de la Foire* and its likelihood of revival (always admitting that complete revival information is impossible). One apparent correlation, however, is that the longest-lived works in *TF* originated during the first period, 1714

---

[70] Martin, 'Un *Dom Juan*'.

Table 8.9 All known records of musical comedies at the Fair theatres, including marionette operas and *parodies* with music, but not ballets. Figures are provisional. FSG = Winter season. FSL = Summer season. No performances occurred in 1719.

Years (inclusive)	Approximate number of new works: FSG	Approximate number of new works: FSL	Currently known revivals: FSG	Currently known revivals: FSL
1714–1718	31	29	9	3
1720–1725	29	47	6	10
1726–1730	19 (no operas in given in 1727–28)	37	6	6
1731–1735	30 (no operas in 1732)	48	11	10
1736–1740	43	47	10	9

to 1718, published in volumes I to III. Yet not everything in these volumes is known to have been reprised: neither *Arlequin Hulla, Le Temple du Destin* nor *Le Temple de l'Ennuy*.

To counteract incompleteness of information, Table 8.9 includes all known records of musical comedies, including marionette theatre. This might lessen the fragility of conclusions. We have no access to day-by-day performance totals, only to evidence that a particular work was revived in a given season.

Revivals within the period 1714 to 1718 include Fuzelier's *La Matrone d'Éphèse* (revived twice or three times), his *Le Pharaon* and also *Pierrot furieux*, 'often repeated', according to Fuzelier's manuscript notes.[71] Seven longer-lived pieces from this first period are shown in Table 8.10.

Under the leadership of Boizard de Pontau in the 1730s favourite scenes could also be programmed as repeats, their details as yet unknown.[72] Other operas which were repeated have been seen in Table 8.1. Lost records of performance for the 1730s should concern us when it comes to *Achmet et Almanzine* (1728) and *Les Pèlerins de la Mecque* (1726), which Desfontaines had singled out for exceptional mention in 1741 (it was also the basis of Gluck's opéra-comique in 1764).[73] Similarly, *La Reine du Barostan* (1730) must have been revived more than the single time affirmed

---

[71] Fuzelier, 'Nouveaux mémoires sur les Spectacles de la Foire', in Cucuel, 'Sources et documents', 255.
[72] 'Several episodic scenes were added [in 1737] which had been successful in earlier Fairs': Parfaict, *Mémoires* (1743), II, 126.
[73] *Les Pèlerins de la Mecque ou La rencontre imprévue*: Brown, *Gluck*, 407–24; Betzwieser, *Exotismus*, 274–84.

Table 8.10 First-period works revived during the 1720s and 1730s, showing original and revival years.

Le Tombeau de Nostradamus (Lesage: 1714/15/21/33)
L'École des amants (Lesage, Fuzelier: 1716/21/26/32)
Le Monde renversé (Lesage, d'Orneval, La Font: 1718/25/31)[a]
Les Funérailles de la Foire (Lesage, d'Orneval, Fuzelier: 1718/21/25/34)
Les Amours de Nanterre (Lesage, d'Orneval, Autreau: 1718/21/31/43/52/55)
L'Isle des Amazones (Lesage, d'Orneval: 1720 [deferred from 1718], 1727/31)
La Statue merveilleuse (Lesage, d'Orneval, Fuzelier: 1720 [deferred from 1719], 1734; rev. as *Le Miroir magique*, 1752)

[a] Also Table 8.4: rev. 1753 by Anseaume. See Brown, 'Christoph Willibald Gluck', 410–23, Barnes, '*Théâtre de la Foire*', 209, Connon, 'Music in the Parisian Fair Theatres', 131.

Table 8.11 Apparent reversal of the ratio between new operas and revived operas at the Fair theatres up to the point of closure in mid-1745.

Year (both FSG and FSL)	New opéras comiques	Currently known revivals
1740	14	0
1741	12	5
1742	11	11
1743	9	15
1744	9	13
1745 (FSG only)	4	6

by Carmody (1734) because we know from the *Mercure* of two revivals in the 1740s and others between 1750 and 1760.

A more radical change of pattern then seemed to occur: see Table 8.11. The ratio of new to revived pieces, year on year, went into reverse. Is this a false observation owing simply to a change in press reporting or the fact that Parfaict's *Mémoires* cease with the 1742 season, or might it be true and attributable to the debt crisis outlined earlier? Hitherto, premieres apparently outnumbered revivals, as in Table 8.9. But from 1740 fewer and fewer new pieces seem to have been matched by more and more revived titles, so that finally there were more of the latter than of the former. This policy, if it was one, cannot be laid at the door of a single entrepreneur since Pontau did not resign until Easter 1743 and his successor Monnet was in the post for only one year.

Table 8.12 Most-frequently revived operas between 1740 and summer 1745. 'Revival' totals refer to the number of seasons in which revival occurred, 'season' meaning a single FSG or FSL.

Favart: *La Chercheuse d'esprit*: premiere 1741 + 5 revivals
Favart: *La Servante justifiée*: premiere 1740 + 3 revivals
Favart: *Les Bateliers de Saint-Cloud*: premiere 1741 + 3 revivals
Favart: *Les Jeunes mariés*: premiere 1740 + 3 revivals
Piron: *Les Jardins de l'Hymen ou La Rose* (1726 but banned): 3 revivals
Pannard: *Le Magazin des modernes* (1736): 2 revivals
Gallet: *Les Coffres / Les Témoins contre eux-mêmes* (1736): 2 revivals
Pannard: *La Fausse ridicule* (1731): 2 revivals
Pannard: *Le Fossé du scrupule/Le Saut du fossé* (1738): 3 revivals
Lesage, d'Orneval: *La Reine du Barostan* (1730): 2 revivals
Pannard: *Pygmalion* (1735): 2 revivals

Only in particular senses does Table 8.11, on analysis, reveal a pattern of repeatable works, an incipient 'core'. This period – 1740 to summer 1745 – contains eleven seasons. If we focus on what was revived in them, to the limits of current knowledge, we find that thirty-five separate titles are involved. Of these, fourteen were entirely or partly the work of Pannard: this was the heyday of his popularity. A further ten revived operas were by Favart. Lesage and d'Orneval were represented by revivals of *Les Amours de Nanterre*, *La Reine du Barostan* and *Achmet et Almanzine*.

But of course, some works were seen more than others; although we lack individual performance figures, we can at least know of some preferred works: see Table 8.12. Because four of these preferred operas were also given their premiere during this period (Favart's *La Chercheuse d'esprit*, *La Servante justifiée*, *Les Bateliers de Saint-Cloud* and *Les Jeunes mariés*) we may claim that these were probably the most frequently seen operas of the period.

Thinking of the longer-term perspective, we can identify other operas which were revived at least once each in the 1740s, and which we have already seen as durable: *Les Amours de Nanterre* (1718), *Achmet et Almanzine* (see Table 8.3) and Pannard's *La Tante rivale* (see Table 8.1).

All this does not necessarily explain the apparently changing ratio of revivals to premieres in the 1740s. Perhaps Pontau's financial straits simply discouraged new writers from coming forward, upon guessing or discovering that he was not covering his existing liabilities. Drouin produced *La Meunière de qualité* but no others; Pierre Rousseau wrote *La Coquette sans le savoir* but no others (Favart revised it); *La Gageure* is by Pannard; and *Marotte, parodie* of *Mérope*, united four authors including Pontau and Pannard.

*

Table 8.13 Ratio of new to revived operas between 1752 and 1762. A 'revival' signifies any given opera revived in any one given season, defined as a single FSG or FSL.

1752–1756	FSG	New operas: 18	Revivals : (at least) 32
1752–1756	FSL	New operas: 26	Revivals : (at least) 35
1757–1761	FSG	New operas: 19	Revivals : (at least) 29
1757–1761	FSL	New operas: 29	Revivals : (at least) 28

During the last decade of Fair theatre a coincident expansion began in the publication of French journals. New sources relevant to us are the *Affiches de province* and *Affiches de Paris* (see note 12). Only in 1752 and 1753 do they add significantly to the *Mercure*'s record, but fortunately the new data concern revivals. This corroborates the supposition that Fair theatre revivals had never been adequately recorded.

In 1753 overall, summer and winter together, there were twelve new operas but as many as eighteen or more revivals. Each of the two fairs saw nine revived operas. These figures should probably be a benchmark guide for this decade, because without the *Affiches* information only six revivals would be known of. Usefully, perhaps, this ratio of new to revived operas, two to three, closely reproduces that observed in Table 8.11 for the years 1743–5. Five-year summaries are set out in Table 8.13: it shows a 2:3 ratio at the winter Fair until 1761, but then a matching of totals for premieres and revivals at the summer Fair during the last quinquennium. This is significant inasmuch as on 5 January 1758 Favart signed a different contract with Moët and Corby that presents us with the first documentary evidence that a policy of revivals was in existence.

[Favart] will choose the new pieces [...] and make selection from those older ones which will be needed to act as fillers. He will correct and improve works from both categories and will encourage their authors; he will instigate rehearsals and train new actors [...] [and] in the month after each Fair has closed he will present a programme and plan of those pieces which he hopes shall be given at the next one.[74]

He was paid as an artistic manager, not a writer, and in fact did not offer any significant works to the Opéra Comique in its last four years.[75]

---

[74] The fee was 4,000 *livres* per annum: AN, Minutier central LXXXIII, 455, cited in Marcetteau-Paul, 'Les Théâtres des Foires', 145–6; terms reiterated on 12 November 1758: F-Po, Fonds Favart, Carton I (11), f° 2ʳ, Art. 8.

[75] *La Parodie au Parnasse* (1759) was just a topical review; *La Bal bourgeois* (1761) added ariettes to the 1738 original (Favart, *Mémoires*, I, 176–7). Before 1758 Favart's works at the OC also consisted of revivals, notably *Les Nymphes de Diane*.

Table 8.14 Revivals of older works between 1752 and 1762 ordered by period of origin, with indication of the number of seasons in which they were revived during the final decade. The revival of 1740s works was seen in Tables 8.4 and 8.5.

1714–18	
Les Amours de Nanterre, Lesage and d'Orneval	3 seasons
La Statue merveilleuse, Lesage and d'Orneval	3
Le Monde renversé, Lesage and d'Orneval	2
1720s	
Les Jardins de l'Hymen, ou La Rose, Piron	6
Le Caprice, Piron	1
La Pénélope moderne, Lesage and Fuzelier	1
1730s	
Le Magazin des modernes, Pannard	3
La Reine du Barostan, Lesage and d'Orneval	2
Le Bal bourgeois, Favart	2
La Répétition interrompue, Pannard, rev. Favart	2
La Fausse ridicule, Pannard, Fagan	1
Le Nouvelliste dupé, Pannard	1

Which, in this turbulent decade, were the operas from before 1740 that still earned revival for a new generation? The sum of present knowledge is found in Table 8.14: twelve titles, mostly encountered in this chapter already. Apparent newcomers were Piron's *Le Caprice* and Lesage and d'Orneval's *La Pénélope moderne*.

Future research might well be directed towards understanding more about updated versions of older pieces, as noted earlier in relation to Moulinghen. Very revealing notes on the historic revival of *Les Amours de Nanterre* were published by Jacques Fleury.

The author of the Prologue [*Le Retour favorable*, 3 February 1752] was also responsible for the numerous changes made to *Les Amours de Nanterre*; this piece, attributed to Monsieur Autreau but printed under the names of MM. Lesage and d'Orneval [...] has always been regarded as a masterpiece of its genre.

But to make it more perfect, or (better) more in agreement with the taste of the times, [I] have removed all the dialogue as well as a proportion of the old *vaudevilles*. In order to rejuvenate the whole, over sixty new *couplets* have been fitted to the best modern *airs* so that today we have an almost new work upon an old, reformed, plan.

It having been successful in a long sequence of performances, we should willingly have had it printed together with the Prologue, had we not feared to displease Monsieur d'Orneval by taking advantage of a treasure over which he and his deceased colleagues shall always have an original and incontestable right of possession.[76]

---

[76] 'Avertissement', *Le Retour favorable* (Paris: Vve Delormel & Fils, 1752), iii–iv.

Fleury also detailed his revisions in 1752 to *Le Miroir magique* (formerly *La Statue merveilleuse*). When rewriting *Le Monde renversé* (April 1753), Anseaume added new *airs* but avoided Italian music; see p. 215, note 29. A revival of *Les Pèlerins de la Mecque* in 1758 included music by Philidor; following this experiment, Julien Corby commissioned the composer to set *Blaise le savetier* (see Table 8.7).[77]

Two sentences found in the *Mercure*'s theatre coverage allude to the policy of selecting operas for revival, and their wording also suggests an emergent form of 'canon'.

October 1759: The public is very satisfied with the care taken to provide variety at this theatre, and to support new works by those older pieces ['Piéces anciennes'] which have been the most appreciated.

March 1761: [The return of Mlle Rosaline] has occasioned the return of several pieces in the older genre ['de l'ancien genre'] which the public has seen again with satisfaction and which it might see there again with pleasure; this genre would seem the most naturally appropriate to this theatre.[78]

Yet Fleury's foregoing evidence compels caution. As with revivals of Lully's operas between 1745 and 1775 which included less and less of that composer's original music, so perhaps popular operas upon revival changed gradually to the same extent.[79]

*

Having juxtaposed institutions and performances in this chapter, we find once again an incomplete historical record. The surest conclusion is that the Opéra Comique ('Théâtre du Fauxbourg Saint-Germain' as Favart called it)[80] was so maturely successful by 1745 that it was suppressed by rival players using unverified arguments, perhaps assisted by the politics of Mme Du Boccage's *Lettre de Madame* +++. As the crisis festered, popular opera went on stage at the Paris Opéra late in 1744. This was not, as in the 1720s, by invitation of the Orléans family, but a prefiguration of the Bouffons eight years later. Both events were brought about by Opéra *directeurs*: Berger in 1744 and Bernage de Saint-Maurice in 1752. For the

---

[77] Laborde, *Essai* (1780), III, 463.
[78] *Mercure*, 1759, Oct./1, 197; *ibid.*, 1761, March, 197. Rosaline was also appearing in *Bertholde à la ville* and *Le Diable à quatre*.
[79] 'What we preserve mainly from Lully's works are the recitatives', as claimed by M. P. G. de Chabanon in *Mercure*, 1773, Jan., 175: see *OAR*, 85–9.
[80] Title pages to *Le Prix de Cythère* (Paris: Clément, 1742), *Le Cocq de village* (Paris: Prault fils, 1743), *Acajou* (Paris: Prault fils, 1744).

Opéra, whose own debt crisis occurred in 1749,[81] the resumption of the Opéra Comique was initially to be welcomed. But the success of the hybrid operas seen in Table 8.6 proved an embarrassment: thanks to their arrangers and singers, the Comédie-Italienne and Opéra Comique profited enormously from Italian music. Taste changed, and a new style of opéra-comique evolved; too late, the Opéra blocked further Italian importations.

A maturity is apparent in the long-lasting status of certain titles; Tables 8.4, 8.5 and 8.14 demonstrate a *de facto* popular repertory. Its existence is unfamiliar, for no recent edition of *Les Amours de Nanterre* has been offered in book form – a work played often and then reworked for the long-anticipated first night in 1752.[82] Popular opera was well aware of its own history, and that awareness would be codified during the 1750s into programming policy. Another type of maturity will be seen in Chapter 9: new roles for new music and some lengthy, virtuosic borrowings from instrumental pieces.

---

[81] Sadler, *Rameau Compendium*, 211–12; *OAR*, 4, 68; Charlton, 'New Light', 38–9.
[82] However, it is found on *Théâtre Classique*: www.theatre-classique.fr (16 Aug. 2020).

9 | Musical Expansion

Overview

'One could ask whether opera exists outside the performance that creates it,'[1] yet when we have sufficient music and text to judge, popular opera comes vicariously alive in imagination. But present conclusions cannot depend on an understanding of progression or on knowing the true internal balance between old and new music. This chapter therefore describes method as well as matter: methods by which old and new musics were made to work together at a time when musical fashion evolved radically. The obsession of the 1730s was for dance and its music, and in Chapter 7 we saw the economic price that opéra-comique paid for trying to negotiate with dance on its own terms. Musical progress as imagined by Favart would consist of change from within. His performative techniques were studied in Chapter 5, and in this chapter we study how it was possible for him to go 'beyond *vaudevilles*', edging the expressive emphasis towards music.

Originally, music was no more important than text, and a good *vaudeville* demanded cleverly turned verse. Quite how extreme that polish could be is shown by an answer sung in the one-act entertainment called *L'Espérance* (*Hope*). A lawyer visits Hope to plead on behalf of prisoners held in Paris.[2] He claims she has broken her

---

[1] Abbate, *In Search of Opera*, ix.
[2] FSL, 1730: *TF* VIII, 318 (R/II/368). Lesage, d'Orneval and Fuzelier wrote a series of scenes linked by the figure of Hope.

word by telling them repeatedly, 'Your woes will end; you will be released tomorrow'. She sings in reply:

Air: 'Nous autres bons Villageois'

Demain est un jour qui suit	*Tomorrow* is a day that stays
Lorsque vous croyez qu'il s'avance:	Behind, when you think it ahead:
Au milieu de chaque nuit,	In the middle of each night, its
Il perd son nom dans sa naissance:	Name is lost when it is born:
Quand on croit se saisir de lui,	Just when you think you have it held
On trouve que c'est aujourd'hui.	You find that it becomes today.
Jusqu'à ce jour aucun Humain	The human race has never seen
N'a pû voir arriver *Demain*.[3]	*Tomorrow*: it has never been.

So, to what extent were audiences attuned to music or to text? Perhaps there was an aesthetic mirror of perceptions at the Paris Opéra, which attracted two types of listener. One favoured its dramatic poetry, delivered in recitative or *air*; they tended to oppose modern music and Italian music. The others were once described as 'true Germans [...]. They have nothing but their ears and, instead of thinking that opera is the imitation of some action, they regard it only as a concert.'[4] Music at the Opéra was divided between conversational *scènes* with recitatives and concise *airs*, and *divertissements* affording expansion in dance, chorus and *ariette*. In opéra-comique, *vaudevilles* were like recitative, giving maximum clarity of text, while other forms of music gave contrast. Pieces ended (as at the Opéra) with dance and *divertissement* featuring a particular composer. There is some evidence that dancers could double as chorus singers: in Act I/9 of *Le Claperman* (*The Nightwatchman*) Piron wrote 'Troupe of women who form a circle, singing and dancing' while in Act II/2, where villagers enter, women 'join hands and form a circle' while men 'form a chorus' singing in a verse-and-refrain finale.

Musical sensibility as such seems obvious in the case of Lesage, d'Orneval, Piron, Pannard and Favart. Writers had individual ways of moulding together dialogue, music, subject matter and performers' skills. The overall picture in Table 9.1 (online) shows basic aspects of musical focus: composers, dances, choruses, cantatas or *cantatilles*. Ceremony and *divertissement* are sometimes found in Lesage and d'Orneval's 'royal

---

[3] Sc. 5: *TF* VIII, 334 (R/II/372). [4] Mably, *Lettres* (1741), 137.

operas'; Piron's *L'Endriague* included two group scenes with Rameau's music.[5] Pannard included group scenes in *L'Impromptu du Pont-Neuf* (*An Impromptu for the Pont-Neuf*) which celebrated the Dauphin's birth in 1729. Resources permitting, dance and ceremony were no strangers to popular opera.

Musical ambitions during the first period of activity, 1714–18, included the commissioning of several cantatas. This practice barely outlasted these years, but an impressive number of composers wrote for the Fairs during the next three decades. Tables 9.1 and 9.2 name fifteen who were involved, including Elisabeth Jacquet de La Guerre and Louis de Lacoste who had already written for the Opéra, and future opera composers like Royer, Rameau and Aubert. We find both familiar and unfamiliar names and a large discrepancy between Gillier's total and those of others.[6] Using his surviving music as a guide we can imagine generous amounts of now-lost music by others, inasmuch as his duet concluding *L'Espérance*, for example, extends to 102 bars.[7]

Table 9.2 Named composers in Fair theatre pieces, ordered by number of works to which identified contributions were made.

Jean-Claude Gillier	79 works[8]
Michel Corrette	8
L'Abbé	6
Jacques Aubert	5
Jean-Philippe Rameau	4
La Croix	3
Pancrace Royer	2
Brou	2
Voisin	2

The following composers were credited with writing for only one opera each: Louis Derochet, Louis-Antoine Dornel, Jacquet de La Guerre, Lacoste, Raillard, Louis-Antoine Travenol.

---

[5] Acts I/7 and II/1: Lurcel, *Théâtre de la Foire*, 449–50, 453–6.
[6] 'Airs [...] de Mr. Gillier' are grouped in *TF* IX, *Table*, 54ff (R/II/550–3). A useful overview: Cook, *Duet and Ensemble*, 34–48; Barnes includes 1750s composers in '*Théâtre de la Foire*', 268–336, 389–447.
[7] Air 139, 'Chantons, chantons, l'agriable *Espérance*!': *TF* VIII, 364–6 and *Table*, 57–60 (R/II/379, 394–5).
[8] Stilwell, 'Gillier', *MGG*, Personenteil, VII, 963–7.

The First Period, 1714–18

Chapter 8 pointed out that many pieces from this period, found in volumes I to III of *TF*, were later revived. One sees an emergence of the whole range of opéra-comique's musical functions and tendencies. For their humour and musical suppleness, works of the first period (as edited in *TF*) stand as an enormous achievement. They cannot be reduced to a formula, but specific operas may reveal how a comedic design used music of any provenance, old or new, to build a greater whole.

Discussion of music has traditionally followed a separation between old and new:

> The name of Lesage or Piron generally brings to mind only a series of *vaudevilles* more or less skilfully connected. This is an error: all these comedies contain an original score, almost always witty and charming; but it passes almost unnoticed, because we can know it only imperfectly and because its authors too often remain unknown [...]. This original music appears in the form of a *divertissement* which concludes the drama itself, or its different acts.[9]

The dynamics of *vaudeville* opera in reality depend on a less stringent separation: *vaudevilles* are constantly selected in order to shape or mould scenes, and new music – especially outside the closing sequence – worked closely with borrowed music. The two main operas chosen to illustrate this will be *La Ceinture de Vénus* (*Venus' Girdle*) and *La Princesse de Carizme* (*The Princess of Carizme*).

La Guerre's 'reconciliation' duet in Act I of *La Ceinture* was the first published music in history written for an opéra-comique: 'Raccommodement comique de Pierrot et de Nicole'. She issued it at the end of her *Cantates françoises*, dateable to *c*. 1715. The domestic singing of cantatas had become a pastime by 1706 which Lesage duly burlesqued in *Le Diable boiteux*:

> [Asmodeus:] Prithee laugh with me at the concert begun after a family supper in a citizen's house hard by there. They are singing cantatas [...]. The symphony consists of a cornemuse and a spinet; an old ungainly chorister with a squeaking pipe sings the treble, and a young girl with a very deep voice the bass.[10]

Operas like *La Ceinture de Vénus* appealed to their educated target audience through parallels with mainstream French opera. Two cantatas, for example, had been sung in Campra's phenomenal success, *Les Fêtes*

---

[9] Cucuel, *Les Créateurs*, 30–1.
[10] *The Devil on Two Sticks* (1707), 17 (modified). Jean-Baptiste Morin's pioneering *Cantates françoises* began in 1706: Tunley, *French Cantata*, 50, 231.

vénitiennes (1710).[11] In the Prologue to *Les Eaux de Merlin* (*Merlin's Waters*, 1715) the two forest springs inducing love or hate reflect Quinault and Lully's *Roland* and Angélique's search for similar fountains. The frame for *La Ceinture de Vénus* is pastoral since, in its Prologue, Cupid and Fortune discuss the destiny of the main characters, Arlequin and Mezzetin. In a classical trope, Arlequin is threatening suicide like a lovelorn pastoral shepherd. The pitying gods supply him and Mezzetin with Venus's girdle to attract new lovers, and a self-replenishing purse of gold.

La Guerre's new music in Act I is motivated by the power of the girdle: Mezzetin tests it in Scene 4 on Nicole, walking to a friend's wedding. She is Pierrot's lover, and the experiment ends when Pierrot finds Mezzetin proposing an elopement with her. Nicole and Pierrot argue in a sequence of *vaudevilles* which grows more heated. That sequence is concluded by the argumentative duet and reconciliation composed by La Guerre.[12] As her publication of this duet reveals, it originally had three sections like a miniature cantata.[13] Section one was repeated to a total of eighteen bars, then after a link section came a fifty-nine-bar 'reconciliation'. In the context of *La Ceinture de Vénus* this proved too long: the link was taken out, the first section shortened to thirteen bars and the 'reconciliation' to twenty-six bars. But Lesage was proud to name La Guerre and courteous enough to admit shortening her work.[14] The latter may have been intended to emulate dialogue duets in early *intermezzi*[15] – see Chapter 10 – since La Guerre's chamber cantatas consciously reconciled French and Italian styles.[16]

---

[11] Harris-Warrick, *Dance and Drama*, 251, 253. [12] Cessac, *Jacquet de La Guerre*, 164–8.

[13] 'Le Raccommodement' was issued at the end of La Guerre's *Cantates françoises* (Paris: Baussen [c.1715]). The composer's objection to the Fair version is given in coded terms: a note explaining 'how it was composed'. 'It is for bass and soprano, proving very difficult to perform with an *haute-contre* without spoiling the harmony': David Tunley (ed.), *The Eighteenth-Century French Cantata*, 17 vols. (New York: Garland, 1990), XIII, xi–xii. The original *TF* version is indeed in the *haute-contre* clef, c3, and certain pitches have been altered in consequence. Beagle, 'Théâtres de la Foire', 118–23, studied a later source not using the *haute-contre* clef.

[14] Note on *TF* I, 311 (R/I/84). La Guerre's name also appears by *Air* 176 itself: Table, 55 (R/I/128).

[15] For example, *Melissa contenta*, 1707–8, ed. by F. Menchelli-Buttini in *Tre Intermezzi* (Drammaturgia Musicale Veneta, 10)(Milan: Ricordi, 2008).

[16] Tunley, *French Cantata*, 116; Rose, 'Jacquet de La Guerre'.

An outstanding point of interest is obvious when we compare the 'Raccommodement' with its predecessor, the 1681 dialogue duet 'Ne veux-tu pas, Perrette' (Examples 3.1 (a–c)). Indeed La Guerre's music echoes the earlier piece, its concerted section also sounding more French than its dialogue section. But whereas the 1681 duet merely entertained the farm-workers, the 1715 duet is sung by named characters who form part of the main action. It is as essential dramatically as are duets in *intermezzi*, though it might have had extra significance for audiences who had sung it themselves: we know that *La Ceinture* was revived in 1727, at least.

Lesage's tightly organised first act concluded with the rustic wedding of Colette and Lucas. Three stanzas of Gillier's song 'Célébrons l'heureux mariage' were followed by dancing and then the *vaudeville* 'Allons gay'.[17] We cannot tell what dance music was heard: the point is that on a functional level there was no difference between borrowed and new music.

In Act II/3 of *La Ceinture de Vénus* a singing-teacher seeks patronage from Arlequin, who has become a rich *bourgeois*. Gillier contrived two musical jokes when the teacher performs a French song followed by an Italian one.[18] Arlequin's Italian preference sides with the 'titled gentlefolk', so 'I'll leave [French styles] to the *Bourgeois*'.[19] The other joke was to make the 'Italian' song a variant of the first, disguised by a new metre and decorated melody; so the episode satirises both ignorance and humbug.

Table 9.3 summarises new music for earlier operas in *TF*, preserved simply as vocal lines. Lesage must have been confident that purchasers would be able to supply a bass part and accompaniment. These loyal patrons were thanked by him when popular opera was suppressed in 1718: 'Ye high and low! The Opéra Comique must shut up shop for earning the custom of honest people.'[20]

Gillier's cantata 'Le Chasseur Actéon' is sung in the character of a musician who is auditioning to perform at the famous fair. His ensemble is requested to play 'une Sonate' as an introduction, and its music and poetry are serious; indeed a trained singer must be used to sustain five

---

[17] 'Célébrons l'heureux mariage', Air 177, is mistakenly printed in *TF* II, Table, 58 (R/I/258). Music at *TF* I, Table, 58–9 contains part of La Croix's music for *Arlequin traitant*.
[18] Airs 178–9: *TF* II, Table, 58–9 (R/I/258).   [19] *TF* I, 327 (R/I/88).
[20] These lines ended *L'Isle des Amazones* with Gillier's music 'En suivant Bellone', Air 223 (mislabelled 228): *TF* III, 374–6 (R/I/355).

Table 9.3 Set pieces in first-period *TF* operas, with vocal clef indications.

FSL, 1714
La Foire de Guibray (*Guibray Fair*)
Jean-Claude Gillier: (a) 'Au son de ma lyre admirable'; (b) *Cantate*, 'Le Chasseur Actéon'. Both use c4 (tenor) clef.[21]

FSG, 1715
La Ceinture de Vénus
(a) Elisabeth Jacquet de La Guerre: 'Le Raccommodement Comique de Pierrot et de Nicole' with c1 (soprano) and c3 (*haute-contre*) clefs; (b) Gillier: 'Ne me reprochez plus, Cruelle' with c1 clef.[22]

FSG, 1716
Le Temple de l'Ennuy (*The Temple of Boredom*)
Gillier: *Cantate*, 'Puissant Dieu de l'Ennuy' with c3 clef.[23]

FSG, 1717
Le Pharaon (*The Game of Faro*)
Nicolas Bernier: *brunette*, 'Prenez les armes' with c1 clef.[24]

FSL, 1718
Le Monde renversé (*The World Upside Down*)
Gillier: *Air*, 'Heureux qui, soir et matin' with c1 clef.[25]

FSL, 1718
La Princesse de Carizme
(a) Louis de Lacoste: *Air*, 'Un Amant d'abord est tout charmant'; (b) *Ibid.*: *Air*, 'Comme les Dieux'; (c) Gillier, *Air*, 'Cessez de vanter mes charmes', all with c1 clefs.[26]

---

sections alternating recitatives and solos, 108 bars in all.[27] Gillier's later cantata 'Puissant Dieu de l'Ennuy', sung in 1716 to the god of Boredom, is serious musically but humorous textually, and the god cuts it off at the repeat of the third section.

Loyal to French music, the Fair readily mocked Italian artists. In Fuzelier's *Le Pharaon*, Bernier's brief 'Prenez les armes' is burlesqued by Pierrot in role as Mlle Fredoniselli ('fredonner' means 'to hum'), specialist in 'fine long cantatas' and the 'cromatique' style, who presumably ruins the beautiful G-minor melody.

---

[21] *Airs* 171–3: *TF* I, *Table*, 50–2 (R/I/127).

[22] *Airs* 176, 179: *TF* I, *Table*, 55–7 and *TF* II, *Table*, 59 (R/I/128–9 and R/I/258).

[23] *Air* 184: *TF* II, *Table*, 60–1 with last bars at *TF* I, *Table*, 62 (R/I/259 and R/I/130). There are three sections: Introduction, 18 bars; first *Air*, 54 bars; final *Air*, 14 bars.

[24] *Air* 186: *TF* I, *Table*, 63 (R/I/130).   [25] *Air* 209: *TF* III, *Table*, 65–6 (R/I/391–2).

[26] Music: (a) *Air* 157: *TF* III, *Table*, 45 (R/I/386); (b) *Airs* 205, 206: *TF* III, *Table*, 62–3 (R/I/391) (c) *Air* 207: *TF* III, *Table*, 64 (R/I/391): incorrectly labelled as '202' in main text.

[27] Absent from Tunley, *French Cantata*, as are the next cantatas mentioned.

Lesage and Gillier together managed to integrate music and philosophy in the Philosopher's *Air* 'Heureux qui, soir et matin' in *Le Monde renversé*. It even advertised its intention to 'ridicule [*airs*] of certain composers'.[28] Eight-bar strains received first a 'simple' and then a decorated performance, or 'double'. Since we are in a dialectical comedy, the ornate form is decried as worldly, and the plain form exemplifies the superior ideals of Merlin's realm. A dialogue-sequence develops an interesting third joke, namely, that in the reversed world philosophers are all 'dancers, poets and musicians'.[29]

A completely new level of achievement was reached in the *La Princesse de Carizme*, one of the 'royal operas' derived from Arabic and Persian tales. Arlequin became *confidant* of the Prince of Persia.[30] Lacoste had composed four works for the Opéra, so it is interesting that Acts I and III conclude with choral and danced scenes lacking special connection to the main plot. Music elsewhere gave articulation to its presiding themes: love and madness. The newly arrived Prince learns that Princess Zélica's beauty, once seen, drives men insane: their cries, in fragmented *vaudevilles*, issue from towers on stage seen on p. 153. He is fascinated, indeed ignores emotive warnings when music first expresses the jocular madness of an Old Man, then the weeping anguish of a Young Girl whose fiancé, also driven to unreason, is to be imprisoned. Arlequin tries to avoid the spectre of tragedy but then the disturbed Young Man enters; the *air* 'Charmante Gabrielle' induces Arlequin's tears and the music of 'Le beau Berger Tircis' with emotive figuration is sung as the Girl 'takes her lover's hand'.[31]

In Act II/2 the Princess's *confidante* Dilara waits alone in the gardens of the Sultan for her friend the Bostangi. As chief palace guard, he will be bribed to allow the Prince and Arlequin to meet Zélica in Scene 11. Dilara's attractive *Air* 157, composed by Lacoste, is not a simple monologue ('Un Amant / D'abord est tout charmant'). Its two strophes are intentionally reflective of Dilara's personal situation:[32] tired of waiting, she expresses incipient jealousy and is latterly overheard by the Bostangi. This is an important moment in opera: a strophic 'impromptu' song is made to work on both particular and general levels.[33] Equally vital to the atmosphere is the preceding folk song, 'O ma bergère, vien seulette', which is also

---

[28] Footnote, *TF* III, 225 (R/I/317), perhaps referring to word-setting ('Catin' becomes 'Ca, Ca, Ca, Catin').

[29] *TF* III, 224 (R/I/317). This episode was retained in 1753 (see Table 8.10): *Le Monde renversé, opéra comique* (Paris: Duchesne, 1753), 13–16 (*Air noté* 1).

[30] From Pétis de La Croix, *Les 1001 jours* (1710–12): Guichemerre, '*Princesse de Carizme*'.

[31] *TF* III, 125 (R/I/292); music: *Table*, 21 (R/I/380).

[32] *TF* III, 141–2 (R/I/296–7); music: *Table*, 45 (R/I/386).

[33] See p. 31 for 'impromptu' song; Heartz, 'Beginnings of the Operatic Romance'.

Example 9.1 Louis de Lacoste, 'Comme les Dieux' in Lesage, *La Princesse de Carizme*, II/9. LE PRINCE: 'As do the Gods whom we silently adore, you receive my vows. The secrets of my heart do not yet dare pass my lips. Alas! what they fear to say can be read in my eyes. But, Philis, would that you might read my heart, as do the Gods.'

in two strophes. Borrowed music and new music once again functioned as a complex in the service of a single dramatic purpose.

Truly extraordinary is the organisation of music in Scenes 9 to 11 of Act II, when the Prince first sees Zélica: set-piece arias by named composers were woven in. Lacoste's *Air* 205 in binary form, 'Comme les Dieux', is the Prince's intended avowal to the Princess which we hear in authentic form when he rehearses it in Scene 9: see Example 9.1.[34] Its courtly mood and unexpected contours require subtle vocal control: he and Arlequin are to be introduced in disguise as 'singers from the Congo Opera'. Zélica enters with six attendants, dancing; a small *divertissement* evolves in which Gillier's *air* 'Cessez de vanter' is sung by Zélica. Thirty-six bars long, in da capo form, it displays her top f''s and g''s. Then the Prince begins performing 'Comme les Dieux' as planned, but his mental distress becomes manifest: the poetic text loses its way and Lacoste composes a distorted version of the 'B' section, which the Prince struggles to finish (Example 9.2). Wagner's *Tannhäuser*, Act II, seems not far away.[35] Recognising a male intruder, the courtiers leave in panic, and the stricken Prince is borne offstage by Arlequin and the Bostangi.

---

[34] *TF* III, 163, *Air* 205 (R/I/302); music: *Table*, 62–3 (R/I/391).
[35] *TF* III, 166, *Air* 206 (R/I/303): music: *Table*, 63 (R/I/391). Tannhäuser's strophic Prize Song becomes exalted.

Example 9.2 Louis de Lacoste, second half of 'Comme les Dieux' distorted by incipient madness in Lesage, *La Princesse de Carizme*, II/11: 'But the sun at which we marvel ... And the moon ... which gleams in your eyes, Make the whole Celestial Empire charm the Gods.'

Operas after 1720 thus built on firm musical foundations. Sometimes opéras-comiques stopped the action and brought in dancers, or familiar figures such as gypsies and fortune tellers. Act II/6 of *La Pénélope moderne* (*The New Penelope*) in 1728 did this using Gillier's music, and the end of the same act introduced a troupe of Pilgrims. But they are not really essential to the plot. On a smaller scale, Pannard's *Les Époux réunis* (*Husband and Wife Reunited*, 1736) brought on gypsies in Act I/10 so that a disguised Julie (the suspicious wife) and her maid Lisette could gain an insight into what was going on between Damon and Hortense.

In the exceptionally sumptuous *La Princesse de la Chine* (*The Princess of China*) a large procession entered in Act I/4. Its function, especially its music, was to alert Prince Noureddin to danger, since it carries the Prince of Basra to execution after he has failed to correctly answer Diamantine's three riddles (this is the Turandot story). The eighteen-person cortège entered to 'a sad march accompanied by bells and gongs' with drummers and criers joining in.[36] Its date (1729) is too early for types of local colour to have infused the music itself, but when Act I closes with another ceremony and a prayer to the Buddha, the surviving music, notated in G minor for choral bass voices, indicates unusual leaps of a minor sixth and a diminished fifth: 'O Jacmouni! Accord us thy favour!'[37]

Table 9.1 (online) shows the extent to which dances ended the acts of operas. But as we see in the following section, music for dance could

---

[36] 1729: no music survives: *TF* VII, 130 (R/II/185): 'Clochettes' and 'tambours Chinois' were specified.
[37] *Air* 73: *TF* VII, *Table*, 31 (R/II/271). 'Jacmouni' is explained in 'Histoire du Prince Calaf', 66th Day, in Pétis de La Croix, *Les 1001 jours* (1710–12), 98.

actually involve the most forward-looking, unexpected styles: pantomime and narrative elements in dance with characteristic, descriptive or completely abstract music.

Corrette and Modern Dance

Sarah McCleave's lucid picture is the best way to imagine the nature of dance in European theatre, for 'Theatrical dance, as an entirely professionalised art, was essentially distinct from social dance by the beginning of the eighteenth century.'[38] Dancers had recourse to four main styles: the 'elegant and earthbound serious style'; the 'brisk and elevated' *demi-caractère* style; a more exaggerated physical version of this ('comic', sometimes caricatural); and the 'grotesque' style, whether acrobatic or for 'exotic or otherworldly characters'.[39] Because dance styles, fashions and music moved around Europe seamlessly, it is relevant to know what was happening at the Comédie-Italienne, which 'by the mid-1730s [...] had expanded its danced offerings to include substantial pantomime ballets'. In May 1732 Italian dancers had brought there 'the more vigorous style' of 'caprioles and entrechats'.[40] Three months earlier the Fair had pioneered a novel attempt to unite theatre and dance in Pannard's *Le Pot-pourri, Pantomime*. Its choreographed prologue offered 'mimed scenes which drew their meaning from different well-known *vaudevilles*. The band played these *airs* and the actors conveyed their meanings and texts through gesture. M. Gillier [...] supplied the music for this.'[41] Narrative impulses meant that gestures had to 'be presented and developed in a successive manner' such as practised by Marie Sallé (1709–56), whose childhood beginnings were seen in *La Princesse de Carizme*.[42]

Gillier's successor was Michel Corrette (1707–95) for whom the first documentary proof of an appointment comes late, in 1739.[43] Corrette was a natural denizen of the commercialised world, teaching, organ-playing, composing and publishing.[44] His dances, *airs* and duets for opérascomiques brought in fresh musical styles, best known from his twenty-five 'Concertos comiques'. Usually in three Italianate movements, they

---

[38] McCleave, *Dance in Handel's Operas*, 15. [39] *Ibid.*, 12.
[40] Harris-Warrick and Marsh, 'The French Connection', 179.
[41] Parfaict, *Mémoires* (1743), II, 76–7. [42] McCleave, *ibid.*, 17–18; Parfaict, *ibid.*, I, 208.
[43] Porot, 'Chants de Momus', 131ff.
[44] D. Fuller, B. Gustafson, 'Corrette, Michel', *Grove*; Jaffrès *et al.*, eds., *Michel Corrette*; Jaffrès, 'Michel Corrette'.

Table 9.4 Selected Fair theatre works correlated with *Concertos comiques* or other music by Corrette, ordered by date. 'TP' indicates title-page dating. Sources: editions in BNF; Rizzoni, *Pannard*; Parfaict, *Mémoires* (1743).

Carolet	*L'Allure, Pièce en un Acte* (TF X)	27 September 1732
Corrette	*L'Allure: IIe Concerto comique*	3 October 1732 (TP)
Pannard	*Le Départ de l'Opéra Comique, opéra-comique en un acte*	28 July 1733
Corrette	*Les Âges, Ballet Pantomime*	28 July 1733 (TP)
Corrette	*Biron: VIIIe Concerto comique*	15 March 1734 (TP)
Pannard	*Divertissement* and 'Concerto pantomime' in Favart's *Les Jumelles* (*The Twins*)	22 March 1734
Pannard	*La Mie Margot, ballet en forme de concerto comique avec prologue*	24 September 1735
Corrette	*Ma mie Margo, Xe Concerto comique*	24 September 1735
Pannard	*La Muse pantomime, pièce en un acte*	14 September 1737
Corrette	*La Béquille du Père Barnaba, XIIIe Concerto Comique*. This 'concerto as Ballet Pantomime on Père Barbabas [...] was much applauded'.	14 September 1737
Laffichard, Valois d'Orville	*La Béquille, opéra-comique* 'followed by the *Concerto*'	21 September 1737

were danced at the Opéra Comique from 1732 and also published for amateur use. Some had titles which advertised various connections with popular opera, thus expanding our musical and conceptual understanding of entertainments involved in Fair theatre. Certain concertos shared or echoed the titles of operas; some used music from *vaudevilles* sung in them. If programmed before or after a linked opera, their costume and choreography might have responded to common themes. Occasional title-pages give dates of premieres, e.g. *Biron*, 'Dancé à l'Opéra Comique le 15 Mars 1734'. Yet title-page dates in 1732–34 rarely match exactly with a known opera premiere, even when a title strongly promotes a link: see Table 9.4.

Corrette soon collaborated in creating theatre-dance forms, notably in *La Mie Margot* (*Little Friend Margot*). For the summer Fair in 1733 he composed a complete ballet-pantomime entitled *Les Âges* (the four ages of Man), inspired by and designed around a popular set of engravings, still unidentified. Its overture is followed by thirty-three dances.[45] D'Argenson thought the Opéra-Comique 'has done very well to introduce long ballets-pantomimes'.[46]

---

[45] Parfaict, *Mémoires* (1743), II, 164. Music: Porot, *ibid.*, 132–4. Only the bass part is on *Gallica*, F-Pn (Mus) Vm7 2514(3). Rizzoni, *Pannard*, 457; *ibid.*, 'Le Geste éloquent'.
[46] Reaction to *Les Âges* in d'Argenson, *Notices* (1725–57) II, 557.

Although the detailed constitution of the Opéra Comique orchestra is unknown, Corrette's solo parts in his concertos offer fascinating suggestions: flute, recorder, hurdy-gurdy, musette. Modern recordings make several of them easily available to hear. They were modelled on *concerto grosso* principles with alternate *tutti* and solo passages, usually with three upper parts and a continuo bass.

Looking at dance music in gestural terms, Vivaldian and pre-classical styles may be seen as trailblazers for modernity. A kind of musical assertiveness becomes noticeable in *vaudevilles*, and even sung *menuets* could adopt disjunct or repeated-note figures, as we shall see. *Contredanse* rhythms were faster, their *timbres* sometimes invoking foreign sources: 'Milord Biron', 'La Gigue Espagnolle', 'Le Carillon Doxfor' or 'Le Prince George'.[47]

The nature of popular dance on stage is suggested by various eyewitnesses.

7 July 1729. Five men and two women, dancing with perfect intelligence to the *airs* of a Scottish composer, gave us steps, attitudes and gestures representing what happens in Dutch 'musicals', a type of beer-hall like our cafés, where sailors and others of different nationalities pursue their love-affairs: these living pictures were entitled *Love and Jealousy*.[48]

Subjects like these were a definite, recurrent taste which Fair theatre audiences must have linked to Dutch genre painting, as journalists and other writers did.[49] We read in the *Mercure* of the length of a danced score, and how ten-year-old Lolotte Cammasse tackled narratives, as well as abstract styles in sonata movements. She could have borrowed music for her storm scene from Corrette's concerto, *The Lucky Shepherd's Journey to the East Indies*,[50] even though her performance was at the Comédie-Française. Its music was already in the public domain.

We shall try to sketch an idea by explaining the sequence of *airs* in differing characters, choreographed by M. Grandval the elder, danced by Lolotte in a manner far beyond her actual years, since she turned ten last September ....

---

[47] These are *contredanses* in Jean-Pantaléon Leclerc's *Premier Recueil de contredanses* (Paris: Le Clerc, n.d.), on *Gallica*.
[48] Parfaict, *ibid.*, II, 53. This account comes from the same year that Roger's company created genre scenes at the FSG: Bergman, 'La grande mode'.
[49] See Chapter 1, n. 93.
[50] *Les Voyages du Berger Fortuné aux Indes Orientales* with 'Earthquake and Tempest' and a 'Storm': Corrette, *IIIe Concerto* (Paris: l'Auteur, etc. [1737]), BNF, Arsenal, M.465. Dated by J.-C. Maillard in Jaffrès, ed., *Regards sur Corrette*, 40.

The second *air* is a type of Sonata or Allegro, spirited in style, in which one sees the enthusiasm of a dancer who creates steps and attitudes to a music that gives her pleasure and stimulates her.

The seventh orchestral *air* is a storm in which the dancer expresses the fear and shock of the tempest at the rolling of thunder; this is followed by calmer hope; with subtle gradation she makes her transition from extreme agitation to eventual tranquillity.

In the ninth *air* the band imitates the songs of birds who return after the storm and celebrate its exhaustion; her steps, movements and eyes all clearly express the pleasure caused by their warbling. Delighted by their approach she tries repeatedly to catch one, with quick steps. This is interrupted first by a hurdy-gurdy melody and then another for bassoons and ends with two lively *tambourins*, choreographed by the dancer herself. She performs this sequence of *airs*, consisting of 244 bars, without interruption and always with equal assurance, graciousness, neatness and exactness.

[In other *divertissements* Lolotte] danced various *airs* of differing characters: first a *concerto* with strings, trumpets and musettes; here, broken up by shorter passages for flutes, she expressed the most difficult, taxing attitudes of *danse noble*, gracious and tranquil. In the *concerto* for musette she conveyed every tenderness that a sarabande can possess; and in the final *concerto* she performed a brisk, imposing dance capturing the authentic spirit of the orchestral music.[51]

To dance a sonata, an Allegro or a concerto was to engage with its modernity; even to answer the famous theoretical question 'Sonate que me veux-tu?': 'What is instrumental music for?'[52] Corrette's concertos were associated with local and anecdotal themes; they could quote *vaudevilles* signifying fashions, or a newsworthy tale about little Margot who ran off to Paris. Robert Darnton found that:

Occasionally, a new song was such a hit that it filled the air everywhere in the city and was adapted to every conceivable subject. 'La Béquille du père Barnabas' [*Father Barnabas' Crutch*], a song about a poor Capuchin friar who endured terrible misery after his crutch was stolen, somehow struck a chord among all sorts of Parisians in 1737. It was copied into all the *chansonniers* for that year and lent itself to the most disparate topics, some political, some plaintive, and some obscene.[53]

The 'Barnabas' melody, Example 9.3, is a twelve-bar song in three-bar phrases, starting on the half-bar: an odd rhythmic gait results. In Corrette's concerto of the same name the audience hears the *vaudeville* instrumentally

---

[51] *Mercure*, 1739, April, 771–2. Essential background information: Burgess, 'From Dance to Poem'.
[52] Attributed to Le Bovier de Fontenelle of the Académie Royale des Sciences.
[53] Darnton, *Poetry*, 89, showing *vaudeville* on 90.

Example 9.3 Anonymous, 'Le Père Barnaba', *vaudeville*: 'All hear me sing this pretty little song about Father Barnabas, which isn't really entertaining.'

Example 9.4 Michel Corrette, *La Béquille du Père Barnaba, XIIIe concerto comique* (Paris: l'Auteur, n.d.), I, showing the 'crutch' theme.

but clearly, developed with semiquaver passages in the solo part. To a dancer it would offer *vaudeville*'s intertextual technique of transferred meaning. At bar 51 of the first movement the composer added a new theme labelled 'La Béquille', 'The Crutch': its disjointed intervals of sixths and sevenths hobble downwards by step, as Example 9.4 shows.

Corrette's central movement is brief, as was usual, so the finale could retain focus on another transformation of the 'Barnabas' tune and the 'crutch' theme (again, with label): see Example 9.5. To us, such reuse of first-movement material sounds modern, like procedures in Bartók's finales; moreover, the dance-like optimism of these concertos prefigures our modern dance-suites.

In one popular opera by Denis Carolet and its matching concerto *L'Allure* (1732) we find a different innovation, elaborating its topic of interest: the word 'allure'. The first and third movements of Corrette's concerto use exactly the same *vaudeville* (seen in Example 9.6) as is found in Carolet's lightweight satire.[54] Set 'in the palace of Allure', the comedy

---

[54] *Vaudeville* is no. 309 in Jean-Pantaléon Leclerc's *Quatrième Recueil de contredanses* (Paris: Le Clerc, n.d.), 99, on *Gallica*. Contextual information: Jaffrès, 'Michel Corrette', 298.

Example 9.5 Michel Corrette, *La Béquille du Père Barnaba*, XIIIe concerto comique, III, opening.

Example 9.6 Michel Corrette, *L'Allure*, IIe concerto comique (Paris: l'Auteur, etc., n.d.), I, opening, words added from Denis Carolet, *L'Allure, Pièce en un acte*, Sc. 1 (*TF* IX/2, 177 (R/II/601)). LA MODE, addressing LE GOUST: 'Thy misfortune is sure, Cousin, It's tiresome and unavoidable, and from morning to night everyone praises Allure.'

mocks Paris's latest obsession about a single word; it may never have meant colloquially what it does now (in English) but what obviously mattered at the time was to capture a mood of innuendo and double meanings.[55]

---

[55] Primarily meaning the gait of an animal like a horse, the word also meant 'the way a person conducts themselves in some affair' (*Dictionnaire de l'Académie française*, 4th ed., 1762).

Starting in Scene 1 and with different words on each rehearing, this *vaudeville* is heard five times throughout the comedy, as follows:

Sc. 1 La Mode (Fashion) sings to Le Goust (Taste): 'allure' is everywhere;
Sc. 5 Le Poëte to L'Allure herself: 'allure' is the way to public fame;
Sc. 8 A provincial actress to L'Allure: sexual politics helps theatre success;
Sc. 10 Drunken coachman to L'Allure: he helps people conducting affairs;
Sc. 11 Dancing master to L'Allure: his pupils will later dance the *divertissement*.

Ninety years before Weber's *Der Freischütz*, recurring music in a popular opera knitted together various events or moral significances over the course of a whole work.[56] The *vaudeville*'s repeated notes seem to connect with gesture and gossip.

The rage for dance in the 1730s led the Opéra to open its doors in 1739 for the first time to Italian virtuosi, Barbara Campanini (Barbarina) and Antonio Rinaldi (Fossano). They came to perform in Royer's *Zaïde*, produced for the Dauphin's marriage.[57] But they brought their own music, which Boivin printed in score.[58] It is extraordinary to think of Parisians studying two- and three-movement pieces built on purely Italian traits – a modern idiom close to the *intermezzi* which helped provoke such ferment thirteen years later. They are 'pre-classical', binary-form movements with modulations to the dominant or the relative major carried out in sharply etched motifs and changes of rhythmic pattern. Octave leaps appear in unison, no different from the accompaniments of such *intermezzi*.[59]

Beyond *vaudevilles*

Fashion does not stay still; when music for dancing changed, it helped to expand the vocal scope of *vaudevilles*. Specialist singers are certainly implied. Clifford Barnes noted that

---

[56] C. M. von Weber, *Der Freischütz* (*The Freeshooter*). Recurring song had been introduced by Piron to *L'Âne d'or* (*The Golden Ass*, 1724): Arlequin has been magically changed into a beast, and a sixfold repeated *air*, music by L'Abbé, expressed various characters' reactions to him. No music survives; see Barnes, 'Théâtre de la Foire', 305.
[57] 3 Sept. 1739: *OAR*, 330–4.
[58] Anon., *Airs Italiens de la 2.eme* [also *Troisième*] *Pantomime dansée par Mr Fossani et Mlle Barbarini dans l'Opera de Zaïde* (Paris: Boivin, Le Clerc, n.d.) (on *Gallica*). Certain pages are transposed between the two sets.
[59] For dance in the 1740s see Lecomte, 'Jean-Baptiste François Dehesse'. Earlier association between Italianate instrumental music and French dancing: Harris-Warrick, *Dance and Drama*, 391–7.

As the new opéra-comique style developed, more and more tunes were used with fewer repetitions and a greater variety in the choice of *vaudevilles*. Volume VII of *TF* is a good example of this. Printed in 1731, it contains nine opéras-comiques written between 1728 and 1730 by Fuzelier, Pannard and Lesage. The 204 tunes printed at the end of the volume are those which Lesage felt were not too well-known. Some of these had appeared in previous volumes. One *timbre*, 'Perrette étant dessus l'herbette', is used five times in the volume; three others are used four times; eight are used three times, thirty-nine are used twice; and the remaining 153 are used once only throughout the nine plays [*sic*]. In addition to the printed tunes, 165 'well-known' *timbres* are called for. However, many of these tunes did not appear in previous volumes, and no music is readily available for them today.[60]

Barnes then calculated that the eighteen most-repeated *timbres* among the 165 whose music is omitted from volume VII appeared 124 times in all, being used between five and eleven times each.

This makes a total of 369 [separate] *timbres* needed for the volume, more than had been required for any previous volume of the series. Although the repetitions seem high, the ratio is considerably lower [than before] since these figures apply to nine plays, one of which is in two acts and another in three acts.[61]

Remarkably, the three-volume collection of *parodies* issued by the Comédie-Italienne, also in 1731, contained almost the same number of melodies: 367.[62] Barnes additionally recorded that 'over 800 *timbres* are used in Favart's works'.[63] The probability is that not all the *airs* in an opéra-comique could have been familiar to every listener. Favart himself compiled an index of *vaudeville* texts, classified by syllabic structure and rhyme.[64] It was surely this abundance that lay behind Fair theatre's clever analysis of what was going on: *Les Couplets en procès* (*The Vaudevilles Go to Law*) by Lesage and d'Orneval in 1729.

In a hidden corner of Mount Parnassus, lawyers acting for the old and the new styles are made to plead before an imaginary court. Older *vaudevilles* are characterised as meant for singing background information and narratives;[65] additionally they are 'very useful for making critiques'. On the other hand, newer melodies taken from ballrooms and concerts evoke

---

[60] Barnes, 'Théâtre de la Foire', 151–2.
[61] *Ibid.*, 153. The commonest melodies were venerable: 'Je ne suis né ni roi ni prince', 'Quand le péril est agréable', 'Quand on a prononcé', 'Comme un coucou', 'Je ferai mon devoir', 'L'autre nuit j'aperçus en songe', 'Des fraises', 'O réguingué', 'Voulez-vous sçavoir qui des deux'.
[62] Falk, *Parodies*, from PNTI (1731).   [63] Barnes, 'Théâtre de la Foire', 158.
[64] The 'Clef de vaudevilles', BNF, Arsenal, Mus.954: Laurence, 'Charles-Simon Favart', II, 655–735.
[65] Heartz, 'Terpsichore at the Fair' (a detailed exegesis which quotes many of the melodies), 155.

'beauty, gaiety, lightness'.[66] The social significance of this is not shirked: older tunes are accused of representing lower-class culture, even of being offensive to certain other people.[67] The newer music, claims its advocate Maître Gouffin, is equally capable of dramatic functions, and honours an institution 'which bears the respectable title of 'Opéra' (!)[68]

If we go by the definitions of *vaudevilles* quoted at the start of Chapter 5, it is apparent that some of the new music in opéras-comiques no longer qualifies for that label. If a true *vaudeville* is easy to sing, remember and transmit orally, it will not be too long or technically difficult. Length and technical difficulty now entered the musical vocabulary of opéra-comique, though without displacing older, more concise *airs*. Even in earlier opéra-comique we can discern something of a future 'showpiece' tradition: 'Je vivrai toujours dans l'allégresse' as sung and danced by the Old Man in Act I of *La Princesse de Carizme*: the audience knew it as the 'Vieillards de Thésée' music from Lully's opera.[69]

Likewise, using a dance-melody twenty-seven bars long, exclusive of repeats or ritornellos, d'Orneval created an ambitious ensemble at the end of *Arlequin traitant* (1716: see p. 157). Twenty people are eventually gathered on stage: the financier Arlequin is being arrested by seven law-enforcement officers watched by Isabelle, Colombine, Léandre, Pierrot and the Doctor. Suddenly a dancing master appears with six dancers; obviously they were summoned earlier for Arlequin's hoped-for wedding. The music begins: 'La Furstemberg' and 'St Martin's Lane' were two of its recognised names.[70] The dancing master, Cabril, sings boastfully to Arlequin and demonstrates his steps. Arlequin, also singing, prevaricates and points towards the officers. Cabril thinks they are his rivals: he pulls his hat down, makes as if to draw his sword and (still singing) challenges them. Then he draws his sword and a fight ensues, allowing Arlequin to escape. The music in question lived on in popular opera through the 1720s and beyond: see the online score of *Le Joueur*, no. 20 (the climax of Act II), described in Chapter 10.

Auguste Font observed that after 1730 *airs* could be 'fifty or sixty' bars long and tended to 'depict the emotions'.[71] His implied teleological drift

---

[66] Sc. 1: *TF* VII, 326 (R/II/235); Sc. 3: *TF* VII, 333 (R/II/237).

[67] In Sc. 2 the *timbre* 'Pierre Bagnolet' appears as a peasant; in Sc. 6 lawyer Gouffin claims that 'modesty is frightened off' by older *vaudevilles*.

[68] Sc. 6: *TF* VII, 340 (R/II/239).

[69] Air 148: *TF* III, 116 (R/I/290); *Table*, 42 (R/I/386) with dotted rhythms. A mocking tone and difficult melismas also characterised 'La Tampone', Air 142 in *Arlequin Thétis*, *TF* I, 79 (R/I/26).

[70] *TF* II, 219 (R/I/186), Act III/13, *air* 162, 'L'autre jour dans un bocage'. See Semmens, '"La Furstemberg"'.

[71] Barberet, *Lesage*, chap. 2; Font, *Favart*, 251, 254.

from 'shorter' to 'longer' melodies is incorrect: as a proportion, 'long' melodies from Opéra *divertissements* and elsewhere never remotely matched the rest. '*Air-vaudeville*' is Judith le Blanc's name for these, since there was no traditional one.[72] What sort of contexts did these more virtuosic types of music serve?

We saw in Chapter 4 how publishers fostered the singing of overtures, *menuets* and chaconnes. The chaconne from *Pyrame et Thisbé* excerpted in Example 4.1 comprised 306 bars of music, at one point demanding eighty-two consecutive semiquavers. How do we know these were meant to be sung? Because in Piron's *Le Fâcheux veuvage* (*The Trials of Widowerhood*) in 1725 the Iman of the Mountain sang Lully's overture to *Bellérophon* 'in a majestic tone', informing Arlequin that no one is permitted to survive a spouse who predeceases them: see Example 9.7.[73] Arlequin repeatedly tries to escape, interrupting the music.

A significant category was that of 'showpiece' *menuets*. They employed repeated-note figures, arpeggios or runs, catchy rhythms that matched clever verses. An early example is the *Menuet des Huit-saoûs* sung by a woman-about-town complaining of poor lovers in *Le Régiment de la Calotte* (*The Calotte Regiment*) in 1721.[74] It shows a common pattern of varied poetic lines, some very short:

Dieu des Plaisirs, Fils de Vénus, / Que devient ta gloire? / On ne voit plus / Que chez Bacchus / Des gens assidus: / On suit trois jours / Les Amours, / Quelle victoire!

A comparable *menuet* in *Les Fêtes grecques et romaines* (*The Festivals of Greece and Rome*) at the Opéra in 1723 quickly migrated to popular opera.[75] New extravagance arose in the *Menuet de la chasse* (Example 9.8) which makes for an unforgettable climax to Piron's *Le Caprice* (1724) when La Folie bursts in, dancing at the same time, to qualify as the bride of Le Caprice: Piron extended it by repetition into a forty-bar duet. Its hilarious horn calls signify craziness and its words celebrated universal folly.[76]

In 1730 Colin de Blamont's 'Deuxième menuet' from *Le Caprice d'Érato* (*Erato's Caprice*) became 'Jupin du grand matin', a favourite. Its thirty-two bars are far more challenging to sing than any *vaudeville* as traditionally

---

[72] Le Blanc, *Avatars*, 539–660 plus Annexe III.
[73] 37 text lines: Piron, *Œuvres* (1776), IV, 42 (Act I/11); music: F-Pn (Mus), X.25, on *Gallica*.
[74] Air 76: *TF* V, 32 (R/I/536); *Table*, 22 (R/I/644).
[75] By Fuzelier and Colin de Blamont: Harris-Warrick, *Dance and Drama*, 301–8, 397–402.
[76] Present in both editions: Piron, *Œuvres* (1776), III, 365 and *TF* VIII, Air 93, *Table*, 39 (R/II/390). He used it again in *Les Chimères* (1726), II: *Œuvres*, IV, 255.

Example 9.7 Alexis Piron, *Le Fâcheux veuvage*, I/11, [*Air*], 'Parodie de l'ouverture de Bellérophon'. L'IMAN DE LA MONTAGNE: 'Glory to you, valiant husband, now summoned back by true fidelity to his spouse's side again. (...) Unwise persons have recently [made known your intentions.]'

Example 9.8 *Air*, 'Menuet de la Chasse' in Alexis Piron, *Le Caprice*, Sc. 12. LA FOLIE: 'Follow my steps, denizens here below! *Reason* has none of my charms. My revelries must command you! Stand up to rats!' LE CAPRICE: 'What beauty! What fecund mutability!'

understood. Example 9.9 illustrates its awkward upward skips through a minor tenth (bars 4, 5) followed by upward arpeggiated figures. As Table 9.5 suggests, performances of 'Jupin du grand matin' went with exaggerated moments requiring vivid acting.[77] Other dances could be

---

[77] *La Caprice d'Érato*, entrée III (Paris: Au Mont-Parnasse, n.d.), 13. Source identified in le Blanc, *Avatars*, 570, 708. See *DOP*, I, 659–61.

Table 9.5 Selected showpiece uses of 'Jupin du grand matin', music from Colin de Blamont's 'Deuxième menuet' in *Le Caprice d'Érato* (1730), III.

FSL 1732	Carolet, *Le Réveil de l'Opéra Comique*, sc. 5: La Folie (Madness) announces her universal influence in society.
FSL, 1732	Carolet, *La Mère jalouse*, sc. 10: Le Financier sings an odiously satirical self-portrait: money buys him women and happiness.
FSG, 1738	Pannard, Prologue to *La Pièce à deux acteurs*: Mlle Julie has seen her boyfriend stabbed by a rival.[a]
FSG, 1740	Favart, *La Servante justifiée*, sc. 13: the nosey neighbour, Commère Cliquet, breathlessly reports something interesting.
FSL, 1742	Pannard, Fagan, *La Foire de Cythère*, sc. 6: Nina, exhibited at a fair as a mute through the cruelty of her parents, reacts to the love-declaration of a young man.[b]

[a] Pannard, *Théâtre* (1763), III, 146. [b] Fagan, *Théâtre* (1760), IV, 198.

Example 9.9 'Jupin du [de] grand matin' in Denis Carolet, *Le Réveil de l'Opéra Comique*, Sc. 5, *TF* IX/2, 13 (R/II/559) and *Table*, 2 (R/II/691). LA FOLIE: 'I am all for you: without me, dear Opéra [Comique] you aren't worth much. When I sing, nobility and bourgeois flock to see me: I want to make you happy. *Abbés*, lawyers, assistants befriend me; painters, musicians, actors [etc.]'.

sung as showpieces too: in Carolet's *L'Allure* a discontented lawyer's wife lists her many complaints to the music of a catchy *rondeau* from Mouret's *Le Triomphe des sens*, sixty-eight bars long.[78]

Gradually changing contexts are revealed in Table 9.5, moving from allegorical madness to human mental disturbance. It seems there was a general widening of contextual use for more difficult music. A rondo from *Pirame et Thisbé*, 'Laissons-nous charmer', targeted hack novellists in

---

[78] Sc. 7: *TF* IX/2, 194 (R/II/605), 'La Syrene du Ballet des Sens'. Mouret's Rondeau is from *Entrée* IV, *L'Ouye*, Sc. 7 (Paris: l'auteur, etc. [1732]), 238.

La Lanterne véridique (*The Truth-telling Lantern*);[79] in Pannard's *Le Fossé du scrupule* (*The Pit of Scruples*) Greed tempts Valère in a forty-four bar duet, 'Viens dans ma cellule'.[80]

The once-famous *Menuet d'Exaudet* (Example 5.5) characterised, among many other things, repugnant or predatory men in Vadé's *Le Suffisant* (*The Self-Satisfied Man*) and *Le Trompeur trompé* (*The Deceiver Deceived*). It is not technically virtuosic, but its showpiece status is confirmed by the multiple parodies it facilitated. The fact that it was published in orchestral score in *Bertholde à la ville* (*Bertoldo in Town*) alongside *intermezzo* pieces demonstrates an actual merging of status between showpiece *airs-vaudevilles* and *bona fide* arias.[81]

*

We saw in Chapter 5 that narrative and sentimental episodes could involve clusters of *vaudevilles*, especially *menuets*. Early 'Minuet-scenes' in Favart's work are found first in *Le Bal bourgeois* (*The Plain Man's Ball*) where dances are both sung and demonstrated, and then in *Les Jeunes mariés* (*The Young Marrieds*) where they convey conjugal warmth in Scene 4.[82] Other comedies might involve one or two key events in the drama that use exceptional musical means. Some of these are set out in Table 9.6.

Even the well-calculated restatement of a *vaudeville* can make this effect: in *La Servante justifiée*, Scene 14, Mme Bertrand's pompous 'De deux cœurs que l'amour engage' clinches the whole comedy when exactly repeated by her 'justified servant' a few pages later.[83] And in *La Chercheuse d'esprit* (*The Girl Who Sought Wit*) high points included Alain's stanzas quoted in Example 5.12: 'Hola, belle Nicette'. *Vaudeville* here became strophic aria. Earlier came another high point: Nicette ended her long search for knowledge in Scene 12 when overhearing L'Éveillé's 'Me promenant à l'écart', which is shown in Example 9.10. These two stanzas adopted a style of amorous *romance*. In *La Princesse de Carizme*, II/2, Dilara's strophic song had linked general plot with individual expression. But Favart embedded L'Éveillé's two stanzas within the action more completely, since the story he narrates is both a personal memory and an unintended lesson to Nicette which leads to the resolution of the whole comedy.

---

[79] *TF* IX/2, 47–8 (R/II/568); also no. 11 of online score of *Le Joueur* (Chap. 10). Carolet used it in *Les Petites maisons*, *TF* IX/2, 446–7 (R/II/667) and *L'Allure*, *TF* IX/2, 211 (R/II/609).
[80] Pannard, *Théâtre* (1763), III, 88.
[81] *Bertholde à la ville. Opéra comique* (Paris: La Chevardière, n.d.); Charlton, '"Minuet-scenes"', 261–4.
[82] Favart, *Les Jeunes mariés* (La Haye: Pierre Gosse, 1751).
[83] Air, 'De tous les Capucins du monde': *La Servante justifiée* (Paris: Prault Fils, 1744), 43, 46.

Table 9.6 Musical and dramatic focus points in Favart.

FSL, 1738	*Le Bal bourgeois*, Sc. 3 and 4: The disguised Frontin performs a set of *menuets* as a dancing master, singing and acting. *Ibid.*, Sc. 10: Julie's 107-bar solo scene paints the delights of attending balls (from Couperin, 'Les Calotins et les Calotines').
FSG, 1741	*La Chercheuse d'esprit*, Sc. 3 and 4: Rameau: Musette en rondeau, 49 bars. *Ibid.*, Sc. 12: L'Éveillé sings a narrative to Finette, two strophes, overheard by Nicette (Example 9.10). *Ibid.*, Sc. 15: Alain presents his bouquet and sings 'Je sommeille' in three strophes as Nicette pretends to sleep (Example 5.12).
FSG, 1742	*Le Prix de Cythère*, Sc. 6: Hébé and two couples sing a quintet set to a 48-bar march from Boismortier, *Les Voyages de l'Amour*, I/2.
FSL, 1743	*Les Bateliers de Saint-Cloud*, Sc. 6: a comic dream-narration for M. Thomas to the *vaudeville* 'Ici sont venus en personne', extended from 28 bars to 38 bars.[a] *Ibid.*, Sc. 9: Climactic quarrel between the Thomas couple, 192 bars from Derochet, *Menuet*.
FSG, then FSL, 1744	*Acajou*, I/5: Two newly composed trios, 40 and 38 bars long, give farcical expression to the lessons provided by Acajou's tutors.[b] *Ibid.*, II/8: Acajou's monologue of sorrow, 68 bars long, rondo form: *Air*, 'Viens, trop insensible Silvie'.

[a] 'Eune nuit ronflant à merveille': see Falk, *Parodies*, no. 102 and *PNTI* (1738), IV, no. 80.
[b] Cook, *Duet and Ensemble*, 46, attributes the second trio to Adolphe Blaise.

Example 9.10 Charles-Simon Favart, *La Chercheuse d'esprit*, Sc. 12, F-V, Mus. Ms. 198, pp. 100-1, *Air*, 'Et la Belle le trouva bon'. L'ÉVEILLÉ: 'Walking a new path, I spied you by chance one day in the depths of a grove; sheltered by thick leaves, you slept quietly.'

The psychologising of *vaudevilles* was a conscious procedure. In Favart's Prologue *Le Génie de l'Opéra Comique* (*The Genius of Opéra Comique*, 1735) a female apprentice learns – i.e. for the audience's benefit – how to write original material.[84] Paul Salvatore explained that

[84] Salvatore, *Favart's Unpublished Plays*, 142–62. The Prologue: BNF Ms Soleinne 9325, ff. 93 *et seq.*(on *Gallica*).

Example 9.11 *Air,* 'Sotto Mettode' = François Couperin, 'Les Calotins et les Calotines', in Charles-Simon Favart, *Le Bal bourgeois* (La Haye: Pierre Gosse Junior, 1750), Sc. 10. JULIE: 'Lovely independence, spending lots of money, ornaments, jewels of every sort, and some lover for amusement all the time – How ravishing her fate! No more teacher, grumbler, stickler, ogler – everywhere a show, nothing in the way when a husband sleeps at night.'

'Le Vaudeville [the teacher] continues to outline the use and importance of the "couplet" not only to convey emotions but also to depict types according to their social status'; 'Favart makes it a general practice to use the "couplet" that best fits the mood of the character as well as the emotion that he is to convey, so that the [musical] dialogue becomes much more lively and interesting'.[85]

Favart did this when virtuosity went well beyond earlier limits, as Example 9.11 shows. Julie's 107-bar solo in *Le Bal bourgeois* was adapted from Couperin's 'Les Calotins et les Calotines' for keyboard.[86] Its motivation is almost the same as Marguérite's in the 'jewel song' from Gounod's *Faust*. Youthful desire, intoxication, the lure of dancing at balls, are all depicted in octave leaps and outrageously difficult figurations requiring control over a *tessitura* of two octaves. It was designed for Mlle le Blanc, a singer absent from later productions when this number was replaced.[87] Favart supplied eighty-nine lines of text, some consisting of a single word.

---

[85] Salvatore, *ibid.*, 155.

[86] F. Couperin, *Troisième Livre de Pièces de Clavecin, Ordre* 19 (Paris: L'Auteur, 1722), 58. Its *timbre* 'Sotto mettode' was identified by Davitt Moroney in 'The *Parodies*'. The keyboard piece is 156 bars long. Favart's *parodie* makes small modifications and returns to the refrain at the end, as the text layout makes clear.

[87] Le Blanc is named in the 1750 libretto: see caption to Example 9.11. For Mlle Luzy later, Favart supplied 'Dans ce verger', 102 bars long: *Théâtre de M. Favart* (Paris: Duchesne, 1763–68), VI.

Outrageous in a different way was a farcical quarrel-duet of 192 bars in *Les Bateliers de Saint-Cloud* (*The Boatmen of Saint-Cloud*). Its music came from social dance, a *menuet* by Louis Derochet.[88] The farmer and his wife, Mr and Mme Thomas, are both ridiculously cross-dressed at this point, and the great length of the duet allows argument to progress through different stages, including a bickering section where short phrases ricochet between them. These had originally been accompaniment phrases. Rather like Corrette's concertos, Favart's piece mixed comedy, everyday life and fashionable music: dance-tunes not from the Opéra but the Comédie-Italienne where Derochet was employed.

Favart's quotations of Rameau's music seem reserved for high points, sometimes expressions of intense love. Rameau's 'Musette en rondeau', familiar since 1724 as a keyboard piece and from *Les Fêtes d'Hébé*, provided a forty-nine-bar episode of sentiment bridging Scenes 3 and 4 of *La Chercheuse d'esprit*.[89] Humiliated by her mother, Nicette sings of 'weeping from dawn to dusk'. But the music continues for the entrance of Monsieur Narquois, the supposed savant: this dignified music is just as apt for him.

Could an entire opera 'beyond *vaudevilles*' be conceived of? Older *vaudevilles* implied ironic content, objectifying urban targets. By situating opérascomiques in villages, Favart rebalanced these expectations. *Les Nymphes de Diane* (*Diana's Nymphs*), discussed in Chapter 7, went further. During 1747–8 Favart was director of the Théâtre de La Monnaie under the protection of the Maréchal de Saxe, whose troops invaded the Austrian Low Countries and occupied Brussels from 1746 to 1748.[90] After this opera's premiere there in 1747 it was published with all the music: eighty-five *airs* plus a duet by Corrette containing florid singing: 'Cruelle Séverine'.[91] The performers were Mlle Durancy (erstwhile Mlle d'Arimath) and M. Rebours, while Justine Favart took centre stage as the nymph Thémire under the name 'Mlle Chantilli'.

As we saw in Chapter 7, the opera is set in Diana's forest like a pastoral, and Favart now employed *vaudevilles* as 'raw material' to make the genre

---

[88] Or 'Desrochers'; first sung by Françoise d'Arimath and M. Rebours. Campardon, *Spectacles*, I, 18; Parfaict, *Dictionnaire*, I, 390. Music ('La mort pour les malheureux'): *Théâtre de M. Favart*, VI. Source: *Recueil des nouveaux menuets de la Comédie Italienne composées par Mr Derochet* (Paris: Boivin, etc., n.d.), 2–5: F-Pn (Mus), Vm7.6763 for strings and bassoon, not on *Gallica*.
[89] See 'Musette en rondeau' in Sadler, *Rameau Compendium*, 137–8.
[90] Haine, 'Charles-Simon Favart'. On Saxe's patronage, the libretto's frontispiece by Boucher, and *La Cythère assiégée*, see Markovits, *Civiliser l'Europe*, 171–84.
[91] First noted by Cook in *Duet and Ensemble*, 42–5, with music example. *Les Nymphes de Diane. Opera Comique du Sr. Favart* (n. p., 1748) is on *Gallica* with its 40-page music supplement. Air 86 is the unattributed duet 'Cruelle Séverine', re-engraved in *Vaudevilles et ariettes de L'Opera Comique Composés par Mr. Corrette. Tome IV* (Paris: Boivin etc., n.d.).

Example 9.12 Jean-Joseph Mouret, *Air* 80, 'Ah! que la forêt de Cythère' parodied in Charles-Simon Favart, *Les Nymphes de Diane* ([Bruxelles], 1748), Sc. 19. L'AMOUR: 'I come to take revenge on the Nymphs of this retreat. In every land my hunt is bounteous, and nothing evades Cupid.'

a kind of directly expressive *collage*. For example, he borrowed Mouret's 'Fanfare' for hunting horns in 'La Terre' (written for the Comédie-Italienne)[92] going so far as to make horns take over the vocal line in both 'À la chasse', *Air* 59, and 'Ah! que la forêt de Cythère' sung by Cupid: see Example 9.12. Scenes 9 to 11 formed the ensemble ritual where Thémire met Agénor. Stage directions describe dance and choral singing; the chorus, as at the Paris Opéra, spread out from the centre.[93] The opera closed with a *Divertissement* in which 'Cupid unties the nymphs' whom he has defeated and who were 'tied together with flowers' as they might have been in any Opéra production. As Cupid paired off the votaries of Diana, Séverine and the Satyr sang Corrette's duet.

Keyboard music by Couperin served as a comic duet between Agénor's friend Cliton, chained up for punishment, and the Satyr who is fooled into taking his place (Scene 8: *Air* 40, 'Des gris vêtus', 34 bars). Séverine sang a da capo *Air* as a warning to the assembled nymphs (Scene 10: *Air* 46, 40 bars). Thémire voiced her feelings for Agénor in Rameau's well-known 'Arrachez de mon cœur' from *Dardanus*, notated in A major like the original (Scene 18: *Air* 77), to which Agénor responded with the *Air*, 'Enfans de la Paix' followed by the couple's final duet, notated in A minor. Analysis of voice-ranges in this source, however, shows that its notated keys could not have been *systematically* used, because individual *tessituræ* are too wide.

*

[92] Mouret, *Le Cahos* IV ('La Terre'), *Troisième recueil des divertissemens*, 203. The *entrée* was written for Marc-Antoine Le Grand's *Le Cahos, parodie* of *Les Éléments*, 23 July 1725.
[93] Favart, *Les Nymphes de Diane*, 34: 'le Tambourin de Jephté [by Montéclair] *que les autres Nymphes reprennent en Chœur, elles finissent en se rangeant sur deux lignes aux côtez de l'Autel.*'

Favart's career took him beyond Fair theatre as well as beyond *vaudevilles*. Even before Jean Monnet first gained the *privilège* of the Opéra Comique in March 1743,[94] the Opéra had taken Favart into its creative orbit by accepting his three-act libretto *Don Quichotte chez la duchesse* (*Don Quixote visits the Duchess*), which Boismortier had agreed to set. Premiered on 12 February 1743, it involved physical acting, comic situations and special effects.[95] Back at the Opéra Comique, Favart employed Boismortier as *Maître de musique* in summer 1744 and winter 1745.[96] Rameau himself was working with a Fair theatre author, Adrien-Joseph Valois d'Orville, on *Platée*;[97] and was invited by Monnet to direct a parody of *Les Indes galantes* at the Opéra Comique in summer 1743.[98]

These facets reflect the 1740s, whose cultural mood favoured relativism. This was to the fore in *Réflexions sur l'opéra* by Rémond de Saint-Mard, for example, when he called for a pluralistic attitude towards all opera, even comic *intermezzi*.[99] The same impulse appeared when Pierre Guyot Desfontaines reviewed *Joseph Andrews* by Fielding: 'we are ridiculous to categorise some things as "low" and others as "noble". The "low" isn't always what we think it is.'[100] Relativism of various kinds was probably perceived in *La Chercheuse d'esprit*, which inspired Desfontaines to suggest an Aristotelian treatise on the 'fine art' of opéra-comique.[101] Obviously, comedy was being seen within a wider agenda. The development and expansion of musical comedy by the Comédie-Italienne is the subject of Chapter 10; the company took what musical advantage it could of the closure of the Opéra Comique in 1745.

---

[94] From *directeur* Louis-Armand-Eugène de Thuret: *DOP*, IV, 817–19.
[95] *OAR*, 36–7, 342–3.
[96] F-Po, Fonds Favart, Carton I, doss. 12, doc. 5, f°.1^r, doc. 8, f°.1^v, doc. 10, f°.2^r, doc.3, f°.1^r.
[97] *DOP*, IV, 198–205.
[98] Favart, *L'Ambigu de la folie*, 31 August 1743; Rameau's presence at the FSL (claimed by Monnet, *ibid.*) is not verified, but accepted by Sadler in 'Rameau, Piron', 28, and Porot in 'Rameau et les théâtres'.
[99] Rémond de Saint-Mard, *Réflexions* (1741), 93; see *OAR*, 162–5.
[100] Desfontaines, *Observations*, 33 (1743), 327.
[101] *Ibid.*, 24 (1741), 144, reporting conversations with an unnamed author, probably Favart.

10 | Italian Inroads: The King's Company

Evolution of Italian Traditions

How can we understand popular opera in all its phases and its evolution in France? These questions arose a century ago in the pioneering work of Georges Cucuel (1884–1918). He defined, in effect, one thread ('a French tradition perceptible above all through its component details') and a series of events, 'an Italian influence which, by sudden revolutions, would determine its general directions'.[1]

Two such 'events' underpin the present chapter: a short visit to the Paris Opéra by two famous *intermezzo* singers in 1729 and an eighteen-month visit there by Eustachio Bambini's company – between three and nine singers – during 1752–54. Both visits produced creative results at the Comédie-Italienne. The first gave rise to two *vaudeville* adaptations, and the second produced hybrid operas adapted from *intermezzi*. A judgement by the writer and composer Johann Mattheson (1681–1764) is relevant here: 'Experience shows that there are many who have never set a foot in Italy who surpass not only others who have been there, but who occasionally surpass native Italian virtuosos themselves.'[2]

During the 1690s Italian music 'became all the rage', was 'sung in *divertissements* at the Court'[3] and was promoted by enthusiasts in special concerts. Mattheson's compatriot J. J. Quantz testified that 'Italian arias, concertos, trios, solos, etc. are privately performed, and Italian singers are brought in and supported'.[4] Corrette adopted the concerto style, as we saw in Examples 9.4 and 9.5. Opening the Opéra Comique in summer 1752, four weeks before Bambini's *intermezzi* began, Mlle Rosaline sang 'Che

---

[1] Cucuel, *Les Créateurs*, 12. See pp. 8–9 for 'threads' and 'events'.
[2] Harriss, trans., *'Der vollkommene Capellmeister'* (1739), 259.
[3] I.e. *Airs italiens composez par les plus celebres autheurs* (Paris, 1695), ed. François Fossard and A. D. Philidor *l'aîné*; *Recueil des meilleurs airs italiens* (Paris: C. Ballard, 1708): Sawkins, 'Lalande's Theatrical Motets', 214. See the opening survey in Lindgren, 'Parisian patronage'.
[4] Quantz, *On Playing the Flute* (1752), 332. See p. 79, n. 16.

desia d'un ver contento', effectively starting a decade of competition with the company we are focusing on.[5]

When Louis XIV died on 1 September 1715, Duke Philippe II d'Orléans took charge as Regent and as an Italophile musician and composer himself. He founded a new Comédie-Italienne, headed by Luigi Riccoboni and his wife Elena Balletti, distinguished and learned actors. This Hôtel de Bourgogne initiative opened on 18 May 1716 with an agreed monopoly of Italian actors but not, as it had wanted, of *commedia* characters. George I, cousin to the Regent, soon requested a London visit for Riccoboni's troupe (it was cancelled at the last moment). The young Louis XV later awarded the Italian players their royal brevet, but 'chronic indebtedness'[6] remained a fact of life, like the struggle for audiences.

Riccoboni's Parisian home served as an Italian cultural centre whose high-level contacts and visitors included musicians. Elena Balletti's sister was married to the opera composer Giovanni Bononcini; he and Riccoboni helped with plans to bring *opera seria* to Paris. These too came to nought, but the *prima donna* Francesca Cuzzoni and her colleagues did give performances for the Prince de Carignan and other wealthy patrons after the 1724 London season.[7] Riccoboni stayed with Cuzzoni and her husband in London four years later; by now he was a government agent as well as a respected historian of theatre.[8]

Another theatre historian wrote: 'Without the desire to put their theatre back in fashion, would the [Italian] actors have thought of giving plays enhanced by music and dancing, [attracting] large crowds?'[9] Their early play by Jacques Autreau, *Le Naufrage au Port-à-l'Anglais*, had three *divertissements* by Jean-Joseph Mouret, official composer from 1717.[10] Such dynamics have sometimes been obscured because of the mixture of genres offered by the Italian company. Historians of spoken comedy discuss the work of Jacques Autreau, Marivaux, Louis de Boissy and others; Italian specialists focus on its *commedia dell'arte* or on Goldoni; limited work on Mouret or singers has been done.[11] Fortunately, music's role emerges in recent literature on *parodies*:

---

[5] She sang it on 30 June at the inauguration of Monnet's new theatre. The music, perhaps by Carlo Sodi, was heard in Jacques Fleury, *Le Temple de Momus*, Prologue nouveau (Paris: Duchesne, 1755), 43.

[6] Brenner, *Théâtre Italien*, 7–9 [9].

[7] Plans for visits: 1723, 1724. Concert performances included Handel's *Giulio Cesare* and *Ottone*: Lindgren, 'Parisian patronage', 22–4.

[8] Courville, *Un Apôtre*, II, 293–304.   [9] D'Origny, *Annales* (1788), I, 55.

[10] *Le Naufrage au Port-à-l'Anglais* (1718) was still given in the 1750s. Mouret's score heads his six-volume collection, *Recueil des divertissemens du Théâtre Italien*.

[11] Nestola, 'L'Air italien'; Viollier, *Mouret*; Coulet and Fajon, eds., *Jean-Joseph Mouret*.

[The Comédie-Italienne] wanted to exploit the genre of opéra-comique and *parodies* of opera, which it claimed by right. [...] The distinction between [*parodies* of spoken tragedy and those of opera] lay in music, spectacle and dancing: at stake in opera *parodies* were their visual and aural components. That meant the possibility of an 'opéra-comique' for the Comédie-Italienne without actually stealing a genre created by the Fair theatres.[12]

To avoid 'stealing', even as late as 1758 with new music by Egidio Duni, *La Fille mal gardée* (*The Girl Who Broke Free*) obeyed the convention. Favart's text works like a modern opéra-comique but was technically a rewrite of *La Provençale* (*The Girl from Provence*), an old *entrée* for the Opéra with music originally by Mouret. Its four scenes were expanded to fifteen; Nicolette's character was developed (Justine Favart); so was that of Lindor (sung by Catherine Foulquier, called Mlle Catinon) who passes her a letter during an action-filled trio.[13]

Given the presence of an orchestra, dancers and singers but under no obligation to observe classical unities or forms, the Comédie-Italienne's artists used music imaginatively. At one end of the spectrum were *commedia* shows, semi-improvised; at the other, a tragicomedy in verse, *Samson*, in which a heavenly voice inspired the hero by singing an arioso including a trumpet obbligato.[14] Writers were encouraged by the genius of Mouret who, in a perfect world, would have continued writing comic operas like *Le Mariage de Ragonde*, composed for the Duchess du Maine in 1714.[15] For the Opéra he composed *tragédies* and *opéras-ballets*, but in spoken theatre his gifts served *divertissements*. Of Marivaux's sixteen plays, nine featured Mouret's music.[16] For *Timon le misanthrope* by Delisle de La Drevetière, Mouret's score reaches thirty-one pages of music; the same playwright's *Arlequin au banquet* opens with a yet longer musical scena for the shipwrecked poet, Arion.

Table 10.1 (online) reveals a strand of sixteen comedies mainly from the 1720s whose *divertissements* contain seventeen arias, three duets and a trio by Mouret, all set in Italian. Certain of these comedies remained on stage

---

[12] Beaucé, *Parodies*, 34.
[13] Favart and Duni, *La Fille mal gardée* (Paris: La Chevardiere, [1759]); see Charlton, 'La Rencontre'.
[14] 'La gloire en d'autres lieux t'appelle' in French style, Act I/3 of the 1730 play by J.-A. Romagnesi; Mouret, *Recueil des divertissemens*, III, 293.
[15] Cessac, 'La duchesse', 97; *DOP*, I, 164–7; reworked as *Les Amours de Ragonde* (*The Loves of Ragonde*, Opéra, 1742).
[16] Particularly integrated in *L'Isle des esclaves* and esp. *Le Triomphe de Plutus*: Fajon, 'Jean Joseph Mouret'.

for decades; the music could be purchased in Mouret's *Divertissemens*.[17] Mostly in da capo form, but also rondo and binary form, these pieces average 120 bars long. From Examples 10.1 (a) and (b) we see something of Mouret's wonderful energy and expression put at the service of Ursula Astori (1694–1739), official singer at this period. Such pieces demonstrate an investment by the troupe, a sub-repertory for the paying public quite separate from the gradual introduction of Italian elements at the Opéra.

As happened in the seventeenth century, leading actors were called upon to sing. Boissy's plays made various musical demands, especially *Le Triomphe de l'intérêt* (*The Triumph of Interest*), *Le je ne sais quoi* (*The I Don't Know What*) and *Les Talents à la mode* (*Fashionable Talents*). In the first, Pierre Théveneau and (probably) Catherine Visentini – see Table 10.2 – sang two extended scenes in *vaudevilles*, representing an aspiring actress and her would-be patron.[18] In the second, Visentini and Théveneau parodied the dancing-master scene in *Les Fêtes vénitiennes* (*Festival in Venice*).[19] An entire cantata, *Le Feu de la ville*, was sung in Act II of *Les Talents à la mode*, Act II, by Visentini and Antoine-François Riccoboni, son of the founder. Supposed in the play to have been written by two sisters, it was actually composed by Mouret's successor Adolphe Blaise, the style sometimes recalling Rameau.[20]

Continuing his efforts to bring Italian opera to Paris, the Prince de Carignan finally succeeded. His close connections with the Opéra evidently made that theatre available for a famous touring team, Rosa Ungarelli and Antonio Ristorini, on 7 June 1729. They gave three *intermezzi* entitled *Serpilla e Baiocco*, 'the gambling husband and the devout wife'.[21] This acclaimed music by Giuseppe Orlandini (1676–1760) had already been

---

[17] The contents of Mouret's *Divertissemens* are in Viollier, *Mouret*, 222–5, and his Italian settings listed on 186–90. Later printings of given *Recueils* unfortunately alter the contents. The source of Ex. 10.1 is *Deuxième Recueil des divertissemens*, 49, Gallica copy from F-Pn (Mus) Vm6.46(2).

[18] *Mercure*, 1730, Nov., 2492–3. The edition by Martial Poirson includes music (Montpellier: Espaces 34, 2007).

[19] Entrée 'Le Bal': Harris-Warrick, *Dance and Drama*, 247, 262–4; *Mercure*, 1731, Sep., 2223.

[20] Music published separately: see *Mercure*, 1739, Oct., 2455; Framery, 'Quelque réflexions' (1770), 5 (R/345).

[21] *Serpilla e Baiocco overo Il marito giocatore e la moglie bacchetona*, libretto by Antonio Salvi. Alternative title: *Il giocatore*. The soloists came via Brussels: *DOP*, II, 253–4. They stayed at Carignan's residence: Lindgren, 'Parisian Patronage', n. 67; *DOP*, I, 682–3; Sadler, 'Carignan', *Rameau Compendium*.

Examples 10.1 (a) Jean-Joseph Mouret, 'Sin dal profondo di flegetonte' in the *divertissement* for Louis-André Riccoboni, *Colombine mari par complaisance* (1719: lost), opening ritornello. Source: Mouret, *Premier Recueil des Divertissemens*, 149. (b) Jean-Joseph Mouret, 'Sin dal profondo di flegetonte', excerpt from middle section of the aria.

heard – with various changes – during ten or more seasons in different countries, always with the same interpreters.[22] Their unique impact was preserved in a long account of visceral reactions to the human drama portrayed: it 'can't be believed by one who hasn't seen them'.[23] A French traveller to Italy described seeing *intermezzi* there, with singers able to interpret physical as well as mental reactions, timed to the music:

The Italians seem to consider the Bouffons mainly as physical actors [*pantomimes*] and to set less store by their music. But any expressive sound claims its due from my heart. Their Bouffons make me understand what they are singing: they have

---

[22] Piperno, 'Buffe e buffi', 274–6. An updated research assessment: Johnston, 'Molière, Descartes'.
[23] In Pistoia, 1725; transl. in Troy, *Comic Intermezzo*, 53, 189.

Table 10.2 Notable singers at the Comédie-Italienne, listed chronologically. Further information is in Nestola, 'Italian music.'

Name	Activity at Comédie-Italienne
Women	
Ursula Astori, 'Isabelle', m. Fabio Sticotti, d. 1739	Official 'cantatrice' from 1716.
Catherine-Antoinette Visentini (1711–74), 'Catine', m. Jean-Baptiste Dehesse (or Deshayes).	Child performer, 1719; doubled Sylvia's roles from 1726; numerous roles up to 1757.
Rosalie Astraudi, daughter of company's cellist.	Child performer as singer and cellist, 1744–5; numerous acting roles in early 1750s; retired 1755.
Marie-Justine-Benoîte Cabaret du Ronceray (1727–72), 'Mlle Chantilly', m. Charles-Simon Favart.	Created 40 roles between 1751 and 1769.[a]
Eulalie Desglands (dates unknown)	Transferred in 1753 from the Opéra Comique; created many roles;[b] retired 1779.
Marie-Thérèse Villette (1744–92), m. Jean-Louis Laruette.	Transferred in 1761 from the Opéra; created many roles; retired 1777.
Men	
Pierre Théveneau, son of company's café manager, d. 1732.	Sang from c.1717; partnered Sylvia in *Le Joueur* and took musical roles in Boissy's plays.
Jean-Antoine Bérard (1710–72)	Transferred from the Opéra in 1733 and returned there in 1736.[c] Took musical roles in plays.
Charles-Raymond Rochard de Bouillac (dates unknown)	Main actor-singer from 1740 to 1764.
Joseph Caillot (1733–1816)	Main actor-singer from 1760 to 1772.

[a] Pougin, *Madame Favart*, 61–2, omitting Sodi's *Baiocco et Serpilla* (1753): see following.
[b] Often more minor roles but also Madame Western in *Tom Jones*.
[c] Sophie Jouve-Ganvert, 'Bérard' in M. Benoit, ed., *Dictionnaire*.

particular sounds which characterise hunger, cold, sorrow, joy; therein lies the true music of a drama. I admit they gave me singular pleasure.[24]

A *résumé* of the story is needed, since *Serpilla e Baiocco* was so influential and long-lived, a point of reference reprised as the second Italian work given at the Opéra in 1752. Yet it dated back to 1715, and therefore was

---

[24] Béthisy de Mézières (1709–81), *Effets de l'air* (1760), 43, n. 2. He identified no titles. 'Since my return to France, Latilla, Pergolesi and several other famous composers have recognised the special advantages of the character and style of the Bouffons': *ibid*.

contemporaneous with *Le Tableau du mariage* (*TF*, 1716), described in Chapter 7. *Serpilla e Baiocco* is also a 'portrait of marriage', a relationship that hangs by a thread owing to the husband's addiction. Baiocco has been out all night and gambled everything away. He denies this until his wife discovers his pack of cards. Serpilla demands a divorce (final duet I). But the 'judge' whom she visits in *intermezzo* II is Baiocco in disguise. He tests her by offering to fast-track her case if she lets him be her *cicisbeo* (gallant). After due doubts, she agrees. Baiocco unmasks in furious mocking revenge, for Serpilla is a *bachettona*, a devout woman. She fails to make him see reason (final duet II). Ejecting her from their house, Baiocco almost kills her in the third *intermezzo*; fortunately she appeals successfully to his better nature.

This dysfunctional husband uses every lever available within the rules of a misogynistic society. So *Serpilla e Baiocco*, like its *vaudeville* adaptation, is a social comment on marriage, though few could express something timeless about human weakness, as Orlandini does.[25]

A heatwave cut short the Opéra performances, but the Comédie-Italienne's parodic version of *Serpilla e Baiocco* (14 July) survived until almost the arrival of the next Bouffons, an unusual length of time for a *parodie*.[26] Entitled *Le Joueur* (*The Gambler*: see the online edition made for this book), it was first performed alongside other Italian music, emulating the Opéra programme of 7 June.[27] Contemporaries like Thomas-Simon Gueullette appreciated the connections between Orlandini's 'extremely singular' music and *Le Joueur* as 'a type of opera'.[28] Whereas routine *parodies* burlesqued their target opera, *Le Joueur* presented an equivalent of *Serpilla e Baiocco*. 'Mr Dominique [Biancolelli] and Mr Romagnesi have imitated the original *intermezzi* very cleverly using mixed Italian and French verses, to which the accompaniment adds new pleasures. [...] The main piece is a comical Chaconne.'[29] Not so differently

---

[25] Recording available (1969); *OAR*, 258–60. Michel Noiray, *DOP*, IV, 631–2, notes that 'Serpilla' means 'little snake', and that a 'Baiocco' was a near-worthless coin.

[26] D. Biancolelli and J. A. Romagnesi, *Le Joueur*, *PNTI*, both eds. The F-Po *Registres* often enter it under *Les Débuts*, the play by these same authors at the end of which it was originally staged.

[27] *Mercure*, 1729, June/1, 1223–30; *ibid.*, July, 1639. Score at www.cambridge.org/9781316515846.

[28] 'cette espèce d'opéra': Gueullette, *Notes* (1750–62), 114.

[29] *Mercure*, 1729, July, 1639–40. An unidentified aria with trumpet was sung by 'Dlle Fabio' [Ursula Astori]; Mouret's entr'acte Chaconne is in *Recueil des divertissements*, IV, 247–53, headed *Les Débuts*.

from the Pistoia witness (see n. 23), the *Mercure* journalist found it 'impossible to describe the admirable artistry' of the actor-singers.

Baiocco's role was taken by Pierre Théveneau and that of Serpilla by the eminent performer Silvia (i.e. Giovanna Rosa Benozzi). She was from Toulouse but of Italian parentage; we know less about her singing than Théveneau's. Although he was French, his performance seems to have influenced Comédie-Italienne tradition through new features of interpretation. 'Mlle Silvia and Théveneau were completely successful in [this] performance and it was in this type of opera that Théveneau established his reputation and merit, which had not so far been properly recognised.'[30] In 1730 he was finally admitted as a royal (Italian) *comédien*, 'in the quality of a singer'.[31] 'The public liked his style of singing and the naturalness and veracity of his acting';[32] 'his voice [was] more graceful than generous, but sufficient in a theatre whose orchestra was not too loud'.[33]

Comparing the online score of *Le Joueur* with opéras-comiques met so far, we find differences as well as similarities. Its musical basis is more diverse, extending south in the case of no. 29 (a Steffani opera) and probably also in numbers 5, 15, 18, 25 (the latter found in Leipzig) and 27. These all have Italian *timbres* while no. 7 is half-Italian, being a song by Giuseppe Fedeli written in French and recently published for those wishing to sing at home in the Italian style. Song-like material is found in nos. 4 and 17, both French. Ten *vaudevilles* of the total twenty-nine have been traced to Fair theatre sources. Mouret's contribution seems to be no. 23 (unattributed), Serpilla's emotive da capo aria beginning *intermezzo* III, thus an equivalent to Orlandini's famous 'A questa Pellegrina' sung by the now-homeless wife.[34]

In fact the dramatic temper of *Le Joueur* respects the ironic power of the original. We cannot know how it was acted or costumed, but only make a judgement through its style. Not only did the authors follow each step of the drama faithfully, but they intensified it by privileging dialogue: out of twenty-nine musical numbers, twenty-one are set as dialogues. Quickfire styles of

---

[30] Gueullette, *ibid.*, 114.
[31] That is, he became a company member, sharing in the profits: d'Origny, *Annales* (1788), I, 117–18.
[32] *Ibid.*, 118.
[33] Parfaict, *Dictionnaire* (1767), V, 460–1. Théveneau died prematurely in November 1732.
[34] *Les Ariettes du Joueur, Opera Bouffon Italien*, by 'Doletti' (Paris: Boivin, Le Clerc, n.d.), 20.

response translate the action in a totally distinct manner, for in the original *intermezzi* duets occur only at the end of each part. *Le Joueur*'s language avoids the neatness or cleverness met in opéra-comique in favour of untidiness and absurdity; but that lends a mocking directness and rawness, modified only at the start of *intermezzo* II. The music is often mellifluous: what gives it freshness and dramatic relevance is its great variety of rhythmic interest.

Vaudevilles in *Le Joueur* sometimes carry over their known effect from Fair theatre, as in number 19 when Baiocco suddenly unmasks, and devastates Serpilla: 'Les filles de Montpellier' regularly appeared in opéras-comiques sung by stressed female characters.[35] But Biancolelli and Romagnesi worked against the grain in numbers 11 and 20, minor-mode equivalents to Orlandini's duos of recrimination and crisis ending *intermezzi* I and II. As we saw in Chapter 9, note 78, 'Laissons-nous charmer' had been understood as a comic showpiece, whereas here Serpilla demands a divorce, leaving Baiocco suddenly repentant. Number 20, with its uncommon octave leaps, had been a showpiece in Piron's *Le Caprice* and *Les Chimères*, whereas in *Le Joueur* it expresses complete betrayal: in fact, the nadir of the couple's relationship.[36]

*

It is worth pausing to take stock of the known differences between Italianate and French singing in comedy. There would be a conscious adjustment of singing styles when another 'event' in this evolutionary process occurred: the merger between the Opéra Comique and the Comédie-Italienne. We have clear evidence that when Italian music was sung in French, the result did not conform to French tradition. Charles Rochard's style in French melody and *vaudeville* was founded on good breath control: 'through adopting my rules' wrote *abbé* Blanchet, 'M. Rochard, so celebrated for his good taste in singing, knows how to perform the lengthiest phrases of music with rare perfection'.[37] But a change in

---

[35] Alternative *timbre* 'Aïe, aïe aïe, Jeanette': *La Statue merveilleuse*, II/3, *Les Trois commères*, Prologue and II/5, *Achmet et Almanzine*, II/8 (Pierrot disguised as a nurse), *Le Mariage du Caprice*, Sc. 13, *Arlequin Endymion*, Sc. 5.

[36] 'L'autre jour dans un boccage', TF VIII, 217 (R/II/342); *Les Chimères*, II/6, *Œuvres* (1776), IV, 291.

[37] Blanchet, *L'Art* (1756), 32. Quotation comes directly after Blanchet links these methods to those of Italian singers. On Rochard's 'delicate taste': *Mercure*, 1747, June/2, 120.

Rochard's technique occurred around 1754, mirroring Théveneau's change twenty-five years before:

Mlle Favart is the delight of all Paris in the leading role [in *La Servante maîtresse* (*The Maid as Mistress*)]; although not the originator of the style, she has at least carried it to undreamt-of degrees of perfection. M. Rochard, who has sometimes been taxed with affectation and a precious style of singing that he perhaps cultivated, was totally different in the role of the old man [Uberto: Pandolfe in the French version]. Everyone was satisfied; Italian music has made him more natural.[38]

Rochard became so identified with this role that he ended his career by singing it for five performances *in Italian* during July 1761: 'Nothing was forced in his acting or vocal expression'; he was 'repaid with the greatest applause'.[39] The archetypal French singer had become 'Italian' at a time when Maria Anna Piccinelli, taking Serpina's role, was made a company member. Duni and Goldoni were guiding a policy of Italian renewal during two years of flux before the union of the companies.[40]

In 1762 five Opéra Comique singers entered the Comédie-Italienne troupe, simultaneously with the removal from the latter's books of several of its own singers. Valuable analysis of the differences between Opéra Comique singers and their new colleagues was published by the *Mercure de France*, whose journalist had been hearing trial selections of works by Duni, Monsigny, Philidor and Dauvergne:[41]

Everyone is agreed about the difficulty of hearing most of the Opéra Comique actors, partly through the vocal quietness of some, which is disproportionate to the size of the hall, and partly through the faulty habit of the others in not pronouncing the words: they are too accustomed merely to articulate their sounds, using a volubility borrowed from Italian music: music analogous to a naturally voluble language [...] very opposed to the moderate character of French.[42]

'Volubilité' meant 'speaking too fast' and 'sounds' recalls Béthisy's 'particular sounds', mentioned earlier: to French ears, the Italian method

---

[38] *Mercure*, 1754, Oct., 165.   [39] *Mercure*, 1761, Oct./1, 192.
[40] Fabiano, 'Le projet Goldoni' in *Histoire*, 48–57, but overlooks Rochard's achievement.
[41] Trial hearings are set out chronologically in Wild*TOC*, 33–4.
[42] *Mercure*, 1762, Mar., 197–8.

conveyed unaccustomed values which were neither primarily linguistic nor in use at the Opéra Comique in earlier times. Its modern singers had evidently adjusted their vocal production in a more radical manner than had Comédie-Italienne singers. One should be 'scrupulous about pronunciation' when singing 'the new music' in French, warned the *Manuel des Châteaux*, because 'Italian pronunciation is a frequently found fault.'[43] Evoking the criticism of Francesco Algarotti (1712–64), Garcin declared that Italian singers 'articulate badly, like a person not wanting to be understood.'[44]

One journalist noticed a compromise worked out by Joseph Caillot, one of the internationally experienced singers of the unified troupe. Court officials had recalled him from the south to strengthen the Comédie-Italienne in 1759; he participated in programmes we saw in Table 8.7.[45] Caillot was an ideal candidate, having sung in crossover French-Italian operas in Parma.[46] Once settled in Paris, he employed a mixed technique to sing opéras-comiques by Philidor:

> [*Le Bûcheron* (*The Woodcutter*)] was found agreeable by the Court. Even those who do not approve of the contours and accents of Italian music being applied to French words judged Mr Philidor's great talents fairly: and Mr Caillot, who possesses the skill to make us like everything he sings, drew the approbation of the supporters of each tradition by softening that musical accent which is foreign to the expression of our language.[47]

Caillot was the perfect singer for the new 'musico-dramatic art'. 'This incomparable actor seems to have been born with two souls, one devoted to the composer, the other to the poet. In *airs* where expression predominates, we have the actor; in those where melody predominates, the actor is eclipsed by the singer. He seems to control these two functions at will.'[48] Caillot's art probably helped Laurent Garcin to conceptualise the claims he made for 'musico-dramatic art', to which we shall return in Chapter 12:

> It is obvious that the actor-singer must completely understand the *accent musical* containing the emotional quality of the music, and that in performance he must

---

[43] Paulmy and Contant d'Orville, *Manuel des Châteaux* (1779), 238.
[44] Garcin, *Traité* (1772), 354, followed by lengthy commentary.
[45] Caillot's first appearance was in *Ninette à la cour* (26 July 1760) followed by roles in *La Fortune au village*, *L'Isle des foux* and *Mazet*.
[46] Butler, *Musical Theater*, 28–9; Bédarida, *Parme*, 486.   [47] *Mercure*, 1763, April, 174.
[48] Garcin, *ibid*., 338.

slide over the *accent oratoire* where this does not receive compositional emphasis, but then should lean more strongly on places where the two types of *accent* coincide.[49]

Italy apparently prevailed: Nougaret complained of not sufficiently understanding the words in *ariettes* as well as ensembles.[50]

'Il soldato valoroso'

> The *Intermezzi* [in Venice] are very comical in their way, which is somewhat low, not much unlike the Farces we see sometimes on our Stage. They laugh, scold, imitate other sounds, as the cracking of a Whip, the rumbling of Chariot Wheels, and all to Musick.[51]

Mouret's aria with trumpet, 'Il soldato valoroso', was written for Théveneau in 1729; we can judge his range and capacity from the edited score that was issued.[52] Mouret was in action as a French composer in *intermezzo* style, exploring significant traits of expression found later in opéra-comique. The aria came in a new parodic *intermède* entitled *Don Micco e Lesbina* which joined *Le Joueur* from 17 August, Silvia taking the part of Lesbina. The Italian original of *Don Micco* had the same title: three *intermezzi* that Ungarelli and Ristorini first gave at the Opéra on 14 June. Lesbina wants to trick Micco, her lover. She will marry him only if he vanquishes her belligerent brother. For the second *intermezzo* the cowardly Micco appears fully armed: 'he works himself up for combat with music perfectly expressing the sounds of drum and trumpet'.[53] Fear strikes him when the supposed brother appears (Lesbina in disguise); after a brief skirmish he declares himself dead. Lesbina takes his ruse as a cue to pretend he really is dead. This situation is prolonged into the third *intermezzo*.

For the *parodie*, Biancolelli and Romagnesi telescoped the three parts into one: an early example of Parisian dramatists perennially trying to bring better order, as they construed it, into the looser structures of

---

[49] *Ibid.*, 336. [50] Nougaret, *Art du théâtre* (1768), II, 311, 332 (blaming the accompaniments).
[51] Wright, *Observations* (1730), I, 85.
[52] Mouret, *Recueil des divertissemens*, IV, 255–60. On *Gallica*, see copy with shelf-mark Vm6.47(3).
[53] *Mercure*, 1729, June/2, 1402.

Italian comedy. Every Franco-Italian comedy mentioned here would be the result of selective redesigning.

Unfortunately, we cannot compare Mouret's music with Don Micco's 'combat' aria at the Opéra: that anonymous *intermezzo* is presumed lost.[54] The text for Mouret's aria, surely modelled on the original, offered the composer the chance to include musically imagined battle sounds. In other words it is not just a description but a series of impressions articulated by a terrified coward: 'la Trombetta, il tamburo, col broulo, il strepito del Canon, les timballes' and 'La bayonetta, zin, zin, zin, Les coups de sabre, flin, flin, flin'. Musical imitations took the form of onomatopœia. But the actor-singer had to work bodily to create the sound-pictures as projections of the character's fearful nature. Similar techniques thirty years hence became part of Philidor's opéra-comique style as debated by Mme d'Entreville and Mme Bouchait de Serée, discussed in Chapter 1. Sonic images surely also qualify as 'sounds' of the type remembered by Béthisy (n. 24). In 1729 everything was arranged by Mouret within a binary form, full of amusement and contrast: the first half modulates from the tonic E minor to the relative G major (where the trumpet can enter) and thence through its dominant, then to A minor, ending on an unexpected B-major chord at the halfway point. Available for purchase, it was perfectly suited to competent amateurs.

Towards *La Servante maîtresse*

Pergolesi's *intermezzi* called *La serva padrona* have been calculated to have been performed in more than sixty theatres in Europe during the two decades following their premiere in 1733.[55] So perhaps it is no surprise that the Comédie-Italienne staged them in 1746. Moreover this was a decade when comic opera, having moved from southern to northern Italy, began to circulate in the wider sphere: Barbara Mackenzie has traced the mutations and dispersal of four key operas, three of which were adapted and given by Bambini's troupe in Paris.[56] These 'events' produced obvious consequences for the evolution of popular opera (Table 8.6). More subtle was the effect of the four performances of Pergolesi's score between 4 and 11 October 1746. These were not related to a production elsewhere – new

---

[54] Piperno, 'Buffe e buffi', 276. [55] In Naples: G. Lazarevich, '*Serva padrona, La*' in *NGO*.
[56] Mackenzie, 'Creation of a genre'; *OAR*, chap. 9.

parodies of opera having been disallowed from 1745 – but parody was obviously not the intention.

At this period conduits for comic works remained Italian singers themselves – 'the most likely agents to carry them abroad'[57] – whereas later, impresarios like Bambini took over that function. Travelling Italian writers, intellectuals and musicians regarded the Comédie-Italienne family network as a focus for news and discussion.[58] Pergolesi's music and Gennaro Federico's text were certainly 'in the air': during the same October, Charles de Brosses, who sometimes visited the Comédie-Italienne, shared a story with his nephew that must have spread to others back in France. We do not know from where he sent this letter:

19 October 1746: [...] in all this I had great need of your advice and revision, for which I could well have recompensed you by bringing you *L'amor platonico*, *Comparisco*,[59] and above all the original of *La serva padrona*, entirely in Pergolesi's handwriting, which I carried off by sheer force of money. Ah! Dear cousin! What a pretty thing, if only you could have seen it acted, as I did.[60]

The importance of *La serva padrona* for popular opera begins in 1746 because spoken dialogue was used instead of recitative at the Comédie-Italienne. This solution was necessary to avoid another enormous fine being imposed, as when *La Fille, la veuve et la femme* (*The Woman, the Wife and the Widow*) was judged to be 'a complete piece with dialogues and singing and divertissements [...] a complete opera in the comic mode'.[61] The Comédie-Italienne actors declaimed Federico's original verses to which Pergolesi's recitatives had been set, while audiences read a French translation in their libretto.[62]

Oddly enough, the singer of the leading role (Serpina) was not a celebrity bearing a copy of Pergolesi's score but Mlle Montigny or Montigni, a beginner, described in the *Mercure* as a 'very likeable Italian woman'.[63] Gueullette noted that the piece was

---

[57] Mackenzie, *ibid.*, 267.
[58] E.g. the Benozzi, the Baletti and the Riccoboni: Casanova, *History of My Life*, vol. III, chap. 8.
[59] These references are untraced.
[60] *Lettres du Président de Brosses*, 171–2. De Brosses' famous 'Letter 51' on Italian opera in 1739–40 also mentions this *intermezzo*: Weiss, *Opera*, 81–90.
[61] See Chap. 8, p. 192: fine of 10,000 l^t plus a ban on new *parodies*: Campardon, *Comédiens*, II, 257–60.
[62] *La Serva padrona, Comedia in duce* [sic] *Atti. La Soubrette Maitresse* (Paris: Vve Delormel & Fils, 1746), copy at BNF, Yth. 50721.
[63] *Mercure*, 1746, October, 162: 'la Signora Monti'. There was a wealthy Montigny clan (Daniel Trudaine de Montigny was *intendant des finances*).

acted, while singing, by Lelio *fils* and an untried actress, very pretty, called Mlle Montigny. [...] The music was excellent and performed four times [before the troupe was obliged to leave for Fontainebleau]. Mlle de Montigny, who had never appeared on stage before, was judged as insufficiently talented and consequently withdrew; she died in Paris several years later.[64]

'Lelio *fils*' was Antoine-François Riccoboni in the role of Uberto: 'actor, dancer, author, he is a true Proteus'.[65] Actors in Italy, even authors, would sing *intermezzo* roles if the need arose.[66]

Montigny's inexperience may be the reason for last-minute changes. In one extant libretto her part included three additional arias: 'Oh che fatica' and 'Di quest'alma' in I/2 and 'Speranza foriera' in II/1.[67] In a different version of the libretto the first two have vanished and the third has been replaced by 'Un aura di speranza'.[68] Both editions have the same permission date for printing (1 October), the same page count and the same title page. Therefore, excision of material is the likely explanation, permitting an almost exact reissue. The title page labels the piece in a politically expedient fashion as *comedia* and *Comédie*: no music is mentioned here, no names of actors follow. The dialogue contains sixty-seven speeches in *intermezzo* I and eighty-seven speeches in *intermezzo* II.

The *Mercure*'s review usefully offered three different descriptions. First (copying the title page) was 'comedy in two acts accompanied by two *divertissements*'; then came a statement that it 'perfectly resembles what the Italian Bouffons gave at the Opéra' in 1729, whether referring to its framing *divertissements* or something else. Finally came the notion that '*La serva padrona* is a type of Italian opéra comique, mixed with spoken dialogue'.[69] The era of conflicting terminology had begun.

*

Various artists already celebrated in popular theatre had the acting skills which they would need when French popular opera became Italianised. It might well have been possible for Catherine Visentini to play Serpina, having doubled Silvia's roles from 1726, including Serpilla in 1731.[70] She remained on stage in the early 1750s with major roles in Favart's new

---

[64] Gueullette, *Notes* (1750–62), 142; Brenner, *Théâtre Italien*, 154 verifies the short run. Four lines honouring 'Mlle Moltini's début': Anon., ed., *Les Étrennes* (1747), 36.
[65] *Les Étrennes*, 26.   [66] Mackenzie, 'Creation of a genre', 299; Weiss, 'Venetian commedia'.
[67] BNF, Yth. 50721.
[68] BNF, ThB.1163; same version on Google books, unidentifiable provenance (Aug. 2019).
[69] The journalist writes 'prose' to mean 'spoken dialogue' (this was a convention): *Mercure*, 1746, Oct., 161.
[70] *Mercure*, 1731, Jan., 148.

parodies, and was a dancer too.⁷¹ She parodied Hippolyte's role in Favart's 1742 *Hippolyte et Aricie*, starting a trend: 'The roles of Hippolyte, Pélée, Iphis, Admète and Acis, all played by the celebrated *haute-contre* Jélyotte [Jéliote] in productions at the Opéra, were played in Favart's *parodies* by women. Each of these roles portrays a young male lover, preferred by the female star to a more masculine suitor, played by a man.'⁷²

To be able to take on various comedic identities was an essential attribute of Italian *intermezzo* singers, and so it is a point of comparison that under Favart's guidance at the Fairs one of the Chéret sisters took the leading role of slow-witted Pierrot in *Le Coq de village* (*The Cock of the Walk*) for example, and Mlle Drouart appeared as Don Carlos and Don Alvar in *L'Ambigu de la Folie* (*The Mad Medley*, 1743), a *parodie* of *Les Indes galantes* (*Love the World Over*). At the Comédie-Italienne in the 1750s Rosalie Astraudi specialised similarly in Favart's *parodies*, as Colin in *Les Amants inquiets* (*The Unquiet Lovers*), Don Carlos in the 1751 *Les Incas*, the *petit-maître* Damon in *Les Amours champêtres* (*Love in the Country*), Raton the farmhand in *Raton et Rosette* and Jolicœur the dragoon in *Les Jumeaux* (*The Twins*).⁷³ Catherine Foulquier was mentioned on page 238.

Italian opera systems made formal links between a given hierarchy of singers and certain types of role that were repeated across different operas, called the *convenienzi*. Within comic roles, contracts typically demanded the ability to 'act and to sing'.

> The highest place was held by the *prime buffe*, the female comic leading roles. [...] To qualify as a *prima buffa*, a singer was expected not only to be a good singer and a good actress but also needed to be attractive or at least charming. The most important required skill, however, was not so much to fit into a single stereotypical role, but to be able to act and to sing in different styles. [...] The *prima buffa* was often expected to perform in disguise (often as a doctor or notary and as other male or female characters), or to speak in different dialects or languages.⁷⁴

Pergolesi's first Serpina, Laura Monti, was expected 'to accomplish all the necessary disguises in the operas, and to play as a man and as a woman, to fence, to dance, etc.'⁷⁵ Fencing in male disguise was featured in *Don Micco*, as we saw. Similar skills were made abundantly clear during the Bouffon residency of 1752–54 when Anna Tonelli was *prima buffa*: in various *intermezzi* she became the skilful psychologist Serpina, a gardener,

---

⁷¹ La Porte, *Anecdotes* (1775), III, 141, under 'De Hesse' (her husband's name).
⁷² Harvey, 'Opera Parody', 296–7. ⁷³ All information taken from early librettos.
⁷⁴ Cicali, 'Roles and Acting', 93. ⁷⁵ *Ibid.*, 93: this translates a quotation from a 1728 document.

a manipulating widow, an upper-class Chinese daughter, a gypsy, a village wife who entrances a prince, an English *bourgeoise* and a Venetian housekeeper. Her stage partner Pietro Manelli represented a mendicant and a quack doctor, Tracollo; Don Calisson, an extravagant; a Chinese lover; and several older eccentrics.[76]

Seeing Bambini's *intermezzi* at the Paris Opéra was a shock for many that either took time to absorb or was too much to accept. 'These extraordinary portrayals' and many reasons for their effects on hearers were described in Wye J. Allanbrook's profound enquiry.[77] Originally only twelve performances had been agreed, as noted on 5 July 1752.[78] Gradually the troupe became a fixture and more singers appeared. In fact, *intermezzi* were seen on every opera night from 1 August (their opening performance) to 9 November, resuming a week later. The first three *intermezzi* had a great following and continued to be given into the new year: *La serva padrona, Il giocatore, Il maestro di musica*: Table 8.6 gives precise dates. By 23 November a year-long contract had been signed and a degree of collaboration with the Opéra ensued, seen most obviously in the presence of choruses and sometimes dancers within *Il maestro di musica* (The Music Master), *La scaltra governatrice* (The Shrewd Governor's Wife), *La zingara* (The Gypsy) and *Bertoldo in corte* (Bertoldo at Court). Table 10.3 offers a time-line for 1753.

Bertoldo in corte's success might well have led to further *intermezzi* under a new contract, but Rousseau's incendiary *Lettre sur la musique françoise* coincided with it and heated up the atmosphere so much that the government made 7 March 1754 the date of the Bouffons' final performance. But two days later the first adaptation of a Bouffon work appeared at the Opéra Comique, *Bertholde à la ville* (Bertoldo in Town). It was to be here and at the Comédie-Italienne that many found what they perceived as a more acceptable form of lyric comedy: 'those who out of pique or partiality never heard *La serva padrona* at the Opéra have become zealous enthusiasts of it at the Comédie-Italienne; they run there in crowds'.[79]

The appointment of Carlo Sodi (c.1710–88) to the Italian company suggests forward musical planning, since he arrived in 1749 – a low period for audience attendance. Sodi would be an orchestral member and all-purpose composer, but also voice coach.[80] Born in Rome, he had served in

---

[76] *OAR*, 273. [77] Allanbrook, *Secular Commedia*, 10: citation from Baron d'Holbach.
[78] Charlton, 'New Light', 43–4. [79] *Mercure*, 1754, Oct., 162–3.
[80] His *ariettes* were sung at the OC (see p. 237, n. 5): Parfaict, *Dictionnaire* (1767), V, 184–5.

Table 10.3 Key premieres in 1753. ARM = Académie royale de musique (Bambini company); CI = Comédie-Italienne; OC = Opéra Comique.

1 March, ARM	Rousseau's *Le Devin du village* (complete version) heard with a *pasticcio*, *Le Jaloux corrigé*. It included four re-texted arias or duets from *La serva padrona*, four from *Il giocatore* and three from *Il maestro di musica*.
24 March, CI	*Raton et Rosette*, C.-S. Favart's *parodie* of *Titon et l'Aurore* by Mondonville, including one *air* falsely attributed to *La serva padrona*, two from *Il giocatore*, the trio 'Come chi gioca' from *Il maestro di musica* and two arias from *La finta cameriera* (*The Counterfeit Chambermaid*).
1 May, ARM	*Tracollo, medico ignorante* (c.12 performances to 2 November).
23 May, CI	*Baiocco et Serpilla*, Carlo Sodi's new setting of the 1729 Franco-Italian libretto of *Le Joueur*.[a] Limited success.
19 June, ARM	*Il cinese rimpatriato* (11 performances to 19 August) and *La zingara* (c.16 performances to 6 November).
30 July, OC	*Les Troqueurs* by J.-J. Vadé and A. Dauvergne, announced as the work of an Italian in Vienna. Extraordinary success all summer.
4 August, CI	*Les Amours de Bastien et Bastienne*, *parodie* of *Le Devin du village* written by Marie-Justine Favart, whose peasant costume as Bastienne was epoch-making.
9 August, CI	*Bastienne et Bastienne*, followed by *Baiocco et Serpilla* (see 23 May) now entirely in French (C.-S. Favart's translation).
17 Sept., CI	*Raton et Rosette* joined the above two works in five performances of a triple-bill.
23 Sept., ARM	*Gli artigiani arricchiti* (17+ performances to 30 Oct.) and *Il paratajo* (8+ performances to 16 Oct.)
9 Nov., ARM	*Bertoldo in corte* (c. 25 performances to 1 Feb.).

[a] F-Po, *Registre*, 23 May.

cathedrals,[81] but had also written an *intermezzo*, *Sorbina e Gialdoni* (Fano, 1737). At the same juncture the Comédie-Italienne made the significant appointment of Marie-Justine-Benoîte Duronceray, later Favart (1727–72) who before long ensured the company's superiority in Italian music. She had trained at Lunéville, where her parents were musicians at the court of Stanislaus, king of Poland.[82] As a dancer and singer she took on early roles we have already discussed in this chapter. Her unusual gifts already polarised public opinion: she was not selected for the 1749 Fontainebleau season and instead joined her husband in Lunéville.[83] Relentlessly pursued in private life by the war-hero Maurice Saxe, she went into hiding before being forcibly confined within different convents.[84]

---

[81] Montefiascone, 1733, Fano, 1737–9, named in his oratorio librettos: Sartori, *Il libretti italiani*, *passim*.
[82] Stanisław I Leszczyński (1677–1766), Louis XV's father-in-law. Marie-Justine's Fair theatre experience was limited to 1745, the year she married Charles-Simon Favart.
[83] Gueullette, *Notes et souvenirs* (1750–62), 49–53.
[84] Gilchrist, 'Favart's Contribution', 47–70.

After Saxe's death in November 1750 Justine Favart returned to the Comédie-Italienne the following March and became a full member a year later, listed as a dancer. Her voice lessons with Sodi might have begun then, or with the advent of the Bouffons.[85] A unique documentary link between teacher and pupil is the score of Sodi's *Baiocco et Serpilla*, written for her and for Rochard, providing the closest record of her much-applauded artistry in May–September 1753.[86]

Baiocco indicates the confidence of the Comédie-Italienne, matching the Bouffons with a new, through-composed operatic comedy. Because the rules still limited them to *parodies*, Sodi made use of their macaronic libretto of *Le Joueur*. The public evidently disapproved: by August it was converted into a completely French text. Its singular nature caused Sodi to write in a somewhat confusing continuum, the first two acts showing little irony or evidence of emotional wars running beneath the surface. Then Act III opens with what might have been an *opera seria* aria in C minor, 'Ah, perfide barbare': a full ABA form, powerful beyond anything else in the work. We witness the hatred of a Serpilla musically defined for the mid-century, no longer the object of pity and powerlessness. A similar aria follows, then an effective rococo aria of remorse ('Souvien-toi, cher époux') where Serpilla pacifies Baiocco through vocal strength and a substantial cadenza. Rochard joined her for the final duet ('Règne sur mon âme') ending with a yet longer cadenza: see Example 10.2.

'Mlle Favart parodied Mlle Tonelli with her usual charms', reported the *Mercure*:[87] Anna Tonelli's interpretation of Orlandini's *Il giocatore* held the Opéra stage until June 1753. Reacting to *La servante maîtresse* the following year, Fréron explained why, for him, Favart was the better artist of the two:

Above all *La Servante maîtresse* owes its brilliant success to Mme Favart and M. Rochard. On both their parts, what liveliness of action! What finesse in the acting! What taste in the singing! No longer do we have the grimaces of the Bouffons Manelli and Tonelli; we have truth, we have Nature itself.[88]

Italian Opera / French Opera

When Justine Favart resumed her career in 1751 the Opéra Comique was still closed. So the Italians apparently linked her return to a commitment by

---

[85] Parfaict, *Dictionnaire* (1767), V, 184–5.
[86] *Baiocco et Serpilla, parodie françoise du Joueur* (Paris: Aux adresses ordinaires, n.d.).
[87] *Mercure*, 1753, June/2, 162–3.   [88] Fréron, *AL*, 1754/6 (15 Oct,), 34–40 [36].

Example 10.2 Carlo Sodi, *Baiocco et Serpilla, parodie françoise du Joueur* (Paris: Aux adresses ordinaires, n.d.), III, 48. Duo, 'Règne sur mon âme', final bars. SERPILLA, BAIOCCO: '[For you my love] will grow.'

Charles Favart to work for them.[89] He would not be able to write opéra-comique but could write music-based *parodies* because the court had reversed its 1745 ban on them. Favart's new *parodies* (Table 8.7) made the Comédie-Italienne into 'the best-attended theatre in Paris',[90] because they were perceived as almost self-sufficient popular operas. Working with a new generation of beautiful songs such as Moncrif's *romances*, Favart moved the balance away from satirising a target opera. *Les Amours champêtres* (*Love in the Country*) transformed 'Les Sauvages' in Rameau's *Les Indes galantes* such that Adario became Philinte, a timorous shepherd sung by Rochard. He wins over Hélène, sung by Justine Favart (Zima in the original), who is entranced by the beauty and sincerity of his musical avowals.

This successful formula was adopted by others, including the civil servant Pierre-Thomas Gondot.[91] Gondot's *Les Bergers de qualité* (The

---

[89] La Porte, *Voyage* (1753), 166–7.
[90] Ibid., 166; see d'Argenson, *Notices* (1725–57), II, 725, 732, 737.
[91] With Favart's advice, according to Gueullette, *Notes et souvenirs* (1750–62), 155.

Well-Born Shepherds) in June 1752 parodied *Daphnis et Chloé* by Boismortier (1747, recently revived). The Bambini troupe was still in Strasbourg, yet Gondot included 'Italian' numbers: Collette's '*air* Italien' and her '*Menuet* Italien' with Zirzis, both in Act II/2, and a tearful B minor duet for Rochard with Justine Favart. It was credited to 'Hendel'.[92]

Only a month after the Bouffons' first night, C. S. Favart's *Tircis et Doristée* (based on Lully's *Acis et Galathée*) began with an *air*, 'De la Serva Padrona', as the lovesick Tircis (Justine Favart) awaits his beloved at dawn: this *galant menuet* may have derived from a motet by either Giuseppe Paganelli or Karl Heinrich Graun.[93] Obviously the authentic Pergolesi could not be far behind, and in *Raton et Rosette* (March 1753) the Favarts displayed seven set pieces from four different Bouffon *intermezzi*.[94] There were also numbers from *Le Devin du village* as well as numerous old and new *vaudevilles*. The intrigue offered a bland reworking of Mondonville's *Titon et l'Aurore*, inserting *divertissements* to accommodate some Italian music. Thus it is hard to say what the whole thing is 'about' except for being a showpiece for Justine Favart as Rosette. Rosalie Astraudi as Raton had no Italian music except the 'echo' part in 'Se giammai da spèco, l'èco'. It was 'la *dlle Favard*' and the ballet sequences by Dehesse that d'Argenson considered the main attractions.[95]

*

Justine Favart meanwhile had been encouraging an original idea by an almost unknown lawyer-turned-dramatist, Pierre Baurans (1710–64).[96] His concept, *comédie mêlée d'ariettes*, was eventually launched in 1754 as *La servante maîtresse*. It combined Pergolesi's music with spoken dialogue in rhyming verse; avoided *vaudevilles*; and eschewed lengthy texts such as Favart's fifty-two lines of French for 'Colà sul praticello'. Baurans' characters would be developed through the kind of dialogue found in theatre comedy. Because the Comédie-Italienne was a variegated company, Charles Rochard and Justine Favart were experienced actors, regularly appearing in plays.

---

[92] Act III/6: 'Ma douleur prend trop d'empire': *Les Bergers de qualité* (Paris: Vve Delormel & fils, 1752), 43–4. Example in *OAR*, 133. The true composer is unknown.

[93] Concordances of incipit on *RISM*, Mss in Warsaw and Prague: binary form, 59 bars of music.

[94] 'Ei mi par' che già' (from 'A Serpina penserete' in *La serva padrona*), 'Se giammai' and 'Netto, netto' (*Il maestro di musica*), 'Si raviva' and 'Spera forsan ch'un dì' (*Il giocatore*), 'La fravoletta' and 'Colà sul praticello' (*La finta cameriera*)

[95] D'Argenson, *Notices* (1725–57), 749.

[96] His play *Pygmalion*, written with Procope-Couteaux, was seen at the CI in 1741, but Justine Favart apparently had to extract *La Servante maîtresse* from him: Anon., 'Éloge historique de M. Baurans' (1767).

What was at stake in taking *intermezzi* seriously? Any non-French work had to please a public aware of its literary heritage and perceived superiority. Some *intermezzi* succeeded better than others in finding points of contact with French taste, reflecting cosmopolitan themes even if their sources were Italian. For example, *Il cinese rimpatriato* (*The Chinese Man Returned*) arrived not long after Voltaire's *Le Siècle de Louis XIV* (1751) whose closing chapters discussed China; both were followed by Voltaire's *L'Orpheline de la Chine* (*The Chinese Orphan*) in 1755.[97] *La serva padrona* had roots in Italian literature,[98] but Paris would have remembered that Serpina's type went back to Gherardi's era: the Biancolelli daughters acted roles where 'the *amoureuse* and [...] the *servetta* have visibly converged', as happens in *La serva padrona*.[99] Soubrettes in spoken comedy were endowed with commanding wit,[100] and this aspect of Serpina could be drawn upon in the dialogue for *La Servante maîtresse*. Crispin, the astute male servant of French tradition, now seemed *passé*:

> It is a fact of nature that an old *monsieur* takes a liking to [a servant], allows himself to be governed; that she should take advantage of the authority she usurps and should be insolent, submissive, disdainful, caring by turns – and that in the end the old man marries her. Such scenes happen every day in the world and we see a thousand examples of it. So it is an excellent comic subject.[101]

There was some resemblance between *La serva padrona* and Richardson's best-seller *Pamela*, a 'fraught dance of conflict and compromise played out between its servant heroine and the predatory master she first resists and finally marries'.[102] Also familiar as a plot type was *La finta cameriera*, which echoed Pannard's *Les deux suivantes* (*The Two Servants*) – both place a cross-dressed lover in the role of a servant. With *Il maestro di musica* the theme seemed only too familiar: a talented young singer is ambitious to find fame and demonstrates her vocal prowess.[103] Lauretta rejects her teacher Lamberto and leaves with the flamboyant impresario Collaggiani. Music-making on stage, as happens here, was known not just from Boissy's

---

[97] Pré, 'Livret d'opéra-comique', 347. On Chinese attitudes to women: La Porte, *Voyage* (1753), I, 10–13.
[98] Toscani, '*La serva padrona*'; Talbot, 'Preface' to Albinoni, *Pimpinone*.
[99] Griffiths, 'Sunset', 102.   [100] Morand, *La Conquête*, 62, 116–17.
[101] Fréron, *AL*, 1754/6 (15 Oct.), 35.
[102] Keymer, 'Introduction', Richardson, *Pamela* (1740), vii. The first French translation was in 1741.
[103] Pasticcio derived from A. Palomba and Pietro Auletta, *Orazio* (1737): Trolese, '*Orazio*'; Walker, '*Orazio*'; Mackenzie, 'Creation of a Genre', *passim*. *NGO*, III, 955 credits three vocal numbers to Pergolesi.

play *Les Talents à la mode* but also from Lesage's *Le Mari préféré* (*The Preferred Husband*) and its singing lesson, music composed by Gillier.[104] Gypsy dancers in the Bouffons' *La zingara* could have reminded Parisians of those in Lesage's *La Pénélope moderne* (*The New Penelope*), again with Gillier's music: this was restaged in winter 1754.[105]

Various 'threads' linked *Bertoldo in corte* with French culture even though it told an ancient Italian tale (a translation had just come out in Paris)[106] in which Bertoldo's peasant family enters a prince's domain. Marivaux's play *La Double inconstance* (*Double Inconstancy*, 1723) had trodden similar territory and was regularly seen at the Comédie-Italienne. Having chosen to make *Bertoldo* an opera rather than a play, Goldoni could 'flirt with [social] themes that he could not raise in his comedies'.[107] As Chapter 11 shows, social themes also characterise C. S. Favart's version of *Bertoldo*, entitled *Ninette à la cour* (*Ninette at Court*). To quote Ted A. Emery,

[*Bertoldo*] repeats the arcadian opposition of a 'pure' agrarian society to a 'corrupt' court, but this motive, common in Italian literature at least as early as Tasso, now seems tinged with sentiments that hint at Goldoni's interest in the liberal philosophy of the Enlightenment. The first and most powerful indication of a conflict between court and country is developed in Act I, scenes 3 to 5, where the symbolic opposition of two ways of life [...] is cast as a face-off between a peasant and his lord. King Alboino sets an arrogant tone before Bertoldo is allowed to enter. [...] Bertoldo, however, proves to be at least as capable of clear reasoning as the aristocrats. His opening lines read like a popularisation of the illuministic notion of the natural quality of man.

In general moral terms, Italian musical comedy offered stronger feelings of personal liberty than was usual on the French stage; there was in Italian comedy, too, a weaker sense of social convention as something inviolable. Italian music created metaphors of feeling and persuasion, whereas in *vaudeville* opera, musical effect was paired with literary effect and allusions to external factors.

With Baurans' and C.S. Favart's *comédies mêlées d'ariettes* the essence was hybridity: engaging with Italian music through French-language comedy. We shall see in Chapter 11 how such adaptations could give Italian

---

[104] FSL, 1736: *TF* IX, 376–81 (R/II/488–90). [105] FSL, 1728: *TF* VII, 59–64 (R/II/167–8).
[106] *Histoire de Bertholde* (La Haye [=Paris], 1752) translated from Giulio Cesare Croce (1550–1609). See Sonneck, 'Ciampi's *Bertoldo*' and Iacuzzi, *European Vogue*, 248–53.
[107] This and the next quotation are from Emery, 'Goldoni as Librettist', 247–8, 252–3. The Paris *Bertoldo* derived from Goldoni's *Bertoldo, Bertoldino e Cacasenno, dramma comico per musica* (Venice, 1749).

music new dramatic roles and how newly imported arias enriched aspects of a particular character. Whereas Goldoni's *Bertoldo* did not survive beyond 1762, *Ninette à la cour* survived for four decades thanks to further adaptations in Denmark, Holland, England, Germany, Sweden and Italy.[108]

In a rare performance of *intermezzi* with spoken dialogue, a 1954 recording on YouTube may be referenced: *Il maestro di musica*, sung and spoken in German.[109] Seen in action here are two principles identified by Chamfort, described in Chapter 1. First we have 'temporal equality, or shared dramaturgy' giving either music or spoken dialogue 'the right to articulate any situation'. Second we find 'the feeling of continuity across music and speech'. Furthermore, hearing German language helps us to imagine the sensation of 'displacement' when *intermezzo* music was heard in French: many Parisians had assumed an exclusive bond between French poetry and its music. As the symphonist Charles-Henri de Blainville thought at the time, 'Is it proposed that we should have an Italian music to French words? One might as well put Italian words to French music. No-one, I take it, is propounding such transformations.'[110] But this is exactly what happened. Blainville's view matched Rousseau's *Lettre sur la musique françoise*, but their positions were overtaken, if not eliminated, by a change in public opinion produced by the hybrid operas we are discussing.

The Vienna recording shows how opéra-comique became European in the wider sense, sharing a variety of languages (even English in many cases). This performance has a lightness and self-conscious humour apt for operetta. And local additions from 1954 – whether jokes, orchestral parts, filling, selection and ordering of *ariettes* or the choice of ending – all illustrate the factors of regionalism and collaboration typical of popular opera.[111]

In Table 10.4 we can see in conclusion how Pierre Baurans and C. S. Favart worked when making hybrid works; the hidden contributions of Justine Favart must also be remembered.[112] Perhaps using musical

---

[108] Iacuzzi, *European Vogue*, 354–6; Loewenberg, *Annals*, 229–30.
[109] Vienna performance with Graziella Sciutti, Fritz Wunderlich, Walter Berry, cond. Hans Swarovsky, who probably made the German translation: www.youtube.com/watch?v=W6IdzyVPRB4.
[110] Blainville, *L'Esprit* (1754), 124.
[111] The Vienna production ends with the trio 'Caro Signor maestro', and Lauretta stays with Lamberto in the end. This is preceded by the duet which ends the work in its 1755 French version ('A celle qui t'engage'), itself imported from *Tracollo*.
[112] Legrand, 'Justine Favart parodiste'; Münzmay, 'Introduction' to Favart and Blaise, *Annette et Lubin* (1762).

Table 10.4 Summary of numerical differences between Bouffon versions of four *intermezzi* at the Opéra and their derived *comédies mêlées d'ariettes* at the Comédie-Italienne. See Table 8.6 for performance details. 'Imported' in the last two columns refers to music borrowed from operas or *intermezzi* quite different from those named in the first column.

Titles of Italian originals and of their French adaptations.	Total of solo numbers and accompanied recitatives in Italian original at the Opéra.	Total of solo numbers and accompanied recitatives in French version at the C.-I.	Total of duets and ensembles (incl. choruses) in Italian original at the Opéra.	Total of duets and ensembles in French version at the C.-I.	Total of newly imported or composed solo numbers in French version.	Total of newly imported or newly created ensembles in French version.
La serva padrona / La Servante maîtresse	7	10	2	3	4	1 (new composition)
Il maestro di musica / Le Maître de musique (1755 version of II)	7	11	4	2	5	1
Il maestro di musica / Le Maître de musique (1757 version of II)	7	17	4	2	10	1
La zingara / La Bohémienne	10	14	5	3	5	1
Bertoldo in corte / Ninette à la cour	19[a]	15	6	11	(11)	(11)[b]

[a] Act II of *Bertoldo* is lost, therefore this figure is derived from the libretto, and the totals in columns 5 and 6 are open to doubt.
[b] Includes Favart's multi-voiced arrangements of solos.

advisers, they rethought material in the manner of Italian impresarios, introducing new arias with increasing confidence. They were willing to improve things as necessary: Baurans made an expanded version of Act II of *Le Maître de musique*,[113] while Favart made changes to *Ninette à la cour*. Table 10.4 shows both versions of *Le Maître de musique*, but for *Ninette*, only the contents of the definitive two-act version (December 1758) are shown.[114]

*

The YouTube recording of once-popular *intermezzi* shows why the Bouffons' residence in Paris could be both an end and a beginning. It was an end because when these singers left Paris, no further Italian operas were imported.[115] The contractual power of the Opéra we saw in Chapter 8 staunched that form of competition. But because the skills of Baurans and C. S. Favart matched performance skills at the Fairs and the Comédie-Italienne, a new beginning emerged through the companies' own strengths.

What was needed were ideas and music that could now stock the popular stage. In the following chapters we shall discover the strategies which resulted from this need. One answer was to invent an overall dramaturgy that favoured dialogue within both speech and music. Another was to absorb the implications of Rousseau's new style in *Le Devin du village*. This and other syntheses led towards the formation of what would be named, among other things, a 'musico-dramatic art'.

---

[113] Revision in 1757: see Chapter 11.
[114] The first version (1755) had three acts: Sonneck, 'Ciampi's *Bertoldo*', 165–76. Sonneck was unaware of *Bertoldo in corte*'s Ms source (Act I only) at F-Po, A.191.
[115] Until the Opéra season of 1778: Fabiano, *Histoire*, 71–103; see 'Caribaldi, Gioacchino', *DOP*, I, 681–2.

11 | Six Methods of Synthesis

Reform of popular opera was obviously as necessary as the reform of serious opera, Paris being an international hub. Historically it is no less important: French reform of comedy happened first, and its legacy was no less significant. History remembers Count Algarotti's deprecation of *opera seria* but forgets his praise of comic *intermezzi*: 'This stile soon obtained the vogue [...] although called plebeian. Why did it succeed? Because it was fraught with truth'.[1] One task of the present chapter is to locate what kinds of 'truth' in *intermezzi* were discovered by reformers of French popular opera.

Parisian embrace of the Bouffons' music took opéra-comique by degrees into completely new territory, so that Italy was left behind. Ideas from *intermezzi* were put to new uses. The reformed genre became an *avant-garde* phenomenon with international appeal. It also answered a need, or a question, that had long been formulated: how should music find a way out of the French–Italian dichotomy? As far back as 1713, some thought that 'one could devise a perfect kind of music' by creating a blend of 'natural and simple' French qualities with 'learned and ingenious' Italian ones'.[2]

Rémond de Saint-Mard proposed that 'poet and composer be joined together in the same person' as a way to improve or reform French opera.[3] We shall discover in this chapter how his proposal actually came about, resulting in operatic comedies for several different theatres. Pierre Baurans, C. S. Favart, Jean-Jacques Rousseau and (in Parma) Egidio Duni joined words to music, making opera individually. In *Les Troqueurs* (*The Swappers*) Dauvergne joined with Vadé and in *Le Peintre amoureux de son modèle* (*The Painter who Loved his Model*) Duni joined with Anseaume, new teams breaking new ground. All 'six methods of synthesis' contributed towards what Grétry later called 'musico-dramatic art'.

---

[1] Algarotti, *Saggio* (1755/63), transl. (1768), 50.
[2] Conclusion of [anon.], 'Dissertation sur la Musique Italienne et Françoise', *Mercure galant*, 1713, Nov., 3–62; trans. in Wood and Sadler, *French Baroque Opera*, 122–5.
[3] Rémond de Saint-Mard, *Réflexions* (1741), 41; *OAR*, 163–4.

Multivocal Elements

In the words of Wye J. Allanbrook, 'Opera buffa's focus on its characters' social rather than interior natures made these [musical] gestures brief and allusive, embedded them in actions, and hence (the most significant musical innovation) deployed them in constant gestural contrasts – in the "dialogued style", the "tone of nature".'[4] On top of this, 'musico-dramatic art' valued an aesthetic quality identified within the debate quoted in Chapter 1, p. 16. Mme d'Entreville, who preferred *vaudeville* opera, had complained that 'this little burlesque monster' [modern opéra-comique] might have some affinity with Italian *intermezzi* if it possessed, like its supposed model, 'a more regular and *univocal* [italics original] way of proceeding'. For her, opéras-comiques were now too irregular, too clever by half, and lacking in proper forms of poetry.[5] If we allow the term '*multi*vocal', we find it fits several aspects of the modern French style: plurality of motifs; new roles for the orchestra; duets and ensembles; descriptive narratives; and interplay between music and speech.

'Multivocal' arias came to Paris with the Bouffons, including the style that had been parodied in 'Un soldato valoroso': see p. 247. Two examples occurred in *Il maestro di musica* (*The Music Master*): both are on the Vienna recording introduced on p. 259. Collaggiani's 'Le virtuose che son famose' is multivocal because it intends to demonstrate, through his singing, the achievements of his pupils. Lauretta's aria 'A un gusto di stordire' conjures up the bright lights of a theatre career, focused through her imagination. Her narrative culminates in a motif imitating applause, something noisily plural (and the second subject of its sonata-binary form). Music like this did not simply imitate something, whether a cartwheel or a whip, but brought the fullness of a character on stage.

The most unusual narrative aria in the surviving Bouffon repertory (for much has been lost) is 'Gli Sbirri già l'aspettano', sung by the credulous Fazio in *La scaltra governatrice* (*The Shrewd Governor's Wife*) in January 1753.[6] Fazio has just overheard a plot being laid to rob him and reacts by imagining and envoicing the arrest and interrogation of the plotters. Detectives and suspects are vocally mimed in turn, then orchestral images are heard representing chains and oars in the prison galleys that

---

[4] Allanbrook, *Secular Commedia*, 16. [5] 'À M. Delagarde', *Mercure*, 1761, November, 167–8.
[6] *Overtur e Scelta d'Arie della Scaltra Governatrice* (n.p., n.d.), 31. Music (1747) by Gioacchino Cocchi, ed. in *La Maestra. Partitura dell' opera in facsimile*, ed. Anna Laura Bellina (Milan: Ricordi, 1987), xli and Table 8.

Example 11.1 Gioacchino Cocchi, *La scaltra governatrice*, III/2, aria 'Gli Sbirri già l'aspettano'. FAZIO: 'Oh, no! I hear the sounds of rusty chains; they're bringing out the oars.'

await his enemies: see Example 11.1. The *Mercure de France* picked this as 'the best aria in the opera'.[7] Gioacchino Cocchi, the composer, had nineteen text lines to set and included a sequence of musical figures to help the actor to project his imagined story, but – exceptionally – without ever returning to the opening text. Thus, Cocchi edged the musico-dramatic balance away from melodic primacy towards a more complete relationship between music, text and meaning, such as the French were later to aim for.

[7] *Mercure*, 1753, March, 155; *OAR*, 237 et seq.

'Gli Sbirri' demonstrates a further connection with French practice: lengthier sung texts allowed for enhanced dramatic content. In Chapter 9 we saw that Favart wrote such texts for instrumental pieces. When Vadé and Dauvergne wrote *Les Troqueurs* (*The Swappers*), longer texts also played their part, affording many multivocal possibilities.[8] Adapting the same technique for hybrid operas, Favart converted 'univocal' Italian arias into multivoiced ensembles.

Multivocal elements had arrived most obviously in the duets, trios and quartets of *intermezzi* and *opere buffe*. Elisabeth Cook identified thirty-six that were actually performed by Bambini's troupe – an average of two new pieces per month for the duration of their stay. Music for only twenty-three of them survives, but sufficient to explain their positive reception. Cook analysed reviews in the *Mercure de France* as follows:

> Three major points arise from these extracts [reviews of *La serva padrona*, *Il giocatore* and *Il maestro di musica*]. The first concerns the musical texture of the duets, all of which were composed in dialogue style, with solos progressing to overlapping and juxtaposed phrases and then to homophonic cadential agreement. Judging from the *Mercure*, French audiences immediately responded to dialogue textures in ensemble composition. They were felt to lend truth and precision (*justesse*) to the drama and translated the poetic text clearly. They had, moreover, style (*finesse*), great naturalness, and an appealing vivacity. [...] A second concern appears to have been the striking musical and dramatic *vérité* of the ensembles in question, their aptness and immediacy of expression, and their matching of music to the situation on stage.[9]

The third element of public approval was that of skilful rendition.

Hybrid Popular Operas

The best theatrical way to involve Italian music took time to determine. Hybrid operas involved Italian music sung in French. Their development was brief because, as mentioned in Chapter 8, the Opéra prevented popular theatre from appropriating more Italian material. But the best of them lived for many years, as Table 8.6 showed. From 1754 to 1757 both rival companies experimented with hybrid materials.

Instinctively, the Opéra-Comique first mixed Italian music with *vaudevilles*: fifty-six of these in *Bertholde à la ville* (*Bertoldo in Town*) were interspersed with five arias from Act I of *Bertoldo in corte* (*Bertoldo at*

---

[8] See Table 11.2 in *OAR*, 290.   [9] Cook, *Duet and Ensemble*, 63.

Court) and one from Cocchi's *La mascherata* (*The Masquerade*).[10] A Paris setting was used, replacing Goldoni's prince by the usual disagreeable money man (*traitant*).[11] In *Le Chinois poli en France* (*The Stylish Chinese Man in France*) sixty-five *vaudevilles* were mixed with a catchy *ariette* from *Il cinese rimpatriato* (*The Chinese Man Returned*), one from *La donna superba* (*The Haughty Woman*) and the closing duet from Act I of *La zingara* (*The Gypsy*).[12] It was witty by comparison with *Bertholde*: the young Nouradden, returning to China, is struck by social and sentimental differences between his home country and France. Italian arias represent foreign influences that the young man likes, heard against *vaudevilles* which represent Chinese norms.

The synthesis then created by Pierre Baurans omitted all *vaudevilles*, and his generic label for the result was *comédie mêlée d'ariettes* ('a play mixed with Italianate music'). He devised two of these and Favart wrote four, all being for the Comédie-Italienne.[13] Spoken verse, freely expanded from the Italian recitative texts, gave elegant life and ironic humour to the characters, as in *La Servante maîtresse*:

PANDOLPHE What the devil? Why is Madame interfering?
                I shall go out.
ZERBINE   You shall not go out.
                And if you disobey I shall go and lock the door.
PANDOLPHE Am I dreaming this?

Audience attention was shared between conversation and music, making for a semi-discrete dramaturgical rhythm. But Pierre Baurans also brought in new music: two accompanied recitatives, two new *ariettes* and one brief dialogue-duet, 'Eh bien! Finiras-tu?' early in Act I, composer unknown.[14] This replaced *secco* recitative in Pergolesi which dramatised the power relations between Pandolphe (Pergolesi's Uberto, the confirmed bachelor),

---

[10] *Bertholde à la ville. Opéra Comique mêlé d'ariettes* (Paris: La Chevardiere etc., n.p.). Attributions in Wotquenne, *Catalogue*, II, 382 except for 'Votre cœur en vain murmure' (=*Bertoldo*, 'Se in me speranza avete') and 'A tant de charmes' (=*Bertoldo*, 'Pupille care'). See Sonneck, 'Bertoldo', 158-62.

[11] Text by Anseaume and Marcouville; the plot is in Iacuzzi, *European Vogue*, 254-6.

[12] Text by Anseaume, incorporating 'Petits maîtres sans cervelle' ('Zerbinotti d'oggi dì'), 'D'une vaine crainte' ('Così mi piacete'), and 'L'amour d'un trait vainqueur' ('Amor, O che dilètto'). The source of the *ariette* 'Ne craigniez rien' remains unidentified.

[13] The other derived works, *Le Charlatan* and *La Pipée*, do not survive in musically complete form.

[14] *La Servante maîtresse. Comédie en deux actes mêlée d'ariettes parodiées de La serva padrona* (Paris, etc.: De La Chevardiere). 'Eh bien! Finiras-tu?' is differently classified in Schneider, '*La serva padrona*', an article important for documenting the influence of Baurans' adaptation outside France.

Zerbine (Serpina, his ward, kept in a servant's role) and Scapin (Vespone, the silent valet). Zerbine is berating Scapin almost violently and countermands Pandolphe's orders; Pandolphe sings brief and ironic remarks. Here, Baurans and his composer were building on a type of aria in *intermezzi* in which a soloist would interact (while singing) with a silent character: an 'implied dialogue' one might say.[15] But 'Eh bien! Finiras-tu?' changed this convention into a short ensemble in actual dialogue, with two people who sing and one who remains silent: an inconspicuous stepping stone towards 'musico-dramatic art'.

At the start of Act II Baurans added the homely *air* 'Vous gentilles jeunes filles' for Zerbine.[16] But eleven spoken lines later he transformed her character completely with a bravura aria, 'Charmant espoir', taken from *Bertoldo in corte* ('Grandi è ver son le mie pene'): in effect, an *opera seria* piece. Sung by Maria Lepri as the queen dowager Armira, it had been heard at the Opéra only months before. Zerbine sings merely the first section of the da capo, but no other cuts were made.[17] If the addition looks unconvincing to us, for others 'the mixing of dialogue, accompanied recitative and *ariettes*' created 'an extremely pleasurable entertainment'.[18]

Thus encouraged, Baurans turned to *Il maestro di musica*, making the impulsive singing-pupil Lauretta into a more thoughtful Laurette and reversing the ending. His substantial dialogue scenes occupied spaces made free by removing 'Splènde fra noi' and 'Qual doppo insano' in Act II: the Comédie-Italienne had no separate chorus as yet.[19] The aria 'Le virtuose', sung at the Opéra by Pietro Manelli as Collaggiani, was allocated to Laurette's teacher, Lambert.[20] In Baurans's version Laurette does not leave home in the end: she rejects the impresario and accepts Lambert. But first she improves Lambert's attitude, articulately forcing him to apologise

---

[15] *Tracollo*, 'Vi stò ben', 'Questo foglio', 'Non si muove'; *La donna superba*, 'Così mi piacete'; *Il paratajo*, 'Chi è bello', 'Io voglio il testamento'; *La zingara*, 'Tu non pensi'; *Bertoldo in corte*, 'Se di me gelosa siete'. Similarly in *La serva padrona* 'Stizzoso mio stizzoso' shows Serpina provoking Uberto and 'Sempre in contrasti' shows Uberto provoking Vespone.

[16] Originally 'Donne belle che bramate', perhaps by Galuppi, in *Amor mascherato* (see *RISM*); Wotquenne, *Catalogue*, II, 382. Roland de la Platière, *Lettres* (1780), VI, 148, attributes it to Galuppi, *Le calamita de' cuori*.

[17] Music of unknown provenance, at F-Po, A.191, f° 5ᵛ (see n. 30). Soloists after Justine Favart also sang it, for example Mlle Victoire: *Mercure*, 1756, Dec., 201.

[18] Fréron, *AL*, 1754/6 (15 Oct.), 39.

[19] Pergolesi, *Le Maître de musique* [= *Il maestro di musica*], *opera bouffon italien* (Paris: Boivin, Leclerc etc., n.d.), 38, 41.

[20] [Pergolesi/Baurans], *Le Maître de musique. Comédie mellé* [sic] *d'ariettes parodiées de L'italien* (Paris: Bailleux, n.d.), 18: 'Le virtuose' became 'Oui, nos chanteuses', sung before Tracolin (Collaggiani) appears.

for his persistent jealousy, caused by having seen the impresario (called Tracolin) kneel to her at the end of Act I. Laurette's persuasive powers are further defined through stage directions in 'Ingrat, je romps ma chaîne' in Act II. This was a newly introduced *ariette* from *I viaggiatori* (*The Travellers*, the Bouffons' final opera) whose character Emilia – sung by Maria Lepri – had displayed two contrasting emotions.[21] With Laurette, things are more complicated: she *pretends* to angrily reject Lambert, who is actually on stage with her. As the music changes (the stage direction instructs this) she sympathises 'tenderly' with him, singing just loudly enough for him to hear. A plain monologue thus became a mixed message, ironic and characterful.

The performance history of *Le Maître de musique* reveals further changes. Initial success was dampened by fewer performances in 1756; Act II seemed 'too serious and unvaried', but by then the score had been published and represents the only version now generally known. Baurans made a thorough revision with two more characters and six further ariettes,[22] this being premiered on 7 March 1757.[23] One *ariette* for Laurette ('Qu'espère un amant': of unknown provenance) involved a thirty-three-line text as she continued to teach Lambert to love respectfully. We await a first edition of this unique Brussels manuscript.

*

The Opéra-Comique's next adaptation, Moustou's *La Bohémienne* (*The Gypsy*) abandoned *vaudevilles* and adopted Baurans's system. Moustou made minimal changes to the Italian plot and its music as found in Rinaldo Di Capua's *La zingara*. Favart's rival version of *La Bohémienne*

---

[21] 'Va pur spergiuro ingrato' in I/8; text: *I viaggiatori, Intermezzo per musica* (Paris: Vve Delormel & Fils, 1754), 26. No original score exists for *I viaggiatori*; this attribution, discovered by Michel Noiray, is in Roland de La Platière, *Lettres* (1780), VI, 152.

[22] Baurans's new version, explained as 'Changemens', is found in some librettos of *Le Maître de musique* (Paris: Vve Delormel & Fils, 1755 [sic]), 41. Copy consulted: F-Pn (Mus), ThB.1664. The only known full score of the second version is Brussels, Conservatoire Royal de Musique, MS 2028. Attributions: Wotquenne, *Catalogue*, II, 386. 'Oh la puissante [score: plaisante] querelle' was taken from Latilla, *Gli artigiani arricchiti* and 'Le badinage' from Davide Perez, 'Se mai perdete l'idolo che amate'. The unattributed 'Ah! Mon cœur' was written specially, because it is a comic demonstration of bad music sung by its supposed composer, Clarinel. An altered version of the work for Dresden is available online (through RISM: D-DL, Mus.2-F-525). The new voice lines, alone, are found in one libretto (Bruxelles: J. J. Boucherie, 1757: on *Gallica*).

[23] Date: Léris, *Dictionnaire* (1763), 274. Five actors, as needed, are recorded in the F-Po *Registre* on this date, lacking names. Another libretto (Didot l'aîné, 1772) gives five singers' names, including Jean-François Lejeune as Lambert. He joined the CI in February 1760, so we know that Baurans's new version was retained: Campardon, *Comédiens*, I, 283–4; Brenner, *Théâtre Italien*, 366.

came out two weeks later. *La zingara* represented a good model for popular opera: its comedy is easy to follow and visual in nature. In order to trick the miser Calcante, the heroine's brother impersonates a bear which he and his sister sell to Calcante for a large sum. The music is up-to-date in style, with repeated-note motifs; oboes and horns participate. Nevertheless the French versions differed between themselves. When Di Capua's heroine Nisa (sung in Paris by Anna Tonelli) performed 'Viverò se tu lo vuoi' the magnetic beauty of the melody, intended to captivate Calcante, was absolute, so Moustou kept the same music.[24] But Favart did not: his Nise sings an imported aria at this important point ('Pauvre Nise', originally 'Vedovella' from *La scaltra governatrice*). Favart's twist, in a new deception, shows the miser respecting Nise's character, not just beauty, because her music and the rewritten spoken dialogue persuade him that she wishes to return his stolen purse even at the cost of self-sacrifice to a devil (her brother in disguise). So Calcante thinks he will save her by marrying her.[25]

Favart's skill lay in so many details, as one more example may show. Unsure of success at the beginning of Act II, Nisa had sung a brisk 3/8 aria, 'È spècie di tormento' ('It is a kind of torment').[26] Moustou's adaptation focused on the same emotional field with words like 'espoir' (hope), 'enflamme' (loves), 'enivre' (desires) and 'plaisir'. But Favart associated the music's image with the swooping motion of a bird in flight, suggesting a metaphor for the wealthy prey that Nise is hoping to catch. Words like 'guette' ('watch closely'), 'avance' and 'piège' ('trap') make the music work harder in illuminating Nise's character: 'He flies off, he comes near, I watch until he's caught': see Example 11.2. Justine Favart must have responded to these suggestions, while C. S. Favart's parodic acuity was long appreciated and, sometimes, even discussed in print.[27]

*

Ninette à la cour (*Ninette at Court*) was pivotal for the history of popular opera both in France and abroad,[28] and Ninette's character was Justine

---

[24] *La Bohémienne* [=*La zingara*] *Intermède en deux actes del signor Rinaldo Da Capua* (Paris: Aux adresses ordinaires, n.d.), 87; discussion and example in *OAR*, 276–7. Moustou's text: 'Si vous méprisez, chère âme'.
[25] *La Bohémienne, comedie en deux actes en vers meslée d'ariettes, traduite de La zingara* (Paris, etc.: De La Chevardiere *et al.*, n.d.), 84.
[26] Text originally from Metastasio's *Temistocle*; the music is by Andrea Bernasconi (1740), as sources on *RISM* reveal.
[27] [Anon.], 'Réflexions sur l'opéra italien', *Journal encyclopédique* (April 1769) tome III, part 2, 285–6, comparing Vinci's setting of Metastasio's 'Vò solcando un mar crudele' with Favart's 'Le nocher loin du rivage' within *Ninette à la cour*.
[28] Iacuzzi, *European Vogue*, 354–6. This is the score's title; its libretto's was *Le Caprice amoureux, ou Ninette à la cour*.

Example 11.2 Andrea Bernasconi, 'È spècie di tormento' as part of Rinaldo Di Capua, *La zingara* (*La Bohémienne*, Paris, Aux adresses ordinaires, n.d.), II/1, 44–9. French text from Favart, *La Bohémienne* (Paris: De la Chevardiere, n.d.), II/2, 53–8. NICE: 'It's a pleasure, an intensity, which would not be believed.' NISE: 'He flies off, he comes near, I watch until he's caught.'

Favart's most complex role to date. Table 10.4 compares the vocal numbers in *Ninette* with its Paris source, *Bertoldo in corte*. Goldoni and Ciampi's Venice original was still a recent work whose popularity had, in the Italian way, wrought many changes already.[29] It was further reconceived for the Comédie-Italienne but without reducing its critical effect or double portrayal of the court and the village.[30] Whereas *Bertoldo* employed scene-changes in each act, however, *Ninette* kept Act I in the village and Act II in the court. Favart reduced the participants to two villagers (Ninette and Colas, to be married next day) and four courtiers (Prince Astolphe; Countess Emilie; Dorine; and Fabrice, a mainly spoken part). The following synopsis follows the definitive two-act score.[31]

Act I: Astolphe, although betrothed to Emilie, has fallen for Ninette. At first incognito, he comes to the village with his confidant Fabrice

---

[29] As described in Sonneck, 'Ciampi's *Bertoldo*'.

[30] The Paris *Bertoldo* survives in F-Po, A.191, Act I only (not on *Gallica*). Pieces probably by Ciampi: 'Quando s'incontrano'; 'Qui si fatica'; 'Ahi, ahi, non farò più'; 'Maledetti quanti siete'; 'Se di me gelosa siete'; 'A riveder ritorno', all texts in the 1749 libretto. Music from Act II may well survive in *Ninette*. The Paris *Bertoldo* had four village characters and two courtly ones: *Bertoldo in corte* (Paris: Vve Delormel, 1753). There had been nine roles in the original 1749 opera: Sonneck, 'Ciampi's *Bertoldo*', 119.

[31] *Ninette à la cour. Parodie de Bertholde à la ville* (Paris: La Chevardiere, etc., n.d [1758]), pp. 73 + 76 (separately paginated). The 1755 premiere was in three acts; the final version was first seen on 8 March 1756.

and declares his love to her. Colas challenges Astolphe, who withdraws: but the latter reappears and discloses his identity when Colas hurts Ninette's arm, trying to pull her inside the house. Ninette agrees to accompany the Prince to his court.

Act II: Now being dressed by Dorine and offered make-up and jewels, Ninette is completely unimpressed by court manners. She continues to reject the Prince's declarations and meets Countess Emilie. The Prince agrees to summon Colas, whose powers of resistance are swiftly tested out by Ninette, disguised as a simpering aristocrat. Ninette gains Emilie's confidence and the two women humiliate Astolphe during a darkened *imbroglio* scene (similarly to Mozart's *Figaro*, Act IV) before the two villagers make to return home.

Favart used music from *Bertoldo in corte* but added much new music, often making solos into dialogued ensembles. He was helped by Ciampi's music, which 'prefigures something of Mozart in his deftness at placing an emphatic, almost defiant musical gesture'.[32] It is impossible not to think of the character Figaro in 'Quando s'incontrano' when Bertoldo scoffs in the Prince's presence at the hypocrisy of all polite behaviour. Favart used this aria, however, to make a dialogue trio in I/5 ('Tu nous perdras, Colas') in which Colas swears at the Prince, still incognito, 'I won't take it. Go to the Devil, you damned seducer'.[33] *Ninette à la cour* also added objections to recreational hunting; in her first spoken scene with Astolphe, Ninette begs for help with the problem. Colas finally tells the Prince to 'stop amusing yourself by hunting on our land' (II/16).

The whole point of the Italian tale was that Bertoldo delivered egalitarian speeches at court. Ninette has the equivalent role, articulating a kind of naïve ridicule against court manners. And in the humiliation scene, Favart involves Astolphe in a dialogue quartet, whereas Goldoni's equivalent *imbroglio* scene had involved no courtly characters, being farcical.[34]

In Act I/4 Goldoni and Ciampi had a chorus of villagers extolling work and toil on one hand, but liberty, nature and beauty on the other. Favart aimed for the same effect with folk-like songs for Ninette and Colas working in Act I/1.[35] Non-singing actors toiled in the background while

---

[32] Heartz, 'Overture', 6.
[33] 'Ce coup m'accable. Va-t-en au Diable, chien d'suborneur': *Ninette*, 47.
[34] *Ninette*, II/16, 67: 'Ce cœur qu'il possède', taken from 'Se giammai da spèco, l'èco' in *Il maestro di musica*.
[35] Favart's 'Travaillons, travaillons', 'Contente je chante' and 'Que le nom de Ninon' resemble 'Chi hà perduto' or 'Vorrei esser uccello' in *Il paratajo*. Work songs in popular opera were mentioned in Chapter 2, pp. 31–2.

the couple's happiness resounded in their 'Duo des cloches' ('Bell duet'), arranged from the roisterous finale I of *La finta cameriera*. But a different mood is projected in Ninette's next song, delivered 'as she pretends to work', knowing that the unknown courtier is watching her: 'Je vois du plus beau jour'.[36] Taken from Cocchi's *La mascherata* (1751), it has simple credentials (6/8 metre, lilting melody, strophic form) but is obviously more artificial than what she has sung before. It makes manifest Ninette's attractiveness to the Prince, who will love her partly for her quickness in mastery of court conventions. Favart builds up his musical picture gradually: Table 11.1 charts the disposition of its ten dialogue ensembles alongside fifteen solos.

All ensembles except one involve Ninette, who has six solos. The prince also has six solos, often in heroic mode, and joins in six ensembles. Favart was choosing arias from a wide swathe of sources, supplying words and giving music the same freedom to incorporate dialogue and action as was traditionally accorded to *vaudevilles*. He could imagine exactly where in an

Table 11.1 Music and action in *Ninette à la cour*.[37]

Location	Music	Action
ACT I: Exposition, Sc. 1–4	Seven solos and one duet, in radically different styles.	Scene-setting; background details; arrival of Astolphe, at first incognito.
Development and crisis, Sc. 4–8	4 dialogue ensembles and one solo.	The Prince tempts Ninette and declares his love. Colas restrains Ninette physically; she decides to visit the court and satisfy her curiosity. Astolphe's huntsmen prevent Colas from following them.
ACT II: Exposition, Sc. 1–3	2 dialogue duets.	Ninette acclimatises to court manners.
Sc. 4–8	1 dialogue duet, 3 solos.	Astolphe and Emilie begin to understand Ninette as a person.
Development, Sc. 9	2 solos, 1 dialogue duet.	Colas arrives, stuffed into a court costume, and suffers a mock-seduction by Ninette in disguise.
Dénouement and resolution, Sc. 10–16	2 solos, 2 quartets, the first in dialogue.	Ninette plots with Emilie; Astolphe declares his love to Emilie, thinking in the darkness that she is Ninette. Humiliated, he agrees to the release of the villagers.

[36] I/4, 27. It had been heard in the Paris *Bertoldo* at the identical point as 'Amore è fatto'.
[37] Detailed sources and attributions listed in Smith, 'Egidio Duni', 56–9 and Sonneck, 'Ciampi's *Bertoldo*'.

aria a new emotional or histrionic contrast might fit; indeed we can easily compare the would-be seducer's first duet with Ninette with the famous duettino between Don Giovanni and Zerlina, 'Là ci darem la mano'. Actually, the music was taken by Favart from an aria in *Il cinese rimpatriato*:[38] see Example 11.3.

In *Le Devin du village* and later popular opera, vocal forms themselves became servants of drama. A virtuoso paradigm of this in *Ninette* was Favart's arrangement of a short aria ('Ahi! Ahi!') that Ciampi had imagined for the young grandson of Bertoldo, Cacasenno: he has been chastised for misbehaving. The piece must have been well known,[39] for an analysis of 'Ahi! Ahi!' detailed Ciampi's image of the boy, whose vexation and anger are found in 'all the accompanying instruments'.[40] Favart devoted the first eighteen bars to the Act I argument between Ninette and Colas, hurting her arm, but suddenly turned the last twenty-two bars into a trio when the Prince appears, making a difficult domestic situation worse.

The finesse with which Favart shared out responsibility between music and dialogue is truly memorable. In her dialogue duet with the Prince in Act II/4 Ninette sings a clever reply to his latest refusal to acknowledge that she misses Colas: 'Give me two hearts, if you are so powerful'. The music of 'Donnez-moi deux cœurs' was taken by Favart from Nicola Porpora's London aria, 'Dall'amor più sventurato' (1736):[41] its catchy theme in A major was brilliantly chosen to suggest Ninette's witty superiority. The prince can hardly believe this rejection. Three scenes later Ninette returns to her taunt with insolent irony within spoken dialogue, upon realising that Emilie – whom she is meeting for the first time – is in a relationship with Astolphe:

Ah, le Prince est son Amoureux.	It seems her lover is the Prince.
Je le vois bien icy l'on a donc l'avantage	Apparently we have the right
De partager son cœur à deux.	At court to make one heart serve two.
C'est encore un plaisant usage.	At least it's a singular thing to do.[42]

---

[38] The aria adapted by Favart, 'Io sono una Donzella', possessed ironic force because it had expressed the fears of Argese when confronted by the impulsive Vexorin: [Sellitto, attrib.], *Arie, e Duetto Del Cinese* (n.p., n.d.), 6.

[39] As used within *Le Diable à quatre* the music is shown in *NOHM*, VII, 205–6.

[40] Lacombe, *Spectacle* (1761), 269–70. He identifies the singer as female since Cacasenno had been sung by Caterina Tonelli.

[41] From the pasticcio *Orfeo*; Mss in Stockholm, Brussels and London: see *RISM*. The idea of 'two hearts' was adapted from Betta's riposte, 'Fate ch'io prender possa due Mariti' in I/9 of *Bertoldo in corte*. CD recording by Vivica Genaux.

[42] *Ninette à la cour*, 22; Ninette's irony can only indirectly be translated.

Example 11.3 Giuseppe Sellitto, *Il cinese rimpatriato*, 'Io sono una Donzella' parodied by Charles-Simon Favart in *Ninette à la cour*, I/4 as a dialogue duet, 'Tout va vous rendre hommage'. LE PRINCE: 'If I am guilty of too much urging, your beauty justifies me.' NINETTE: 'Not so fast, Monsieur. You embarrass me with so much esteem.' LE PRINCE: 'Ninette rejects me.'

Le Devin du village

Rousseau's *intermède* was the most regularly performed work of its time at the Opéra and was generously noted for its achievements by contemporaries and their successors. Courtly as well as popular roots helped to form its synthesis, including Mouret's *Les Amours de Ragonde* but also short pastoral works commissioned between 1747 and 1750 by the Marquise de Pompadour for her private company.[43] Pierre de La Garde's *Æglé* and Rebel and Francœur's *Ismène* had a songlike intimacy that matched intense emotional encounters between lovers.[44] Both had entered the Opéra by 1751 and had been published. All this helps to explain why *Le Devin du village* scored an instant success at Fontainebleau (1752) and at the Opéra (1753).[45] Colin and Colette are already friends, but Colin has been found attractive by the Lady of the Manor. The Soothsayer gets the villagers back together by persuading Colette to feign affection for a gentleman in the town. A *devin* (as in the English 'soothsayer') was able to discover a troubling truth – this is its meaning here – not simply to tell the future.

Le Devin du village must be celebrated for its complexity as a project, not just for the singability of its melodies, suited for performance at home and re-texted by others as *vaudevilles*.[46] Although not containing any spoken dialogue, it counts as a popular opera for at least three reasons: it escaped the poetic and musical languages of the court and the Opéra; it gained international familiarity; and its stage directions are linked to Fair theatre (see following).[47] Its special freedoms arise because it was written and composed by one single person, meaning that text, music and action served mutually. Gradually, Rousseau's example instilled awareness that *any* opera could aim for tighter collaboration: '*Le Devin du village* makes us always wish that a *Poème-Lyrique* might need but one author. Where shall we find a more perfect match, a more complete accord, between words and music?'[48] In popular opera this became a serious aim, at least for some.

---

[43] Kaehler, 'Operatic Repertoire'; *OAR*, 14–20, 118–29.
[44] Pompadour's repertory: *OAR*, Table 1.3. La Garde, notably, was a song composer.
[45] At the Fontainebleau premiere, or a rehearsal, some melodies were taken down aurally and issued in a pirate edition: Charlton, 'Spying on Rousseau'. The extended final scene was completed in 1753.
[46] *OAR*, 130–57. The following arguments are developed in Charlton, 'The Melodic Language'.
[47] Rousseau's place in pre-Revolution culture: Blanning, *Culture of Power*, 357–74. In London it was promoted by David Garrick and Charles Burney (Drury Lane, 1766). Fanny Burney thought it would 'refine the public taste amongst the middle classes': Kerry S. Grant, 'Introduction' to *The Cunning Man* (Burney's version) issued with *Le Devin du village* (1753), ed. Kaufman, vii.
[48] Nougaret, *De l'art* (1768), II, 294, and following sections.

A librettist like Sedaine and a composer like Monsigny would speak of themselves metaphorically as a married couple, committed to one artistic purpose.[49]

Rousseau's account of the conception of *Le Devin du village* was unequivocal: '[François Mussard and I] had a long talk about [Italian music] before going to bed, and especially about *opera buffa*, which we had both seen in Italy. [...] I began musing as to how one might go about introducing this kind of drama into France.'[50] His answer was to suggest modern French characters in rural guise. Events begin shortly before curtain-up with the kind of dalliance staged in *Bertoldo* and *Ninette*, for the Lady of the Manor has made Colin the gift of a fine ribbon. The Soothsayer knows that Colin has doubts and has returned to the village. The final truth-seeking reconciliation scene – discussed later – is reminiscent of emotional encounters in the Pompadour *entrées* and it distantly recalls those from 1681 and 1715 which we have documented on pp. 55–7 and 211–12.

Sometimes the music is Italian-inflected, though most is in what Charles Burney heard as 'a familiar pleasing ballad style, neither entirely French nor Italian'.[51] Removing Baroque idioms such as mixed time signatures, Rousseau adopted Italianate phrase-structures involving half the chord-changes per bar as were normally found at the Opéra. Most influentially, he evoked some specific *vaudeville* features, or simply improvised them, so that his melodies could seem rather *vaudeville*-like. In particular, the second melody in Example 11.4 may be compared with Example 5.3. Five of these *vaudeville* traits are seen in Example 11.4: gavotte rhythm; stepwise movement; smaller leaps (thirds and fourths, not fifths, sixths or octaves); limited variety of rhythms; continuous lines (i.e. melodies often extended while avoiding any rests). These are the facets that Egidio Duni (see following) would adopt in *Le Retour au village*. They are opposites of normative Italian features that he had employed up to then in *opera seria*.

The phrase 'Unity of melody' would be debated by Rousseau in his 1768 musical dictionary.[52] So one might observe that all melodies in Example 11.4 include four notes descending by step. We are never aware of this unity when listening because these *airs* all begin in other ways; but the four notes release their full effect in the chorus 'Colin revient à sa Bergère' when Colin and Colette have reunited and returned to their

---

[49] 'M. Sedaine has in this way married M. Monsigny': *Corr. litt.* (Furne ed.), VI, 61 (1 Nov. 1768).
[50] *Confessions*, Book 8, 365; Heartz, 'Italian by Intention'.
[51] Grant, 'Introduction', vii; Charlton, 'The melodic language'.
[52] Rousseau, *Écrits sur la musique*, 1143.

Example 11.4 Jean-Jacques Rousseau, *Le Devin du village*, opening bars of six solos showing five characteristic style features (see main text) and the prevalence of a falling stepwise figure.

community. Over simple chord-textures, sopranos enter on high g" and descend by four notes, without decoration; the harmony also makes us feel we have reached a concluding statement.[53]

Proposing new research on *Le Devin*, Jacqueline Waeber insisted on its connections with popular opera and acting styles.[54] She showed that several stage directions linked to Fair theatre tradition were somehow edited out of Rousseau's manuscript and are missing from the printed libretto and score. Thus *Le Devin* staged a 'confrontation' with traditional practices, linking acting and comedy to 'the legacies and potentialities of the "bas comique" [low comedy] and its related uses of music.'[55]

---

[53] Sc. 8: *Le Devin*, ed. Kaufman, 69. The 2nd-inversion chord would normally lead to a concluding cadence.
[54] Waeber, '"Le Devin de la Foire?"'   [55] *Ibid.*, 156.

Comedic stage directions at the Opéra had been used in Favart and Boismortier's *Don Quichotte chez la duchesse* and Rameau's *Platée*. But Rousseau, when describing the Soothsayer's exaggerated 'contortions' in Scene 4, introduced this word for the first time at the Opéra even though *devins* had been seen in Campra (*Les Fêtes vénitiennes*) and Rameau (*Dardanus*).[56] 'The term was heavily loaded [...] as characterising certain usages in the repertoire of the Fair theatres'.[57] The actor Saurin in 1714 had twisted his body, but Louis Cuvillier did no differently, as Waeber pointed out:

Nostradamus waves his wand like a cabbalist. He moves his lips and seems agitated by convulsive movements.[58]

The Devin takes from his pocket a book of spells and a small sextant with which to make a charm. Young peasant girls coming to consult him drop their gifts and rush away in fright, seeing his contortions.[59]

The distinction between these examples lies in Rousseau's planned, mimetic uses of music. Together with the above instruction was another which became erased: '*The actor must invent mysteriously comic gestures which are to be exactly timed to the music.*'[60] Similarly, Colette was to express movements of heartbroken sorrow '*so that, without caricature, they will be precisely timed with the music*', in the ritornello of her opening *ariette*. Only a shortened version of these words found its way into the printed sources.[61]

These cases of control, matching music with gestural meaning, were also developed in figurative dance within Scene 8, where the pantomimic directions allowed the work's social messages to emerge.[62] A courtier arrives in a village and propositions a young woman first with a purse, then a necklace which she tries on. The theme anticipated *Ninette à la cour* because there is then a confrontation with a young man, but it ends with a reconciliation between the courtier and the village couple.

Colin and Colette's reconciliation is in Scene 6, where Rousseau's unconventional use of musical forms dramatises the complexity of human relations. Colette is wearing an ornament or similar token to

---

[56] *Ibid.*, 164. Earlier stage-directions discussed: *OAR*, 31–40.
[57] Waeber, '"Le Devin de la Foire?"', 166–7.
[58] *Le Tombeau de Nostradamus*, Sc. 5: *TF* I, 182 (R/I/52).
[59] *Le Devin du village*, ed. Kaufman, Sc. 4, 38. The sextant ('bâton de Jacob') is shown in Waeber, *ibid.*, Plate C. Louis Cuvillier's brother had been cast as Momus in Rameau's *Platée* and his father as Sancho Pança in *Don Quichotte chez la duchesse*: *DOP*, I, 933–6.
[60] Waeber, *ibid.*, 164–6. [61] *Le Devin du village*, ed. Kaufman, 11; Waeber, *ibid.*, 167.
[62] See translation in Blanning, *Culture of Power*, 363 and *OAR*, 156–7; *Le Devin du village*, ed. Kaufman, 84–100.

remind Colin of her threat to leave him behind; he still wears the Lady's ribbon. The music first dramatises their physical distancing and nervousness. Each realises that the other is capable of making alternative choices involving wealth and social status.

(a) Recitative with mimed reactions during orchestral phrases. No conversation, only separate statements.
(b) Recitative and *air*: Colette rejects Colin, who is penitent.
(c) Recitative and first duet, G minor: Colin resolves to leave the village. The duet ends in disharmony: it dissolves as they try to avoid an affected separation neither wants.
(d) Second duet, G major, preceded by a ritornello-mime: here, Colette removes the Lady's ribbon, replacing it with one of hers.[63]

An even bolder rethinking of convention occurs in the subsequent *Romance* for Colin, 'Dans ma cabane obscure' (the penultimate melody in Example 11.4). At the Opéra, virtuoso singing normally followed after the main action.[64] Colin instead has a very simple melody – merely two strophes with four descending notes, describing hard labour in the open air. Perhaps, even as it became a *vaudeville* itself, this reminded people of how Voltaire also had measured truth against sentimentality:

Vois-tu dans ces vallons ces esclaves champêtres	See those slaves of the fields
Qui creusent ces rochers, qui vont fendre ces hêtres,	Smashing rocks, cleaving wood,
Qui détournent ces eaux …	Digging waterways …
Ils ne sont point formés sur le brillant modèle	Little have they to do with the well-dressed swains
De ces pasteurs galants qu'a chantés Fontenelle.	In the much-admired poems of great Fontenelle.[65]

Les Troqueurs

Like *The Beggar's Opera*, *Les Troqueurs* (see pp. 95 and 170) has the double distinction of being both a prototype and a masterpiece. Like *Le Devin du*

---

[63] Rousseau's mimes are omitted from Kaufman's ed. at 56.
[64] I.e. the traditional *ariette*. Colette sings 'Avec l'objet de mes amours', but this was added under duress.
[65] 'De la liberté' in *Discours en vers sur l'homme* (1738–9), which was inspired by Alexander Pope's *An Essay on Man*.

village, it was labelled '*Intermède*', or French *intermezzo*, and used recitative. Technically, both fall outside our definition of 'popular opera' and remain unique cases.[66] But while *Le Devin* echoed older *vaudeville* traits, Dauvergne's melodic style echoed *intermezzo* characteristics like wide-ranging intervals, varied rhythms and broken-up phrases. Where Dauvergne coincided with Rousseau, apart from the use of recitative, was in his free approach to musical forms, intended to follow the action. His duets and ensembles, helped by Vadé's brilliant ground plan, also benefited from his command of sonata-form technique. Equally important, the gestures of the participants were inscribed, not just implied, within the score. For example, when Lucas and Lubin decide in Scene 2 to exchange fiancées without warning, '*They tear up their [marriage] contracts*' during 'Troquons, troquons'.[67] Stage-directions were constantly followed through into real-time features within the music, as was shown in Figure 4.3, p. 96.

Gesture and multi-voicing are found everywhere. Thus in Scene 7, 'Sans rire', Dauvergne found the ideal ironic tone to capture Lubin's inappropriate bluffing: a *menuet*. This emphatically non-Italian element symbolises the synthesis achieved by this work. Margot's monosyllabic disgust deflates all attempts to curry favour and coerce her into forgiveness. Her punning sequence of answers (an idea from *vaudeville* comedy) is effortlessly maintained in tension as Dauvergne marks each one with a cadence to a new key. Or one might point to *ariettes* where Dauvergne changed from slow music to fast, implying vivid acting, never returning to the first tempo. Margot thus turns furiously on Lucas in Scene 4 ('Ah! Qu'il me tarde'), and in Scene 5 Lucas suddenly loses resolve, deciding to try and regain the trust of Fanchon. The complete trust shown between Vadé and Dauvergne, and their fusion of traditions, were abiding models for 'musico-dramatic art'.

Duni's Journey

In Table 8.7 the first Paris works of Egidio Duni are listed. He was almost fifty when he and Anseaume created the paradigm that is *Le Peintre amoureux de son modèle*. Table 8.8 shows that it held the stage until the Revolution. Duni would have included in his luggage for Paris a mixed-genre court opera in French, recently given in Parma. This original score,

---

[66] OAR, 287–92 discusses *Les Troqueurs*.
[67] *Les Troqueurs*, *Intermède* (Paris: L'Auteur, etc. n.d.), 22: as was usual, stage directions appear only in the libretto. In Cook, *Duet and Ensemble*, 76, 89–91, this stage direction should appear at the third bar before the end of Ex. 2.4.

brought to light by Kent M. Smith, was *Le Retour au village* (*Return to the Village*).[68]

Duni had been moderately successful with *opera seria* commissions for Rome, Milan, London and Genoa. But he had also spent time convalescing in Paris in 1733: 'France and the French pleased him so well that, walking on the Quai du Louvre, he said he would be happy to die there'.[69] It was through French contacts that Duni later found support in Genoa, thereafter entering the service of the incoming duke of Parma and his music-loving consort Louise-Elisabeth (1727–59), one of Louis XV's musical daughters. *Le Retour au village* was dedicated to her, having been 'written for her'.[70]

Duni's 'French' credentials included *La semplice curiosa*, derived from Favart's *La Chercheuse d'esprit*, which reached the Florentine stage in 1751.[71] The music is lost, but the libretto claims it was 'all in the French style', 'La Musica è tutta alla francese'.[72] With recitatives rather than spoken dialogue, Favart's plot was disposed over ten duets, two trios, eight cavatinas and five arias. It has been identified as the first example of a French libretto being adapted for Italian use.[73]

'False facts' took early hold when historians wrongly decided that Duni helped to write *Ninette à la cour*. But he had taken no part in Favart's operation, as was fully proven by Kent Smith. The reason for confusion – still propagated in reference books – is understandable: *Le Retour au village* was (textually) an arrangement of the libretto of Favart's first, three-act version of *Ninette à la cour* (1755), so this was the name by which Duni's piece was referred to at the time and in his obituary.[74] Having reached Paris, he gave it a new name and issued the score. This had no function except to document Duni's role in the evolution of a popular genre newly welcomed by the French court, and we will use it precisely for that purpose. Publication must have been carried out on Louise-Elisabeth's instructions as duchess, since her mission was to promote the cause of Parma at Versailles, where she lived for extended periods.

Rameau's brother-in-law J.-S. Mangot directed and sang the role of Colas in *Le Retour au village* at its only performances, 3 and

---

[68] Smith, 'Egidio Duni', 76–87.   [69] Anon., 'Éloge de Monsieur Duni' (1767), 22.
[70] Dedication of *Le Retour au village, opéra comique Pantomime et Ballet tiré de Ninette à la Cour, comédie de Mr Favart. Mis en Musique par Mr Duny* (n.p., n.d.) [c.1759], on *Gallica*.
[71] Teatro in Via del Cocomero, 4 Sept. 1751: Marica, 'Rappresentazioni', 432.
[72] Sartori, *I libretti italiani* no. 21599 (Firenze, G. B. Stecchi, 1751), performed in that autumn.
[73] Russo, 'Duni: l'opéra-comique'; Marica, 'Rappresentazioni', 430–34.
[74] These versions of *Ninette* are compared in Sonneck, 'Bertoldo', 163ff. Reference books classify *Le Retour* variously, even as a dubious attribution.

5 October 1756.⁷⁵ This music rejects Italian norms; instead, Duni adopted the stylistic ingredients we earlier identified in *Le Devin du village*: stepwise figures, smaller intervals, limited rhythmic variety, few rests. He matched Favart's interactively conceived libretto to forms of notes suiting a particular circumstance and character on stage. In 1756, therefore, the skills later celebrated by Diderot had already been worked out:

> Is it not rather odd that a foreigner, an Italian, one Duni, should be the one to come and teach us how to put accents into our music, how to make our melody fit every movement, tempo, interval, declamation, without harming the prosody? It really shouldn't have been all that difficult.⁷⁶

When the sense is forward-moving, as seen in Example 11.5, Duni spins out new motifs to match new words. Because he used Favart's texts, already non-repeating and sometimes extensive, Duni was free to try things out. Sometimes he shortened them, sometimes he retained most of them, finally adopting between four and thirty-three lines in his set pieces.⁷⁷

The addition of stage directions and the absence of verbal repetition are notable. We find new stage directions (presumably Duni's own: no librettist is mentioned anywhere) in ten solos and ensembles. They show that he was working like Rousseau, composing music for stage actions that were his own to imagine and determine.⁷⁸ The most vivid stage direction occurs in Act I/6 after the quarrel when Colas is prevented from following after Ninette and the Prince:

> Colas attempts to follow at a distance. He returns downstage, morose and in a dream. The Prince's men remain upstage. [Five bars of recitative follow.] The Prince's men gradually approach Colas and lay their hands on his shoulders whenever Colas sings 'Poor Colas, poor Colas' in the next piece.⁷⁹

And that phrase 'Pauvre Colas', seen in Example 11.5, is well distinguished from its musical surroundings. In fact it had been added by Duni: it was taken from the spoken lead-in, not the sung French text which Favart had written for 'Maledetti quanti siete'.⁸⁰ When we compare Duni's vocal line

---

⁷⁵ At the ducal summer residence, Colorno. Russo, 'Duni a Parma', 109–11; Butler, *Musical Theater*, 19–20, 26; Charlton, 'Duni's *Le Retour*'.
⁷⁶ Diderot, *Rameau's Nephew*, 72 (modified).
⁷⁷ Exact figures: Charlton, 'Duni's *Le Retour*', 153–4.
⁷⁸ Duni, *Le Retour au village*, 1, 7, 11, 23–4, 34, 39, 45, 56, 62, 77; also the instruction on 66.
⁷⁹ Duni, *Le Retour au village*, 38–9.
⁸⁰ The composer of 'Maledetti', Act I/8 of *Bertoldo in corte*, is unknown: Bertoldino's aria was not part of *Bertoldo* in 1749. Favart made it into 'Auroit-on cru cela', the dialogue between Colas and Fabrice.

Example 11.5 Egidio Duni, *Le Retour au village*, I/6, 'Auroit-on cru cela?', 40. COLAS: 'Poor Colas! Poor Colas! I'm her husband, or nearly. It's sheer cruelty. Ah!, Messieurs, I beg you.'

with the music which is its equivalent in Act I/8 of *Ninette à la cour*, the dramatic value of 'Pauvre Colas' becomes clear. Favart had made Fabrice, the Prince's valet, sing 'Quiet now, Colas', instructing 'several hunters [to] block Colas's way'. Since Fabrice was not included in Duni's opera, the orchestra supplies what is needed to connect Colas's desperation with the *force majeure* he feels, emotionally and physically.

*

Duni's move to Paris was made in February 1757: in Monnet's account, 'One of my friends, a musician and man of taste attached to the Parma court [Mangot?] wrote and asked me to send a French text for Duni to set.

This skilful composer, who was also there, had the greatest desire to write an *intermède* for my theatre.'[81] Duni's obituary claimed that *Le Peintre amoureux de son modèle* was written in Parma while Monnet claimed it was written in Paris: the truth surely lies in between. Monnet presumably selected the subject, just as he had overseen *Les Troqueurs*.[82] At the head of its printed score Duni wrote, 'I have come here to render homage to the language that has furnished me with melody, sentiment and images', and he made his debt to Rousseau equally public.[83]

Melchior Grimm later called the new style of word-setting 'manier la parole', 'handling the words', asserting that Philidor learnt it from Duni: 'The revolution [in public taste] is being uniquely driven by Duni. [...] *Le Peintre amoureux de son modèle* and *L'Isle des foux* (*The Island of the Mad*) might not have been greatly popular in Italy but they are teaching French composers how to set words to music.'[84] 'In *Le Maréchal* you will find [that] M. Philidor has made noticeable progress in handling the words, an art perfectly unknown to French composers, whose primary elements [...] M. Duni has shown them in his works.'[85]

Le Peintre amoureux de son modèle is set in a working household in Paris, but Alberti the painter is not unlike the Italian type of the Doctor. Its comic ambience draws from *intermezzi*: for example, there is a breathtaking quartet at the end of Act I involving the word 'fracas'.[86] Anseaume knew he should supply ample text-lines for Duni to set, devising the greatest number (thirty-two) for the highly original *dénouement* sequence described subsequently. As various *intermezzi* involved arias of frustration addressed to a silent character, Act I opened with Alberti berating his silent pupil Zerbin in 'Oh! Pour le coup'. We see in a moment how different Duni's music was from the expected idiom. When a new model is introduced in Act I/4, Zerbin recognises her as Laurette, a stranger to whom he was recently attracted by chance in the street. He describes this coincidence to the housekeeper Jacinthe in Scene 2 ('Me promenant près du logis'). Jacinthe decides in her own interest to

---

[81] Monnet, *Mémoires* (1772), 181.
[82] Anon., 'Éloge de Monsieur Duni' (1767). Final Italian trace of Duni on 24 February 1757: Russo, 'Duni a Parma', 114–15. The interpreters would be Mlle Deschamps (Jacinthe), Jean-Louis Laruette (Alberti), Bouret (Zerbin) and Mlle Rosaline (Laurette). Rosaline (extreme left), Bouret and Deschamps are shown in Fig. 7.3, p. 172.
[83] Smith, 'Egidio Duni', 93; Heartz, *Music in European Capitals*, 731.
[84] Grimm, *Corr. litt.*, ed. Tourneux, IV, 456–7 (Aug. 1761).   [85] *Ibid.*, IV, 501 (Dec. 1761).
[86] The fictional source, *Il pittore innamorato*, was a ruse by Monnet. The first libretto pretends that Duni's *ariettes* had been translated from Italian (Paris: Duchesne, 1757, 3).

protect Laurette from the amatory fantasies of Alberti and encourages her to see a prospective lover in the shy Zerbin. Jacinthe finally marries Alberti.

If the new 'musico-dramatic art' was 'apt for our superior faculties' as Garcin would write in 1770,[87] proof that it had already arrived is Fréron's review dated 8 March 1758. As a leading intellectual journalist, Fréron had written highly perceptive appreciations of *La Servante maîtresse* and *Ninette à la cour*.[88] Reviewing *Le Peintre amoureux*, he made the exceptional claim of having studied the musical score as well as having witnessed performances.[89] The new art gripped him, as Diderot and others were gripped: he described six *ariettes*, a duet for Jacinthe and Alberti in Act II/4, and the closing Act I quartet. On each occasion he drew attention to multi-voicing and the mimetic function of orchestral music: in Alberti's 'La fortune se présente', Act I/5, 'the orchestra explains all that the painter promises [to Laurette] such as jewels, a carriage, a table, and so on.'

Thanks to Fréron we understand perfectly how Duni conceived the opening solo as a double picture. Alberti grumpily criticises while Zerbin paints at his easel, as the stage direction says. It is Zerbin whom Duni depicts in the opening ritornello, seventeen bars long. Fréron observed:

In Alberti's first *ariette* the composer expresses two different things. The first is the distraction and embarrassment of the pupil, painting, and the second is the impatience of the master who surprises him [this detail is not found elsewhere]. These two heavily opposed features are united and contained in the music without change of tone or speed.

Zerbin's studious music returns in the middle (thirteen bars) and at the end: perhaps Jean-Louis Laruette as Alberti devised a mime for these passages; 'he was long famous for his musical talent and the inimitable way he acted ridiculous characters'.[90] Nevertheless Duni's concept ensures that the interesting character of Zerbin gains strength.

The point at which Duni's genius fully awoke was Zerbin's narrative in Scene 2, describing the effect on him of the young woman later revealed as Laurette. 'A remarkable piece', wrote Fréron: 'Although an *ariette*, it becomes both a speech *vis-à-vis* the Governess [Jacinthe] by virtue of its narration, and a description of the person who enchanted him.' That is, the perky accompaniment rhythm suggests Laurette's physical motion whereas Zerbin's emotional confession has different figures and a 'hook' with four repeated notes, 'without a thought my heart was struck': Example 11.6. The

---

[87] Garcin, *Traité* (1772), 92.
[88] Fréron, *AL*, 1754/6 (15 Oct.), 34–9, and *AL*, 1755/3 (5 May), 41–7.
[89] Ibid., 1758/4 (8 Mar.), 97–109.   [90] Campardon, *Comédiens*, I, 278.

Example 11.6 Egidio Duni, *Le Peintre amoureux de son modèle*, I/2, 17, 'Me promenant près du logis'. ZERBIN: 'As I was walking near the house, without a thought my heart was struck. My poor heart!'

whole context was different from 'Il soldato valoroso' or 'Gli Sbirri', whose narratives were fantasies. Zerbin's *ariette* offers a remembered impression; consequently, he receives a past as well as a character.

Exactly the same mixture of narrative planes follows when Jacinthe boasts to Zerbin of her past lovers.[91] 'In "Quand j'étois jeunette, fillette"', noted Fréron, 'connoisseurs praised [Duni's] transformations of tone and the agreeable, well-turned melody'. These 'transformations' are the main point, because Jacinthe reproduces the words and tones of her old admirers. Amazingly, the insinuations of one envoiced suitor ('feel my anguish, have pity on my passion!') called forth a texture in the orchestra which in later decades developed into a common signifier of love: oscillating strings over sustained harmonies, shown in Example 11.7.[92]

As Chapter 12 illustrates, Sedaine was also well attuned to the potential of narrated memories.[93] Others too used this effect of 'conflicting diegetic spaces', as Jacqueline Waeber called them.[94] Perhaps they originated in Pergolesi with the 'secret voice' that Uberto tells us he hears in the desperate aria, 'Son imbrogliato io già'.[95]

---

[91] Mlle Deschamps' earlier roles included Zaïde in Anseaume's *Le Chinois poli* (1754), singing 'Petits maîtres sans cervelle' ('Zerbinotti d'oggi dì' from *Il cinese*); she created at least twenty-nine roles to 1766, latterly under the name Mme Bérard.

[92] 'Expressive medium' discussed in Charlton, 'Orchestra and Image'.

[93] Cf. Jenny's narration in *Le Roi et le fermier*, I/8, 'Le Milord m'offre des richesses' and Courchemin's narration in *Le Déserteur*, III/6, 'Le Roi passait'; see pp. 302, 318.

[94] In Weigl's *Die Schweizerfamilie* (1809) the shepherd's pipe causes 'oscillation between the external reality and another diegetic dimension marked by introspection': Waeber, 'Afterword', 196.

[95] 'Uberto, pensa a te': *La serva padrona* (Paris, Aux adresses ordinaires, [1752]), 52, 54–5. This passage is discussed in Allanbrook, *Secular Commedia*, 19–22.

Example 11.7 Egidio Duni, *Le Peintre amoureux de son modèle*, I/2, 24, 'Quand j'étois jeunette, fillette'. JACINTHE: '"My queen, feel my anguish, have pity on my passion!"'.

Alberti's downfall comes in Act II/5 with 'the Picture scene: a fine effect, very well performed'.[96] It involves stage directions, mime, thirty-two lines of sung text and an unfolding musical span of 147 bars conceived purely for the requirements of the action, and without repetition. While he sings, Alberti paints at a large easel with the silent Laurette posing as 'Venus

---

[96] 'Chère Laurette': see *Affiches de Province*, 24 Aug. 1757, 136.

Receiving Mars'. She surreptitiously makes eye contact with Zerbin as he creeps in; her face flushes and Alberti imagines himself in the role of Mars. But Laurette is 'receiving' Zerbin instead, since he is found in the act of kissing her hand when Alberti moves closer. Fréron observed:

'Chère Laurette' has charmed both the connoisseurs and the ordinary public: the former because of the harmony and the transformations of tone, the latter because of the aptness of the vocal line while Alberti suffers and declares his love. This *ariette* is completely novel and unique by reason of its special compositional nature.

Many times in the future would popular opera tailor its music according to the action, most ambitiously in the 1790s with the 'rescue' sequences of Cherubini, Méhul and Kreutzer.

Fréron's report ignored the work's twelve *vaudevilles*,[97] and also Laurette's *opera seria* aria 'De l'amour je sens la flamme'.[98] The *vaudevilles* added to the multi-voicing, especially since Anseaume used them for dialogue and character depiction. When Laurette and Zerbin become friends under the protective eye of Jacinthe in Act II/3, *vaudevilles* like 'Dite la belle, le voulez-vous' conveyed an innocence which Duni echoed when composing the *amoroso* solo for Zerbin, 'Mon trouble et mon silence'. When Mlle Nessel took over Laurette's part, she proved that 'by the nature of her acting [...] one may succeed at this theatre in affectionate roles without resorting to indecency'.[99] With speeches in verse and appropriate music, the young lovers might have reminded audiences of Colin and Colette, finding truth in Scene 6 of *Le Devin du village*.

*

If the historical initiative for reform came from Italy, its consequence – a new operatic language – was defined in France. In the operas we have seen, common pivotal concerns are clear. There was the drive to conceive and guide actors' movements on stage, binding these to the drama while the music translated the required gestures. A need was felt to unify such ingredients, giving a spontaneous, realistic effect, rather as *intermezzo*

---

[97] Reduced by three when Duni revised the score in 1758.
[98] Act II/1: Duni took this from his own *L'Olimpiade* (1755). Mlle Rosaline here had to negotiate between low e' and top c'''. In *Bertholde à la ville* she had sung 'Tel qu'un petit oiseau' ('Amore è fatto come un uccelleto' by Cocchi), 'Votre cœur en vain murmure' ('Se in me la speranza avete' from *Bertoldo in corte*) and 'À tant de charmes' ('Pupille care', from the same work). In Anseaume's *Le Chinois poli en France* she had sung 'D'une vaine crainte' ('Così mi piacete' from *La donna superba*).
[99] *Mercure*, 1759, July/2, 198–99.

artists had given. An urge towards multivocality and the pursuit of dialogue as such was the obvious inheritance of *vaudeville* opera. Multivocal writing now occurred in the exceptional multiplication of ensembles in opéra-comique, as well as the constructive interplay of music and spoken language.

In Chapter 12 we discover how these initiatives played out in the most unexpected product of the early collaboration between the 'married' artistic partners, Sedaine and Monsigny.

12 | A 'Musico-Dramatic Art'

Introduction

Almost by definition, an ambitious opera seeks an ambitious synthesis. This chapter focuses on *Le Roi et le fermier* (*The King and the Farmer*), the most ambitious popular opera of the decade preceding *Le Déserteur*. It was intended to break with current limits and caused a break with Sedaine's first musical associate, Philidor.[1] Monsigny's score was written speedily, but the project was not staged until November 1762. It dealt with social class in the same spirit as *Bertoldo in corte* and *Ninette à la cour*: a ruler meets ordinary people, and abusive behaviour is punished. But it also aligns with other popular operas in which ordinary people encountered the body politic: *Arlequin traitant*, *Les Mariages de Canada* or *Annette et Lubin*. Kingship was a sensitive subject; Louis XV ruled personally, and his role took on extra importance during the Seven Years War, 1756 to 1762. For his part, Sedaine determined to exploit the full possibilities of 'musico-dramatic art', which will be discussed later in this chapter: it began to be theorised at around the time of *Le Déserteur*.

Monsigny and Sedaine looked for synthesis between serious opera and popular opera. The composer had imagined, in principle, some blend of styles around 1755 when offering *Les Aveux indiscrets* (*Indiscreet Confessions*) to the Opéra (see p. 198): a village comedy based on La Fontaine. This avoided Italianate music and the need for subtle or ironic acting; its style was fairly unoriginal, and its libretto favoured solos rather than ensembles. Presumably rejected by the Opéra – confessions of premarital sexual relations would never have found acceptance as a theme there – it held the popular stage well enough.

---

[1] 'Philidor [...] returned it, saying it was unfeasible': Sedaine, 'Quelques réflexions', 507. The music of this opera is recorded on CD, cond. by Ryan Brown.

Regarding *Le Roi et le fermier*, Rameau's *Platée* (1745) and *Les Paladins* (1760) seem to have offered ideas.[2] Rameau had long been interested in connecting musical motifs with meaning. A free type of thematic cross-referencing could even bind together different melodies relating to a particular ingredient of the plot: *Les Paladins* thus employed an illustrative motif referring to the all-powerful Fairy Manto. The connection is explained in La Fontaine's Tale forming its source, *The Little Dog That Shakes out Silver and Jewels*.[3]

Although first performed ten months after the merger of the Opéra Comique and the Comédie-Italienne, *Le Roi et le fermier* seems to have been completed earlier. Sedaine remembered that Jenny's role had begun to be learned by Mlle Nessel, a favourite Opéra Comique singer. Although appointed as a new member of the Comédie-Italienne, she retired before matters there had been legally finalised. Indeed, no Opéra Comique singer actually performed at the Hôtel de Bourgogne before Easter 1762.[4]

Exactly why did the merger take place? The event is partially explained through a series of letters by Favart to Count Durazzo in Vienna, suggesting one of two possible motivations: either that of money (regarding Julien Corby) or that of ministerial planning (regarding La Vrillière, Count de Saint-Florentin, Interior Minister with responsibility for the City of Paris, including the Opéra). Corby was the major partner in the 1758 contract mentioned in Chapter 8, along with Moët, Champeron, Dehesse and Favart. On 12 December 1761, Favart told Durazzo that Corby 'was the first to urge that it [the merger] should take place. An annuity of eight thousand *livres* was enough of a bait for him to dispose of everyone's stake'.[5] Indeed Corby was apparently raising the price: weeks before, the 'bait' had been only six thousand *livres*.[6]

At the time when his partnership had taken control, at a price of 83,000 *livres*, Corby had mortgaged some property and borrowed some money.[7] Fees payable to the Opéra had been agreed at 15,000 *livres* per annum, but

---

[2] Monsigny made a near-quotation from *Les Paladins* in *Aline, Reine de Golconde* (Opéra, 1766): *OAR*, 371.

[3] 'Le Petit chien qui secoue de l'argent et des pierreries'. See *OAR*, 323–4 and 360–1 (the 'shaking' idea). Other, more symbolic, representations are discussed in Burgess, 'Enlightening Harmonies'.

[4] Sedaine, 'Quelque réflexions' (1778), 507–8. OC personnel received what appear to be two indemnity payments totalling 9,224 *livres* in this transition period: F-Po, *Registre* for 1761–2. At the Fairs Nessel had taken leading parts in *Le Peintre amoureux de son modèle*, *Le Cadi dupé*, *Le Maître en droit*, *On ne s'avise jamais de tout*, etc.

[5] Favart, *Correspondance* (1808), I, 184.   [6] *Ibid.*, 204–5 (11 Nov.)

[7] Cucuel, 'Sources et documents', 259–60.

from 1761 they rose to 20,000 *livres* per annum: Corby may have decided to liquidate his assets and retire. On the other hand, Favart mentions that Corby was 'the creature of the Minister' (obviously La Vrillière),[8] thus could have been part of an existing plan to strengthen the Comédie-Italienne. The latter, after all, had quietly been allowed to give self-sufficient operas (see pp. 195–6); so a merger may have been in view, justified by the Louis XIV tradition. That was not all good news for the Italians,[9] and not for the public either, which had enjoyed rich fruits of competition but henceforth had no chance to see popular opera at either of the Fairs.

Once Paris realised that the future of the Opéra Comique was uncertain, everyone offered plans: courtiers favoured an alliance with the Comédie-Italienne; the Opéra wanted it for itself; the Comédie-Française wanted to 'exterminate' it.[10] Perhaps in the spirit of compromise, the court mounted a trial. *Les Troqueurs* (*The Swappers*) and *On ne s'avise jamais de tout* (*Impossible to Think of Everything*) were given at Versailles, but with players exclusively from the Opéra and the Comédie-Italienne. Sedaine remembered taking rehearsals: 'I have never seen or heard anything more ridiculous. [...] For all the skills of [Henri] Larrivée, [Nicolas] Gélin, [Charles] Rochard and the great Opéra orchestra, the court saw what it was: detestable.' Favart, concealing the advisory role he must have played all along, wrote differently to Vienna: 'the entertainment gave pleasure and is to be repeated tomorrow'.[11]

But Sedaine's and Favart's reports converge in one detail: the king's tolerance of Fair theatre, which we noted on pp. 7–8. Sedaine recalled how tired he grew of discussions about the merger; Favart noted, 'the king is not especially fond of this great project: he showed his indifference to it'.[12]

Certain basic choices were faced by the genre at this crossroads. Contant d'Orville's assessment, following, preceded his account of *Le Roi et le fermier*.

Considering the preference of the public for pieces with *ariettes*, connoisseurs of the new genre felt that it could be given noble status, but no author dared to take the necessary step. It was said that for dramas in which music formed the main and sole

---

[8] As for n.5. Corby's wife was lady-in-waiting to the Duchess de Choiseul (Campardon, *Spectacles*, I, 216) who had apparently advanced 10,000 *livres* for this purchase. But Choiseul, Minister of Foreign Affairs, was officially indifferent to the merger: Favart, *ibid.*, 214 (25 Dec.).
[9] Brenner, 'Introduction', *Théâtre Italien*, 9, shows that existing CI debts were modest. From 1762 it had to pay burdensome dues to the Opéra, and also Corby's pension.
[10] Favart, *ibid.*, 204.
[11] Sedaine, 'Quelques réflexions' (1778), 506–7; Favart, *ibid.*, 184–5 (12 Dec.).
[12] Favart, *ibid.*, 214 (25 Dec.); Sedaine, *ibid.*, 507.

attraction, complementary materials should consist of a hackneyed and amusing plot, exaggerated characters drawn from people of low estate, and a witty or else dubiously suggestive style. Anyone who tried to include matters of greater importance, nobility or genuine feeling would incur the risk of a humiliating failure: the aim must be to provoke mirth, to delight the ears; anything else would be futile.

Others however, while not harbouring any illusions concerning the strange co-existence of spoken and sung dialogue, argued that nothing might exceed the scope of this mixed genre were it to be prepared by two creative artists dedicated to knowing and portraying motions of the soul and subtleties of feeling; that one could, in that case, banish triviality and low humour in order to speak to the mind and the heart.[13]

The future led to expansion; popular opera developed along both these paths.

Politics and Kingship

Having successfully adapted one favourite English play in *Le Diable à quatre*, Sedaine returned to *Choix de petites pièces* and selected Patu's translation of Robert Dodsley's *The King and the Miller of Mansfield*. Why did he think that a king of England could interest the French after seven years fighting the English?[14] The marquis d'Argenson provides a clue. He personally liked Patu's translations and saw Comédie-Italienne traditions as the nearest equivalent to English practice, where 'changes of place and use of machines are more permitted': 'what better way to correct and amuse?' 'The morality is good', he wrote of *Le Diable à quatre*, while *The King and the Miller of Mansfield* was 'a subject which ought to be given on our stage, even with scene-changes. [...] We like these tender and virtuous subjects, the goodness of a king, the depiction of the vices of his courtiers, something our nation deplores.'[15]

The King and the Miller of Mansfield was a success right from its first showing at Drury Lane, 29 January 1737. It held the stage until 1765 and survived sporadically until 1794. Two years earlier Dodsley had made a mark in theatre with *The Toy-Shop*, a 'Dramatick Satire' whose shopkeeper moralises wittily over each sale so that, together with the lack of plot, the overall style resembles opéras-comiques from the same decade: Pannard's *Le Magazin des modernes* (*The Fashion-Store*), mocking city-based fashions,

---

[13] Contant d'Orville, *Histoire* (1768), I, 251–2.
[14] McLynn, *1759*: France was defeated in the East and West Indies.
[15] D'Argenson, *Notices* (1725–57), II, 767–8, 773–4.

or plays with music like Boissy's *Le Triomphe de l'intérêt* (*The Triumph of Interest*).

Dodsley was born in 1704, the son of a Mansfield schoolmaster. Like Sedaine, who was the son of a housebuilder, he began his career by publishing a collection of poems.[16] One link between *The King and the Miller* and many pieces mentioned in Chapter 7 is their connection with older popular literature. French writers plundered La Fontaine, while Dodsley found 'A pleasant Ballad of King *Henry* the II^d, and the Miller of *Mansfield*' in *A Collection of Old Ballads*. This tale, and that of King Alfred and the Shepherd, showed a 'King who has wander'd *incognito* amongst his Subjects, to discover their Humours, Affection, and Manner of Living'.[17] Ballads and popular English operas alike generated 'a broad-based ideology of nationhood'.[18] King Henry becomes lost when hunting near Nottingham; he meets the Miller, John Cockle, and is lodged by him (still incognito) though he must share a bed with Cockle's son Richard. Next morning, he is identified when nobles come searching. The Miller is knighted for his 'kind courtesy' and given a pension.

Parallel to this 'good king' myth, Dodsley adopted another strand: the 'corrupt courtier'. Cockle's son Richard has returned to Mansfield from London after an absence of four years. He left home as a result of the machinations of the neighbouring Lord Lurewell, a courtier who persuaded Richard's fiancée Peggy that Richard had been unfaithful and fathered someone else's child. Richard has grown disenchanted with courtiers whilst waiting on another aristocrat in the hope of gaining a position. Peggy has been seduced by Lurewell and is pregnant. But she has written to Richard explaining Lurewell's deceit.

In Dodsley's play there are scene-changes involving four sets: Sherwood Forest (seen twice) where the king has become lost during a hunt; Mansfield town; a house where Peggy is reunited with Richard; and finally the mill. Cockle, as Keeper of the royal forest, orders his gamekeepers to arrest apparent poachers (in fact, Lurewell and two friends, members of the royal hunt). Lurewell is unaware that Peggy has contacted Richard, but the still-incognito king, brought by Richard to the mill, learns of Lurewell's behaviour and meets Peggy. Two surprises make for an effective *dénouement*. The king's identity is revealed when Lurewell recognises him, then Lurewell's denials of wrongdoing are disproved when Peggy is

---

[16] Dodsley, *A Muse in livery*, 1732; Sedaine, *Pièces fugitives*, 1752.
[17] *A Collection of Old Ballads*, 2nd ed., 3 vols. (London: J. Roberts, 1723–5), I, 43, 53. See Aspden, 'Ballads and Britons', 44–5.
[18] Aspden, 'Ballads and Britons', 25.

Figure 12.1 Robert Dodsley, *The King and the Miller of Mansfield*, final scene. John Cockle is knighted by the king, watched by Lurewell and another courtier; Peggy and Richard are on the right. © The British Library Board.

summoned from the adjoining room to bear witness: Lurewell had even promised to marry her. The king orders him to settle an annuity on Peggy, who turns it over to Richard, who agrees to marry Peggy. Cockle is knighted by the king, as shown in Figure 12.1.

Dodsley's king is a just monarch who rewards human value and loyalty and is taught – more than once – the low regard in which his court is held by ordinary people. In the forest Cockle says to him 'What! Do you live at Court, and not lie! that's a likely Story indeed.' In the mill, the following conversation takes place in the king's presence:

MILLER: Zoons! Do the Courtiers think their Dependants can eat Promises!
DICK: No, no, they never trouble their Heads to think, whether we eat at all or not. [...]
MILLER: Poor *Dick*! And is plain Honesty then a Recommendation to no Place at Court?
DICK: It may recommend you to be a Footman, perhaps, but nothing further, nothing further indeed. If you look higher, you must furnish yourself with other Qualifications: [...] Flattery, Insinuation, Dissimulation, Application, and (*Pointing to his Palm*) right Application too, if you hope to succeed.[19]

These speeches obviously appealed to Dodsley's translator. Casanova, having met Patu by chance in 1750, reported on his views and political character:

Everything that happens in France [said Patu] makes foreigners believe that the nation adores its King; but those among us who think, see that this love of the nation for the monarch is only tinsel. How can one base anything on a love which has no basis? [...] Everyone cries 'Long live the King' because some idler has begun shouting it. It is a cry which comes from high spirits, or perhaps from fear, and which the King himself, believe me, does not take seriously. He cannot wait to get back to Versailles.[20]

Although Patu translated plays that contained music, he had no apparent inkling of the potential of opera. If he envisaged musical productions, they would have involved the Comédie-Italienne, not the Opéra Comique, which he elsewhere denigrated. He intended *Choix de petites pièces* to be read, prefacing the second volume with long extracts from Jonathan Swift's defence of *The Beggar's Opera*, including the following sentences. In their original context, Swift's words followed the quotations we saw in Chapter 3 (p. 51) where he invoked Gherardi's *Théâtre Italien*.

Although some things are too serious, solemn or sacred to be turned into ridicule, yet the abuses of them are certainly not, since it is allowed that corruption in religion, politics, and law, may be proper topics for this kind of satire.

---

[19] Robert Dodsley, *The Toy-Shop* [and] *The King and the Miller of Mansfield*, facs. ed. Harry M. Solomon (Los Angeles: UCLA, 1983)(Augustan Reprint Society 218–19), 15, 28–9.
[20] Casanova, *History of My Life*, III, 131.

> There are two ends that men propose in writing satire, one of them [...] regarding nothing further than personal satisfaction [...]. The other is a public spirit, prompting men of genius and virtue to mend the world, as far as they are able.[21]

When Sedaine redesigned the translated play for operatic purpose, he made Richard the leading male character: Cockle has died, and Richard is Keeper of Sherwood Forest. Peggy (now called Jenny) has not been seduced but has been tricked and briefly confined by Lurewell. The king is never named, but French audiences loved to make connections. Charles Collé's play on this subject was not given in public until after Louis XV's demise.[22] Sedaine's preface to *Le Roi et le fermier* mentioned censorship: unnamed authorities had provoked changes during the rehearsals even though everyone knew that the source was English:

> I had made my Farmer speak of the truths about courts, concerning every period; but certain persons motivated by a zeal that I perhaps might have shown had I been in their position, believed these to be attacks; they enforced changes which were duly adopted in that scene. However [out of self-defence] I wish to offer this scene to the public just as I had made it; I hope people will simply perceive what an angry English farmer would have said in such circumstances to an unjust Courtier.[23]

The scene in question is Act III/10 where, after a toast, the (incognito) king questions Richard about his sojourn in London.

RICHARD: I don't see how a king can be good.
KING: Why not?
RICHARD: Because certain people sometimes prefer it otherwise.
KING: The idea ... surprises me. But there are honest people at court. [...]
  I assure you, Richard, that a king who understands affection has faithful friends and trustworthy ministers.
RICHARD: Perhaps so, but ...
KING: Again, you surprise me: who can have taught you all this?
RICHARD: Well, one idea at court is to believe that thinking only happens there; I wager you believe it too.

Contrary to the reader's assumption, these lines are nowhere to be found in Dodsley's play, whose king never refers to royal duties or ministers;

---

[21] Swift, 'Vindication of Mr Gay' (1728), 318. Translated text: Patu, *Choix* (1756), II, v–xi, followed by Patu's commentary.
[22] Brown, *A Field of Honor*, 249–53, traces the fortunes of Collé's *La Partie de chasse de Henri IV*.
[23] Sedaine, 'Avertissement', *Le Roi et le fermier*, ed. in Charlton and Ledbury, *Michel-Jean Sedaine*, 243.

perhaps it was this element which aroused French suspicion behind the scenes, or else the idea of open debate concerning 'thinking'. Yet Sedaine balances the 'good king' motif strongly against the 'corrupt courtier' one and gave his monarch a solo dilating on the subject of good governance, described later.

The New Art in Action

In a preface to *Rose et Colas* (1764) Sedaine defined his understanding of opera with spoken dialogue:

> [It] aims to present an authentic drama that forms a unity with pieces of music bound to the action by necessity, and thus false whenever the happy assistance of music fails to give rise to tension, excitement, movement and preciseness, especially during moments of rapid action that cannot be shown in spoken tragedy and comedy.[24]

Much of consequence lies behind this sentence: for example, every musical number in *Le Roi et le fermier* has a built-in 'trigger' of some sort, an explicit justification. Ensembles, duets and solos carry the action. Some older justifications for music that we saw in Chapter 2 still held good, namely Auden's 'called-for' and 'impromptu' songs.[25] Sedaine added several others, the simplest being the answer to a spoken question. When the principle of the 'impromptu' musical utterance extended to duets, opera inevitably supervened. Perhaps learning from Duni, Monsigny could suggest speech-characteristics within the vocal line, so that we hear a blend of meaning with expression.

Crucial to Sedaine's plan was the use of prose dialogue, utterly realistic in style, deftly sketching in certain essentials and leaving imagination to fill in the detail. This was his response to the 'English' method that La Place had outlined in 1746: 'style is always fitted to the matter'.

Librettist and composer worked hard to reshape Dodsley's play. Some aspects seem related to *Ninette à la cour*, presumably in order to rival Favart's success, but Monsigny's score contains not a single Italian-sounding phrase. For *Ninette*, two settings had sufficed: the village and

---

[24] Sedaine, 'L'Auteur au lecteur', *Rose et Colas* in Charlton and Ledbury, *ibid.*, 246. He then justified his practice with reference to the recognition scene in *Le Roi et le fermier* (III/14), whose ensembles had been criticised in the journal *Avant-Coureur* fairly harshly: Cook, *Duet and Ensemble*, 272–4.

[25] See p. 30. Auden, 'Music in Shakespeare', 511, 522.

the court. Sedaine reduced Dodsley's scene changes likewise: one forest view for the first two acts and a farmhouse interior for Act III. In other words, Sedaine rejected what d'Argenson would have defended, and remained near the rules prescribing an Aristotelian unity of place. The elimination of John Cockle in favour of his son was explained in a wonderfully ironic speech in Act I/4 from the gamekeeper Rustaut, chiding the irritable Richard – irritable because Jenny has gone missing: 'Your late father made you study and travel, for God's sake, brought you up like a lord; you run a nice farm, you're Inspector of the Hunt, Jenny loves you and is ready to marry you – what more do you want? To be king?'

Lurewell has inveigled Jenny that same morning by trapping her flock of sheep; she enters his property. When a summons to the king's hunt arrives, he detains her under the orders of a housekeeper. Described by Jenny in Act I, the housekeeper obviously resembles Mrs Jewkes in Richardson's *Pamela*.[26] Jenny is not physically harmed, but the serious incident is given full expressive quotient in that its ramifications occupy all of Act I from the distraught opening *ariette* of Richard through to Jenny's arrival (after escaping through a window), her explanations and their reconciliation.

What follows this moment is a new episode of turmoil that brings Lurewell closer: a storm approaches (subtle references have prepared this) and leads to the breaking up of the lovers' duet, 'Ah! Richard, ah! Mon cher ami'. Discordant orchestral sounds occur, three times, with increasing violence; during the third interruption the hunt is heard approaching and receding. The duet is drowned out, and the tempest expands into an entr'acte. This 'royal hunt and storm' with lovers sheltering under a rock was conceived a century before that of Berlioz, who surely remembered it when writing *Les Troyens*.[27] But two current French operas could have been inspirations: the entr'acte between Acts II and III of Royer's *Zaïde*, whose offstage actions impact on the main plot; and the storm in Rameau's *Platée* between Acts I and II, approaching gradually and even better woven into the action.[28]

To understand the principles whereby music and dialogue were shared out in Sedaine's operas we can follow Raphaëlle Legrand.[29] First, he reduced basic events to a workable minimum, focusing on certain

---

[26] *Le Roi et le fermier*, I/10; Richardson, *Pamela*, Letter 32, 98–219, *passim* (the ambiguous Mrs Jewkes was placed in charge of the confined Pamela).
[27] Berlioz regularly mentioned *Le Déserteur* in reviews but never the present opera.
[28] The three-act *Zaïde* (1739) had thirty-eight performances in 1756–7; the three-act *Platée* (1745/1749) had eight performances in 1754.
[29] Legrand, '"Risquer un genre nouveau"'.

interesting scenes. Next, he identified a primary group of characters with whom we identify the most. Then he imagined a secondary group of characters whose music would provide for variety: their scenes do not require emotional involvement, allowing focus on the principal plot. Music assists the 'larger-scale articulation of dramatic progress', especially at the start and finish of an act. In *Le Roi et le fermier* the concluding ensemble of Act II involves more characters than that of Act I, and that of Act III involves more characters than that of Act II. Explanations in Act I that would take only a short time in a play are slowed down by musical events. And the king's actual existence is only gradually sketched in.

*

Rameau's later overtures sometimes introduce the drama;[30] Monsigny's overture does the same. A Presto is followed by a minor-mode Andante Allegretto. But its expected finale is denied: we move seamlessly into Richard's desperate monologue 'Je ne sais à quoi me résoudre'. Sedaine's expositions often 'plunge the audience into an emotional climate' whose precise meaning is explained only later in dialogue. Overall, 'Sedaine will exploit and sustain [tension] up to a delayed *dénouement* which we can anticipate, prolonged by various comic, picturesque or affecting interventions'.[31]

The 'royal hunt and storm' avoids spoken dialogue completely, starting with Jenny's duet with Richard and ending at Act II/3, after the lost king's substantial opening *scena*: a total sequence of 533 bars lasting fifteen minutes. In *The King and the Miller of Mansfield* the king's scene opened the play: 'What is a King? Is he not wiser than another Man? Not without his counsellors I plainly find. [...] When lost in a Wood, alas! what is he but a common Man?'[32] Comparing *Le Roi et le fermier* with *Il re alla caccia*, an opera which Goldoni created from the same materials, Marvin Carlson observed:

Sedaine and Goldoni both made the most not only of the political implications of the lost king but also of the powerful emotional, musical and scenic possibilities in the depiction of a frightened and helpless individual lost in a dark wood [...]. The King lost in the woods [exemplifies] its democratic message of the disappearance of social distinctions in common human situations of fear and danger.[33]

---

[30] Sadler, *Rameau Compendium*, 150. [31] Legrand, '"Risquer un genre nouveau"', 139.
[32] Dodsley, *The King and the Miller*, ed. Solomon, 11–12.
[33] Carlson, '*Il re alla caccia*', 87, 91. See also Noiray, 'Quatre rois'.

That type of fear and danger, so effectively conveyed by orchestral music, was completely new in popular opera.

Technically, action-finales in Italian opera were in the course of development during the 1750s.[34] The Act II ending of *Le Roi et le fermier* uses music in a related way, dramatising the surprise arrest of the courtiers in darkness and confusion.[35] Sedaine also introduced violence whereas Dodsley had plain dialogue. English and French traditions became reversed. Thirty-two bars of slowish music depict two gamekeepers prowling round the stage while Lurewell and the other courtier try to locate them in the dark; all sing completely different phrases. Then a sudden *mêlée* takes place during the last twenty-eight bars, coordinated by a stage direction:

At the Presto section of this quartet Miraut and four other gamekeepers join up with their fellow guards. They attack the lords who defend themselves with their hunting-knives; the guards push them and arrest them, whereupon the act ends. (Score, p. 110)

An illusion of extra voices was created by these five non-singing actors. This is the sequence referred to by Sedaine in the preface to *Rose et Colas* quoted earlier (i.e. when 'moments pass by quickly'). To use singing here, he argued, was preferable to using speech because in a play every character must react separately, slowing down stage time. Thus, Dodsley's equivalent scene required twenty-one speeches after '*The Keepers rush upon them*' to reach its end, during which the courtiers claim they mistook the gamekeepers for robbers, a lame excuse that the gamekeepers find unconvincing. Dodsley's courtiers never explain that they were following the king's hunt, whereas Monsigny's ensemble 'explains' the fact that Lurewell does not assert his authority at the key moment.

Even more ambitious was the ensemble for eight characters in Act III when the monarch is revealed. Monsigny and Sedaine created a scene of ambitious modernity, 105 bars long, expanding the shock moment with an impression of barely controlled chaos. The king demands explanations, his courtiers prevaricate and the locals react in wonderment. It actually ends on the wrong chord as the king orders 'Quiet!' Then come spoken explanations, Jenny's entrance and the disgrace of Lurewell. After king and courtiers have departed, the 'Chœur' (six people, 44 bars) sings 'May Heaven's happiness grant the king long life' for which Monsigny supplied a rhetoric we might associate with Beethoven. It leads to a *vaudeville*-finale

---

[34] Heartz, '*Vis comica*' and 'Creation of the Buffo Finale'.
[35] A 'progressive ensemble of the physical type' such as this normally occurred within the course of an act: Cook, *Duet and Ensemble*, 129, 133.

reflecting both the calm after the storm and the return of national peace with Britain:

Ne perdons jamais l'espérance	Let us never forsake hope;
L'orage écrase nos forêts	The storm lays waste to our forests
Mais l'orage amène la paix	But then the storm brings us the peace
Et de là ton bonheur commence.	And from that your contentment starts.
Il ne faut s'étonner de rien,	The lesson easily is taught:
Il n'est qu'un pas du mal au bien.	From bad to good the way is short.

Monsigny's music can be seen in many lights, and yet its linear style was built on *Le Devin du village* (*The Village Soothsayer*) and its development by Duni: melodies with few rests but a continuous response to words; straightforward rhythms. When Jenny wants to calm Richard's lingering worries, her phrases all begin with the same rhythm: 'Ce que je dis est la vérité même' (I/8). The *Mercure* praised 'beautiful, ingenious, rational images in the orchestra, and the sagacity by which [the composer] has found a way to make his melody speak'.[36] Another type of musical speech passes between the gamekeepers: 'Did you hear that the king is lost in this part of the forest?' 'Bad luck. Did you hear that Richard has found Jenny?'

Examples 11.6 and 11.7 have shown envoicing of remembered characters and speeches in Duni's work. In *Le Roi et le fermier*, I/8, the same approach articulates Jenny's distressed account of detention, 'Le Milord m'offre des richesses'. Music follows the curve of emotional pressure from reported speech to urgent quasi-recitative as she envoices the words and tones of both assailant and victim. Again, *Le Devin du village* had offered a model: Colette's opening *ariette* contains a dramatic recitative whose 'envoiced' questions (to herself) are given their own stage directions.[37]

Various linear and tonal threads seem to resolve in Jenny's *Romance* in Act III/12: see Example 12.1. Like Colin's Romance in *Le Devin du village* it expresses human love in the face of rural toil.[38] Yet the rhythm and shape of its opening phrases have appeared five times before in *ariettes* and ensembles linked to unease or stress; so there is a subtle dialectic within this 'unity of melody'. The key of G major relates to the unresolved G minor of the storm sequence; and those who studied and experienced the opera would see that the Romance's text makes the same link: 'When the sun on the fields scorches shepherds and flocks, When sudden storms cause floods in

---

[36] *Mercure*, 1763, Jan./1, 182.   [37] *Le Devin du village*, Sc. 1, bars 86–98.
[38] The form is original: ABCBDB, with 'B' as the memorable refrain.

Example 12.1 Pierre-Alexandre Monsigny, *Le Roi et le fermier*, III/12, 148, 'Que le Soleil dans la plaine'. JENNY: 'When the sun on the fields scorches shepherds and flocks, when sudden storms [cause floods in our orchards].'

our orchards, Nothing is difficult, all is pleasure for those who are bound by affection'.

Such lines might have reflected national as well as personal meaning. Support for Louis XV revived in France as the Seven Years War drew to an end. Writers in 1762, that is, theorised a 'new' patriotism whose supposed antiquity and purity were declared 'superior to the English variety'. It would bind together 'the glory of the Prince and the honour of the nation'.[39] At this historical moment, Sedaine's king could represent that prince. Prevailed upon to sing in Act III/2, the still-unidentified guest offers an *ariette* supposed to be from another opera, whose words reproduce (as he claims) advice given by a tutor to a prince. 'Can there be greater happiness than that of a sovereign who says to himself: "All that Heaven has made obedient to me, all the subjects of my empire, are my children and my friends"?' Monsigny surrounds the singer with a 'halo' of benevolence by which the audience – knowing the character's identity – may feel that sentiment and transfer it to its chosen monarch over the heads of the other characters. Some may have realised that these words were actually an echo: see p. 124.

Definitions

To theorise ambitions for the genre which we have just seen in action on the page, we must lend an ear to literate observers who saw the art in action. Two of them, Nicolas-Étienne Framery (1745–1810) and Jean-Laurent Garcin (1733–81), were music journalists. Garcin wrote a book about the new 'mélo-drame', and Framery analysed 'the new genre'. It was André Grétry (1741–1813), writer as well as composer, who coined the phrase 'musico-dramatic art': 'A ritornello in Italy announces musical phrases that the singer will perform, or repeats something already sung: it is restful, not the continuation of a discourse. In France, where musico-dramatic art was born, ritornellos should have a dramatic character'.[40]

---

[39] Louis Basset de La Marelle, *La Différence du patriotisme national chez les François et chez les Anglois* (Lyon, 1762) cited in Grieder, *Anglomania*, 124 and Dziembowski, *Nouveau patriotisme*, 465, alongside Claude-François Millot, *Discours sur le patriotisme françois* (Lyon, 1762).

[40] Grétry, *Mémoires* (1797), III, Bk 6 Chap. 9, 319; Garcin, *Traité* (1772); Framery, 'Quelques réflexions' (1770), 13. Garcin was based in Switerland but familiar with music in Paris. His *Traité* was excerpted in the *Mercure*, 1771, Sept., 133–59: Sgard, ed., *Dictionnaire des journalistes*, digital ed.

He could have been thinking of *Le Peintre amoureux de son modèle* (*The Painter Who Loved his Model*), described in Chapter 11. Today we are more familiar with such concepts from Gluck's preface to *Alceste*: 'I have thought to restrict music to its true office of serving poetry [i.e. the libretto] through expression and by following the circumstances of the plot'.[41] Or as the dedication of *Orphée et Eurydice* put it: 'I have observed with satisfaction that the accent of nature is a universal language. M. Rousseau has used it with the greatest success in the simpler genre. His *Le Devin du village* is a model [here Gluck sidesteps the work of Duni] which no author has yet imitated.'[42]

Garcin defined opéra-comique's new resources by the phrase 'compound music' ('*chant composé*'), music which 'is but an auxiliary of her mistress, poetry'.[43] Metaphors of servitude were doubtless necessary but could mislead: what Garcin and Gluck meant was that opera should be able to realise the complex implications of a libretto.

> *Chant composé* can extend to far more subjects [than *chant simple*], depict different aspects of nature, different feelings of the soul, make us feel progression and change.
>
> Since dramatic music is not intended solely to flatter the ear, and since on the contrary its main aim is to offer our minds the whole, complex expression of emotions affecting every character on stage, it must of necessity be a music compounded of as many ideas, images and different expressions as are contained in all the other parts of the dramatic poem.[44]

Grétry's later explanation complemented this:

> Your music is always inappropriate if, as one might say, it does not marry the drama it embellishes. [...] It will be a nonsense if the orchestral sound stops us understanding the words, or if the music is pointlessly complicated, or it extends an emotion or internal feeling beyond their limits, if it fails to give each character their suitable form of language [...] and, finally, if it is not so unified with the text that one cannot distinguish the poet from the composer, as it were.[45]

The main notion was that operatic music should evince permanent awareness of dramatic necessity.

Framery and the others were not narrowly partisan, having no need to defend a national tradition. Garcin recognised Italian opera as an 'inexhaustible treasure' and Italians as 'the true masters of the school of *chant*

---

[41] Text drafted anonymously by Ranieri de' Calzabigi: *Alceste* (Vienna: Trattnern, 1769), xi–xii.
[42] Gluck, *Orphée et Euridice* (Paris: M. Lemarchand, n.d. [1774]), [3].
[43] Garcin, *Traité* (1772), 349. [44] Garcin, *Ibid.*, 4, 6. [45] Grétry, *Mémoires* (1797), III, 326–7.

simple', where melody had primacy.⁴⁶ Neither would he exclude the latter from popular opera, for lyrical *ariettes* should (and did) have their place. But *chant composé* had already proven 'as wide-ranging as our ideas, as complicated as our emotions, as rich as our imaginations; it is apt for our superior faculties, for the needs of our minds'.⁴⁷ Perhaps the sweeping rhetoric reflected chauvinism, but nowhere did Garcin argue that Italian librettos lack complexity: in fact, he uses Metastasio's 'Se cerca, se dice' from *L'Olimpiade* (*The Olympic Games*) and its conflicted emotions to make comparison between settings by Pergolesi and Galuppi.⁴⁸ Yet popular opera for him led to a new level of aspiration: it should emulate novelists like Fielding and Richardson by giving music responsibility for conveying better knowledge of characters. Rich and poor could be understood in a novelistic, rounded way. From Philidor's work he selected Blaise the woodcutter in *Le Bûcheron* (*The Woodcutter*) and Squire Western in *Tom Jones*. The woodcutter's exposition 'Dès le matin' offers contextual details that Richardson might have provided; without them, Garcin says, we should not have reason to feel sympathy for the woodcutter's predicament: the work would leave us cold.⁴⁹ In *Tom Jones*, Squire Western's hunting-aria 'D'un cerf dix cors' shows us an obsessive quality (Garcin argues) that explains Western's decisions and judgements elsewhere.⁵⁰

There was an ideal fusion between text and music within *Le Roi et le fermier*:

If music be destined only for the service of the libretto, this type of servitude augments the composer's prestige rather than diminishes it. The more he is challenged by the number of ideas the more he is master of his art, supposing every idea has been encompassed, enlivened, made beautiful. Then his music bears the stamp of real skill: what it forgoes in charm it will acquire in strength: it becomes a music of depiction. When [in Act I/1, Monsigny] was given these well-known words,

> I cannot make up my mind,
> I don't know which way to go

to limit the music to one single motif was not possible. Too many incoherent ideas met together in this piece: but how was this incoherence, so to speak, made musical? What haste and collision of shifting thoughts! What disorder in the pent-up emotion! The poet's whole soul is on display and is seemingly transported by music into that of the hearer.⁵¹

---

⁴⁶ Garcin, *Traité*, 24, 91. But he misses progressive aspects as discussed here and tends towards essentialism, e.g. on 269.
⁴⁷ Garcin, *ibid.*, 92. ⁴⁸ Garcin, *ibid.*, 110–2; see Heartz, *Music in European Capitals*, 118.
⁴⁹ Garcin, *ibid.*, 119–21. See p. 163. ⁵⁰ Garcin, *ibid.*, 121–22.
⁵¹ 'Je ne sçais à quoi me résoudre': Garcin, *ibid.*, 108.

We can easily put this in modern terms. Monsigny mixes innate confidence on Richard's part with terrible doubt, using (in our language) sonata form with full tonic reprise of the second subject. There is musical dissonance and disruption, but also a building up of new melodic segments that convey new turns of thought in Sedaine's text; these are, however, kept contained within the sonata form. Older 'spinning out' as implied in Rousseau's theories of the 'unity of melody' would not have had nearly as much effect.

Omitted by Garcin was any mention of stage directions, tying music to specific purposes within the 'compound' effect. Those which survive are not comprehensive enough: rare clues show how much information has been lost. Writing of *L'Ami de la maison* (*The Family Friend*) Grétry described a heightened moment in Agathe's 'Je suis de vous très-mécontente' (Act I/1), pointing to a four-note motif in the orchestra: 'The actress who fails to indicate several signs of ironic pity when these four notes are heard, does not understand my music.'[52] Interpretation might be difficult today, but perhaps Grétry signalled a lack of comprehension even in his own lifetime.

Framery's chief admiration was for the works of Philidor. Duni and Monsigny had merely begun a synthesis, he claimed; *Les Troqueurs* was not too alien and what followed were 'many things easy to sing', 'a mere assemblage whose harmony had acquired less perfection than its melody'.[53] But then

A person appeared whose first work [*Blaise le savetier* (*Blaise the Cobbler*)] seemed extraordinary rather than likeable. Ears, filled for the first time, believed they were being deafened. Words were expressed in a new way, which could not be appreciated. Those emotions which [Philidor] wished to depict were given to the orchestra in order to allow a simpler melodic line, so people denied that he was capable of expression. Because he did not give all his *ariettes* the foursquare monotony of a *brunette* or a *romance*, critics denied that he could be melodic.

Following *Le Maréchal ferrant* – which was 'sung by all, even when they denied the composer melody' –

[Other] composers adopted this new genre, which was not at all that of Italy; its turns of phrase, each dependent on the last, in no way resembled the former stylistic mixture; this was the model on which different musicians formed their own work. The transformation came about without anyone noticing it [...]. This style has kept the name 'Italian manner', and yet it is obvious that it hardly resembles such a thing at all.[54]

---

[52] Grétry, *Mémoires* (1797), I, 232. [53] Framery, 'Quelques réflexions' (1770), 11–12.
[54] *Ibid.*, 13–14.

That phrase, 'each dependent on the last', is the signal which tells us that what Framery was hearing was 'the classical style' in formation.

Orchestral Coda

A hidden casualty of the merger of 1762 was the Opéra Comique orchestra. Monnet's publicity had identified 'the beauty of the theatres [he] has constructed, the fine quality of the orchestra, the excellence of the pieces staged and the acting of certain members, especially Mlle Rosaline.'[55] On p. 98, its use of clarinets was mentioned. Another casualty was the chance to hear symphonies. For ten years, opéra-comique overtures like *Les Troqueurs* helped to set the pace for the Parisian symphony. The decade of the Bouffons, of hybrid operas and *Le Devin du village* was also that of symphonic evolution. Two orchestral players wrote symphonies: François Martin (1727–57) at the Opéra,[56] and Étienne Mangean (c.1710–c.1756), leader of the Opéra Comique.[57]

The expensive Concert Spirituel encouraged symphonic music, followed by other subscription series directed by Johann Stamitz (Stamič) in 1754–55 and François-Joseph Gossec from 1756. But a different public could hear symphonies at the Fairs when opéras-comiques began with them. Symphonies had in effect been democratised when played as overtures; perhaps they were played between stage-works too. Three-movement symphonies by Philidor opened *Le Jardinier et son seigneur* and *Le Maréchal-ferrant*; another by Monsigny opened *Le Cadi dupé*. None appears in the opera's score, only in special publications.[58] Symphony-overtures in three movements precede the scores of Monsigny's *Les Aveux indiscrets* and *On ne s'avise jamais de tout*.

Recordings of Philidor's symphonic overtures give us the shock of the musical new: drama, glitter, simplicity of effect, self-sufficient means. Some – as *Le Roi et le fermier* showed – became poetically linked with their operas. Duni's *Les Deux chasseurs et la laitière* (*Two Hunters and a Milkmaid*) made its overture develop into a storm; the curtain rises while it plays, revealing the wild night-time forest where Colas waits for the bear

---

[55] *Les Spectacles de Paris ... Troisième Partie* (Paris: Duchesne, 1754), 171.
[56] Brook, *La Symphonie française*, I, 78–84, 110–12. Five Concerts Spirituels in 1751 contained Martin's symphonies, one of which has been recorded.
[57] Seven symphonies: Brook, *ibid.*, II, 456–62.
[58] On scores, see p. 85. Symphonies in part-books available by subscription were introduced by La Chevardière (1760) and Venier (1761).

in freezing cold: see pp. 171–3. As had occurred in the 1730s when Corrette and his colleagues linked orchestral music with operas, so in the 1750s came a new linkage.

Michael Robinson observed that 'advances in orchestration had their influence over advances in operatic characterisation', and quoted Philidor's *Tom Jones* to illustrate his point in detail.[59] Framery's observations concerning Philidor's style relate to similar consequences: the adoption of symphonic methods. In a cogent modern assessment, Paul Bekker summed up the historical importance of the new balance:

In the course of [Italian opera's] migration into northern lands, the primacy of singing yielded to instrumental music. The ideas of the drama issued from the sound-world of the orchestra, and with them came all the other associated constituents capable of being illustrated: action, staging, representation.[60]

---

[59] Robinson, *Opera Before Mozart*, 159.
[60] Paul Bekker, *Wandlungen der Oper* (Zurich, 1934), 5, transl. in Dahlhaus, 'What is a musical drama?', 103, with commentary.

13 | Conclusions

The late Philip Gossett addressed the question 'What is opera?' as follows: 'Without looking for compositions that have already been accepted in today's opera houses, but allowing a more flexible – and inclusive – definition of what opera might mean, one already increases the number of acceptable works and sees a very different picture of the genre today.' 'A definition that embraces more works from the late seventeenth century to today would allow us to include [...] works with spoken dialogue (written in Paris as *opéras comiques* or for Germany as *melodramas* [...].)' His vision was wholly positive, understanding the totality of 'new or older forms of the interaction between music and theatre'.[1]

Writers quoted at the end of Chapter 1 may stand for anyone who, coming across a French popular opera, finds the unfamiliar. I have been concerned to write about 'a reality that operatic historiography has not yet fully fathomed' (these words were conceived for Rebecca Harris-Warrick's *Dance and Drama in French Baroque Opera*).[2] Her study concludes with other words that I could happily co-opt: 'Once we look and listen, we discover a vast dramatic repertoire, richly deserving of study and performance' (*ibid.*, 449). Consequently, 'the time seems ripe for an integrative model for French opera' (*ibid.*, 1). Such a model would reveal cross-currents; to focus on underexplored comedy at the Opéra would, for example, require knowledge of the popular stage. Harris-Warrick demonstrates this when using Fair theatre history as the only way to prove that in 1711 Françoise Prévost danced to a new 'Caprice', music by Rebel.[3] The evidence is 'eye-opening' because Rebel's music consisted of 'through-composed movements in a violinistic Italian style', shown in her book. That account can be linked with Chapter 9 of the present book, which mentions another Opéra work, *Zaïde*. And the question of dancing to instrumental sonatas (*Dance and Drama*, 392) is expanded by evidence we saw on pages 218–23.[4]

---

[1] Philip Gossett, 'Writing the History of Opera', in Greenwald, ed., *Oxford Handbook*, 1032.
[2] Harris-Warrick, *Dance and Drama*, 1.   [3] *Ibid.*, 391–2.
[4] An analogous case concerns Giovanni Servandoni: *TF*'s engraving of the décor for *La Pénélope moderne* (see p. 150) augments his modest total of archival designs of Opéra commissions: *DOP*, IV, 639–40.

Parallel connections in the financial domain progressed to the administrative sphere. Charles-Simon Favart became an Opéra librettist when comedy was being built up in the 1740s and then worked as manager of the Opéra Comique under the control of the Opéra *directeur*, François Berger. As a supremely interesting figure linking Opéra and Fair theatre, Louis Fuzelier demands attention. Author or part-author of 206 stage works in various genres, including *Les Indes galantes*,[5] he was a cultural insider with a professional portfolio including an editorship at the *Mercure de France*. Rotation of singers between Opéra and popular stages involved, as we saw, Mlle Petitpas, Mlle Antheaume (or Antiaume), M. Desjardins and Jean-Antoine Bérard, among others.

Knowledge of Rameau is certainly incomplete without knowledge of Fair theatre, where his first known stage work was heard. *Les Paladins* and the evolution of Opéra repertory cannot be understood without knowing that La Fontaine was a longstanding source for popular opera. Opéra and Opéra Comique became competitors after the Bouffon residency, although contractual clauses restricted popular theatre's freedom to compete, beginning in January 1758.

*

But there is no special reason to view popular opera through the lens of classical opera. To discover the former's independent identity has always been the motivation of the present project. Dispassionate observers could see that the commercial, generically free home of opera with spoken dialogue was a major attraction. It began as a seasonal institution capable of attracting writers, musicians and singers known already for their work elsewhere (Lesage's fame as a prose writer and dramatist, for example). By 1743 the Opéra Comique was the subject of a two-volume history written by the most respected of theatre historians, the Parfaict brothers. To visit this company in summer or winter meant entering a building of significant size. The only one whose capacity is known (see p. 139) accommodated at least 1,262 persons in the 1720s. In order to understand that better, we can visit (online or in person) later theatres still in use: the Richmond Theatre, west of London, which in 1899 held 1,500 people though now seats only 807; and the Theatre Royal, Bury St Edmunds (1819) which originally held 800 people.[6]

---

[5] Brenner, *Bibliography*; Trott, *Théâtre du XVIIIe siècle*.
[6] *Theatres Database*: database.theatrestrust.co.uk (13 Feb. 2021).

Singer-actors in the French eighteenth century were known for restrained or even quiet modes of delivery; the Paris Opéra itself was modest in size and capacity. The first dedicated opera houses in Paris remained in use for popular opera and/or spoken theatre. Anyway, there must have been less contrast than we imagine now between sung and spoken modes of delivery: actors slipped between *vaudeville* and speech, regularly improvising some spoken dialogue. French singers were said by visitors to be superior actors, and popular opera certainly demanded those.

Eyewitnesses whom we have quoted in Chapter 6 and elsewhere came from five different countries (France, England, Ireland, Italy and Germany). Popular opera needed to be made known to those able to travel. Anne-Marie Du Boccage's pamphlet, intended to destroy it, ironically gave us the best descriptions known to us. They revealed green room, main stage and audience; the pressures placed on female audience members; the raffish behaviour of aristocrats and their friends. Its atmosphere seems recognisable to us because it prefigures descriptions and fictions fully a hundred years later. Boccage was moved to attack the institution *precisely* because it was such a socially accepted venue and a danger to the ever-inimical Comédie Française.

On stage, as Boccage noted, degrees of obscenity were expected in earlier popular opera. This was improvised as well as insinuated, especially perhaps in *parodies*. Joachim Nemeitz reported on both vulgarity and on its enjoyment. On the page, of course, Pannard's opéras-comiques are inoffensive society comedies, and *Le Théâtre de la Foire* was marketed in print as family entertainment. D'Argenson also confirmed the suggestive *doubles entendres* of all kinds.[7] Registering a change when reviewing Vadé's *Le Trompeur trompé* (*The Deceiver Deceived*) in 1754, Fréron liked the fact that it avoided obscene allusions or puns, thus seeming less an 'opéra comique' than a 'comedy sung in *vaudevilles*'.[8] Yet Sedaine asserted that although he wrote *Les Femmes vengées* (*The Women Avenged*) in prose, he published it in verse (1775) 'so that the actors might put in the least possible amount of their own invention'.[9]

Visitors to France took librettos home with them, even sent them back to friends. Research has focused recently on a near-torrent of stage performances of French theatre and opera in London, a consistent familiarity that lasted the whole century and beyond.[10] Vanessa Rogers' published list includes 186 productions, including many titles discussed in this book,

---

[7] D'Argenson, *Notices* (1725–57), II, 535.   [8] *AL*, 1754/2 (8 April), 71.
[9] Sedaine, *Réflexions*, 514.   [10] Rogers, 'John Gay, Ballad Opera'.

especially from *Le Théâtre italien de Gherardi* and *Le Théâtre de la Foire*. Erica Levenson identified over 175 specifically musical plays that toured to London, and went on to enquire how French materials in many different media affected public and private experience in English culture, where France represented supposedly inimical values.[11] As we saw in Swift's commentary on *The Beggar's Opera*, public familiarity with social satire and humour in Gherardi's collection was to be taken for granted. In their attitudes to cronyism, inequality, greed, officialdom, aspects of marriage and so on, critics and satirists on both sides of the Channel engaged in a meeting of minds. Whether on the stage or at home, the messages could be very effectively carried in music.

The acquaintance of John Gay with French theatre continues to fascinate, and the evidence we have seen helps to suggest specific aspects of *The Beggar's Opera* that relate to those sources. An abiding rhetoric of ironic inversion drives the social commentary in each: in Chapter 3 we quoted the conversation in Hades between the career thief and the legal officer ('There is too much similarity in our professions for there not to be at least some in our tastes'). *The Beggar's Opera* immediately comes to mind: 'Through the whole piece you may observe such a similitude of manners in high and low life, that it is difficult to determine whether (in the fashionable vices) the fine gentlemen imitate the gentlemen of the road, or the gentlemen of the road the fine gentlemen' (Act III/16).

Specifically French dramaturgy was used by Gay in his musical setting of dialogue and the design of ensembles. Like *vaudeville* authors, Gay often made borrowed melodies into agents within a conversation – part of the operatic dialogue, in French terms. In Act I alone, airs 8, 9, 12, 13 and 15 come into this category; in Act II, airs 31 (Lucy's question), 32 (Lockit's answer) and 37 (Polly's indignant riposte to Lucy). Furthermore, all Gay's duets and his final trio (*air* 68) avoid any simultaneous singing, whether when moralising (*air* 49) or actively exchanging phrases (*airs* 36 and 52) or arguing (*air* 9): the characters' voices, as in France, never sing together.[12]

However, Gay's conception of opera was wider, helping us to understand what the Beggar means when saying in the Introduction that he presents 'an opera in all its forms'. Gay looked backwards to spoken tradition and sideways to Italian opera. From the former he used three basic motivations for music we saw in Chapter 2: 'impromptu' (as in Macheath's soliloquy, *air* 21); 'called-for'

---

[11] Levenson, 'Traveling Tunes'.
[12] Editors relate Macheath's disjointed sequence of nine songs in III/12 (as he awaits execution) to Italian opera or to Handel. Gay also knew *La Princesse de Carizme* (and Figure 6.4), where disturbed suitors sing fragments of *vaudevilles*.

(especially in *airs* 19, 20 and 22); and answering a question (Polly's *air* 8). He used music to mark the end of a scene or an act. Yet he frequently went against *vaudeville* convention by employing music in an 'Italian' way, namely as an expression of feeling or as a digression, without any immediate prompting from a narrative point of view.

Such an eclectic approach must have helped Bertolt Brecht when thinking about music in *Die Dreigroschenoper*. For Brecht, the dialogic continuity of *vaudeville* was the opposite of the needs of his own theatre method. He used the three basic motivations mentioned just now ('impromptu', 'called-for', question/answer), plus finale-like functions. Like Gay, he included spontaneous non-dramatic functions such as the 'Interlude' sung by Jenny and Mrs Peachum between II/1 and II/2. As it happens, the primary effect Brecht sought – radical non-dialogic participation of music, sung with texts that objectified the subject matter – was wholly French in conception; for, as is apparent in performance (see p. 120) *vaudevilles* in popular opera can sound like *de facto* quotations, added to which French dramatic authors had dealt in objectification since the time of Gherardi, especially 'double-operational irony' (see p. 65).

*

If we accept that the Opéra Comique was an established, relatively stable 'third force' in music theatre (beside the Opéra and the Comédie-Italienne) it can be claimed on present knowledge that there were three periods of growth: 1714 to 1718, 1723 to 1745 and 1752 to 1762. Excellent, varied works arrived in the first period and some were revived over several decades. Lesage originally regarded them as a beginning; he and d'Orneval edited their best results (as they defined them) as a memorial to Fair theatre following its suppression in autumn 1718. Thus the title page to *Le Théâtre de la Foire* depicts a sarcophagus whose Latin epitaph links the new genre's fate to that of Arachne, the low-born weaver of genius; she was metamorphosed into a spider by the jealous, less talented goddess Athene (in other terms, the Comédie-Française).[13]

Opéra-comique expanded in subject matter and tone when new writers contributed to *vaudeville* opera: Piron, Pannard, Favart. But it depended on new music too: incoming fashions included – after the financial crash of 1720 – a range of zany melodies, and thereafter (as we saw in Chapter 9) some difficult-to-sing extended numbers inspired by danced music deriving from the Opéra. Too little space has been available for these topics in the preceding chapters; whoever takes them up will find great rewards awaiting them.

---

[13] See vol. I (1721) and its epigraph from Ovid's *Metamorphoses*.

Perhaps the most startling evidence from Lesage and d'Orneval's volumes concerns the existence of a developed operatic dramaturgy. Moments highlighted in this book stand for many others: the climactic scenes of *Arlequin traitant* (p. 226); the distorted music of the suffering Prince (Example 9.2); the dramatic meeting between Almoraddin and the Queen of Barostan (p. 123). Sung in ways and with accompaniments not yet fully known, this was an interactive kind of dramaturgy. Other such evidence stems from the Versailles manuscript of *La Chercheuse d'esprit*, suggesting that *vaudevilles* were subtly altered in performance under Favart's guidance in order to respond to the aesthetics of opera: the mood and motive of a stage character communicated in song. The evidence implies, too, that *vaudevilles* were always subject to improvised changes. But here the subtle adjustments taking place made *vaudevilles* seem to be being 'acculturated'. Analogous phenomena are observable slightly later in *Le Devin du village*: Rousseau's novel melodies favoured not only regular phrase structures but also *vaudeville* characteristics, which were illustrated in Example 11.4, p. 277. Favart and Rousseau ask us to backdate negotiations between bourgeois and popular idioms that used to be attributed to, say, Haydn in later decades.

This was, culturally speaking, an age of universal pleasure in singing. Popular opera included not just dialogue but also musical expansion and melodic beauty found in *menuets* and other songs. Solo cantatas could be brought within the action; the role of dancers was established from the start (such features differed little in essence from those of all-sung French opera). *Vaudevilles* – always set to rhyming verse – may have been heard at the time as a type of recitative. Then the style changed, but these basic qualities remained in place. Joseph Caillot, after working in Italy, adopted at the Comédie-Italienne one nuance of style for dialogic numbers such as ensembles and another for lyrical *ariettes*. The question remains whether his approach might have been used by earlier singers.[14]

The fact that people staged excerpts, arrangements or even whole operas at home before the Revolution is not sufficiently known. The case put by Thomas Christensen should be supported and backdated: 'Operatic music heard outside the theatre in the guise of these domestic and salon arrangements for piano was as important a part of operatic history as that experienced during

---

[14] Even in the mid-twentieth century, opéra-comique singers made their musical line sound 'through the words', perhaps a remnant of these binary modes: cf. the French Radio (ORTF) recording of Monsigny's *Le Déserteur* mentioned in Chapter 1, n. 111.

a staged live performance.'[15] Of musicals, Scott McMillin wrote, 'We are looking outside the theatre now, but that is where the most successful songs are meant to go.'[16] In the eighteenth century a cottage industry grew up extremely early around set pieces for home performance, including Lully's overtures and chaconnes in sung versions; these were in addition to monthly issues of songs and occasional issues of music for plays. When Macheath refers to 'the French tune that Mrs Slammekin was so fond of' (*air* 22) Gay reminds us of an age of singing both in his own country and the one 'over the water'. The long history of musical circulation between theatre and home was easily continued by popular opera. *We* might not sing or act at home, but that hardly invalidates the past status of opera as having had a 'binary identity'. Paris was the world's publication centre for music and, therefore, of opera scores and arrangements. After these became collectable, they dispersed knowledge of popular opera far and wide across Europe to Russia, and westwards towards the Americas.

Many chapters have shown how Charles-Simon Favart advanced the comic genre in numerous ways. Like Lesage he made it part of public debate, using new sources like *Acajou* or older ones as in *Les Nymphes de Diane*, whose underlying subject was 'forced immurements in convents'.[17] As poet and musician combined, he wished to make popular opera a moral vehicle, no less than Lesage had done. Favart followed Baurans's lead when *comédie mêlée d'ariettes* arrived with *La Servante maîtresse*: Italian music, no *vaudevilles*, a polite style of spoken verse. Then Favart made Italian arias into ensembles so that, as in the *vaudeville* era, dialogue could continue across the musical numbers. Without Favart's *Ninette à la cour*, Duni could not have written *Le Retour au village* as a test bed for a new musical language. Duni's own 'musico-dramatic art' was celebrated by his contemporaries and by Diderot in *Le Neveu de Rameau* (published much later). Reassessed in our own time by Kent M. Smith and now by Italian researchers, Duni can be freed of former misunderstandings. Why should he be thought any less important to history than, say, Traetta or Stamitz?

*

Thomas Betzwieser's work demonstrated how essentially different are the aesthetic assumptions we need to make when theorizing popular opera.[18] For instance, more remains to be done in studying spoken dialogue itself.

---

[15] Christensen, 'Soundings offstage' in Greenwald, ed., *Oxford Handbook*, 900.
[16] McMillin, *The Musical as Drama*, 37.   [17] Birberick, 'From World to Text', 198.
[18] Betzwieser, *Sprechen und Singen*; ibid., 'Verisimilitude' in Greenwald, ed., *Oxford Handbook*, 296–317.

Comédie mêlée d'ariettes did not remain wedded to the spoken verse principle used in hybrid operas; it mostly returned to prose (as used in *vaudeville* comedy) partly under the influence of English theatre where 'style is always fitted to the matter' (p. 178). Popular opera retained what Mikhail Bakhtin later termed 'heteroglossia', defined as 'The totality of the world of objects and ideas depicted and expressed in [the novel] by means of the social diversity of speech types and by the differing individual voices'.[19] Popular opera after 1752 could partake of a general cultural movement, in the sense that texts like Richardson's *Pamela* were not always polite in tone:

> In the original text of 1740 [...] Pamela's deviations from polite usage are at their most frequent and marked. The opening letter introduces such colloquialisms as 'a Clog upon my dear Parents', 'wrapt close in Paper, that it mayn't chink', and 'I did nothing but curchee and cry'. [...] They also work [...] as strident lexical markers of her subaltern status.[20]

Prose dialogue, Chamfort would write, was 'more rapid, [it] gave greater movement and warmth to the action' (p. 19). It also evoked the outside world. Sedaine prefaced *Le Jardinier et son seigneur* as follows: 'The first [objection made to my text] is that my comedy is written in a common and vulgar style [...] but I believe I have used the style which suits the manners, the morals and the station in life of the person talking.'[21]

Such aims, which we recognise today, should not lead to false conclusions about the music's role. A theory of modern musicals has observed that 'two orders of time' operate: 'the time of the numbers, as opposed to the time of the book'.[22] This does not apply automatically to popular operas in pre-Revolution France: they aimed for a different kind of aesthetic switching and the audience was accustomed to following on different levels. One level related to external factors brought in to the comedic narrative, such as social ideas connected to a *vaudeville* (see Chapter 5) or personal knowledge related to an *air* or *romance*. The comedy – the dramatic vehicle – also switched between speech and music, but this was not intended to produce a stop-start process: rather, because multivoicing was natural, continuity itself was multilayered.

---

[19] Bakhtin, 'Discourse in the Novel', 263.
[20] Keymer, 'Introduction', Richardson, *Pamela*, xvii. Some of these markers reached French ears, for Desfontaines wrote of the first translation, 'were it "better written" it would be less touching and less natural': Desfontaines, *Observations* 29, Letter 429 (28 July 1742), 209–10.
[21] Carroll, 'Philidor', 139 (modified). [22] McMillin, *The Musical*, 31.

Familiar opera forms used in 'musico-dramatic art' were made to interact with different narrative elements. At the end of Act I of *Le Roi et le fermier* (see Chapter 12) Richard and Jenny begin a conventional duet, rendered unstable by discordant music representing the approaching storm. These are abrupt sound effects entering from outside the conventional level; as they overwhelm the duet, the latter's aesthetic level is replaced by the external level. Act III/1 opens with a trio for Jenny, Betsy and Richard's mother; each sings a different song as she works at a different task. Their music is appreciated as a definite part of an outside level because these characters have (within the fiction) memorised their music. At first the songs fit together, as if by chance. But they develop with a degree of complexity that overtakes our belief in 'borrowed' or 'exterior' music: the piece becomes a trio on the operatic level.

Near the end of *Le Déserteur*, Courchemin narrates in music certain offstage events which the audience needs to know: Louise's petitioning of the king. In 'Le Roi paraît' he sings the words of her petition itself, changing his delivery in multivoiced fashion; the orchestration alters and the music modulates to the unexpected key of A major. After this narrative, his *ariette* returns to its opening music, completing a ternary structure: the aesthetic has switched again as the 'exterior' level is overtaken by conventional form.[23]

An idea by Grétry was used by Thomas Betzwieser in his account of operatic verisimilitude, an essay which has much to do with opéra-comique. Popular opera, said Grétry, contained both 'singing for singing' and 'singing for speaking'.[24] If we interpret Grétry's distinction within the tradition of aesthetic switching as described earlier, to which his audiences were accustomed, its message will be as helpful for the eighteenth-century field as for later periods discussed in Betzwieser's research.

*

Looking similarly forward, Ruth Müller's comparative work on opéra-comique given after 1762 is comprehensive, combining historical, cultural and musical levels. Money, marriage and love were three main themes studied.[25] Müller looked at friendship, gender, family, fortune, nobility versus bourgeois values, and wealth versus poverty. Opera plots, she found,

---

[23] *Le Déserteur*, III/6. Herbert Schneider discussed this *ariette* and its contexts in 'L'Air narratif'.
[24] Grétry, *Mémoires* (1797), I, 439–40; Betzwieser, 'Verisimilitude' in Greenwald, *ibid.*, 304.
[25] Müller, '"Il faut s'aimer"' and 'Weinen und Lachen'. The 1991 study covered some 70 works, and the 2001 study covered 112 works from France between 1757 and 1789 plus 75 from Italy between 1746 and 1792: see her Tables 1 and 2, 263–7.

disclose a gradual mutation in areas of sentimental conflict: up to the later 1750s, obstacles to marriage often took the form of an authority figure defeated by deception or disguise; lovers focused more on mutual longing.[26] This exact duality motivated, for example, Sedaine and Monsigny's *On ne s'avise jamais de tout* (*Impossible to Think of Everything*), consciously descended from Molière, as we saw. But it had entered many opéras-comiques *en vaudevilles*, also mentioned in Chapter 7: the adolescents constituting Favart's *Les Jeunes mariés* (*Young Marrieds*) or Nicette and Alain in *La Chercheuse d'esprit*. The young family in Pannard and Fagan's *La Foire de Cythère* (*The Fair at Cythera*), working in the field of entertainment, overcome a father's opposition (their dilemma anticipating Marmontel and Grétry's *Silvain*).

A swing towards social issues around 1762, noted Müller, was coincident with the disappearance of comic figures like older servants. In *Annette et Lubin* the *bailli* figure, traditionally rather ridiculous, becomes more of a threat. Confrontations between nobility and bourgeois, or between town and country, or palace and cottage, came to define the central conflict. These confrontations, Müller found, displaced the theme of money, that is, the problem of insufficient funds to permit marriage (*Annette and Lubin* again); and the existence of social class was interpreted in a moral sense.[27] Future work could readily take forward Müller's structural discoveries.

*

Topics like 'What is opera?' or 'What makes an opera an opera?' therefore continue to be relevant.[28] Neglect of *Le Déserteur*'s music was one explicit warrant for the present study (p. 25), together with the need to make popular opera better known, whether to cultural historians or even music specialists. To quote Thomas Bauman, introducing the 'neglected terrain' of North German opera in 1985: 'We often judge as trivial that for which we have not yet found a context.'[29] 'Received wisdom' betrays fact if readers are told that 'In France and England before the television age, opera was an expensive taste' and not a provincial one either.[30] Future readers deserve to know that the opposite was true, even before the Revolution; *popular* opera was affordable, it was available for home performance; and the building of regional and colonial theatres mushroomed after 1760 to the great benefit of opéra-comique.[31]

---

[26] Müller, '"Il faut s'aimer"', 154.   [27] Müller, *ibid.*, 161.   [28] Greenwald, *ibid.*, 15, 53.
[29] Bauman, *North German Opera*, 1.   [30] Sutcliffe, *Believing in Opera*, 69.
[31] Clay, *Stagestruck*.

Later on, Sutcliffe more correctly observed, 'The operatic past is still not properly in focus'.[32] Even if we cannot see many popular operas at the moment, we ought to grant their right to consideration. Mahler's stage designer Alfred Roller was proposing a century ago, 'Could it not be that the travelling theatre was healthy and right, and that all permanently established theatre is merely decadent? [...] A thespis-van, what fun!'[33] This is the kind of epistemological shift I have made in recognising opera with spoken dialogue as historically authentic and different.

---

[32] Sutcliffe, *ibid.*, 417.
[33] Alfred Roller, *Bühnenreform* (*Theatre Reform*), *Der Merker*, 1 (1909–10), 193–7, trans. by Meredith Oakes in Sutcliffe, *ibid.*, 427–8.

Stage Works Cited

Note: A comma separates writers; an ampersand [&] announces composer(s). Dates for *intermezzi* apply to Parisian performance. Dates in parentheses indicate premiere outside France.

Académie bourgeoise, L' (*The Urban Academy*: Pannard) 1735
Acajou (Favart) 1744
Achmet et Almanzine (Lesage, d'Orneval, Fuzelier & Gillier) 1728
Adieux des officiers, Les (*The Officers' Farewells*: Dufresny) 1693
Alceste (Quinault & Lully) 1674
Allure, L' (Carolet & Corrette) 1732
Amante ennemie, L' (*The Lover as Enemy*: Sallebray) 1642
Amants inquiets, Les (*The Unquiet Lovers*: Favart) 1751
Amants magnifiques, Les (*The Splendid Lovers*: Molière & Lully) 1670
Ambigu de la folie, L' (*The Mad Medley*: Favart) 1743
Ami de la maison, L' (*The Family Friend*: Marmontel & Grétry) 1771
Amour au village, L' (*Love in a Village*: Favart) 1745
Amour désœuvré, L' (*Cupid Unemployed*: Carolet) 1734 (rehearsed only)
Amours champêtres, Les (*Love in the Country*: Favart) 1751
Amours d'Apollon et de Daphné, Les (*The Loves of Apollo and Daphne*: Dassoucy) 1650
Amours de Gonesse, Les (*The Loves of Gonesse*: Favart, Chamfort & La Borde) 1765
Amours de Nanterre, Les (*The Loves of Nanterre*: Lesage, d'Orneval, Autreau) 1718
Amours de Ragonde, Les (*The Loves of Ragonde*: La Font & Mouret) 1714 / 1742
Animaux raisonnables, Les (*The Animals Endowed with Reason*: Fuzelier, Legrand & Aubert) 1718
Anneau perdu et retrouvé, L' (*The Ring Lost and Found*: Sedaine & Chardiny) 1764
Annette et Lubin (Justine Favart & Blaise) 1762
Annette et Lubin (Marmontel & La Borde) 1762
Arlequin baron allemand (*Harlequin German Baron*: Fuzelier, Lesage, d'Orneval) 1712
Arlequin comédien aux Champs Elisées (*Harlequin Actor in the Heavenly Fields*: Bordelon) 1691
Arlequin défenseur d'Homère (*Harlequin Takes Homer's Side*: Fuzelier) 1715
Arlequin devin par hasard (*Harlequin Soothsayer by Chance*: Fuzelier) 1716
Arlequin empereur dans la lune (*Harlequin Emperor in the Moon*: Fatouville) 1684

Arlequin Énée ou La prise de Troyes (*Harlequin-Aeneas or the Siege of Troyes*: Fuzelier) 1711
Arlequin Ésope see *Ésope à la cour*
Arlequin et Mezzetin morts par amour (*Harlequin and Mezzetin Die for Love*: Lesage) 1712
Arlequin et Scaramouche vendangeurs (*Harlequin and Scaramouche Grape-Pickers*: anon.) 1681
Arlequin Grapignan (Fatouville) 1682
Arlequin homme à bonne fortune (*Harlequin the Lucky*: Regnard) 1690
Arlequin Hulla (Lesage, d'Orneval) 1716
Arlequin Mahomet (*Harlequin-Mahomet*: Lesage) 1714
Arlequin misanthrope (*Harlequin Misanthropist*: Brugière de Barante) 1696
Arleqin Phaéton (Palaprat) 1692
Arlequin Roland furieux (*Harlequin the Raging Roland*: Bordelon) 1694
Arlequin Roy de Serendib (*Harlequin King of Serendib*: Lesage) 1713
Arlequin sultane favorite (*Harlequin Sultana and Favourite*: Letellier) 1715
Arlequin Thétis (Lesage) 1713
Arlequin traitant (*Harlequin the Financier*: d'Orneval & La Croix) 1716
Artigiani arricchiti, Gli (*The Artisans Grown Rich*: Barlocci [attrib.] & Latilla [et al.]) 1753 (1738)
Attendez-moi sous l'orme (*Just Don't Count on It*: Dufresny) 1695
Aventures des Champs-Elisées, Les (*Adventures in the Elysian Fields*: L.C.D.V.[1]) 1693
Aveux indiscrets, Les (*Indiscreet Confessions*: La Ribadière & Monsigny) 1759
Baguette de Vulcain, La (*Vulcan's Wand*: Regnard, Dufresny) 1693
Bains de la Porte Saint-Bernard, Les (*Swimming at Porte-Saint-Bernard*: Boisfranc) 1696
Baiocco et Serpilla (Favart & Sodi) 1753
Bal bourgeois, Le (*The Plain Man's Ball*: Favart) 1738
Bateliers de Saint-Cloud, Les (*The Boatmen of Saint-Cloud*: Favart) 1743
Beggar's Opera, The (Gay & Pepusch) (1728)
Bellérophon (T. Corneille, Fontenelle, Quinault & Lully) 1679
Béquille du Père Barnaba, La (*Father Barnabas' Crutch*: Laffichard) 1737
Bergers de qualité, Les (*The Well-Born Shepherds*: Gondot) 1752
Bertholde à la ville (*Bertoldo in Town*: Anseaume, Marcouville) 1754
Bertoldo in corte (*Bertoldo at Court*: Goldoni et al. & Ciampi et al.) 1753 (1748)
Biron, VIIIe Concerto Comique (Corrette) 1734
Blaise le savetier (*Blaise the Cobbler*: Sedaine & Philidor) 1759
Bohémienne, La (*The Gypsy*: Moustou & Rinaldo Da Capua et al.) 1755
Bohémienne, La (*The Gypsy*: Favart & Rinaldo Da Capua et al.) 1755
Bon soldat, Le (*The Good Soldier*: Dancourt) 1691

---

[1] Only the initials are known today.

Bourgeois gentilhomme, Le (*The Would-be Gentleman*: Molière & Lully) 1670
Bûcheron, Le (*The Woodcutter*: Guichard, Castet & Philidor) 1763
Cadi dupé, Le (*The Cadi Deceived*: Lemonnier & Monsigny) 1761
Camille, ou Le souterrain (*Camille, or The Dungeon*: Marsollier & Dalayrac) 1791
Caprice, Le (*The Caprice*: Piron) 1724
Caprice d'Érato, Le (*Erato's Caprice*: Fuzelier & Colin de Blamont) 1730
Ceinture de Vénus, La (*Venus' Girdle*: Lesage & Gillier & Jacquet de La Guerre) 1715
Cendrillon (*Cinderella*: Anseaume & Duni & Laruette) 1759
Chercheuse d'esprit, La (*The Girl Who Sought Wit*: Favart) 1741
Chinois, Les (*The Chinese People*: Regnard, Dufresny) 1692
Chinois, Les (*The Chinese People*: Favart, Naigeon & Sellitto et al.) 1756
Chinois poli en France, Le (*The Stylish Chinese Man in France*: Anseaume & Sellitto et al.) 1754
Cinese rimpatriato, Il (*The Chinese Man Returned*: anon. & Sellitto) 1753
Circé (T. Corneille, Donneau de Visé & Charpentier) 1675
Claperman, Le (*The Nightwatchman*: Piron) 1724
Coffres, Les (*The Coffers*: Gallet) 1736
Collier de perles, Le (*The Pearl Necklace*: Girardin & Beauchamps) 1672
Comédie de chansons, La (*The Comedy in Song*: Sorel (attrib.)) 1640
Comédiens du Mans en Flandres (*The Actors of Le Mans in Flanders*: Favart) 1745
Comédie sans hommes, La (*The Women-Only Comedy*: Pannard) 1732
Comte d'Albert, Le (*Count d'Albert*: Sedaine & Grétry) 1786
Contessina, La (*The Count's Daughter*: Goldoni) 1743
Coq de village, Le (*The Cock of the Walk*: Favart) 1743
Coquette, La (*The Coquette*: Regnard) 1691
Coquette sans le savoir, La (*The Innocent Coquette*: P. Rousseau, Favart) 1744
Corsair de Salé, Le (*The Pirate of Salé*: Lesage, d'Orneval) 1729
Couplets en procès, Les (*The Vaudevilles Go to Law*: Lesage, d'Orneval) 1729
Crispin rival de son maître (*Crispin His Master's Rival*: Lesage) 1707
Critique de La Cause des femmes, La (*Critique of The Women's Lawsuit*: Delosme de Montchesnay) 1687
Dare-Devil Rides to Jarama (Neil Gore) (2017)
Débuts, Les (*The Débuts*: Biancolelli, Romagnesi) 1729
Départ de l'Opéra Comique (*Opéra-Comique's Farewell*: Pannard) 1733
Départ des comédiens, Le (*The Actors' Farewell*: Dufresny) 1694
Déserteur, Le (*The Deserter*: Sedaine & Monsigny) 1769
Désespérés, Les (*Entertainers in Despair*: Lesage) 1732
Deux amies, Les (*Two Women Friends*: Bret & Papavoine) 1761
Deux Arlequins, Les (*The Two Harlequins*: Le Noble) 1691
Deux chasseurs et la laitière, Les (*Two Hunters and a Milkmaid*: Anseaume & Duni) 1763
Deux Pierrots, Les (*The Two Pierrots*: Biancolelli) 1714

Deux suivantes, Les (*The Two Servants*: Pannard) 1730
Devin du village, Le (*The Village Soothsayer*: J. J. Rousseau) 1752–3
Diable à quatre, Le (*The Hell-Raiser*: Sedaine) 1756
Docteur Sangrado, Le (*Doctor Sangrado*: Anseaume, Lourdet de Santerre & Duni & Laruette) 1758
Don Micco et Lesbina (Biancolelli, Romagnesi) 1729
Don Quichotte chez la duchesse (*Don Quixote visits the duchess*: Favart & Boismortier) 1743
Donna superba, La (*The Haughty Woman*: Barlocci & Rinaldo Di Capua) 1752 (1738)
Double inconstance, La (*Double Inconstancy*: Marivaux) 1723
Dreigroschenoper, Die (Brecht & Weill) (1928)
Eaux de Merlin, Les (*Merlin's Waters*: Lesage) 1715
École des amants, L' (*The School for Lovers*: Lesage, Fuzelier) 1716
École des amours grivois, L' (*Love on the Battlefield*: Favart & Boismortier) 1744
École des femmes, L' (*The School for Wives*: Molière) 1662
Effets du hazard, Les (*Just by Chance*: Laffichard) 1735
Endriague, L' (*The Dragon*: Piron & Rameau) 1723
Entführung aus dem Serail, Die (*Abduction from the Seraglio*: Bretzner, Stephanie & Mozart) (1782)
Époux réunis, Les (*Husband and Wife Reunited*: Pannard) 1736
Ercole amante (*Hercules in Love*: Buti & Cavalli) 1662
Ésope à la cour (*Æsop at Court*: Le Noble) 1691
Espérance, L' (*Hope*: Lesage, d'Orneval, Fuzelier) 1730
Fâcheux veuvage, Le (*The Trials of Widowhood*: Piron & Royer) 1725
Fausse ridicule, La (*Misplaced Ridicule*: Fagan) 1731
Fée Urgèle, La (*Fairy Urgèle*: Favart & Duni) 1765
Fées, Les (*The Fairies*: Dufresny, Brugière de Barante) 1697
Femme orgueilleuse, La (*The Haughty Woman*: Quétant & Sodi) 1759
Femmes vengées, Les (*The Women Avenged*: Sedaine & Philidor) 1775
Festin de pierre, Le (*The Stone Guest*: Letellier) 1713
Fêtes de Thalie, Les (*Thalia's Festival*: La Font & Mouret) 1714
Fêtes grecques et romaines, Les (*The Festivals of Greece and Rome*: Fuzelier & Colin de Blamont) 1723
Fêtes parisiennes, Les (*Festival in Paris*: Fuzelier) 1712
Fêtes vénitiennes, Les (*Festival in Venice*: Danchet & Campra) 1710
Fille capitaine, La (*The Girl-Commander*: anon.) 1709
Fille, la veuve et la femme, La (*The Woman, the Wife and the Widow*: Laujon, Parvi) 1745
Fille mal gardée, La (*The Girl Who Broke Free*: Favart & Duni) 1758
Filles errantes, Les (*Girls Astray*: Regnard) 1690
Finta cameriera, La (*The Counterfeit Chambermaid*: Barlocci & Latilla *et al.*) 1752 (1738)

Finta pazza, La (*The Fake Madwoman*: Strozzi & Sacrati) 1641
Fleuve Scamandre, Le (*The River Scamander*: Laffichard, Pannard) 1734
Foire de Bezons, La (*The Bezons Fair*: Favart) 1735
Foire de Cythère, La (*The Fair at Cythera*: Pannard, Fagan) 1742
Foire de Guibray, La (*The Guibray Fair*: Lesage & Gillier) 1714
Foire Saint-Germain, La (*The Saint-Germain Fair*: Regnard, Dufresny) 1695
Folies amoureuses, Les (*Crazy Loves*: Regnard & Gillier) 1704
Fontaine de sapience, La (*The Fountain of Wisdom*: Brugière de Barente) 1694
Forêt de Dodône, La (*The Forest of Dodona*: Lesage, Fuzelier, d'Orneval) 1721
Fossé du scrupule, Le (*The Pit of Scruples*: Pannard) 1738
Foux divertissans, Les (*The Amusing Madmen*: Poisson) 1680
Funérailles de la Foire, Les (*The Fair's Funeral*: Lesage, d'Orneval, Fuzelier) 1718
Gageure, La (*The Wager*: Pannard) 1740
Génie de l'Opéra Comique, Le (*The Genius of Opéra Comique*: Favart) 1735
Georget et Georgette (Harny de Guerville & C. G. Alexandre) 1761
Gilles garçon-peintre (*Gilles, Assistant Painter*: Poinsinet & La Borde) 1758
Giocasta regina d'Armenia (*Jocasta Queen of Armenia*: Moniglia & Grossi) (1676)
Giocatore, Il (*The Gambler*: Salvi & Orlandini et al.) 1729, 1752 (1715)
Grand'mère amoureuse, La (*The Amorous Grandmother*: d'Orneval, Fuzelier) 1726
Guy de chêne, Le (*The Oak and the Mistletoe*: Junquières & Laruette) 1763
Harlequin à la guinguette (*Harlequin at the Tavern*: Pellegrin) 1711
Homme à bonne fortune, L' (*The Lucky Man*: Regnard) 1690
Huître et les plaideurs, L' (*The Oyster and the Litigants*: Sedaine & Philidor) 1759
Impromptu du Pont-Neuf, L' (*An Impromptu for the Pont-Neuf*: Pannard) 1729
Inconnu, L' (*The Stranger*: T. Corneille, Donneau de Visé & Charpentier) 1675
Inconstant vaincu, L' (*The Defeat of the Cheat*: anon.) 1660
Indes galantes, Les (*Love the World Over*: Fuzelier & Rameau) 1735
Isle des Amazones, L' (*Amazon Island*: Lesage, d'Orneval & Gillier) 1720
Isle des foux, L' (*The Island of the Mad*: Anseaume, Marcouville & Duni) 1760
Ismène (Paradis de Moncrif & Rebel & Francœur) 1747
Jaloux corrigé, Le (*The Jealous Husband Cured*: Collé) 1753
Jardinier et son seigneur, Le (*The Gardener and His Lord*: Sedaine & Philidor) 1761
Jardins de l'Hymen ou La Rose, Les (*Hymen's Garden, or The Rose*: Piron, rev. Favart
    & Rameau) 1726
Je ne sais quoi, Le (*The I Don't Know What*: Boissy) 1731
Jeune-Vieillard, Le (*The Old Young Man*: Lesage, Fuzelier, d'Orneval) 1722
Jeunes mariés, Les (*The Young Marrieds*: Favart) 1740
Joueur, Le (*The Gambler*: Biancolelli, Romagnesi) 1729
Jugement de Paris, Le (*The Judgement of Paris*: Dassoucy) 1648
Jumeaux, Les (*The Twins*: Guérin de Frémicourt) 1754
Jumelles, Les (*The Female Twins*: Favart) 1734
King and the Miller of Mansfield, The (Dodsley) (1737)
Lanterne véridique, La (*The Truth-Telling Lantern*: Carolet) 1732

Lucile (Marmontel & Grétry) 1769

Maestro di musica, Il (*The Music Master*: Palomba *et al.* & Auletta *et al.*) 1752 (1737)

Magazin des modernes, Le (*The Fashion-Store*: Pannard) 1736

Maître de musique, Le (*The Music Master*: Baurans & Auletta *et al.*) 1755

Maître en droit, Le (*The Master at Law*: Lemonnier & Monsigny) 1760

Mal-assortis, Les (*The Ill-Matched Couples*: Dufresny) 1693

Malade imaginaire, Le (*The Hypochondriac*: Molière & Charpentier) 1673

Maréchal-ferrant, Le (*The Blacksmith*: Quétant, Anseaume & Philidor) 1761

Mari préféré, Le (*The Preferred Husband*: Lesage) 1736

Mariage du Caprice et de la Folie, Le: see *Caprice, Le*

Mariages de Canada, Les (*The Marriages in Canada*: Lesage & Gillier) 1734

Mary sans femme, Le (*The Wifeless Husband*: Montfleury) 1663

Mascherata, La (*The Masquerade*: Goldoni & Cocchi) 1751

Matrone d'Éphèse, La (*The Widow of Ephesus*: Fatouville) see *Arlequin Grapignan*

Matrone d'Éphèse, La (*The Widow of Ephesus*: Fuzelier) 1714

Mazet (Anseaume & Duni) 1761

Médecin de l'amour, Le (*The Love-Doctor*: Anseaume, Marcouville & Laruette) 1758

Médecin de village, Le (*The Village Doctor*: anon. & Gillier) 1704

Médecin malgré lui, Le (*The Unwilling Doctor*: Molière) 1666

Mère embarrassée, La (*The Embarrassed Mother*: Pannard, Pontau) 1734

Mère jalouse, La (*The Jealous Mother*: Carolet) 1732

Mie Margot, La (*Little Friend Margot*: Pannard & Corrette) 1735

Momies d'Egypte, Les (*The Egyptian Mummies*: Regnard, Dufresny) 1696

Monde renversé, Le (*The World Upside Down*: Lesage, d'Orneval, La Font & Gillier) 1718

Moulinet Premier (*Moulinet the First*: Favart) 1739

Muse pantomime, La (*The Pantomime Muse*: Pannard) 1737

Naissance d'Amadis, La (*The Birth of Amadis*: Regnard) 1694

Naufrage au Port-à-l'Anglais, Le (*Shipwreck at Port-à-l'Anglais*: Autreau & Mouret) 1718

Nicaise (Vadé) 1756

Nina ou La folle par amour (*Nina or The Woman Crazed by Love*: Marsollier & Dalayrac) 1786

Ninette à la cour (*Ninette at Court*: Favart) 1755–6

Nopce de village, La (*The Village Wedding*: Brécourt & Charpentier) 1681

Nouvelliste dupé, Le (*The Newsmonger Deceived*: Pannard) 1732

Nymphes de Diane, Les (*Diana's Nymphs*: Favart & Corrette) 1747

Olimpiade, L' (*The Olympic Games*: Metastasio & Duni) 1755

Olivette juge des enfers (*Olivette, Judge of the Underworld*: Piron) 1726

On ne s'avise jamais de tout (*Impossible to Think of Everything*: Sedaine & Monsigny) 1761

Opéra de campagne, L' (*Opera in the Country*: Dufresny) 1692

Originaux, Les (*The Eccentrics*: Houdar de La Motte) 1693
Paladins, Les (*The Paladins*: Duplat de Monticourt, *attrib.* & Rameau) 1760
Paratajo, Il (*The Fowler's Net*: anon. & Jommelli *et al.*) 1753 (1750)
Pasquin et Marforio (Dufresny, Brugière de Barante) 1697
Peines et les plaisirs de l'amour, Les (*The Pains and Pleasures of Love*: Gilbert & Cambert) 1672
Peintre amoureux de son modèle, Le (*The Painter Who Loved his Model*: Anseaume & Duni) 1757
Pèlerins de la Mecque, Les (*The Pilgrims from Mecca*: Lesage, d'Orneval & L'Abbé) 1726
Pénélope moderne, La (*The New Penelope*: Lesage, Fuzelier, d'Orneval) 1728
Petits-maîtres, Les (*The Fops*: Lesage) 1712
Pharaon, Le (*The Game of Faro*: Fuzelier) 1717
Phénix, Le (*The Phœnix*: Delosme de Montchesnay) 1691
Pièce à deux acteurs, La (*The Two-Hander*: Pannard) 1738
Platée (Autreau, Valois d'Orville & Rameau) 1745
Poirier, Le (*The Pear Tree*: Vadé) 1752
Prétendu, Le (*The Intended Husband*: Riccoboni & Gaviniès) 1760
Princesse de Carizme, La (*The Princess of Carizme*: Lesage & Gillier & Lacoste) 1718
Princesse de la Chine, La (*The Princess of China*: Le Sage, d'Orneval & Giller) 1729
Prix de Cythère, Le (*The Cytherean Prize*: Antoine-René de Paulmy (*attrib.*), Favart) 1742
Promenades de Paris, Les (*Paris Walks*: Mongin) 1695
Proserpine (Quinault & Lully) 1680
Provençale, La (*The Girl from Provence*: La Font & Mouret) 1722
Psyché (Molière, Quinault, T. Corneille & Lully) 1671
Pygmalion (Pannard) 1735
Pyrame et Thisbé (La Serre & Rebel & Francœur) 1726
Quiproquo, Le (*The Misunderstanding*: Moustou & Philidor) 1760
Racoleurs, Les (*The Press-Gang*: Vadé) 1756
Rappel de la Foire à la vie, Le (*The Fair Summoned back to Life*: Lesage, d'Orneval) 1721
Raton et Rosette (Favart) 1753
Régal des dames, Le (*The Ladies' Delight*: anon.) 1668
Régiment de la Calotte, Le (*The Calotte Regiment*: Fuzelier, Lesage, d'Orneval) 1721
Reine du Barostan, La (*The Queen of Barostan*: Lesage, d'Orneval & Gillier) 1730
Rémouleur d'amour, Le (*The Sharpener of Love*: Lesage, Fuzelier, d'Orneval) 1722
Re pastore, Il (*The Shepherd King*: Metastasio) 1751
Répétition interrompue, La (*The Interrupted Rehearsal*: Pannard, rev. Favart) 1735 / 1757
Retour au village, Le (*Return to the Village*: anon. & Duni) 1756
Retour de la Foire de Bezons, Le (*Return from the Bezons Fair*: Gherardi or Fatouville) 1695
Réveil de l'Opéra Comique, Le (*The Opéra Comique Awakens*: Carolet) 1732

Richard Cœur de lion (*Richard Lionheart*: Sedaine & Grétry) 1784
Roger de Sicile (Lesage, d'Orneval & Gillier) 1731
Roi et le fermier, Le (*The King and the Farmer*: Sedaine & Monsigny) 1762
Rose, La: see *Jardins de l'Hymen*
Routes du monde, Les (*Ways through the World*: Lesage, Fuzelier, d'Orneval) 1730
Saut du fossé, Le (*The Leap over the Pit*: Pannard) 1742
Scaltra governatrice, La (*The Shrewd Governor's Wife*: Palomba & Cocchi *et al.*) 1753 (1747)
Serpilla e Baiocco: see *Giocatore, Il*
Serrurier, Le (*The Locksmith*: Quétant & Kohaut) 1764
Servante justifiée, La (*The Justified Servant*: Favart) 1740
Servante maîtresse, La (*The Maid as Mistress*: Baurans & Pergolesi *et al.*) 1754
Serva padrona, La (*The Maid as Mistress*: Federico & Pergolesi) 1746, 1752 (1733)
Sicilien, Le (*The Sicilian*: Molière & Lully) 1667
Siège de Cythère, Le (*The Siege of Cythera*: Favart, Fagan) 1743
Soldat magicien, Le (*The Soldier-Magician*: Anseaume, Serrière & Philidor) 1760
Sophie et Sigismond (Lesage, d'Orneval) 1732
Sorcier, Le (*The Sorcerer*: Poinsinet & Philidor) 1764
Statue merveilleuse, La (*The Magic Statue*: Lesage, Fuzelier, d'Orneval) 1720
Suffisant, Le (*The Self-Satisfied Man*: Vadé) 1753
Tableau du mariage, Le (*A Portrait of Marriage*: Lesage, Fuzelier) 1716
Talents à la mode, Les (*Fashionable Talents*: Boissy & Blaise) 1739
Tante rivale, La (*The Aunt as Rival*: Pannard, Thierry) 1729
Témoins contre eux-mêmes, Les (*The Self-Incriminators*: Gallet) 1736 (= *Coffres, Les*)
Temple de l'Ennui, Le (*The Temple of Boredom*: Lesage, Fuzelier & Gillier) 1716
Temple du Destin, Le (*The Temple of Destiny*: Lesage & Gillier) 1715
Temple du Sommeil, Le (*The Temple of Sleep*: Pannard, Fagan) 1731
Thésée, parodie (Favart, Laujon, Parvi) 1745
Tircis et Doristée (Favart) 1752
Tirésias (Piron & L'Abbé) 1722
Tombeau de Nostradamus, Le (*Nostradamus' Tomb*: Lesage) 1714
Tonnelier, Le (*The Cooper*: Audinot, Quétant & various composers) 1761
Tracollo, medico ignorante (Mariani & Pergolesi *et al.*) 1753 (1734)
Triomphe de l'interêt, Le (*The Triumph of Interest*: Boissy) 1730
Triomphe des dames, Le (T. Corneille & Charpentier) 1676
Troc, Le (*The Exchange*: Hautemer) 1756
Trois cousines, Les (*The Three Cousins*: Dancourt) 1700
Trois commères, Les (*Three Married Women*: Lesage, Piron, d'Orneval) 1723
Trois fermiers, Les (*The Three Farmers*: Monvel & Dezède) 1777
Trompeur trompé, Le (*The Deceiver Deceived*: Vadé) 1754
Troqueurs, Les (*The Swappers*: Vadé & Dauvergne) 1753
Ulisse et Circé (*Ulysses and Circe*: L.A.D.S.M.) 1691

Union des deux opéras, L' (*The Two Operas United*: Dufresny) 1692
Veuve coquette, La (*The Coquettish Widow*: Desportes) 1721
Veuve indécise, La (*The Indecisive Widow*: Vadé, Anseaume & Duni) 1759
Viaggiatori, I (*The Travellers*: Palomba & Latilla) 1754 (1743)
Voyage de Scaramouche, Le (*Scaramouche's Journey*: anon.) 1676
Zauberflöte, Die (*The Magic Flute*: Schikaneder & Mozart) (1791)
Zingara, La (*The Gypsy*: anon. & Rinaldo Di Capua *et al.*) 1753

Bibliography

Pre-1800 Authors and Works[1]

Addison, Joseph, Richard Steele, and others, *The Spectator* (1711–14), ed. Gregory Smith, 4 vols. (London: J. M. Dent, 1907).

Algarotti, Francesco, *Saggio sopra l'opera in musica* [1755, rev. 1763], anon. trans. as *An Essay on the Opera* (Glasgow: R. Urie, 1768).

Anon., 'Éloge historique de M. Baurans', *Le Nécrologe des hommes célèbres de France* (Paris: Moreau, 1767), 117–25; repr. in Desboulmiers, *Histoire anecdotique* (1769), VI, 231–8.

Anon., 'Éloge de Monsieur Duni', *Le Nécrologe des hommes célèbres de France* XI (1776), 163–79; ed. Dinko Fabris in Russo, ed., *I due mondi di Duni*, 20–5.

Anon., ed., *Les Étrennes des acteurs des théâtres de Paris* (Paris: Delormel, 1747).

Aristotle, *On the Art of Poetry*, in *Classical Literary Criticism*, ed. T. S. Dorsch (Harmondsworth: Penguin Books, 1987).

Ballard, Jean-Baptiste-Christophe, *La Clef des chansonniers* [1717], ed. Herbert Schneider (Hildesheim: Olms, 2005).

Barbier, Edmond Jean François, *Chronique de la Régence et du Règne de Louis XV (1718–1763) ou journal de Barbier*, 8 vols. (Paris: Charpentier, 1857).

Bentley, Thomas, *Journal of a Visit to Paris, 1776*, ed. Peter France (Falmer: University of Sussex Library, 1977).

[Béthisy de Mézières, Eugène-Éléonore de], *Effets de l'air sur le corps humain, considérés dans le son* (Amsterdam: Duchesne, 1760).

Blainville, C. H., *L'Esprit de l'art musical* (Geneva: n. p., 1754).

[Blanchet J.], *L'Art, ou Les principes philosophiques du chant*, 2nd ed. (Paris: Lottin, 1756).

Boislisle, A. de, ed., *Lettres de M. de Marville, lieutenant général de police, au Ministre Maurepas (1742–1747)*, 3 vols. (Paris: H. Champion, 1896–1905)

Brosses, Charles de, *Lettres du Président de Brosses à Ch.-C. Loppin de Gemeaux*, ed. Yvonne Bezard (Paris: Firmin-Didot, 1929).

Burney, Charles, *The Present State of Music in France and Italy* (London: T. Becket, 1771).

Casanova, Giacomo, chevalier de Seingalt, *History of My Life*, trans. Willard R. Trask, 12 vols. (London: Longmans, Green, 1966–8; R/1997 in 6 vols.).

---

[1] Including later editions but not digital reproductions or photo-reprints.

[Chamfort, Sébastien-Roch-Nicolas and Joseph de La Porte], *Dictionnaire dramatique*, 3 vols. (Paris: Lacombe, 1776).

Chevrier, François-Antoine, *Observations sur le theatre. Dans lesquelles on examine avec impartialité l'état actuel des spectacles à Paris* (Paris: Debure le Jeune, 1755).

Choderlos de Laclos, Pierre Ambroise François, *Les Liaisons dangereuses* [1782], trans. P. W. K. Stone (Harmondsworth: Penguin Books, 1961).

Collé, Charles, *Journal et Mémoires* [1748–72], ed. Honoré Bonhomme, 3 vols. (Paris: Firmin-Didot Frères, 1868).

[Contant d'Orville, André Guillaume], *Histoire de l'opéra bouffon*, 2 vols. (Amsterdam: Grangé, 1768).

D'Argenson, René-Louis de Voyer de Paulmy, *Journal et mémoires du Marquis d'Argenson publiés pour la première fois*, ed. E. J. B. Rathery, 9 vols. (Paris: Veuve Jules Renouard, 1859–67).

Notices sur les œuvres de théâtre [1725–57], ed. Henri Lagrave, 2 vols. (Geneva: Institut et Musée Voltaire, 1966).

[Desboulmiers, Jean-Auguste Jullien], *Histoire anecdotique et raisonnée du Théâtre Italien*, 7 vols. (Paris: Lacombe, 1769).

Desfontaines, Pierre-François Guyot, *Observations sur les écrits modernes*, XXIV (Paris: Chaubert, 1741) and XXXIII (1743).

Diderot, Denis, *The Nun* [1760, published 1796], trans. Russell Goulbourne (Oxford: Oxford University Press, 2005).

Œuvres complètes, XIX: *Musique*, ed. Jean Mayer and Pierre Citron (Paris: Hermann, 1983).

Œuvres Esthétiques, ed. Paul Vernière (Paris: Garnier, 1988).

Rameau's Nephew. A Multi-Media Edition, ed. Marian Hobson, trans. Kate E. Tunstall and Caroline Warman, with Pascal Duc (Cambridge: Open Book Publishers, 2014). DOI: https://doi.org/10.11647/OBP.0044

Diderot, Denis, and Jean Le Rond d'Alembert, eds., *Encyclopédie ou Dictionnaire raisonné des sciences, des arts et des métiers*, 17 vols. (Paris: 1751–72).

D'Origny, Antoine, *Annales du Théâtre italien depuis son origine jusqu'à ce jour*, 3 vols. (Paris: Vve Duchesne, 1788).

Dryden, John, 'The Preface' to *Albion and Albanius: An Opera* [1685], in *Of Dramatic Poesy and Other Critical Essays*, ed. George Watson, 2 vols. (London: J. M. Dent, 1962), II, 34–43.

[Du Boccage, Anne-Marie Le Page], *Lettre de Madame* +++ *à une de ses amies sur les spectacles et principalement sur les Opéra-Comique* (Paris: n. p., 1745).

Duclos, Charles, *Acajou et Zirphile* [1744], ed. Jean Dagen (Paris: Desjonquères, 1993).

Fagan de Lugny, Barthélemy-Christophe, *Théâtre de M. Fagan*, 4 vols. (Paris: N. B. Duchesne, 1760).

Favart, Charles-Simon, *Mémoires et correspondances dramatiques et anecdotiques*, ed. A. P. C. Favart, 3 vols. (Paris: Léopold Collin, 1808).

Théâtre de Monsieur Favart, ou Recueil des Opéra-Comiques & Parodies qu'il a données depuis quelques années, 2 vols. (Paris: Prault fils, 1746), works paginated separately.

Favart, Marie-Justine-Benoîte and Adolphe Benoît Blaise, *Annette et Lubin* (Paris, 1762), ed. Andreas Münzmay (*Opera: Spektrum des europäischen Musiktheaters in Einzeleditionen*, II) (Kassel: Bärenreiter, 2016).

Framery, Nicolas-Étienne, 'Quelques réflexions sur la musique moderne', *Journal de musique*, I (May 1770), 3–18; R/ Geneva, 1972, I, 343–58.

'Sur le genre larmoyant dans les Drames en Musique', *Journal de musique*, I (Sept. 1770), 3–13; R/ Geneva, 1972, I, 697–707.

[Fréron, Elie-Catherine], *L'Année littéraire ou Suite des Lettres sur quelques Écrits de ce Temps, par M. Fréron* (Amsterdam, Paris: Lambert, 1754–90).

Lettres sur quelques écrits de ce tems, 13 vols. (Amsterdam, Paris: Duchesne, 1749–50, 1752–4).

[Garcin, Laurent], *Traité du Mélo-Drame, ou Réflexions sur la musique dramatique* (Paris: Vallat-la-Chapelle, 1772).

Garrick, David, *The Diary of David Garrick. Being a Record of His Memorable Trip to Paris in 1751*, ed. Ryllis Clair Alexander (New York: Oxford University Press, 1928).

Gherardi, Evaristo, ed., *Le Théâtre italien de Gherardi*, 6 vols. (Paris: Jean-Baptiste Cusson and Pierre Witte, 1700).

Grétry, André Ernest Modeste, *Mémoires, ou Essais sur la musique*, 3 vols. (Paris: Imprimerie de la République, Pluviôse An V [Jan.–Feb. 1797]).

Grimm, Friedrich Melchior, *Correspondance littéraire*, ed. Maurice Tourneux, 16 vols. (Paris: Garnier Frères, 1877–82).

Correspondance littéraire, 15 vols. (Paris: Furne, 1829–31).

Gueullette, Thomas-Simon, *Notes et souvenirs sur le Théâtre-Italien au XVIIIe siècle* [1750–62], ed. J.-E. Gueullette (Paris: Droz, 1938).

Harriss, Ernest C. (trans., ed.), *Johann Mattheson's 'Der vollkommene Capellmeister'* [1739]. *A Revised Translation with Critical Commentary* (Ann Arbor: UMI Press, 1981).

La Borde, Jean-Benjamin de, *Essai sur la musique ancienne et moderne*, 4 vols. (Paris: Eugène Onfroy, 1780).

La Bruyère, Jean de, *Les Characters* [1688] (Paris: Emler Frères, 1829) trans. by Henri Van Laun (New York: Howard Fertig, 1992).

Lacombe, Jacques, *Le Spectacle des beaux arts* (Paris: Vincent, 1761).

[La Dixmerie, Nicolas Bricaire de], *Lettres sur l'état présent de nos spectacles* (Amsterdam, Paris: Duchesne, 1765).

La Fontaine, Jean de, *Contes et nouvelles en vers* [1665–74], ed. Alain-Marie Bassy (n. p.: Gallimard, 1995).

Selected Fables [1668–94], trans. Christopher Wood, ed. with introduction by Maya Slater (Oxford: Oxford University Press, 1995).

Some Tales of La Fontaine, trans. C. H. Sisson (Manchester: Carcanet, 1979).

La Harpe, Jean-François de, *Correspondance littéraire*, 6 vols. (Paris: Migneret, 1801–7).

La Place, Pierre-Antoine de, 'Discours sur le Théâtre anglois', *Le Théâtre anglois*, 2nd ed., 8 vols. (Londres, n.p., 1746–49).

La Porte, Joseph de, *Voyage en l'autre monde ou nouvelles littéraires de celui-cy* (Londres, n.p., 1753).

La Porte, Joseph de, and Jean-Marie Clément, *Anecdotes dramatiques*, 3 vols. (Paris: Duchesne, 1775).

Lebeau de Schosne, Augustin-Théodore, *Lettre à Monsieur de Crébillon sur les spectacles de Paris* (Paris: Cailleau, 1761).

[Le Cerf de La Viéville, Jean Laurent], *Comparaison de la musique italienne et de la musique françoise*, 2nd ed., 3 vols. (Brussels: Foppens, 1705–06).

Léris, Antoine de, *Dictionnaire portatif, historique et littéraire des théâtres*, 2nd ed. (Paris: Jombert, 1763).

Lesage, Alain-René, *The Adventures of Gil Blas of Santillane* [1715, 1724, 1735], trans. B. H. Malkin, 2 vols. (London: J. M. Dent, 1910).

Devil on Two Sticks [*Le Diable boiteux, 1707/1726*], trans. William Strange (London: Navarre Society, 1927).

and Jacques-Philippe d'Orneval, eds., *Le Théâtre de la Foire, ou L'Opéra comique. Contenant les meilleurs Piéces qui ont été représentées* [...], 10 vols. (Paris: Pierre Gandouin, 1737) originally issued successively by various publishers in Paris in 1721, 1724, 1728, 1731, 1734 and 1737. Reprint edition, shown in the footnotes as 'R', 2 vols. (Geneva: Slatkine, 1968).

Lister, Martin, *A Journey to Paris in the Year 1698* (2nd ed., London: Jacob Tonson, 1699).

[Mably, Gabriel Bonnot de], *Lettres à Madame la Marquise de P .... sur l'opéra* (Paris: Didot, 1741).

Marmontel, Jean-François, *Mémoires* [1799] ed. Jean-Pierre Guicciardi and Gilles Thierriat (n. p., Mercure de France, 1999).

Mémoires secrets pour servir à l'histoire de la République des Lettres en France, depuis 1762 jusqu'à nos jours [credited to 'de Bachaumont': Londres: John Adamson, 1777–89], ed. Christophe Cave and Suzanne Cornand, 5 vols. [in progress] (Paris: Champion, 2009–10).

Molière, *Œuvres complètes* (Oxford: Imprimerie de l'Université, 1926).

Monnet, Jean, *Mémoires de Jean Monnet, Directeur du Théâtre de la Foire* [1772] ed. Henri d'Alméras (Paris: Louis-Michaud, [1908]).

Montesquieu, Charles-Louis, *Lettres persanes* [1721] ed. Jacques Roger (Paris: Garnier-Flammarion, 1964).

Mouret, Jean-Joseph, *Recueil des divertissemens du Théâtre Italien*, 6 vols., (Paris: L'Auteur, etc., n.d. [1722–*c*. 1738]), issued successively: see Viollier, *Mouret*, 221–5.

[Nemeitz, Joachim Christophe], *Séjour de Paris, oder Getreue Anleitung Welchergestalt Reisende von Condition sich zu erhalten haben* (Frankfurt am Main: F. W. Förster, 1718).

Séjour de Paris, c'est à dire, Instructions fidèles pour les Voiageurs de Condition, 2nd ed., 2 vols. (Leyden: Jean Van Abcoude, 1727).

[Nougaret, Pierre Jean], *De l'Art du théâtre en général, où il est parlé des spectacles de l'Europe*, 2 vols. (Paris: Cailleau, 1768).

Pannard, Charles-François, *Théâtre et œuvres diverses*, 4 vols. (Paris: Duchesne, 1763).

Parfaict, Claude and François Parfaict, *Dictionnaire des théâtres de Paris*, 2nd ed., 7 vols. (Paris: Rozet, 1767).

Mémoires pour servir à l'histoire des spectacles de la Foire, 2 vols. (Paris: Briasson, 1743).

Parodies du Nouveau Théâtre Italien, Les: 1st ed., 3 vols. (Paris: Briasson, 1731); expanded ed., 4 vols. (Paris: Briasson, 1738).

Patu, Claude-Pierre, *Choix de petites pièces du théâtre anglois, traduites des originaux*, 2 vols. (Londres: Prault, 1756).

Paulmy, Antoine-René de Voyer de and André-Guillaume, Contant d'Orville, *Manuel des châteaux (Mélanges tirés d'une grande bibliothèque, II)* (Paris: Moutard, 1779).

[Perrault, Charles], *Critique de l'Opéra, ou Examen de la tragédie intitulée Alceste, ou le Triomphe d'Alcide* (Paris: Claude Barbin, 1674).

Pétis de La Croix, François, *Les Mille et un jours* [1710–12] (Paris: Desrez, 1840).

Piron, Alexis, *Œuvres complettes d'Alexis Piron*, ed. Jean-Antoine Rigoley de Juvigny, 7 vols. (Paris: Lambert, 1776).

Quantz, Johann Joachim, *On Playing the Flute* [1752], trans. Edward R. Reilly, 2nd ed. (London: Faber, 1985).

Raguenet, François, *Parallèle des Italiens et des François* [1702], trans. as *A Comparison between the French and Italian Musick and Opera's* (London, 1709), ed. Charles Cudworth (Farnborough: Gregg International, 1968).

Rémond de Saint-Mard, Toussaint, *Réflexions sur l'opéra* (La Haye: J. Neaulme, 1741).

Richardson, Samuel, *Pamela; or, Virtue rewarded* [1740], ed. Thomas Keymer and Alice Wakely (Oxford: Oxford University Press, 2001).

[Roland de La Platière, Jean-Marie], *Lettres écrites de Suisse, d'Italie, de Sicile et de Malthe*, 6 vols. (Amsterdam, 1780).

Rousseau, Jean-Jacques, *Confessions* [1782–9], trans. Angela Scholar (Oxford: Oxford University Press, 2000).

'Dictionnaire de musique' [1768] and 'Lettre sur la musique françoise' [1753], in *Écrits sur la musique, la langue et le théâtre (Œuvres complétes de Jean-Jacques Rousseau, V)*, ed. Bernard Gagnebin, Marcel Raymond, Jean-Jacques Eigeldinger, Olivier Pot (n. p., Gallimard, 1995).

Le Devin du village [1753], ed. Charlotte Kaufman (Madison, WI: A-R Editions, 1998).

Sedaine, Michel-Jean, 'Quelques réflexions inédits de Sedaine sur l'opéra comique' [1778] in René Charles Guilbert de Pixérécourt, *Théâtre choisi*, 4 vols. (Paris: L'Auteur, 1841–3), IV, 501–16.

Smollett, Tobias, *Peregrine Pickle* [1751], ed. James Clifford (Oxford: Oxford University Press, 1969).

Sterne, Laurence, *A Sentimental Journey through France and Italy* [1768], ed. Ian Jack (Oxford: Oxford University Press, 1984).

Swift, Jonathan, 'A Vindication of Mr Gay, and the Beggar's Opera', *The Intelligencer*, III (25 May 1728), ed. Temple Scott in *The Prose Works of Jonathan Swift*, IX (London: G. Bell, 1902).

Voltaire, *Candide, or Optimism* [1759], trans. John Butt (Harmondsworth: Penguin Books, 1970).

Wright, Edward, *Some Observations Made in Travelling through France, Italy, etc.*, 2 vols. (London: Ward & Wicksteed, 1730).

Post-1800 Works

Abbate, Carolyn, *In Search of Opera* (Princeton: Princeton University Press, 2001).

Achenwall, Max, *Studien über die komische Oper in Frankreich im 18. Jahrhundert und ihre Beziehungen zu Moliere* (Eilenburg: C. W. Offenhauer, 1912).

Albert, Maurice, *Les Théâtres de la Foire (1660–1789)* (Paris: Hachette, 1900).

Allanbrook, Wye Jamison, *The Secular Commedia. Comic Mimesis in Late Eighteenth-Century Music*, ed. Mary Ann Smart and Richard Taruskin (Oakland: University of California Press, 2014).

Anthony, James, *French Baroque Music from Beaujoyeulx to Rameau* (rev. ed., London: Batsford, 1974).

   'A Source for Secular Vocal Music in 18th-Century Avignon: MS 1182 of the Bibliothèque du Muséum Calvet', *Acta Musicologica* 54/1–2 (1982), 261–79.

Antoine, Michel, *Louis XV* (Paris: Fayard, 1989).

Arnold, R. J., *Grétry's Operas and the French Public* (Farnham: Ashgate, 2016).

   Musical Debate and Political Culture in France, 1700–1830 (Woodbridge: Boydell, 2017).

Aspden, Suzanne, 'Ballads and Britons: Imagined Community and the Continuity of "English" Opera', *Journal of the Royal Musical Association* 122/1 (1997), 24–51.

Astbury, Katherine, *The Moral Tale in France and Germany 1750–1789* (Oxford: Voltaire Foundation, 2002).

Auden, W. H., 'Music in Shakespeare', *The Dyer's Hand and Other Essays* (London: Faber & Faber, 1963), 500–27.

Audéon, Hervé, 'Des arrangements purement instrumentaux des opéras de Grétry à la fin du XVIIIe siècle' in Duron, ed., *Grétry, musicien*, 123–63.

Baggio, Pauline, 'The Ambiguity of Social Characterization in Lesage's *Théâtre de la Foire*', *The French Review* 55/5 (1982), 618–24.

Bakhtin, Mikhail Mikhailovich, 'Discourse in the Novel', in *The Dialogic Imagination*, ed. and trans. Michael Holquist with Caryl Emerson (Austin: University of Texas Press, 1981).

Barberet, Vincent, *Lesage et le Théâtre de la Foire* (Nancy: Sordoillet, 1887).

Barbier, Pierre and France Vernillat, *Histoire de France par les chansons, III: Du Jansénisme au Siècle des Lumières* (Paris: Gallimard, 1957).

Barnes, Clifford R., 'The Théâtre de la Foire (Paris, 1697–1762), Its Music and Composers', dissertation, University of Southern California, 1965.

Barthélemy, Maurice, 'La Critique et l'actualité musicales dans le *Théâtre italien* de Gherardi', *Revue d'Histoire Littéraire de la France* 59/4 (Oct.–Dec. 1959), 481–90.

  'L'Opéra-comique des origines à la Querelle des Bouffons', in Vendrix, ed., *L'Opéra-comique en France*, 8–78.

Bauman, Thomas, *North German Opera in the Age of Goethe* (Cambridge: Cambridge University Press, 1985).

Beagle, Nancy Sue, 'The Théâtres de la Foire in Early Eighteenth-Century France: Analysis of *La Ceinture de Vénus* by Lesage', dissertation, Stanford University, 1985.

Beaucé, Pauline, *Parodies d'opéra au siècle des Lumières. Évolution d'un genre comique* (Rennes: Presses Universitaires de Rennes, 2013).

  and Françoise Rubellin, eds., *Parodier l'opéra: pratiques, formes et enjeux* (Les Matelles: Espaces 34, 2015).

Beaurepaire, Pierre-Yves, Philippe Bourdin, and Charlotta Wolff, eds., *Moving Scenes. The Circulation of Music and Theatre in Europe, 1700–1815* (Oxford: Voltaire Foundation, 2018).

Bédarida, Henri, *Parme et la France* (Paris: Champion, 1928).

Bellina, Anna Laura, 'Bertoldo, Bertoldino e Cacasenno. Arie legittime, adottate, spurie e adulterine', *Atti del XIV Congresso della Società Internazionale di Musicologia*, ed. Angelo Pompilio et al., 3 vols. (Torino: EDT, 1990), III, 275–84.

Benoit, Marcelle, ed., *Dictionnaire de la musique en France aux XVIIe et XVIIIe siècles* (Paris: Fayard, 1992).

  Musiques de cour. Chapelle, Chambre, Écurie. Recueil de documents 1661–1733 (Paris: Picard, 1971).

Bergman, Gösta, 'La grande mode des pantomimes à Paris vers 1740 et les spectacles d'optique de Servandoni', *Theatre Research. Recherches théâtrales*, 2/2 (1960), 71–81.

Berlioz, Hector, *Critique musicale 1823–1863*, ed. Yves Gérard, Anne Bongrain, and Marie-Hélène Coudroy-Saghaï, 10 vols. (Paris: Buchet/Castel; Société française de musicologie, 1996–2020).

Betzwieser, Thomas, *Exotismus und 'Türkenoper' in der französischen Musik des Ancien Régime. Studien zu einem ästhetischen Phänomen* (Laaber: Laaber-Verlag, 1993).

'Funktion und Poetik des Vaudevilles im Théâtre de la foire' in Schneider, ed., *Chanson und Vaudeville*, 157–84.

Sprechen und Singen: Ästhetik und Erscheinungsformen der Dialogoper (Stuttgart: J. B. Metzler, 2002).

'Verisimilitude' in Greenwald, ed., *Oxford Handbook of Opera*, 296–317.

'Zu einer Theorie des Vaudevilles in der Opéra-comique', *Tanzdramen / Opéra-comique*, ed. Gabriele Buschmeier and Klaus Hortschansky (Gluck-Studien, 2) (Kassel: Bärenreiter, 2000), 135–52.

Biget, Michelle, and Rainer Schmusch, eds., *'L'Esprit français' und die Musik Europas. Festschrift für Herbert Schneider* (Hildesheim: Olms, 2007).

Birberick, Anne L., ed., *Reconfiguring La Fontaine: Tercentenary Essays* (Charlottesville: Rookwood Press, 1996).

'From World to Text: The Figure of the Nun in La Fontaine's *Contes*' in Birberick, ed., *Reconfiguring La Fontaine*, 181–201.

Blanning, T. C. W., *The Culture of Power and the Power of Culture* (Oxford: Oxford University Press, 2002).

Boaden, James, ed., *The Private Correspondence of David Garrick*, 2nd ed., 2 vols. (London: Henry Colburn, 1835).

Bouissou, Sylvie, Pascal Denécheau, and France Marchal-Ninosque, eds., *Dictionnaire de l'Opéra de Paris sous l'Ancien Régime*, 4 vols. (Paris: Garnier, 2019–20).

Brenner, Clarence D., *A Bibliographical List of Plays in the French Language 1700–1789* (New York: AMS Press, 1979).

'Dramatizations of French Short Stories in the Eighteenth Century with Special Reference to the "Contes" of La Fontaine, Marmontel and Voltaire', *University of California Publications in Modern Philology* 33/1 (Berkeley: University of California Press, 1947), 1–34.

The Theatre Italien. Its Repertory, 1716–1793. With a Historical Introduction. University of California Publications in Modern Philology, 63 (Berkeley: University of California Press, 1961).

Brereton, Geoffrey, *French Comic Drama from the Sixteenth to the Eighteenth Century* (London: Methuen, 1977).

Brockett, Oscar G., 'The Fair Theatres of Paris in the Eighteenth Century: The Undermining of the Classical Ideal' in *Classical Drama and Its Influence. Essays presented to H. D. F. Kitto*, ed. M. J. Anderson (London: Methuen, 1965), 249–70.

Brook, Barry S., *La Symphonie française dans la seconde moitié du XVIIIe siècle*, 3 vols. (Paris: Institut de musicologie, 1962).

Brown, Bruce Alan, 'Christoph Willibald Gluck and opéra-comique in Vienna, 1754–1764)', dissertation, University of California, Berkeley, 1986.

'La Diffusion et l'influence de l'opéra-comique en Europe au XVIIIe siècle', in Vendrix, ed., *L'Opéra-Comique en France*, 283–343.

Gluck and the French Theatre in Vienna (Oxford: Clarendon Press, 1991).

'Sedaine, le vaudeville, et l'opéra-comique: la composition du *Diable à quatre* (1756/57)', in le Blanc et al., eds., *Le Théâtre de Sedaine* [online: in press].

Brown, Gregory S., *A Field of Honor: Writers, Court Culture and Public Theater in French Literary Life from Racine to the Revolution* (New York: Columbia University Press, 2005).

Bruford, W. H., *Theatre, Drama and Audience in Goethe's Germany* (London: Routledge & Kegan Paul, 1950).

Buch, David J., *Magic Flutes and Enchanted Forests. The Supernatural in Eighteenth-Century Musical Theater* (Chicago: University of Chicago Press, 2008).

Burden, Michael, 'The lure of aria, procession and spectacle: opera in eighteenth-century London' in Keefe, ed., *Cambridge History of Eighteenth-Century Music*, 385–401.

Burgess, Geoffrey, 'Enlightening Harmonies: Rameau's *corps sonore* and the Representation of the Divine in the *tragédie en musique*', *JAMS* 65 (2012), 383–462.

'From Dance to Poem: Jean-Féry Rebel, Françoise Prévost and the Character of Dance in Early Eighteenth-Century France', *Early Music* 46/1 (2018), 103–22.

Butler, Margaret, *Musical Theater in Eighteenth-Century Parma* (Rochester: Rochester University Press, 2019).

Campardon, Emile, *Les Comédiens du roi de la troupe italienne pendant les deux derniers siècles*, 2 vols. (Paris: Berger-Levrault, 1880).

Les Spectacles de la Foire. Documents inédits recueillis aux Archives nationales, 2 vols. (Paris: Berger-Levrault, 1877).

Carlson, Marvin, '*Il re alla caccia* and *Le Roi et le fermier*: Italian and French Treatments of Class and Gender', in *Opera buffa in Mozart's Vienna*, ed. Mary Hunter and James Webster (Cambridge: Cambridge University Press, 1997), 82–97.

Carmody, Francis James, 'Le Répertoire de l'opéra-comique en vaudevilles de 1708 à 1764', *University of California Publications in Modern Philology* 16/4 (1933), 373–438.

Carroll, Charles Michael, 'Francois-André-Danican Philidor: His Life and Dramatic Art', dissertation, Florida State University, 1960.

Cash, Arthur H., *Laurence Sterne. The Later Years* (London: Routledge, 1992).

Castelvecchi, Stefano, *Sentimental Opera. Questions of Genre in the Age of Bourgeois Drama* (Cambridge: Cambridge University Press, 2013).
Censer, Jack R., and Jeremy D. Popkin (eds.), *Press and Politics in Pre-Revolutionary France* (Berkeley: University of California Press, 1987).
Cessac, Catherine, *Elisabeth Jacquet de La Guerre* (n.p.: Actes Sud, 1995).
  'La duchesse du Maine et la musique' in *La Duchesse du Maine (1676–1753)*, ed. C. Cessac and M. Couvreur (Brussels: Éditions de l'Université, 2003), 97–107.
Charlton, David, 'Duni's "Le Retour au village" and the Politics of Parma' in Russo, ed., *I due mondi di Duni*, 119–154.
  French Opera 1730–1830: Meaning and Media (Aldershot: Ashgate, 2000).
  Grétry and the Growth of Opéra-Comique (Cambridge: Cambridge University Press, 1986).
  'La Borde's ironic pastoral: *Annette et Lubin*' in Biget, ed., *'L'Esprit français'*, 404–19.
  'The melodic language of *Le Devin du village* and the evolution of *opéra-comique*' in Maria Gullstam and Michael O'Dea, eds., *Rousseau on Stage: Playwright, Musician, Spectator* (Oxford: Voltaire Foundation, 2017), 178–207.
  '"Minuet-Scenes" in Early *opéra-comique*', in *idem, French Opera 1730–1830*, VI.
  'New Light on the Bouffons in Paris (1752–1754)', *Eighteenth-Century Music* 11/1 (2014), 31–54.
  Opera in the Age of Rousseau: Music, Confrontation, Realism (Cambridge: Cambridge University Press, 2013).
  'Orchestra and Chorus at the Comédie-Italienne (Opéra Comique), 1755–1799' in *idem, French Opera 1730–1830*, III.
  'Orchestra and Image in the Later Eighteenth Century', *Proceedings of the Royal Musical Association*, cii (1975–6), 1–12.
  'La Rencontre de l'ancien et du nouveau dans *La Fille mal gardée* de Duni et Favart' in *Rire et sourire dans l'opéra-comique en France aux XVIIIe et XIXe siècles*, ed. Charlotte Loriot (Lyron: Symétrie, 2015), 33–51.
  'Sedaine's Prefaces: Pretexts for a New Musical Drama' in Charlton and Ledbury, eds., *Michel-Jean Sedaine*, 196–272.
  'Sight Meets Sound: Fifty Years of Musical Scenography at the Opéra-Comique' in Frassà, ed., *The Opéra-comique*, 37–79.
  'Sodi's Opera for Mme Favart: *Baiocco et Serpilla*' in Fabiano, ed., *"Querelle des Bouffons"*, 205–18.
  'Spying on Rousseau: Le Devin at Fontainebleau in 1752' in Reynaud, ed., *Noter, annoter, éditer*, 337–49.
Charlton, David, and Mark Ledbury (eds.), *Michel-Jean Sedaine (1719–1797): Theatre, Opera and Art* (Aldershot: Ashgate, 2000).
Christensen, Thomas, 'Public Music in Private Spaces. Piano-Vocal Scores and the Domestication of Opera', in *Music and the Cultures of Print*, ed. Kate van Orden (New York: Garland Publishing, 2000), 67–93.

Cicali, Gianni, 'Roles and Acting' in DelDonna, ed., *The Cambridge Companion to Eighteenth-Century Opera*, 85–98.

Clarke, Jan, 'Aile, coulisse et cantonade: l'évolution de trois termes de théâtre', *La Scène et la coulisse dans le théâtre du XVIIIe siècle en France*, ed. G. Forestier and L. Michel (Paris: PUPS, 2011), 87–95.

Clarke, Janet, 'Music at the Guénégaud Theatre 1673–1680', *Seventeenth-Century French Studies* 12 (1990), 89–110.

Clay, Lauren, *Stagestruck. The Business of Theater in Eighteenth-Century France and Its Colonies* (Ithaca and London: Cornell University Press, 2013).

Connon, Derek, *Identity and Transformation in the Plays of Alexis Piron* (London: Legenda, 2007).

'Music in the Parisian Fair Theatres: Medium or Message?', *Journal for Eighteenth-Century Studies*, 31/1 (2008), 119–35.

and George Evans, eds., *Anthologie de pièces du Théâtre de la Foire* (Egham: Runnymede Books, 1996).

Cook, Elisabeth, *Duet and Ensemble in the Early Opéra-comique* (New York: Garland, 1995).

Cordier, Henri, *Essai bibliographique sur les œuvres d'Alain-René Lesage* (Paris: Henri Leclerc, 1910).

Cotticelli, Francesco and Paologiovanni Maione, 'Metastasio: The Dramaturgy of Eighteenth-Century Heroic Opera' in DelDonna, ed., *The Cambridge Companion to Eighteenth-Century Opera*, 66–84.

Coulet, Henri, and Robert Fajon, eds., *Jean-Joseph Mouret et le théâtre de son temps* (Aix-en-Provence: University of Provence, 1983).

Courville, Xavier de, *Un Apôtre de l'art du théâtre au XVIIIe siècle, Luigi Riccoboni*, 2 vols. (Paris: E. Droz, 1945).

Couvreur, Manuel, *Jean-Baptiste Lully. Musique et dramaturgie au service du Prince* (n.p.: Marc Vokar, 1992).

and Philippe Vendrix, 'Les Enjeux théoriques de l'opéra-comique' in Vendrix, ed., *L'Opéra-comique en France*, 213–81.

'Les Opéras-comiques de Marmontel' in Girou-Swiderski et al., eds., *Ris, masques et tréteaux*, 117–35.

Cowart, Georgia, 'Carnival in Venice or Protest in Paris? Louis XIV and the Politics of Subversion at the Paris Opéra', *JAMS* 54/2, 265–301.

Cronk, Nicholas, ed., *The Cambridge Companion to Voltaire* (Cambridge: Cambridge University Press, 2009).

'Molière–Charpentier's *Le Malade imaginaire*: The First opéra-comique?', *Forum for Modern Language Studies* 29/3 (1993), 216–229.

'The Play of Words and Music in Molière–Charpentier's *Le Malade imaginaire*', *French Studies* 47/1 (Jan. 1993), 6–19.

Cross, W. L., *The History of Henry Fielding*, 3 vols. (New Haven: Yale University Press, 1918).

Cucuel, Georges, *Les Créateurs de l'opéra-comique français* (Paris: Félix Alcan, 1914).
  'Sources et documents pour servir à l'histoire de l'opéra-comique en France', *L'Année musicale*, 3 (1913), 247–82.
Dahlhaus, Carl, 'What Is a Musical Drama?', *COJ* I/2 (1989), 95–103.
Darlow, Mark, '"Peindre sa voix pour soutenir son rôle": The Use of écriteaux in Lesage's *Théâtre de la Foire*, and the Transgressionary Nature of the Aesthetic' in *Les Lieux interdits: Transgression in French Literature*, ed. L. Duffy and A. Tudor (Hull: Hull University Press, 1998), 114–45.
Darnton, Robert, *Poetry and the Police. Communication Networks in Eighteenth-Century Paris* (Cambridge, MA: Belknap, 2010).
Davies, Peter, 'Heir to Anacreon: Charles Simon Favart in the Theatrical Life of Eighteenth-Century France', dissertation, Yale University, 1968.
Davis, Natalie Zemon, *Society and Culture in Early Modern France* (London: Gerald Duckworth, 1975).
DeJean, Joan, *Ancients against Moderns. Culture Wars and the Making of a Fin de Siècle* (Chicago: University of Chicago Press, 1997).
  The Reinvention of Obscenity. Sex, Lies, and Tabloids in Early Modern France (Chicago: University of Chicago Press, 2002).
DelDonna, Anthony R., and Pierpaolo Polzonetti, eds., *The Cambridge Companion to Eighteenth-Century Opera* (Cambridge University Press, 2009).
Della Seta, Fabrizio, 'Some Difficulties in the Historiography of Italian Opera', *COJ* 10/1 (1998), 3–13, repr. in *Not without Madness: Perspectives on Opera* (Chicago: Chicago University Press, 2013).
De Luca, Emanuele, *Il repertorio della Comédie-Italienne di Parigi (1716–1762). Le répertoire de la Comédie-Italienne de Paris (1716–1762)* (Paris: IRPMF, 2011). Accessed at https://hal.inria.fr/IRPMF.
Denby, David J., *Sentimental Narrative and the Social Order in France, 1760–1820* (Cambridge: Cambridge University Press, 1994).
Dickie, Simon, *Cruelty and Laughter. Forgotten Comic Literature and the Unsentimental Eighteenth Century* (Chicago: Chicago University Press, 2011).
Doe, Julia I., 'French Opera at the Italian Theater (1762–93): Opéra-Comique and the Development of National Style in France', dissertation, Yale University, 2013.
  'Two Hunters, a Milkmaid and the French "Revolutionary" canon', *Eighteenth Century Music* 15/2 (2018), 177–205.
Dompnier, Bernard, Catherine Massip, and Solveig Serre, eds., *Musiques en liberté. Entre la cour et les provinces au temps des Bourbons* (Paris: École nationale des chartes, 2018).
Dratwicki, Benoît, *Antoine Dauvergne (1713–1797)* (Wavre: Mardaga, 2011).

Duron, Jean, ed., *Grétry, musicien de Marie-Antoinette* (Versailles: Centre de Musique Baroque, 2009); repr. as *Grétry en société* (Sprimont: Mardaga, 2009).

Dziembowski, Edmond, *Un nouveau patriotisme français 1750–1770* (Oxford: Voltaire Foundation, 1998).

Emery, Ted, 'Carlo Goldoni as Librettist: Theatrical Reform and the "Drammi giocosi per musica"', dissertation, Brown University, 1985.

Evstratov, Alexeï, *Les Spectacles francophones à la cour de Russie (1743–1796): l'invention d'une société* (Oxford: Voltaire Foundation, 2016).

Fabiano, Andrea, *Histoire de l'opéra italien en France (1752–1815)* (Paris: CNRS Editions, 2006).

 ed., *La 'Querelle des Bouffons' dans la vie culturelle française du XVIIIe siècle* (Paris: CNRS Editions, 2005).

Fader, Don, 'The "Cabale du Dauphin", Campra, and Italian Comedy: the Courtly Politics of French Musical Patronage around 1700', *Music and Letters* 86/3 (2005), 380–413.

 'The *Goûts-réunis* in French Vocal Music (1695–1710) through the Lens of the *Recueil d'airs sérieux et à boire*', *Revue de musicologie* 96/2 (2010), 321–63.

Fairchilds, Cissie, 'Masters and Servants in Eighteenth-Century Toulouse', *Journal of Social History* 12/3 (1979), 368–93.

Fajon, Robert, 'Jean Joseph Mouret: Musicien de Marivaux' in Coulet and Fajon, eds., *Jean-Joseph Mouret et le théâtre*, 59–85.

Falk, Marguerite, *Les Parodies du Nouveau Théâtre Italien (1731). Répertoire systématique des timbres* (Bilthoven: A. B. Creyghton, c. 1973).

Fend, Michael, 'An Instinct for Parody and a Spirit for Revolution' in Keefe, ed., *Cambridge History of Eighteenth-Century Music*, 295–330.

Finscher, Ludwig, ed., *Die Musik in Geschichte und Gegenwart*, 2nd edition, 26 vols. (Kassel: Bärenreiter, 2002).

Font, Auguste, *Favart, l'opéra-comique et la comédie-vaudeville aux XVIIe et XVIIIe siècles* (Paris: Fischbacher, 1894).

Frantz, Pierre, *L'Esthétique du tableau dans le théâtre du XVIIIe siècle* (Paris: Presses Universitaires de France, 1998).

Frassà, Lorenzo, ed., *The Opéra-comique in the Eighteenth and Nineteenth Centuries* (Turnhout: Brepols, 2011).

Frostin, Charles, 'Du peuplement pénal de l'Amérique française aux XVIIe et XVIIIe siècles: hésitations et contradictions du pouvoir royal en matière de déportation', *Annales de Bretagne et des pays de l'Ouest* 85/1 (1978), 67–94; accessed 8 Oct. 2018 at www.persee.fr/doc.

Furbank, P. N., *Diderot. A Critical Biography* (London: Secker & Warburg, 1992).

Gagey, Edmond, *Ballad Opera* (New York: Blom, 1937/1968).

Ganim, Russell, 'Scientific Verses: Subversion of Cartesian Theory and Practice in the "Discours à Madame de La Sablière"' in Birberick, ed., *Refiguring La Fontaine*, 101–25.

Garrioch, David, *The Making of Revolutionary Paris* (Berkeley: California University Press, 2002).

Gelbart, Matthew, *The Invention of 'Folk Music' and 'Art Music'* (Cambridge: Cambridge University Press, 2007).

Gelbart, Nina Rattner, 'The *Journal des dames* and Its Female Editors', *Press and Politics in Pre-Revolutionary France*, ed. Jack R. Censer and Jeremy D. Popkin (Berkeley: University of California Press, 1987), 24–74.

George, David J., and Christopher J. Gossip, eds., *Studies in the Commedia dell'arte* (Cardiff: University of Wales Press, 1993).

Gétreau, Florence, 'Philippot le Savoyard – Portraits d'un Orphée du Pont-Neuf mêlés de vaudevilles, d'images et de vers burlesques' in Biget, ed., '*L'Esprit français*', 269–88.

Gilchrist, Ingrid Kyler, 'Charles Simon Favart's Contribution to Eighteenth-Century French Comedy', diss., Columbia University, 1975.

Giles, Roseen, 'A Natural Voice?', *COJ* 29/2 (2017), 240–51.

Gill-Mark, Grace, *Une Femme de lettres au XVIIIe siècle: Anne-Marie Du Boccage* (Paris: Champion, 1927).

Girou-Swiderski, Marie-Laure, Stéphanie Massé, and Françoise Rubellin, eds., *Ris, masques et tréteaux. Aspects du théâtre du XVIIIe siècle* (Québec: Presses de l'Université Laval, 2008)

Golder, John, 'The Hôtel de Bourgogne in 1760: Some Previously Unpublished Drawings by Louis-Alexandre Girault', *Journal for Eighteenth-Century Studies* 32/4 (Dec. 2009), 455–91.

Gougon, Jean-Philippe, 'Les *Recueils d'airs sérieux et à boire* des Ballard (1695–1724)', *Revue de musicologie* 96/1 (2010), 35–72.

Goulbourne, Russell, 'Introduction' to Diderot, *The Nun* (Oxford: Oxford University Press, 2005).

'Voltaire's Masks: Theatre and Theatricality', in Cronk, ed., *The Cambridge Companion to Voltaire*, 93–108.

Goulet, Anne-Madeleine, *Poésie, musique et sociabilité au XVIIe siècle. Les 'Livrets d'airs de différents auteurs' publiés chez Ballard de 1658 à 1694* (Paris: Champion, 2004).

Gousset, Jean-Paul and Raphaël Masson, 'Les décors historiques pour *Le Roi et le fermier*', *Opéra royal de Versailles. Programme janvier–février 2012*, 76–7.

Greenwald, Helen, ed., *The Oxford Handbook of Opera* (New York: Oxford University Press, 2014).

Grewar, Andrew, 'Shakespeare and the Actors of the Commedia dell'arte' in George, ed., *Studies in the Commedia dell'arte*, 13–47.

Grieder, Josephine, *Anglomania in France 1740–1789. Fact, Fiction and Political Discourse* (Geneva: Droz, 1985).

Griffiths, Bruce, 'Sunset: from *commedia dell'arte* to *comédie italienne*', in George, ed., *Studies in the Commedia dell'arte*, 91–105.

Griffiths, Wanda R., 'Critical Report' in Elisabeth-Claude Jacquet de La Guerre, *Céphale et Procris* (Madison, WI: A-R. Editions, 1998).

Grisé, Catherine, 'The Optics of Relativism in the Fables of La Fontaine' in Birberick, ed., *Refiguring La Fontaine*, 126–56.

Grosrichard, Alain, *The Sultan's Court. European Fantasies of the East*, trans. Liz Heron (London: Verso, 1998),

Grout, Donald J., 'The Music of the Italian Theatre at Paris, 1682–97', *Papers of the American Musicological Society* 1941, 158–70.

'The Origins of the Opéra-comique', dissertation, Harvard University, 1939.

A Short History of Opera (New York: Columbia University Press, 1947).

Guichemerre, Roger, '*La Princesse de Carizme* de Lesage. L'adaptation d'un conte persan au *Théâtre de la Foire*' in *L'Art du théâtre. Mélanges en hommage à Robert Garapon*, ed. Yvonne Bellenger, Gabriel Conesa, and Jean Garapon (Paris: PUF, 1992), 371–9.

Guillo, Laurent, 'L'Édition musical française avant et après Lully' in Terrier, ed., *L'Invention*, 79–98.

'La musique de scène, un produit invendable?' in Dompnier et al., ed., *Musiques en liberté*, 487–500.

Habermas, Jürgen, *The Structural Transformation of the Public Sphere* (Cambridge: Polity Press, 1989).

Hahn, Franz, *François Pétis de La Croix et ses Mille et Un Jours* (Amsterdam: Rodopi, 2002).

Haine, Malou, 'Charles-Simon Favart à la tête du Théâtre des armées du maréchal de Saxe à Bruxelles (janvier 1746–décembre 1748)' in Vendrix, ed., *Grétry et l'Europe*, 281–330.

Harris, Frances, 'Jean-Claude Gillier, Theatre Musician of the Early Eighteenth Century', dissertation, University of Minnesota, 1975.

Harris-Warrick, Rebecca, *Dance and Drama in French Baroque Opera. A History* (Cambridge: Cambridge University Press, 2016).

'Staging Venice', *COJ*, 15/3 (2003), 297–316.

and Bruce Alan Brown (eds.), *The Grotesque Dancer on the Eighteenth-Century Stage. Gennaro Magri and His World* (Madison: University of Wisconsin Press, 2005).

and Carol G. Marsh, 'The French Connection' in Harris-Warwick and Brown, eds., *The Grotesque Dancer*, 173–98.

Harvey, Susan, *La Grand-mére amoureuse, parodie d'Atys. A Marionette Parody of Lully's 'Atys' by Louis Fuzelier and Dorneval from 1726* (Middleton, WI: A-R Editions, 2008).

'Opera Parody in Eighteenth-Century France: Genesis, Genre, and Critical Function', dissertation, Stanford University, 2002.

Hayward, John, ed., *The Letters of Saint Evremond* (London: George Routledge, 1930).

Heartz, Daniel, 'The Beginnings of the Operatic Romance: Rousseau, Sedaine, and Monsigny', *Eighteenth-Century Studies*, 15 (1981–2), 149–78 and in *idem*, *From Garrick to Gluck*, 188–209.
 'The Creation of the Buffo Finale' in *idem*, *From Garrick to Gluck*, 40–51.
 From Garrick to Gluck. Essays on Opera in the Age of Enlightenment, ed. John A. Rice (Hillsdale, NY: Pendragon Press, 2004).
 'Hasse, Galuppi and Metastasio' in M. T. Muraro, ed., *Venezia e il melodramma nel settecento*, vol. I (Firenze: Olschki, 1978), 309–39.
 'Italian by Intention, French of Necessity: Rousseau's *Le Devin du village*' in *idem*, *From Garrick to Gluck*, 225–37.
 Music in European Capitals. The Galant Style, 1720–1780 (New York: Norton, 2003).
 'Overture: Les Lumières' in *idem*, *From Garrick to Gluck*, 1–9.
 'Terpsichore at the Fair' in *idem*, *From Garrick to Gluck*, 146–58.
 '*Vis comica*: Goldoni, Galuppi and *L'arcadia in Brenta*', in *idem*, *From Garrick to Gluck*, 11–39.
 'Watteau's Italian Comedians' in *idem*, *From Garrick to Gluck*, 159–77.
Hennebelle, David, *De Lully à Mozart. Aristocratie, musique et musiciens à Paris (XVIIe–XVIIIe siècles)* (Seyssel: Champ Vallon, 2009).
 'La Vie musicale sur les théâtres de société au XVIIIe siècle' in Plagnol-Diéval, ed., *Les Théâtres de société*, 53–62.
Heyer, John Hajdu, ed., *Lully Studies* (Cambridge: Cambridge University Press, 2000).
Highfill, Philip H. Jr, Kalman A. Burnim, and Edward A. Langhans, eds., *A Biographical Dictionary of Actors, Actresses, Musicians, Dancers, Managers and Other Stage Personnel in London, 1660—1800*, 16 vols. (Carbondale: Southern Illinois University Press, 1973–93).
Hirschmann, Wolfgang, 'The British Enchanters and George Granville's Theory of Opera', in *Music in the London Theatre from Purcell to Handel*, ed. Colin Timms and Bruce Wood (Cambridge: Cambridge University Press, 2017), 38–48.
Hitchcock, H. Wiley, 'Marc-Antoine Charpentier and the Comédie-Française', *JAMS* 24 (1971), 255–81.
Hobson, Marian, *The Object of Art* (Cambridge: Cambridge University Press, 1982).
Howarth, W. D., 'The Playwright as Preacher: Didacticism and Melodrama in the French Theatre of the Enlightenment', in *The Theatre of the French and German Enlightenment*, ed. Samuel S. B. Taylor (Edinburgh: Scottish Academic Press, 1979), 1–19.
Hume, Robert, 'The Politics of Opera in late seventeenth-century London', *COJ* 10/1 (1998), 15–43.

Hüttler, Michael, and Hans Ernst Weidinger, eds., *Ottoman Empire and European Theatre, I: The Age of Mozart and Selim III (1756–1808)* (Vienna: Höllitzer, 2013).

Hytier, Adrienne D., 'The Decline of Military Values: The Theme of the Deserter in Eighteenth-Century French Literature', *Studies in Eighteenth-Century Culture*, 11 (Cleveland, OH: Case Western Reserve University, 1982), 147–62.

Iacuzzi, Alfred, *The European Vogue of Favart. The Diffusion of the opéra-comique* (New York: Institute of French Studies, 1932).

Isherwood, Robert M., 'The Centralization of Music in the Reign of Louis XIV', *French Historical Studies* 6/2 (1969), 156–71.

Farce and Fantasy: Popular Entertainment in Eighteenth-Century Paris (Oxford: Oxford University Press, 1986).

Music in the Service of the King. France in the Seventeenth Century (Ithaca: Cornell University Press, 1973).

Jaffrès, Yves, 'Michel Corrette, sa vie, son œuvre', dissertation, Lumière University Lyon 2, 1989.

ed. with Pierre Saby and Gérard Streletski, *Regards sur Michel Corrette. Lyon, 26 avril 2007* (Lyon: Lumière University Lyon 2, 2011).

Johnston, Keith, 'Molière, Descartes, and the Practice of Comedy in the Intermezzo', *Music & Letters* 94/1 (2013), 38–77.

Jouve-Ganvert, Sophie, 'Bérard et l'art du chant en France au XVIIIe siècle', *RMFC* XXIX (1998), 103–62.

Kaehler, Winston Haverland, 'The Operatic Repertoire of Madame de Pompadour's Théâtre des Petits Cabinets (1747–1753)', dissertation, University of Michigan, 1971.

Kavanagh, Thomas M., *Enlightened Pleasures. Eighteenth-Century France and the New Epicureanism* (New Haven: Yale University Press, 2010).

Keefe, Simon P., ed., *The Cambridge History of Eighteenth-Century Music* (Cambridge: Cambridge University Press, 2009).

Kennedy, Emmet, Marie-Laurence Netter, James P. McGregor and Mark V. Olsen, *Theatre, Opera, and Audiences in Revolutionary Paris* (Westport, CT: Greenwood Press, 1996).

King, Richard and Saskia Willaert, 'Giovanni Francesco Crosa and the First Italian Comic Operas in London, Brussels and Amsterdam, 1748–1750', *Journal of the Royal Musical Association* 118 (1993), 246–75.

Kirkness, W. John, *Le Français du Théâtre Italien d'après le Recueil de Gherardi* (Geneva: Droz, 1971).

Kleinertz, Rainer, 'Zur Rezeption der Opéra comique in Spanien im 18. und frühen 19. Jahrhundert', in Biget, ed., *'L'Esprit français'*, 446–57.

La Gorce, Jérôme de, '*Le Collier de perles* et la musique de Pierre Beauchamps', in *Histoire, humanisme et hymnologie*, ed. Pierre Guillo and Louis Jambou (Paris: PUP, 1997), 99–107.

and Herbert Schneider, eds, *Jean-Baptiste Lully. Actes du colloque Saint-Germain-en-Laye/Heidelberg, 1987* (Laaber: Laaber-Verlag, 1990).

Lagrave, Henri, 'La Pantomime à la Foire, au Théâtre-Italien et aux Boulevards (1700–1789). Première approche', *Romanistische Zeitschrift fur Literaturgeschichte*, 3/3–4 (1979), 408–30.

Le théâtre et le public à Paris de 1715 à 1750 (Paris: Klincksieck, 1972).

Lancaster, Henry Carrington, 'The Comédie Française 1701–1774. Plays, Actors, Spectators, Finances', *Transactions of the American Philosophical Society*, new series, 41/4 (1951), 593–849.

A History of French Dramatic Literature in the Seventeenth Century. Part V. Recapitulation 1610–1700 (New York: Gordian Press, 1966).

Sunset. A History of Parisian Drama in the Last Years of Louis XIV, 1701–1715 (Baltimore/London: Johns Hopkins Press/Oxford University Press, 1945).

Lanson, Gustave, *Nivelle de La Chaussée et la comédie larmoyante*, 2nd rev. ed. (Paris: Librairie Hachette, 1903).

Laurence, Marinette. 'Charles-Simon Favart: Théâtre et vaudevilles. Édition critique de manuscrits inédits', dissertation, University of Nantes (2015).

Leathers, Victor, *British Entertainers in France* (n. p.: Toronto University Press, 1959).

Le Blanc, Judith, *Avatars d'opéras. Parodies et circulation des airs chantés sur les scènes parisiennes* (Paris: Garnier, 2014).

and Clemence Monnier, 'Le Devenir des airs-vaudevilles de l'opéra lullyste sur la scène des théâtres parisiens jusqu'en 1745' in le Blanc and Schneider, eds., *Pratiques du timbre et de la parodie d'opéra en Europe* (Hildesheim: Olms, 2014), 317–36.

and Raphaëlle Legrand with Marie-Cécile Norbelly-Schang, eds., *Le Théâtre de Sedaine: une œuvre en dialogue* (Paris: PUF, online ed. in press).

Lecomte, Nathalie, 'Jean-Baptiste François Dehesse. Chorégraphe à la Comédie Italienne et au Théâtre des Petits Appartements de Madame de Pompadour', *RMFC* XXIV (1986), 142–91.

Ledbury, Mark, *Sedaine, Greuze and the boundaries of genre* (Oxford: Voltaire Foundation, 2000).

'Sedaine and the Question of Genre' in Charlton and Ledbury, eds., *Michel-Jean Sedaine*, 20–2.

Legrand, Raphaëlle, 'Justine Favart parodiste' in Beaucé and Rubellin, eds., *Parodier l'opéra*, 235–53.

'Libertines et femmes vertueuses: l'image des chanteuses d'opéra et d'opéra-comique en France au XVIIIe siècle', *Emancipation sexuelle ou contrainte des corps*, ed. Hélène Marquié and Noel Burch (Paris: L'Harmattan, 2006), 157–75.

'"Risquer un genre nouveau en musique": l'opéra-comique de Sedaine et Monsigny' in Charlton and Ledbury, eds., *Michel-Jean Sedaine*, 119–45.

'La Scène et le public de l'Opéra-Comique de 1762 à 1789', in Vendrix, ed., *L'Opéra-comique en France*, 178–212.

and Nicole Wild, *Regards sur l'opéra-comique. Trois siècles de vie théâtrale* (Paris: CNRS Editions, 2002).

Levenson, Erica Pauline, 'Traveling Tunes: French Comic Opera and Theater in London, 1714–1745', dissertation, Cornell University, 2017.

Levin, David J., ed., *Opera through Other Eyes* (Stanford: Stanford University Press, 1993).

Lindenberger, Herbert, *Opera the Extravagant Art* (Ithaca, NY: Cornell University Press, 1984), 52.

Lindsay, Frank Whiteman, *Dramatic Parody by Marionettes in Eighteenth-Century Paris* (New York: King's Crown Press, 1946).

Linton, Marisa, *The Politics of Virtue in Enlightenment France* (Basingstoke: Palgrave, 2001).

Locke, Ralph, *Music and the Exotic from the Renaissance to Mozart* (Cambridge: Cambridge University Press, 2015).

Loewenberg, Alfred, *Annals of Opera*, 3rd ed. (London: Calder, 1978).

Lough, John, *Paris Theatre Audiences in the Seventeenth and Eighteenth Centuries* (London: Oxford University Press, 1957).

Lurcel, Dominique, ed., *Le Théâtre de la Foire au XVIIIe siècle* (n.p.: Union Générale d'Éditions, 1983).

Mackenzie, Barbara Dobbs, 'The Creation of a Genre: Comic Opera's Dissemination in Italy in the 1740s', dissertation, University of Michigan, 1993.

Marcetteau-Paul, Agnès, 'Les Auteurs de la foire à Paris au XVIIIe siècle', *Bibliothèque de l'école des chartes* 141/2, (1983), 307–35.

'*L'Obstacle favorable*, ou comment Louis XIV inventa l'opéra-comique', *Littéraires classiques* 21 (1994), 265–75.

'Les Théâtres des Foires Saint-Germain et Saint-Laurent', dissertation, École nationale des chartes, Paris, 1983.

Marica, Marco, 'Rappresentazioni, traduzioni e adattamenti operistici di *comédies en vaudevilles* in Italia (1750-1815)' in Schneider, ed., *Timbre und Vaudeville*, 379–459.

Markovits, Rahul, *Civiliser l'Europe. Politiques du théâtre français au XVIIIe siècle* (n.p.: Fayard, 2014).

Martin, Isabelle, *Le Théâtre de la Foire. Des tréteaux aux boulevards* (Oxford: Voltaire Foundation, 2002).

'Un *Dom Juan* au Théâtre de la Foire', *XVIIe Siècle*, 194 (1997) (49e année), 157–71.

Martinuzzi, Paola, *Le 'Pièces par écriteaux' nel teatro della Foire (1710–1715)* (Venice: Cafoscarina, 2007).

Mason, Laura, *Singing the French Revolution. Popular Culture and Politics 1787–1799* (Ithaca, NY: Cornell University Press, 1996).

Matthes, Lothar, *Vaudeville. Untersuchungen zu Geschichte und literatursystematischem Ort einer Erfolgsgattung* (Heidelberg: Carl Winter/ Universitätsverlag, 1983).

Maza, Sarah, *Private Lives and Public Affairs. The Causes Célèbres of Prerevolutionary France* (Berkeley: University of California Press, 1993).

Mazouer, Charles, *Le Théâtre d'Arlequin. Comédies et comédiens italiens en France au XVIIe siècle* (Fasano/Paris: Schena Editore/The Sorbonne University Press, 2002).

McCleave, Sarah, *Dance in Handel's London Operas* (Rochester, NY: University of Rochester Press, 2013).

McLynn, Frank, *1759. The Year Britain Became Master of the World* (London: Pimlico, 2005).

McManners, John, *Church and Society in Eighteenth-Century France*, 2 vols. (Oxford: Clarendon Press, 1998).

McMillin, Scott, *The Musical as Drama. A Study of the Principles and Conventions behind Musical Shows from Kern to Sondheim* (Princeton: Princeton University Press, 2006).

Moindrot, Isabelle, 'The "Turk" and the "Parisienne": From Favart's *Soliman Second ou les Trois sultanes* (1761) to *Les Trois Sultanes* (Pathé, 1912)' in Hüttler, ed., *Ottoman Empire*, 427–63.

Mongrédien, Georges, *Daily Life in the French Theatre at the Time of Molière*, trans. Claire Eliane Engel (London: George Allen and Unwin, 1969).

Moore, A. P., *The 'genre poissard' and the French Stage of the Eighteenth Century* (New York: Institute of French Studies, 1935).

Morand, Yves, *La Conquête de la liberté de Scapin à Figaro. Valets, servantes et soubrettes de Molière à Beaumarchais* (Paris: PUF, 1981).

Moroney, Davitt, 'The Parodies of François Couperin's Harpsichord Pieces' in Biget, ed., *'L'Esprit français'*, 608–33.

Moureau, François, *De Gherardi à Watteau. Présence d'Arlequin sous Louis XIV* (Paris: Klincksieck, 1992).

   'Lully en visite chez Arlequin', in La Gorce and Schneider, eds., Jean-Baptiste Lully, 235–50; repr. in Moureau, *De Gherardi à Watteau*, 63–75.

   'Parties et parodie musicales à la Comédie Française sous Louis XIV' in Delia Gambelli and Letizia Norci Cagiano, eds., *Le Théâtre en musique et son double (1600–1762)* (Paris: Champion, 2005), 85–103.

   'Un singulier moderne: Dufresny', dissertation, University of Paris IV, 1977, pub. as *Dufresny auteur dramatique* (Paris: Klincksieck, 1979).

Müller, Ruth, '"Il faut s'aimer pour s'épouser": Das dramaturgische Konzept der Opéra-comique zwischen 1752 und 1769', *Jahrbuch des Staatlichen Instituts für Musikforschung Preussischer Kulturbesitz 1978/88*, (Kassel 1991), 139–83.

'Weinen und Lachen: Dramaturgie und musikalisches Idiom der Opéra-comique im Vergleich zur Opera buffa (1750–1790)', dissertation, University of Bayreuth, 2001.

Müller-Lindenberg, Ruth, *Weinen und Lachen: Dramaturgie und musikalisches Idiom der Opéra-comique im Vergleich zur Opera buffa (1750–1790)* (Berlin: Lit, c.2006).

Nancy, Sarah, *La Voix féminine et le plaisir de l'écoute en France au XVIIIe siècle* (Paris: Garnier, 2012).

Nestola, Barbara, 'L'Air italien sur la scène des théâtres parisiens (1687–1715)', dissertation, François Rabelais University of Tours, 2015.

'Italian Music, French Singers. Reception and performance practice on the Parisian Stage at the beginning of the eighteenth Century', in Damien Colas and Alessandro di Profio, eds., *D'une Scène à l'autre. L'Opéra italien en Europe* (Collines de Wavre: Mardaga, 2009), I, 253–67.

Noiray, Michel, 'Quatre Rois à la chasse: Dodsley, Collé, Sedaine, Goldoni' in Charlton and Ledbury, eds., *Michel-Jean Sedaine*, 97–118.

'Un opéra-comique "bourgeois": *L'École de la jeunesse* d'Anseaume et Duni (1765)' in Russo, ed., *I due mondi di Duni*, 155–90.

Oreglia, Giacomo, *The Commedia dell'arte*, trans. Lovett F. Edwards (London: Methuen, 1968).

Pach, Walter, ed., trans., *The Journal of Eugéne Delacroix* (New York: Covici, Friede, 1937).

Parakilas, James, 'The Power of Domestication in the Lives of Musical Canons', *Repercussions* 4/1 (1995), 5–24.

Paul, Agnès, 'Les Théâtres des Foires Saint-Germain et Saint-Laurent dans la première moitié du XVIIIe siècle (1697–1762)', dissertation, École nationale des chartes, Paris, 1983.

Piperno, Franco, 'Buffe e buffi', *Rivista italiana di musicologia* 18 (1982), 240–84.

Pitou, Spire, '*Le Médecin de village* (1704) exhumed', *Romance Notes* 6/1 (Autumn 1964), 50–4.

Plagnol-Diéval, Marie-Emmanuelle, and Dominique Quéro, eds., *Les Théâtres de société au XVIIIe siècle* (Études sur le 18e siècle, 33) (Brussels: Free University of Brussels, 2005).

Porot, Bertrand, 'Aux origines de l'opéra-comique: étude musicale du *Théâtre de la Foire* de Lesage et d'Orneval (1713–1734)', in Frassà, ed., *The Opéra-comique*, 283–329.

'Les Chants de Momus et de la Folie: pour une histoire institutionnelle et artistique du premier opéra-comique', dissertation, University of Paris-IV, 2012.

'L'organisation d'un spectacle de marionnettes en 1722: à propos d'archives méconnues de Fuzelier' in *Parodier l'opéra: pratiques, formes et enjeux*, ed. Pauline Beaucé and Françoise Rubellin (Les Matelles: Espaces 34, 2015), 127–53.

'Rameau et les théâtres de la Foire: nouvelles perspectives' in *Rameau, Entre Art et Science*, ed. Sylvie Bouissou et al. (Paris: École nationale des chartes: 2016), 51–67.

Pougin, Arthur, *Madame Favart. Étude theâtrale 1727–1772* (Paris: Fischbacher, 1912).

Powell, John S., 'Appropriation, parody, and the birth of French opera: Lully's Les Festes de l'Amour et de Bacchus and Molière's Le Malade imaginaire', *RMFC* XXIX (1998), 3–26.

'Charpentier's Music for Molière's *Le Malade imaginaire* and Its Revisions', *JAMS* 39/1 (1986), 87–142.

Music and Theatre in France, 1600–1680 (Oxford: Oxford University Press, 2000). Also consultable on www.personal.utulsa.edu/~john-powell/Music_and_Theater_in_France/contents.htm (7 Oct. 2020).

'Music, Fantasy and Illusion in Molière's *Le Malade imaginaire*', *Music & Letters* 73/2 (May 1992), 222–43.

Pré, Corinne, 'Le Livret d'opéra-comique en France de 1741 à 1789', dissertation, University of Paris III, 1982.

Prod'homme, Jacques-Gabriel, 'La Musique à Paris, de 1753 à 1757, d'après un manuscrit de la Bibliothèque de Munich', *Sammelbände der Internationalen Musik-Gesellschaft*, VI (1904–1905), 568–83.

and E. de Crauzat, *Les Menus-Plaisirs du Roi: l'École Royale et le Conservatoire de Musique* (Paris: Delagrave, 1929).

Raine, Craig, *T. S. Eliot* (Oxford University Press, 2006).

Ranum, Patricia, 'Lully Plays Deaf: Rereading the Evidence on His Privilege', in Heyer, ed., *Lully Studies*, 15–31.

Rasch, Rudolf, 'Soixante ans de réception de la musique de Lully en Hollande (1655–1715)' in Terrier, ed., *L'Invention*, 99–111.

Ravel, Jeffrey S., *The Contested Parterre. Public Theater and French Political Culture 1680–1791* (Ithaca, NY: Cornell University Press, 1999).

Ray, Marcie, *Coquettes, Wives, and Widows. Gender Politics in French Baroque Opera and Theater* (Rochester: University of Rochester Press, 2020).

Rex, Walter E., 'Inversions and Subversions in the *théâtre de la Foire*', in idem, *The Attraction of the Contrary* (Cambridge: Cambridge University Press, 1987), 49–72.

Reynaud, Cécile, and Herbert Schneider, eds., *Noter, annoter, éditer la musique. Mélanges offerts à Catherine Massip* (Paris: Bibliothèque Nationale; Geneva, Droz, 2012).

Rizzoni, Nathalie, *Charles-François Pannard et l'esthétique du 'petit'* (Oxford: Voltaire Foundation, 2000).

'Inconnaissance de la Foire' in Terrier (ed.), *L'Invention*, 119–151.

'Le Geste éloquent: la pantomime en France au XVIIIe siècle' in Waeber, ed., *Musique et Geste*, 129–47.

Robinson, Michael F., *Opera before Mozart* (London: Hutchinson, 1966).

'Two London Versions of *The Deserter*' in *Report of the Twelfth Congress of the International Musicological Society*, ed. Daniel Heartz and Bonnie Wade (Kassel: Bärenreiter, 1981), 239–45.

Robinson, Philip, 'Les Vaudevilles: un médium théâtrale', *Dix-huitième siècle* 28 (1996), 431–47.

Roche, Daniel, *A History of Everyday Things. The Birth of Consumption in France, 1600–1800*, trans. Brian Pearce (Cambridge: Cambridge University Press, 2000).

Rodmell, Graham E., 'Sedaine's *Le Diable à quatre*: an English source', *British Journal for Eighteenth-Century Studies* 2/1 (1979), 66–8.

Rogers, Katharine, ed., *Eighteenth and Nineteenth-Century British Drama* (New York: Signet Classics, 1979).

Rogers, Vanessa L., 'John Gay, Ballad Opera and the *Théâtres de la Foire*', *Eighteenth-Century Music*, 11/2 (2014).

Rollin, Monique, 'À propos des recherches sur les timbres avant le XVIIIe siècle' in Schneider, ed., *Das Vaudeville*, 3–12.

Romey, John, 'Songs that Run in the Streets: Popular Song at the Comédie-Italienne, the Comédie-Française, and the Théâtres de la Foire', *Journal of Musicology* 37/4 (2020), 415–58.

Rose, Adrian, 'Élisabeth-Claude Jacquet de La Guerre and the Secular *cantate françoise*, *Early Music* 13 (1985), 529–41.

Rosow, Lois, 'The Articulation of Lully's Dramatic Dialogue' in Heyer, ed., *Lully Studies*, 72–99.

Rubellin, Françoise, ed., *Le Théâtre de la Foire: Anthologie* (Montpellier: Espaces 34, 2005).

Runte, Roseann, 'Parallels between Lesage's Theatre and His Novels', in *Enlightenment Studies in Honour of Lester G. Crocker*, ed. Alfred J. Bingham and Virgil W. Topazio (Oxford: Voltaire Foundation, 1979), 283–99.

Russo, Paolo, 'Duni a Parma. Tracce d'archivio tra opera italiana e teatro francese' in Russo, ed., *I due mondi di Duni*, 87–117.

'Duni: l'*opéra-comique* prima dell'*opéra-comique*', *Recercare* 22/1-2 (2010), 147–56.

ed., *I due mondi di Duni. Il teatro musicale di un compositore illuminista fra Italia e Francia* (Lucca: Libreria Musicale Italiana, 2014).

Sadie, Stanley, ed., *The New Grove Dictionary of Music and Musicians*, 2nd ed., 29 vols. (London: Macmillan, 2001).

ed., *The New Grove Dictionary of Opera*, 4 vols. (London: Macmillan, 1992).

Sadler, Graham, 'Rameau, Piron and the Parisian Fair Theatres', *Soundings* (University College Cardiff), 4 (1974), 13–29.

The Rameau Compendium (Woodbridge: Boydell Press, 2014).

Sakhnovskaia, Anastassia, 'Sur la trace des Italiens à la Foire pendant les années de disgrace (1697–1716): *CESAR* Colloque 21–22 June 2004 (https://cesar.huma-num.fr/cesar2/conferences/index.php).

Sakhnovskaia-Pankeeva, Anastasia, 'Théâtre de la Foire et inspiration italienne: *L'Opéra de campagne* et *La Parodie de Psyché* à la Foire Saint-Laurent de 1713' in Girou-Swiderski et al., eds., *Ris, masques et tréteaux*, 163–96.

Salvatore, Paul J., *Favart's Unpublished Plays. The Rise of the Popular Comic Opera* (New York: Institute of French Studies, 1935).

Sartori, *I libretti italiani a stampa dalle origini al 1800*, 7 vols. (Cuneo: Bertola & Locatelli, 1990–94).

Sawkins, Lionel, 'Lalande's Theatrical Motets: Did the Sun King Approve?', in Dompnier, et al., ed., *Musiques en liberté*, 213–26.

Scherer, Jacques, *Théâtre et anti-théâtre au XVIIIe siècle. Inaugural Lecture, University of Oxford, 13 February 1975* (Oxford: Clarendon Press, 1975), 7.

Schiedermair, Ludwig, *Der junge Beethoven* (Leipzig: Quelle & Meyer, c.1925).

Schmidt, Carl B., 'The Amsterdam Editions of Lully's Music: A Bibliographical Scrutiny with Commentary' in Heyer, ed., *Lully Studies*, 100–65.

Schneider, Herbert, 'L'Air narratif dans l'opéra-comique' in Dompnier, et al., ed., *Musiques en liberté*, 539–53.

'Airs de comédie de J.-Cl. Gillier pour différentes pièces de la Comédie-Française' in Charles Mazouer, ed., *Théâtre et musique au XVIIe siècle: Littératures Classiques* 21 (Spring, 1994), 175–92.

ed., *Chanson und Vaudeville. Gesellschaftliches Singen und unterhaltende Kommunikation im 18. und 19. Jahrhundert* (St. Ingbert: Röhrig UniversitätsVerlag, 1999).

'Das Finalvaudeville bei Charles-Simon Favart: Gestalt und Funktion' in Thomas Betzwieser, Richard Erkens, Arnold Jacobshagen and Peter Ross, eds, *Festschrift für Jürgen Maehder zum 70. Geburtstag* (Frankfurt am Main: Peter Lang, 2021).

'Publier la musique dans le livret', in Reynaud, ed., *Noter, annoter*, 307–35.

'Die Revitalisierung des Vaudeville in der vorrevolutionären Opéra comique durch Barré und de Piis (1780–1789)' in Schneider, ed., *Das Vaudeville*, 75–164.

Die Rezeption der Opern Lullys im Frankreich des Ancien regime (Tutzing: Schneider, 1982).

'*La serva padrona* traduite et arrangée', *Studi pergolesiani* 6 (2011), 121–55.

ed., *Timbre und Vaudeville. Zur Geschichte und Problematik einer populären Gattung im 17. und 18. Jahrhundert* (Hildesheim: G. Olms, 1999).

'Übersetzungen französischer Opéras-comiques für Marchands *Churpfälzische Deutsche Hofschauspielergesellschaft*', in *Mannheim – Ein 'Paradies der Tonkünstler'? Kongressbericht Mannheim 1999*, ed. Ludwig Finscher et al. (Frankfurt: Peter Lang, 2002), 387–434.

ed., *Das Vaudeville. Funktionen eines multimedialen Phänomens* (Hildesheim: G. Olms, 1996).

Scott, Derek B., 'Musical Theater(s)' in Greenwald, ed., *Oxford Handbook of Opera*, 53–72.

Scott, Virginia, *The Commedia dell'arte in Paris, 1644–1697* (Charlottesville: University Press of Virginia, 1990).

Women on the Stage in Early Modern France, 1540–1750 (Cambridge: Cambridge University Press, 2010).

Sgard, Jean, ed., *Dictionnaire des journalistes, 1600–1789*, 2 vols. (Oxford: Voltaire Foundation, 1999). For revised digital ed., see p. xxii.

Shapiro, James, *1606. Shakespeare and the Year of 'Lear'* (London: Faber, 2015).

Smith, Kent M., 'Egidio Duni and the Development of the *opéra comique* from 1753 to 1770', dissertation, Cornell University, 1980.

Smith, Simon, *Musical Response in the Early Modern Playhouse, 1603–1625* (Cambridge: Cambridge University Press, 2017).

Sonneck, Oscar George Theodore, 'Ciampi's *Bertoldo, Bertoldino e Cacasenno* and Favart's *Ninette à la cour*. A Contribution to the History of Pasticcio' [1911] in ibid., *Miscellaneous Studies in the History of Music* (New York: Macmillan, 1921), 111–79.

Stevens, John, 'Introduction' to musical works, *Catalogue of the Pepys Library at Magdalene College Cambridge* IV, ed. Robert Latham (Cambridge: D. S. Brewer, 1989), v–viii.

Stilwell, Jama Liane, '"A Story Altogether Foolish, Bizarre, and Buffoonish": the *Théâtres de la Foire* and the Eighteenth-Century Captivity Opera', dissertation, University of Iowa, 2003.

'A New View of the Eighteenth-Century "Abduction" Opera: Edification and Escape at the Parisian Théâtres de la Foire', *Music and Letters* 91/1 (Feb. 2010), 51–82.

Striker, Ardelle, 'The Theatre of Alain-René Lesage', dissertation, Columbia University, 1968.

Strohm, Reinhard, *Dramma per Musica. Italian Opera Seria of the Eighteenth Century* (New Haven, CT: Yale University Press, 1997).

Strunk, Oliver, *Source Readings in Music History, 3: The Baroque Era* (London: Faber, 1981).

Stuurman, Siep, *François Poulain de la Barre and the Invention of Modern Equality* (Cambridge: Harvard University Press, 2004).

Sutcliffe, Tom, *Believing in Opera* (London: Faber & Faber, 1996).

Talbot, Michael, 'Preface' to Tomaso Albinoni, *Pimpinone. Intermezzi comici musicali* (Madison, WI: A–R Editions, 1983), vii–xvii.

Tancock, Leonard, 'Introduction' to Diderot, *The Nun* (Harmondsworth: Penguin Books, 1974).

Terrier, Agnès, and Alexandre Dratwicki, eds., *L'Invention des genres lyriques français et leur redécouverte au XIXe siècle* (Lyon: Symétrie, 2010).

Thomas, Downing A., *Aesthetics of Opera in the Ancien Régime, 1647–1785* (Cambridge: Cambridge University Press, 2002).

Music and the Origins of Language. Theories from the French Enlightenment (Cambridge: Cambridge University Press, 1995).

Tissier, André, *Les Spectacles à Paris pendant la Révolution*, 2 vols. (Geneva: Droz, 1992, 2002).

Tocqueville, Alexis de, *The Ancien Régime and the French Revolution* [1856], trans. Gerald Bevan (London: Penguin Classics, 2018).

Tomlinson, Robert, *La Fête galante: Watteau et Marivaux* (Geneva: Droz, 1981).

Toscani, Bernard, '*La serva padrona*: Variations on a Theme', *Studi Pergolesiani* 2 (Florence: Nuova Italia Editrice, 1988), 185–94.

Trolese, Alessandra, '*Orazio* de Naples à Paris' in Fabiano, ed., '*Querelle des Bouffons*', 103–15.

Trott, David, *Théâtre du XVIIIe siècle: jeux, écritures, regards* (Montpellier: Editions Espaces 34, 2000).

Trouille, Mary, 'Buried Alive: Genlis's Gothic Tale of Marital Violence in "Histoire de la Duchesse de C***"', *Studies on Voltaire and the Eighteenth Century* (Oxford: Voltaire Foundation, 2005) (*SVEC* 2005: 12), 77–113.

Troy, Charles E., *The Comic Intermezzo* (Ann Arbor: UMI, 1979).

Tunley, David, *The Eighteenth-Century French Cantata* (London: Dobson, 1974).

Vallas, Léon, *Un Siècle de musique et de théâtre à Lyon, 1688–1789* (Lyon: P. Masson, 1932).

Velde, François R., 'John Law's System and Public Finance in 18th-Century France': www.researchgate.net/publication/237596844 (30 May 2019).

Venard, Michèle, *La Foire entre en scène* (Paris: Librairie Théâtrale, 1985).

Vendrix, Philippe, ed., *Grétry et l'Europe de l'Opéra-Comique* (Liège: Mardaga, 1992).

L'Opéra-Comique en France au XVIIIe siècle (Liège: Mardaga, 1992).

Vernet, Thomas, 'Théâtre, musique et société dans les résidences du prince de Conti', in Plagnol-Diéval, ed., *Les Théâtres de société*, 75–84.

Viollier, Renée, *Jean-Joseph Mouret, le musicien des grâces, 1682–1738* (Paris: Librairie Floury, 1950).

Waeber, Jacqueline, 'Afterword' in *The Melodramatic Moment*, ed. Katherine Hambridge and Jonathan Hicks (Chicago: Chicago University Press, 2018), 191–8.

'"Le Devin de la Foire"? Revaluating the Pantomime in Rousseau's *Devin du Village*' in Waeber, ed., *Musique et Geste*, 149–72.

ed., *Musique et Geste en France de Lully à la Révolution* (Berne: Peter Lang, 2009).

Wåhlberg, Martin, 'L'opéra-comique dans *Les Liaisons dangereuses*', *Romanistische Zeitschrift für Literaturgeschichte / Cahiers d'Histoire des Littératures Romanes* 42/3-4 (2018), 289–304.

Walker, Frank, '*Orazio*: The History of a Pasticcio', *Musical Quarterly* 38/3 (1952), 369–83.

Ward, Adrienne, *Pagodas in Play. China on the Eighteenth-Century Italian Opera Stage* (Lewisburg, PA: Bucknell University Press, 2010).

Weber, William, '"La musique ancienne" in the Waning of the Ancien Régime', *The Journal of Modern History*, 56 (1984), 58–88.

 'Lully and the Rise of Musical Classics in the 18th Century' in La Gorce, ed., *Jean-Baptiste Lully*, 581–90.

Weiss, Piero, *Opera: A History in Documents* (New York: Oxford University Press, 2002).

 'Venetian commedia dell'arte "operas" in the age of Vivaldi', *Musical Quarterly* 70 (1984), 195–217.

Weisstein, Ulrich, 'Librettology: the fine art of coping with a Chinese twin', *Komparatistische Hefte* 5/6 (1982): *Literatur und die anderen Künste*, 23–42.

Wellesz, Egon, and Frederick Sternfeld, eds., *The New Oxford History of Music*, VII (London: Oxford University Press, 1973).

Wild, Nicole, *Dictionnaire des théâtres parisiens au XIXe siècle* (Paris: Aux amateurs de livres, 1989).

 and David Charlton, *Théâtre de l'Opéra-Comique, Paris: Répertoire 1762–1972* (Sprimont: Mardaga, 2005).

Willett, John, ed. and trans., *Brecht on Theatre. The Development of an Aesthetic*, 2nd ed. (New York: Hill & Wang, 1974).

Wolff, Charlotta, 'Lyrical Diplomacy: Count Gustav Philip Creutz (1731–1785) and the opera', in Beaurepaire *et al.*, eds., *Moving Scenes*, 143–56.

Wood, Caroline and Graham Sadler, *French Baroque Opera: A Reader* (rev. ed., London: Routledge, 2017).

Wotquenne, Alfred, *Catalogue de la Bibliothèque du Conservatoire Royal de Musique de Bruxelles*, 4 vols. (Bruxelles: J. J. Coosemans, 1898).

Wyngaard, Amy S., *From Savage to Citizen. The Invention of the Peasant in the French Enlightenment* (Newark: University of Delaware Press, 2004).

Zupančič, Alenka, *The Odd One In. On Comedy* (Cambridge, MA: Massachusetts Institute of Technology Press, 2008).

Index

Abduction, theme of, 181–2, 299
Académie bourgeoise, La, 116
Acajou, 189–92, 206, 231
Achmet et Almanzine, 117, 124–6, 152, 186–8, 201–3
Acting. *See* Stage directions
  and Théveneau at Comédie-Italienne, 243
  by *intermezzo* players, 247
  in domestic operas, 93–9
  in Gherardi's troupe, 50
  in Italian comedy, 251
  of Justine Favart and Charles Rochard, 254
Adaptation. *See* Parodies
  from *intermezzi* to popular opera, 262–73
  from Italian sources, 262–73
  from popular opera to Italian opera, 281
  of earlier literary material, 156–62
Adieux des officiers, Les, 52, 57, 58, 59, 61
Aigremont, d', Mlle, 113, 167
Alard (troupe), 108
Alceste, 6, 45, 72, 79
Allanbrook, Wye Jamison, 252, 263, 286 n. 95
Allure, L', 219, 224
Amante ennemie, L', 28
Amants inquiets, Les, 118, 193, 196, 251
Amants magnifiques, Les, 101
Ambigu de la Folie, L, 251
Ami de la maison, L', 307
Amour au village, L', 142
Amour désœuvré, L', 149
Amours champêtres, Les, 196, 251, 255
Amours d'Apollon et de Daphné, Les, 28
Amours de Gonesse, Les, 85, 88
Amours de Nanterre, Les, 8, 152, 205
  and formation of repertory, 201–5
  influence on Favart, 166
  popularity of, 189
  shown in Figure 7.2, 168
Amours de Ragonde, Les, 238, 275
Amsterdam, 83
Ancien Théâtre Italien
  and Italian music, 46–55
  and music, 36
  establishment and nature of, 46–55
Animaux raisonnables, Les, 138, 163, 188
Anneau perdu et retrouvé, L', 15
Annette et Lubin (Favart & Blaise), 92, 120, 146, 181
Annette et Lubin (Marmontel & La Borde), 92, 96, 181
Anseaume, Louis. *See Bertholde à la ville; Chinois poli, Le; Deux chasseurs et la laitière, Les; École de la jeunesse, L'; Femme orgueilleuse, La; Maréchal-ferrant, Le; Mazet; Médecin de l'amour, Le; Peintre amoureux de son modele, Le; Soldat magicien, Le; Veuve indécise, La*
Antheaume, Mlle, 115, 311
Anti-theatre, 12
Argenson, Marc-René de Voyer, marquis d', 6, 114, 138, 139, 156, 166, 186, 199, 255, 256, 293
Arimath, d', Françoise, 115, 233
Arlequin baron allemand, 110
Arlequin comédien aux Champs Élisées, 86
Arlequin défenseur d'Homère, 149, 157
Arlequin empereur dans la lune, 59, 61, 147
Arlequin Énée, 108
Arlequin et Mezzetin morts par amour, 110
Arlequin et Scaramouche vendangeurs, 33, 55, 56
Arlequin Grapignan, 53, 158
Arlequin homme à bonne fortune, 67
Arlequin Hulla, 114, 177, 201
Arlequin Mahomet, 117, 140, 151, 154, 188
Arlequin misanthrope, 54, 62
Arlequin Phaéton, 55, 64
Arlequin Roland furieux, 46, 86, 87
Arlequin sultane favorite, 104, 181
Arlequin Thétis, 112, 226
Arlequin traitant, 149, 213, 226, 290, 315
  and contemporary politics, 157
Arrangements (musical), 77–84
Artigiani arricchiti, Gli, 253, 268
Astori, Ursula, 239, 241, 242
Astraudi, Rosalie, 241, 251, 256

357

Attendez-moi sous l'orme, 53, 59, 68
Auden, W. H., 298
  classification of song types, 30
Audiences
  and perceptions, 209
  as Fair theatre singers, 107–11
  as singers, 80
  at Comédie-Italienne, 143–4
  at Fair theatres, 136, 141
Audinot, Nicolas-Médard. See *Tonnelier, Le*
  in Figure 7.3, 172
Autreau, Jacques. See *Amours de Nanterre, Les*; *Naufrage au Port-à-l'Anglais, Le*
Aventures des Champs-Élisées, Les, 70, 72
Aveux indiscrets, Les, 85, 196, 198, 290, 308
  longevity of, 200
  offered to the Opéra, 198

Baculard d'Arnaud, François-Thomas, 125
Baguette de Vulcain, La, 52, 64, 68
Baillis
  in *Annette et Lubin*, 98, 181
  in Gherardi's repertory, 55
  in *Le Médecin de l'amour*, 13
Bains de la Porte Saint-Bernard, Les, 54, 158
Baiocco et Serpilla, 194, 241, 253–4
Bal bourgeois, Le, 189, 205, 230, 231, 232
Bambini, Eustachio, 193, 236, 248, 249, 253, 256, 265
Bateliers de Saint-Cloud, Les, 189, 203, 233
Baurans, Pierre, 256–61, See *Maître de musique, Le*; *Servante maîtresse, La*
Baxter, Richard, xv, 108, 140
  works with Lesage, 111–13
Beauchamps, Pierre, 35, 41
Beethoven, L. van
  hears Monsigny's music, 23
Beggar's Opera, The, 179, 296, 313
Bellérophon, 43, 44, 63, 83, 227
Bentley, Thomas, 145
Béquille du Père Barnaba, La, 219
Berger, Francois, 191–2, 206
Bergers de qualité, Les, 196, 255
Bergiron, Nicolas, 116
Berlioz, Hector, 23–4, 299
Bertholde à la ville, 194, 230, 265, 288
Bertoldo in corte, 154, 194, 252, 258, 267, 270
Betzwieser, Thomas, 9, 316
  and Grétry's theory, 318
Biancolelli, Domenico, 4, 46, 156
Biancolelli, Pierre-François, 76, 242
Biron, VIIIe Concerto Comique, 219–20
Blaise le savetier, 171, 196, 200, 206, 307

Blaise, Adolphe. See *Annette et Lubin* (Favart & Blaise)
Bohémienne, La (Favart), 194, 260, 268
Bohémienne, La (Moustou), 194, 268
Boismortier, Joseph Bodin de, 235, 256, 278
Boissy, Louis de, 239, 294
Boizard de Pontau, Florimon-Claude. See Pontau, Boizard de
Bon soldat, Le, 161
Bordelon, Laurent, 85–7, see *Arlequin Roland furieux*
Bouchait de Serée, Mme, 16, 17
Bouret, Claude-Antoine
  in Figure 7.3, 172
Bourgeois gentilhomme, Le, 34, 38
Brecht, Bertolt, xvi, 113, 314
Bûcheron, Le, 163, 246, 306
Burney, Charles, xv, 197

Cadi dupé, Le, 92, 96, 159, 196, 200, 308
Caillot, Joseph, 146, 181, 241, 246, 315
  'born with two souls', 246
Camille, ou Le souterrain, 182
Cammasse, Lolotte, 220
Cantatas
  in *Les Talents à la mode*, 239
  in popular opera, 209, 211–14
Caprice d'Érato, Le, 227
Caprice, Le, 189, 205, 227
Carolet, Denis, 78, 140, 149, 150, See *Allure, L'*; *Amour désœuvré, L'*; *Lanterne véridique, La*; *Mère jalouse, La*; *Petites maisons, Les*; *Réveil de l'Opéra Comique, Le*
  collaboration with Corrette on *L'Allure*, 222
  uses 'Jupin du grand matin', 229
Casanova, Giacomo, 144, 249, 296, 330
Catinon, Mlle, 238
Ceinture de Vénus, La, 211, 214
Cendrillon, 196
Chaconnes
  arranged for domestic performance, 83
Chamfort, Sébastien-Roch Nicolas de, 17–19, 259, 317
Charpentier, Marc-Antoine. See *Circé*; *Foux divertissans, Les*; *Malade imaginaire, Le*
Chauvon, Francois, 91
Chercheuse d'esprit, La
  adapted as *La semplice curiosa*, 281
  and strophic song, 230
  Favart's 1741 manuscript, 126–33
  in Lyons, 116
  La Fontaine source, 166
  performances, 189, 203

Chéret, Mlles, 115, 251
Chinois poli en France, Le, 194, 196
Chinois, Les (Dufresny), 52, 54
Chinois, Les (Favart, Naigeon), 12, 194, 196
Chorus. *See* Table 9.1 (online)
  in *La Princesse de la Chine*, 217
  in *Le Claperman*, 209
  in *Le Roi et le fermier*, 301
  in *Les Aventures des Champs-Élisées*, 70–2
Ciampi, Vincenzo. *See Bertoldo in corte*
Cinese rimpatriato, Il, 253, 257, 266
Circé, 41
Clairval, Jean-Baptiste
  in Figure 7.3, 172
Claperman, Le, 209
Cocchi, Gioacchino. *See Scaltra governatrice, La*
Coffres, Les, 188, 203
Collé, Charles, 133, 297
Collier de perles, Le, 33, 35, 41
Comédie de chansons, La, 28, 29
Comédie sans hommes, La, 116, 188
Comédie-Française. *See Folies amoureuses, Les; Foux divertissans, Les*
  and dance, 220
  establishment of, 5
  in the crisis of 1744-5, 191–2
Comédie-Italienne
  at Saint-Laurent Fair, 7
  competition with Opéra Comique, 194–7
  establishment of, 9–10
  green room described, 144
  in development of popular opera, 236–61
  La serva padrona at, 248–50
  merger with Opéra Comique, 291–2
  parodies and *vaudevilles*, 225
  parodies forbidden, 192
Comédie-Italienne (17th century), 46, *see* Ancien Théâtre Italien
Comédiens du Mans, Les, 79
commedia [dell'arte]
  in Ancien Théâtre Italien, 46–50
  in domestic use, 85–7
Comte d'Albert, Le, 15
Concertos
  danced in popular opera, 218–22
Contessina, La, 14
Contrast
  and 'binary opposition', 29
  and *vaudevilles*, 66
  as constitutive of comedy, 29
  in musical plays, 31
Cook, Elisabeth, 265

Coq de village, Le, 189, 251
Coquette sans le savoir, La, 189
Coquette, La, 54
Corby, Julien, 197, 198, 204
  role in 1762 merger, 291–2
Corrette, Michel, 224, *See Allure, L'; Béquille du Père Barnaba, La; Biron; Mie Margot, La; Nymphes de Diane, Les*
  and concertos for operas, 218–24
Corsair de Salé, Le, 177
Costantini, Angelo
  in Figures 3.1 and 3.2, 47–8
Couplets en procès, Les, 188
Crispin rival de son maître, 110
Critique (including social satire)
  and theme of marriage, 176–7
  as basic to Fair theatre, 156–9
  in Gherardi's repertory, 49–51
  in *Moral Tales*, 180
  in popular opera, 12–14
  in Sedaine's comedies, 171–3
  of policy of deportation, 178
Critique de La cause des femmes, La, 59
Cross-dressed roles
  in Fair theatre, 250–1
  in *intermezzi*, 251–2
  in *La finta cameriera* and *Les deux suivantes*, 257
  in *Le Soldat magicien*, 161
  in *Les Bateliers de Saint-Cloud*, 233
  in *Les Nymphes de Diane*, 167
Cucuel, Georges, 236
Cuvillier, Louis, 278

D'Orneval, Jacques-Philippe. *See* [the following collaborative works are a selection] *Achmet et Almanzine; Amours de Nanterre, Les; Isle des Amazones, L'; Mariages de Canada, Les; Monde renversé, Le; Pélerins de la Mecque, Les; Pénélope moderne, La; Rémouleur d'amour, Le; Trois Commères, Les*
  and *Arlequin traitant*, 157
Dalayrac, Nicolas, 182
Dancers
  as 'gypsies', 217
  doubling as chorus, 209
  English, 151, 190
  in 1744, 140
  in *Arlequin traitant*, 226
  in Bouffon repertory, 252
  in early Fair theatre, 107, 112, 114
  in *Le Bourgeois gentilhomme*, 38

Dancers (cont.)
    in *Le Devin du village*, 278
    in *Le Malade imaginaire*, 40
    in *Le Sicilien*, 37
    in *Les Foux divertissans*, 43
    in *Les Originaux*, 70
    in 'lyric pantomime', 110
    Italian, 218
    styles of, 218
Danneret, Elisabeth, 57–62
Dare-Devil Rides to Jarama, 31
De Lisle [Delisle], Mlle, 114
Débuts, Les, 242
Départ de l'Opéra Comique, Le, 115, 219
Départ des comédiens, Le, 63
Derision
    and vaudevilles, 64–7
Des Aigles, Mlle, 115
Deschamps, Mlle, 54, 160, 284, 286
    in Figure 7.3, 172
Déserteur, Le, 22–6, 318
Désespérés, Les, 78
Desfontaines, Pierre Francois Guyot, 132, 184, 235
Desjardins, M., 114
Deux amies, Les, 195
Deux Arlequins, Les, 53, 62
Deux chasseurs et la laitière, Les, 18, 171, 188, 308
Deux Pierrots, Les,
Deux suivantes, Les, 257
Devin du village, Le, 133, 253, 302
    named by Gluck, 305
    style and form in, 275–9
Diable à quatre, Le, 92, 179, 196, 200, 273
Dialogue
    and continuity, 121–3
    and English influence, 180
    and heteroglossia, 316
    and proportion, 19
    improvised, 11, 117
    in *vaudeville* performance, 116–17
Diderot, Denis
    and 'conditions', 19
    and Duni, 282
    and *Les Deux chasseurs*, 173
    La Religieuse, 169
    tableau, 14
Docteur Sangrado, Le, 196, 200
Dodsley, Robert. See *King and the Miller of Mansfield, The*
Don Micco e Lesbina, 247
Don Quichotte chez la duchesse, 235, 278

Donna superba, La, 194, 266
Double inconstance, La, 258
Dreigroschenoper, Die, 314
Drouart, Mlle, 251
Du Boccage, Anne-Marie
    and *Lettre de Madame +++*, 142–4, 155, 191, 192, 206, 312
    polemic against Opéra Comique, 142–3
Duets
    discussed in the *Mercure de France*, 265
    in *Arlequin et Scaramouche vendangeurs*, 57
    in *La Ceinture de Vénus*, 211–13
    in *Le Devin du village*, 279
    in *Le Roi et le fermier*, 300
    in *Les Fêtes parisiennes*, 110
    in *Les Folies amoureuses*, 89
    in *The Beggar's Opera*, 313
Duni, Egidio, 280–8, See *Deux chasseurs et la laitière, Les*; *Fille mal gardée, La*; *Mazet*; *Peintre amoureux de son modele, Le*; *Retour au village, Le*
Durancy, Mlle. See Arimath, d'
Duval, Mlle *l'ainée*, 116

Eaux de Merlin, Les, 149, 212
École des amants, L', 187
École des amours grivois, L', 149
École des femmes, L', 159
Écriteaux (sign-boards or scrolls)
    in 'lyric pantomime', 107–10
Effets du hazard, Les, 115
Emplois (character-types), 115
Endriague, L', 7, 153, 210
Ensembles
    as tableaux, 15
    in *Arlequin traitant*, 226
    in *Le Maître en droit*, 170
    in *Le Prix de Cythère*, 231
    in *Le Roi et le fermier*, 300–2
    in *Le Troc*, 95
    in *Les Momies d'Égypte*, 58
    in *Les Troqueurs*, 280
    in *On ne s'avise jamais de tout*, 161
Entführung aus dem Serail, Die, 29, 31
Entr'actes
    as Chaconne in *Le Joueur*, 242
    as storm in *Le Roi et le fermier*, 299
    in *Le Malade imaginaire*, 39
    mentioned in 1673 edict, 4
Entreville, Mme Gastin d', 16, 17, 248, 263
Époux réunis, Les, 188, 217
Ercole amante, 34
Ésope à la cour, 53

Espérance, L', 208
Exaudet, André-Joseph
    and *menuets*, 118, 119, 230

Fâcheux veuvage, Le, 154, 176, 227
Fagan, Barthélemy. *See Fausse ridicule, La; Foire de Cythère, La; Isabelle Arlequin; Répétition interrompue, La; Siège de Cythère, La; Temple du Sommeil, Le*
Fairs (Saint-Germain and Saint-Laurent)
    annual dates, 5
    theatre descriptions, 142–5
    theatres in, 134–41
Fatouville, Anne Mauduit de, 49, *See Arlequin Grapignan*
Fausse ridicule, La, 116, 189, 203, 205
Favart, Charles-Simon. *See Acajou; Bal bourgeois, Le; Bohémienne, La; Don Quichotte chez la duchesse; École des amours grivois, L'; Jeunes mariés, Les; Ninette à la cour; Nymphes de Diane, Les; Raton et Rosette; Servante justifiée, La; Thésée*, parodie
    and *Chercheuse d'esprit, La*, 126–33
    and *comédies melées d'ariettes*, 259–60
    and hybrid operas, 268–73
    and *Le Soldat magicien*, 162
    and musical focus points, 230–4
    and psychologising *vaudevilles*, 231
    and the contract of 1758, 198
    and the merger of 1762, 291–2
    and virtuoso *vaudevilles*, 232–5
    as OC manager, 191
    describes *Annette et Lubin*, 146
Favart, Marie-Justine. *See Annette et Lubin*
    and Carlo Sodi, 252–4
    and *Ninette à la cour*, 269–73
Fée Urgèle, La, 151
Fées, Les, 52, 57
Femme orgueilleuse, La, 194
Femmes vengées, Les, 117
Festin de pierre, Le, 188, 200
Fêtes de Thalie, Les, 192
Fêtes grecques et romaines, Les, 227
Fêtes parisiennes, Les, 110
Fêtes vénitiennes, Les, 212, 239
Fielding, Henry
    and *Tom Jones*, 14
Fille capitaine, La, 107
Fille mal gardée, La, 196, 238
Fille, la veuve et la femme, La, 192, 249
Filles errantes, Les, 52, 53, 71

Finta cameriera, La, 253, 257
Finta pazza, La, 36
Fleuve Scamandre, Le, 165
Foire de Bezons, La, 187
Foire de Cythère, La, 178, 229, 319
Foire de Guibray, La, 151, 214
Foire Saint-Germain, La, 50, 53, 59
Folies amoureuses, Les, 89
Fontaine de sapience, La, 57
Forêt de Dodône, La, 152
Fossé du scrupule, Le, 187, 203, 230
Foux divertissans, Les, 33, 42–5
    adapted as *Le Bon soldat*, 161
Fréron, Élie
    analysis of Duni's *Le Peintre amoureux*, 285–8
    and spoken dialogue, 12
    defines *Le Trompeur trompé*, 312
    praise of Justine Favart, 254
Funérailles de la Foire, Les, 120, 187
Fuzelier, Louis. *See Achmet et Almanzine; Amours déguisés, Les; Animaux raisonnables, Les; Arlequin défenseur d'Homère; Arlequin Énée; Caprice d'Érato, Le; École des amants, L'; Espérance, L'; Fêtes parisiennes, Les; Forêt de Dodône, La; Funérailles de la Foire, Les; Grand'mère amoureuse, La; Matrone d'Éphèse, La; Pénélope moderne, La; Pharaon, Le; Routes du monde, Les; Tableau du mariage, Le; Temple de l'Ennuy, Le*
    adapts La Fontaine, 163–5
    and 'anti-comedy', 174
    and marionette theatre, 134
    and return of solo singing, 113
    and scenic demands, 152
    as 'cultural insider', 311
    experiments in 'lyric pantomime', 110
    revises earlier plays, 76
    updates *L'Opéra de campagne*, 113

Gageure, La, 203
Garcin, Laurent
    and *Le Roi et le fermier*, 306
    Traité, 246, 285, 304
Garrick, David
    corresponds with Patu, 179
    describes green room, 144
Gastin d'Entreville, Mme. *See Entreville, Mme Gastin d'*
Gaviniès, Pierre. *See Prétendu, Le*
Gay, John. *See Beggar's Opera, The*
    and *The Beggar's Opera*, 313–14

Gender roles
  explored in popular opera, 175–7
Génie de l'Opéra Comique, Le, 231
Georget et Georgette, 196, 200
Gherardi, Evaristo
  career in Paris, 49–52
  in Figures 3.1 and 3.2, 47–8
Gilles Garçon-peintre, 98
Gillier, Jean-Claude. See *Ceinture de Vénus, La*; *Foire de Guibray, La*; *Foire de Saint-Germain, La*; *Folies amoureuses, Les*; *Isle des Amazones, L'*; *Mari préféré, Le*; *Médecin de village, Le*; *Monde renversé, Le*; *Pénélope moderne, La*; *Pot-pourri, Le*; *Princesse de Carizme, La*
  dramatic music of, 59
  local colour anticipated in, 89
  music in first-period Fair theatre, 213–15
  summary of contributions, 210
Giocasta regina d'Armenia, 59
Giocatore, Il, 194, 253
Gluck, Christoph Willibald
  and 'musico-dramatic art', 305
Goldoni, Carlo. See *Bertoldo in corte*
  theory of comedy, 14
Gondot, Pierre-Thomas. See *Bergers de qualité, Les*
Grand-mère amoureuse, La, 10
Grétry, André-Ernest-Modeste. See *Comte d'Albert, Le*; *Lucile*; *Richard Cœur de lion*; *Silvain*
  and 'musico-dramatic art', 304–7
  scores studied in London, 26
Grimm, Friedrich Melchior
  describes Duni's word-setting, 284
  describes unaccompanied *vaudevilles*, 119
  reports on private theatre, 96
Grout, Donald J.
  analysis of *vaudeville* functions, 62–4
  scope of dissertation, 55
Guénégaud, theatre, 4
Guy de Chêne, Le, 92

Hamoche, Jean-Baptiste
  as soloist, 113
  in *Pierrot furieux*, 87
Harlequin à la guinguette, 108
Harvey, Susan, 10
Hautemer, Farin de
  and the domestic opera *Le Troc*, 93–6
Homme à bonne fortune, L', 54, 64
Hôtel de Bourgogne theatre, 5, See Chapter 3
  and musical comedy, 237–43
  and vocal projection, 245
Huître et des plaideurs, L', 54
Hybrid popular operas, 258–261, 265–74

Impromptu du Pont-Neuf, L', 188, 210
Inconnu, L', 42, 110
Inconstant vaincu, L', 28, 30
Indes galantes, Les, 251, 255
Intermezzi. See *Don Micco e Lesbina*; *Serpilla e Baiocco*; *Serva padrona, La*; Hybrid operas; online score of *Le Joueur*
  as described, 247
  as parodied in *Le Joueur*, 242
  at Opéra in 1729, 236
  in descriptions, 240
Isle des Amazones, L', 8, 175, 188
Isle des foux, L', 196, 246
Ismène, 275

Jaloux corrigé, Le, 253
Jardinier et son seigneur, Le, 92, 171, 196, 200, 308
Jardins de l'Hymen ou La Rose, Les, 8, 189, 203
Je ne sais quoi, Le, 239
Jeunes mariés, Les, 189, 203, 230
Jeune-Vieillard, Le, 152, 154
Joueur, Le, 59, 68, 118, 242–4
Jugement de Paris, Le, 28
Jumeaux, Les, 251
Jumelles, Les, 219

King and the Miller of Mansfield, The, 182, 293–8, 300
Kingship
  and 'new patriotism' of 1762, 304
  in *Le Roi et le fermier*, 293–8
Kohaut, Josef
  described by Quétant, 79

La Borde, Jean-Benjamin de. See *Amours de Gonesse, Les*
  Annette et Lubin and private theatre, 96–9
La Bruyère, Jean de
  describes amateur singers, 80
La Fontaine, Jean de. See *Mazet*; *Paladins, Les*; *Quiproquo, Le*
  operas derived from his *Fables and Tales*, 162–73
La Guerre, Elisabeth Jacquet de
  and Fair theatre, 210
  duet in *La Ceinture de Vénus*, 211–13
La Harpe, Jean-Francois de
  theory of opéra-comique, 15

La Motte, Houdar de, 88
  divertissement in *Les Originaux*, 69
La Place, Pierre-Antoine de, 298
  essay on English theatre, 178
Lacoste, Louis de, 210
  achievements in *La Princesse de Carizme*, 215–17
Laffichard, Thomas. See *Effets du hasard, Les*; *Fontaine de Sapience, La*; *Pygmalion*
  and *Fleuve Scamandre, Le*, 165
  La Béquille and Michel Corrette, 219
Lanterne véridique, La, 230
Laujon, Pierre
  and *La Fille, la veuve et la femme*, 192
  co-authors *Thésée, parodie*, 142
  describes domestic theatre, 93
Law, John
  and his 'system', 13
Le Cerf de La Viéville, Jean Laurent
  on *vaudevilles* sung in society, 80
Le Noble, Eustache. See *Deux Arlequins, Les*
Legrand, Charlotte
  farewell season memorialised, 115
Lepri, Maria, 267, 268
Lesage, Alain-René. See [selection only:] *Achmet et Almanzine*; *Amours de Nanterre, Les*; *Arlequin Hulla*; *Ceinture de Vénus, La*; *Eaux de Merlin, Les*; *École des amants, L'*; *Funérailles de la Foire, Les*; *Isle des Amazones, L'*; *Mariages de Canada, Les*; *Monde renversé, Le*; *Pèlerins de la Mecque, Les*; *Rémouleur d'amour, Le*; *Roger de Sicile*; *Routes du monde, Les*; *Tableau du mariage, Le*; *Tombeau de Nostradamus, Le*; *Trois commères, Les*
  and 'lyric pantomime', 110–13
  and music 1714-18, 211–18
  and vaudeville dramaturgy, 121–6
  social critique in *Le Diable boiteux*, 158
Letellier, Jean-Francois. See *Arlequin sultane favorite*; *Festin de pierre, Le*
Levenson, Erica, xvii, 313
London
  and popular opera, 293
  and *The Devil to Pay*, 179
  burlettas in, 197
  Italian players in, 4
  Jean Monnet in, 195
  opéra-comique in, 50
  Patu in, 179
Louis XIV
  and theatre organisation, 3
  destroys Italian troupe, 50

Louis XV
  and Fair theatre, 7, 292
  and 'new patriotism', 304
Lucile, 180
Lully, Jean-Baptiste. See *Arlequin Roland furieux*; *Bellérophon*; *Filles errantes, Les*; *Opéra de campagne, L'*; *Proserpine*; *Sicilien, Le*; *Thésée, parodie*
  and arrangements, 83
  and vaudevilles, 80, 101–5
  music in Pepys's library, 90
  music parodied in Italian theatre, 71
Lyons
  operas in, 116
Lyric pantomime
  in Fair theatre, 108–13

Madness
  and *La Princesse de Carizme*, 215–16
  and music sung by La Folie, 227–9
  pretended in *Les Folies amoureuses*, 89
Maestro di musica, Il, 194, 252, 259–61, 263, 267
Magazin des modernes, Le, 187, 189, 203, 205
Maître de musique, Le, 194, 196, 261, 268
Maître en droit, Le, 170, 196, 200
Malade imaginaire, Le, 34, 35
Mal-assortis, Les, 54, 59, 62
Mangot, Jacques-Simon
  and *vaudeville* in Parma, 119
  sings in *Le Retour au village*, 281
Maréchal-ferrant, Le, 16, 200, 308
Mari préféré, Le, 258
Mariages de Canada, Les, 178
Marionette theatres, 6, 10, 134, 201
Marmontel, Jean-François
  and *Annette et Lubin*, 99
  and *Moral Tales*, 180
Marriage (theme of), 173–81
Mary sans femme, Le, 28, 33
Mascherata, La, 266, 272
Matrone d'Éphèse, La (Fuzelier), 151, 152, 163
Mazet, 195, 196
Mazouer, Charles, 36
Médecin de l'amour, Le, 13, 200
Médecin de village, Le, 88
Médecin malgré lui, Le, 30
Menuets
  and expressiveness, 120, 124–6
  as showpieces, 227–30
  as signifier of love, 102
  as *vaudevilles*, 101–3

Mercier, Louis-Sébastien
  and *Le Déserteur*, 24
Mère embarrassée, La, 188
Mère jalouse, La, 229
Metastasio, Pietro
  and themes in popular opera, 124
Mie Margot, Ma, 219
Minart, Charles
  in Figure, 80–1
Molière
  and forms of opera, 35
Momies d'Égypte, Les, 57, 69
Monde renversé, Le, 152, 175, 189, 205, 215
Mondonville, Jean-Joseph Cassanéa de
  Titon et l'Aurore parodied, 256
Monnet, Jean
  and *Les Troqueurs*, 197
  contract with Bernage, 195
  excludes liveried servants from OC, 141
  hires Rameau, 235
  initial tenure of OC, 190
Monsigny, Pierre-Alexandre. *See Aveux indiscrets, Les*; *Cadi dupé, Le*; *Déserteur, Le*; *On ne s'avise jamais de tout*; *Roi et le fermier, Le*
  and composition of *Le Roi et le fermier*, 298–304
  and Rameau's music, 291
  and success of *Le Déserteur*, 25
  and symphony-overtures, 308
  as 'married' to Sedaine, 276
  longevity of stage works, 200
  offers comedy to the Opéra, 198
  setting of *Le Maître en droit*, 170
  setting of *On ne s'avise jamais de tout*, 161
Montéclair, Michel Pignolet de
  'Boute var la tasse en mair', 88
Montfleury, Antoine de
  and *Le Mary sans femme*, 33
Montigny [Montigni], Mlle
  and *La serva padrona*, 249
Moral Tales
  as source, 97, 125, 180
Moulinet Premier, 106
Moulinghen, Jean-Baptiste
  and added accompaniments, 189
Mouret, Jean-Joseph
  arias in Italian, 238, *See* Table 10.1 (online)
  'Il soldato valoroso', 247
  'La Terre' parodied, 234
  music in *Le Joueur*, 243
  rondeau parodied, 229
Moustou

  and *La Bohémienne*, 268
Multivocality
  and definitions, 263
  in *Le Maître de musique*, 268
  in *Le Peintre amoureux de son modèle*, 285–8
  in 'musico-dramatic art', 317–18
  in *Ninette à la cour*, 271, 272
Muse pantomime, La, 189, 219
'Musico-dramatic art'
  defined by observers, 304–9
  in *Le Roi et le fermier*, 298–304

Naissance d'Amadis, La, 58, 60
Narrative
  and appropriate *vaudevilles*, 225
  in dance forms, 220–2
  in *Il maestro di musica*, 263
  in *La Chercheuse d'esprit*, 230, 231
  in *La scaltra governatrice*, 263
  in *Le Peintre amoureux de son modèle*, 286
  in Lesage, 124
Naufrage au Port-à-l'Anglais, Le, 237
Nemeitz, Joachim
  observation of Fair theatre, 135
Nessel, Mlle, 79, 98, 288, 291
Nestola, Barbara
  and sources of Italian music, 62
Nicaise, 170, 200
Nina ou La folle par amour, 125
Ninette à la cour, 89, 154, 194, 259, 269–73, 281
Nopce de village, La, 56
Nougaret, Pierre Jean
  and *De l'art du théâtre*, 20–2
Nouvelliste dupé, Le, 187, 189, 205
Nuns
  in La Fontaine's Tales, 169
  own *La Comédie de chansons*, 30
Nymphes de Diane, Les, 93, 166, 189, 233–4

Olimpiade, L', 288
Olivette juge des Enfers, 120
On ne s'avise jamais de tout, 159–161, 196, 200, 292, 308
Opéra (Académie Royale de Musique)
  and Bambini's troupe, 252
  and Opéra Comique, 6, 198
  and opéra-comique, 8
  opéras-comiques on stage of, 191
Opéra Comique
  and policy before the merger, 197–9
  and programming. *See* Chapter 8
  enforced closure of, 190–4
  establishment of, 5

theatres and ticket prices, 134–42
Opéra de campagne, L', 54, 64, 69
Opera, popular
  and definitions, 2–3
  and origins, 11
  as 'musico-dramatic art'. See Chapter 12
  defended by Nougaret, 19–22
  for domestic performance, 93–9
  reform of. See Chapter 11
  studied in London, 25
Originaux, Les, 54, 69
Orlandini, Giuseppe
  Il giocatore (Serpilla e Baiocco), 254
  parodied in *Le Joueur*, 239
Overtures
  and *Le Roi et le fermier*, 300
  arranged for singers, 83
  as symphonies, 308
  sung in popular opera, 227

Paladins, Les, 291
Palaprat, Jean
  and 'double-operational irony', 64
  and Molière, 41
Pannard, Charles-François. See *(selection only)*
  Comédie sans hommes, La; *Deux suivantes, Les*; *Fleuve Scamandre, Le*; *Fossé du scrupule, Le*; *Magazin des modernes, Le*; *Mie Margot, Ma*; *Muse pantomime, La*; *Nouvelliste dupé, Le*; *Pygmalion*; *Répétition interrompue, La*
  longevity of opéras-comiques, 187
  revivals 1752–62, 189
  works revived in 1740s, 203
Parakilas, James, 82
Paratajo, Il, 194, 253, 267
Paris
  as comic subject, 55
  Fair theatre in, 6
  private theatre groups in, 78
  song activity in, 80
  theatre organisation in, 7
Parodies
  as hybrid operas, 254–61
  at Comédie-Italienne, 238
  defined, 10
  of *intermezzi*, 239
  of Lully, 42, 63, 67, 69, 71
  permitted at Comédie-Italienne, 9
  suppressed in 1745, 192
Pasquin et Marforio, 49, 53, 72–5
Patu, Claude-Pierre

  and *The King and the Miller of Mansfield*, 293–6
  and translations of English theatre, 179
  described by Casanova, 296
Peines et les plaisirs de l'amour, Les, 35
Peintre amoureux de son modèle, Le, 196, 200, 284–8
Pèlerins de la Mecque, Les, 8, 124, 176, 184
Pénélope moderne, La, 150, 205, 217
Pepys, Samuel, 90
Performance
  of *Il maestro di musica* in German, 259
  of Italian actors, 47
  of Joseph Caillot, 246
  of Justine Favart, 254
  of Opéra Comique in 1761. See Figure 7.3
  of *vaudevilles*, 113–17
Pergolesi, Giovanni Battista. See *Serva padrona, La*; *Servante maîtresse, La*
Perrault, Charles
  and *Critique de l'Opéra*, 79
  and *Le Bûcheron*, 163
Petitpas, Mlle, 7, 115
Petits-maîtres, Les, 111
Pharaon, Le, 201, 214
Phénix, Le, 53
Philidor, François-André Danican
  additions to *Les Pèlerins de la Mecque*, 206
  and Framery's analysis, 307
  and 'handling the words', 284
  and *Le Jardinier et son seigneur*, 171
  and *Le Soldat magicien*, 161
  and public discussion of *Le Maréchal-ferrant*, 17
  and symphonic style, 308–9
  dedicates *Le Sorcier* to 'The Public', 85
  judgements of *Le Bûcheron*, 246
  longevity of stage works, 200
Philippe II d'Orléans, Regent of France
  and musical patronage, 237
Pièce à deux acteurs, La, 189, 229
Piron, Alexis. See *Claperman, Le*; *Caprice, Le*; *Endriague, L'*; *Fâcheux veuvage, Le*; *Olivette, juge des Enfers*; *Rose, La, ou Les Jardins de l'Hymen*; *Tirésias*; *Trois commères, Les*
  and Rameau, 7
  and use of chorus, 209
  longevity of stage works, 189, 205
  themes of gender, identity, marriage, 176
Platée, 235, 278
Poirier, Le, 200

Poisson, Raymond
    and *Les Foux divertissans*, 42–5
Pontau, Boizard de
    and debt crisis, 190
    and programming, 203
    and theatre construction, 138
    approved by d'Argenson, 6
Powell, John S.
    research on music in plays, 27–34
Prétendu, Le, 154, 195
Princesse de Carizme, La, 8, 214, 215–17
    and Figure 3.1, 152
Princesse de la Chine, La, 217
Prix de Cythère, Le, 231
Promenades de Paris, Les, 54
Proserpine, 43
Provençale, La, 238
Psyché, 35
Pygmalion, 187–9, 203
Pyrame et Thisbé, 227
    chaconne arranged for solo voice, 83

Quétant, Antoine-François. See *Maréchal-ferrant, Le*; *Tonnelier, Le*
    and libretto prefaces, 15
Quiproquo, Le, 173, 195

Racoleurs, Les, 196, 200
Rameau, Jean-Philippe
    and composition of *L'Endriague*, 8
    and Piron's *La Rose*, 8
    returns to Fair theatre, 140
    thematic recurrence in *Les Paladins*, 291
Rappel de la Foire à la vie, Le, 7
Raton et Rosette, 196, 253, 256
Re pastore, Il, 124
Reboul
    cantata, *Le Mauvais ménage*, 88
Rebours, M., 115, 233, See Figure 7.3
Régal des dames, Le, 36
Régiment de la Calotte, Le, 7, 227
Regnard, Jean-François, 49, See *Baguette de Vulcan, La*; *Chinois, Les*; *Coquette, La*; *Filles errantes, Les*; *Foire Saint-Laurent, La*; *Folies amoureuses, Les*; *Homme à bonne fortune, L'*; *Momies d'Égypte, Les*
    as composer, 59
Reine du Barostan, La, 123, 126, 177, 189, 203, 205
Rémouleur d'amour, Le, 120
    in Figure 2.1, 31–2
Répétition interrompue, La, 189, 205
    heard in 1991, 120

Retour au village, Le, 276, 281
Retour de la Foire de Bezons, Le, 55
Réveil de l'Opéra Comique, Le, 229
Riccoboni, Antoine-François. See *Prétendu, Le*
    sings in *La serva padrona*, 250
Riccoboni, Luigi [Louis]
    establishes Comédie-Italienne, 237
Richard Cœur de lion, xvi, 22
Richardson, Samuel
    as a standard for 'musico-dramatic art', 163, 306
    dialogue in *Pamela*, 317
Ristorini, Antonio
    in *Don Micco e Lesbina*, 247
    in *Serpilla e Baiocco*, 239
Rizzoni, Nathalie, 115, 186
Rochard, Charles-Raymond
    breath control of, 114, 244
    career at Comédie-Italienne, 241
    in *Baiocco et Serpilla*, 254
    in *Les Bergers de qualité*, 256
    sings *La serva padrona* in Italian, 245
Roger de Sicile, 115, 124, 125, 151
Roi et le fermier, Le, 14, 77, 148, 290–304, 306, 318
Romance. See Example 9.10
    in *Le Devin du village*, 279
    in *Le Prétendu*, 132, 155
    in *Le Roi et le fermier*, 302
    in *Sancho Pança*, 92
    theatre origins, 132
Rosaline, Mlle
    and the 'older genre', 206
    as leading soprano of the OC, 308
    sings 'Che desia d'un ver contento', 236
    vocal range in *Le Peintre amoureux*, 288
Rose, La. See *Jardins de l'Hymen, Les*
Rousseau, Jean-Jacques
    and *Le Devin du village*, 275–9
    describes *vaudeville* performance, 117
    Duni's testimony (*Le Devin du village*), 284
    Gluck's testimony (*Le Devin du village*), 305
    Le Devin du village in early circulation, 91
    Paris premiere of *Le Devin du village*, 253
Routes du monde, Les, 126, 149, 156
'Royal' operas, 124–6

Saint-Évremond, Charles de, 32
Saurin, Joseph
    and return of solo singing, 113
    as actor, 111
    builds theatre, 140
    in role as Nostradamus, 278

issues policy statement, 156
Saut du fossé, Le, 187, 203
Scaltra governatrice, La, 252, 263, 269
Schneider, Herbert, 188, 266, 318
Sedaine, Michel-Jean
    adaptations from La Fontaine, 171
    adapts Dodsley's play for *Le Roi et le fermier*, 299
    and *Le Diable à quatre*, 179–80
    and musico-dramatic design, 299–304
    and Prefaces, 15
    and reception of *Le Déserteur*, 22–5
    as 'married' to a composer, 276
    designs libretto of *On ne s'avise jamais de tout*, 159–161
    dramaturgy viewed by La Harpe, 15
    verse dialogue in *Les Femmes vengées*, 117
Serrurier, Le, 15
Serva padrona, La, 194, 252, 257, 260
    with dialogue spoken, 248–50
Servandoni, Jean-Nicolas
    design for *La Pénélope moderne*, 150
Servante justifiée, La, 166, 167, 189, 203, 229
Servante maîtresse, La, 188, 245, 254, 256, 260, 266–7
Shakespeare, William
    as point of critical reference, 15, 24
Sicilien, Le, 35, 37–8
    and recycled motifs, 159
Siège de Cythère, Le, 189
Singers. *See* Aigremont, Antheaume, Astraudi, Baxter, Chéret, Cuvillier, Danneret, Desjardins, Drouart, Arimath, d', Duval, Favart, Hamoche, Lepri, Montigny, Nessel, Petitpas, Rebours, Riccoboni, Ristorini, Rosaline, Saurin, Théveneau, Tonelli, Ungarelli, Visentini
    and their careers, 113
    Caillot's career, 246
    Rochard's career, 245
Singing. *See* Performance
    enthusiasm for, 77–82
    in *intermezzo* style, 240, 247
    in Italian style, 245
    of chaconnes, overtures and *menuets*, 83
    of *vaudevilles*, 100–3
Smith, Kent M.
    and Duni's *Le Retour au village*, 281
Soldat magicien, Le, 92, 200
    derived from *Le Bon soldat*, 161
Sonata form, 307–8
Songs
    in domestic use. *See* Chapter 4

    in *Le Théâtre italien de Gherardi*, 57–62
    in plays, 30
    obscene, 108
    rustic, 88
    strophic, 131, 215, 230, 231
Sophie et Sigismond, 126, 154
Sorcier, Le
    dedicated to 'Le Public', 85
Sorel, Charles
    and *La Comédie de chansons*, 29
Stage directions
    in *Le Devin du village*, 277
    in *Le Maître de musique*, 268
    in *Le Retour au village*, 282
    in *Le Roi et le fermier*, 301
    in *Le Troc*, 95
    in *Les Troqueurs*, 280
    in *L'Opéra de campagne*, 69
Statue merveilleuse, La, 124, 125, 151, 189, 205
Sterne, Laurence
    account of the Comédie-Italienne, 145–6
Stilwell, Jama
    and 'abduction' theme, 182
    and 'singing the unspeakable', 104
Suffisant, Le, 230
Swift, Jonathan
    and defence of *The Beggar's Opera*, 296
    and 'true humour', 51
Symphonies
    as overtures, 308

Tableau
    and Diderot, 14
    in *La Chercheuse d'esprit*, 146
    in opéra-comique, 19
Tableau du mariage, Le, 174
Talents à la mode, Les, 239
Tante rivale, La, 187
Témoins contre eux-mêmes, Les, 188, 203
Temple de l'Ennuy, Le, 120, 214
Temple du Destin, Le, 201
Temple du Sommeil, Le, 158
Teniers, David (I and II), 20
Théâtre de la Foire, Le
    and intended uses, 77
    brief description, 105–6
Theatre, English
    approved by d'Argenson, 293
    known in France, 13
    promoted by La Place, 178
    translations adopted by Sedaine, 293

Theatres
   and capacity, 311
   and ticket prices, 141
   descriptions of. *See* Chapter 6
Thésée, parodie, 142
Théveneau, Pierre
   as solo singer, 239–43
'Threads', 9, 89, 162, 236, 258
Tircis et Doristée, 196, 256
Tirésias, 175–6
Tombeau de Nostradamus, Le, 151, 187
   and improvised dialogue, 117
   and lighting effect, 154
   and Richard Baxter, 111
Tonelli, Anna, 251, 254
Tonelli, Caterina, 273
Tonnelier, Le, 171, 200
Toscano, Angela
   as solo singer, 52, 61, 62, 69
Tracollo, medico ignorante, 194, 253
Triomphe de l'intérêt, Le, 239
Triomphe des dames, Le, 42
Troc, Le, 93–6
Trois commères, Les, 151
   and La Fontaine, 165
   and moral reform, 174
   and *vaudeville* dialogue, 122
   circumstances of first performance, 7
Trois cousines, Les, 34
Trois fermiers, Les, 89
Trompeur trompé, Le, 196, 230, 312
Troqueurs, Les, 196, 200, 253
   and Jean Monnet, 197
   and La Fontaine, 170
   and *Le Troc*, 94–7
   and overtures, 308
   as synthesis, 279–80
   given at Versailles, 292

Ulisse et Circé, 62–4
   and parody of Lully, 71
Ungarelli, Rosa
   in *Don Micco e Lesbina*, 247
   in *Serpilla e Baiocco*, 239
Union des deux opéras, L'
   and parody, 63

Vadé, Jean-Joseph. *See Nicaise; Poirier, Le; Racoleurs, Les; Suffisant, Le; Trompeur trompé, Le; Veuve indécise, La*
   adaptations from La Fontaine, 170
   and *Les Troqueurs*, 94, 197
   Les Troqueurs assessed by Framery, 307
   longevity of *Les Troqueurs*, 200
   musical dramaturgy in *Les Troqueurs*, 279–80
Vaudeville-finales, 55, 62, 67
   in *Le Roi et le fermier*, 302
Vaudevilles
   accompaniment and continuity. *See* Chapter 5
   altered by Favart in *La Chercheuse d'esprit*, 127
   and 'singing the unspeakable', 103
   as expressive. *See* Chapter 5
   as 'unitary' compositions, 76
   as virtuosic. *See* Chapter 9
   at Comédie-Italienne. *See* Chapter 10
   characteristics in *Le Devin du village*, 276
   in plays, 29
   irony in, 64
   keys selected freely, 106, 129
Veuve coquette, La, 127
Veuve indécise, La, 196
   longevity of, 200
Viaggiatori, I
   source for *Le Maître de musique*, 268
Visentini, Catherine-Antoinette
   as soloist, 239
   career of, 241
   doubles Silvia's roles, 250
Voltaire
   and amateur acting, 78
   and interest in China, 257
   Candide and theme of deserters, 24
   Discours en vers sur l'homme, 279
Voyage de Scaramouche, Le, 36

Waeber, Jacqueline, 277–8, 286
War, Seven Years
   and *Le Roi et le fermier*, 293

Zauberflöte, Die
   and stylised work-songs, 31
Zingara, La
   and French adaptations, 268
   compared with *La Bohémienne*, 260

For EU product safety concerns, contact us at Calle de José Abascal, 56–1°,
28003 Madrid, Spain or eugpsr@cambridge.org.